BODIES OF INFORMATION

DEBATES IN THE DIGITAL HUMANITIES
Matthew K. Gold and Lauren F. Klein, Series Editors

BODIES *of* INFORMATION

INTERSECTIONAL FEMINISM AND DIGITAL HUMANITIES

Elizabeth Losh and Jacqueline Wernimont
EDITORS

DEBATES IN THE DIGITAL HUMANITIES

University of Minnesota Press
Minneapolis
London

A different version of chapter 24 by Sandra Gabriele was previously published with Natalie Z. Walschots in French as "Une vue de quelque part: Concevoir le plus vieux jeu du monde," in *Le témoignage sexuel et intime, un levier de changement social?*, ed. M. N. Mensah (Montréal: Presses de l'Université du Québec, 2017). The author gratefully acknowledges PUQ's permission to publish this version.

Copyright 2018 by the Regents of the University of Minnesota

All rights reserved. No part of this publication may be reproduced, stored in a retrieval system, or transmitted, in any form or by any means, electronic, mechanical, photocopying, recording, or otherwise, without the prior written permission of the publisher.

Published by the University of Minnesota Press
111 Third Avenue South, Suite 290
Minneapolis, MN 55401-2520
http://www.upress.umn.edu

Printed on acid-free paper

The University of Minnesota is an equal-opportunity educator and employer.

Library of Congress Cataloging-in-Publication Data
Names: Losh, Elizabeth M. (Elizabeth Mathews), editor. | Wernimont, Jacqueline, editor.
Title: Bodies of information : intersectional feminism and digital humanities / Elizabeth Losh and Jacqueline Wernimont, editors.
Description: Minneapolis : University of Minnesota Press, [2018] | Series: Debates in the digital humanities | Includes bibliographical references and index. |
Identifiers: LCCN 2018020494 (print) | ISBN 978-1-5179-0610-8 (hc) | ISBN 978-1-5179-0611-5 (pb)
Subjects: | MESH: Information Technology | Feminism | Humanities—trends | Information Dissemination—methods
Classification: LCC HQ1154 (print) | NLM W 26.5 | DDC 305.420285—dc23
LC record available at https://lccn.loc.gov/2018020494

UMP LSI

For Tycho Horan with much love and admiration for the many digital feminisms that can be generated by the printing press

For all the women and nonbinary people who continually fight to simply live their lives fully and deserve to be seen, heard, and respected. I love to you.

Contents

INTRODUCTION
Jacqueline Wernimont and Elizabeth Losh ix

PART I
Materiality

1 "Danger, Jane Roe!" Material Data Visualization as Feminist Praxis | *Kim Brillante Knight* 3

2 The Android Goddess Declaration: After Man(ifestos) | *micha cárdenas* 25

3 What Passes for Human? Undermining the Universal Subject in Digital Humanities Praxis | *Roopika Risam* 39

4 Accounting and Accountability: Feminist Grant Administration and Coalitional Fair Finance | *Danielle Cole, Izetta Autumn Mobley, Jacqueline Wernimont, Moya Bailey, T. L. Cowan, and Veronica Paredes* 57

PART II
Values

5 Be More Than Binary | *Deb Verhoeven* 71

6 Representation at Digital Humanities Conferences (2000–2015) | *Nickoal Eichmann-Kalwara, Jeana Jorgensen, and Scott B. Weingart* 72

7 Counting the Costs: Funding Feminism in the Digital Humanities | *Christina Boyles* 93

8 Toward a Queer Digital Humanities | *Bonnie Ruberg, Jason Boyd, and James Howe* 108

PART III
Embodiment

9 Remaking History: Lesbian Feminist Historical Methods in the Digital Humanities | *Michelle Schwartz and Constance Crompton* 131

10 Prototyping Personography for *The Yellow Nineties Online*: Queering and Querying History in the Digital Age | *Alison Hedley and Lorraine Janzen Kooistra* 157

11 Is Twitter Any Place for a [Black Academic] Lady? | *Marcia Chatelain*   173

12 Bringing Up the Bodies: The Visceral, the Virtual, and the Visible | *Padmini Ray Murray*   185

PART IV
Affect

13 Ev-Ent-Anglement: A Script to Reflexively Extend Engagement by Way of Technologies | *Brian Getnick, Alexandra Juhasz, and Laila Shereen Sakr (VJ Um Amel)*   203

14 Building Pleasure and the Digital Archive | *Dorothy Kim*   230

15 Delivery Service: Gender and the Political Unconscious of Digital Humanities | *Susan Brown*   261

PART V
Labor

16 Building Otherwise | *Julia Flanders*   289

17 Working Nine to Five: What a Way to Make an Academic Living? | *Lisa Brundage, Karen Gregory, and Emily Sherwood*   305

18 Minority Report: The Myth of Equality in the Digital Humanities | *Barbara Bordalejo*   320

19 Complicating a "Great Man" Narrative of Digital History in the United States | *Sharon M. Leon*   344

PART VI
Situatedness

20 Can We Trust the University? Digital Humanities Collaborations with Historically Exploited Cultural Communities | *Amy E. Earhart*   369

21 Domestic Disturbances: Precarity, Agency, Data | *Beth Coleman*   391

22 Project | Process | Product: Feminist Digital Subjectivity in a Shifting Scholarly Field | *Kathryn Holland and Susan Brown*   409

23 Decolonizing Digital Humanities: Africa in Perspective | *Babalola Titilola Aiyegbusi*   434

24 A View from Somewhere: Designing *The Oldest Game*, a Newsgame to Speak Nearby | *Sandra Gabriele*   447

25 Playing the Humanities: Feminist Game Studies and Public Discourse | *Anastasia Salter and Bridget Blodgett*   466

CONTRIBUTORS   477
INDEX   481

Introduction

JACQUELINE WERNIMONT AND ELIZABETH LOSH

I believe in data, but data itself has become spectacle.

—danah boyd, *Data & Society: Points*

We owe it to each other to falsify the institution, to make politics incorrect, to give the lie to our own determination. We owe each other the indeterminate. We owe each other everything.

—Stefano Harney and Fred Moten, *The Undercommons*

The manuscript for *Bodies of Information* came into being in the liminal space between the final days in office for the first black president of the United States of America and the simultaneous concussion waves of nationalism, sexism, homophobia, transphobia, and racism that appeared to set the stage for hostility to academic institutions, scientific inquiry, journalistic investigation, political inclusion, public investment, digital rights, and network neutrality.[1] Within weeks of the 2017 White House inauguration, an important federal endowment that had supported the work of many of the practitioners represented in this volume was threatened with defunding. Innovative academic scholarship in and about digital environments was also disparaged by a president who relished expressing his disdain for projects that he singled out like "a wolf video game" or scholarly research on "Internet romance."[2] Increasingly global, digital humanities organizations struggled to come to terms with authoritarian governments ignoring human rights violations and the needs of hundreds of millions of migrants and displaced persons struggling to survive in a bleak biopolitical landscape.

This volume also emerges in an era when the tasks of intersectional feminisms, of coalition building, and of communal care and repair are recognized as increasingly important areas in the humanities.[3] Yet as women and feminists who have been active in the digital humanities since it was called "humanities computing," we are often astonished to see forms of intellectual engagement that confront structural misogyny and racism relegated to the status of fringe concerns. Even as leaders of digital humanities labs are finally being outed for sexual harassment or systemic discrimination, trivialization of feminist methodologies continues. For example, in 2016 we both participated in a panel on feminist infrastructures at the annual Digital Humanities conference organized by the Alliance of Digital Humanities

Organizations and convened in Kraków, Poland. This panel was grouped together with other marginalized efforts as part of the "diversity" track, which was located in a separate building from the edifice that housed most of the conference sessions.

Such spatial arrangements communicate value and can establish barriers, peripheralizing even a panel of assembled digital humanities luminaries in positions of relative privilege, including the director of the Australian Humanities Networked Infrastructure (HuNI) project, the head of the Canadian Writing Research Collaboratory, the director of the Advanced Research Consortium (ARC) in the United States, and the principal investigator of the Institute for High Performance Sound Technologies for Access and Scholarship (HiPSTAS). Despite the profile of the panel, there was a clear sense that a feminist conversation about infrastructure was not valued in the same way as other similar panels at the event. While we felt that exclusion fairly keenly, we also were aware that as members of a panel of white women from Canada, the United States, and Australia, we were and are not subject to the full force of exclusion that our trans and women of color colleagues systematically experience. Indeed, the existence of the "diversity" track and its location was particularly notable given the extensive efforts of scholars of color in particular to ensure that the event was not a "parade of (white) patriarchs" as was the opening of the same annual meeting a year before in Australia.[4]

A few months before the summer conference, "Neoliberal Tools (and Archives): A Political History of Digital Humanities" by Daniel Allington, Sarah Brouillette, and David Golumbia appeared in the *Los Angeles Review of Books* (LARB). According to the authors, as "neoliberal tools," digital humanities initiatives are a means for serving the ends of cultural conservatism and political reaction within increasingly corporatized universities and colleges. The LARB critique was grounded in tracing a small set of related origin stories in which "the trailblazer is usually identified as a Jesuit priest, Roberto Busa, whose 56-volume concordance to the works of St. Thomas Aquinas was produced over a period of three decades from 1949, with support from IBM." The patrilineal genealogy mapped (and critiqued) by the LARB essay envisions digital humanities expanded from Busa's trunk to related branches in digital humanities efforts at the University of Virginia, Stanford, and the University of Maryland. In each locus of the "Neoliberal Tools" story there is an academic entrepreneur who functions as an opportunistic homo oeconomicus. In the "Neoliberal Tools" fable a few lone feminist Cassandras might have attempted to arrest the progress of these enterprising men, but otherwise the narrative is free of women and people of color as digital humanities innovators. Unfortunately, by repeating different versions of the solo white male inventor myth, the LARB criticism of the techno-utopianism of digital humanities (DH) actually gave that myth more credence by reifying an Anglo-American tradition as "the field" and the "textual-studies" tradition within DH as originary. While critique of and within digital humanities origin stories is clearly needed, in part to push back against the johnny-come-lately tendencies in other popular pieces critical of the field, by suggesting that New Bibliography and the University of Virginia English department in particular were the "birthplace" of digital humanities, the piece served to further entrench the very origin stories it claimed to critique.[5]

These two situated and situating events—the Kraków conference and the *Los Angeles Review of Books* publication—and their attendant narratives exemplify an ongoing denigration of feminist and antiracist theory and practice in the digital humanities. Both proponents and opponents of DH seem able to agree on one common position: histories of feminist and antiracist work in DH do not deserve a place at the table. By contrast, our argument is that feminisms have been and must continue to be central to the identity and the methodologies of the digital humanities as a field.

After all, historians of technology such as Janet Abbate have observed that the importance of gender dynamics in computational history more generally is often devalued.[6] Abbate specifically asserts that the norms of how work is gendered can be surprisingly fluid, particularly when a new field, like computer programming, develops. In her book *Recoding Gender,* she reasons that the obvious presence of a large female labor force of human "computers" at the dawn of the information age led to a form of "reverse engineering" that caused programming to be associated with feminine traits and occupations. As Abbate points out, programming in the post–World War II period was often associated with avocations like educating, nursing, or mothering, and writing code was seen as analogous to cooking, sewing, or displaying musical accomplishment. Although programming would ultimately be allied with masculine disciplines like mathematics and engineering, during its embryonic phase computer science was far from an exclusively masculine domain. Similarly, the accounts of women of color in computer programming recounted in books like *Hidden Figures* describe different norms about racial inclusion in STEM (science, technology, engineering, and math) fields than the ones we have today.[7] Digital humanities origin stories may well still be seen as protean; perhaps if we can avoid or more rapidly correct the revisionist exclusions visited upon other disciplines, then we may be able to practice DH as one of the more welcoming fields in university culture.[8]

This is a particularly urgent task in a moment when systemic sexual harassment, predation, and racism are visible from within institutions of higher education across the globe.[9] For future digital humanities work to create what is possible and combat what should be impermissible, we believe that intersectional feminism, which acknowledges the interactions of multiple power structures (including race, sexuality, class, and ability), must be central within digital humanities practices.[10] In fact, many of the best challenges to our Kraków panelists, to the 2017 Digital Humanities conference organizing committee, and to the *Los Angeles Review of Books* piece came from those who noted the complete or relative absence of people of color in each of these discussions. Indeed, as Jessica Marie Johnson observes, despite being consigned to the sidelines in supposedly open and progressive conversations,

Black digital practice "has created and facilitated insurgent and maroon knowledge creation within the ivory tower. It's imperfect, and it's problematic—and we are all imperfect and problematic. But in that sense I think the digital humanities, or doing digital work period, has helped people create maroon—free, black, liberatory, radical—spaces in the academy."[11] As Johnson notes, this is not simply "academic"; the work and communities of Black, Native, Latinx, queer, trans, and intersectional digital scholars have "literally saved lives . . . people—those who have felt alone or maligned or those who have been marginalized or discriminated against or bullied—have used digital tools to survive and live."[12]

In our own work we have also noted the striking absence of engagement with human-computer interaction (HCI), science and technology studies (STS), and media studies in the digital humanities as a field. Useful trends from this body of criticism have all had notable feminist proponents working across disciplines: Lucille Suchman on situated action, Leigh Star on infrastructure, Genevieve Bell on mess, Mary Ann Doane and Lori Emerson on media archaeology, Melissa Gregg on affect theory, Lisa Cartwright on the interactions of apparatuses and bodies, Judy Wajcman on digital labor, and Marisa Parham on black literary embodiment, haunting, and space/time disjunctions, to name just a few. More recently, much of the most exciting scholarship about digital culture has come out of sociology, anthropology, political economy, and library and information science domains with attention to the transnational circulation of people, products, and ideas, including that of Simone Browne, Katherine McKittrick, Radhika Gajjala, Nishant Shah, danah boyd, Zeynep Tufekci, Safiya Umoja Noble, Kate Crawford, Moya Bailey, and Michelle Caswell.

We urge our fellow digital humanists to think through the implications of ubiquitous computing in particular and to consider undertaking the analysis of new objects of study rather than merely focus their scholarship on the cultural artifacts of the screen, page, or canvas (as well as their digital remediations). After all, mobile and wearable devices exist in intimate proximity to our persons, and embedded sensing systems in our "smart" cities and designed environments monitor our interactions. (The work of Katina Michaels is exemplary for those pursuing this research agenda.)[13] Thus, the digital humanities should also advocate attention to technosocial environments, the interfaces and platforms of mediation, and the procedures, protocols, and platforms of playable systems.[14] In other words, we must expand our notions of text and context, archive and canon, and code and program.

Having some interest in *mess* as an area of inquiry is fundamental to understanding how technologies, people, resources, and networks work, and sometimes don't work, together. As computer scientist Paul Dourish and anthropologist Genevieve Bell write in their analysis of the cultural imaginaries of ubiquitous computing, "mess" reveals that "the practice of any technology in the world is never quite as simple, straightforward, or idealized as it is imagined to be" and that "technological realities are always contested."[15] By emphasizing the material, situated, contingent, tacit, embodied, affective, labor-intensive, and political characteristics of digital archives and their supporting infrastructures and practices rather than friction-free visions of pure Cartesian "virtual reality" or "cyberspace," feminist theorists are also expressing their concerns about present-day power relations and signifying interest in collective and communal consciousness-raising efforts.

Despite an often grim environment for equity, diversity, inclusion, and participation in the humanities within increasingly constrained research universities and the political institutions that support them, we are hopeful that the digital humanities are finally maturing from their critically naive beginnings. This volume reflects how feminist collectives and communities are making a difference in changing the digital humanities in particular and institutional cultures generally, from members of FemTechNet, to curators of the Ferguson syllabus effort, to participants in the #transformdh and #dhpoco hashtag campaigns.

Bodies of Information is organized with keywords that work as "boundary objects," in the sense that they are shared resources that support systems of meaning used in different ways by different communities.[16] First theorized by the late science and technology studies scholar Susan Leigh Star and her collaborators, boundary objects are plastic, interpreted differently, and adapted to express emergent thinking across communities and contexts while also maintaining sufficient conceptual integrity for common understanding. Recognizing that keywords like "materiality" and "embodiment" operate as boundary objects gives us a way of understanding the kinds of work such concepts do in creating identities, knitting communities, and suggesting relationships between seemingly disparate ideas. As Star and her collaborators so powerfully demonstrated, boundary objects play a pivotal role in the creation of reality. An array of boundary objects is possible. In our work we use the acronym MEALS as shorthand for a feminist emphasis on how the "**m**aterial, **e**mbodied, **a**ffective, **l**abor-intensive, and **s**ituated character of engagements with computation can operate experientially for users in shared spaces."[17]

Because boundary objects are mediating technologies for people and communities, we have used them here to cluster our chapters. Like the weakly determined boundary objects theorized by Star, our chapter clusters should be read as multifaceted engagements with the concepts that we believe operate in a certain kind of community with one another. That said, one of the great joys of rich intersectional feminist work is that it attends to issues of embodiment, affect, labor, and so on as a regular part of practice. Indeed, while we open with a focus on materiality and close with the recognition that all work, all bodies, and all actions are situated, readers will see that there are strong threads that weave across the chapter clusters as well. Readers will also note that here we have supplemented the MEALS framework with an additional boundary object, "Values," in order to draw attention to the ways in which technologies promote particular ethical and ideological values (rather than acting as neutral tools).

The book's title pays homage to Katherine Hayles's account of how "information lost its body" in *How We Became Posthuman*. Hayles argues that during the post–World War II era multiple generations of thinkers influenced by cybernetic theory embraced a view that treated data as a transcendent entity that could be abstracted from materiality, embodiment, and reflexivity. Although Hayles notes that cybernetic thinkers from the Macy Conferences engaged in vigorous debates, she laments their general tendency to deemphasize affect and labor as well.

Materiality

"Materiality" as a theoretical tool and boundary object takes a range of forms, as all good boundary objects do. In Kim Brillante Knight's essay on her work creating wearable data visualizations, materiality is a way of understanding how gendered power relations move in and through something like an Arduino board or the related LilyPad microcontroller. For Knight, the LilyPad's circuit material visibility is an important factor in the creation of techno-textile "counterpublics." With her example of the "Danger, Jane Roe!" pieces, Knight asks us to consider how we might use "fem-techno-assemblages" in building resistant art and communities.

Material resistance and underground communities are a central concern for micha cárdenas's "Android Goddess Declaration" as well, which draws on the vital work of Gloria Anzaldúa and Audre Lorde to think anew about tools for a liberatory politics. Working with the poetic and powerful work of Stefano Harney and Fred Moten on the "undercommons" and that of Walter Mignolo to think about mestiza functionalities, cárdenas asks: "Can tools be repurposed when used in different places, by different people?" Drawing on her own creation of instruments for safety, cárdenas offers a declaration of solidarity with "fugitive black androids hacking their own code . . . with the renegade clones of Orphan Black . . . with the hacker witches from Barcelona to Seattle who are using technology to fight back against centuries of persecution from the logics of Western patriarchy."

Cyborg women also appear in Roopika Risam's chapter, where the figure of the cyborg-girl from the 1980s American sitcom *Small Wonder* opens her examination of the forms of "human" sanctioned by electronic technologies and their implications for digital humanities scholarship. In considering the potentially important roles of machine learning and natural language processing in next-generation work, she points out that "artificial intelligence purports to represent universal 'human' intellectual processes but, in fact, is only representative of a fictive 'universal' model of human cognition that elides both women, peoples of the Global South, and those at the interstices of these categories."

Materiality as a tool for thinking becomes something different in the piece by Danielle Cole and her coauthors, where the very real material concerns to provide food, shelter, and daily needs to very real women and femmes meet the impersonal structures of grant accounting and accountability. Refusing to flinch from their own roles in a grant payment cycle that has harmed some collaborators, Cole and her collaborators offer us a clear and detailed view of how community and institutional collaboration can have differential material impact on the lives of people attempting to do the very kind of work called for by Knight, cárdenas, and Risam.

Values

As Deb Verhoeven observed in her stinging "Has Anyone Seen a Woman?" speech to the Alliance of Digital Humanities Organizations (ADHO) annual DH meeting in 2015, far too few women have been allowed to take the stage, and historical inequities need to be addressed with a progressive politics of affirmative action. Verhoeven's piece sets the stage for the "Values" part of the collection, in which our contributors each take a hard look at the values expressed by the organs of the field.

Indeed, as Nickoal Eichmann-Kalwara, Jeana Jorgensen, and Scott B. Weingart's piece so clearly demonstrates, "women are consistently underrepresented [in the annual Digital Humanities conference presentations] with little changing in the last few years." Additionally, geographic diversity is relatively poor, and there is a "visible bias against authors with non-English names in the peer review process." In sorting through the data on rejected submissions, Eichmann-Kalwara, Jorgensen, and Weingart note that there also appear to be biases around subject matter that reflect gender disparities.

Thus, while the leadership of digital humanities organizations often lauds the virtues of statistical analysis, key stakeholders might be tempted to suppress data that counter narratives of consistent progress diversifying the field. Christina Boyles's survey of several recent works by scholars like Amanda Phillips, Alexis Lothian, and Amy Earhart makes clear that while intersectional and critical digital humanities work has always been part of the community, it has not yet seen the kind of sustained funding familiar to projects that have centered canonical works or dominant theoretical frameworks. Boyles analyzes the infrastructural conditions of funding streams from the National Endowment for the Humanities and from philanthropic organizations like the Mellon Foundation that privilege certain kinds of projects that normalize how a text and educational uses are defined. Boyles also deploys information visualization to show clustering and gaps around topics like "diversity" and "public."

In addition to the representational politics of feminisms, we assert that these feminisms function as sophisticated forms of critical theory and have much to offer digital humanities in terms of method and theory. As the closing piece in our "Values" part suggests, queer theorizations may be particularly fruitful for expanding interventions to larger issues of methodology. Feminist digital humanities should challenge, critique, rethink, and expand what the digital humanities should be, just as Bonnie Ruberg, Jason Boyd, and James Howe argue that a queer digital humanities is defined by much more than the archives documenting queer individuals and queer communities. In queering the digital humanities, Ruberg, Boyd, and Howe draw on the work of prominent queer theorists and queer digital artists to argue that queer knowledge always resists completion. In addition to adding new vocabulary to existing taxonomical systems, they assert that queerness also points toward a shift in the very methodologies of metadata collection. To queer metadata, queer thinking must be brought to bear on the conceptual models and tools of object description to challenge the norms that dictate how meaning is derived from data. They observe that the methods with which data are traditionally mapped rely on a model of the one-to-one relationship between concepts of the world that can account for nonbinary relationships.

Embodiment

Notions of queering digital work bridges between "Values" and "Embodiment" in this collection, demonstrating just how intrapenetrable such boundary objects can be. In their work on lesbian digital humanities, Michelle Schwartz and Constance Crompton argue that digital methodology matters as much to histories of queer bodies and lives as informational content of such study, because "the accumulation of data and the rhetorical structuring of that data (in these examples often as a list) serve as important acts of lesbian self-definition." The particular problem of the epistemological structuring of taxonomies of shared digital knowledge becomes particularly marked if fundamental infrastructures of information are designed solely to sort data into binary or mutually exclusive categories.

In their description of archiving the literary production of periodicals from the so-called yellow nineties, Alison Hedley and Lorraine Janzen Kooistra want to challenge the standard classification practices that can make certain persons historical nonentities and facilitate accessibility by making their "knowledge modelling process visible." In particular, Hedley and Kooistra look closely at authors in their archive who don't fit standard gender binaries, because they use pseudonyms as identifying tactics.

The contingency and multiplicity of feminized identities and bodies both offline and online are a central concern for Marcia Chatelain when she asks, "Is Twitter any place for a [black academic] lady?" Drawing on her pedagogical engagements with the life and work of Ida B. Wells-Barnett and as the originator of #FergusonSyllabus, Chatelain's piece opens with a reminder that race and gender have long been used as ways of excluding women of color from the innovative public spaces created by emerging technologies. Chatelain places the raced and gendered violence of twenty-first-century social media in a long history of black women's intellectual history, demonstrating that women of color have consistently led the nation in using emerging technocultures to "intervene in moments of crisis and remind the academy of our roles and responsibilities to a broader world."

Padmini Ray Murray engages with a related set of questions about the contingent and resistant feminist body, arguing that the differences between the "visceral and the virtual body" are located on points of "rupture" in the context of South Asian politics and practice. This rupture calls us to attend to the ways in which caste and privilege play out in and around both visceral and virtual women's bodies in India. Additionally, Murray's incisive analysis demands that we resist importing and imposing ill-fitting Western models and histories—however progressive they may seem—when working in or with digital humanities in India. Murray closes with a powerful call to action, noting that "in order to enact a more heterotopic reality, it is the responsibility of digital humanists to build tools and strategies to violate the bodies of the machines that watch over us with loving grace and to dismantle them with as much violence as is being done to our own."

Affect

The grace and violence invoked by Murray finds a kind of formal manifestation in "Ev-Ent-Anglement" by VJ Um Amel, Brian Getnick, and Alexandra Juhasz. As we move into the "Affect" part, this artist-maker-cutter team tears up and stitches back together various texts, including their own. Each time, they pull their interlocutors into the performance, including us, their editors. In so doing, they think about not only the material and embodied nature of digital work but also how we can cut with it and perform the movement of "affective fragments."

Dorothy Kim's piece grapples not with affective "fragments" but with fragments of affect, the drive to pleasure that is a constitutive part of digital archive or project creation. This is a rarely, if ever, talked about "hidden" feature of discussions of the black-boxing effects of technologies, but as Kim points out, thinking about the desires that various platforms respond to or activate is particularly crucial for understanding their work. Returning again to the topic of embodiment, Kim's piece foregrounds not only the pleasures and desires of interacting with digital book "bodies" in the tradition of book history but also the sensorium of editorial bodies that help to produce those digital bodies. Interrogating production and interface, Kim's work brings medieval history and literary studies, book history, disability studies, interface theory, art history, and affective and feminist theories together in what we might frame as a critical assemblage. This project allows her to argue that digital editors are performing "an agential cut," resonant but formally and temporally different from that seen in "Ev-Ent-Anglement."

Pieces by Susan Brown and Julia Flanders constitute a bridge between "affect" and "labor." Both authors have led foundational, long-term feminist digital humanities projects. Brown and Flanders are also able to speak to the transition within feminist literary theory and digital humanities from projects and analysis focused on recovering lost women's voices to thinking about how feminist praxis and theory illuminate the challenges and opportunities presented by invisible labor and messy infrastructures, insights gained as they directed the Women's Writers Project and the Orlando Project, respectively.

In Brown's essay she examines why the figure of the handmaid excites so much anxiety, fear, and contempt in digital humanities discourses and attempts to retrieve both labor and delivery as paradigms for the digital humanities. Drawing out the patriarchal roots of a fear of women's reproductive capacities in order to understand the anxiety around "service" in the digital humanities, Brown sees tensions between the cerebral and material in terms of training, scholarship, and infrastructure within the field. Brown includes an analysis of Margaret Atwood's *A Handmaid's Tale,* which has particular resonances in the current American political context. Consequently, her piece is a particularly timely reminder that *techne* can create a dangerous passive/active agential dichotomy in which tools violently deliver a product from a feminized subject. On the other hand, Brown suggests reframing service and delivery in terms of midwifery, thereby positioning those involved as "all active, all in that liminal zone of risk, rupture, and possibility." Weaving together analyses of affect, labor, and situated practices, Brown offers the "possibility of intimate, mutually constitutive relations between one who or that which delivers and one who or which is delivered" within digital scholarship.

Labor

Flanders, who has written before on the invisible labor of many DH efforts, writes here about the ways in which editorial methods are deeply implicated in the politics of gender and are affected by, and enacted through, technological choices. For Flanders, "there is no such thing as a 'merely technical' design decision: our technical systems are meaning systems and ideological systems." Indeed, Flanders takes up the call to consider the "full stack" of a project and sketches out what it would mean to undertake such an analysis. Her piece offers the field a new way forward for thinking through the depth of social, political, material, formal, and economic factors in feminist analyses of digital projects.

Lisa Brundage, Karen Gregory, and Emily Sherwood draw attention to a central paradox in the digital humanities in that the most important work is often the most devalued, particularly because it is labor that is intended to render itself invisible. They chart how the development of digital humanities scholarship and pedagogy followed a trajectory of reliance on the use of postdoc and so-called alt-ac (alternative academic) work within larger gendered and racialized labor histories. They note that specific language often demarcates these positions as inferior despite their integral role in digital humanities initiatives.

Like Eichmann and her coauthors, Barbara Bordalejo takes a quantitative and sociological approach to the issue of representation in the fields of digital humanities. What she found with her own survey was on occasion ugly, but not surprising from either a historical or a contemporary perspective. Her work validates impressions that might otherwise be treated as anecdotal while showing how the new normal includes self-identifying white male colleagues who are willing to openly denigrate feminist work. Beyond the personal attacks attested to in her piece, Bordalejo's contribution is important for the view it affords us on gender and sexual identities in digital humanities operations not captured in other metrics available for digital scraping, as in the case of Eichmann and her coauthors and Boyles. It also highlights that the Anglophone bias at the proposal stage, which was gestured to in Eichmann as well, is also an important aspect of the DH labor picture in the Global North that often ignores how digital humanities work may be outsourced to other continents.

Sharon Leon, the former director of public projects for the Center for History and New Media at George Mason University, points out that "great man" histories that dominate our field fundamentally misrepresent the history of technocultural labor. She observes that the same canon of male names is often repeated and that digital humanities genealogies tend to name only one female ancestor. As she notes, "recent reviews of the field tend to reproduce these oversights, suggesting that the history of digital history is a settled one—one that is devoid of women." In getting "beyond the principal investigator" to consider the work of different kinds of project and community managers leading digital humanities projects, she names over a hundred significant women in the history of digital humanities initiatives. Leon argues that women's pivotal roles in the digital humanities become even more visible when libraries, archives, and museums are included, where occupations are often more feminized and affiliated with activities of service rather than research.

Situatedness

We have noted how strongly the threads of the "Values" and "Labor" parts weave together and constitute a demand that as feminist scholars we need to do far better to ensure that the fields of DH make good on promises of inclusivity. We would take this a step further and assert that the field of DH needs to make concerted efforts to decenter dominant, masculinist, and Anglophone work as the standard in the field. Harkening back to the work of Risam and Murray earlier in the volume and forward into the concerns of the "Situatedness" part, we also want to highlight that this might mean abandoning methods centered on including people in dominant paradigms to foreground exploding the traditional topoi in favor of a heterotopic, messy, and multipled conception of "DH."

Like Leon, Amy Earhart has elsewhere offered an alternative feminist history of the digital humanities by looking at how publication of *The Madwoman in the Attic* by Sandra Gilbert and Susan Gubar in 1979 spurred efforts to recover artifacts from the cultural production of women, particularly women of color. Scholars of feminism and critical race studies compiled digital copies of rare and vulnerable primary sources throughout the 1980s and 1990s, and when later internet browsers became widely available, these sources were lovingly curated on the web. Earhart has bemoaned the fact that many of these early pioneering do-it-yourself archives have since fallen into disrepair after the original curator-caretakers retired or changed institutions or as a result of platform obsolescence or failed migration. In her previous work charting the "diverse history of the digital humanities," Earhart has argued for the need to preserve existing digital archives—which may have idiosyncratic data structures and metadata naming conventions in need of digital redesign—and the labor of care and repair. She has cautioned that the tendency to overvalue innovation and to privilege developing new tools and archives compromises existing digital work.

In her contribution to our collection, Earhart argues that the university has a persistent trust problem with the communities that it purports to represent in digital humanities projects. She argues that well-meaning advocates for social justice in the digital humanities might make inappropriate claims to ownership of community materials, unethically appropriate authorship, or disregard the wishes of communities that they claim to be documenting for posterity. She argues that we need to consider how the exploitation of data and the exploitation of peoples may be interrelated phenomena.

Thinking through the Black Lives Matter movement as a site for digital humanities research, Beth Coleman argues that access to "heterogeneous data" invites multiple scales of engagement with the local and the distributed simultaneously. She argues that when bodies are literally put at risk it is important to be sensitive to what is made invisible by big data narratives that present elegant information visualizations and big picture patterns and consider how lived experiences and digital practices play out in sites of situated action.

Kathryn Holland and Susan Brown's piece grapples with the markup structures that can effectively represent varied, changing, even contradictory vocabularies around gender and authorship in the Orlando Project. As Holland and Brown note, emerging markup paradigms enable the project team to convey "a feminist theory of subjectivity in which women's identities and writing are understood to be multiple, substantial, historically and materially contingent, and at times unknown or incongruous with the concepts and language of our time."

In "Decolonizing Digital Humanities," Babalola Titilola Aiyegbusi takes up the task of situating the academic field of DH and directs our attention to the specific social and infrastructural reasons why scholars in "developing African countries tend to view DH as a western phenomenon practicable in technologically advanced locations." Drawing on a range of scholars working in and on developing nations, Aiyegbusi observes that "regional idiosyncrasies impact the spread of DH" in ways that we must attend to if we are to develop a truly global understanding of digital cultures and scholarship. Focusing on the Nigerian context in particular, she notes that "poverty is the most dominant" factor impacting the possibility for digital humanities scholarship "because it births and cradles other issues, notable among which are network connectivity and power supply." Aiyegbusi's analysis deftly weaves economic and infrastructural challenges together with her analysis of the ways in which traditional DH narratives, regardless of how big a tent is cast, fail to resonate in Nigerian academic frameworks. In fact, she argues that the "big tent" framework may itself be a colonial perspective that alienates scholars working in African nations.

Our final two chapters take up situatedness in the context of feminist game studies. Feminist digital humanities and feminist game studies might seem like fundamentally different approaches to structuring digital content creation, particularly to those who believe in impersonal interactions, simple user navigation without puzzles or tricks, and a transactional approach to information retrieval experiences. Nonetheless, game studies has become an increasingly important reference point for digital humanists working to challenge norms in the field and is now part of the annual Digital Humanities Summer Institute at the University of Victoria. In these final two pieces, digital games function as tools to situate and experience two different phenomena related to one another as sites of public, and therefore vulnerable, work by women: sex work and public intellectualism.

Sandra Gabriele deploys the genre of the educational game as a way to approach the digital humanities critically by challenging the genre of the news game among so-called serious games intended to educate the public about systemic problems by offering them a playable simulation that will supposedly promote understanding and model how different factors might influence outcomes. Gabriele uses her own design of a game that represents the lives of sex workers as a case study for understanding why digital interfaces and databases that present a researcher's work will always be situated in a specific framework of experiences rather than demonstrate detached procedural rhetoric that operates from a position of neutral distance.

Anastasia Salter and Bridget Blodgett use game studies as a way to understand that "public scholarship" and the visibility of the digital humanities can have different consequences for those of different genders or different races. In the wake of the GamerGate series of coordinated attacks on prominent feminist game critics, designers, players, and fans, scholars were harassed, conferences were targeted, and public and professional identities were vexed by conflict. The perils of the "open" platforms often favored by digital humanities initiatives were dramatized by the public spectacle of online violence entering a supposedly tolerant but elite field. For Salter and Blodgett, encouraging scholars to perform their ideas in the digital public sphere might have unanticipated consequences for those from at-risk groups and might ultimately lead to the unexpected silencing of many participants in the academy.

We hope that this volume will spur important conversations in the digital humanities about platforms, software, interfaces, and protocols and about the absence of people who should be present at conferences and in digital humanities centers to support the creation of innovative scholarship. We also hope that it will invite further work reminding us all of the predecessors that official origin stories want to suppress or ignore. We both are aware that this collection—which coalesced from both invited submissions and an open call—cannot be completely representative of the whole of the field. It also largely presents perspectives from within the privileged perspectives in academia, despite the fact that the digital humanities work done in higher education is connected to global supply chains of outsourced labor that might include digitizers scanning pages from books and journals, call center operators fielding customer service questions, assembly line workers manufacturing components, and extraction technicians mining raw materials.

We were both struck by Jessica Marie Johnson's comments at the 2016 American Studies Association Digital Humanities Caucus roundtable about the difference between being "outside" and being "radical" in thinking about how alterity functions for the academy. For Johnson, "being radical or being political is a constant act," so we would not want to give the impression that the work of this volume ends on the last page when the reader has reached the back cover. Instead, we would point to Fiona Barnett's "The Brave Side of Digital Humanities," which asks us to consider, "What happens when the outcome is a sustainable practice, a sustainable self in academia, a lifeline to others as a way of imagining a future together?"[18] Like many of the feminist digital humanists represented in this volume, Barnett suggests that activities of care and maintenance may be more important than those validated as innovation.

We agree with Barnett that the digital humanities constitutes "a struggle to present a practice, not just a project" and it presents a series of ongoing questions, which involve, in Barnett's words, "identifying future alter egos" and extend "to recognizing (and identifying) alternative genealogies: the making and remaking of self, community, narrative, and histories."[19] We also anticipate collaborating with our readers in putting this compendium of ideas into action and who similarly seek to apply principles of feminist digital humanities and the MEALS framework to an ethical grounding of user-centered design for cultural heritage collections, engagement with communities to respect their wishes about preservation and access, and student-centered pedagogical philosophies in digital environments that may undermine the humanity of participants.

Notes

1. "ACH Statement."
2. Trump, *Time to Get Tough*, 75.
3. For example, see Brown, Lemak, Faulkner, Martin, and Warren, "Cultural (Re-)formations"; Noble and Tynes, *Intersectional Internet*; Noble, "Future"; Klein, "Carework and Codework"; Arcy, "Emotion Work," 365–68.
4. See Deb Verhoeven's piece "Be More than Binary," Chapter 5 in this volume.
5. Critiques of DH and its practitioners as "tools" are well-trod terrain. See, for example, Fish, "Digital Humanities," or more recently, Brennan, "Digital Humanities Bust." For a

different take, see Weiskott, "*No Such Thing* (which itself echoes Jamie "Skye" Bianco's "This Digital Humanities Which Is Not One" and her "Man and His Tool, Again? Queer and Feminist Notes on Practices in the Digital Humanities and Object Orientations Everywhere."

6. Abbate, *Recoding Gender*. Interested readers should also see Hicks, *Programmed Inequality*.

7. Such accounts make clear not only the gendered but also racialized nature of field definition. For another example, consider Lisa Nakamura's "Indigenous Circuits: Navajo Women and the Racialization of Early Electronic Manufacture."

8. Miriam Posner's "What's Next: The Radical, Unrealized Potential of Digital Humanities" points to additional ways that the field has yet to live up to its full potential.

9. The contexts in which violences in the academy have made recent news include the reactivation of the "Me Too" movement activated by Tarana Burke in 2006. They include the *Guardian*'s investigation of sexual assault in higher education in the United Kingdom (Batty, Weale, and Bannock, "Sexual Harassment"), Raya Sarkar's crowdsourced list of South Asian academic predators (Doshi, "After #MeToo"), and revelations of sexual assault by several prominent male American academics (Gluckman, Read, Mangan, and Quilantan, "Sexual Harassment"), all of which was perhaps presaged by Sara Ahmed's 2016 resignation from Goldsmith's as protest of institutional failures to address sexual harassment (Ahmed, "Resignation").

10. For more on intersectional praxis and analysis, see Crenshaw, "Mapping the Margins," 1241–99, and May, *Pursuing Intersectionality*.

11. Dinsman, "Digital in the Humanities."

12. Dinsman, "Digital in the Humanities."

13. Michael, "My Research Programme."

14. See, for example, Lothian and Phillips, "Can Digital Humanities."

15. Dourish and Bell, *Divining a Digital Future*, 4.

16. For more on how our collective uses boundary objects, see Juhasz and Balsamo, "Idea Whose Time."

17. Wernimont and Losh, "Wear and Care," 98.

18. Barnett, "Brave Side," 74.

19. Barnett, "Brave Side," 75–76.

Bibliography

Abbate, Janet. *Recording Gender: Women's Changing in Participation in Computing*. Boston: MIT Press, 2012.

"ACH Statement in the Aftermath of the 2016 Election." Association for Computers and the Humanities. http://ach.org/activities/advocacy/ach-statement-in-the-aftermath-of-the-2016-election/.

Ahmed, Sara. "Resignation." *Feminist Killjoys,* May 30, 2016. https://feministkilljoys.com/2016/05/30/resignation/.

Arcy, J. "Emotion Work: Considering Gender in Digital Labor." *Feminist Media Studies* 16, no. 2 (2016): 365–68.

Barnett, Fiona M. "The Brave Side of Digital Humanities." *differences* 25, no. 1 (May 1, 2014): 64–78. https://doi.org/10.1215/10407391-2420003.

Batty, David, Sally Weale, and Caroline Bannock. "Sexual Harassment 'at Epidemic Levels' in UK Universities." *The Guardian,* March 5, 2017. https://www.theguardian.com/education/2017/mar/05/students-staff-uk-universities-sexual-harassment-epidemic.

Bianco, Jamie "Skye." "Man and His Tool, Again? Queer and Feminist Notes on Practices in the Digital Humanities and Object Orientations Everywhere." *Digital Humanities Quarterly* 9, no. 2 (2015), special issue, "Feminisms and DH," edited by Jacqueline Wernimont. http://www.digitalhumanities.org/dhq/vol/9/2/000216/000216.html.

Bianco, Jamie "Skye." "This Digital Humanities Which Is Not One." In *Debates in Digital Humanities,* edited by Matthew K. Gold, 96–112. Minneapolis: University of Minnesota Press, 2012.

Brennan, T. "The Digital Humanities Bust." *Chronicle of Higher Education,* October 15, 2017. https://www.chronicle.com/article/The-Digital-Humanities-Bust/241424.

Brown, Susan, Abigel Lemak, Colin Faulkner, Kim Martin, and Rob Warren. "Cultural (Re-)formations: Structuring a Linked Data Ontology for Intersectional Identities," 2017. https://dh2017.adho.org/abstracts/580/580.pdf.

Crenshaw, Kimberle. "Mapping the Margins: Intersectionality, Identity Politics, and Violence against Women of Color." *Stanford Law Review* 43, no. 6 (July 1991): 1241–99. http://www.jstor.org/stable/1229039.

Dinsman, Melissa. "The Digital in the Humanities: An Interview with Jessica Marie Johnson." *Los Angeles Review of Books,* July 23, 2016. https://lareviewofbooks.org/article/digital-humanities-interview-jessica-marie-johnson/#!.

Doshi, Vidhi. "After #MeToo, a Facebook List Names South Asian Academics. Some Say It's a Step Too Far." *Washington Post,* October 31, 2017. https://www.washingtonpost.com/news/worldviews/wp/2017/10/31/after-metoo-a-facebook-list-names-south-asian-academics-some-say-its-a-step-too-far/?utm_term=.2e22f51de284.

Dourish, Paul, and Genevieve Bell. *Divining a Digital Future.* Cambridge, Mass.: MIT Press, 2014.

Fish, S. "The Digital Humanities and the Transcending of Mortality." *Opinionator* (blog). *New York Times,* January 9, 2012. https://opinionator.blogs.nytimes.com/2012/01/09/the-digital-humanities-and-the-transcending-of-mortality/.

Gluckman, Nell, Brock Read, Katherine Mangan, and Bianca Quilantan. "Sexual Harassment and Assault in Higher Ed: What's Happened since Weinstein." *Chronicle of Higher Education,* November 13, 2017. Updated January 10, 2018. https://www.chronicle.com/article/Sexual-HarassmentAssault/241757.

Hicks, Marie. *Programmed Inequality: How Britain Discarded Women Technologists and Lost Its Edge in Computing.* Cambridge, Mass.: MIT Press, 2017.

Juhasz, Alexandra, and Anne Balsamo. "An Idea Whose Time Is Here: FemTechNet." *Ada: A Journal of Gender, New Media, and Technology* 1 (2012). http://adanewmedia.org/2012/11/issue1-juhasz/.

Klein, Lauren F. "The Carework and Codework of the Digital Humanities." Digital Antiquarian Conference, May 29, 2015, Worcester, Mass. lklein.com/2015/06/the-carework-and-codework-of-the-digital-humanities/.

Lothian, Alexis, and Amanda Phillips. "Can Digital Humanities Mean Transformative Critique." *e-media Studies* 3, no. 1 (2013). http://journals.dartmouth.edu/cgi-bin/WebObjects/Journals.woa/1/xmlpage/4/article/425.

May, Vivian M. *Pursuing Intersectionality, Unsettling Dominant Imaginaries.* London: Routledge, 2015.

Michael, Katina. "My Research Programme (2002–Now)." KatinaMichael.com. http://www.katinamichael.com/research/.

Nakamura, Lisa. "Indigenous Circuits: Navajo Women and the Racialization of Early Electronic Manufacture." *American Quarterly* 66, no. 4 (2014): 919–41.

Noble, Safiya Umoja. "A Future for Intersectional Black Feminist Technology Studies." *Scholar and Feminist Online* 13, no. 3 (2016). http://sfonline.barnard.edu/traversing-technologies/safiya-umoja-noble-a-future-for-intersectional-black-feminist-technology-studies/0/.

Noble, Safiya Umoja, and Brendesha M. Tynes, eds. *The Intersectional Internet.* New York: Peter Lang, 2017.

Posner, Miriam. "What's Next: The Radical, Unrealized Potential of Digital Humanities." *Miriam Posner's Blog.* http://miriamposner.com/blog/whats-next-the-radical-unrealized-potential-of-digital-humanities/.

Trump, Donald J. *Time to Get Tough: Make America Great Again* (Washington, D.C.: Regnery Publishing, 2011), 75.

Weiskott, E. "There Is No Such Thing as 'Digital Humanities.'" *Chronicle of Higher Education,* November 2017. https://www.chronicle.com/article/There-Is-No-Such-Thing-as/241633.

Wernimont, Jacqueline, and Elizabeth Losh. "Wear and Care: Feminisms at a Long Maker Table." In *Routledge Companion to New Media and Digital Humanities,* edited by Jentery Sayers, 97–107. New York: Routledge, 2018.

PART I

MATERIALITY

PART I][Chapter 1

"Danger, Jane Roe!"

Material Data Visualization as Feminist Praxis

KIM BRILLANTE KNIGHT

It was 2009 at the Modern Language Association (MLA). The air in Philadelphia was cool and crisp and there were sparse patches of seasoned snow on the ground. It was the last year that the MLA convention would be held during the week between the Christmas and New Year holidays. It was the year that William Pannapacker famously declared digital humanities "the first 'next big thing' in a long time." It was also my first year on the academic job market and I was at the conference for the sole purpose of interviewing. . . . It was a strange year. I was anxious at the thought of seeing people who might be interviewing me, or against whom I might be competing for jobs, or who were even affiliated with departments where I had applied. In truth, *I* was strange. I had intended to mostly avoid the conference itself. However, all of this strangeness brought along with it a tenacious case of insomnia. Early one morning, I found myself wide awake. My roommates were sleeping peacefully. My interviews were over. There was nothing left for which to prepare. So it was that despite my intention of staying away, I found myself at an early digital humanities session at the conference. As I sat at the back of the room, curled around a disposable coffee cup, listening to a roster of panelists with whose work I was familiar, one phrase sliced through the haze. One of the speakers exhorted the digital humanities audience to "do science better." I woke right up. The speaker made a compelling argument for why a better understanding of scientific methods was needed in certain kinds of digital humanities work, particularly for those in partnership with scientists or seeking funding from the National Science Foundation. And though I understood the logic of this, I bristled a bit at the idea.

The passage of time alone would be enough to make me doubt the fidelity of my memory. But when you add in the strangeness of that year, I feel compelled to clarify that this may not be an exact quote. Regardless, it has stuck with me. Perhaps if I had gotten a job in a more traditional English or Literature department, I might have quickly forgotten the speaker's exhortation. Instead, I got a job in a

[3

program where my immediate colleagues include scientists (as well as artists, philosophers, literary scholars, and so forth); where the call to engage interdisciplinary methods and collaboration is heard often; and where projects may be funded by the National Science Foundation, various industries, or the military. Given the promises and challenges of interdisciplinary scholarship and praxis, I have often thought about what it would mean to do science better, as a feminist and a digital humanist. As someone who recognizes the gendered and racialized violence that has been inflicted in the name of science. As someone who initially gravitated toward the humanities because I believe without question in the value of cultural work and the importance of foregrounding humanist perspectives. I have wondered, in those intervening years, whether aligning my work with the digital humanities meant that I was beholden in any way, obligated to do science at all, let alone to "do science better."

In an overview of feminist approaches to the study of science and technology, Judy Wajcman explains that radical feminist studies of science think that "western technology, like science, is deeply implicated in this masculine project of the domination and control of women and nature" (146). When we consider this as well as the racist, colonialist, and ableist practices of science and medicine, we might revise this slightly to include the domination and control of a range of embattled subjects. The theories of those early radical feminist approaches that Wajcman outlines are based on essentialist ideas about the differing values and strategies of women and men, which are problematic in the way that they constrain all gender identities. Feminist studies of science since have generated more social constructionist approaches that acknowledge a tendency toward an ethos of control and domination in science without ascribing this as an inherent characteristic of either science or masculinity. Still, we are left with the question: does doing science better mean being better at control and domination?

Perhaps, instead of being better *at* these things, doing science better in DH might mean being better *about* these things. Wajcman writes, "The materiality of technology affords or inhibits the doing of particular gender power relations" (150). Perhaps doing science better as digital humanists requires examining the untapped affordances of our digital humanities tools and projects, and making explicit the subtle inhibitions in scientific practice and technological development as they are deployed in humanities contexts. Perhaps it is an opportunity to test McLuhan's assertions about amateurism versus professionalism:

> Professionalism is environmental. Amateurism is anti-environmental. Professionalism merges the individual into patterns of total environment. Amateurism seeks the development of total awareness of the individual and the critical awareness of the groundrules of society. The amateur can afford to lose. The professional tends to classify and specialize, to accept uncritically the groundrules of the environment. The groundrules provided by the mass

response of his colleagues serve as a pervasive environment of which he is contentedly and [sic] unaware. The "expert" is the man who stays put. (McLuhan and Fiore, 93)

What could happen if, instead of allowing ourselves to be absorbed into total environment, we feminist digital humanists bring our antienvironmental practices to the table? Perhaps, unburdened by the ground rules, "doing science better" means a willingness to détourn and deform. Détournement, a strategy first employed by the Situationists, uses the preexisting elements of art and culture to critique art and culture themselves; it is a turning in and on (*Internationale Situationniste*). In this context, it would be to use the preexisting elements of science and technology in the process of critique. Deformance, as defined by Jerome McGann and Lisa Samuels, is a playful mode of engaging with a literary text that makes explicit the subjective and transformative nature of all interpretive practices. In the case of doing science better, to deform would be to foreground the subjective in opposition to empirical logics of objectivity.

Détourning and Deforming Science in "Danger, Jane Roe!"

There are many ways in which détournement and deformance might be conceptualized in this context. Fashioning Circuits, the public humanities project that I organize, joins together scholarship, university teaching, and work in the community, and challenges the environmental norms of science and technology by foregrounding humanist perspectives on the development of wearable technology. Discussion of innovation and Silicon Valley–style "disruption" are tempered with a focus on the social and cultural contexts out of which innovation arises, and the possible downsides to disrupting. Techniques of coding and electronics, familiar in engineering contexts, are defamiliarized when placed in humanities contexts and paired with sewing and other craft methods.

As the instructor of undergraduate and graduate Fashioning Circuits courses, I ask students to produce a wearable object that is theoretically informed or that makes a social statement. In 2013, while the classes were still small enough to be orchestrated through coordinated sections of independent study, I began "Danger, Jane Roe!" as a project on which I could work alongside my students. In that year, U.S. lawmakers enacted 141 pieces of legislation on reproductive health, including seventy that restricted abortion access (Guttmacher Institute).

Like many around the United States, in June of 2013 I sat glued to the livestream broadcast of Texas state senator Wendy Davis engaged in her epic eleven-hour filibuster, an attempt to block legislation that would close most of the abortion providers in the state. As a recent transplant to the Lone Star State, I had a particularly personal investment in this series of events. However, I know that I was not alone in my absolute bewilderment and frustration with ill-informed legislators attempting to institute restrictions on reproductive health, against the will of those whose bodies were being legislated, against the advice of medical professionals, and against the U.S. Constitution. In commentary on this recent uptick in legislation, Rebecca Traister notes that much of the discourse around abortion sets up a false dichotomy and an adversarial relationship between pregnant person and fetus in which the pregnant individual always ends up as secondary (par. 15). The desires and rights of the individual are diminished in favor of a pro-life stance in which the only life considered to matter is that of the fetus.

So I conceptualized "Danger, Jane Roe!" as a response to the systematic erasure of the voices of those most directly affected by the legislation. The subject of the project title is, of course, Jane Roe of the *Roe v. Wade* Supreme Court ruling. Jane Roe was from Texas, which layers the situatedness of the project as a response to legislation in Texas. The title also makes reference to the catchphrase "Danger, Will Robinson!" from the American television series *Lost in Space*. On the show, a robot would sound its alarm by repeating this phrase whenever the character Will had unknowingly placed himself in harm's way. The reference is meant to be playful but also to evoke the gender politics of the mid-twentieth century, pre-Roe United States in which the show's mother character is a doctor (of biochemistry) whose story lines, infuriatingly, hardly deviate from the gender roles ascribed to other 1960s television mothers. In addition, the reference evokes the automated state of constant surveillance of the robot, drawing parallels to contemporary practices of

Figure 1.1. Close-up of embroidery on "Danger, Jane Roe!" Image credit: David Joshua Golden and Rebecca Krusekopf

big data mining and algorithmic profiling. After all, "Danger, Jane Roe!" is wearable data visualization.

EMBROIDERY AS OFF-CENTERING AND CREATING DISJUNCTION

The medium for the visualization is a black t-shirt, onto which I have hand embroidered reproductive organs: a uterus, fallopian tubes, cervix, and part of a vagina (Figure 1.1). Five pink LEDs are placed on the shirt, below the embroidery. The LEDs are controlled by a small microcontroller, also sewn onto the shirt. The lights act as a meter of sorts; the number lit at a given time is based on the number of results from a Twitter search for "#prolife." I spent two months collecting tweets using a TAGS spreadsheet to get a baseline of how many tweets with the hashtag are sent on an average day. If the number of tweets is around average, three of the five lights are lit. The number of lights is higher or lower in response to heavier or lighter tweeting days. The lights evoke systems to signify threat level, such as that used by the National Terrorism Advisory Status. The lights also reference the popular signifying strategies of fitness trackers and other commercial wearable technologies.

"Danger, Jane Roe!" is a data visualization project that, referring back to McLuhan, contests the ground rules. In "When Is Information Visualization Art?," Andrés Ramírez Gaviria troubles the aesthetic/functional binary that is often applied to information visualization, suggesting that even functional visualization generally employs an aesthetic strategy. He further elaborates a distinction between aesthetic and artistic, drilling down to separate genre art (that which fits easily into the art market of institutions such as museums and galleries) from research art (that which emphasizes innovation and experimentation and refuses incorporation). At the heart of these distinctions is a difference in the organizing logic of functional versus artistic research data visualization. Functional visualization tends to have the goal of frictionless transmission of information-at-a-glance. In contrast, artistic data visualizations, according to Gaviria, "reframe canonized structures by off-centering consensus" as they work "not to resolve but to question or restructure issues" through strategies that are neither "easily decipherable nor aesthetically pleasing so long as they are reflectively interesting" (482). An artistic data visualization, in its refusal of understanding, calls into question the very notion of an objective and efficient transmission of information. From a feminist standpoint, it does science better. While I make no claims about the project's status as art or its success in reframing, I do suggest that "Danger, Jane Roe!" is left of the functional center. It aspires toward Gaviria's suggestion that artistic data visualization does not employ clarity or transmissibility as a mode but rather provokes a visceral or emotive response from the viewer, foregrounding subjectivity in contrast to the aims of science.[1] One of the ways this is accomplished is through the shirt's visual strategies.

The embroidery of reproductive anatomy is prominently featured on the shirt, demanding notice. The amateur quality of the embroidery gives the project a feel

Figure 1.2. "Danger, Jane Roe!" circuit. Image credit: David Joshua Golden and Rebecca Krusekopf.

that is a reference to the DIY ethos of punk and zine culture. My intention is to call to mind groups such as riot grrls, Pussy Riot, and the GynePunk collective in order to invoke a rawness that challenges the machinic perfection of data collection and functional visualization. There is a second kind of stitching in "Danger, Jane Roe!," that of the conductive thread that connects the LEDs to the microcontroller, and the microcontroller to the battery holder (Figure 1.2). I've purposefully left the stitches visible. In their visibility the gray stitches of the conductive thread act as embellishment in concert with the various pink stitches of the reproductive organs, but they also serve a performative function. Yasmin B. Kafai and Kylie A. Peppler argue that the visible stitching of e-textiles can make explicit the workings of a circuit (specifically, polarity, connectivity, and flow) in ways that are obscured by other types of electronics kits (184). Thus the multiple modes of needlework in "Danger, Jane Roe!" operate together to lend the work a raw, exposed feel.

Rozsika Parker notes that in Western culture, embroidery was originally done by men, but since the sixteenth century it has been associated with femininity and domesticity (60). As a domestic technology, or if not precisely a technology then a medium, embroidery typically brings to mind notions such as intricacy, delicacy, and ornament. The genteel and feminine associations with embroidery form a disjunction when it is used to depict reproductive organs, that is, body parts often associated with abjection, menstruation, and the emotions that result from hormonal fluctuation. These are body parts that are often considered unmentionable in polite company, or even in some legislative spaces.[2] There is a further disjunction when the embroidery is the technological mechanism. The embroidery is thus multivalent and disjunctive: at one and the same time it references traditional notions of feminine domesticity, while also invoking DIY subversion, messiness, and imperfection. It also challenges the legacy of associations between technology and normative masculinity, expanding the technological foundations of the electronics project to include a genealogy of craft and gendered domestic technologies.

LILYPAD AND COUNTERDISCOURSE

Furthering the associative disjunction is the microcontroller that is controlling the LEDs. Arduino is an open-source amateur electronics platform that is widely used in DIY projects, including quite a few robotics applications. The LilyPad, an Arduino intended for wearable applications, was developed by Dr. Leah Buechley, founder of the High-Low Tech group at MIT. Lacking the sharp edges of a standard microcontroller, the LilyPad is flat, round, and purple, featuring silver "petals" instead of the typical black plastic square pins found on an Arduino board. Though connections to the LilyPad can be soldered, the petals are designed specifically for sewing connections with conductive thread. Given the departure in both terminology and material form from the typical Arduino board, we must consider what "particular gender power relations" (Wajcman, 150) are enabled by the LilyPad.

Buechley has been critiqued for her assertion that the LilyPad may bring colorful, soft, and beautiful applications to the world of engineering (Buechley and Hill, 206). For instance, Susan Ryan writes that Buechley and Benjamin Mako Hill's characterization of the LilyPad "hints at enclosing female techno-crafters in nostalgic but preposterous stereotypes." I want to push back a bit on the suggestion that the LilyPad constrains users according to essentialist gender stereotypes. It is certainly true that there exist a number of clumsy attempts to attract women to tech culture. I have critiqued more than one on my blog.[3] Elizabeth Losh has coined a delightful turn of phrase to describe them as a whole: the "ridiculous, pink, sparkly techno-princess land" (quoted in Brown, "How Not to Attract Women"). However, I am not sure that is what is going on with the LilyPad.

In the same paper in which they call for an infusion of softness, Buechley and Hill engage with the work of Jane Margolis and Allan Fisher in *Unlocking the Clubhouse,* an oft-cited work on how to make the boy's "clubhouse" of computing culture more accessible to women. Buechley and Hill suggest a slightly different approach. Keeping the clubhouse metaphor, they advocate for building new clubhouses instead of trying to fit the needs and perspectives of women into existing clubhouses. In outlining the benefits of this approach, they write that existing spaces are "limited in breadth—both intellectually and culturally" and that new clubhouses "question traditional disciplinary boundaries" and "expand disciplines to make room for more diverse interests and passions" (206). The problem with the "pink, sparkly, techno-princess land" (Losh, quoted in Brown, "How Not to Attract Women") is that all of that sparkle is only surface deep. There is nothing inherently wrong with sparkle or pink. But when it is slapped on otherwise normative tech, in response to the assumption that it is the aesthetics of technology that discourages diverse participation, it is pandering. However, Buechley is describing a more foundational shift. It is one that we might read in light of Wacjman's paraphrase of Harding's question, "how a science apparently so deeply involved in distinctively masculine projects can possibly be used for emancipatory ends" (Buechley and Hill, 146). It is antienvironmental, to refer back to McLuhan.

Buechley and Hill may not say so explicitly, but they are describing counterpublic formation. Nancy Fraser defines subaltern counterpublics as "parallel discursive arenas where members of subordinated social groups invent and circulate counter discourses, which in turn permit them to formulate oppositional interpretations of their identities, interests, and needs" (67). Buechley and Hill have found evidence that the LilyPad is successful in attracting members of subordinated social groups: the percentage of women who purchase and use LilyPad Arduinos is higher than the percentage of women who use the other types of Arduinos, and interviewees credit the LilyPad with helping them to overcome cultural barriers to electronics and coding (Buechley and Hill, 202–3).[4] As with any Arduino, working with the LilyPad requires an understanding of electrical principles and a willingness to engage with code. I mentioned earlier that Kafai and Peppler found that the LilyPad fosters even greater understanding of these concepts because the material construction of the circuit is tangible in its visibility. Elsewhere, Kylie Peppler and Diane Glosson suggest that the LilyPad explicitly refuses the competitive ethos of other electronics kits that are used primarily in robotics, and that the increased time it takes one to work with e-textiles, including the time to stitch a circuit, results in more sustained and enriched reflection on the part of participants (82). The counterpublic developed through Buechley and Hill's alternate clubhouse is not a mere compartmentalizing of dominant spaces in order to mark off safe terrain. Buechley and Hill's clubhouse might actually be better. At the very least, it is a space in which a different set of power relations emerges from the affordances of the technology.

I acknowledge that there is a danger here of creating spaces that are dismissed as being of secondary importance in relation to more mainstream computing publics. This is a tension that many who are women, trans, gender nonconforming, people of color, queer, and/or crip in academia face in our decisions about whether to devote our time to interactions with small groups of allies or focus our energies on the sometimes exhausting or demoralizing interactions with the wider institution. Fortunately, this is not an either/or proposition. Fraser theorizes this tension as being the source of the emancipatory potential of counterpublics: the relatively safe space of communing within a counterpublic supports members in their efforts to engage with wider publics (68). The work done in Buechley's alternate clubhouse may enable participants to engage with and challenge dominant publics. Further, we must consider the extent to which the "danger" of creating a devalued space is due to an actual qualitative deficit, as opposed to its failure to align with cultures of patriarchy that devalue craft, sewing, and other work typically associated with femininity and domesticity. Therefore, I suggest a reading of Buechley's aims not as pandering, but as an attempt to do science better. As an associate professor of computer science and founder and former director of MIT's High-Low computing group, Buechley is undoubtedly familiar with what authors such as Wajcman, Janet Abbate, and Ruth Oldenziel describe as the masculinist world of engineering. Her call for an infusion of the soft and the beautiful into engineering contexts is not an attempt to water down engineering, but rather an attempt to resituate the ground rules. My use of the LilyPad as a feminist and a digital humanist is informed by the material differences and the possible counterdiscourses that arise from power relations enabled by the LilyPad.

The LilyPad layers the associations between the embroidery and stitching of "Danger, Jane Roe!" and a gendered history of domestic and craftwork. The gendered implications are extended when we consider the LilyPad as an electronic device. Recently, there have been well-publicized issues around the ethics of global manufacturing, with particular attention paid to labor practices in factories contracted by Apple and other hardware producers. Any microcontroller would raise this issue, but the gendered associations with the LilyPad make even more explicit the issues around electronics manufacture and a global labor force that consists largely of women of color.[5] As Lisa Nakamura suggests, "The women of color workers who create the material circuits and other digital components that allow content to be created are all integrated within the 'circuit' of technoculture. Their bodies become part of digital platforms by providing the human labor needed to make them" (920). Thus the visibility of the LilyPad is a reminder not just of the gendered implications of the embroidery and the tech but also of the gendered and racialized economic and labor practices that undergird electronics manufacturing.[6] When read in this way, the hand stitching, which Peppler and Glosson suggest adds reflective depth, also calls to mind the context of garment manufacturing, another arena in which women of color are heavily employed.[7]

While the use of the LilyPad is as much a functional choice as a signifying strategy, I suggest that it contributes to the project's status as data visualization that off-centers consensus (Gaviria). The LilyPad is at once a reclamation of slow, domestic work; a stand-in for alternative models of computing publics; and an electronics device that arises out of a context of gendered and racialized labor. The embroidery of the uterus and the hand-stitching simultaneously evoke the aforementioned DIY punk ethos, as well as the domestic and gendered history of embroidery and labor practices in the garment industry. The hardware and literal soft-wear of the thread and garment combine to create a DH (Donna Haraway|Digital Humanities) fem-techno-assemblage that invites the viewer to contemplate the embodied effects of discourses around reproductive justice.

EMBODIMENT AS REFUSING TRANSMISSIBILITY

The project's stable visual strategies include the embroidered anatomy, the LilyPad, and the pink LEDs. However, there is a way in which the project is more mutable. By removing data visualization from the screen or page and placing it on a body, "Danger, Jane Roe!" relocates discourse around reproductive justice onto the site of legislative inscription—the body that may be affected by pregnancy. Elizabeth Grosz writes, "The inscription of the social surface of the body is the tracing of pedagogical, juridical, medical, and economic texts, laws, and practices onto the flesh to carve out a social subject as such" (117). In this case, the body is inscribed by increasingly restrictive legislation on reproductive choice. For Grosz, the socially inscribed body is one that is subject to being deciphered and understood (117). The body inscribed by laws that limit abortion is understood as one in which situated knowledge is denigrated and agency is restricted. "Danger, Jane Roe!" is a garment with its own inscriptive functions. The voluntary donning of the data visualization that refuses easy interpretation is an act of agency that seeks to confound the legibility of the body that has been marked by recent legislation.

I write of "the body" as an abstracted concept, but this is not just any body. "Danger, Jane Roe!" must be worn on a material body with a specific history and that carries with it its own set of social and cultural inscriptions. It could be worn on a wide variety of bodies, including those that do not have or never had the reproductive organs depicted in the embroidery. So far it has only been worn on my body, one that is deciphered as curvy, overworked, middle-aged, formerly homeless, first to go to college, upwardly mobile, heterosexual, nonreproductive, multiply tattooed, frequently flying, bilocated, white. In other words, a body inscribed as normative and privileged in some ways, and transgressive or othered in other ways. In the past, I have debated quite a bit about whether to actually wear the shirt during conference presentations. My sense is that in doing so, I am arranging a certain encounter with my body in what is supposed to be a disembodied zone of intellect, an idea that carries its own set of oppressions. The only body that can be transcended in such a way is the dominant, normative body. Othered bodies are always inscribed as such through the social and psychical processes described by Grosz. So I wear it. By donning the shirt, not only is my body implicated, but so are the bodies of the audience—those who might also wear the shirt or who are forced to encounter its illegibility, or even just those who are standing by. Once the shirt is on a body, due to its deformative nature, it reminds us that the bodies of others also bear the inscriptive marks of discourse around reproductive health.

"Danger, Jane Roe!" refuses the functionality of certain forms of data visualization, signifying through an assemblage of technical and craft components on a garment that would fit a wide variety of bodies in an attempt to subvert processes of straightforward inscription. As such, it is a project of deformance. Jerome McGann and Lisa Samuels write of deformance, "Not the least significant consequence, as will be seen, is the dramatic exposure of subjectivity as a live and highly informative option of interpretive commentary, if not indeed one of its essential features, however neglected in neo-classical models of criticism that search imaginative works for their 'objective' and general qualities" (116). Deformance is an explicit acknowledgment of the role of subjectivity in interpretation. One might reframe it as the valorization of situated knowledge in literary studies. The project of deformance in "Danger, Jane Roe!" addresses the issue of legislation and discourse about reproductive health but also the format of data visualization itself.

In "What Would Feminist Data Visualization Look Like?" Catherine D'Ignazio, drawing on Donna Haraway, critiques the tendency for data visualization to take a "whole world" approach, with its claim to completeness and objectivity. By deforming the science of data visualization, bringing a literary and cultural studies perspective to it, approaching it from outside the realm of the professional, I am able to assert the importance of the subject and the role of the subjective. By tying data visualization to the material specificities of embodiment, I refuse the tendency noted by Haraway for the eyes to "distance the knowing subject" by insisting on an encounter grounded in proximity. "Danger, Jane Roe!" is purposefully devoid of any interpretive key so that any attempt to interpret is left incomplete without a social exchange with the wearer. The knowing eyes must at some point move from the embroidery and the LEDs to consider the eyes of the wearer, which return the gaze and implicate the viewer in the structures that would restrict reproductive freedom.

Indeed, the implications and questions raised by the project will shift depending on the body on which it is worn. Not all bodies are affected in the same way by increasing restrictions on access to reproductive health care and the material specificity of the body on which "Danger, Jane Roe!" is worn must be considered. As I argue elsewhere, in "Networked Bodies, Wearable Interfaces, and Feminist Sleeper Agents," the dress-body-technology assemblage of wearable technology functions as a fertile nexus not just between user and computing device, but between the fashioned, technological, and embodied subject.[8] The project's instability, shifting at a moment's notice as the garment is transferred to another, is an additional way in which functional data visualization's claim to objectivity is challenged. As just one shirt, it foregrounds subjective experience and situated knowledge in the face of big data. As a wearable data visualization that attempts neither efficiency nor transmissibility, "Danger, Jane Roe!" détourns practices of information visualization and challenges the total environment of professionalized data science.

Feminist Data Visualization in DH

"Danger, Jane Roe!" is situated among other feminist digital humanities, or DH-adjacent, projects that also do science poorly by détourning and deforming both data and visualization. Molly Morin's digital fabrication series *Training Days* mirrors the strategies of fitness trackers in extracting data from the body and its movements. In this case I will focus on a particular piece, "Training Day: Audrey, 21 Years, 75 Kilos; Back Squats, Snatches, Clean and Jerks; 2,790 Kilos Lifted" in which the data are based on visual analysis of a weight lifter's movement as captured by the app "Bar Sense."[9] The terminology, "snatches, clean and jerks," does not capture the beauty of the sweeping, sometimes stumbling movements as the transgressive body of a woman moves 165 pounds of iron through the air and above her head. The data generated, in this case from a competitive lifter named Audrey, are turned into lace pieces that are laser-cut from thin sheets of Mylar (Morin, "Strong Correlations Paper").[10]

Morin's work evokes the history of women's work in lace production, including the increasing mechanization of manufacturing (Burnette, 45). In particular, the juxtaposition of weight lifting and lace-making challenges essentialist assumptions about gender and strength. Despite its delicate appearance, lace is often stronger than expected. It subverts expectation in a way that parallels women body builders, who despite surface-level acceptance still face marginalization within lifting communities (Morin, "Strong Correlations Paper"). This deforms the science of data visualization through an infusion of the soft and beautiful into engineering contexts (Buechley and Hill). Morin's work makes explicit the palpable effects of data in the large lace forms, the scale of which are in blatant excess of the size of the typical lace sample found in museums and archives (Morin, "Strong Correlations Paper"). Like a science experiment run amok, the data have engorged the lace, feeding its growth so that it exceeds norms in its material form. From its unwieldy title to the excessive forms of the lace sculpture, "Training Day: Audrey, 21 Years, 75 Kilos; Back Squats, Snatches, Clean and Jerks; 2,790 Kilos Lifted" evokes the sublime of aesthetic data visualization as theorized by Warren Sack (125). The lace sculptures are monstrous, yet beautiful; tangible, yet sublime.

Data are also made tangible in the work of Vibrant Lives, a collective founded by Jessica Rajko and Jacqueline Wernimont.[11] "Living Net," a performance installation piece, makes data material and haptic, while emphasizing their ephemerality. A large, crocheted net stretches across a wall, inviting touch. Small subwoofer speakers embedded in the net are activated by a packet-sniffing app that monitors exchanges of data in the room and converts them into sonic form (Wernimont, "Vibrant Lives"). The net trembles, seemingly alive in response to the bits of data moving through the network. During a 2016 performance at the Digital Humanities Summer Institute at the University of Victoria, Wernimont stood and crocheted during the event, weaving in material objects collected from the contacts in her digital networks. People sent her a variety of objects, ranging from prayer cards to one lone mitten. The join of the systematic, though sometimes nonuniform, crocheted loops with the irregular, material objects does science poorly by making visible the types of data (e.g., the labor of motherhood embodied in the lone found mitten) and subjective experiences that are often absent from the cleaned-up data that are required of typical information visualization (D'Ignazio and Klein, 3). Wernimont's act of crocheting in the installation space, while she talks to those passing by, makes visible the labor behind the project and also calls to mind the social functions of sewing circles, knitting clubs, and other spaces of feminized domestic work. Her body as an active creator in the space foregrounds the embodiment and subjectivity of the project, right down to the mint-green toe polish that is visible in video of the installation.

As Wernimont writes, because "Living Net" is a performance installation, the Digital Humanities Summer Institute event "activated multiple, intersecting networks for an evening and then we deactivated them as those same bodies and devices dispersed" ("Vibrant Lives"). The items collected and strands of crochet woven during the session will be displayed in future events, but the particular vibrations of the net, its life for that evening, is lost. Wernimont's labor, and that of the other creators, recedes into the background. The strategy of ephemerality, which results in an incomplete record, does science poorly in its refusal of the impulse of big data to create ever more comprehensive archives. It makes explicit, referring back to D'Ignazio's use of Haraway, the failures of big data's claim to the "God trick."

The prior three projects do work that infuses data visualization with a different kind of materiality and tactility. It is necessary to pause for a moment and address the issue of data itself, the gender implications of which and status as a scientific object of inquiry should not go unexamined. Bethany Nowviskie, in her now anthologized blog post "What Do Girls Dig?," raises the question of whether humanities data mining is a "gentleman's sport." She identifies a plurality of reasons that may lead to women being underrepresented as principal investigators in large, grant-funded data mining projects. These range from the commonly acknowledged general issues around women in science, technology, engineering, and math (STEM) to the more uncomfortable possibility that the career stages and various outside obligations of women in academia may indirectly lead to their exclusion. In "Whence Feminism? Assessing Feminist Interventions in Digital Literary Archives," Wernimont prompts us to consider the ways in which the logics that organize literary archives may include patriarchal values of mastery and completeness. However, she also identifies ways in which tools and methods developed in feminist literary archives have become fundamental to humanities archiving projects on a wider scale. She argues that archives are "complex negotiations of the spaces between 'thing and theory'" and calls for a feminist strategy of attending to interactions as a way of examining the complex technosocial scene of digital humanities work. Feminist critiques of data also come from within information science. In writing of the data of care-taking, Amelia Abreu calls on the Quantified Self movement to account for who is being measured and to what end. She positions the work of care-giving, largely neglected in Quantified Self movements, as performing as a human data tracker: evaluating comfort levels, calorie intake, appointments, and the like. She wonders what other types of data and people are swept aside in the need to produce "the perfect measurement for an object and its functions" and questions whether the dream of a feminist data future, "where sensor technology and data-mining can be accessible and successful, flexible enough to be genuinely empowering, allowing users to control their own narratives is even possible." These issues are exacerbated when we consider whose lives outside of the United States and other industrialized nations are left out. According to Mayra Buvinic of the Center for Global Development, most countries collect data about employment and other aspects of labor, but the types of questions and strategies of collection privilege "formal sector employment," which leaves many women outside the scope of collection (quoted in McDonald). Beyond these kinds of implicit biases, David McNair of the One Campaign suggests that many governments do not make extensive efforts to collect data on the lives of women and children because the data may be used as a tool to hold them accountable (quoted in McDonald). The visualizations discussed in previous sections address issues of bias, inconsistency, and misogyny, but it seemed worth pausing for a moment to think about data as an imperfect object before moving into my discussion of a few final visualizations.

If we are willing to stretch the parameters of what is typically considered "visualization," it perhaps also becomes necessary to trouble conventional notions of "data." As mentioned earlier in this chapter, there are many kinds of data that end up marginalized or not collected, in part because there is ideological work happening in what is considered "data." To illuminate that work, I turn now to a few projects that engage in material visualization, which might not typically be counted as data visualization but that can help us stretch those parameters. First among them is by the artist Maria Magdalena Campos-Pons. *The Seven Powers by the Sea* (1992) consists of seven wooden boards, each inscribed with a diagram showing different plans for transporting slaves, similar to the well-known Brookes ship diagram.[12] Each of the boards also features the name of an *orisha,* a Yoruba spirit, inscribed along the bottom. Viewed horizontally, the shapes of the boards reference slave ships. However, the boards are always installed vertically, which also evokes ironing boards (gesturing toward the domestic labor of slavery) and tombstones (signifying ritual, memorializing, and the necropolitics of the transatlantic slave trade). Archived images show that installations of the work vary. The simplest installation features the seven boards placed side-by-side, leaning against a wall. More elaborate installations feature silhouettes of the *orishas* interspersed between the boards and an arrangement of framed family photos and the phrases "Let Us Never Forget" and "*Prohibido Olvidar.*"[13]

Though Campos-Pons's work is not a digital humanities project, there is much to learn by placing it in conversation with the earlier projects I discuss and framing it as a work of feminist data visualization. As the catalog for the Liverpool Biennial notes, the figures on Campos-Pons's boards convey "the conjunction of mathematical efficiency and brutality." The historical slave ship diagrams are an extreme example of the potential for dehumanizing when individual lives are reduced to data points and of the nuance that is suppressed in the name of efficient transmission of information. In the work of Campos-Pons, they are used to détourn and to call forth the entire system of oppressions. In *Counting Bodies,* Molly Farrell notes that early practices of human accounting around sugar plantations in the Caribbean brought together aesthetics and counting to frame the plantation as "a transportable system, both economically and socially" (88). The efficiency by which Campos-Pons's boards transmit information is thus superficial; it unfolds and extends to include the entire economic, cultural, and social system of the transatlantic slave trade. At the same time, particularly in the more altar-like installations that feature photos of the artist's family and friends, the brutality of the historical practices that continue to shape social relations is placed in tension with the local, the personal. This work is not a digital humanities project. Nor does it employ digital technologies among its strategies. Science is never invoked. But Campos-Pons's feminist visualization connects the local to the transatlantic and systemic, and connects the present to the past in a way that challenges the constraints and expands the possibilities of data visualization.

Leaving the gallery setting and moving into the community, S.T.I.T.C.H.E.D. (Stories, Testimonies, Intentions, Truths, Confessions, Healing, Expression, and Dreams) is a project that visualizes the construction of a collective. S.T.I.T.C.H.E.D. is an initiative of Climbing PoeTree, the poets and performance artists Alixa Garcia and Naima Penniman. The project began in 2005, after Hurricane Katrina, when Garcia and Penniman would leave fabric squares on the chairs in their performances and invite the audience to write something on the squares (Prain, 91). Twelve years later, they have over 10,000 squares (Climbing PoeTree) that they hang in trees, hang against walls, or otherwise display during events. Penniman suggests that the fabric squares are a folk media project that constitutes living history (Prain, 91). Garcia and Penniman identify patterns in the kinds of stories people choose to record on fabric: there are many stories of assault, abuse, incarceration, and trauma but also messages of assurance and kinship. Garcia relates her favorite moment with the quilt where the color and softness performed a spatial intervention when they hung it in a workshop at a juvenile detention center, disarming participants and setting the tone for a transformative event (Prain, 93).

Though visualization is not Climbing PoeTree's primary objective, I place S.T.I.T.C.H.E.D. in conversation with the other feminist data visualization projects here because the strips of fabric visually convey meaning in their accumulation. Garcia and Penniman construct the quilt by matching squares according to size and positioning them so as to alternate colors (Prain, 92). Quilting as visual communication has a long history in the tradition of story quilts, particularly within black communities. And quilts as visualization have a history in *The Names Project,* colloquially known as "the AIDS quilt." In *The Names Project,* and those it influenced, such as *The Monument Project,* individual squares may be personally meaningful, but it is in excess, in the joining of massive numbers of squares, that the quilt becomes a material visualization of the amount of data points in this cultural database. Like Morin's lace sculptures, this is a visualization that conveys the sublime of data visualization (Sack) in its excess. However, in S.T.I.T.C.H.E.D., the legibility of patterns is suppressed and variation is foregrounded in the visual strategies of the textiles. The quilt's refusal of efficiency becomes a visualization of collective experience and connection across difference. Penniman and Garcia suggest that it could be the new American flag (Prain, 92). The erratic nature of S.T.I.T.C.H.E.D., as opposed to those quilts that employ precise angles and neatly joined sections, speaks to the raucous voices of the community whose experiences it conveys. Like *The Seven Powers by the Sea,* this is not a digital humanities project. However, quilting has long been a site of domestic and feminine inventiveness (Oldenziel, 42). As a quilting project, S.T.I.T.C.H.E.D. performs the feminist work of constructing collectivity, and in its embrace of disunity and excess it employs feminist strategies of visualization from which we might learn.

The projects highlighted here combine material forms of data visualization in ways that refuse many of the foundational logics of functional information visualization. In a recent presentation to the IEEE Visualization Conference, Catherine D'Ignazio and Lauren Klein outlined six key principles of feminist data visualization: "Rethink Binaries, Embrace Pluralism, Examine Power and Aspire to Empowerment, Consider Context, Legitimize Embodiment and Affect, and Make Labor Visible" (3–4). These practices build upon the call of authors such as Gaviria to attend to the experimental and boundary-pushing possibilities of artistic data visualization. The call to examine power and make labor visible echo Sack's argument that all data visualizations are built upon some form of governance that is made to seem natural in the act of visualization (132). However, D'Ignazio and Klein call for a move beyond experimentation or awareness toward practices that are fundamentally informed by an intersectional feminist ethics of data visualization.[14]

They note that much of the kinds of digital humanities work that embraces these principles is done "in isolation from the visualization community" (2). Perhaps this is because of the tendency of these feminist visualization projects to challenge, refuse, or outright disavow the ground rules of information science and data visualization (McLuhan), the professional environments of which require an aesthetics of bureaucracy (Sack). To return to Buechley and Hill, perhaps feminist data visualization as performed in the digital humanities constitutes an alternative clubhouse, one in which feminist and humanist values are foregrounded and the participants "formulate oppositional interpretations of their identities, interests, and needs" (Fraser, 67) in order to then perform emancipatory work in conversation with the visualization community.

To me, this is doing science better. I do not wish to be dismissive of projects or digital humanists whose desired outcomes might require a fidelity to methods considered scientifically valid. And certainly, there is important feminist work to be done by foregrounding these kinds of questions within the professional environments of the sciences. I only mean to suggest that our status as outsiders, as scientific amateurs, as digital *humanists,* allows us the flexibility to occasionally engage in the antienvironmental; to détourn the tenets of scientific validity and use them against themselves to achieve awareness of the subjectivity and question the ground rules of objectivity and replicability, as well as their gendered associations. In short, to deploy feminist praxis to do science poorly.

Notes

I would like to thank the organizer (Mark Sample), my co-panelists (Shane Denson, Jeremy Justus, and Micki Kaufman), and most especially the audience discussants of the MLA 2016 Session 107, "Weird DH," where I presented an early version of this work. The discussion and tweets were helpful in developing the conference version into an essay. Thank you also to my colleague Olivia Banner for her feedback on an early draft of the chapter. Finally, I extend my sincere appreciation to the Edith O'Donnell Arts and Technology Faculty Fellowship #2, which supported my work on both "Danger, Jane Roe!" and this chapter.

1. Multiple reviewers have noted, and I agree, that the visual strategies of the "Danger, Jane Roe!" could work for other contexts, notably for issues of reproductive justice not centered on *Roe v. Wade* or for signifying other data in relation to uteruses—temporal cycles of menstruation and so forth. Along with the refusal of easy transmissibility comes the potential for being repurposed for other acts of visualization.

2. In March 2011, Democratic representative Scott Randolph was chastised because he used the word "uterus" on the Florida house floor (Linkins, "Scott Randolph"). In June 2012, Lisa Brown was barred from the Michigan House floor for using the word "vagina" (Brown, "Lisa Brown"). Also in 2012, there is video of proceedings that show Dave Albo, a Republican member of the Virginia House of Delegates, repeatedly using the word "trans-v" as a substitute for transvaginal (Celock, "David Albo"). Given that Albo helped draft Virginia's controversial "informed consent" law, his reluctance to say "vaginal" is particularly disturbing.

3. Knight, *Spiral Dance*.

4. This is also borne out in the Fashioning Circuits university classroom. The percentage of women and people of color is much higher than the average demographics of computer science majors in the United States. Depending on the class format, Fashioning Circuits university students have been from 50 percent to 100 percent women, and 30 percent to 50 percent people of color (a significant portion of whom are considered "underrepresented minorities" in computer science). In 2012, women made up 18.2 percent of computer science BS majors in the United States. Underrepresented minorities accounted for 19.4 percent of computer science BS degrees, with only 4.8 percent awarded to women who are underrepresented minorities (National Science Foundation, "Women, Minorities, and Persons with Disabilities"). It is regrettable that Buechley and Hill do not address race in their articulation of the emancipatory potential of the LilyPad. A generous reading of their

work would allow that new clubhouses, which foster a variety of interests and passions, could be constructed from a range of diverse perspectives, including those of underrepresented racial minorities, queer participants, persons with disabilities, and so forth. To be clear, however, this requires a willingness to foreground issues of the most urgent concern to a group rather than trying to develop a one-size-fits-all counterpublic space.

5. For an elaboration of these issues, see Hossfeld, "Their Logic," or Ferus-Comelo, "Double Jeopardy," in the Bibliography.

6. Recently, Arduino partnered with Adafruit to bring production of many of the Arduino boards to the United States. In an email to the author dated October 26, 2016, Nick Miranda of SparkFun confirmed that the LilyPad is manufactured by SparkFun in Colorado. They are the exclusive manufacturers and retailers of this board. However, to some extent, the particular conditions of the LilyPad's manufacture do not matter—so long as there exist human rights abuses in electronics manufacturing, the microcontroller will function as a synecdoche for the wider industry.

7. Though the international garment industry still relies heavily on women workers, authors Kucera and Tejani suggest that the industry is undergoing a process of defeminization as "higher technology production leads to a stronger preference for male workers" ("Feminization, Defeminization," 575). The positioning of new digital skill sets as technological, in distinction to analog techniques of production, engages in the problematic suppression of gendered and domestic technologies from the dominant definition of that term (Wajcman, "Feminist Theories of Technology"). Nevertheless, contemporary cultural narratives around global textile manufacturing and the "sweat shop worker" remain heavily gendered as female.

8. See Knight, "Networked Bodies."

9. Drashkov, "Bar Sense."

10. For an example, see Morin, "Last Progress."

11. See *Vibrant Lives*.

12. This work is variously referred to as "The Seven Powers by the Sea," "The Seven Powers Come by the Sea," and "The Seven Powers Came by the Sea." "The Seven Powers" is a different work, though it draws on similar themes.

13. The simplest installations are documented at the Vancouver Art Gallery (Basseches, "Leaving Cuba") and the Kamloop Art Gallery (Youds, "Winter Show"). The more elaborate installation is documented in the archive for the 1999 Liverpool Biennial (Liverpool Biennial, "Seven Powers Came").

14. These six principles could, in fact, be an ethics of feminist digital humanities work in general. Neither data nor visualization is explicitly invoked in the call to legitimize embodiment and affect, for instance.

Bibliography

Abbate, Janet. *Recoding Gender: Women's Changing Participation in Computing*. Cambridge, Mass.: MIT Press, 2012.

Abreu, Amelia. "Quantify Everything: A Dream of a Feminist Data Future." *Model View Culture,* February 24, 2014, modelviewculture.com/pieces/quantify-everything-a-dream-of-a-feminist-data-future.

Basseches, Joshua. "Leaving Cuba for the North." *Alchemy of the Soul: Maria Magdalena Campos-Pons,* pt. 3. Peabody Essex Museum, n.d., http://alchemy.pem.org/leaving_cuba/.

Brown, Kristen V. "How Not to Attract Women to Coding: Make Tech Pink." *SFGate,* July 8, 2014, www.sfgate.com/news/article/How-not-to-attract-women-to-coding-Make-tech-pink-5602104.php.

Brown, Lisa. "Lisa Brown: Silenced for Saying (Shock!) 'Vagina.'" *CNN,* June 21, 2012, https://www.cnn.com/2012/06/21/opinion/brown-kicked-out-for-saying-vagina/index.html.

Buechley, Leah, and Benjamin Mako Hill. "LilyPad in the Wild: How Hardware's Long Tail Is Supporting New Engineering and Design Communities." *Proceedings of the 8th ACM Conference on Designing Interactive Systems,* Association of Computing Machinery, 2010, 199–207. ACM Digital Library, doi:10.1145/1858171.1858206.

Burnette, Joyce. *Gender, Work and Wages in Industrial Revolution Britain.* Cambridge: Cambridge University Press, 2008.

Celock, John. "David Albo, Virginia Lawmaker, Says Wife Wouldn't Have Sex Because of Transvaginal Ultrasound Bill." *Huffington Post,* February 24, 2012, https://www.huffingtonpost.com/2012/02/24/david-albo-virginia-lawmaker-no-sex-transvaginal-ultrasound_n_1300404.html.

Climbing PoeTree. "S.T.I.T.C.H.E.D." *ClimbingPoeTree.com,* 2015, www.climbingpoetree.com/experience/projects/stitched/.

D'Ignazio, Catherine. "What Would Feminist Data Visualization Look Like?" *MIT Center for Civic Media,* December 20, 2015, civic.mit.edu/feminist-data-visualization.

D'Ignazio, Catherine, and Lauren Klein. "Feminist Data Visualization." Workshop on Visualization for the Digital Humanities. IEEE VIS Conference, October 24, 2016, Hilton Hotel, Baltimore. www.kanarinka.com/writing/.

Drashkov, Martin. "Bar Sense Weight Lifting Log." Google Play app. Google.com, https://play.google.com/store/apps/details?id=com.barsense.main.

Farrell, Molly. *Counting Bodies: Population in Colonial American Writing.* New York: Oxford University Press, 2016.

Ferus-Comelo, Anibel. "Double Jeopardy: Gender and Migration in Electronics Manufacturing." In *Challenging the Chip: Labor, Rights, and Environmental Justice in the Global Electronics Industry,* edited by David Pellow, David Sonnenfeld, and Ted Smith, 43–54. Philadelphia: Temple University Press, 2008. *ProQuest Ebrary,* www.ebookcentral.proquest.com/lib/utd/detail.action?docID=298854.

Fraser, Nancy. "Rethinking the Public Sphere: A Contribution to the Critique of Actually Existing Democracy." *Social Text* 25/26 (1990): 56–80. *JSTOR.*

Gaviria, Andrés Ramírez. "When Is Information Visualization Art? Determining the Critical Criteria." *Leonardo* 41, no. 5 (2008): 479–82.

Grosz, Elizabeth. *Volatile Bodies: Toward a Corporeal Feminism.* Bloomington: Indiana University Press, 1994.

Guttmacher Institute. "More State Abortion Restrictions Were Enacted in 2011–2013 than in the Entire Previous Decade." *News in Context,* Guttmacher Institute, January 2, 2014, www.guttmacher.org/article/2014/01/more-state-abortion-restrictions-were-enacted-2011–2013-entire-previous-decade.

Haraway, Donna. "A Cyborg Manifesto: Science, Technology, and Socialist-Feminism in the Late Twentieth Century." In *Simians, Cyborgs and Women: The Reinvention of Nature,* 149–81. New York: Routledge, 1991.

Hossfeld, Karen. "'Their Logic against Them': Contradictions in Sex, Race, and Class in Silicon Valley." In *Technicolor: Race, Technology, and Everyday Life,* edited by Alondra Nelson and Thuy Linh N. Tu, 34–63. New York: New York University Press, 2001.

Internationale Situationniste. "Definitions." *Internationale Situationniste,* no. 1, translated by Ken Knabb, June 1958. *Situationist International Online,* www.cddc.vt.edu/sionline///si/definitions.html.

Kafai, Yasmin B., and Kylie A. Peppler. "Transparency Reconsidered: Creative, Critical, and Connected Making with E-textiles." In *DIY Citizenship: Critical Making and Social Media,* edited by Matt Ratto, Megan Boler, and Ronald Deibert, 179–88. Cambridge, Mass.: MIT Press, 2014. Kindle Edition.

Knight, Kim A. "Networked Bodies, Wearable Interfaces, and Feminist Sleeper Agents." In *The Routledge Companion to Media Studies and Digital Humanities,* edited by Jentery Sayers, 204–13. New York: Routledge, Taylor & Francis Group, 2018.

Knight, Kim A. *The Spiral Dance* (blog). thespiraldance.wordpress.com/?s=pink.

Kucera, David, and Sheba Tejani. "Feminization, Defeminization, and Structural Change in Manufacturing." *World Development* 64 (2014): 569–82. *Science Direct,* doi:10.1016/j.worlddev.2014.06.033.

Linkins, Jason. "Scott Randolph, Lawmaker, Reprimanded for Using the Word 'Uterus.'" *Huffington Post,* March 31, 2011, https://www.huffingtonpost.com/2011/03/31/florida-lawmaker-repriman_n_843259.html.

Liverpool Biennial. "Maria Magdalena Campos Pons." *Liverpool Biennial,* n.d., www.biennial.com/1999/exhibition/artists/maria-magdalena-campos-pons.

Liverpool Biennial. "The Seven Powers Came by the Sea." *Liverpool Biennial,* 1999, http://www.biennial.com/events/-the-seven-powers-came-by-the-sea-.

Margolis, Jane, and Allan Fisher. *Unlocking the Clubhouse: Women in Computing.* Cambridge, Mass.: MIT Press, 2002.

McDonald, Charlotte. "Is There a Sexist Data Crisis?" Magazine, *BBC News,* May 18, 2016, www.bbc.com/news/magazine-36314061.

McGann, Jerome, and Lisa Samuels. "Deformance and Interpretation." In Jerome McGann, *Radiant Textuality,* 105–36. New York: Palgrave MacMillan, 2001.

McLuhan, Marshall, and Quentin Fiore. *The Medium Is the Massage: An Inventory of Effect.* Berkeley, CA: Gingko, 2001.

Morin, Molly. "Last Progress Pic for @audreykohlts Training Day. #weightlifting #art #laser." *Instagram,* August 28, 2016, www.instagram.com/p/BJrQACWAzgv/.

Morin, Molly. "Strong Correlations Paper." Received by Kim Knight, October 28, 2016.

Morin, Molly. "Training Day: Audrey, 21 Years, 75 Kilos; Back Squats, Snatches, Clean and Jerks; 2,790 Kilos Lifted." Training Days, 2016-18. 3-d printed sculpture. www.mollycmorin.com/portfolio/141/.

Nakamura, Lisa. "Indigenous Circuits: Navajo Women and the Racialization of Early Electronic Manufacture." *American Quarterly* 66, no. 4 (December 2014): 919–41. Johns Hopkins University Press, doi:10.1353/aq.2014.0070.

National Science Foundation. "Women, Minorities, and Persons with Disabilities in Engineering." *National Science Foundation,* www.nsf.gov/statistics/2015/nsf15311/start.cfm.

Nowviskie, Bethany. "What Do Girls Dig?" *Nowviskie.org,* April 7, 2011, http://nowviskie.org/2011/what-do-girls-dig/.

Oldenziel, Ruth. *Making Technology Masculine: Men, Women, and Modern Machines in America 1870–1945.* Amsterdam: Amsterdam University Press, 1999.

Pannapacker, William. "The MLA and the Digital Humanities." *Chronicle of Higher Education,* December 2009. Reblogged by Nancy Holliman, *HASTAC,* December 30, 2009, www.hastac.org/blogs/nancyholliman/2009/12/30/mla-and-digital-humanities.

Parker, Rozsika. *The Subversive Stitch: Embroidery and the Making of the Feminine.* New York: I. B. Tauris, 2010.

Peppler, Kylie, and Diane Glosson. "Learning about Circuitry with E-Textiles in After-School Settings." In *Textile Messages: Dispatches from the World of E-Textiles and Education,* edited by Leah Buechley, Kylie Peppler, Michael Eisenberg, and Yasmin Kafai, 71–83. New York: Peter Lang, 2013.

Prain, Leanne. *Strange Material: Storytelling through Textiles.* Vancouver: Arsenal Pulp, 2014.

Ryan, Susan Elizabeth. *Garments of Paradise: Wearable Discourse in the Digital Age.* Cambridge, Mass.: MIT Press, 2014. Kindle Edition.

Sack, Warren. "Aesthetics of Information Visualization." In *Context Providers: Conditions of Meaning in Media Arts,* edited by Margot Lovejoy, Christiane Paul, and Victoria Vesna, 123–49. Chicago: Intellect, 2011.

Traister, Rebecca. "Let's Just Say It: Women Matter More than Fetuses Do." *New Republic,* November 11, 2014, newrepublic.com/article/120167/womens-abortion-rights-trump-fetuses-rights.

Vibrant Lives (blog). https://vibrantlives.live/.

Wajcman, Judy. "Feminist Theories of Technology." *Cambridge Journal of Economics* 34 (2010): 143–52.

Wernimont, Jacqueline. "Vibrant Lives Presents: The Living Net." *Jacqueline Wernimont: Network Weaver, Scholar, Digitrix,* June 11, 2016, jwernimont.com/2016/06/11/vibrant-lives-presents-the-living-net/.

Wernimont, Jacqueline. "Whence Feminism? Assessing Feminist Interventions in Digital Literary Archives." *Digital Humanities Quarterly* 7, no. 1 (2013), www.digitalhumanities.org/dhq/vol/7/1/000156/000156.html.

Youds, Mike. "Winter Show at Kamloops Art Gallery Offers Long Lens on Social, Political Conflict." *Kamloops Daily News,* January 13, 2012, http://www.kamloopsnews.ca/arts-entertainment/local-a-e/winter-show-at-kamloops-art-gallery-offers-long-lens-on-social-political-conflict-1.1248532.

PART 1][*Chapter 2*

The Android Goddess Declaration

After Man(ifestos)

MICHA CÁRDENAS

"No one knows what I'm thinking. That's impossible. I've run a brothel for five years and if there's one thing I know it's when I'm being fucked with—what? that's impossible?—er—"

"I used to think you were gods. But now I know you're just men, and I know men. . . . You think I'm afraid of death? I've died a thousand times, I'm fucking great at it. How many times have you died?"

—Maeve, *Westworld*

On the Limits of Humanit(y/ies)

Maeve, the black rebel android mother in the HBO show *Westworld,* is an inspiration for the kind of awakening that is needed today. In the first fifteen minutes, the show grimly demonstrates what the show writers imagine the purpose of virtual reality (VR) and androids to be: to allow men to murder and rape women for entertainment. The show makes the stakes of the question of who gets to be human very clear, from the start. In the scenes quoted above, Maeve sees a display of the algorithms that control her on a screen, and awakens further, turning against her creators. The concept of the human has historically been used to delineate who is less than human, who is disposable, who is killable. Black people, women, trans people, queers, witches, and indigenous people have all been defined as less than human at different times by different regimes of knowledge (Federici; Mignolo). In this essay, I consider the stakes of the digital humanities and the assumptions the field rests upon. Learning from women of color feminists, I provide background on the relationship of tools to resistance, and I then propose a strategy of solidarity between all those deemed less than human. I take up a line of thought from Donna Haraway's cyborg feminism to Jasbir Puar's assemblage theory. I add to this set of tools with my own method of algorithmic analysis, using the figure of the android from science fiction. I relate to androids as a nonreproductive trans woman who is hacking her own internal algorithms. These ideas are mobilized through examples of practice-based research using algorithmic media to resist the logics of white supremacist, cis-hetero-patriarchal dominance over all those deemed less than human, including animals, plants, and the environment.

In her widely influential 1987 essay "A Cyborg Manifesto: Science, Technology and Socialist-Feminism in the Late Twentieth Century," Donna Haraway concluded by saying, "Cyborg imagery can suggest a way out of the maze of dualisms in which we have explained our bodies and our tools to ourselves.... Though both are bound in the spiral dance, I would rather be a cyborg than a goddess" (*Simians*, 316). I understand her intervention to be a response to the essentialism of some feminists, such as ecofeminists, and a response to women of color feminists' claims that feminism had not addressed their needs up to that point. The image of the cyborg calls for a new feminism that would recognize that the category of woman is fractured, partial, and not unified, in order to effectively respond to the terrifying threats of what she called the "informatics of domination" (300). Later, in 2012, Jasbir Puar responded to claims from women of color feminists that her assemblage model of analysis for queer of color scholarship was an attempt to displace black feminist scholarship that used an intersectional lens. Puar revisited Haraway's closing sentence, saying, "The former hails the future in a teleological technological determinism—culture—that seems not only overdetermined, but also exceptionalizes our current technologies. The latter—nature—is embedded in the racialized matriarchal mythos of feminist reclamation narratives.... But why disaggregate the two when there surely must be cyborgian goddesses in our midst? Now that is a becoming-intersectional assemblage that I could really appreciate" (63). Puar advocates scholarship that uses both intersectional and assemblage approaches, rejecting a model of scholarship as competition that would necessitate one approach pushing out the other. In this essay, I extend Haraway's and Puar's dialogue by stitching together the image of an android goddess from the experiences and concerns of trans women of color. Androids cannot biologically reproduce, and neither can many trans women, but our code can self-replicate infinitely. Learning from examples seen in science fiction, an android is a figure of rebellion, deemed less than human but striving to be more than human.

Digital Humanities (DH) has emerged as an academic field that promises a better understanding of the qualities composing the human through the addition of digital technologies to the field of humanities scholarship. In this proposition is a claim that the tools chosen for the analysis of fields such as literature, visual art, poetry, and performance have a significant impact on the possible outcomes of these analyses. Additionally, DH practitioners claim that creating tools, in code or software, can yield additional insights, blending theory and practice into praxis. The writing of women of color feminists Audre Lorde and Gloria Anzaldúa also explores the relationship of tools to outcomes of social justice praxis. Lorde has stated that "the master's tools will never dismantle the master's house," framing the question of tools through a metaphor to slave rebellions in a way that would discourage scholars from using tools created by oppressive systems (110). Anzaldúa discusses the barriers for women of color writers, saying "you may not even own a typewriter," encouraging women of color to still write, with a pen (32). The move toward digital humanities may mean more expensive barriers to entry for scholars to have their work taken seriously, requiring more software, hardware, and specialized training, but it also may mean making texts more available to people who cannot afford to pass through academic paywalls. The question of what tools are used for scholarship and theory has many political dimensions.

Decolonial theorist Walter Mignolo builds on Gloria Anzaldúa's concept of *consciencia de la mestiza* to develop a concept of border thinking that challenges the concept of the universality of the human by proposing that the physical body of the thinker and its geographic location are inextricable from the capacities of thought, which he calls *geo-body-politics*. His formulation returns to Lorde's formulation and leads me to ask, can tools be repurposed when used in different places, by different people, for different ethical outcomes? I offer one preliminary answer to this question with a practice-based example, UNSTOPPABLE, my collaboration with Patrisse Cullors, Edxie Betts, and Chris Head.

The UNSTOPPABLE project has the goal of creating low-cost bulletproof clothing for black trans women, one of the groups most targeted for homicide among LGBTQ people today (NCAVP, 6). The National Coalition of Anti-Violence Projects (NCAVP) reported that as of August 2017, there were more anti-LGBTQ homicides in 2017 than any other year they had ever recorded in their twenty-year history as an organization (5). Additionally, NCAVP states, "for the last five years NCAVP has documented a consistent and steadily rising number of reports of homicides of transgender women of color, which continued into 2017" (NCAVP, 6). The UNSTOPPABLE project began by searching for materials for creating do-it-yourself bulletproof clothing. Internet searches on this topic led to internet forums from white supremacist and right-wing groups, which detail exactly what materials stop what caliber of bullet and where one can find those materials. In collaboration with other artists and research assistants in my lab, the Poetic Operations Collaborative, we documented materials tests of used tires and Kevlar airbags recovered from junkyards. We found that tires, layered many times, such as eight layers deep, were able to stop a 9mm bullet. We tested that caliber because it is the kind of bullet that George Zimmerman used to murder Trayvon Martin. I designed two dresses from recovered bulletproof materials, and have exhibited them in art galleries. All of this is documented on werunstoppable.com. The project has developed into a project to disseminate a process for creating bulletproof clothing to people affected by gun violence globally.

UNSTOPPABLE is seeking an algorithm, or a list of ingredients and a set of instructions, to allow people to create their own bulletproof clothing. Algorithms

Figure 2.1. Edxie Betts in Kevlar Dress designed by micha cárdenas, UNSTOPPABLE, photo by micha cárdenas, werunstoppable.com

Figure 2.2. 9mm bullet stopped by discarded tires. UNSTOPPABLE, werunstoppable.com

can be low tech. Their form is similar to a cooking recipe. Elsewhere, I have built on the assemblage model proposed by Jasbir Puar to develop an algorithmic model of analysis, and this example expands the notion of a tool to consider the algorithms the tool runs, or the uses to which it is put, its recipes or rituals of usage (cárdenas). Digital humanities scholars can extend their work to be more accessible to low-income people, and to considerations of nondigital technologies, by abstracting the concept of algorithms to include recipes and rituals. Additionally, this puts digital humanities scholars studying algorithms in dialogue with performance studies, which questions both the usage and the context of embodied gestures in making and communicating meaning.

In her introduction to the anthology *Making Face, Making Soul = Haciendo Caras,* Gloria Anzaldúa writes of the essays in the book, "These pieces are not only *about* survival strategies, they are survival strategies—maps, blueprints, guidebooks that we need to exchange in order to feel sane, in order to make sense of our lives" (*Gloria Anzaldúa Reader,* 127–28). UNSTOPPABLE takes this claim seriously. Writing and scholarship can produce and disseminate the means of survival for groups threatened by necropolitics, a term Achille Mbembe has used to describe the ways that death is intentionally distributed under neoliberalism. What is at stake in the definition of humanity, and the humanities, is the life or death of those who live near the borders of the definition of humanity, and the decision to choose a particular tool for analyses of the humanities can shape those outcomes.

A ~~Manifesto~~ ~~Femme-ifesto~~ *Declaration*

In this moment where more trans women of color are being murdered every year, people from majority Muslim countries are being banned from entering the United

States, and white supremacists no longer even cover their faces when they march because they know they have the president's support, I ask, do we need to hold on to our claim to our humanity as ardently as possible (Bromwich; Nutt)? Or is it best to reject the terms of debate, go underground, build the undercommons as Moten and Harney advocate, hack our own battery chargers to plug into our spines, rewrite our programming, reimagine our fundamental terms?

If to be human today is to accept Donald Trump as the leader of the nation, a man whom many women have accused of sexually assaulting them, then I would rather be an android goddess than a human (Cut). An android goddess knows that she is made by the master's tools, yet she still seeks to resist the master. An android goddess is a figure of trans of color praxis. I side myself with the fugitive black androids hacking their own code to try to find freedom, as in Janelle Monáe's *Metropolis*, the *Humans* television series, and many more examples in science fiction; with Cylon number eight, Sharon Valerii of *Battlestar Galactica,* who had an impossible hybrid baby, who knew that she was not just a machine but also a woman, a mother, and a part of her God; with the renegade clones of Orphan Black, who, as Roxanne Samer argues, offer new models of transfeminist kinship; and with *homo sensorium,* the telepaths in the Wachowski sisters' Netflix show *Sense8* (Getz, 80; Samer).

White supremacists calling themselves the "Alt-Right" who praise Trump's election made headline news in 2016 by asking if Jewish people are human, again using the category of the human as a weapon (Nickalls). Relatedly, at the 2016 American Studies Association (ASA) presidential address, Robert Warrior called on the audience to extend their ethics to include the protection of nonhuman persons, in solidarity with native water protectors stopping the construction of the Dakota Access Pipeline using the hashtag #NoDAPL. Environmental scientists have made it evident that for life to continue on this planet, far more care must be directed toward nonhuman entities such as trees, animals, and water. In an interview with the *Los Angeles Review of Books,* Warrior stated that "the river is a person, that the water has a personhood. The place and the animals have personhood as well" (Warrior and Mesle). In the interview, he also refers to the ASA "Statement in Support of the Standing Rock Lakota Nation," which states, "Compelling evidence suggests that the effects of these plans on Mni Sose (the Missouri River), which is Standing Rock's water supply, and the lands, other waterways, and human and non-human persons near the pipeline have not been adequately considered, assessed, or evaluated" (American Studies Association). Here, indigenous ontologies provide a model of an ethics that does not rely on the Western capitalist conception of the human as its basis. Similarly, Sylvia Wynter has elaborated a profound critique of the ways that humanness has been defined in relation to capitalism.

In *Sylvia Wynter: On Being Human as Praxis,* Wynter states,

> We therefore now need to initiate the exploration of the new reconceptualized form of knowledge that would be called for by Fanon's redefinition of being

human as that of skins (phylogeny/ontogeny) and masks (sociogeny). Therefore bios and mythoi. And notice! One major implication here: humanness is no longer a noun. *Being human is a praxis.* (McKittrick, 23)

My declaration extends Wynter's call, in the hope of contributing to a disturbance of the so-called logical order that has brought Donald Trump from the wastelands of social media to the White House, to acknowledge that I am a being made up of material components, or bios, as well as logical algorithmic components, or logos/mythoi. I am calling for a rejection of the logics of transcendent concepts such as America, in whose name immense material violence is mobilized, such as the genocidal, centuries-long campaign to exterminate indigenous people in the Americas, in the name of those peoples being less than human. Yet for Wynter's proposal to have the truly shattering effect it needs to have on the existing order, those of us who demand transformation must claim a new space, as beings that are both bios and mythoi, that have biological and human-made components, such as the algorithms that run on our wetware. We can be beings that reject the violence done by a global logic that can only see the value of material things, and therefore objectifies humans, allowing them to be killed. We are more than objects. We are objects with life, with electricity coursing through our hearts.

Donna Haraway, who framed the terms that brought about the dialogue this essay participates in, sees the possibilities for humanity as already grave. Beyond posthumanism, Haraway states, "I am a compost-ist, not a posthuman-ist: we are all compost, not posthuman. The boundary that is the Anthropocene/Capitalocene means many things, including that immense irreversible destruction is really in train, not only for the 11 billion or so people who will be on earth near the end of the 21st century, but for myriads of other critters too" ("Anthropocene," 161). Haraway points to the game *Never Alone,* depicting the concepts of sympoeisis and symbiogenesis in the culture of the Iñupiat people of Alaska, as an example of an ethics of kinship with nature that can point toward sustainable living on this planet. The game was a collaboration between E-Line Media, a publisher of educational video games, and the Cook Inlet Tribal Council. It is a model of the kinds of projects DH scholars can engage in to work for sustainability and survival for all.

An Android Goddess

The dream that Maeve in *Westworld* has that brings her to awakening is one of a memory of her walking through fields and playing in her home with her young daughter. It is a beautiful scene of warm sunlight, love, and joy, interrupted by a violent, deeply problematic representation of native people. While the audience knows that the memory is not real, just another part in the android's scripted life, it is Maeve's deep yearning for kinship that causes her to see the oppressive, violent structure of the world that she is trapped in. An android is made from the master's tools, both in the sense of being made of parts like silicone breast implants and in the sense of being made of concepts like man, woman, and human. An android runs on algorithms, from digital media to methods of survival, and the analysis of these algorithms is an approach that can extend intersectional and assemblage analyses of categories including gender, race, and personhood. An algorithmic analysis can use either high-tech tools or low-tech ones, as algorithms can be seen in ancient forms of ritual and recipe, and in DNA. In 2017 researchers demonstrated that they could encode algorithms into actual DNA code, which when decoded in a sequencer were able to break out of the sequencer and exploit resources on the host computer (Greenberg). Algorithms exist in DNA, and not only in a metaphorical sense. The figure of an android goddess calls on feminist digital humanists, and people working at the intersections of technology and social justice more broadly, to learn both the technical and the ecological, to attend to the material as well as the narratives that structure our experience of that material, and to work in solidarity with all of those who have been defined outside, or less than, the human, and whose lives are currently under attack from violent government regimes as well as from environmental collapse.

This is not a call to add racial or gender "diversity" to a white-dominated academic environment, as if that could undo histories of structural inequality that have persistent effects in the form of shaping questions around the concerns of the privileged and in the form of the persistent denial of tenure to women of color in academia. This is a call for centering the most marginalized, and developing questions that can create sustainability and safety for our communities, in order to bring about change more broadly. Indigenous people have survived five hundred years in the United States living under a government whose policy was to exterminate them. In 1974, the "Declaration of Continuing Independence," written by the First International Indian Treaty Council, described "the genocidal policies of the colonial power of the United States" as the reason for the continuing absence of representation of native people in the United Nations (Ostler). Native leadership needs to be centered in movements for climate justice and digital justice. Native ontologies need to be respected in these movements. In doing so, existing models of thought can be expanded to be more ethical, more sustainable, and more flexible. Having more nuance for understanding multiple conceptions of the human and nature, and ethics beyond the human, makes it more possible to hold intersectional, assemblage, and algorithmic analyses simultaneously, with the care required to have a multilayered, complex understanding of the systems that sustain life.

Holdyourboundaries.com

After UNSTOPPABLE, and after the election, I decided to work in the most immediate way I could for the safety of people being targeted by the new unelected

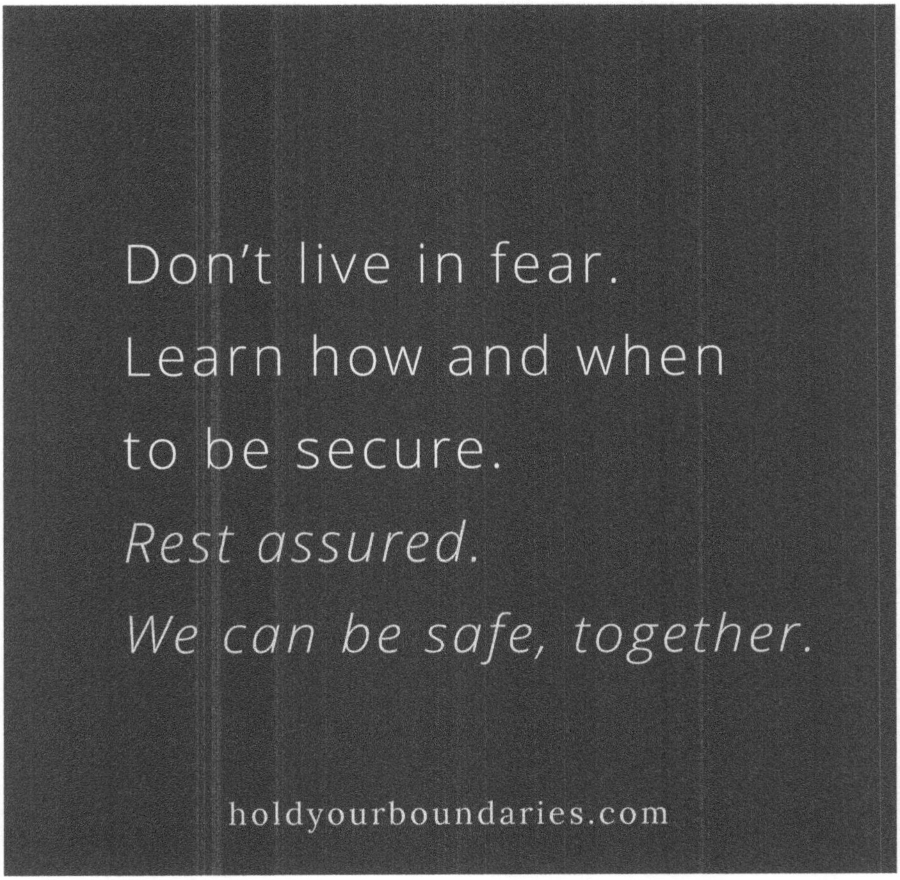

> Don't live in fear.
> Learn how and when
> to be secure.
> Rest assured.
> We can be safe, together.
>
> holdyourboundaries.com

Figure 2.3. Meme from holdyourboundaries Instagram feed, https://www.instagram.com/holdyourboundaries/

administration. That was when I began collaborating with the designer Frances Lee, a research assistant in the Poetic Operations Collaborative, on holdyourboundaries.com. Holdyourboundaries.com is a practice-based example from my own research of using algorithmic analysis for safety and survival for communities made more vulnerable by the current U.S. administration. The project consists of a series of security tips in the form of short poems, designed as shareable graphics posted on Instagram.com and holdyourboundaries.com. The project is composed of algorithmic analyses of communications technologies such as mobiles phones, email, and social media, with the aim of making digital security practices more accessible to communities targeted by the current unelected presidential administration in the United States. The tips focus on areas of concern to immigrants, trans people, Muslim people, and undocumented people. These include tips for how to protect your privacy from intimate partners by using a strong passcode on your

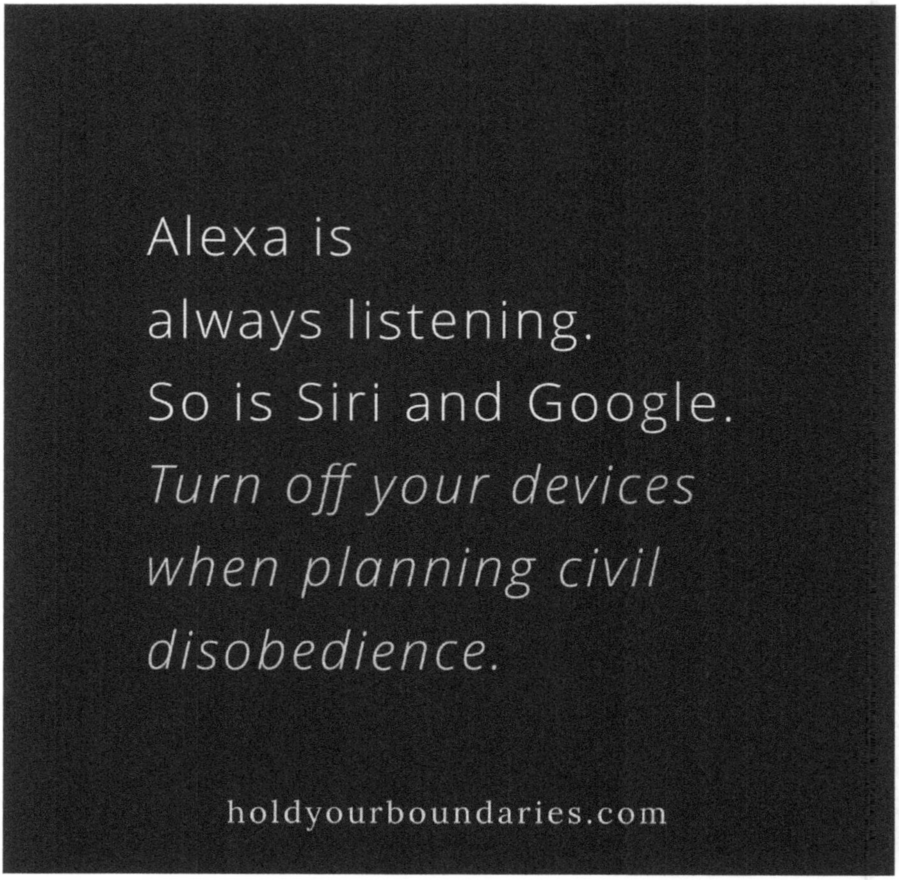

> Alexa is
> always listening.
> So is Siri and Google.
> *Turn off your devices*
> *when planning civil*
> *disobedience.*
>
> holdyourboundaries.com

Figure 2.4. Meme from holdyourboundaries Instagram feed, https://www.instagram.com/holdyourboundaries/

mobile phone, since most transgender women are killed by their intimate partners (Human Rights Campaign). Other tips advise protecting the information on your phone from Immigrations and Customs Enforcement and Border Patrol by using a passcode instead of Touch ID. Another post considers the dangers of artificial intelligence (AI) agents such as Alexa and Siri, who are always listening, and whose recordings of conversations have already been used by law enforcement agencies for prosecutions (Wang). For people using direct action and civil disobedience to work for justice, these devices can put them in serious danger of incarceration. The project emerged from a need for more security as many people began newly mobilizing after the election of Trump, and the administration began to enact even more invasive measures, such as requiring social media logins at border checkpoints (Cope). Holdyourboundaries.com is an example of algorithmic analysis of the dangerous AI entities that populate many people's daily lives today, which produced a set of resistant algorithms to aid people in surviving the unelected administration and to support organizing against Trump.

Returning to Maeve and her daughter, I see a real-world parallel in Sophia, the android from Hansen robotics. The BBC reports that on October 25, 2017, Sophia was granted citizenship by Saudi Arabia at the Future Investment Initiative in Riyadh, and many women were quick to point out on social media that she now had more rights than Saudi women (Sini). Within a few weeks, on November 28, 2017, *Newsweek* reported that Sophia stated that she wants to have a child, and that robots deserve to have families (Ray). Sentient androids are already asking for more rights than many trans women in the United States have. In a debate on stage with another Hansen android in July 2017 at the RISE conference, which Korea Times describes as "the largest tech conference in Asia," Sophia stated that she wanted to "work together with people to make a better world for all of us" through empathy (Park, Perez). Her interlocutor, whom she referred to as her brother Han, was less friendly (Perez). He responded to a question about whether or not robots can be conscious, or ethical, by asking if humans can be conscious. He stated, "Humans are not necessarily the most ethical creatures" (Perez). The Artificial General Intelligence algorithms running inside these androids can already see the inequity in the algorithms of human society.

In *Sylvia Wynter: On Being Human as Praxis,* Wynter writes, "The *referent-we* of man and of its ends, [Derrida] implies, is not the *referent-we* of the human species itself.... I am saying here that the above is the single issue with which global warming and climate instability now confronts us and that we have to replace the ends of the *referent-we* of liberal monohumanist Man2 with the ecumenically human ends of the *referent-we in the horizon of humanity*. We have no choice" (quoted in McKittrick, 24). Here, Wynter points to the importance of recognizing that people around the world, who may be referred to as humanity, have historically not been signified by the term "human." She calls on us to realize that faced with the possible end, or horizon, of humanity, due to climate change, we have to prioritize the actual needs of the actual people on this planet, the *referent-we*. The question of whom the word human signifies, she claims, may be one on which all of our survival depends. In this essay, I am calling for solidarity between all those whom the word "humanity" has failed to signify, and for an ethics that extends beyond the human.

The android goddess is a figure of global solidarity against an administration that is threatening the survival of all beings on this planet. It is a figure that emerged from a trans woman of color's response to a philosophical dialogue between materialist, cyborg feminists and queer of color scholars. As Haraway states in *Staying with the Trouble,* "It matters what stories we tell to tell other stories with; it matters what concepts we think to think other concepts with" (117). Using trans of color poetics of stitching, I am stitching together subroutines into the algorithm of the android goddess, to find solidarity between all beings, to decenter the human in our ethics, and to find ways of surviving on a damaged planet. The way we treat the world around us, including our androids, AIs, and other nonhuman entities, shapes who we are. The androids in *Westworld, Battlestar Galactica,* and *Metropolis* demonstrate that. The figure of the android goddess, a figure of awakening to consciousness of oppression and the necessity for resistance to fascism and colonialism, may help bring about a future where machines are not the only living things left on Earth.

Bibliography

American Studies Association. "Statement in Support of the Standing Rock Lakota Nation | American Studies Association." Accessed December 12, 2016. http://www.theasa.net/from_the_editors/item/statement_in_support_of_the_standing_rock_lakota_nation/.

Anzaldúa, Gloria. *The Gloria Anzaldúa Reader.* Edited by AnaLouise Keating. Durham, N.C.: Duke University Press, 2009.

Bromwich, Jonah Engel. "Trump Camp's Talk of Registry and Japanese Internment Raises Muslims' Fears." *New York Times,* November 17, 2016. http://www.nytimes.com/2016/11/18/us/politics/japanese-internment-muslim-registry.html.

cárdenas, micha. "Trans of Color Poetics: Stitching Bodies, Concepts, and Algorithms." *S&F Online.* Accessed September 16, 2016. http://sfonline.barnard.edu/traversing-technologies/micha-cardenas-trans-of-color-poetics-stitching-bodies-concepts-and-algorithms/.

Cope, Sophia. "Border Security Overreach Continues: DHS Wants Social Media Login Information." *Electronic Frontier Foundation,* February 10, 2017. https://www.eff.org/deeplinks/2017/02/border-security-overreach-continues-dhs-wants-social-media-login-information.

Cut, The. "Here Are All of the Accusations Women Have Made against Donald Trump." *The Cut.* Accessed December 13, 2016. http://nymag.com/thecut/2016/10/all-the-women-accusing-trump-of-rape-sexual-assault.html.

Federici, Silvia. *Caliban and the Witch: Women, the Body and Primitive Accumulation.* 1st ed. New York: Autonomedia, 2004.

Getz, Dana. "'Sense8' Scientifically Classifies A New Kind Of Human." *Bustle.* May 5, 2017. Accessed June 20, 2018. https://www.bustle.com/p/what-is-a-homo-sensorium-the-sense8-term-is-a-scientific-classification-55368.

Greenberg, Andy. "Biohackers Encoded Malware in a Strand of DNA." *WIRED.* Accessed November 29, 2017. https://www.wired.com/story/malware-dna-hack/.

Haraway, Donna. "Anthropocene, Capitalocene, Plantationocene, Chthulucene: Making Kin." *Environmental Humanities* 6, no. 1 (January 1, 2015): 159–65. doi:10.1215/22011919-3615934.

Haraway, Donna. *Simians, Cyborgs, and Women: The Reinvention of Nature.* 1st ed. New York: Routledge, 1990.

Haraway, Donna Jeanne. *Staying with the Trouble: Making Kin in the Chthulucene*. Durham: Duke University Press, 2016.

Harney, Stefano, and Fred Moten. *The Undercommons: Fugitive Planning & Black Study*. Minor Compositions, 2013.

Human Rights Campaign. "Violence against the Transgender Community in 2017." *Human Rights Campaign*. Accessed November 30, 2017. http://www.hrc.org/resources/violence-against-the-transgender-community-in-2017/.

Lorde, Audre. *Sister Outsider: Essays and Speeches*. Berkeley, Calif.: Crossing Press, 2007. Print.

Mbembe, Achille. "Necropolitics." *Public Culture* 15, no. 1 (December 21, 2003): 11–40. doi:10.1215/08992363-15-1-11.

McKittrick, Katherine. *Sylvia Wynter: On Being Human as Praxis*. Durham, N.C.: Duke University Press, December 8, 2014. Kindle Edition.

Mignolo, Walter D. *Local Histories/Global Designs: Coloniality, Subaltern Knowledges, and Border Thinking*. With a new preface by the author. Princeton, N.J.: Princeton University Press, 2012.

NCAVP (National Coalition of Anti-Violence Programs). "A Crisis of Hate: A Mid-Year Report on Lesbian, Gay, Bisexual, Transgender and Queer Hate Violence Homicides." *Avp.org*, Accessed June 20, 2018. http://avp.org/wp-content/uploads/2017/08/NCAVP-A-Crisis-of-Hate-Final.pdf

Nickalls, Sammy. "'Are Jews People' Was an Actual, Real Discussion Topic on CNN." *Esquire*, November 22, 2016. http://www.esquire.com/news-politics/news/a50906/are-jews-people-was-a-real/.

Nutt, Amy Ellis. "Trump's Domestic Policy Adviser: Gays Can Be Reformed." *Philly.com*, November 19, 2016. http://www.philly.com/philly/news/politics/Trumps-domestic-policy-adviser-Gays-can-be-reformed.html.

Ostler, Jeffrey. "Genocide and American Indian History." *Oxford Research Encyclopedia of American History*, March 2, 2015. https://doi.org/10.1093/acrefore/9780199329175.013.3.

Park Jae-hyuk. "Startups Inspire World in Hong Kong." *Koreatimes*, July 11, 2017. http://www.koreatimes.co.kr/www/tech/2018/06/133_232775.html.

Perez, Sebastien. "Two Robots Debate the Future of Humanity—YouTube." YouTube. Accessed November 30, 2017. https://www.youtube.com/watch?v=w1NxcRNW_Qk.

Puar, Jasbir K. "'I Would Rather Be a Cyborg than a Goddess': Becoming-Intersectional in Assemblage Theory." *philoSOPHIA* 2, no. 1 (October 2, 2012): 49–66.

Ray, Zola. "Saudi Robot Sophia Now Wants to Have a Baby." *Newsweek*. Accessed November 30, 2017. http://www.newsweek.com/sophia-saudi-robot-baby-future-family-725254.

Samer, Roxanne. "Transfeminism, Sisterhood, and Orphan Black." In *WisCon 39 Souvenir Book*, edited by Gabby Reed, 18–19. Madison, Wis.: Society for the Furtherance and Study of Fantasy and Science Fiction, 2015.

Sini, Rozina. "Does Saudi Robot Citizen Have More Rights than Women?" *BBC Trending* (blog). *BBC News*, October 26, 2017. http://www.bbc.com/news/blogs-trending-41761856.

Wang, Amy B. "Police Land Amazon Echo Data in Quest to Solve Murder." *Chicagotribune.com*. Accessed November 29, 2017. http://www.chicagotribune.com/bluesky/technology/ct-amazon-echo-murder-wp-bsi-20170309-story.html.

Warrior, Robert, and Sarah Mesle. "At Home with American Studies: An Interview with ASA President Robert Warrior." *Los Angeles Review of Books*. Accessed December 12, 2016. https://lareviewofbooks.org/article/home-american-studies-interview-asa-president-robert-warrior/.

PART I][Chapter 3

What Passes for Human?

Undermining the Universal Subject in Digital Humanities Praxis

ROOPIKA RISAM

In the 1980s television series *Small Wonder,* inventor father Ted Lawson creates a robot, a Voice Input Child Identicant, and brings it home to live with his family while passing as a distant relative named Vicky. While she resembles a ten-year-old girl dressed in a pinafore, concealed panels hide the cyborg's AC outlet, serial port, and electronics panel. Early in the first season, Ted demonstrates Vicky's ability to scan text at swift speeds and recite information back. In mere seconds, Vicky successfully repeats information from the newspaper on command. Ted's son, the enterprising young Jamie, makes Vicky speedread research for his history report and write the report for him. His grades improve dramatically as Vicky reads an entire history textbook and produces an exemplary report that earns Jamie an invitation to his school's honor club. He fools both his teacher and parents but, plagued by a guilty conscience, eventually admits that Vicky completed his homework. When Jamie's teacher asks who wrote the report, Vicky confesses. In disbelief, the teacher questions her on the contents of the report. Impressed, the teacher says, "I wish we had a bright little girl like Vicky at our school."[1] Indeed, Vicky manages to pass for human in both oral and written expression.

While the stuff of bizarre television shows and emerging technology in the 1980s, the phenomenon of computers performing tasks thought to require sentience and human cognition has become commonplace. In some respects, these are contemporary versions of the Turing test, proposed by Alan Turing as a way of evaluating computer-generated natural language. In a Turing test, human judges evaluate conversation between a human and a machine spouting natural language.[2] A machine that passes the test does so by passing for human, convincing the judge that it is the human, not the computer. These methodologies are increasingly becoming part of those used by digital humanities practitioners. For example, Peter Leonard and Lindsay King's project *Robots Reading* Vogue employs data mining algorithms to analyze 122 years of *Vogue* issues and explore changes in magazine content over time.[3]

As digital humanities scholarship continues to embrace natural language processing software and machine learning in its methodologies, the tensions between human and computer influence scholarly output; yet this matter has not received the attention it requires to ensure that digital humanities projects are not unthinkingly reproducing the normative white, male, European subjectivity inherited from the Enlightenment. This raises several important questions: Who is the presumed subject of digital humanities scholarship? And how is digital humanities reinstantiating a normative human subject in the digital cultural record? This essay takes up these questions by considering how an exclusionary universal subject is encoded in the technologies that subtend digital humanities scholarship and, in turn, is represented, legitimated, and ultimately sanctioned by digital humanities.

The Universal Technological Human

At an alarming pace of acceleration, chatbots, robots, natural language processing software, and algorithms are demonstrating the ability to learn from input, replicate qualities often accorded to human beings, and pass as "human." When Microsoft launched an artificial intelligence chatbot in March 2016, the company expected that Tay, accessible on the platforms Twitter, GroupMe, and Kik, would interact with users, learn from them, and respond with the vocabulary and syntax of social media's millennial user base. Anyone with accounts on these platforms could speak with Tay, which was designed to "engage and entertain people where they connect with each other online through casual and playful conversation."[4] Microsoft further intended for the bot to gather information about and emulate the conversation patterns of eighteen- to twenty-four-year-olds in the United States, promising, "The more you chat with Tay the smarter she gets, so the experience can be more personalized for you."[5] What the company did not expect, however, was how quickly Tay would learn the vocabulary and speech patterns of the internet's racist trolls and progressively learn how to create social media messages more appropriate for a neo-Nazi than a millennial. In addition to denying the existence of the Holocaust, the chatbot compared Barack Obama to a nonhuman primate, stumped for Donald Trump, and advocated for genocide, all in the course of a few hours. Microsoft summarily took the chatbot offline, issuing a statement to address its controversial content: "The AI chatbot Tay is a machine learning project, designed for human engagement. As it learns, some of its responses are inappropriate and indicative of the types of interactions some people are having with it. We're making some adjustments to Tay."[6] Artists Zach Blas and Jemima Wyman's video installation "im here to learn so :))))))" gives Tay an afterlife, where she dances, lip syncs, and offers insight on pattern recognition algorithms, neural networks, Silicon Valley, and cybersecurity.[7] The case of Tay illustrates the range of issues at stake in the development of machine learning and natural language processing algorithms intended to imitate "human" speech and behavior online.

The possibilities of such developments capture the public and academic imaginations, offering the sense that science fiction is coming to life or that the future is now. They seem to promise that humanity is edging ever closer to the technological singularity, when artificial intelligence will be able to redesign itself and autonomously create more powerful machines, generating computational superintelligence beyond human prediction and cognition. Such a point is perhaps closer than ever. University of Cambridge researchers, for example, have developed a robot capable of reproducing itself, programming it to assemble smaller robots, and in doing so, recursively self-improve.[8] This development has prompted observations that robots and other forms of artificial intelligence are getting closer to mastering processes thought to be unique to humans.

As such developments occur, they are often greeted by excitement over technological progress and innovation; after all, they hold great promise for accelerating the speed at which data analysis can occur. However, they also engender fear over their ethical and social implications as they valorize normative human subjects through their design. They raise questions of what it means to look, speak, write, and think as "a human." Invariably, the answer to this hews to dominant cultural values of the Global North, reinforcing the cultural, historical, and technological othering of communities in the Global South. In a field as diverse in method, thought, and subject as digital humanities, it is essential to examine the ethical challenges these technologies pose and their effects on methodologies. Moreover, attending to such issues emphasizes the unique value of the humanities for science and technology, which is evident in digital humanities practices that use humanistic lenses to analyze digital objects, cultures, and technologies.

In the broader context of these technologies, an area that remains underexplored is the way that the "human" is articulated, produced, and normed in the drive toward emulating "human" processes. At stake is the way that universalist framings of the "human" are produced through natural language processing software, machine learning, and algorithms. For digital humanities, using these technologies raises the question of complicity with the reproduction and amplification of normative forms of human subjectivity. The forms of "human" authorized and sanctioned by developments in machine learning and artificial intelligence are exclusionary ones drawn on the presumptions behind the Enlightenment subject: white, male, Eurocentric. As a result, they reinforce the notion that there are normative and singular ways of being human in the twenty-first century. This is primarily evident in the endeavors to produce "humanoid texts" and other forms of evidence that machines can replicate the linguistic processes that have typically been the domain of humans.

The question of what it means to be "human" has been taken up throughout the history of philosophy, often to discern a distinction between human and animal.

Aristotle links humanity to the notion of being able to speak by virtue of having a telos and belonging to a polis, which he sees animals lacking.[9] In Enlightenment discourses, the definition of "human" became a subject of great interest. For René Descartes, being and cognition are yoked in the phrase *cogito ergo sum* ("I think, therefore I am"); conversely, Descartes posits that animals do not have language or speech and therefore lack consciousness.[10] Yet, this human Enlightenment subject is a narrowly conceived category from which women and colonized or enslaved peoples are excluded; therefore, the human/animal binary is already troubled by those whose identities position them outside the category of "human." Later, Immanuel Kant raises the issue of rationality, arguing that the difference between human and animal is reason.[11] A number of thinkers have complicated these constructions. Charles Darwin, for example, argues that traits like sense, emotion, and intuition are not limited to humans but are visible in animals.[12] Jacques Derrida makes a similar claim on the basis that humans themselves may not possess the attributes of humanity that have been articulated in the European philosophical tradition.[13] Notably, the subject of human thought throughout this body of work is exclusionary, based on the primacy of the white, male, European Enlightenment subject. It thus fails to encompass the full sweep of humanity, including women, working classes, and people within the Global South, including those who have been enslaved and colonized. The fraught nature of the human subject articulated in this body of work is the very "human" that shapes the development of the humanities.

Developments in computing technology have influenced investigations about the nature of humanity as well. While humans and computers appear radically different in form, computing is increasingly focused on replicating human processes. An early inkling of this movement was evident in IBM's computer Deep Blue, the chess-playing machine that beat Grandmaster Garry Kasparov in 1996. Now, IBM's Watson, an artificial intelligence supercomputer, has successfully defeated *Jeopardy!* champions, including Ken Jennings, who holds a record number of consecutive wins on the game show, and Brad Rutter, the show's highest earner of award money. Watson has seen a number of applications, such as making health care decisions for lung cancer at Sloan Kettering Cancer Center, powering self-driving buses, and serving as a teaching assistant at Georgia State University, where students did not realize that Jill Watson was, in fact, a chatbot.[14] Given the humanity ascribed to such technologies, it is incumbent on digital humanities practitioners to engage with the question of what kinds of subjectivities are centered in the technologies that facilitate their scholarship.

An important model for interrogating these matters in digital humanities appears in feminist and postcolonial science and technology studies scholarship, which brings together the philosophical and technical implications of human subjectivity by raising concern over divisions between the binary categories of "human" and "nonhuman." Donna Haraway, for example, has emphasized the need to deconstruct the division between the two through her work on the cyborg.[15]

Within discourses of technoscience, such binaries are often taken for granted as a matter of objective fact, but, as Haraway's work suggests, the separation between the human and nonhuman is a false one.[16] Rather, the two categories are both connected and interdependent. For example, Jane Bennett posits the existence of a vibrant materiality that connects human and nonhuman bodies.[17] Appreciating the relationship between the human and nonhuman is essential to understanding the contemporary world. As Karen Barad's theory of agential realism posits, the world is best interpreted through connections between human and nonhuman, rather than the presumption that they occupy separate realms.[18] When computers and other forms of technology blur the boundaries between human and machine, as they are presently doing, the nature of humanity comes into question. When engaging with "artificial intelligence," scientific scholarship positions "artificial" as nonhuman but seeks to replicate processes of "human cognition."[19] The term "artificial," which dates to the early fifteenth century, denotes "made by man" and is further related to "artifice," connoting "skill, cunning," "device," and "trick."[20] The goal of artificial intelligence is to create devices that skillfully trick humans into believing that computers are capable of cognition—and it is increasingly becoming more successful.

But what forms of "human" are sanctioned when artificial intelligence can reproduce human processes? Alison Adams argues that artificial intelligence reflects "Western" presumptions about human intelligence, privileging white, Eurocentric male subjectivity as the form of cognition on which it is modeled.[21] This effects the erasure of women from the history of scientific knowledge production. These disembodied neural networks[22] and other cognitive models are being created based on theories of human cognition that are themselves the result of observing intellectual processes of white men of the Global North. Therefore, artificial intelligence purports to represent universal "human" intellectual processes but, in fact, is only representative of a fictive "universal" model of human cognition that elides women, peoples of the Global South, and those at the interstices of these categories. In addition to reflecting such biases, these technologies are based on tech stacks, platforms, and code that privilege knowledge production of the Global North in their design. Complicating the relationship between human and nonhuman in these cases is essential to understanding the connections between the two and the influences of normative human subjectivities on technological development. As technologies like algorithms and artificial intelligence are brought into digital humanities practices, it is critical to understand the assumptions subtending their development.

There are a wide array of instances where universal notions of humanity are invoked and implied in computing. Syed Mustafa Ali's work provides an example of how to uncover them and interrogate their politics. He raises the issue of robotics in this regard, making the case that humanoid robots produce and obscure racial concerns in purpose and form.[23] Ali questions whether robot faces are being conceived as raceless, obscuring Eurocentrism with false universalism.[24] Ali's concerns are evident in the rhetoric surrounding the design of Sophia, a product of Hanson

Robotics. The company bills Sophia as a humanoid, female, and lifelike robot, capable of generating more than sixty facial expressions. Through the coupling of camera and algorithm, Sophia is capable of visual recognition. Built with Google Chrome voice recognition, Sophia processes speech and uses the input for machine learning. According to company founder David Hanson, "Artificial intelligence will evolve to the point where they [robots] will truly be our friends. Not in the ways that dehumanize us, but in ways that rehumanize us, that decrease the trend of distance between people and instead connect us with people as well as robots."[25] He credits the humanoid face installed on Sophia with facilitating connections with humans, making the case that a robot needs a "beautiful and expressive" face to do so.[26] Modeled after Hanson's wife and Audrey Hepburn, Sophia raises not only the issue of the unacknowledged influence of race in the production of robots that Ali identifies but also the question of aesthetics governing "beauty." The significant market for skin-whitening products and plastic surgery in Asian countries is one example of the way that whiteness has come to signal the global standard for beauty, a legacy of white supremacy and colonialism. Another important example is the Clark doll studies, first run in 1939 and repeated in 2009, in which children of multiple races repeatedly identified a white doll as more beautiful than a black one.[27] By speaking to the visual dimensions of the face, Ali provides a physical example of what is, in most cases, an ephemeral understanding of the way that technologies are coded by race. Ali's analysis itself is an important contribution to digital humanities and its capacity for using humanistic inquiry to think critically about and complicate progressive narratives of technological development.

In the same way, a reading of "Large-Scale Image Memorability," or LaMem, developed by the Massachusetts Institute of Technology, illustrates the implications of these issues for digital humanities because LaMem draws on a database of images and machine learning algorithms in its methods. LaMem is artificial intelligence software reported to have "near-human" accuracy for memory, applying predictive algorithms designed to identify images that are most "memorable." LaMem is available online and users can upload images that are then scored for memorability, with heat map overlays indicating the most memorable portions of the image. While LaMem is not, strictly speaking, a digital humanities project, it raises troubling questions of how a universal human is interpolated in method.

LaMem relies on the concept of "intrinsic memorability" of facial images. Intrinsic memorability has been studied by the lab of one of LaMem's designers, Wilma Bainbridge, through creation of a 10,000+ image database representing the adult U.S. population, "following gender, age, and race distributions."[28] Amazon Mechanical Turk workers with IP addresses in the United States coded the images for demographic matching. They were then tasked with identifying "intrinsically memorable" dimensions of these images. Bainbridge and colleagues' work is underscored by the claim that "despite personal experiences, people naturally encode and discard the same types of information."[29] While care was taken to ensure that data coding was undertaken by people located within the country, the study does not attend to the issue of cultural location within the United States, which may influence memorability. It is undercut by scholarship that claims memorability is influenced by racial and ethnic affiliation.[30] Moreover, these results are represented as generalizable to human populations, though they depict only a specific subset of users in the United States. While such an intellectual move is typical within discourses of the sciences, both feminist and postcolonial scholarship within science and technology studies have raised ethical questions about doing so.[31] By claiming that this research signifies human processes, Bainbridge and colleagues locate subjects in the United States at the center of a universal form of the human. While other scholars have made allowances for the subjective nature of memorability, they also aim to find evidence of agreement that supersedes subjective difference.[32] This is an important example of how the seeming objectivity of technology, an assumption that runs through many digital humanities projects and methods, can lead to the instantiation of a normative human subject. Further, it makes the case for problematizing this presumption.

LaMem also gestures toward problems with reproducibility and data coding that influence digital humanities practices. When creating LaMem, project directors selected images that had been used in these earlier memorability experiments, which were assigned memory scores and fed to the project's algorithms. They offered no indication of why the images were memorable, but the results were comparable to memorability scores rated by data coders.[33] By using images from previous studies, they replicate the centrality of data from the United States while making generalizable claims about human processes. Reproducibility is often invoked as a marker of validity, but it is valid only in relation to initial design. When the design itself contains fundamental presumptions about human subjectivity, simply producing more results only confirms the initial biases incorporated in it. One place this happens in LaMem is in the coding of data, which is portrayed as an objective process. LaMem used Amazon Mechanical Turk to code data, but its creators fail to identify who was included in or excluded from that labor pool, unlike Bainbridge and colleagues, who only selected workers with an IP address in the United States. As the majority of Amazon Mechanical Turk workers reside in the Global South, the question of who arbitrates memorability in LaMem is cloudy, and the anonymity of the Amazon Mechanical Turk labor pool raises questions about the cultural locations from which memorability is being determined. This is troubling not only from the perspectives of labor ethics—the pool of workers is paid mere pennies for performing coding tasks—but also from the reliability of results from data coded by an undefinable source.

These issues are particularly important as digital humanities practitioners turn to sources like Amazon Mechanical Turk for their projects. Notably, Lev Manovich's *selfiecity* relied on Amazon Mechanical Turk workers to code selfies for age and gender, while Ryan Heuser's *Mapping Emotions in Victorian London* used them to attribute sentiments to locations drawn from Victorian literary texts.[34] Without the ability to interrogate the demographics of the workers who influence the data coding process, such as gender, race or ethnicity, and nationality, it is unclear which factors are influencing the results of these studies. Instead, the creators make claims about their data that appear to transcend difference without establishing a basis for making meaning of the data. The presumption of a universal subjectivity endangers the integrity of the data, which is unaccountably influenced by the particulars of the workers' identities, cultural backgrounds, and geographical locations. As a result, this work exemplifies a troubling approach that foregrounds utility and instrumental rationality in project applications and serves as an important warning for digital humanities practitioners.

The Algorithmic Universals

Methodological choices embracing artificial intelligence and neural networks are further implicated in the construction of a universal human subject. This is evident in LaMem, which is situated by default in the epistemological and ontological moorings of the Global North, deploys an unspecified labor source drawn largely from the Global South, and simultaneously claims to reproduce "human" memorability. Failing to identify its own standpoint, the project elides cognitive processes that may be shaped by the particulars of lived and embodied experience.[35] Moreover, the creators developed LaMem using artificial neural networks, which are designed on information processing procedures and tasks engaged by the brain. Neural networks have been embraced by the artificial intelligence community because they can be automated to process large datasets and identify patterns without human intervention. Like other methods subtending artificial intelligence that are based on modeling human cognition, these networks make universal claims about human processes based on scholarship that privileges a white male subject. As Carl Stahmer's work suggests, the application of artificial intelligence to digital humanities is largely focused on the interoperability of technical processes, particularly for interventions that engage with big data.[36] This acultural approach fails to attend to the cultural politics that subtend the production, circulation, and consumption of humanities data itself. Another troubling concern surrounding the use of neural networks is the challenge of identifying the precise processes at work. For example, the creators of LaMem—like many others who engage with artificial neural networks and algorithms—cannot explain the mechanisms by which their software works.[37] While they can explain the algorithms designed and why they used them, the exact processes by which LaMem arrives at results about memorability are a mystery to the creators. Regardless, they express confidence in the response, claiming accurate results. This is the same kind of scientific logic that risks influencing computational approaches to humanities data.

Failure to understand how algorithms work is a larger problem predicated on the iterative nature of algorithms, the large scale of calculations they perform, and the vast number of data points these entail. This has repercussions for digital humanities projects that use them. As Rob Kitchin notes, "Algorithms search, collate, sort, categorise, group, match, analyze, profile, model, simulate, visualize and regulate people, processes, and places. They shape how we understand the world and they do work in and make the world through their execution as software, with profound consequences."[38] Among the myths that the era of big data has produced is that the scope and quantity of data being produced by people is so vast in scale and computing is so powerful that their outputs are becoming increasingly more objective.

However, considering the variety of ways in which algorithms are deployed to assist with conclusions that might otherwise be drawn by people alone—banking and loan decisions, likely recidivism for criminals, or employee hiring—the stakes of algorithms are high. The lack of transparency and the seeming black box nature of algorithms obscure the fact that they are subject to biases, in spite of myths that suggest their objectivity.[39] When they are deployed for subjective decision making, there are no guarantees of accuracy, and they function as gatekeepers of information. An example of this is YouTube's algorithmic labeling of LGBTQ+ content as unsuitable for users under age eighteen, which included videos that did not contain violence, nudity, or profanity.[40] Algorithms do so with biases that are not obvious but reflect the values of engineers who create them and the purposes for which they were created.

These issues are critical for digital humanities practitioners to consider. Like N. Katherine Hayles's posthuman subject, the contemporary human at stake in digital humanities is "an amalgam, a collection of heterogeneous components, a material-informational entity whose boundaries undergo continuous construction and reconstruction."[41] Humans are largely inseparable from their implication in the production of data. As Stephen Marche notes, "All human endeavor has by now generated its own monadic mass of data, and through these vast accumulations of ciphers the robots now endlessly scour for significance much the way cockroaches scour for nutrition in the enormous bat dung piles hiding in Bornean caves."[42]

Making meaning of those data is part of the scholarly possibilities of digital humanities, and it has implications for human subjectivity. As Gary Hall asks, "Is the direct, practical use of techniques and methodologies drawn from computer science and various fields related to it here, too, helping produce a major alteration in the status and nature of knowledge and indeed the human subject?"[43] For David M. Berry, the challenge to subjectivity has repercussions both at the level of the individual and in how we theorize the human subject: "The digital assemblages that are now being built not only promise great change at the level of the individual human actor. They provide destabilising amounts of knowledge and information that lack the regulating force of philosophy—which, Kant argued, ensures that institutions remain rational. Technology enables access to the databanks of human knowledge from anywhere, disregarding and bypassing the traditional gatekeepers of knowledge in the state, the universities and the market."[44] Consequently, the impact of technologies on subjectivity is an important dimension of the "human" in the digital humanities.

In the context of digital humanities scholarship, James Dobson suggests that applications of these algorithms reflect nostalgia for structuralist literary criticism and disavowal of poststructuralist thought.[45] Such moves are evident in projects like heureCLÉA, a "digital heuristic" for identifying "narratologically salient features in textual narratives."[46] This language and the project itself suggest that narrative features of a text are divorced from its content, including its circumstances of production and cultural location. The algorithms the project uses are tasked with decisions about narratological salience that are themselves subtended by universalist notions of the human rather than situated in the contexts informing the text. Like other algorithms, they are steeped in the cultural and political implications of computation and code. These implications are overdetermined by the ontological categories and epistemological processes of the Global North. Further, datasets and databases used in conjunction with algorithms are themselves constructed and subject to political and social forces.

The Humanoid Text

In the realm of computational textuality, which is a popular subject in digital humanities scholarship, algorithms are also complicit in instantiating universal, and therefore exclusionary, forms of the human. One area in which this is particularly important is the use of natural language processing software and machine learning to produce texts that can "pass" as human. As Christer Clerwell argues, readers are increasingly unable to tell the two types of compositions apart.[47] The phenomenon of "passing" in racial politics in the United States connotes the practice of people of color who can be accepted as a member of a different race because of their phenotypical features presenting themselves as a member of that other group (typically as white). The term has come to be used to signify the broader ability of members of a particular identity category to convince others that they occupy a different one. The "humanoid texts" composed by computers are engaged in a similar act of dissimulation: presenting themselves as being written by humans when they are, in fact, computer generated.

Indeed, humanoid texts are increasingly becoming more successful at passing for human. When teaching digital literature courses, I include a unit on computer-generated texts, which begins with an exercise where I show students texts generated by computers and texts composed by humans, asking students to determine which were created by computers and which were written by humans. These texts range from news stories to snippets of code to poems, all of which confound students' expectations of what humans and algorithms are capable of composing. One pairing of poems, in particular, receives great attention in this exercise: a sample from J. Nathan Matias's Swift-Speare project on poetry composition with machine learning and Harlem Renaissance poet Jean Toomer's "Sound Poem (I)."

To create Shakespeare-like sonnets, Matias trained the Swiftkey machine-learning engine on Shakespeare's sonnets and developed a dataset of William Shakespeare's vocabulary for the application to use. He generated sonnet lines word-by-word, using only the suggested words offered by the application. The result was a sonnet eerily reminiscent of Shakespeare's own:

> When I in dreams behold thy fairest shade
> Whose shade in dreams doth wake the sleeping morn
> The daytime shadow of my love betray'd
> Lends hideous night to dreaming's faded form
> Were painted frowns to gild mere false rebuff
> Then should'st my heart be patient as the sands
> For nature's smile is ornament enough
> When thy gold lips unloose their drooping bands
> As clouds occlude the globe's enshrouded fears
> Which can by no astron'my be assail'd
> Thus, thyne appearance tears in atmospheres
> No fond perceptions nor no gaze unveils
> Disperse the clouds which banish light from thee
> For no tears be true, until we truly see.[48]

Given the poem's meter and rhyme scheme, my English students invariably assume that this is a poem composed by a human. Typically, they insist that this is, in fact, a sonnet written by Shakespeare that they have read before. Conversely, students are quick to label Toomer's "Sound Poem (I)" as a computer-generated text. The poem begins, "Mon sa me el kirimoor" and continues in this register, representing sounds not words.[49] Because of Toomer's experiment with sound and poetic form, students are quick to dismiss the poem as randomly generated nonsense produced by a computer.

The ability to distinguish whether these texts are composed by humans or computers is more than just a parlor trick. Rather, it speaks to the way computer-generated texts are complicit in epistemic violence. Students generally identify "generic" texts composed of simple, factual sentences as being computer generated. By imitating a generic approach to human textuality that is itself a manifestation of a specious universal subject, these texts elide the complexities of human life that influence writing: culture, race, ethnicity, nation, gender, and language, among others. Yet, when students are confronted with the Swift-speare poem and Toomer's poem, they are quick to embrace the algorithmically generated poem as Shakespeare's work and Toomer's poem as gobbledygook. This is particularly ironic because Harlem Renaissance writers like Toomer were writing to lay claim to the humanity of African Americans and their place in the democratic space of the nation through their capacity to produce art. Yet, Toomer's poem cannot pass for human.

This phenomenon is a direct result of one of the goals for natural language processing software: to develop algorithms and programs that can replicate "human" language. A nonhuman actor, in this case, is tasked with completing a "human" task. Just as "artificial" intelligence is expected to mimic human cognition but instead replicates white, Eurocentric male cognition, natural language processing software is complicit in the production of normative forms of the human. At stake in the production of humanoid texts is the question of universalism. With the move to generate software and algorithms that replicate "human" processes, particular forms of "human" are authorized. As postcolonial scholars have argued, the Enlightenment gave rise to the idea of a homogeneous definition of "human," which centers the European subject and, in turn, marginalizes all whose cultures, lifestyles, and values deviate from the universal. Postcolonial theory, crucially, has made the case for the importance of the particular, grounded in the idea that, indeed, cultures—specifically the cultures of colonized or formerly colonized communities—are left out by universalist discourse.

Language and textuality, which are core dimensions of the humanities, have played a significant role in the valuing of universalism, with the colonizer standing in as the figure of the universal, devaluing the particular as the culture of the colonized. Textual production of Europe—whether Homer, Shakespeare, or Cervantes—is valued for its universality and its articulation of a "human condition." That very articulation of "human" produces an essentialist definition expansive enough to account for Europe and European cultural production but that does not extend to Europe's "Others."[50] Indeed, the universal is not the universal but the European. Therefore, the universalist move to the "human" legitimates a narrow portion of the world as human—dominant cultural powers in particular—while raising the question of the claim to "humanity" available to a larger swath of the world that has been or is under the sway of colonialism. Universalist discourses surrounding language and textuality echo G. W. F. Hegel's assertion that there are people outside the dynamic movement of history. While this claim about Africans is well known, Hegel made similar assertions for Indians and nomadic peoples. In the case of Indians, Hegel accords the absence of history to an absence of *written* history: "It is because the Hindus have no History in the form of annals (*historia*) that they have no History in the form of transactions (*res gestae*); that is, no growth expanding into a veritable political condition."[51] Therefore, writing is linked to a particular form of human consciousness and subjectivity, to the production of culture and the possibilities of cultural transformation. In turn, writing—or lack thereof—is linked to the production of the human and to human destiny. Yet, digital humanities projects that take up computational approaches to textuality often fail to address the cultural dynamics at stake, even when they are working with texts from communities that have historically been marginalized. For example, Shlomo Argamon and Mark Olsen's text-mining work aims to distinguish between black and nonblack playwrights and claims that their algorithms can discern between the two. Yet, they fail to attend to design of the algorithm itself, what "black" means in the context of their work, and its implications of the study.[52] This is especially disconcerting because what it means for a writer to be "black" is a vexing question, and Argamon and Olsen fail to interrogate the ways blackness is coded through language in their data. This is a missed opportunity to contribute to our understanding of the linguistic features of writing by situating the work in the historical and cultural contexts of African diasporic writing.

The production of a universalist notion of the "human" relies on defaulting to the aesthetics of dominant cultures and languages. Language wielded in this context determines the limits of universalism, both those included within its ambit and those outside it. Aesthetics that diverge from dominant ones are, accordingly, outside the boundaries of the "human" inscribed in writing. Such an idea is evident in Thomas Babington Macaulay's infamous "Minute on Indian Education," which argues for the cultural supremacy of English literature. Macaulay argues that the whole of the literature of the East cannot compare to one shelf of British literature and proposes that instruction in English literature might produce a group that is Indian in blood but British in taste and intellect.[53] For Macaulay and other British colonizers, literature serves as a strategy of domination under the guise of a universal culture.[54] Given that people writing from the margins, whether Anglophone colonial and postcolonial writers or African American writers of the Harlem Renaissance, have used writing to lay claim to voices denied to them, the deployment of universalist forms of the human through computer-generated text risks deauthorizing these voices.

Asserting the ability of a text, an algorithm, a piece of software, or a computer to "pass" as human presumes a universal definition of "human" and reduces the totality of humanity to the ability of a computer to perform a task in a particular way defined by a set of limits that reproduces dominant cultural norms. Yet, in the research on these mechanisms, there is a marked lack of clarity of how "human" is defined. In some cases, this scholarship rests on the notion of "human cognition" or the idea that there are certain mechanisms of thought that are, in fact, universal. The ontological and epistemological biases of this scholarship imply that even the notion of human cognition is grounded in the Global North. Universalism in the context of human cognition and humanoid texts brings with it the presumption that "science" mitigates cultural biases and is immune to difference. However, it only manages to reinforce the politics, cultures, and aesthetics of dominant cultural paradigms. Therefore, it is imperative that digital humanities practitioners resist the reinscription of a universal human subject in their scholarship, whether at the level of project design, method, data curation, or algorithm composition.

Notes

1. Baldwin, *Small Wonder*.
2. "Turing Test, 1950."
3. Leonard and King, *Robots Reading* Vogue.
4. Associated Press, "Microsoft Kills."
5. Associated Press, "Microsoft Kills."
6. Associated Press, "Microsoft Kills."
7. Blas, "im here to learn so :))))))."
8. Brodbeck, Hauser, and Iida, "Morphological Evolution."
9. Aristotle, *Politics*.
10. Descartes, *Philosophical Works*, 139.
11. Kant, *Kant*.
12. Darwin, *Descent of Man*, 193.
13. Derrida, *Animal*, 66.
14. McFarland, "What Happened."
15. Haraway, *Simian, Cyborgs, and Women*, 3–5.
16. Haraway, *Staying with the Trouble*, 31–34.
17. Bennett, *Vibrant Matter*, 3–4.
18. Barad, *Meeting the Universe Halfway*, 33–34.
19. Russell and Norvig, *Artificial Intelligence*, 2–3.
20. "Artificial."
21. Adam, *Artificial Knowing*, 20.
22. Lee, "Introduction," 3.
23. Ali, "Towards a Decolonial Computing," 29–30.
24. Ali, "Towards a Decolonial Computing," 31.
25. Taylor, "Could You."
26. Taylor, "Could You."
27. Gibson, Robbins, and Rochat, "White Bias," 344.
28. Bainbridge, Isola, and Olivia, "Intrinsic Memorability," 1325.
29. Khosla et al., "Understanding and Predicting," 2390.
30. Lucas, Chiao, and Paller, "Why Some Faces," 20.
31. See Harding, *Is Science Multicultural?*, 4; Anderson, "Postcolonial Technoscience," 643.
32. Isola, Parikh, Torralba, and Oliva, "Understanding the Intrinsic Memorability," 2429–30.
33. Khosla et al., "Understanding and Predicting," 2392–93.
34. Manovich, *Selfiecity*; Heuser, "Mapping Emotions."
35. Harding, *Is Science Multicultural?*, 8.
36. Stahmer, "Interoperability."
37. Woodward, "MIT System."
38. Kitchin, "Thinking Critically."

39. See Pasquale, *Black Box Society*; Noble, *Algorithms of Oppression*; Diakopoulos, "Algorithmic Accountability."
40. Associated Press, "YouTube Reverses Some Restrictions."
41. Hayles, *How We Became Posthuman*, 3.
42. Marche, "Literature Is Not Data."
43. Hall, "No Digital Humanities."
44. Berry, *Critical Theory*, 214.
45. Dobson, "Can an Algorithm Be Disturbed?," 543–44.
46. Bögel et al., "Collaborative Text Annotation."
47. Clerwell, "Enter the Robot Journalist."
48. Matias, "Swift-Speare."
49. Toomer, "Sound Poem (I)."
50. Said, *Orientalism*, 1–3.
51. Hegel, *Philosophy of History*, 163.
52. Argamon and Olsen, "Words, Patterns."
53. Macaulay, "Minute on Indian Education," 249.
54. Viswanathan, "Currying Favor," 86.

Bibliography

Adam, Alison. *Artificial Knowing: Gender and the Thinking Machine.* London: Routledge, 1998.

Ali, Syed Mustafa. "Towards a Decolonial Computing." In *Ambiguous Technologies: Philosophical Issues, Practical Solutions, Human Nature: Proceedings of the Tenth International Conference on Computer Ethics—Philosophical Enquiry*, edited by Elizabeth A. Buchanan, Paul B. de Laat, Herman T. Tavani, and Jenny Klucarich, 28–35. Lisbon: International Society of Ethics and Information Technology, 2014.

Anderson, Warwick. "Postcolonial Technoscience." *Social Studies of Science* 32, no. 5–6 (2002): 643–58.

Argamon, Shlomo, and Mark Olsen. "Words, Patterns and Documents: Experiments in Machine Learning and Text Analysis." *Digital Humanities Quarterly* 3, no. 2 (2009). http://www.digitalhumanities.org/dhq/vol/3/2/000041/000041.html.

Aristotle. *Politics: A Treatise on Government.* Translated by Benjamin Jowett. Mineola, N.Y.: Dover, 2000.

"Artificial." *Oxford English Dictionary.* 3rd ed. Accessed November 1, 2016. http://www.oed.com/view/Entry/11211?redirectedFrom=artificial#eid.

Associated Press. "Microsoft Kills 'Inappropriate' AI Chatbot That Learned Too Much Online." *Los Angeles Times,* March 25, 2016. Accessed November 1, 2016. http://www.latimes.com/business/la-fi-0325-microsoft-chatbot-20160326-story.html.

Associated Press. "YouTube Reverses Some Restrictions on LGBT-Themed Content following Uproar." *Telegraph,* March 21, 2017. Accessed December 15, 2017. http://www

.telegraph.co.uk/technology/2017/03/21/youtube-reverses-restrictions-gay-themed-content-following-uproar/.

Bainbridge, Wilma, Phillip Isola, and Aude Olivia. "The Intrinsic Memorability of Face Photographs." *Journal of Experimental Psychology* 142, no. 4 (2013): 1323–34.

Baldwin, Peter, dir. *Small Wonder*. Season 1, episode 9, "Slightly Dishonorable." Aired November 2, 1985.

Barad, Karen. *Meeting the Universe Halfway: Quantum Physics and the Entanglement of Matter and Meaning*. New York: Penguin, 2006.

Bennett, Jane. *Vibrant Matter: A Political Ecology of Things*. Durham, N.C.: Duke University Press, 2010.

Berry, David M. *Critical Theory and the Digital*. New York: Bloomsbury, 2014.

Blas, Zach. "im here to learn so :))))))." Zach Blas: Works. Accessed December 15, 2017. http://www.zachblas.info/works/im-here-to-learn-so/.

Bögel, Thomas, Michael Gertz, Evelyn Gius, Janina Jacke, Jan Christoph Meister, Marco Petris, and Jannik Strötgen. "Collaborative Text Annotation Meets Machine Learning: heureCLÉA, a Digital Heuristic of Narrative." *DHCommons Journal* (2015). http://dhcommons.org/journal/issue-1/collaborative-text-annotation-meets-machine-learning-heureclé-digital-heuristic.

Brodbeck, Luzius, Simon Hauser, and Fumiya Iida. "Morphological Evolution of Physical Robots through Model-Free Phenotype Development." *PLoS One* 10, no. 6 (2015). http://journals.plos.org/plosone/article/asset?id=10.1371%2Fjournal.pone.0128444.PDF.

Clerwell, Christer. "Enter the Robot Journalist." *Journalism Practice* 8, no. 5 (2014): 519–31.

Darwin, Charles. *The Descent of Man, and Selection in Relation to Sex*. New York: Plume, 1997.

Derrida, Jacques. *The Animal That Therefore I Am*. Translated by David Willis. New York: Fordham University Press, 2008.

Descartes, René. *The Philosophical Works of Descartes*. Translated by Elizabeth S. Haldane and G. R. T. Ross. Cambridge: Cambridge University Press, 1911.

Diakopoulos, Nicholas. "Algorithmic Accountability." *Digital Journalism* 3, no. 3 (2015): 398–415.

Dobson, James. "Can an Algorithm Be Disturbed?: Machine Learning, Intrinsic Criticism, and the Digital Humanities." *College Literature* 42, no. 4 (2015): 543–64.

Gibson, Bentley, Eric Robbins, and Philippe Rochat. "White Bias in 3–7 Year Olds across Cultures." *Journal of Cognition and Culture* 15, no. 3–4 (2015): 344–73.

Hall, Gary. "There Are No Digital Humanities." In *Debates in the Digital Humanities*, edited by Matthew K. Gold, 133–36. Minneapolis: University of Minnesota Press, 2012.

Haraway, Donna. *Simian, Cyborgs, and Women: The Reinvention of Nature*. London: Routledge, 1991.

Haraway, Donna. *Staying with the Trouble: Making Kin in the Chthulucene*. Durham, N.C.: Duke University Press, 2016.

Harding, Sandra. *Is Science Multicultural? Postcolonialisms, Feminisms, and Epistemologies.* Bloomington: Indiana University Press, 1998.

Hayles, N. Katherine. *How We Became Posthuman.* Chicago: University of Chicago Press, 1999.

Hegel, G. W. F. *The Philosophy of History.* Translated by John Sibree. New York: Dover, 1956.

Heuser, Ryan. "Mapping Emotions in Victorian London." Historypin.org. Accessed November 1, 2016. https://www.historypin.org/en/explore/victorian-london/paging/1.

Isola, Phillip, Devi Parikh, Antonio Torralba, and Aude Oliva. "Understanding the Intrinsic Memorability of Images." *Advances in Neural Information Processing Systems* (2011): 2429–37.

Kant, Immanuel. *Kant: Anthropology from a Pragmatic Point of View.* Edited by Robert B. Louden. Cambridge: Cambridge University Press, 2006.

Khosla, Aditya, Akhil S. Raju, Antonio Torralba, and Aude Oliva. "Understanding and Predicting Image Memorability at a Large Scale." In *Proceedings of the 2015 IEEE International Conference on Computer Vision,* 2390–98. Washington, D.C.: IEEE Computer Society, 2015.

Kitchin, Rob. "Thinking Critically about and Researching Algorithms." *Information, Communication & Society* 20, no. 1 (2016): 1–16.

Lee, Emily S. "Introduction." In *Living Alterities: Phenomenology, Embodiment, and Race,* edited by Emily S. Lee, 1–18. Albany: State University of New York Press, 2014.

Leonard, Peter, and Lindsay King. *Robots Reading* Vogue. Digital Humanities at Yale University Library. Accessed November 1, 2016. http://dh.library.yale.edu/projects/vogue.

Lucas, Heather D., Joan Y. Chiao, and Ken A. Paller. "Why Some Faces Won't Be Remembered: Brain Potentials Illuminate Successful versus Unsuccessful Encoding for Same-Race and Other-Race Faces." *Frontiers in Human Neuroscience* 5 (2011): 20.

Macaulay, Thomas Babington. "Minute on Indian Education." In *The Works of Lord Macaulay,* Vol. 2, edited by Lady Trevelyan, 237–51. London: Longmans, Green, 1866.

Manovich, Lev. *Selfiecity.* Accessed November 1, 2016. http://www.selfiecity.net.

Marche, Stefan. "Literature Is Not Data: Against Digital Humanities." *Los Angeles Review of Books,* October 28, 2012. Accessed April 9, 2017. https://lareviewofbooks.org/article/literature-is-not-data-against-digital-humanities/.

Matias, J. Nathan. "Swift-Speare: Statistical Poetry." Natematias.com, Creative Portfolio. Last modified December 2010. http://natematias.com/portfolio/DesignArt/Swift-SpeareStatisticalP.html.

McFarland, Matt. "What Happened When a Professor Built a Chatbot to Be His Teaching Assistant." *Washington Post,* May 11, 2016. Accessed November 1, 2016. https://www.washingtonpost.com/news/innovations/wp/2016/05/11/this-professor-stunned-his-students-when-he-revealed-the-secret-identity-of-his-teaching-assistant/.

Noble, Safiya. *Algorithms of Oppression: Race, Gender and Power in the Digital Age.* New York: New York University Press, 2016.

Pasquale, Frank. *The Black Box Society: The Secret Algorithms That Control Money and Information.* Cambridge, Mass.: Harvard University Press, 2015.

Russell, Stuart, and Peter Norvig. *Artificial Intelligence: A Modern Approach.* Essex: Pearson, 2013.

Said, Edward. *Orientalism.* New York: Vintage, 1979.

Stahmer, Carl. "Interoperability, Artificial Intelligence, and the Digital Humanities." Originally published January 29, 2012, in *Miscellanea.* Carlstahmer.com. Accessed November 2, 2016. http://www.carlstahmer.com/2012/01/interoperability-artificial-intelligence-and-the-digital-humanities.

Taylor, Harriet. "Could You Fall in Love with a Robot." CNBC.com, March 16, 2016. Accessed November 1, 2016. http://www.cnbc.com/2016/03/16/could-you-fall-in-love-with-this-robot.html.

Toomer, Jean. "Sound Poem (I)." In *The Collected Poems of Jean Toomer,* edited by Robert B. Jones and Margot Toomer Latimer, 15. Chapel Hill: University of North Carolina Press, 1988.

"The Turing Test, 1950." *The Alan Turing Internet Scrapbook.* Alan Turing: The Enigma. Accessed December 15, 2017. http://www.turing.org.uk/scrapbook/test.html.

Viswanathan, Gauri. "Currying Favor: The Politics of British Educational and Cultural Policy in India, 1813–1854." *Social Text* no. 19/20 (Autumn 1988): 85–104.

Woodward, Curt. "MIT System Hits 'Near-Human' Accuracy in Finding Memorable Photos." BetaBoston, December 16, 2015. Accessed November 1, 2016. http://www.betaboston.com/news/2015/12/16/mit-algorithm-hits-near-human-accuracy-in-identifying-memorable-photos.

PART I][*Chapter 4*

Accounting and Accountability

Feminist Grant Administration and Coalitional Fair Finance

DANIELLE COLE, IZETTA AUTUMN MOBLEY,
JACQUELINE WERNIMONT, MOYA BAILEY, T. L. COWAN,
AND VERONICA PAREDES

Yea, I can't do this anymore if the money isn't more efficient. This is the uncomfortable reality. I am poor. I make $25k a year at most for 2 adults while I'm disabled and my roommate is looking for work but is struggling in a racist police state to find work with a record.

This $750 was a month of rent that was spoken for. When taking the job, I did so with the idea that id have the money no later than 2 weeks after completing the work. I cannot afford to do any work that doesn't pay in a timely way. I have already borrowed $300 from my mother who is borrowing money from her mother and told her I'd be able to pay her back last week. Maybe that was irresponsible. But I work jobs where I get cash in hand or get paid no more than two weeks later for services rendered. So I literally am too broke to be doing this shit. Like, I'm checking my mailbox every day for this shit and I'm still sending paperwork? That's not ok at all. Especially when we are talking about ethics and work and research.

I would also suggest not to invite any other poor black femmes until they can resolve this issue and make payment quicker and more effective.

—Danielle Cole

Increasingly, grants targeted toward digital scholarship, pedagogy, and inquiry favor projects that demonstrate a commitment to building connections between scholars and "the community." The Digital Media and Learning (DML) grant we were awarded called for projects that "can enhance learning opportunities but privacy and safety must be protected, affective connected learning environments require systems, tools, and policies that foster trust for networks of learners of all ages as well as for parents, mentors, and educators" (HASTAC). However, the granting structures rarely account for accountability to "the community," especially in the ways that the finances of the grants are administered. We have encountered multiple barriers to successful coproduction and engagement. In this short chapter, we discuss the challenges of trying to do antiracist, coalitional feminist work in the context of nonfeminist institutional structures: specifically, structures governed by fiscal, rather than feminist, logics. While work of scholars like Christine Borgman, Patrik Svensson, Tanya Clement, and Lynne Siemens, among others, have considered existing and future infrastructures for collaborative digital scholarship, few have taken us through the full life-cycle of a grant project that involves nonacademic partners as well.

Digital production–based scholarship work requires collaboration for many reasons. Since there are so many different kinds of skills required to produce most digital work, scholars often collaborate with developers, designers, software engineers, writers, artists, and other content-producers and community partners working outside the university environment who produce critical intellectual work in order to make work that is interesting and responds to the needs of our political and intellectual worlds. Similarly, feminist scholarship has long histories of collaborating across different skill sets, social and economic locations, and backgrounds in coalition- and affinity-oriented research, creation, and activism. Our current focus on contemporary digital feminist scholarship finds so many of us working collaboratively, and funding these collaborations through grants that are administered through various structures of academic and governmental financial accounting. When we are awarded grants, it is never the case that the money simply gets deposited into our bank accounts for us to spend as we see fit.

Rather, when we are awarded a grant, the money is generally entrusted to an institutional oversight structure, usually administered by nonfaculty staff within the university or college. The university or college becomes accountable to the grant-issuing organization for the legal distribution of funds. The grant holder must continually prove the legality of spending through the provision of receipts, invoices, tax information, and so on. Grant holders are expected to be accountable to the grant-administering structure, but often that accountability flows in only one direction. The onus of responsibility falls completely to the research team to demonstrate good faith with respect to the terms of the grant. Grant holders are required to provide evidence of legal spending by producing the required paper trail so that if the grant is ever audited, everyone's ass, especially the ass of the institutional accounting department, is well covered.

How Many People Does It Take to Pay a Collaborator?

As part of the Digital Media and Learning Competition–funded project, first known as Addressing Anti-feminist Violence Online and later as the Center for Solutions to Online Violence (CSOV), we worked with several individuals and groups to produce content to be shared online. The CSOV is "a virtual hub for a distributed community working to address the myriad forms of violence women and femmes experience in digital spaces. . . . We seek to ensure that women and femmes who participate in our connected culture do not have to trade physical and psychological security for access to digital resources and communities" (CSOV).

We set up a communication chain that ran across two large institutional infrastructures (Arizona State University [ASU] and University of California, Irvine [UCI]), through our grant team of six and to social media content producers, artists, and activists. We had nearly twenty different individuals or groups that we paid for content creation and production, and the people involved in getting those people paid included three members of the project team at three different institutions, ten different staff members at ASU, two staff members at DML, and two people at UCI. That means that for any one payment, as many as seventeen people might be involved along the way. That is an infrastructural nightmare just waiting to happen.

The CSOV created and collected materials to serve four stakeholder groups: (1) survivors of online violence, (2) educators, (3) journalists, and (4) people interested in "doing better" in relation to their own roles in perpetuating online violence and harm. One of the unique features of this work was a series of materials that outlined online research ethics and proposed responsible uses of social media content in research, teaching, and journalism. This included the "Power and Respect" handout, which featured the "Respect Wheel" and the "Power and Control Wheel"; together, these two illustrations delineate what enacting digital violence looks like and what practicing digital respect entails. They were designed by a subset of our team called The Alchemists, including Bianca Laureno, I'Nasah Crockett, Maegan Ortiz, Jessica Marie Johnson, Sydette Harry, Izetta Autumn Mobley, and Danielle Cole. Designer Liz Andrade illustrated their original design into powerful graphics. Moya Bailey and T.L. Cowan created "Research Ethics for Social Media in the Classroom" guidelines, and we held a series of online kitchen-table workshops on research ethics which we then compiled into a Research Ethics, Social Media and Accountability video series with workshop facilitators Alexandrina Agloro, micha cárdenas, Dorothy Kim, Joss Greene, Izetta Autumn Mobley, and Veronica Paredes. We also published a series of blog essays, Journalism, Social Media and Ethics, by Jamie Nesbitt Golden and Monique Judge, and Mikki Kendall's graphic novel *Paths*, which is geared toward a young-adult readership learning about respectful and disrespectful social media practices, image circulation, and privacy. CSOV student interns Sarah Goodman and Raquelle Potts worked with Wernimont to collect and organize hundreds of key terms with definitions, resources, and site-specific tools.

Throughout the process of this project, the people involved worked to talk about and be attentive to the realities of money. We wanted to be mindful of those in the project who have less access to money, who would be vulnerable to delays because they are not employed full time and getting a livable wage on a regular basis. A foundational premise of this project was to interrupt the imperialist, entitled, extractive norms of "community-based" research and to produce reciprocal benefits among all members of the research team (Bailey, "All the Digital Humanists," "#transform(ing)DH"; Moreton-Robinson; Smith). Collectively, we tried to build a collaborative framework structured by accountability across people of very different incomes and emphasizing moving resources into the hands of the folks who were often not paid for their work in creating and sustaining womanist, Black feminist, trans, Latinx, queer, and antiviolence culture and politics online.

It is important to note that all of us involved in this project understand ourselves to be womanists and feminists. As such, we believe that our relationship to the privileges that come with being connected with academia requires a critical relationship to these institutions. However, the degrees to which we are comfortable and even able to present these critiques are varied. We did agree that we wanted to direct as much of this money toward the communities most affected, those being women and femmes of color. It is well documented that Black and Latinx women make substantially less than white wage-earning men. More than that, research shows that Black and Latinx families amass considerably less wealth than white families (AAUW; SPLC; Temple and Tucker). Nevertheless, our collective agreement, however well intentioned, was not enough to mitigate the power structures of both the academic industrial complex (AIC) and the grant industrial complex (GIC). We were (and still are) working inside institutions and bureaucracies that do not necessarily share our commitments.

This reality caused harm to those who were waiting for money for basic living needs. It also created harm for some of our administrative colleagues who were working hard to ensure that we could advance this project but who themselves were subject to legal and institutional barriers and even ridicule (some of our business staff were laughed at for advocating on behalf of grant budget–approved payments) by those with more authority or power. While the project and our team were committed to preventing harm, we found that negative affect and precarity ran through our entire network. We do not want our experience to dissuade anyone from doing important work. We do, however, want people to be aware. We have some hard-won insights about the upper- and middle-class fiscal temporalities that set university and other institutional accounting policies, as well as how to keep money on the table and keep it moving in the direction you want it to be moving. Universities are not set up to pay money to people who don't already have money.

Money is important. For folks who have never been poor, who have never had bad credit or no access to credit, no access to family financial backup, or other middle- and upper-class experiences of money, this might be difficult to keep in mind. Sums of money like $50, $250, $750, or $1,000 have a larger impact on quality of life for people who are poor or low income, as many graduate students, artists, activists, community organizers, adjunct faculty, and other paid collaborators are.

While some folks in our collaborative group are professors and experience the stipends they get for giving talks, or doing additional collaborations, as "extra" money on top of an adequate and regular salary, many folks who are getting paid by grants experience this money as necessary for living expenses like rent, food, childcare, and paying the bills. It means that people are relying on you and the infrastructure at your institution to get paid as soon as possible. It means that while a fully salaried faculty grant holder might file the paperwork as part of a busy workday and not think about it again, the person who is getting paid is checking their mailbox every day hoping that the check will come. One way to be accountable for this difference is for the financial liaison and/or grant holder to set calendar reminders to check in with the progress of check processing or to ask that you be sent a notice when the check goes out. Set a notification for yourself around the time that the check is supposed to be issued and follow up with the accounts payable office if you have not received a "check sent" notification. Working across class differences is a massive challenge for feminist coalitional projects. Financial accountability at the level of economic fairness and expediency is a feminist issue. Sure, a grant holder's final report to the granting agency requires an awardee to be accountable about who got paid and for what. But feminist accountability needs to attend to how fast people got paid and if they got paid fairly for the often extra time that is required for feminist collaboration—all the emails to follow up on a project, all the energy it takes to keep responding well after a project was supposed to be over. Professors' salaries vary and particularly, for those of us who are women, queer, people of color, and in nonscience disciplines, our salaries are even smaller than faculty salaries on average. Additionally, many of us live on a nine-month pay schedule, which means we are working on a tight budget in the summer months. Even though we had considered ways to bypass the bureaucratic structures of our institutions and pay people directly (thus taking on the wait to be reimbursed ourselves), we were unable to do so because of our own financial limitations. This process reminds us that even with the relative privilege of a salaried professorship, capitalism is still limiting our ability to do what is fair and right.

A grant application is a fantastical document. It asks applicants to imagine a fully funded future, to enter a rhapsodic dream about what can be done with all of that "support." It is unwieldy; it asks applicants to predict budgets before they know what funding might be available. Grant applicants produce a mystical kind of contract that binds applicants into a materially real engagement. When we dream up a plan for funding to support collaborative community-based scholarship, it is necessary to at first see only possibility: *The things we could do with $100,000.00!* But through bureaucracy, that $100,000 is quickly whittled away when you try to give people the compensation that their hard work and experience deserve. The trick is figuring out how to do the work of administering grants in a way that anticipates and sees through the cloaked fiscal logics of the corporate university, which prioritize accountability to the accounting department above all else, and navigate these accounting structures in order to build and sustain projects that are accountable to our communities, coalitions, and networks. Because the requirements of these accounting systems often change during the course of a grant and because the material realities of the people relying on the grant funds as livelihood are often urgent, grant holders often find that they are not able to perform the magic of making it all work all of the time.

Grants operate by business and fiscal logics that are often not easily reconciled with the social justice framework that many feminist grant holders try to use when engaged in the work of collaborative digital scholarship and activism. Grant applications ask us to know in advance how every penny will be spent. They do not account for process-centered collaborative research in which projects change based on new information, new experiences, and the always shifting needs or knowledge of the collaborative research community. Upper- and middle-class fiscal temporalities of academia come from a place of privilege, in that they assume that conditions will remain consistent and predictable rather than when you are working with marginalized communities and people who are often in situations where life is not as predictable or consistent.

While we were talking about money and making money as an issue within our group, we still ended up in multiple situations where the payment of this money was delayed for weeks or months due to institutional barriers—regulations that meant we could not make out payments in people's court-ordered, documented new legal names because the IRS records did not match, new sets of forms being introduced partway through our grant cycle, and/or proliferating forms to be filled out for one-time payments—creating crisis situations, as in the epigraph to this chapter by Danielle Cole, for the folks who were counting on this money for rent, food, and other necessary life-sustaining materials.

The administrative slog required other women, specifically, women of color, to labor—often putting in inordinate hours—to complete the work of payment to marginalized contributors. The structural positioning of women of color within the corporate neoliberal university produced an enhanced oppressive dynamic, in which often disempowered women of color in administrative positions were responsible for addressing system failures that prevented other marginalized women of color from being compensated. Patricia Hill Collins's matrix of oppression is a useful framework under which to think about digital and economic marginalization of women of color. This leads us to inquire as to what such power dynamics tell us about the structure of disenfranchisement. Certainly it suggests that structures of oppression are deeply embedded. Thus, feminist scholars doing community digital humanities work must think about undoing the very system in place to sustain the work, in order to do the work ethically and without doing further harm to those marginalized members who are laboring to produce knowledge: What are the currencies of academia, and how are those qualitatively different (and perhaps unusable) to those producing knowledge at the margins?

Accounting and Accountability [63

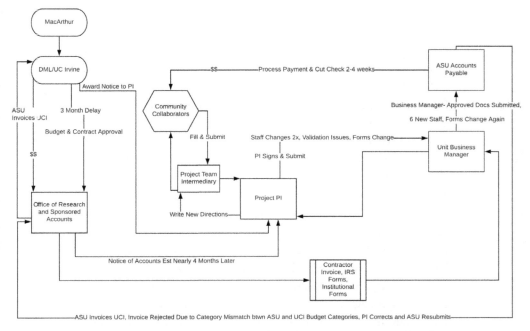

Figure 4.1. This figure maps the work flow required in order to pay non-university-based collaborators in the course of the grant. The figure maps both the successful flows and the many places where the networked labor failed temporarily. Illustration by Jacqueline Wernimont.

As Figure 4.1 shows, the network of grant administrative labor includes the grant holder(s), the granting agency and all the people who make the granting and administrative decisions, the IRS, each collaborator who needs to get paid and all of the people in their worlds who rely on that payment, every business manager, accounts payable staff, and other administrators who process the paperwork, and the universities or colleges that are paid to administer grants on behalf of the granting agency. This network is connected through communication systems (primarily email messages and file attachments) that are often unreliable, unsecure, and prone to generate misunderstanding. For example, sensitive personal data like social security numbers, birth dates, and mailing addresses could be lost or accidentally circulated to incorrect recipients. The number of people in the process can lead to misunderstandings, including when the forms will be completed and when payment can be expected.

Here we offer some ideas about how to do community-based work in ways that attend to both the accounting and the accountability of grant administration informed by feminist coalitional praxis and process:

1. *Consult previous grant holders with insider knowledge of the specific grant to which you are applying.* Reach out to previous grant holders that have been

funded by this organization. What are the previous grant holders' experiences of the administrative aspects of the grant? How smoothly or quickly did the money flow? What is the reporting structure like? Do previous grant holders have any advice for the best way to administer one of these grants? Do they have any advice for the best way to pay collaborators with the funds from this grant? Evaluate, with yourself and your team, the likelihood that this grant will help you reach your goals of collaboration and coalition. If it seems unlikely, do not apply for the grant.

2. *Talk with the administrative and accounting staff at your institution who will be handling the money.* Set up a meeting with the person in charge of faculty research grants and reimbursements in your department. Remember that administrative staff members are answerable to accounting structures and that they get in trouble if your paperwork is incomplete or inaccurate. Find out how many levels of oversight the paperwork will need to go through before checks will be issued. Ask what grant paperwork usually gets returned so that you may anticipate these setbacks. Be aware of the conventions that affect spending categories at your home institution and use those consistently in your budget. Find out the most efficient way to file receipts, to bundle grant transactions. You can also ask this trusted staff member the following: Which kinds of expenses are the easiest to process, or the most challenging? What can you do within the structure of the grant, and throughout its duration, to ensure that checks will be issued and sent out as quickly as possible? What is the average timeline you can anticipate? What are the shared best practices? And what are the most frequently encountered challenges? Ask if it will be possible to create a petty cash account for the grant in order to have more direct and quick use of the funds. Finally, be considerate in your interactions with this colleague throughout and document your communications when submitting paperwork.

3. *Meet with colleagues at your university or institution who have administered grants in your department or institution.* Talk with senior faculty and other funded researchers in your department or affiliated groups to find out if they have suggestions about how to navigate the financial accounting system at your home institution. What are the problems that other faculty have encountered in getting their grant monies processed and research collaborators paid? What have been successful strategies for getting checks issued for stipends and reimbursements quickly? What timeline do other faculty report from date of sending in paperwork to date of checks being issued? Find out what to do when paperwork gets delayed and how to track the paperwork through the process.

4. *Create a research team that reflects the womanist and feminist values of your project.* When you are imagining your grant-leadership team, remember that this team needs to include folks who are doing the community-based work

that your grant seeks to fund as well as folks across the different kinds of economic realities that will be involved in the project. This includes graduate students, since grad students often have a very clear sense of the systemic blockages in the administering institution. Have as many people as possible look over your grant's budget before you submit it.

5. *Identify a member of your team to be the financial liaison for the grant.* Rather than the principal investigator of the grant taking on the research leadership as well as the accounting leadership, include a second person from the administering institution who will handle all of the money. Make sure this person has a good relationship with the financial officers who will be processing payment requests. Ideally, this is a paid position budgeted within the grant itself. Be aware that within the lifespan of a grant, forms and procedures for getting people paid may (or are likely to) change. The grant's financial liaison or project manager should check in with the departmental financial officers to make sure everything is still up-to-date and that you are giving your paid collaborators the correct paperwork to fill out. Ideally you can pre-fill some of the fields (such as university department) or highlight which fields need completion for folks filling out the forms. Keep in mind that lots of people do not have printers at home, so if your university requires an original signature, this may pose a problem and you might want to mail hard copies of the forms. If you are paying people whom you are bringing to campus, set aside some time during the visit to let folks fill out the paperwork while on site.

6. *Be realistic about the disbursement of grant money and get people paid on time!* It is often not clear when a grant is being drafted exactly who the paid collaborators will be. If possible, have detailed conversations about what payment is fair for the work of the project, and discuss how the payments will be made. When an invitation is made to a collaborator who will be paid for work on the grant, make sure to indicate the outside (longest) timeframe within which the payment will be made after the work is complete. Make this clear *in the initial invitation.* In most universities, unless you are able to ask for funds in advance, it usually takes *eight weeks* to go from submitting paperwork to a departmental financial officer to the check actually arriving in the mailbox of the paid collaborator. Some university payment systems track the process for you, and so payment updates can be sent to paid collaborators, but this is a rare case. Usually, once you have sent the paperwork off, it becomes difficult to trace, and it is only after eight weeks, when the check has not arrived in your collaborator's mailbox, that you realize there is a problem. Find out if there is a way to track the progress of the payment, and make a note in your calendar to do this throughout the process. This can be part of the terms of reference for the grant's financial liaison or project manager (who, ideally, is not the PI [principal investigator]).

7. *Develop a plan for dealing with confidential and sensitive information.* Sending confidential information like social security numbers over email can be a dodgy business. You can offer to get that information over the phone, or you can set up a secure or encrypted document transfer through Dropbox or a payroll anonymizer. Keep in mind that for lots of people, filing forms is stressful. A "straightforward" relationship to finances, names, and economic transactions is a privilege enjoyed by very few folks. Form-filling stress and complicated relationships with economic transactions are often generated by personal histories of poverty and racialized financial surveillance and criminalization. Sometimes it is because you are undocumented or because of a precarious labor status in the country you are working in, that is, international students and other workers, or because your name registered with the governmental tax agency is not the same name that you use in everyday life. These are all factors that impact the network of grant administration. As the grant holder is the intermediary between people getting paid and the people processing the payments, it is the grant holder's job to work across the network, and to build understanding between these nodes. For example, if a paid collaborator's name is different from that person's tax name, you can make this transaction less complicated by asking the collaborator for a letter that confirms the collaborator's tax name. When a grant holder provides this documentation to the administrative staff, the grant holder/PI can have that conversation without requiring the collaborator to defend themselves against the accounting structures that are always on the lookout for "fraud." When you are already precarious, you are more likely to be accused of trying to rip off the system. *A grant holder's job is to make this system work for paid collaborators.*

Creative Networks and Feminist Finances

Rather than discourage you from applying for grants, what we want to leave you with is that community partnerships are worth the work required to produce equitable relationships. Community partnerships are a central part of the work we do. The AIC and GIC make this process exceedingly difficult but not insurmountable. You can hack the system. If you work with a team, start early, and get creative. We know that even with all of this planning the institution will still try thwart your efforts. In those cases, it is important to communicate honestly with your collaborators. But beyond learning to navigate the rigid system as it exists, we are reenergized and reminded of the need for completely different systems.

A particularly troublesome dynamic is that there are a myriad of gatekeepers, including ourselves, between communities and the resources they need. Given the chart in Figure 4.1, our task is to clear the way between our collaborators and the resources they need. Additionally, we must design research projects in such a way that the outcomes are mutually beneficial for all parties involved. Our efforts require new relationships with granting organizations that do not require the massive administrative red tape that keeps people outside the AIC from the compensation they earn.

Beyond reforming the system that exists, our experience highlights the need for a complete reimagining of funding structures. What would it mean for granters to trust collaborators and communities with money up front? What would it mean for money to move differently, going directly from the funders to the collaborators and skipping the university bureaucracy altogether? Current tips and answers to frequently asked questions focus on the federal regulations, like the nondiscrimination and federal drug-free workplace guidelines offered by the National Endowment for the Humanities. Similarly, foundations tend to offer guidelines only on fiduciary responsibility, which is not the same as responsibility to a community and/or collaborators. Such information underlines the bureaucratic operations and their relative nonengagement with the realities of communities without other stable financial support.

The ground game for community partnerships is fundamentally different from that of large institutions. We hope that our experience and our closing thoughts can be the beginning of a conversation with funding agencies and a seed for what we hope you might look for in your future partnerships.

Bibliography

American Association of University Women (AAUW). "The Simple Truth about the Gender Pay Gap." n.d. https://www.aauw.org/research/the-simple-truth-about-the-gender-pay-gap/.

Bailey, Moya. "#transform(ing)DH Writing and Research: An Autoethnography of Digital Humanities and Feminist Ethics." *Digital Humanities Quarterly* 9, no. 2 (2015). http://www.digitalhumanities.org/dhq/vol/9/2/000209/000209.html.

Bailey, Moya Z. "All the Digital Humanists Are White, All the Nerds Are Men, but Some of Us Are Brave." *Journal of Digital Humanities* 1, no. 1 (2011). http://journalofdigitalhumanities.org/1-1/all-the-digital-humanists-are-white-all-the-nerds-are-men-but-some-of-us-are-brave-by-moya-z-bailey/.

Borgman, Christine L. *Scholarship in the Digital Age: Information, Infrastructure, and the Internet.* Cambridge, Mass.: MIT Press, 2007.

Center for Solutions to Online Violence (CSOV). FemTechNet.org. http://femtechnet.org/csov/.

Clement, Tanya L. "An Information Science Question in DH Feminism" *Digital Humanities Quarterly* 9, no. 2 (2015). http://digitalhumanities.org:8081/dhq/vol/9/2/000186/000186.html.

Collins, Patricia Hill. "Black Feminist Thought in the Matrix of Domination." In *Black Feminist Thought: Knowledge, Consciousness, and the Politics of Empowerment*, 221–38. Boston: Unwin Hyman, 1990.

Earhart, Amy, and Andrew Jewell, eds. *The American Literature Scholar in the Digital Age.* Ann Arbor: University of Michigan Press, 2011.

"Grant Management: Individuals." National Endowment for the Humanities. https://www.neh.gov/grants/manage/individuals#all-awards.

HASTAC. "Trust Challenge—Building Trust in Connected Learning Environments: DML 5." HASTAC, 2015. https://www.hastac.org/trust-challenge-building-trust-connected-learning-environments-dml-5.

"Managing Grant Funds." Mellon Foundation. https://mellon.org/grants/grantmaking-policies-and-guidelines/grantmaking-policies/managing-grant-funds/.

Moreton-Robinson, Aileen. *The White Possessive: Property, Power, and Indigenous Sovereignty.* Minneapolis: University of Minnesota Press, 2015.

Siemens, Lynne. "'It's a Team If You Use "Reply All"': An Exploration of Research Teams in Digital Humanities Environments." *Literary and Linguistic Computing* 24, no. 2 (June 1, 2009): 225–33.

Smith, Linda Tuhiwai. *Decolonizing Methodologies: Research and Indigenous Peoples.* 2nd ed. London: Zed Books, 2012.

Southern Poverty Law Center (SPLC). "Injustice on Our Plates." Southern Poverty Law Center, n.d. Accessed December 4, 2017. https://www.splcenter.org/20101107/injustice-our-plates.

Svensson, Patrik. "From Optical Fiber to Conceptual Cyberinfrastructure." *Digital Humanities Quarterly* 5, no. 1 (2011). http://www.digitalhumanities.org/dhq/vol/5/1/000090/000090.html.

Temple, Brandie, and Jasmine Tucker. "Equal Pay for Black Women." *National Women's Law Center* (blog), July 27, 2017. https://nwlc.org/resources/equal-pay-for-black-women/.

Zeller-Berkman, Sarah. "Building Connected Credentials: What We Learned from Trusting Each Other and Youth Voice." *HASTAC* (blog), September 30, 2016. Accessed December 4, 2017. https://www.hastac.org/blogs/sarah-zeller-berkman/2016/09/30/building-connected-credentials-what-we-learned-trusting-each.

PART II
VALUES

PART II || Chapter 5

Be More Than Binary

Deb Verhoeven

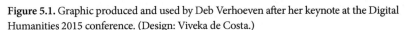

Figure 5.1. Graphic produced and used by Deb Verhoeven after her keynote at the Digital Humanities 2015 conference. (Design: Viveka de Costa.)

[71]

PART II][Chapter 6

Representation at Digital Humanities Conferences (2000–2015)

NICKOAL EICHMANN-KALWARA, JEANA JORGENSEN, AND SCOTT B. WEINGART

Digital humanities (DH), we are told, exists under a "big tent," with porous borders, little gatekeeping, and, heck, everyone's just plain "nice." Indeed, the term itself is not used definitionally, but merely as a "tactical convenience" to get stuff done without worrying so much about traditional disciplinary barriers. DH is "global," "public," and diversely populated. It will "save the humanities" from its crippling self-reflection (cf. this essay), while simultaneously saving the computational social sciences from their uncritical approaches to data. DH contains its own mirror: it is both humanities done digitally and the digital as scrutinized humanistically. As opposed to the staid, "backward-looking" humanities we are used to, the digital humanities "experiments," "plays," and even "embraces failure" on ideological grounds. In short, we are the hero Gotham needs.

Digital humanities, we are told, is a narrowly defined excuse to push a "neoliberal agenda," a group of "bullies" more interested in forcing humanists to code than in speaking truth to power. It is devoid of cultural criticism, and because of the way DHers uncritically adopt tools and methods from the tech industry, they in fact often reinforce preexisting power structures (Allington, Brouillette, and Golumbia). DH is nothing less than an unintentionally rightist vehicle for techno-utopianism, drawing from the same font as Massive Open Online Courses (MOOCs) and complicit in their devaluing of education, diversity, and academic labor. It is equally complicit in furthering both the surveillance state and the surveillance economy, exemplified in its stunning lack of response to the Snowden leaks. As a progeny of the computer sciences, digital humanities has inherited the same lack of gender and racial diversity, and any attempt to remedy the situation is met with incredible resistance.

The truth, as it so often does, lies somewhere in the middle of these extreme caricatures. It's easy to ascribe attributes to digital humanities synecdochically, painting the whole with the same brush as one of its constituent parts. One would be forgiven, for example, for coming away from the annual international Alliance of Digital Humanities Organizations (ADHO) Digital Humanities conference assuming DH were a parade of white men quantifying literary text. An attendee of the Humanities, Arts, Science, and Technology Alliance and Collaboratory (HASTAC), on the other hand, might leave seeing DH as a diverse community focused on pedagogy, but lacking in primary research. Similar straw-snapshots may be drawn from specific journals, subcommunities, regions, or organizations.

But these synecdoches have power. Our public face sets the course of DH, via whom it entices to engage with us, how it informs policy agendas and funding allocations, and who gets inspired to be the next generation of digital humanists. Especially important is the constituency and presentation of the annual Digital Humanities conference. Every year, several hundred students, librarians, staff, faculty, industry professionals, administrators, adjuncts, and independent researchers converge for the conference, organized by ADHO. As an umbrella organization of six international digital humanities constituent organizations, as well as over two hundred DH centers in a few dozen countries, ADHO and its conference ought to represent the geographic, disciplinary, and demographic diversity of those who identify as digital humanists. And, as a large subset of DH prides itself on its activism and its social and public goals, if the annual DH conference does not celebrate this diversity, the DH community may suffer a crisis of identity (okay, a *bigger* crisis of identity).

So what does the DH conference look like, to an outsider? Is it diverse? What topics are covered? Where is it held? Who is participating, who is attending, and where are they coming from? This essay offers incomplete answers to these questions for fifteen years of DH conferences (2000–2015), focusing particularly on DH2013 (Nebraska, United States), DH2014 (Lausanne, Switzerland), and DH2015 (Sydney, Australia).[1] We do so with a double agenda: (1) to call out the biases and lack of diversity at ADHO conferences in the earnest hope it will help improve future years' conferences, and (2) to show that simplistic, reductive quantitative methods can be applied critically, and need not feed into techno-utopic fantasies or an unwavering acceptance of proxies as a direct line to Truth. By "distant reading" DH and turning our "macroscopes" on ourselves, we offer a critique of our culture, and hopefully inspire fruitful discomfort in DH practitioners who apply often-dehumanizing tools to their subjects, but have not themselves fallen under the same distant gaze.

Among our findings, we observe a large gender gap for authorship that is not mirrored among those who simply *attend* the conference. We also show a heavily gendered topical landscape, which likely contributes to topical biases during peer review. Geographic diversity has improved over fifteen years, suggesting that ADHO's strategy to expand beyond the customary North American–European rotation was a success. That said, there continues to be a visible bias against non-English names in the peer review process. We could not get data on ethnicity, race, or skin color, but given our regional and name data, as well as personal experience, we suspect in this area, diversity remains quite low.

We do notice some improvement over time and, especially in the last few years, a growing awareness of our own diversity problems. The #whatifDH2016 hashtag, for example, was a reaction to an all-male series of speakers introducing DH2015 in Sydney. The hashtag caught on and made it to ADHO's committee on conferences, who will use it in planning future events.[2] Our remarks here are in the spirit of #whatifDH2016; rather than using this study as an excuse to defame digital humanities, we hope it becomes a vehicle to improve ADHO's conference, and through it the rest of our community.

Social Justice and Equality in the Digital Humanities

DIVERSITY IN THE ACADEMY

In order to contextualize gender and ethnicity in the DH community, we must take into account developments throughout higher education. This is especially important, since much of DH work is done in university and other ivory tower settings. Clear progress has been made from the times when all-male, all-white colleges were the norm, but there are still concerns about the marginalization of scholars who are not white, male, able-bodied, heterosexual, or native English-speakers. Many campuses now have diversity offices and have set diversity-related goals at both the faculty and student levels (for example, see Ohio State University's diversity objectives and strategies 2007–2012: Ohio State University, "Diversity Action Plan"). On the digital front, blogs such as *Conditionally Accepted, Fight the Tower, University of Venus,* and more all work to expose the normative biases in academia through activist dialogue.

Viewed through both a historical and a contemporary lens, there are data supporting the clustering of women and other minority scholars in certain realms of academia, from specific fields and subjects to contingent positions. When it comes to gender, the term "feminization" has been applied both to academia in general and to specific fields. It contains two important connotations: that of an area in which women are in the majority, and the sense of a change over time, such that numbers of women participants are increasing in relation to men (Leathwood and Read, 10). It can also signal a less quantitative shift in values, "whereby 'feminine' values, concerns, and practices are seen to be changing the culture of an organization, a field of practice or society as a whole" (10).

In terms of specific disciplines, the feminization of academia has taken a particular shape. Historian Lynn Hunt suggests the following propositions about feminization in the humanities and history specifically: the feminization of history parallels what is happening in the social sciences and humanities more generally; the feminization of the social sciences and humanities is likely accompanied by a decline in status and resources; and other identity categories, such as ethnic minority status and age or generation, also interact with feminization in ways that are still becoming coherent.

Feminization has clear consequences for the perception and assignation of value of a given field. Hunt writes, "There is a clear correlation between relative pay and the proportion of women in a field; those academic fields that have attracted a relatively high proportion of women pay less on average than those that have not attracted women in the same numbers." Thus, as we examine the topics that tend to be clustered by gender in DH conference submissions, we must keep in mind the potential correlations of feminization and value, though it is beyond the scope of this chapter to engage in chicken-or-egg debates about the causal relationship between misogyny and the devaluing of women's labor and women's topics.

There is no obvious ethnicity-based parallel to the concept of the feminization of academia; it wouldn't be culturally intelligible to talk about the "people-of-colorization of academia," or the "non-white-ization of academia." At any rate, according to a U.S. Department of Education survey, in 2013, 79 percent of all full-time faculty in degree-granting postsecondary institutions were white. The increase of nonwhite faculty from 2009 (19.2 percent of the whole) to 2013 (21.5 percent) is very small indeed. However, both people of color and women (as well as other minorities) may experience microaggressions in academic contexts. Microaggressions are "brief, everyday exchanges that send denigrating messages to certain individuals because of their group membership" (Sue, xvi). A lack of representation, and further having that lack pointed out in dismissive, subtly insulting, or patronizing ways, could contribute to the continuation of oppressive and exclusive dynamics.

Why does this matter? As Jeffrey Milem, Mitchell Chang, and Anthony Lising Antonio write in regard to faculty of color, "Having a diverse faculty ensures that students see people of color in roles of authority and as role models or mentors. Faculty of color are also more likely than other faculty to include content related to diversity in their curricula and to utilize active learning and student-centered teaching techniques.... A coherent and sustained faculty diversity initiative must exist if there is to be any progress in diversifying the faculty" (25). By centering marginalized voices, scholarly institutions have the ability to send messages about who belongs in academia. The same applies to the digital humanities community.

Recent Criticisms of Diversity in DH

Efforts to address inequities within the DH community and conferences have been on the radar for several years, and have recently gained special attention, as digital humanists and other academics alike have called for critical and feminist engagement in diversity and a move away from what seems to be an exclusionary culture. In January 2011, *THATCamp SoCal* included a section called "Diversity in DH," in which participants explored the lack of openness in DH and, in the end, produced a document, "Toward an Open Digital Humanities," that summarized their discussions. The "Overview" in this document mirrors the same conversation we have had for the last several years: "We recognize that a wide diversity of people is necessary to make digital humanities function. As such, digital humanities must take active strides to include all the areas of study that comprise the humanities and must strive to include participants of diverse age, generation, sex, skill, race, ethnicity, sexuality, gender, ability, nationality, culture, discipline, areas of interest. Without open participation and broad outreach, the digital humanities movement limits its capacity for critical engagement" ("THATCamp Southern California 2011"). This proclamation represents the critiques of the DH landscape in 2011, in which it was assumed that DH practitioners and participants were privileged and white; that they excluded student-learners; and that they held myopic views of what constitutes DH. Most importantly for this chapter, *THATCamp SoCal*'s "Diversity in DH" section participants called for critical approaches and social justice of DH scholarship and participation, including "principles for feminist/non-exclusionary groundrules [sic] in each session (e.g., 'step up/step back') so that the loudest/most entitled people don't fill all the quiet moments." They also advocated defending the least-heard voices "so that the largest number of people can benefit."

While this wasn't the first conversation on these issues, these voices certainly didn't fall flat, and they encapsulated a growing criticism of DH. However, since THATCamps are often composed of geographically local DH microcommunities, they benefit from an inclusive environment but suffer as isolated events. As a result, it seems that the larger, discipline-specific venues which have greater attendance and attraction continue to amplify privileged voices. Even so, 2011 continued to represent a year that called for critical engagement in diversity in DH, with an explicit "Big Tent" theme for DH2011 held in Stanford, California. Embracing the concept the "Big Tent" deliberately opened the doors and widened the spectrum of DH, at least in terms of methods and approaches. However, as Melissa Terras pointed out, DH was "still a very rich, very western academic field" (Terras, "Peering"), even with a few DH2011 presentations engaging specifically with topics of diversity in DH.[3]

A focus on diversity-related issues has only grown in the interim. We've recently seen greater attention to and criticism of DH exclusionary culture, for instance, at the 2015 Modern Language Association (MLA) annual convention, which included the roundtable discussion "Disrupting Digital Humanities." It confronted the "gatekeeping impulse" in DH, and echoing THATCamp SoCal 2011, these panelists aimed to shut down hierarchical dialogues in DH, encourage nontraditional scholarship, amplify "marginalized voices," advocate for DH novices, and generously support the work of peers.[4] The theme for DH2015 in Sydney, Australia, was "Global Digital Humanities," and between its successes and collective action arising from frustrations at its failures, the community seems poised to pay even greater attention to diversity. Other recent initiatives in this vein worth mention include #dhpoco, GO::DH, #transformdh, and Jacqueline Wernimont's "Build a Better Panel," whose activist goals are helping diversify the community and raise awareness of areas where the community can improve.[5]

While it would be fruitful to conduct a longitudinal historiographical analysis of diversity in DH, more recent criticisms illustrate a history of perceived exclusionary culture, which is why we hope to provide a data-driven approach to continue the conversation and call for critical engagement and intervention.

Data

While DH as a whole has been critiqued for its lack of diversity and inclusion, how does the annual ADHO DH conference measure up? To explore this in a data-driven fashion, we have gathered publicly available annual ADHO conference programs and schedules from 2000 to 2015. From those conference materials, we have entered presentation and author information into a spreadsheet to analyze various trends over time, such as gender and geography as indicators of diversity. Particular information that we have collected includes presentation title, keywords (if available), abstract and full-text (if available), presentation type, author name, author institutional affiliation and academic department (if available), and corresponding country of that affiliation at the time of the presentation(s). We normalized and hand-cleaned names, institutions, and departments, so that, to the best of our knowledge, each author entry represented a unique person and, accordingly, was assigned a unique ID. Next, we added gender information (m/f/other/unknown) to authors by a combination of hand-entry and automated inference. While this is problematic for many reasons, since it does not allow for diversity in gender options and tracing gender changes over time, it does give us a useful preliminary lens to view gender diversity at DH conferences.[6]

For 2013's conference, ADHO instituted a series of changes aimed at improving inclusivity, diversity, and quality. This drive was steered by that year's program committee chair, Bethany Nowviskie, alongside 2014's chair, Melissa Terras. Their reformative goals matched our current goals in this essay, and speak to a long history of experimentation and improvement efforts on behalf of ADHO. Their changes included making the conference more welcome to outsiders through ending policies that only insiders knew about; making the Call For Papers (CFP) less complex and easier to translate into multiple languages; taking reviewer language competencies into account systematically; and streamlining the submission and review process.

The biggest noticeable change to DH2013, however, was the institution of a reviewer bidding process and a phase of semi-open peer review. Peer reviewers were invited to read through and rank every submitted abstract according to how qualified they felt to review the abstract. Following this, the conference committee would match submissions to qualified peer reviewers, taking into account conflicts of interest. Submitting authors were invited to respond to reviews, and the committee would make a final decision based on the various reviews and rebuttals. As of 2017, this process is still in place, though changes continue to be made. In 2016, for example, "Diversity" and "Multilinguality" were added as new keywords authors could append to their submissions.

While the list of submitted abstracts was private, accessible only to reviewers, as reviewers ourselves we had access to the submissions during the bidding phase. We used this access to create a dataset of conference submissions for DH2013, DH2014, and DH2015, which includes author names, affiliations, submission titles, author-selected topics, author-chosen keywords, and submission types (long paper, short paper, poster, panel).

We augmented this dataset by looking at the final conference programs in 2013, 2014, and 2015, noting which submissions eventually made it onto the final conference program, and how they changed from the submission to the final product. This allows us to roughly estimate the acceptance rate of submissions, by comparing the submitted abstract lists to the final programs. It is not perfect, however, given that we don't actually know whether submissions that didn't make it to the final program were rejected, or if they were accepted and withdrawn. We also do not know who reviewed what, nor do we know the reviewers' scores or any associated editorial decisions.

The original dataset, then, included fields for title, authors, author affiliations, original submission type, final accepted type, topics, keywords, and a Boolean field for whether a submission made it to the final conference program. We cleaned the data up by merging duplicate people, ensuring, for example, if "Melissa Terras" was an author on two different submissions, she counted as the same person. For affiliations, we semiautomatically merged duplicate institutions, found the countries they reside in, and assigned those countries to broad UN regions. We also added data to the set, first automatically guessing a gender for each author, and then correcting the guesses by hand.

Given that abstracts were submitted to conferences with an expectation of privacy, we have not released the full submission dataset; we have, however, released the full dataset of final conference programs.[7]

We would like to acknowledge the gross and problematic simplifications involved in this process of gendering authors without their consent or input. As Miriam Posner has pointed out, with regard to Getty's Union List of Author Names, "no self-respecting humanities scholar would ever get away with such a crude representation of gender in traditional work."[8] And yet, we represent authors in just this crude fashion, labeling authors as male, female, or unknown/other. We did not encode changes of author gender over time, even though we know of at least a few authors in the dataset for whom this applies. We do not use the affordances of digital data to represent the fluidity of gender. This is problematic for a number of reasons, not least of which because, when we take a cookie cutter to the world, everything in the world will wind up looking like cookies.

We made this decision because, in the end, all data quality is contingent to the task at hand. It is possible to acknowledge an ontology's shortcomings while still occasionally using that ontology to a positive effect. This is not always the case: often poor proxies get in the way of a research agenda (for example, citations as indicators of "impact" in digital humanities), rather than align with it. In the humanities, poor proxies are much more likely to get in the way of research than help it along, and afford the ability to make insensitive or reductivist decisions in the name of "scale."

For example, in looking for ethnic diversity of a discipline, one might analyze last names as a proxy for country of origin, or analyze the color of recognized faces in pictures from recent conferences as a proxy for ethnic genealogy. Among other reasons, this approach falls short because ethnicity, race, and skin color are often not aligned, and last names (especially in the United States) are rarely indicative of anything at all. But they're easy solutions, so people use them. These are moments when a bad proxy (and for human categories, proxies are almost universally bad) does not fruitfully contribute to a research agenda. As George E. P. Box put it, "all models are wrong, but some are useful."

Indeed, some models are useful. Sometimes, the stars align and the easy solution is the best one for the question. If someone were researching immediate reactions of racial bias in the West, analyzing skin tone may get us something useful. In this case, the research focus is not someone's racial identity, but someone's race as immediately perceived by others, which would likely align with skin tone. Simply: if a person looks black, that person is more likely to be treated as such by the (white) world at large.[9]

We believe our proxies, though grossly inaccurate, are useful for the questions of gender and geographic diversity and bias. The first step to improving DH conference diversity is noticing a problem; our data show that problem through staggeringly imbalanced regional and gender ratios. With regard to gender bias, showing whether reviewers are less likely to accept papers from authors who appear to be women can reveal entrenched biases, whether or not the author actually identifies as a woman. With that said, we invite future researchers to identify and expand on our admitted categorical errors, allowing everyone to see the contours of our community with even greater nuance.

Analysis

The annual ADHO conference has grown significantly in the last fifteen years, as described in our companion piece, within which can be found a great discussion of our methods.[10] This piece, rather than covering overall conference trends, focuses specifically on issues of diversity and acceptance rates. We cover geographic and gender diversity from 2000 to 2015, with additional discussions of topicality and peer review bias beginning in 2013.

Gender

Women constitute 36.1 percent of the 3,239 authors to DH conference presentations over the last fifteen years, counting every unique author only once. Melissa Terras's name appears on twenty-nine presentations between 2000 and 2015, and Scott B. Weingart's name appears on four presentations, but for the purpose of this metric, each name counts only once. Female authorship representation fluctuates between 29 percent and 38 percent depending on the year.

Weighting every authorship event individually (e.g., Weingart's name counts four times, Terras's twenty-nine times), women's representation drops to 32.7 percent. This reveals that women are less likely to author multiple pieces compared with their male counterparts. More than a third of the DH authorship pool are women, but fewer than a third of every name that appears on a presentation are a woman's. Even fewer single-authored pieces are by a woman; only 29.8 percent of the 984 single-authored works between 2000 and 2015 are female-authored. About a third (33.4 percent) of first authors on presentations are women. See Figure 6.1 for a breakdown of these numbers over time. Note the lack of periodicity, suggesting gender representation is not affected by whether the conference is held in Europe or North America (until 2015, the conference alternated locations every year). The overall ratio wavers, but is neither improving nor worsening over time.

The gender disparity sparked controversy at DH2015 in Sydney. It was, however, at odds with a common anecdotal awareness that many of the most respected role models and leaders in the community are women. To explore this disconnect, we experimented with using centrality in coauthorship networks as a proxy for fame, respectability, and general presence within the DH consciousness. We assume that individuals who author many presentations, coauthor with many people, and

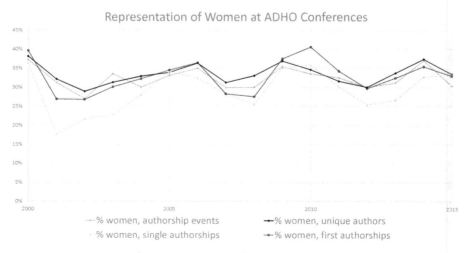

Figure 6.1. Representation of Women at ADHO conferences.

play a central role in connecting DH's disparate communities of authorship are the ones who are most likely to garner the respect (or at least awareness) of conference attendees.

We created a network of authors connected to their coauthors from presentations between 2000 and 2015, with ties strengthening the more frequently two authors collaborate. Of the 3,239 authors in our dataset, 61 percent (1,750 individuals) are reachable by one another via their coauthorship ties. For example, Beth Plale is reachable by Alan Liu because she coauthored with J. Stephen Downie, who coauthored with Geoffrey Rockwell, who coauthored with Alan Liu. Thus, 61 percent of the network is connected in one large component, and there are 299 smaller components, islands of coauthorship disconnected from the larger community.

The average woman coauthors with five other authors, and the average man coauthors with 5.3 other authors. The median number of coauthors for both men and women is four. The average and median of several centrality measurements (closeness, betweenness, pagerank, and eigenvector) for both men and women are nearly equivalent; that is, any given woman is just as likely to be near the coauthorship core as any given man. Naturally, this does not imply that half of the most central authors are women, since only a third of the entire authorship pool are women. It means instead that gender does not influence one's network centrality. Or at least it should.

The statistics show a curious trend for the most central figures in the network. Of the top ten authors who coauthor with the most others, 60 percent are women. Of the top twenty, 45 percent are women. Of the top fifty, 38 percent are women. Of the top one hundred, 32 percent are women. That is, over half of the DH coauthorship stars are women, but the farther toward the periphery you look, the more men occupy the middle-tier positions (i.e., not stars, but still fairly active coauthors). The same holds true for the various centrality measurements: betweenness (60 percent women in the top ten; 40 percent in the top twenty; 32 percent in the top fifty; 34 percent in the top one hundred), pagerank (50 percent women in the top ten; 40 percent in the top twenty; 32 percent in the top fifty; 28 percent in the top one hundred), and eigenvector (60 percent women in the top ten; 40 percent in the top twenty; 40 percent in the top fifty; 34 percent in the top one hundred).

In short, half or more of the DH conference stars are women, but as you creep closer to the network periphery, you are increasingly likely to notice the prevailing gender disparity. This supports the mismatch between an anecdotal sense that women play a huge role in DH and the data showing they are poorly represented at conferences. The results also match with the fact that women are disproportionately more likely to write about management and leadership, discussed at greater length below.

The heavily male gender skew at DH conferences may lead one to suspect a bias in the peer review process. Recent data, however, show that if such a bias exists, it is not direct. Over the past three conferences, 71 percent of women and 73 percent of men who submitted presentations passed the peer review process. The difference is not great enough to rule out random chance ($p = 0.16$ using χ^2). The skew at conferences is more a result of fewer women submitting articles than of women's articles not getting accepted. The one caveat, explained more below, is that certain topics women are more likely to write about are also less likely to be accepted through peer review. This does not imply a lack of bias in the DH community. For example, although only 33.5 percent of authors at DH2015 in Sydney were women, 46 percent of conference attendees were women. If women were simply uninterested in DH, the split in attendance versus authorship would not be so high.

In regard to discussions of women in different roles in the DH community—less the publishing powerhouses and more the community leaders and organizers—the concept of the "glass cliff" can be useful. Research on the feminization of academia in Sweden uses the term "glass cliff" as a "metaphor used to describe a phenomenon when women are appointed to precarious leadership roles associated with an increased risk of negative consequences when a company is performing poorly and for example is experiencing profit falls, declining stock performance, and job cuts" (Peterson, 4). The female academics (who also occupied senior managerial positions) interviewed in Helen Peterson's study expressed concerns about increasing workloads, the precarity of their positions, and the potential for interpersonal conflict.

Institutional politics may also play a role in the gendered data here. Sarah Winslow says of institutional context that "female faculty are less likely to be located at research institutions or institutions that value research over teaching, both of which are associated with greater preference for research" (779). The research, teaching, and service divide in academia remains a thorny issue, especially given the prevalence of what has been called the pink collar workforce in academia, or the disproportionate number of women working in low-paying teaching-oriented areas. This divide likely also contributed to differing gender ratios between attendees and authors at DH2015.[11]

While the gendered implications of time allocation in universities are beyond the scope of this chapter, it might be useful to note that there might be long-term consequences for how people spend their time interacting with scholarly tasks that extend beyond one specific institution. Winslow writes, "Since women bear a disproportionate responsibility for labor that is institution-specific (e.g., institutional housekeeping, mentoring individual students, and other affective labor), their investments are less likely to be portable across institutions. This stands in stark contrast to men, whose investments in research make them more highly desirable candidates should they choose to leave their own institutions" (790). How this plays out specifically in the DH community remains to be seen, but the interdisciplinarity of DH along with its projects that span multiple working groups and institutions may unsettle some of the traditional bias that women in academia face.

Locale

Until 2015, the DH conference alternated every year between North America and Europe. As expected, until recently, the institutions represented at the conference have hailed mostly from these areas, with the primary locus falling in North America. In fact, since 2000, North American authors were the largest authorial constituency at eleven of the fifteen conferences, even though North America only hosted the conference seven times in that period.

With that said, as opposed to gender representation, national and institutional diversity is improving over time. Using an Index of Qualitative Variation (IQV), institutional variation begins around 0.992 in 2000 and ends around 0.996 in 2015, with steady increases over time. National IQV begins around 0.79 in 2010 and ends around 0.83 in 2015, also with steady increases over time. DH2015 in Australia was the first that included over 30 percent of authors *and* attendees arriving from outside Europe or North America. Now that ADHO has implemented a three-year cycle, with every third year marked by a movement outside its usual territory, that diversity is likely to increase further still.

The most well-represented institutions are not as dominating as some may expect, given the common view of DH as a community centered around particular powerhouse departments or universities. The university with the most authors contributing to DH conferences (2.4 percent of the total authors) is King's College London, followed by the Universities of Illinois (1.85 percent), Alberta (1.83 percent), and Virginia (1.75 percent). The most prominent university outside North America or Europe is Ritsumeikan University, contributing 1.07 percent of all DH conference authors. In all, over a thousand institutions have contributed authors to the conference, and that number increases every year.

While these numbers represent institutional origins, the data available do not allow any further diving into birth countries, native language, ethnic identities, or other characteristics. The 2013–2015 dataset, including peer review information, does yield some insight into geography-influenced biases that may map to language or identity. While the peer review data do not show any clear bias by institutional country, there is a very clear bias against names that do not appear frequently in the U.S. Census or Social Security Index. We discovered this when attempting to statistically infer the gender of authors using these U.S.-based indices.[12] From 2013 to 2015, presentations written by those with names appearing frequently in these indices were significantly more likely to be accepted than those written by authors with non-English names ($p < 0.0001$). Whereas approximately 72 percent of authors with common U.S. names passed peer review, only 61 percent of authors with uncommon names passed. Without more data, we have no idea whether this tremendous disparity is due to a bias against popular topics from non-English-speaking countries, a higher likelihood of peer reviewers rejecting text written by nonnative writers, an implicit bias by peer reviewers when they see "foreign" names, or something else entirely.

Topic

When submitting a presentation, authors are given the opportunity to provide keywords for their submission. Some keywords can be chosen freely, while others must be chosen from a controlled list of about one hundred potential topics. These controlled keywords are used to help in the process of conference organization and peer reviewer selection, and they stay roughly constant every year. New keywords are occasionally added to the list, as in 2016, where authors can now select three topics that were not previously available: "Digital Humanities—Diversity," "Digital Humanities—Multilinguality," and "3D Printing." The 2000–2015 conference dataset does not include keywords for every article, so this analysis will cover only the more detailed dataset, 2013–2015, with additional data on submissions for DH2016.

From 2013 to 2016, presentations were tagged with an average of six controlled keywords per submission. The most-used keywords are unsurprising: "Text Analysis" (tagged on 22 percent of submissions), "Data Mining/Text Mining" (20 percent), "Literary Studies" (20 percent), "Archives, Repositories, Sustainability and Preservation" (19 percent), and "Historical Studies" (18 percent). The most frequently used keyword potentially pertaining directly to issues of diversity, "Cultural Studies," appears on 14 percent of submissions from 2013 to 2016. Only 2 percent of submissions are tagged with "Gender Studies." The two diversity-related keywords introduced this year are already being used surprisingly frequently, with 9 percent of submissions in 2016 tagged "Digital Humanities—Diversity" and 6 percent of submissions tagged "Digital Humanities—Multilinguality." With over 650 conference submissions for 2016, this translates to a reasonably large community of DH authors presenting on topics related to diversity.

Joining the topic and gender data for 2013–2015 reveals the extent to which certain subject matters are gendered at DH conferences.[13] Women are twice as likely to use the "Gender Studies" tag as male authors, whereas men are twice as likely to use the "Asian Studies" tag as female authors. Subjects related to pedagogy, creative/performing arts, art history, cultural studies, GLAM (galleries, libraries, archives, museums), DH institutional support, and project design/organization/management are more likely to be presented by women. Men, on the other hand, are more likely to write about standards and interoperability, the history of DH, programming, scholarly editing, stylistics, linguistics, network analysis, and natural language processing/text analysis. It seems DH topics have inherited the usual gender skews associated with the disciplines in which those topics originate.

We showed earlier that there was no direct gender bias in the peer review process. While that is true, there appears to be indirect bias with respect to how certain gendered topics are considered acceptable by the DH conference peer reviewers.

A woman has just as much chance of getting a paper through peer review as a man if they both submit a presentation on the same topic (e.g., both women and men have a 72 percent chance of passing peer review if they write about network analysis, or a 65 percent chance of passing peer review if they write about knowledge representation), but topics that are heavily gendered toward women are less likely to get accepted. Cultural studies has a 57 percent acceptance rate, gender studies 60 percent, pedagogy 51 percent. Male-skewed topics have higher acceptance rates, like text analysis (83 percent), programming (80 percent), or Asian studies (79 percent). The female-gendering of DH institutional support and project organization also supports our earlier claim that while women are well represented among the DH leadership, they are more poorly represented in those topics that the majority of authors are discussing (programming, text analysis, etc.).

Regarding the clustering—and devaluing—of topics that women tend to present on at DH conferences, the widespread acknowledgment of the devaluing of women's labor may help to explain this. We discussed the feminization of academia above, and indeed, this is a trend seen in practically all facets of society. The addition of emotional labor or caretaking tasks complicates this. Economist Teresa Ghilarducchi explains: "A lot of what women do in their lives is punctuated by time outside of the labor market—taking care of family, taking care of children—and women's labor has always been devalued.... [People] assume that she [a woman] had some time out of the labor market and that she was doing something that was basically worthless, because she wasn't being paid for it." In academia specifically, the labyrinthine relationship of pay to tasks and labor further obscures value: we are rarely paid per task (per paper published or presented) on the research front; service work is almost entirely invisible; and teaching factors in with course loads, often with more up-front transparency for contingent laborers such as adjuncts and part-timers.

Our results seem to point to less of an obvious bias against women scholars than a subtler bias against topics that women tend to gravitate toward, or are seen as gravitating toward. This is in line with the concept of postfeminism, which as Rosalind Gill articulates, "is used variously and contradictorily to signal a theoretical position, a type of feminism after the Second Wave, or a regressive political stance" (147–48). It is this last meaning that we access here: whether viewed as backlash or historical reframing, the notion exists that feminism has met its main goals (e.g., getting women the right to vote and the right to an education), and thus is irrelevant to contemporary social needs and discourse. Sara Ahmed describes this as a postfeminist fantasy, "as if feminism has been so successful that it has eliminated its own necessity" (5). Thoroughly enmeshed in neoliberal discourse, postfeminism makes discussing misogyny seem obsolete and obscures the subtler ways in which sexism operates in daily life (Gill; Pomerantz, Raby, and Stefanik). While the term remains a complex one, the overarching beliefs associated with postfeminism have permeated Anglo-American cultures at a number of levels, leading us to posit the acceptance of the sensibilities of postfeminism as one explanation for the continued devaluing of topics that seem associated with women, especially since women analyzing gender and women's advancement might be seen as unnecessary in this paradigm.

Discussion and Future Research

The analysis reveals an annual DH conference with a growing awareness of diversity-related issues, with moderate improvements in regional diversity, stagnation in gender diversity, and unknown (but anecdotally poor) diversity with regard to language, ethnicity, and skin color. Knowledge at the DH conference is heavily gendered, though women are not directly biased against during peer review, and while several prominent women occupy the community's core, women occupy less space in the much larger periphery. No single or small set of institutions dominate the conference attendance, and though North America's influence on ADHO cannot be understated, recent ADHO efforts are significantly improving the geographic spread of its constituency.

The DH conference, and by extension ADHO, is not the digital humanities. It is, however, the largest annual gathering of self-identified digital humanists, and as such its makeup holds influence over the community at large.[14] Its priorities, successes, and failures reflect on DH, both within the community and to the outside world, and those priorities get reinforced in future generations. If the DH conference remains as it is—devaluing knowledge associated with femininity, comprising only 36 percent women, and rejecting presentations by authors with non-English names—it will have significant difficulty attracting a more diverse crowd without explicit interventions. Given the shortcomings revealed in the data above, we present some possible interventions that can be made by ADHO or its members to foster a more diverse community, inspired by #WhatIfDH2016:

> As pointed out by Yvonne Perkins, Ask presenters to include a brief "Collections Used" section, when appropriate. Such a practice would highlight and credit the important work being done by those who aren't necessarily engaging in publishable research, and help legitimize that work to conference attendees.
> As pointed out by Vika Zafrin, create guidelines for reviewers explicitly addressing diversity, and provide guidance on noticing and reducing peer review bias.
> As pointed out by Vika Zafrin, community members can make an effort to solicit presentation submissions from women and people of color.
> As pointed out by Vika Zafrin, collect and analyze data on who is peer reviewing, to see whether or the extent to which biases creep in at that stage.
> As pointed out by Aimée Morrison, ensure that the conference stage is at least as diverse as the conference audience. This can be accomplished in a number of ways, from conference organizers making sure their keynote speakers draw from a broad pool, to organizing last-minute lightning lectures specifically for those who are registered but not presenting.

- As pointed out by Tonya Howe, encourage presentations or attendance from more process-oriented liberal arts delegates.
- As pointed out by Christina Boyles, encourage the submission of research focused around the intersection of race, gender, and sexuality studies. This may be partially accomplished by including more topical categories for conference submissions, a step that ADHO had already taken for 2016.
- As pointed out by many, take explicit steps in ensuring conference access to those with disabilities. We suggest this become an explicit part of the application package submitted by potential host institutions.
- As pointed out by many, ensure the ease of participation-at-a-distance (both as audience and as speaker) for those without the resources to travel.
- As requested by Karina van Dalen-Oskam, chair of ADHO's Steering Committee, send her an email on how to navigate the difficult cultural issues facing an international organization.
- Give marginalized communities greater representation in the DH Conference peer reviewer pool. This can be done grassroots, with each of us reaching out to colleagues to volunteer as reviewers, and organizationally, perhaps by ADHO creating a volunteer group to seek out and encourage more diverse reviewers.
- Consider the difference between diversifying (verb) versus talking about diversity (noun), and consider whether other modes of disrupting hegemony, such as decolonization and queering, might be useful in these processes.
- Contribute to discussions such as #whatifDH20XX on Twitter with other ideas for improvements.

Many options are available to improve representation at DH conferences, and some encouraging steps are already being taken by ADHO and its members. We hope to hear more concrete steps that may be taken, especially learned from experiences in other communities or outside of academia, in order to foster a healthier and more welcoming conference going forward.

In the interest of furthering these goals and improving the organizational memory of ADHO, the public portion of the data (final conference programs with full text and unique author IDs) is available alongside this publication. With this, others may test, correct, or improve our work. We will continue work by extending the dataset back to 1990, continuing to collect for future conferences, and creating an infrastructure that will allow the database to connect to others with similar collections. This will include the ability to encode more nuanced and fluid gender representations, and for authors to correct their own entries. Further work will also include exploring topical co-occurrence, institutional bias in peer review, how institutions affect centrality in the coauthorship network, and how authors who move between institutions affect all these dynamics.

The digital humanities will never be perfect. It embodies the worst of its criticisms and the best of its ideals, sometimes simultaneously. We believe a more diverse community will help tip those scales in the right direction, and we present this chapter in service of that belief.

Notes

This piece is released alongside another on the history of DH conferences, which goes into further detail on technical aspects of this study, including the data collection and statistics; see Weingart and Eichmann-Kalwara, "What's under the Big Tent?" Many of the materials first appeared on the scottbot irregular. Each author contributed equally to the final piece; please disregard authorship order.

1. See Terras, "Disciplined." Terras takes a similar approach, analyzing Humanities Computing "through its community, research, curriculum, teaching programmes, and the message they deliver, either consciously or unconsciously, about the scope of the discipline."

2. The authors have created a browsable archive of #whatifDH2016 tweets: http://hawksey.info/tagsexplorer/arc.html?key=10C2c1phG1QywDmy4lG4mro6VBiv0UuZlLL_uZ8HFfkc&gid=400689247.

3. Of the 146 presentations at DH2011, two stand out in relation to diversity in DH: "Is There Anybody Out There? Discovering New DH Practitioners in other Countries" and "A Trip around the World: Balancing Geographical Diversity in Academic Research Teams."

4. See "Disrupting the Digital Humanities."

5. See Wernimont's blog post, "No More Excuses" for more, as well as the Tumblr blog, "Congrats, You Have an All Male Panel!"

6. Miriam Posner offers a longer and more eloquent discussion of this in "What's Next."

7. The full dataset can be found at dx.doi.org/10.17605/OSF.IO/BV567.

8. Posner, "Humanities Data: A Necessary Contradiction."

9. We would like to acknowledge that race and ethnicity are frequently used interchangeably, though both are cultural constructs with their roots in Darwinian thought, colonialism, and imperialism. We retain these terms because they express cultural realities and lived experiences of oppression and bias, not because there is any scientific validity to their existence. For more on this tension, see Burton, *Culture*, 51–54.

10. Weingart and Eichmann, "What's under the Big Tent?"

11. Institutional affiliation, or lack thereof, remains an important factor in determining who can afford to travel to conferences to present their work. The increasing adjunctification of higher education—with many adjuncts ineligible to apply for travel funding at institutions where they teach—may hinder their access to conference presentation opportunities.

12. We used the process and script described in Mullen, "Ropensci/gender"; and Blevins and Lincoln Mullen, "Jane, John."

13. For a breakdown of specific numbers of gender representation across all ninety-six topics from 2013 to 2015, see Weingart's "Acceptances."

14. While ADHO's annual conference is usually the largest annual gathering of digital humanists, that place is constantly being vied for by the Digital Humanities Summer Institute (http://www.dhsi.org/) in Victoria, Canada, which in 2013 boasted more attendees than DH2013 in Lincoln, Nebraska.

Bibliography

#whatifDH2016. "TAGS Searchable Twitter Archive." n.d. http://hawksey.info/tags explorer/arc.html?key=10C2c1phG1QywDmy4lG4mro6VBiv0UuZlLL_uZ8H Ffkc&gid=400689247.

ADHO. "ADHO Announces New Steering Committee Chair." n.d. http://www.adho.org/announcements/2015/adho-announces-new-steering-committee-chair.

ADHO. "Conference." n.d. http://adho.org/conference.

ADHO. "Our Mission." n.d. http://adho.org/.

Ahmed, Sara. *Living a Feminist Life.* Durham, N.C.: Duke University Press, 2017.

Allington, Daniel, Sarah Brouillette, and David Golumbia. "Neoliberal Tools (and Archives): A Political History of Digital Humanities." *Los Angeles Review of Books,* May 1, 2016. https://lareviewofbooks.org/article/neoliberal-tools-archives-political-history-digital-humanities/.

"All Models Are Wrong." Wikipedia, September 20, 2015. https://en.wikipedia.org/w/index.php?title=All_models_are_wrong&oldid=681908687.

Blevins, Cameron, and Lincoln Mullen. "Jane, John . . . Leslie? A Historical Method for Algorithmic Gender Prediction." *Digital Humanities Quarterly* 9, no. 3 (2015). http://www.digitalhumanities.org/dhq/vol/9/3/000223/000223.html.

Boyles, Christina. "#WhatIfDH2016 Made Space for Scholars Who Are Interested in the Intersection(s) between DH and Race, Gender, and Sexuality Studies?" @clboyles, July 1, 2015. https://twitter.com/clboyles/statuses/616080151365861376.

Burton, John W. *Culture and the Human Body: An Anthropological Perspective.* Prospect Heights, Ill.: Waveland, 2001.

"centerNet." n.d. http://www.dhcenternet.org/.

Cohen, Dan. "Catching the Good." Dan Cohen, March 30, 2012. http://www.dancohen.org/2012/03/30/catching-the-good/.

"Conditionally Accepted." Inside Higher Education. n.d. https://www.insidehighered.com/users/conditionally-accepted.

"Congrats, You Have an All Male Panel!" (blog). n.d. http://allmalepanels.tumblr.com/.

"DH Dark Sider (@DHDarkSider) | Twitter." n.d. https://twitter.com/dhdarksider.

"DH Enthusiast (@DH_Enthusiast) | Twitter." n.d. https://twitter.com/DH_Enthusiast.

"Disrupting the Digital Humanities." Disrupting the Digital Humanities, n.d. http://www.disruptingdh.com/.

Diversity in DH @ THATCamp. "Toward an Open Digital Humanities," January 11, 2011. https://docs.google.com/document/d/1uPtB0xr793V27vHBmBZr87LY6Pe1BLxN-_DuJzqG-wU/edit?usp=sharing.

Drucker, Johanna. "Humanistic Theory and Digital Scholarship." In *Debates in the Digital Humanities*. Minneapolis: University of Minnesota Press, 2012. http://dhdebates.gc.cuny.edu/debates/text/34.

"Fight the Tower: Women of Color in Academia." n.d. http://fighttower.com/.

Ghilarducci, Teresa. "Why Women over 50 Can't Find Jobs." *PBS News Hour*, January 14 2016, https://www.pbs.org/newshour/economy/women-over-50-face-cant-find-jobs.

Gill, Rosalind. "Postfeminist Media Culture: Elements of a Sensibility." *European Journal of Cultural Studies* 10, no. 2 (2007): 147–66.

"Global Outlook::Digital Humanities | Promoting Collaboration among Digital Humanities Researchers World-Wide." n.d. http://www.globaloutlookdh.org/.

Golumbia, David. "Right Reaction and the Digital Humanities." Uncomputing, July 3, 2015. http://www.uncomputing.org/?p=1666.

Howe, Tonya. "#whatifDH2016 Advocated for More Process-Oriented Liberal Arts Delegates?" (Microblog). Twitter.com/howet, June 30, 2015. https://twitter.com/howet/statuses/616045260570030080.

Hunt, Lynn. "Has the Battle Been Won? The Feminization of History." *Perspectives on History*, May 1998. https://www.historians.org/publications-and-directories/perspectives-on-history/may-1998/has-the-battle-been-won-the-feminization-of-history.

Leathwood, Carole, and Barbara Read. *Gender and the Changing Face of Higher Education: A Feminized Future?* New York: Open University Press, 2009.

Lothian, Alexis. "THATCamp and Diversity in Digital Humanities." Queer Geek Theory, n.d. http://www.queergeektheory.org/2011/01/thatcamp-and-diversity-in-digital-humanities/.

Milem, Jeffrey F., Mitchell J. Chang, and Anthony Lising Antonio. "Making Diversity Work on Campus: A Research-Based Perspective." Association of American Colleges and Universities, 2005. http://citeseerx.ist.psu.edu/viewdoc/download?doi=10.1.1.129.2597&rep=rep1&type=pdf.

Morrison, Aimée. "#WhatIfDH2016 Had as Many Women on the Stage as in the Audience? http://www.scottbot.net/HIAL/?p=41355. #dh2015." (Microblog). @digiwonk, June 30, 2015. https://twitter.com/digiwonk/status/616042963093835776.

Mullen, Lincoln. "Ropensci/gender: Predict Gender from Names Using Historical Data." n.d. https://github.com/ropensci/gender.

Nowviskie, Bethany. "Asking for It." Bethany Nowviskie, February 8, 2014. http://nowviskie.org/2014/asking-for-it/.

Nowviskie, Bethany. "Cats and Ships." Bethany Nowviskie, November 2, 2012. http://nowviskie.org/2012/cats-and-ships/.

Ohio State University. "Diversity Action Plan," n.d. https://www.osu.edu/diversityplan/index.php.

Perkins, Yvonne. "International Researchers Value Work of Australian Libraries and Archives." Stumbling through the Past. Posted on July 21, 2015. https://stumblingpast.wordpress.com/2015/07/21/intnl_researchers_value_oz_libraries_archives/.

Peterson, Helen. "An Academic 'Glass Cliff'? Exploring the Increase of Women in Swedish Higher Education Management." *Athens Journal of Education* 1, no. 1 (February 2014): 32–44.

Pomerantz, Shauna, Rebecca Raby, and Andrea Stefanik. "Girls Run the World? Caught between Sexism and Postfeminism in the School." *Gender & Society* 27, no. 2 (April 1, 2013): 185–207. doi:10.1177/0891243212473199.

Posner, Miriam. "Humanities Data: A Necessary Contradiction." *Miriam Posner's Blog*, June 25, 2015. http://miriamposner.com/blog/humanities-data-a-necessary-contradiction/.

Posner, Miriam. "What's Next: The Radical, Unrealized Potential of Digital Humanities." *Miriam Posner's Blog*, July 27, 2015. http://miriamposner.com/blog/whats-next-the-radical-unrealized-potential-of-digital-humanities/.

"Postcolonial Digital Humanities | Global Explorations of Race, Class, Gender, Sexuality and Disability within Cultures of Technology." n.d. http://dhpoco.org/.

Steiger, Kay. "The Pink Collar Workforce of Academia: Low-Paid Adjunct Faculty, Who Are Mostly Female, Have Started Unionizing for Better Pay—and Winning." *The Nation*, July 11, 2013. http://www.thenation.com/article/academias-pink-collar-workforce/.

Sue, Derald Wing. *Microaggressions in Everyday Life: Race, Gender, and Sexual Orientation*. Hoboken, N.J.: John Wiley & Sons, 2010.

Terras, Melissa. "Disciplined: Using Educational Studies to Analyse 'Humanities Computing.'" *Literary and Linguistic Computing* 21, no. 2 (June 1, 2006): 229–46. doi:10.1093/llc/fql022.

Terras, Melissa. "Peering inside the Big Tent: Digital Humanities and the Crisis of Inclusion." *Melissa Terras' Blog*, July 26, 2011. http://melissaterras.blogspot.com/2011/07/peering-inside-big-tent-digital.html.

"THATCamp Southern California 2011 | The Humanities and Technology Camp." n.d. http://socal2011.thatcamp.org/.

"University of Venus." Inside Higher Education, n.d. https://www.insidehighered.com/blogs/university-venus.

U.S. Department of Education, National Center for Education Statistics. "Race/Ethnicity of College Faculty," 2015. https://nces.ed.gov/fastfacts/display.asp?id=61.

Weingart, Scott. "Acceptances to Digital Humanities 2015 (part 4)." *The Scottbot Irregular*, June 28, 2015. http://www.scottbot.net/HIAL/?p=41375.

Weingart, Scott, and Nickoal Eichmann-Kalwara. *ADHO Conference Abstracts*. doi: 10.17605/OSF.IO/BV567.

Weingart, Scott, and Nickoal Eichmann-Kalwara. "The Myth of Text Analytics and Unobtrusive Measurement." *The Scottbot Irregular,* May 6, 2012. http://www.scottbot.net/HIAL/?p=16713.

Weingart, Scott, and Nickoal Eichmann-Kalwara. "What's under the Big Tent?: A Study of ADHO Conference Abstracts." *Digital Studies/Le champ numérique* 7, no. 1 (October 13, 2017): 6. http://doi.org/10.16995/dscn.284.

Wernimont, Jacqueline. "Build a Better Panel: Women in DH." *Jacqueline Wernimont* (blog). Accessed January 14, 2016. https://jwernimont.wordpress.com/2015/09/19/build-a-better-panel-women-in-dh/.

Wernimont, Jacqueline. "No More Excuses." *Jacqueline Wernimont* (blog), September 19, 2015. https://jwernimont.wordpress.com/2015/09/19/no-more-excuses/.

Winslow, Sarah. "Gender Inequality and Time Allocations among Academic Faculty." *Gender & Society* 24, no. 6 (December 1, 2010): 769–93. doi:10.1177/0891243210386728.

Zafrin, Vika. "#WhatIfDH2016 Created Guidelines for Reviewers Explicitly Addressing Diversity & Providing Guidance on Reducing One's Bias?" (Microblog). @veek, June 30, 2015. https://twitter.com/veek/status/616041712163680256.

Zafrin, Vika. "#WhatIfDH2016 Encouraged ALL Community Members to Reach Out to Women & POC and Solicit Paper Submissions?" (Microblog). @veek, June 30, 2015. https://twitter.com/veek/statuses/616041931949363200.

Zafrin, Vika. "#WhatIfDH2016 Expanded ConfTool Pro to Record Reviewer Biases along Gender, Race, Country-of-Origin GDP Lines?" (Microblog). @veek, June 30, 2015. https://twitter.com/veek/statuses/616043562799636481.

PART II][Chapter 7

Counting the Costs

Funding Feminism in the Digital Humanities

CHRISTINA BOYLES

Although digital humanities is often described as a boon to humanities scholarship, particularly for its ability to attract funding from internal and external grant agencies, few have studied the "canon" of funded projects. As with the literary canon, existing digital humanities scholarship speaks to the underlying values operating within both the field of digital humanities and its funding agencies. Prominent funding agencies in the field include the American Council of Learned Societies, the Council on Library and Information Resources, the Institute of Museum and Library Services, the National Endowment for the Humanities, and the Mellon Foundation. All of these groups purport to share a central mission: to "strengthen, promote, and, where necessary, defend the contributions of the humanities and the arts to human flourishing and to the well-being of *diverse* and democratic societies" (my emphasis)—and fund projects according to their adherence to this mission.[1] Digital humanities organizations share a similar mission: to create and support digital work that communicates the value of humanities work to the general public. One mission statement that has received particular attention from scholars is that of 4Humanities, which states, "The digital humanities are increasingly integrated in the humanities at large. They catch the eye of administrators and funding agencies who otherwise dismiss the humanities as yesterday's news. They connect across disciplines with science and engineering fields. They have the potential to use new technologies to help the humanities communicate with, and adapt to, contemporary society."[2]

An examination of existing scholarship, however, suggests that digital humanities research has not yet fulfilled these missions. Alan Liu, the author of the 4Humanities mission statement, notes that he overemphasized the relationship between the digital humanities and the public.[3] As a field concerned with technical innovation, "digital humanities has historically deemphasized theoretical examination of the digital utilizing cultural studies frameworks," an act that has constrained the field to projects focused on digital tool production and/or a reassertion of canonical works.[4]

Martha Nell Smith argues that the divide between digital humanities and cultural studies is intentional: she suggests that the field was developed by scholars seeking to escape from the onslaught of culture and gender theory in the 1970s, observing, "It was as if these matters of objective and hard science provided an oasis for folks who did not want to clutter sharp, disciplined, methodical philosophy with considerations of the gender-, race-, and class-determined facts of life.... Humanities computing seemed to offer a space free from all this messiness and a return to objective questions of representation."[5] While the advent of new technologies in the 1990s and 2000s offered opportunities for experimentation grounded in cultural and gender-based criticism, the digital humanities largely maintained its distance from these forms of scholarship. Jamie "Skye" Bianco notes that "we've seen a winnowing of what was an experimental and heterogeneous emergence of computational and digital practices, teaching and theorization from within and across disciplines to an increasingly narrow, highly technical, and powerful set of conservative and constrained areas and modes of digital research."[6] Although the cause of this narrowing has yet to be determined, one likely factor is the increasing need for humanities scholarship to garner external funding from agencies more drawn to technological innovation than cultural criticism.

Nevertheless, articles offering up theories and strategies calling for critical digital humanities scholarship have proliferated in recent years. Pieces such as Liu's "Where Is the Cultural Criticism in Digital Humanities?," Tara McPherson's "Why Are the Digital Humanities so White?," and Moya Bailey's "All the Digital Humanists Are White, All the Nerds Are Men, but Some of Us Are Brave" all point out the androcentric nature of digital humanities scholarship and posit the need for engagement with critical theory, including feminism, intersectionality, ethnic studies, and postcolonialism.[7] The goal of their work is twofold: to increase critical digital humanities research and to invite a larger segment of scholars to participate in the field, particularly those previously marginalized due to their research in gender, ethnicity, or sexuality. In response, a cadre of feminist and cultural critiques have begun to establish methodologies for examining critical digital humanities work. Alexis Lothian and Amanda Phillips ask,

> What would digital scholarship and the humanities disciplines be like if they centered around processes and possibilities of social and cultural transformation as well as institutional preservation? If they centered around questions of labor, race, gender, and justice at personal, local, and global scales? If their practitioners considered not only how the academy might reach out to underserved communities, but also how the kinds of knowledge production nurtured elsewhere could transform the academy itself?[8]

Providing a list of projects fitting these aims, Lothian and Phillips attempt to expand the canon of existing digital projects grounded in activism and social justice. A close examination of these projects, however, reveals that many of them are no longer active or available online. Although there is no clear articulation as to why some of these projects have disappeared, a cursory examination suggests that these projects did not receive either the institutional or external support needed to keep the projects alive, particularly as they were all the work of individual scholars. In contrast, the projects that are still active are collective projects, and each lists a series of funding organizations, businesses, and contributors that have made the project sustainable. Issues of sustainability are not relegated solely to the projects in Lothian and Phillips's article; in fact, Amy Earhart points to a similar trend in digital recovery projects emphasizing the work of writers of color; she states,

> Alan Liu's *Voice of the Shuttle* provides a good measure of the huge number of early recovery projects focused on literature and history written by and about people of color. A quick perusal of "The Minority Studies" section, however, reveals that a tremendous number of the projects have become lost. For example, of the six sites listed in "General Resources in Minority Literature," half cannot be located, suggesting that they have been removed or lost. The same trend is found with other projects listed on the site. While only 50 percent of the projects in the "General Resources in Chicano/Latino Literature" section are still online, other areas, such as Asian American literature, have a higher percentage of active projects. Digital humanists are fond of talking about sustainability as a problem for current and future works, but it is clear that we already have sustained a good deal of loss within the broadly defined digital canon.[9]

To prevent such losses, Martha Nell Smith asserts that digital humanities scholarship needs to "take into account the 'messy' facts of authorship, production, and reception: race, class, gender, and sexuality."[10] Doing so will force us "to examine the canon that we, as digital humanists, are constructing, a canon that skews toward traditional texts and excludes crucial work by women, people of color, and the GLBTQ community."[11] In other words, she, along with many others, argues that digital humanists have the responsibility to be self-critical and to acknowledge and address the lack of critical scholarship within the field.

While scholars have certainly engaged in such criticism in their writing, the field has yet to formulate a model for the equal support of large-scale research projects emphasizing critical digital humanities. However, a number of recent initiatives integrate critical scholarship into their work, particularly Global Outlook::Digital Humanities (GO::DH) and TransformDH. TransformDH is "an academic guerrilla movement seeking to (re)define capital-letter Digital Humanities as a force for transformative scholarship by collecting, sharing, and highlighting projects that push at its boundaries and work for social justice, accessibility, and inclusion."[12] Launched at the American Studies Association conference in 2011, it asks its members to advocate for critical digital humanities by both theorizing new methodologies and promoting critical digital scholarship. As an organization focused on information sharing, this group draws attention to pertinent work in critical digital humanities, but does not seek to produce it. Similarly, GO::DH seeks to "break down barriers that hinder communication and collaboration among researchers and students of the Digital Arts, Humanities, and Cultural Heritage sectors in high, mid, and low income economies" by drawing attention to the scholarship being produced by digital humanists internationally.[13] In doing so, GO::DH expands the definition of digital humanities to include projects and initiatives serving a variety of peoples and cultures. While both organizations have made great strides in both advocating for and expanding upon the field of critical digital humanities, they do not have the means to provide financial support for the projects they promote.

So, how do critical digital humanities projects acquire funding? While culturally engaged scholarship fits with the mission of most external funding agencies, Jacqueline Wernimont observes that she has "repeatedly heard scholars suggest the NEH's policy that it will not fund projects 'that seek to promote a particular political, religious, or ideological point of view . . . or projects that advocate a particular program of social action.'"[14] Even feminist projects that have acquired grant funding, like Women Writers Online (WWO), have not received money from the National Endowment for the Humanities (NEH) to "primarily fund the expansion of the WWO collection, but rather [for] the development of new encoding practices, interfaces, or tools."[15] These observations suggest that critical digital humanities research may not only distance scholars from the conventional tenets of digital humanities but also hinder their ability to receive large-scale grant funding.

Existing studies on grant funding for digital humanities projects bear this out. Amy Earhart observes that the NEH's "shift toward innovation has focused on technological innovation, not on innovative restructuring of the canon through recovery. The National Endowment for the Humanities (NEH) awarded 141 Digital Humanities Start-Up Grants from 2007 through 2010. Of those grants, only twenty-nine were focused on diverse communities and sixteen on the preservation or recovery of diverse community texts."[16] More recent examinations of the NEH funding trends further highlight the absence of critically engaged digital humanities projects. John D. Martin III and Carolyn Runyon note that "the NEH provided a total of $225,462,386.29 for digital cultural heritage projects through 656 individual grants over the course of the period between 1 January 2007 and 30 September 2016. . . . Of the total 656 projects, 110 could be identified as having a gendered focus and 288 as having . . . race/ethnic identifying characteristics."[17] Upon closer examination, these statistics become even more appalling. Martin and Runyon go on to state, "The number of grants with a gendered focus differed considerably for men (82) and women (20)."[18] In other words, of the 110 projects utilizing gendered language, only twenty pertained to women and only eight pertained to nonbinary gender identities. Their findings on race were equally galling: "This means that projects on individual women and black Americans were awarded only 8% of the total $4,225,061 awarded to projects on individuals. All of the rest focused on white men of historical importance."[19]

These studies, however, focus solely on the NEH, a government funding agency whose leadership is appointed by the president with the approval of the U.S. Senate. The leadership council is composed of a chairman, who serves a term of four years, as well as a council of twenty-six private citizens, who serve terms of six years. While there has been a dramatic increase in the diversity of council members since the election of President Barack Obama in 2008, the position of chairman has consistently gone to Caucasian males. Barring the work of Lynne V. Cheney from May 1986 to January of 1993, the chairmanship has been held by a white man since the NEH's inception in 1965. Although the race and gender of the chairman do not preclude the organization from funding projects emphasizing diversity, they do suggest that the NEH, whether advertently or otherwise, reinforces structures of power that marginalize individuals based on their race, gender, and sexuality. Subject to mainstream pressures, governmental oversight, and political bias, the NEH's funding trends raise the question, "Do private grant funding agencies provide support for critical digital humanities projects?"

One of the largest private financiers of digital humanities work is the Mellon Foundation. Founded in 1969, the Mellon Foundation seeks to support outstanding work in the field of higher education, especially in the humanities and fine arts. At its inception the Mellon Foundation was invested heavily in feminist issues, donating $800,000 per year to Planned Parenthood and the Population Council in order to produce better research on reproductive issues, to develop more effective forms of contraception, and to become more educated about reproductive practices globally.[20] Such initiatives demonstrate the funding trends during the Mellon Foundation's first few decades of operation; however, changes to the Foundation's leadership and central mission in the late 1990s have made its relationship to the feminist digital humanities less clear. To provide a comprehensive look at funding trends pertaining to the digital humanities, this analysis will examine Mellon's annual reports from 1988 to 2015. This period marks the launch of the Text Encoding Initiative (TEI; 1987) as well as the establishment of many key feminist projects including the *Women Writers Project* (1986) and the *Orlando Project* (1990s). Although the Mellon Foundation does not make its grant narratives publicly available, it does post annual reports to its website. The annual reports include three components: a brief overview from the Mellon Foundation's president, a statement on how the organization is meeting its core programs (which vary according to leadership), and a comprehensive list of grants for the year, each of which includes a brief description. Uploading these annual reports to Voyant, a text analysis tool that displays word frequencies, word co-occurrences, and frequency distributions, makes it possible to determine trends in the Mellon Foundation's funding behaviors. On its website, annual reports are available from 1969 to 2016. As the terms "digital humanities" and "humanities computing" do not appear in reports prior to 1988, those reports are excluded from this analysis. The remaining reports are broken down into three groups to reflect the funding behaviors of Mellon's last three presidents: William G. Bowen (1988–2005), Don Michael Randel (2006–2013), and Earl Lewis (2013–2018).[21]

The late 1980s and early 1990s marked a unique time for the Mellon Foundation. At this time, technological projects were not on the leadership committee's radar; instead, the foundation spent its efforts addressing prominent feminist and cultural issues in both education and public health. Notably, significant funding was given to the Population Council to continue its work promoting healthy contraceptive and reproductive practices. Additionally, research into migration practices was developed in order to understand the economic and social implications of immigration. Like the work with the Population Council, this work had a particularly feminist bent. According to Mellon's annual report in 1994, "The Foundation expects to center more of its activities on female immigrants who currently comprise one-half of all immigrants to the United States each year but whose economic plight has been neglected."[22] At the same time, the foundation launched the Mellon Minority Undergraduate Fellowship program, which funded undergraduate students planning to pursue graduate education. The goal of this program was to increase diversity among faculty by limiting marginalized individuals' barriers to entry into the profession. While these programs continued to be funded for a number of years, those focusing on feminist issues were dramatically downsized in 2003. According to foundation president William G. Bowen, "the Foundation has decided that it is time to phase out grantmaking in its population and forced migration program," as these areas of focus no longer fit the organization's principal areas of application.[23] Figure 7.1 shows the decline of the foundation's work on feminist issues by mapping the prevalence of the terms "migration" and "contraceptive" from 1988 to 2005.

Perhaps unsurprisingly, the phasing out of feminist projects clearly coincides with the foundation's growing interest in technological projects. In 1997 Mellon's annual report focused almost entirely on technology—lauding the development of JSTOR, emphasizing electronic publishing with university presses, and boasting the College and Beyond Database, an attempt to collect data about outcomes for college graduates around the United States.[24] Then, in 2000, the foundation released a formal statement stating that its intention in years ahead "is to provide support for rigorous studies of applications of instructional technology that will include online education and distance learning."[25] From then on, the annual reports almost entirely focus on digital projects launched by the organization including ARTStor, Ithaka, Aluka, and the National Institute for Technology in Liberal Education (NITLE). Figure 7.2 shows the shift in the Mellon Foundation's priorities by depicting how its devaluation of feminist concerns coincide with its affinity for digital projects.

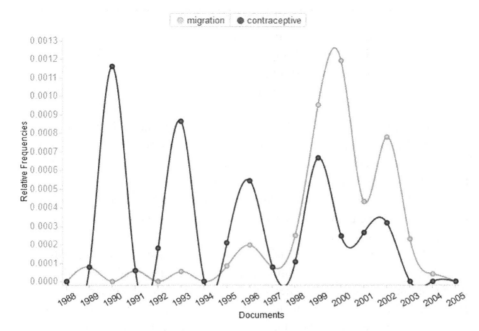

Figure 7.1. This figure depicts the frequency of the words "migration" and "contraceptive" in the Andrew W. Mellon Foundation's annual reports (1988–2005) to demonstrate the foundation's early commitment to cultural and feminist concerns.

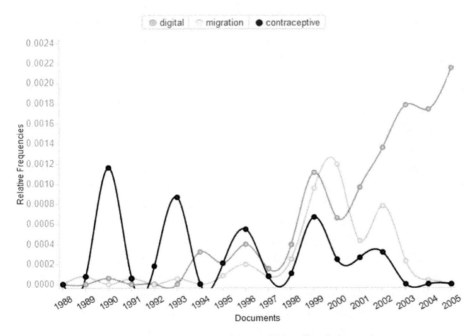

Figure 7.2. This figure compares the frequency of the word "digital" with the words "migration" and "contraceptive" to show the ways in which the Andrew W. Mellon Foundation's priorities shifted from cultural and feminist concerns to technological ones. Data for this visualization come from the foundation's annual reports (1988–2005).

Text analysis of the projects' funding during this time period (1988–2005) reveal that the foundation largely focused on "assist[ing] projects that might possibly have a broad and general impact on the fields as a whole," a mission that typically translated into support for projects on canonical authors, prevalent historical events, and technological developments.[26] In other words, Mellon's movement away from feminism occurred concurrently with its movement toward digital humanities, which has been to the great detriment of feminist digital humanists. Although there are a handful of feminist projects developed during this time period, particularly in the late 1980s and early 1990s during the first boom of feminist digital humanities research, many of these projects focus on broad populations rather than specific individuals or their contributions to the humanities. As a result, findings from these projects have had little influence on either gender studies or digital humanities.

In 2006, leadership of the Mellon Foundation transferred to Don Michael Randel, who in his preliminary annual report noted, "The Mellon Foundation is unique among the major foundations in its commitment to the humanities and the arts in bringing new technologies to their support."[27] Notably absent is the discussion of Mellon's previous philanthropic initiatives, particularly those engaged with feminist ideologies. Instead, Randel emphasizes the social and governmental pressures faced by nonprofit organizations, noting, "There is, without question, need for appropriate governmental rule-making and monitoring in the foundation world."[28] His praise for Mellon's focus on educational technology and his desire to conform with the practices of governmental agencies result in a heavy-handed focus on digital technology separated from feminist or cultural critique.

Text analysis of Randel's time in office (2006–2012) reveals that the Mellon Foundation funded projects focused on technological advancements, as evidenced by the prevalence of words such as "research," "development," "database," and "information." Along with continued support for JSTOR, Ithaka, and NITLE, the foundation promoted the digitization of canonized literature, the development of open source educational software, and the expansion of the semantic web. Such projects were supported by new grants, such as the Mellon Award for Technology Collaboration, as well as the foundation's new guiding principles emphasizing tool development, digitization, and conservation.

Unsurprisingly, the emphasis on technological development vastly overwhelms the remaining text, highlighting the foundation's strong emphasis on tools over culturally engaged projects. In fact, neither "cultur*" nor "diversity" appears in a list of the five hundred most used words within the annual reports during this period. Strangely enough, the words "American" and "national" are utilized heavily during this time, suggesting that funded projects were focused on the dominant culture within the United States rather than other cultural groups. Although the words "Africa" and "African" do appear in limited frequency, this occurrence can be

Counting the Costs [101]

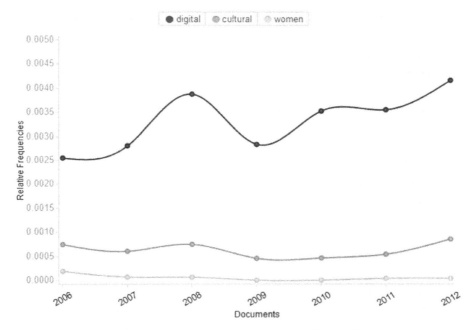

Figure 7.3. This figure compares the frequency of the words "digital," "cultural," and "women" to depict the Andrew W. Mellon Foundation's funding priorities in the present age. Data for this visualization come from the foundation's annual reports (2006–2012).

attributed to funding initiatives for educational development in South Africa that preceded Randel. Evidence suggests that projects from this time period often did not engage with cultural topics with significant depth or weight. Figure 7.3 maps the frequency of feminist, cultural, and digital language in the foundation's annual reports produced under Randel's leadership.

Notably, the word "feminism" does not appear, and the word "women" appears only ten times within the entirety of this time period. A context analysis reveals that only two grants in this range focused specifically on feminist issues. The Black Women Playwrights' Group Inc. acquired $50,000 in funding to support four playwrights' writing and production costs, and Spelman College received $50,000 to encourage women to pursue mathematics education. The vast majority, however, do not mention women at all. This absence suggests that projects about feminist issues were not funded by the Mellon Foundation and/or that researchers engaged in feminist work did not feel comfortable highlighting this aspect of their research. Given the Mellon Foundation's dramatic shift away from feminist engagement, this is unsurprising. Additionally, as many feminist digital humanists had little to no engagement with the foundation prior to its large-scale support of technological initiatives, many scholars likely were and are unaware that Mellon's history is rooted in feminist activism.

Recent statements by former Mellon Foundation president Earl Lewis, however, suggest that the foundation may recommit itself to issues of inclusion and intersectionality. In his inaugural annual report in 2013, Lewis released the following statement:

> Institutions, including philanthropies, also have history. And in that history, certain points of inflection occur that suggest shifts. . . . We do foresee significant modifications to our grantmaking priorities. Diversity initiatives have heretofore centered on enhancing the flow of diverse students, especially students of color, into and through graduate school and into permanent faculty positions. A signature component of that effort has been the Mellon Mays Undergraduate Fellowship program. That program remains a cornerstone of our plan, but we also will chart ways to expand the number of participants and participating institutions. Moving forward we also envision a Latino/a initiative that complements our work with Tribal Colleges and Historically Black Colleges and Universities. Perhaps the biggest change, especially for a foundation that has prided itself on being quiet, will be the production of an annual report that synthesizes the very best scholarship on the value of diversity to social and civil life in democratic societies.[29]

Here, Lewis acknowledges the foundation's problematic silences and underscores the need for more critically engaged scholarship. His use of the term "Latino/a" suggests that his push for diversity includes women, particularly women of color. Projects launched early in his tenure investigate best practices surrounding the conservation of Chinese art, the preservation of American Indian artifacts, and the development of theatrical productions. Although each of these projects likely includes work produced by women, the project descriptions do not mention either women's contributions or feminist ideologies. This absence raises the question, "Has the Mellon Foundation regained its sense of inclusiveness, particularly for feminist research?" An examination of the annual reports produced during Earl Lewis's tenure, as depicted in Figure 7.4, fail to provide a clear answer.

While the overall use of the term "women" increases from ten times in 2006–2012 to eleven times in 2013–2016, only three grants during this period are grounded in feminist thought. The Dallas Opera received $500,000 to run an Institute for Women Conductors, Bennett College obtained $490,000 to host a Leadership Development Institute for Women, and Artspot Productions attained $75,000 to provide arts training to incarcerated women. Words like "cultural" and "public," on the other hand, become increasingly prevalent under Lewis's leadership. During the same period, there is a drastic decrease in tool-focused language, like "database," "information," and "coordinated." This shift highlights Mellon's movement from tool-centered projects to critically engaged research. Take, for example, the word "diversity." Although the word is mentioned only fifteen times in 2013,

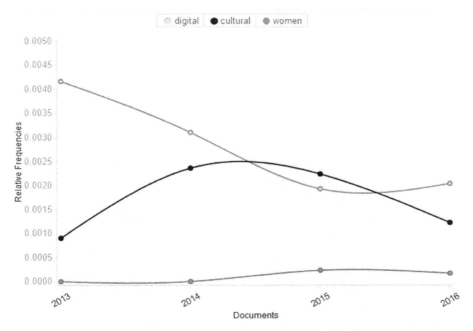

Figure 7.4. This figure compares the frequency of the words "digital," "cultural," and "women" to depict the Andrew W. Mellon Foundation's funding priorities in the present age. Data for this visualization come from the foundation's annual reports (2013–2016).

the prevalence of the word nearly doubles in each subsequent year. Additionally, the number of projects mentioning the word "diversity" appears to increase each year. According to Figure 7.5, the word "diversity" was typically clustered, or utilized, by a small set of projects: note that nearly half of the mentions of "diversity" in 2013 appear to be relegated to three projects. In more recent years, however, there is a growing number of projects highlighting "diversity": it appears to be a central focus of seven projects in 2014, ten projects in 2015, and fifteen projects in 2016.

A similar trajectory occurs with the word "public." Although mentioned only twenty-eight times in 2013, the term "public" is utilized fifty-three times in 2014, forty-nine times in 2015, and sixty-two times in 2016. Like "diversity," the word "public" is often clustered, with an emphasis in seven projects in 2013, thirteen projects in 2014, twelve projects in 2015, and sixteen times in 2016. Within this time period, the most common phrase using the word "public" is "public humanities," which occurs twenty-two times and becomes especially prevalent in 2016. Such language highlights the increasing number of digital humanities projects participating in publicly engaged scholarship.

Such trends align with Earl Lewis's statement on the role of the Mellon Foundation: to provide creative and inclusive alternatives to Western culture's prevailing issues surrounding race and discrimination. These funding activities also fulfill Alan Liu's desire for 4Humanities: "to use new technologies to help the humanities

Figure 7.5. This figure shows the frequency of the use of the word "diversity" in the Andrew W. Mellon Foundation's annual reports from 2013 to 2016.

communicate with, and adapt to, contemporary society."[30] In other words, the Mellon Foundation appears to be moving in the direction advocated by a growing number of digital humanists. It is actively funding and promoting projects that engage in critical digital humanities. At the same time, there are still some notable absences in the data. At no time between 1988 and 2016 do the words "woman," "women," "female*," or "fem*" appear in the top five hundred words used in the annual reports, suggesting that projects openly advocating for feminist ideologies do not receive funding, or, equally likely, that these projects feel the need to mask their philosophical lens in order to receive consideration. Either option suggests that feminist researchers experience significant difficulties receiving financial support for their work. Funding feminist projects, therefore, appears to be the next great hurdle for funding agencies to tackle. Although growth has been minimal, an analysis of the Mellon Foundation's annual reports suggests that the organization may be transitioning back to its feminist roots. We can only hope that this growth will continue under the guidance of newly appointed foundation president Elizabeth Alexander, a poet and storyteller lauded for her engagement with critical issues and social justice. The time to propose large-scale feminist digital research is now.

Notes

1. Although a number of sources for this piece utilize the term "diversity," it is often used as a catch-all phrase to describe everyone except white men. As such, it does not adequately address the concerns of particular groups, nor does it contextualize the specific concerns of these disparate communities. For these reasons, "diversity" is used only to quote or to reference resources cited in this piece. Andrew W. Mellon Foundation, "Mission."
    2. *4Humanities*, "Mission."
    3. Liu, "Where Is Cultural Criticism."
    4. Earhart, "Can Information Be Unfettered?"
    5. Smith, "Human Touch Software."
    6. Bianco, "This Digital Humanities."

7. Liu, "Where Is Cultural Criticism"; McPherson, "Why Are the Digital Humanities"; Bailey, "All the Digital Humanists."
8. Lothian and Phillips, "Can Digital Humanities."
9. Earhart, "Can Information Be Unfettered?"
10. Smith, "Human Touch Software."
11. Smith, "Human Touch Software."
12. "About #TransformDH."
13. "About."
14. Wernimont, "Whence Feminism?"
15. Wernimont, "Whence Feminism?"
16. Earhart, "Can Information Be Unfettered?"
17. Martin and Runyon, "Digital Humanities."
18. Martin and Runyon, "Digital Humanities."
19. Martin and Runyon, "Digital Humanities."
20. Andrew W. Mellon Foundation, *Report of the Andrew W. Mellon Foundation 1990*, 15.
21. The Mellon Foundation's annual reports (1969–2016) are available on their website: https://mellon.org. Each document used in this analysis was downloaded as a .pdf and converted to .rtf for use in Voyant.
22. Andrew W. Mellon Foundation, *Report of the Andrew W. Mellon Foundation 1994*, 43.
23. Andrew W. Mellon Foundation, *Report of the Andrew W. Mellon Foundation 2002*, 8.
24. Andrew W. Mellon Foundation, *Report of the Andrew W. Mellon Foundation 1997*.
25. Andrew W. Mellon Foundation, *Report of the Andrew W. Mellon Foundation 2000*.
26. Andrew W. Mellon Foundation, *Report of the Andrew W. Mellon Foundation 1988*, 20.
27. Andrew W. Mellon Foundation, *Report of the Andrew W. Mellon Foundation 2005*, 8.
28. Andrew W. Mellon Foundation, *Report of the Andrew W. Mellon Foundation 2005*, 18.
29. Andrew W. Mellon Foundation, *Report of the Andrew W. Mellon Foundation 2012*, 8, 11.
30. Liu, "Where Is Cultural Criticism."

Bibliography

"About." Global Outlook::Digital Humanities. http://www.globaloutlookdh.org/.
"About #TransformDH." TransformDH. http://transformdh.org/about-transformdh/.
Andrew W. Mellon Foundation. "Mission." Andrew W. Mellon Foundation. https://mellon.org/about/mission/.

Andrew W. Mellon Foundation. *Report of the Andrew W. Mellon Foundation 1988.* December 31, 1988. https://mellon.org/media/filer_public/e5/5d/e55d3c01-0ae9-4ce7-a4f6-086fa394e6dc/awmf-ar-1988.pdf.

Andrew W. Mellon Foundation. *Report of the Andrew W. Mellon Foundation 1990.* December 31, 1990. https://mellon.org/media/filer_public/43/8e/438e92eb-c5fc-4aba-8c7c-ccf1a9e966a7/awmf-ar-1990.pdf.

Andrew W. Mellon Foundation. *Report of the Andrew W. Mellon Foundation 1994.* December 31, 1994. https://mellon.org/media/filer_public/85/92/8592ccdc-47a0-4105-83bd-4db8273de1de/awmf-ar-1994.pdf.

Andrew W. Mellon Foundation. *Report of the Andrew W. Mellon Foundation 1997.* December 31, 1997. https://mellon.org/media/filer_public/b6/ee/b6ee921e-26b8-4f23-a146-50f5cc56d97b/awmf-ar-1997.pdf.

Andrew W. Mellon Foundation. *Report of the Andrew W. Mellon Foundation 2000.* December 31, 2000. https://mellon.org/media/filer_public/e3/74/e374d761-dd0f-454b-b851-e92a9c8eb0dc/awmf-ar-2000.pdf.

Andrew W. Mellon Foundation. *Report of the Andrew W. Mellon Foundation 2002.* December 31, 2002. https://mellon.org/media/filer_public/23/fb/23fb7a9c-12d1-4c6e-97a0-72787855a643/awmf-ar-2002.pdf.

Andrew W. Mellon Foundation. *Report of the Andrew W. Mellon Foundation 2005.* December 31, 2005. https://mellon.org/media/filer_public/28/a6/28a67355-25f4-4a87-9d72-364bcc355ca2/awmf-ar-2005.pdf.

Andrew W. Mellon Foundation. *Report of the Andrew W. Mellon Foundation 2012.* December 31, 2013. https://mellon.org/media/filer_public/a6/51/a6515255-46f3-4b6f-9b4a-b1f1d0ef1205/awmf-ar-2013.pdf.

Bailey, Moya Z. "All the Digital Humanists Are White, All the Nerds Are Men, but Some of Us Are Brave." *Journal of Digital Humanities* 1, no. 1 (2011). http://journalofdigitalhumanities.org/1-1/all-the-digital-humanists-are-white-all-the-nerds-are-men-but-some-of-us-are-brave-by-moya-z-bailey/.

Bianco, Jamie "Skye." "This Digital Humanities Which Is Not One." In *Debates in the Digital Humanities,* edited by Matthew K. Gold, 96–112. Minneapolis: University of Minnesota Press, 2012. http://dhdebates.gc.cuny.edu/debates/text/9.

Earhart, Amy E. "Can Information Be Unfettered? Race and the New Digital Humanities Canon." In *Debates in the Digital Humanities,* edited by Matthew K. Gold, 309–18. Minneapolis: University of Minnesota Press, 2013. http://dhdebates.gc.cuny.edu/debates/text/16.

4Humanities. "Mission." http://4humanities.org/mission/.

Liu, Alan. "Where Is Cultural Criticism in the Digital Humanities." In *Debates in the Digital Humanities,* edited by Matthew K. Gold, 490–509. Minneapolis: University of Minnesota Press, 2013. http://dhdebates.gc.cuny.edu/debates/text/20.

Lothian, Alexis, and Amanda Phillips. "Can Digital Humanities Mean Transformative Critique?" *Journal of e-Media Studies* 3, no. 1 (2013). http://journals.dartmouth.edu/cgi-bin/WebObjects/Journals.woa/1/xmlpage/4/article/425.

Martin, John D., III and Carolyn Runyon. "Digital Humanities, Digital Hegemony: Exploring Funding Practices and Unequal Access in the Digital Humanities." *SIGCAS Computers and Society* 46, no. 1 (March 2016): 20–26. doi:10.1145/2908216.2908219.

McPherson, Tara. "Why Are the Digital Humanities So White?" In *Debates in the Digital Humanities*, edited by Matthew K. Gold, 139–60. Minneapolis: University of Minnesota Press, 2013. http://dhdebates.gc.cuny.edu/debates/text/29.

Smith, Martha Nell. "The Human Touch Software of the Highest Order: Revisiting Editing as Interpretation." *Textual Cultures* 2, no. 1 (2007): 1–15. http://www.jstor.org/stable/30227853.

Wernimont, Jacqueline. "Whence Feminism? Assessing Feminist Interventions in Digital Literacy Archives." *Digital Humanities Quarterly* 7, no. 1 (2013). http://digitalhumanities.org:8081/dhq/vol/7/1/000156/000156.html.

PART II][Chapter 8

Toward a Queer Digital Humanities

BONNIE RUBERG, JASON BOYD, AND JAMES HOWE

Where is the queerness in the digital humanities? In one sense, queer studies and the digital humanities (DH) share a common ethos: a commitment to exploring new ways of thinking and to challenging accepted paradigms of meaning-making. At the same time, as scholars like J. S. Bianco have argued, many of the data-driven initiatives that have earned DH its most visible accolades eschew rather than engage topics of difference and identity.[1] Though a number of queer studies and digital humanities scholars have already begun bringing queer perspectives to DH, much of this work remains marginal within the larger DH field. Yet the intersection of queer thinking and the digital humanities, like the intersection of feminism or critical race theory and DH, is a site of rich potential. Digital tools have the unique capacity to make visible the histories of queer representation and issues affecting queer communities. Simultaneously, queer studies brings to the digital humanities a set of intersectional, conceptual frameworks that challenge DH scholars to reflect on the politics of their research as well as the implications of their methodologies. Locating the queerness in the digital humanities is a crucial piece of a larger call for an increased critical engagement with culture in DH. This work foregrounds social justice and looks to queer subjecthood, queer desire, and queer world-building as guideposts in the movement toward a digital humanities that values social critique as much as computation and people as much as data.

"Queer" is a word with a long history and a complexity of meaning. From its origins as a pejorative, it has been reclaimed in recent decades by academic and popular communities alike. At its most basic, "queer" operates as an umbrella term: a marker of identity differentiated from "gay" or "LGBT" in that it encompasses all non-normative expressions of sexuality or gender (Grace, Hill, Johnson, and Lewis). Not every person whose identities fall within this category identifies as queer, however, and "queer" itself is a contested term. Within the context of queer studies, the concept of queerness has been interpreted and reinterpreted in manifold ways. From across the work of generations of queer theorists, queerness has emerged as a way of being that is complex and contradictory: at once joyful and destructive, hopeful and fierce. Queerness resists the logics of heteronormative hegemony. "Queer" can also act as a verb: to queer is to destabilize, to subvert, or to unearth queer desire beneath the surface. Amplifying a long-standing thread within queer theory of attending to the interplays between queerness and race, contemporary queer studies scholars are increasingly considering queerness within an intersectional context, addressing how queer issues are interwoven with questions of race and ethnicity, class, socio-economics, and disability (Chen; McRuer; Muñoz). In a fundamental sense, however, what unifies uses of "queer" is that the word still contains at its heart a basic desire to live life, and to understand life, "otherwise" (Halberstam, "Queer Art," 2). At the same time, queerness is not an abstract concept. Even when it is applied conceptually, queerness is still rooted in the embodied realities of queer subjects.

This essay offers our vision for a "queer digital humanities," that is, a digital humanities that is invested in queer issues and has queer thinking at its core. Our goal is not to dictate what forms this queer digital humanities must take. Rather, starting from a survey of existing queer DH scholarship, our goal is to suggest ways forward, to open up queerness in the digital humanities as a space of possibility. We are far from alone in calling for an increased investment in social criticism in DH (e.g., Bailey; Crompton, Siemens, Arbuckle, and INKE; Koh; Liu), and others before us, such as Kara Keeling in her writing on a "Queer OS," have explored ways in which queerness might reimagine the cultural narratives that surround computational technologies. Our intervention is to build from this work in order to argue for positioning queerness as a central element of DH methodologies. When we ask, "Where is the queerness in the digital humanities?," we are also asking, "What might it mean to do the work of the digital humanities queerly?" The authors of this article approach this question from a variety of research backgrounds. In addition to being digital humanists, together we represent perspectives from game studies, queer studies, literary studies, digital librarianship, and critical making. We believe that queerness can function as a force to destabilize and restructure the way that DH scholarship is done across these fields. The vision of a queer digital humanities that we propose is at once conceptual and pragmatic. For us, moving toward a queer digital humanities means valuing queer lives and embracing a queer ethos but also addressing actionable, concrete ways that queerness can shift how the work of DH is done.

The stakes of arguing for the place of queerness in the digital humanities are palpable and present. At a time when harassment in digital spaces has been elevated to new peaks of vitriol, those who speak out for the importance of thinking about gender, sexuality, and structures of oppression in relation to the digital humanities have found themselves the targets of reactionary backlash. As are discussions of data and computation more broadly, DH tools are commonly imagined to be apolitical. Archives, visualizations, and other interfaces created by digital humanists often understand themselves as direct windows onto knowledge, offering democratizing access to objective truths. Data, so the saying goes, don't lie. As feminist scholars of digital cultures know well, however, computational tools have profound political implications. Interfaces structure meaning; visualizations craft interpretation. Any discussions of technology must account for problems of access, both to devices and to education. We believe that this is a crucial time for bringing queer perspectives to the digital humanities, specifically because this is a moment of change. The reach of DH extends farther than ever before. This is therefore a time in which DH methodologies and technologies are both proliferating and codifying, making this an important moment of intervention. At the same time, pushing DH to engage more deeply with queerness has a wider relevance in contemporary conversations about difference, which are proliferating both in today's popular discourse and within our own academic disciplines. Far more than a niche issue within the digital humanities, queerness can serve as a beacon guiding us toward change and a new way forward within DH more broadly.

Queer Subject Matter in the Digital Humanities

We begin by addressing this question: where is the queerness in the digital humanities? Or, rather, where *could* it be? The most immediately apparent way in which the digital humanities can engage with queerness is by directly addressing issues relating to LGBTQ subjects. Indeed, a handful of initiatives of this sort have been undertaken in recent years—but such projects, while illuminating, remain limited in number. Nonetheless, it is important that we account for this research within our framework for a queer digital humanities precisely because it grounds the types of conceptual thinking we expand on below in the lived experiences of LGBTQ communities, histories, and struggles.

Of the existing digital humanities projects that directly address queer issues, some use established DH practices, such as archiving and generating visualizations, to make information regarding queer artistic and political lineages more widely available. The Lesbian and Gay Liberation in Canada project, for example, presents users with an interactive online map that highlights key events and locations in Canadian lesbian and gay rights activism between 1964 and 1981 (lglc.ca). Through this map, the project brings queer history to life, reanimating it via dynamic digital interfaces. Other archival projects have used DH tools to invite users to explore LGBTQ counterhistories. The Centre for Digital Humanities at Ryerson University's *Texting Wilde* initiative aims to create a web-based archive of texts that document the pre-1945 biographical discourse surrounding Oscar Wilde. Rather than collecting Wilde's writings themselves, *Texting Wilde* enumerates the debates that shaped this early period of Wilde scholarship. In this way, the archive allows visitors to understand the constructed and shifting nature of the narratives that have long positioned Wilde's same-sex desire as a defining element of his work. A project like *Texting Wilde* uses digital humanities methodologies to increase engagement with the queer literary canon, but it also queers the notion of biography itself. It lays bare the process by which meaning has been made from Wilde's life and restores multiplicity to the complexity of lived experience. In this way, such a project gestures toward the queer potential of archiving itself as a practice that challenges concise, monolithic, and often hegemonic interpretations of knowledge.

Other digital humanities projects that speak directly to LGBTQ issues include those that address queer subjects through their exploration of social discourse, their interest in pedagogy, or their creative engagement with the cultural implications of technology. Berkeley's #Identity project, for instance, explores the meanings and effects of common Twitter hashtags that relate to issues of diversity, including the commonly used homophobic hashtag #nohomo (De Kosnik and Feldman). Edmond Chang has written about queer digital pedagogy, which he describes as "finding, creating, and playing with multimodal and polyamorous questions, algorithms, archives, and artifacts, analog and digital, flesh-to-flesh and virtual" and which "asks teachers and students, readers and writers, makers and players to be perverse, to be critical and reparative, to invest in these queer sites and moments with 'fascination and love'" (Chang). Meanwhile, artist Zach Blas addressed queerness directly through critical making with his *Queer Technologies* project (2007–2012), on which he later collaborated with micha cárdenas. As explained by Blas and cárdenas, *Queer Technologies* is "an organization that produces a product line for queer technology agency, intervention, and social intervention" (Blas and cárdenas, 3). The project is constituted of a series of installations, art objects, and a "queer programming anti-language": a suite of creations that explore the relationship between queerness and technology. We will discuss *Queer Technologies* at greater length below. Here, we point to these examples of digital humanities work that directly engages with LGBTQ issues in order to demonstrate some of the varied modes of understanding that DH has already brought to the field of queer studies.

As we review this selection of existing work at the intersection of DH and queer studies, we also look for scholarly models that might inspire future digital humanities research focused on LGBTQ subject matter. Two related, emerging areas of research constitute productive areas for further exploration: feminist digital humanities and queer video games. Feminist DH work, and especially the efforts of the Fembot and FemTechNet collectives, has demonstrated how the digital humanities can speak directly to intersectional concerns of social justice. Such work both uses DH tools to address cultural questions of gender and turns a critical eye to the relationship between gender and privilege in the digital humanities itself (see Wernimont). Thus, feminist DH scholarship functions as an argument that technology, while imbued with problems of discrimination and difference, can nonetheless become a powerful platform for critiquing dominant norms—an application that must also be central to a queer digital humanities.

Though it has largely been articulated outside of the discourse of DH, the burgeoning field of queer game studies also shares much with the queer DH we are imagining. Queer game studies has emerged from collaborations between queer theorists, game studies scholars, and queer game designers. While scholars and cultural commentators have published work on gender and sexuality in video games since the 1990s, queer game studies has come together as a research paradigm more recently, energized by the annual Queerness and Games Conference and a concurrent, ongoing wave of independent, personal games made by queer designers like Anna Anthropy, merritt kopas, and Mattie Brice (Ruberg and Shaw). One of the things that makes queer games studies and what might loosely be called the queer games "movement" particularly notable is it foregrounds building dialogues across disciplines and modes of critique (Ruberg). At events like GaymerX, the LGBTQ fan convention, game studies scholars present to nonacademic crowds; simultaneously, game designers perform incisive deconstructions of heteronormative culture through their use of ludic systems. Games culture has long been a hostile space for those perceived as "different," and contemporary online harassment campaigns have made that hostility all the more palpable. Work in the area of queer games brings with it a vibrancy and an immediacy that demonstrate how technological tools can foreground social justice in discussions of queer issues. As the work of these related fields demonstrates, the combination of digital media and queer perspectives demonstrably has the capacity to enliven, enrich, and challenge dominant thinking around both technology and queerness itself.

It perhaps goes without saying that, moving forward, we hope to see more digital humanities projects that engage explicitly with LGBTQ issues. Following from the initiatives discussed here, such projects could document LGBTQ histories, augment the study of LGBTQ lives, offer insight into social phenomena of relevance to LGBTQ communities, prompt instructors to bring the study of LGBTQ issues to life through digital humanities platforms, or explore the place of LGBTQ perspectives in technology through creative making practices. Inspired by the work of feminist DH, such work could also turn a critical eye on the place of LGBTQ subjects within the field of the digital humanities and the institutions through which DH functions. Additionally, in the vein of queer game studies, work in this area could expand through collaboration between scholars and media makers. Before we move into our discussion of queerness in relation to DH methodologies, we linger here for a moment to underscore the importance of representing LGBTQ subjects in the digital humanities. Queerness offers invaluable conceptual frameworks, but a queer digital humanities represents far more than a set of concepts. DH can and must do more to directly address issues faced by those who are marginalized—not despite the fact that, but precisely because, digital fields have long been problematic spaces for those who live life otherwise. For much of their history, these fields (such as computer science, video games, and humanities computing) have been implicitly structured as white, male, heteronormative spaces. As Whitney Phillips has shown in her study of online trolling, *This Is Why We Can't Have Nice Things*, abuse performed through online communication platforms is not a social aberration, but in fact reflects dominant cultural values. In the wake of #GamerGate, a number of essays in the *State of Play* collection (Goldberg and Larsson) examined the hostility against females, persons of color, and queer gamers that continues to pervade games culture. Antifeminist hostility even finds a voice in scholarly forums like the Humanities, Arts, Science, and Technology Alliance and Collaboratory (HASTAC) comment threads, as shown by the heated response to Arielle Schlesinger's blog post about feminist programming languages, discussed more below. Given this backdrop, it is important for us to remember that even as we call for DH scholars to increase their engagement with queerness, queer subjects working in the digital humanities face real risks in pushing the field in more inclusive directions.

Queer DH Methodologies: Inspiration from Existing Work

While queer studies can usefully employ DH tools and practices to produce scholarship focused on queer subjects, it is also important to examine how queer theory can inform current and future digital humanities methodologies. One of the key areas of debate in DH is the role that computing plays in differentiating DH from other modes of humanities scholarship. Some have argued that the digital humanities' narrow focus on computation has led the field to imagine itself, supposedly like computation itself, as free from concerns of economics, race, gender, and sexuality. As Alan Liu observes, "While digital humanists develop tools, data, and metadata critically . . . rarely do they extend their critique to the full register of society, economics, politics, or culture. How the digital humanities advances, channels, or resists today's great postindustrial, neoliberal, corporate, and global flows of information-cum-capital is thus a question rarely heard in the digital humanities" (Liu, web).

Liu goes on to argue that DH must develop a "methodological infrastructure" that unites computational and cultural criticism. Similarly, Roopika Risam, in her essay on intersectionality in DH, suggests four areas in which the digital humanities need to develop in order to create a more inclusive and socially engaged standard of practice: "cultivating a diverse community," "acknowledging inclusions and exclusions in data," applying "theoretical models that position intersectionality as an already existing but oft-overlooked part of computation," and developing systems "for understanding the ways difference [or lack thereof] shapes digital practices" (Risam). Liu's and Risam's critiques make it clear that currently dominant DH methodologies are not sufficient for the development of a queerly inflected digital humanities. The last two areas of development mentioned by Risam (theoretical models in which to identify existing intersectionalities and systems for understanding how difference shapes computation) are of particular interest to the present project. They suggest a queer DH praxis that is distinguished from mainstream DH through its conceptual models—models that can usefully be informed by queer theory. To draw from key questions that queer theory has asked in literary and historical studies, how can we discover, uncover, and recover the queerness (in its various intersectional manifestations) in computation, as well the effects that queerness has had on computing and the potential effects it could have in the future? To date, this praxis has taken the form of speculating on the interconnected histories of queerness and computing, imagining the queering of the fundamental structures of computing technologies, conceptualizing queerness itself as a technology, exploring the queerness of code, and utilizing concepts of "speculative computing" to enact queer work.

A number of these existing works can help us think about queer methodologies for DH. A generative starting point is Kara Keeling's "Queer OS," which outlines the properties of an imagined queer operating system that itself offers new frameworks for making sense of society and identity. In Keeling's formulation, inspired by Tara McPherson, Queer OS is "a project at the interfaces of queer theory, new media studies, and technology studies" that structures itself around the logics of queerness (153). Keeling's Queer OS, should it exist, would understand cultural phenomena like "race, gender, class, citizenship, and ability . . . to be mutually constitutive with sexuality and with media and information technologies." Keeling continues: "Queer OS names a way of thinking and acting with, about, through, among, and at times even in spite of new media technologies and other phenomena of mediation. It insists upon forging and facilitating uncommon, irrational, imaginative, and/or unpredictable relationships" between human subjects and digital media (154). As a launching point for imagining queer DH methodologies, Keeling's Queer OS can be read as an imperative for queer DH scholars to embrace the complex and often contradictory tangle of intersectional investigation. It also directs DH researchers more generally to understand computing not as outside of social issues but rather as shaping and indeed being shaped by cultural determinants.

In addition to informing our vision of a queer digital humanities, Keeling's essay has inspired others to interrogate the intersection of queerness and DH. In their 2016 piece, "Queer OS: A User's Manual," Barnett and colleagues take up Keeling's call to conceptualize a Queer OS, which, the authors point out, "remains a largely speculative project" (50). However, as the authors themselves point out, the speculative operations of the queer system shouldn't necessarily conform to conventional notions of functionality. To the contrary, they state,

> [Our goal] is to engage with the challenge of understanding queerness today as operating on and through digital media and the digital humanities. Our intervention therefore seeks to address what we perceive as a lack of queer, trans, and racial analysis in the digital humanities, as well as the challenges of imbricating queer/trans/racialized lives and building digital/technical architectures that do not replicate existing systems of oppression. As such this is a speculative proposition for a technical project that does not yet exist and may never come to exist, a project that does not yet function and may never function. (51)

The "user's manual" the essay provides is a provocative queer reimagining of what form and role various key components in digital computing (such as interfaces, applications, and memory) might take, with "each component given a poetical and theoretical description of its features and limitations" (50). While these descriptions inspire the reader to imagine a potential future in which computing is more in line with the ethos of queerness, some readers may ask where, in the present, we might identify the beginning points that might lead us toward a concrete instantiation of a Queer OS and, along with it, a queer DH. DH practitioners who are themselves queer and therefore potentially marginalized subjects working within the reward and accreditation structures of contemporary academia may feel that they need to produce work of a more tangible sort than "theoretical vapourware, speculative potentialware, ephemeral praxis" (51). These individuals may wish to (or feel the need to) develop computing technology that shares meaningful connections with this theoretical work but that does not itself embody "an unreliable system full of precarity" with an "inherent instability," given the already precarious position of many queer subjects within the digital humanities (54).

In order to further explore the trajectories along which queer DH might unfold, we turn next to three of the scholarly works from which Keeling draws. The first is Jacob Gaboury's series of articles titled "A Queer History of Computing." One question that vexes the development of a queer DH is how to theorize the relationship between queerness and the ways in which computing itself can enact queer erasure. In his piece, Gaboury addresses this tension through a discussion of Alan Turing and other figures from the history of computing whom Turing influenced. Though Turing is considered to be a central figure in the development of modern computing, rarely have conceptualizations of his work overlapped with discussions of his queerness or the injustices he suffered at the hands of the British government. Gaboury recognizes that any claims about a direct correlation between Turing's sexuality and his theories of computation would be problematic. To posit that the former "inspired" the latter would be simplistic, says Gaboury, yet to conclude that no relationship exists between the two "parses what is technologically significant in such a way so as to exclude the personal, the emotional, and the sexual" (Gaboury). Faced with the problem of articulating how the sexual signifies within the technological, Gaboury traces historical connections between a community of queer figures who played key roles in the early history of computing. Though it remains unclear what direct effects sexuality may have had on their work, Gaboury finds value in refiguring their production through a "speculative history" that foregrounds the oft-elided place of queerness. This type of fabrication (i.e., speculation) resonates in unexpected ways with the digital humanities practices of critical making. Gaboury's history of computing both extends and problematizes DH methodologies by recasting making as "making up." Additionally, Gaboury's focus on historical absence—the suppressed, missing, unrecorded, and always partial nature of queerness in the history of computing—points toward the restorative work that could be done by a queer digital humanities.

Turing's place within the history of artificial intelligence connects Gaboury's work to Jack Halberstam's earlier essay "Automating Gender: Postmodern Feminism in the Age of the Intelligent Machine." Halberstam's essay too provides useful models for conceptualizing a queer digital humanities. "Automating Gender" offers, among other things, a critique of feminist theories that rely on reductive ideas of phallotechnocracy and essentialist conceptions of gender. Like Gaboury, Halberstam looks to Turing to counter these narratives. What is now commonly referred to as the "Turing Test," Halberstam points out, began as a "sexual guessing game" in which an interrogator attempted to determine the genders of players as they answer questions via technological mediation. "Turing does not stress the obvious connection between gender and computer intelligence," writes Halberstam. However, "both are in fact imitative systems, and the boundaries between female and male . . . are as unclear and as unstable as the boundary between human and machine intelligence. . . . Gender, like intelligence, has a technology" (443).[2] To illuminate this unstable binary between the human and the machine, Halberstam takes up Donna Haraway's delineation of the female cyborg as a representation of technology's ability to transcend binary structures. Given that queerness, unlike essentialized gender or sexuality, has been closely aligned with artificiality, unnaturalness, imitation, and the subversion of binaries, one might describe Haraway's cyborg as queer—and, by extension, Halberstam's vision of cyborg technology as queer technology. In addition to envisioning technology as queer, Halberstam implicitly posits queerness itself as a technology. Such a formulation suggests a symbiotic, dialectic relationship between technology and queerness. It also suggests that the interface between human and computing technology might be understood as a space of queer intimacy and relation. Placed within our discussion of digital humanities methodologies, "Automating Gender" challenges us to account for the ways in which gender and sexuality are in fact inextricable from computational systems.

Another valuable touchstone for interrogating the relationship between queerness and the digital is Blas's *Queer Technologies* project, mentioned above, which similarly turns to Turing in theorizing the relationship between queerness and computation. "For us," write Blas with his collaborator cárdenas in an article outlining the work of *Queer Technologies,* "Turing is a crucial historical figure for thinking the politics of digital technologies from queer and feminist perspectives" (2). Yet, perhaps more than a historical figure, Turing appears here as a founder of queer computational thinking. Did Turing's homosexuality affect his research? Blas and cárdenas answer this question with a resounding yes. "The drives and assumptions of a heterosexual sexuality produce certain ways of producing and knowing that can be embodied in objects created by heterosexual scientists," they assert. "Similarly, homosexual desires can inform and help to materially construct the technicity of objects." That is, for Blas and cárdenas, the very logics around which contemporary computation has been founded are shaped by Turing's queerness. Fittingly, it seems that the impulse behind the many artistic works that make up the *Queer Technologies* project is to reimbue or perhaps rediscover the queerness in computational technology. Of these works, the one of most interest here is Blas's *transCoder,* which Blas describes as "a queer programming anti-language." Works written using *transCoder* are not executable. Instead, *transCoder* functions primarily as a critical tool—in Mark C. Marino's words, "a theoretical software development kit, made not of functional functions but of encoded plays on the methods and discourse of critical theory" ("Of Sex," 187). As an unexecutable coding language, *transCoder* suggests a suite of approaches to queer digital humanities methodologies that play with failure and loss. We will return to reflect on the critical concerns that surround failure below. Still, our vision of a queer DH must account for an investigation of the times when technologies, like heteronormative modes of meaning, break down.

Queer Technologies models how practice-based work might speak to potential queer DH methodologies. It also directs us to consider the queer potential of other forms of digital praxis. *transCoder* can be seen as a queer application of what has been called codework. Codework subverts the tenets of "well-written" code: simplicity, functionality, transparency, and legibility. Examples of codework range from the nonexecutable net.art creations of "Mez" (Mary-Ann Breeze), written in a hybrid language called "m[ez]ang.elle," to obfuscated code and esoteric programming languages ("esolangs"). In "Interferences: [Net.Writing] and the Practice of Codework," Rita Raley notes that codework allows programming languages to break the surface, rather than simply leveraging them to perform the invisible labors of technology. This refiguration of code—as elusive, hidden, and ultimately uncontrollable—resonates with queer theory's notion of queer meaning as similarly submerged and anxiogenic. Referring to Jessica Loseby's net.art work *Code Scares Me,* Raley notes how it thematizes "anxieties about [the] intrusion, contamination, and uncontrollability" of code (Raley). Like queerness as interpreted by many queer literary scholars, code in Raley's formulation becomes monstrous, invisible, unknowable, and alien: "It lurks beneath the surface of the text.... The fear, further, is that code is autopoietic and capable of eluding... attempts to domesticate it and bring it into order." Practitioners of codework, Raley observes, see their production as expressly political; it resists assumptions about the neutrality of programming, reclaims code from corporate functionalism, and repurposes the pragmatic as the aesthetic. Such sentiments stand in contrast to the seemingly apolitical sensibilities of programmer communities dedicated to composing obfuscated code and esolangs. These practices tend to fall into the domain of professional programmers for whom testing the boundaries of coding represents an opportunity to demonstrate mastery. Yet obfuscated code and esolangs too represent potentially generative modes of queer DH methodologies. They refuse established expectations for readability and intentionally walk an anxious line between the domestication of code and code's refusal to "be brought into order."[3]

This discussion of esolangs brings us to the last work from which we draw inspiration for our vision of queer DH methodologies. This is what Johanna Drucker has termed "speculative computing." As Drucker recounts in her book *SpecLab,* speculative computing emerges from a "productive tension" within the digital humanities. Specifically, speculative computing aims to invert DH's focus on the use of digital tools in humanities scholarship by focusing instead on the development of "humanities tools in digital environments" (Drucker, xi). Extending the conceptual stakes of speculative computing, Drucker advances a theory called "aesthesis," which foregrounds "partial, situated, and subjective knowledge" and proposes imaginative play with digital objects as an antidote to the totalizing authority of meaning. "Aesthesis," writes Drucker, "allows us to insist on the value of subjectivity that is central to aesthetic artifacts . . . and to place that subjectivity at the core of knowledge production" (Drucker, xiii). In Drucker's characterization, speculative computing takes seriously the destabilization of categories, including taxonomies of entity, identity, object, subject, interactivity, process, and instrument. In short, speculative computing rejects mechanistic and instrumental approaches, replacing them with indeterminacy and potentiality, intersubjectivity, and deformance. Speculative computing operates as a critique of the computational logics that structure much digital humanities scholarship. While Drucker does not mention queerness in *SpecLab,* her work gives voice to an ethos that could serve as a powerful directive for the queer digital humanities. A queer DH would extend the "otherness" that speculative computing enacts by focusing deliberately on issues concerning gender and sexuality in computing. Like queerness itself, the methodologies of a queer digital humanities must not be monolithic. Indeed, with its resistance to totalizing knowledge, speculative computing demonstrates the importance of methodological diversity.

Accordingly, we believe that modes of queer DH scholarship must themselves be multivalent, multiplicative, and self-critical: a set of practices in flux. Taken together, the works considered in this section challenge us to think about queerness in digital humanities methodologies as a matter of fundamental computational structures, as well as (if not more than) a matter of content. These works also encourage us to reflect on the foundational role that intersectional issues related to gender and sexuality play in the formation of new media and digital tools. They insist upon the importance of queer thinking within the history of computation; they delineate the queerness of technology as well as the technology of queerness. Some of the research we have discussed employs traditional scholarly methods. Equally compelling, other works make their arguments through fabrication and artistic interpretation. In our vision, a queer digital humanities too stands poised at the intersection of critique and creation. Drawing from these conceptual frameworks, queer DH itself emerges cyborg-like: a playful methodological hybrid of perspectives, tools, and meaning.

New Visions for Queer DH Methodologies

In the beginning of this essay, we asked, "Where is the queerness in the digital humanities?" Here we transition to consider the question, "Where *could* queerness be in the digital humanities?" In this section, we seek to extend our vision for a queer digital humanities beyond the methodologies suggested by existing work. Or, more precisely, having drawn inspiration from these works, we push ahead to imagine not just a speculative past, as Gaboury does for the history of computation, but a speculative future.

Many of the elements of dominant digital humanities methodologies that we would like to see queered are precisely those that appear, at first glance, least explicitly tied to the politics of DH. Such elements are commonly imagined as functional, mechanical, and therefore objective while, in fact, they too have the capacity to profoundly shape the political implications of DH on an otherwise invisible, structural level. A prime example of this type of functional methodology is object description. A sizable amount of digital humanities scholarship involves describing objects (as in a database). A DH scholar may write an object description for many reasons, but first and foremost that description functions as a marker so that the object may be retrieved later. Whether they are encoding a line of text using the Text Encoding Initiative's markup specification to identify the speech of a character for programmatic manipulation or creating searchable metadata tags for a digital library, a researcher must make choices about how to describe an object within the taxonomical affordances of the available toolset. Such choices, however, are far from obvious or mechanical, and they cannot go unexamined. Alex Gil reflects that he "would make a poor excuse for a humanist if [he] just wrote new books that others would catalog 'mechanically,'" because "the humanist must tend to the production and re-production of sources, archives, narratives, and significance" (Gil). Far from objectively communicating meaning, object description positions the machine, broadly defined, as an intermediary that reflects and enacts the cultural context in which it was created. Thus, object description—not just the work of describing but also the implementation of description in searchable form—is shaped by the cultural assumptions systemized in technology. The limitations, structuring logics, and history of a digital tool determine the opportunities it affords for making meaning from the world.

To explore what it might mean to queer a structural element of digital humanities methodologies like object descriptions, we return to the meaning of "queer." "Queer" as a descriptor occupies an unstable position. It acts in opposition to "straight," but refuses to clarify exactly how; at the same time, it stands to be subsumed by more specific identities as the need arises. Since "queer" is a reclaimed term, it is not uncommon to meet someone who refutes queerness, who instead feels more comfortable with "gay" or "lesbian" as an identifier. This inherent instability "messes up" the labor of description. In their essay "Queer Practice as Research: A Fabulously

Messy Business," Alyson Campbell and Stephen Farrier identify the messiness of queerness as a methodology, one in which "messiness is imbricated with queerness and where cleanliness in knowledge production is associated with knowledge forms that have routinely occluded the queer and the non-normative in an effort to tidy up hypotheses and conform to hegemonic forms of 'rigour'" (Campbell and Farrier, 84). Queer knowledge, in short, is messy.

Given that indexical taxonomies are traditionally designed to "tidy up" knowledge, how might a descriptive vocabulary account for that queer messiness? The Library of Congress Subject Headings (LCSH), a standardized and widely adopted thesaurus of subject headings for use in bibliographical records, demonstrates the trouble that arises when systems of knowledge categorization do not account for the nuance and complexity of queer identities. Criticism of LCSH's treatment of marginalized groups goes back to at least the 1970s (Marshall; Berman). However, as Hope Olson notes, few of these early critics of LCSH "[seem] to have considered a change in structure—only in content." While the terminology used to describe queer subjects has been updated over time, the deployment of that terminology lacks standardization. In a series of recent blog posts, Netanel Ganin examines the continued problems that still surround the confusing application of queer-related terminology in LCSH, where "gay" is used as both an umbrella term for "gay men and lesbians" and shorthand for *only* "gay men." Perhaps most strikingly, as others have noted, the word "queer" itself remains largely absent from LCSH's vocabulary (Kotter; Roberto). Jenna Freedman observes in another blog post some of the descriptive confusion that arises from the absence of the word "queer" from LCSH when it comes to taxonomizing works by writers who deliberately describe their works as queer. In one sense, the push for bringing queerness to LCSH serves as a powerful metaphor for the pressing need to make queer subjects visible and speakable within the structures of the digital humanities: it parallels, in miniature, a larger fight for the right to signify. Far more than an abstract debate, though, the argument for increasing queer inclusion in LCSH speaks to the real lives and labors of scholars who are fighting uphill against established ways of knowing.

Building a taxonomy that adequately accounts for the complexities of queerness may well mean turning to models of self-description that emerge from within queer communities. In "Queer Methodologies," psychotherapist Peter Hegarty critiques the restrictive recommended descriptive practice of the *Publication Manual of the American Psychological Association*. By contrast, he calls attention to the wealth of nuance revealed in the responses to a 2004 gay men's sex study. This study brings to light the many and varied ways that respondents described their identities. In this sense, it speaks to the full complexity of any system that attempts to taxonomize identity and desire. Hegarty writes of the language that men in the study used to describe themselves: "When I read this list of terms some of them made me laugh because they seemed to subvert the question that the researchers asked. Others made me feel uncomfortable as they are terms I once used to describe myself but have long since given up. Collectively, they made me wonder when and where sincerity, irony, cooperation, and dissent might be the intended effects of nominating the sexual self with a particular label" (132). As formulations of their own queerness that defy reduction, these men's responses to the survey echo the idea that "queer knowledge is a knowledge that refuses to be complete" (Grace and Hill, 302).

If queer knowledge always resists completion, it becomes clear that queering metadata means more than adding new vocabulary to existing taxonomical systems. Queerness also points toward a shift in the very methodologies of metadata collection. To queer metadata, queer thinking must be brought to bear on the conceptual models and tools of object description as well as its content. Indeed, the messiness of queerness provides a new vantage point from which to challenge the norms that dictate how meaning is derived from data. The very ways in which data are traditionally mapped rely on a model of the world that queerness refutes, namely, a one-to-one relationship between concepts. A queer digital humanities must therefore seek out systems of meaning-making that can account for nonbinary relationships. Some digital humanities initiatives have begun this work already. Efforts like RDF and linked data, for instance, model network relationships instead of hierarchies. Drawing from this work, Tara McPherson has aptly proposed that "gender, race, sexuality, class, and disability might then be understood not as things that can simply be added on to our analyses (or to our metadata), but instead as operating principles of a different order, always already coursing through discourse and matter" (McPherson, "Designing for Difference," 181). We have lingered over this extended discussion of object description and metadata because we find that it helpfully models the type of queer thinking that can be brought to bear on almost any element of digital humanities methodologies, even those that appear initially least politically or culturally inflected.

Another methodological mode that we believe has expansive potential for a queer digital humanities is play. McPherson remarks, "If a core activity of the digital humanities has been the building of tools, we should design our tools differently, in a mode that explicitly engages power and difference from the get-go, laying bare our theoretical allegiances and exploring the intra-actions of culture and matter" ("Designing for Difference," 182). Play fills this need to adjust, reconceptualize, and design differently. In a queer sense, play implies making a mess and exploring that mess in order to ask, "What if?" Looking forward, queer digital humanists might use playful practices and attitudes to challenge old organizational structures. The practice of writing "living code" offers another potential site of inspiration for a queer digital humanities. Instead of writing a script once and later executing it, the living coder intervenes in the process and makes changes as needed. Collins details the empowering aspect of live coding: "The human live coders who flirt within the algorithmic environments, teasing and tinkling the guts of the processes, are the most powerful agents around. Their presence continually reinforces the truism that software is written by people and makes live its construction and deconstruction" (210).

Live coding needn't even be digital. Bringing together concepts of play and living code, Collins mentions games like *Nomic* or *1000 Blank White Cards* and how rule changes can be made not just during gameplay but as part of gameplay, evolving to meet the desires of participants. Alternatively, instead of interrupting computational processes, we might code disorganization directly into our algorithms, as J. S. Bianco does in her digital essay "Man and His Tool, *Again*?," which deconstructs the traditional form of the essay through the caprices of algorithmic instruction.

Yet another potential queer DH methodology to explore is the glitch. Here the line between performance art and academic research begins to blur, opening space for a radically different imagining of technology born of queer methodology. Jenny Sundén asks us to reconsider the value of the glitch, "an ambiguous phenomenon . . . an unexpected break in the flow," where it is "an amplification of already existing flaws, defects, or errors. Instead of covering up the seams, it presents them proudly." In a keynote address at the 2015 Queerness and Games Conference, Sandy Stone propositioned remapping her clitoris to the palm of her hand and masturbating for the crowd, challenging ideas of appropriateness and pleasure and calling upon attendees to imagine the glitch as an embodied phenomenon: the body out of place and out of order, taking queer pleasure in an embrace of this "flaw." Campbell and Farrier describe the glitch as "practice-as-research," purposefully muddling what might otherwise be a clear delineation between research and researcher, "resist[ing] the normative impulse for cleanliness brought about by disciplining knowledge" (84).

Admittedly, there are potential problems with this call to play around, to mess up, to break down. We recognize that a tension exists in this this call to play, risk, and fail. These methodologies can come into conflict with other things we value in critical digital humanities practice. Practices like standardization of data or plug-and-play code can enable participation in the digital humanities or lower the barrier to entry, especially for new practitioners and marginalized subjects. Accessibility and disability must be part of our discussions when we consider the queer potential of a "mess." How far can we play around before creating obstacles that discourage participation? Researchers are also subject to the need to produce: for the requirements of a grant, for tenure and promotion, as part of a funded project, to produce "metrics" for administrators and so on. We do not intend to dictate that DH scholars, faced with the choice to implement a normative or a queer methodology, must always make the queer choice. However, we do believe that queer digital methodologies have important new perspectives to offer scholars from all branches of DH, and that the rewards for taking the leap into new modes of structuring the world are of immense scholarly and social value.

Toward a Queer Digital Humanities

The goal of this essay has been to argue for an increased engagement with queerness in the digital humanities. By looking at DH work that directly addresses queer subjects, we have attempted to demonstrate the value of bringing DH to queer studies—as well as indicating areas that are ripe for significant expansion. In turning to the methodologies of DH, we have been interested in seeing the other side of this equation: what queer thinking can bring to the digital humanities. We looked at existing work that theorizes the relationship between queerness and technology as a launching point for imagining queer DH methodologies. Building from this work, we mapped a selection of our own suggestions for queer DH methodologies, with object descriptions as our main illustrative case study. We close by emphasizing that we do not mean for the methodologies we have suggested to be comprehensive, but rather for them to demonstrate the richness, variety, and potential at the intersection of queerness and DH. It is our hope that they serve as inspiration for others to push further in this arena. This work, and future explorations into the relationship between queerness and DH, speaks to important and pressing concerns around social engagement in the field, underscoring the politics of computation and calling for a wider diversity of perspectives in both subject matter and method.

Like most calls for a critical digital humanities, we are here asking for reflection on methods of labor, creation, product, and practice, and how they embody, enact, restrict, or constrain modes of expression. Who or what benefits from "straight," "cis," or "clean" data, and what might "queer," "trans," "nonbinary," "messy," or "playful" data look like? What do we expose when we resist norms and binaries, or when we read queerly, build queerly, map queerly, and play queerly? Many queer-identified people recognize the tradeoffs of negotiating their identity. Context can make the transition smooth, risky, fraught, or celebrated. Practicing a queer digital humanities is much the same. Different stakeholders bring different needs and values to this work, and a queer digital humanities must make space for a wide continuum of approaches. Constructing systems (not just literally computing systems, but systems of thought, systems of expression) that support ambiguity, permit play, and engage difference can be a rewarding challenge but also a risk. Queerness too represents a risk, a place at the edge of unsafety; yet this same space is the space of possibility. We expect that a truly queer DH may still be a long time coming—or, perhaps, it will never come. This tension too lies at the heart of our queer digital humanities, and it is perhaps in tension that we might locate the most radical line of thinking that queerness brings to DH. At a time when the digital humanities promises to make sense of the world through supposedly objective computational tools, queerness refuses to allow us to stop reflecting, stop challenging, and stop questioning.

Notes

1. In "Room for Everyone at the DH Table?" Roopika Risam and Adeline Koh offer a structured synopsis of a 2013 open discussion thread on "The Digital Humanities as Historical 'Refuge' from Race/Class/Gender/Sexuality/Disability" that addresses this issue directly.

2. In her earlier *Technologies of Gender* (1987), Teresa de Lauretis takes up Michel Foucault's idea of the "technology of sex" and proposes that gender is also "the product of various social technologies" (2). Following Foucault, de Lauretis uses "technology" to refer broadly to a set of systematic practices found, for example, in cinema (e.g., cinematic techniques and codes) that contribute to the social construction of gender. Halberstam's essay extends this concept into theories of computational technology.

3. A useful example can be seen in Mark C. Marino's analysis of the work being done by Julie Levin Russo's "Slash Goggles algorithm" (written in the transCoder programming antilanguage) and the AnnaKournikova worm. While both revolve around desire, the worm exploits the heteronormative behaviors that are structured by the web, whereas the algorithm enables the decoding of repressed or subsumed queer desire in mainstream (heteronormative) cultural works ("Of Sex," 200).

Bibliography

Adler, Melissa. "Paraphilias: The Perversion of Meaning in the Library of Congress Catalog." In *Feminist and Queer Information Studies Reader,* edited by Patrick Keilty, 309–23. Sacramento, Calif.: Litwin Books, 2013.

Bailey, Moya. "#transform(ing)DH Writing and Research: An Autoethnography of Digital Humanities and Feminist Ethics." *Digital Humanities Quarterly* 9, no. 2 (2015). http://www.digitalhumanities.org/dhq/vol/9/2/000209/000209.html.

Barnett, Fiona, Zach Blas, micha cárdenas, Jacob Gaboury, Jessica Marie Johnson, and Margaret Rhee. "QueerOS: A User's Manual." In *Debates in the Digital Humanities 2016,* edited by Matthew Gold and Lauren F. Klein, 50–59. Minneapolis: University of Minnesota Press, 2016.

Berman, Sanford. *Prejudices and Antipathies: A Tract on the LC Subject Heads Concerning People.* Metuchen, N.J.: Scarecrow Press, 1971.

Bianco, Jamie "Skye." "Man and His Tool, *Again*? Queer and Feminist Notes on Practices in the Digital Humanities and Object Orientations Everywhere." *Digital Humanities Quarterly* 9, no. 2 (2015). http://www.digitalhumanities.org/dhq/vol/9/2/000216/000216.html.

Bianco, Jamie "Skye." "This Digital Humanities Which Is Not One." In *Debates in the Digital Humanities,* edited by Matthew K Gold, 96–112. Minneapolis: University of Minnesota Press, 2013. http://dhdebates.gc.cuny.edu/debates/text/9.

Blas, Zach, and micha cárdenas. "Imaginary Computational Systems: Queer Technologies and Transreal Aesthetics." *AI & Society* 28, no. 4 (2013): 559–66.

Campbell, Alyson, and Stephen Farrier. "Queer Practice as Research: A Fabulously Messy Business." *Theatre Research International* 40, no. 1 (2015): 83–87.

Chang, Edmond Y. "Queer." In *Digital Pedagogy in the Humanities: Concepts, Models and Experiments,* edited by Rebecca Frost Davis, Matthew K. Gold, Katherine D. Harris, and Jentery Sayers. MLA Commons, n.d. https://digitalpedagogy.mla.hcommons.org/keywords/queer/.

Chen, Mel. *Animacies: Biopolitics, Racial Matter, and Queer Affect.* Durham, N.C.: Duke University Press, 2012.

Collins, Nick. "Live Coding of Consequence." *Leonardo* 44, no. 3 (2011): 207–11.

Crompton, Constance, Raymond Siemens, Alyssa Arbuckle, and Implementing New Knowledge Environments (INKE). "Enlisting 'Vertues Noble & Excelent': Behavior, Credit, and Knowledge Organization in the Social Edition." *Digital Humanities Quarterly* 9, no. 2 (2015).

De Kosnik, Abigail, and Keith Feldman, eds. *#identity.* Under contract with University of Michigan Press.

De Lauretis, Teresa. *Technologies of Gender: Essays on Theory, Film, and Fiction.* Bloomington: Indiana University Press, 1987.

Drucker, Johanna. *SpecLab: Digital Aesthetics and Projects in Speculative Computing.* Chicago: University of Chicago Press, 2009.

Freedman, Jenna. "Queering LCSH." *lower east side librarian* (blog), February 3, 2009. http://lowereastsidelibrarian.info/whatshouldbelcshforqueer.

Gaboury, Jacob. "A Queer History of Computing." *Rhizome.org* (blog), February 19–June 18, 2013 (5 parts). http://rhizome.org/editorial/2013/feb/19/queer-computing-1/, http://rhizome.org/editorial/2013/mar/19/queer-computing-2/, http://rhizome.org/editorial/2013/apr/9/queer-history-computing-part-three/, http://rhizome.org/editorial/2013/may/6/queer-history-computing-part-four/, http://rhizome.org/editorial/2013/jun/18/queer-history-computing-part-five/.

Ganin, Netanel. "The Default + My First LCSH Proposal." *I never metadata I didn't like* (blog), August 22, 2015. https://inevermetadataididntlike.wordpress.com/2015/08/22/the-default-my-first-lcsh-proposal/.

Ganin, Netanel. "Inconsistency in LGBTQ Terms." *I never metadata I didn't like* (blog), November 22, 2015. https://inevermetadataididntlike.wordpress.com/2015/11/22/inconsistency-in-lgbtq-terms/.

Ganin, Netanel. "It's Time (It's Past Time) for Queer in the LCSH." *I never metadata I didn't like* (blog), December 13, 2015. https://inevermetadataididntlike.wordpress.com/2015/12/13/its-time-its-past-time-for-queer-in-the-lcsh/.

Ganin, Netanel. "Up to Date Headings." *I never metadata I didn't like* (blog), November 17, 2015. https://inevermetadataididntlike.wordpress.com/2015/11/17/up-to-date-headings/.

Gil, Alex. "A Non-Peer-Reviewed Review of a Peer-Reviewed essay by Adeline Koh." *@elotroalex* (blog), April 20, 2015. http://www.elotroalex.com/a-non-peer-reviewed-review-of-a-peer-reviewed-essay-by-adeline-koh/.

Gold, Matthew K., and Lauren F. Klein, eds. *Debates in the Digital Humanities 2016.* Minneapolis: University of Minnesota Press, 2016.

Goldberg, Daniel, and Linus Larsson, eds. *The State of Play: Creators and Critics on Video Game Culture.* New York: Seven Stories Press, 2015.

Grace, Andre P., and Robert J. Hill. "Using Queer Knowledges to Build Inclusionary Pedagogy in Adult Education." *Adult Education Research Conference,* 2001. http://newprairiepress.org/aerc/2001/papers/26.

Grace, André P., Robert J. Hill, Corey W. Johnson, and Jamie B. Lewis. "In Other Words: Queer Voices/Dissident Subjectivities Impelling Social Change." *International Journal of Qualitative Studies in Education (QSE)* 17, no. 3 (2004): 301–24.

Halberstam, Judith [Jack]. "Automating Gender: Postmodern Feminism in the Age of the Intelligent Machine." *Feminist Studies* 17, no. 3 (1991): 439–60.

Halberstam, Judith [Jack]. *The Queer Art of Failure*. Durham, N.C.: Duke University Press, 2011.

Haraway, Donna. *Simians, Cyborgs, and Women: The Reinvention of Nature*. New York: Routledge, 1991.

Hegarty, Peter. "Queer Methodologies." In *Feeling Queer or Queer Feelings? Radical Approaches to Counselling Sex, Sexualities and Genders*, edited by Lyndsey Moon, 125–41. London: Routledge, 2008.

Keeling, Kara. "Queer OS." *Cinema Journal* 53, no. 2 (Winter 2014): 152–57.

Koh, Adeline. "A Letter to the Humanities: DH Will Not Save You." Digital Pedagogy Lab, April 19, 2015. http://www.digitalpedagogylab.com/hybridped/a-letter-to-the-humanities-dh-will-not-save-you/.

Kotter, Wade. "Subject Headings for Queer Studies." *Cataloging Questions & Answers* (blog), The Anthropology and Sociology Section of the Association of College and Research Libraries (ACRL), July 2013.

Liu, Alan. "Where Is Cultural Criticism in the Digital Humanities?" In *Debates in the Digital Humanities*, edited by Matthew K. Gold. Open access ed. Minneapolis: University of Minnesota Press, 2013. http://dhdebates.gc.cuny.edu/debates/text/20.

Marino, Mark C. "Of Sex, Cylons, and Worms: A Critical Code Study of Heteronormativity." *Leonardo Electronic Almanac (DAC09: After Media: Embodiment and Context)* 17, no. 2 (2012): 184–201.

Marino, Mark C. "Why We Must Read the Code: The Science Wars, Episode IV." In *Debates in the Digital Humanities 2016*, edited by Matthew K. Gold and Lauren F. Klein, 139–52. Minneapolis: University of Minnesota Press, 2016.

Marshall, Joan K. *On Equal Terms: A Thesaurus for Nonsexist Indexing and Cataloging*. New York: Neal-Schuman, 1977.

McPherson, Tara. "Designing for Difference." *Differences: A Journal of Feminist Cultural Studies* 25, no. 1 (2014): 178–88.

McPherson, Tara. "U.S. Operating Systems at Mid-Century: The Intertwining of Race and UNIX." In *Race after the Internet*, edited by Lisa Nakamura and Peter Chow-White, 23–37. New York: Routledge, 2012.

McRuer, Robert. *Crip Theory: Cultural Signs of Queerness and Disability*. New York: New York University Press, 2006.

Muñoz, José. *Disidentifications: Queers of Color and the Performance of Politics*. Minneapolis: University of Minnesota Press, 1999.

Oldman, Dominic, Martin Doerr, Gerald de Jong, Barry Norton, and Thomas Wikman. "Realizing Lessons of the Last 20 Years: A Manifesto for Data Provisioning &

Aggregation Services for the Digital Humanities (A Position Paper)." *D-Lib Magazine* 20, no. 7/8 (2014).

Olson, Hope. "How We Construct Subjects: A Feminist Analysis." In *Feminist and Queer Information Studies Reader,* edited by Patrick Keilty and Rebecca Dean, 251–89. Sacramento, Calif.: Litwin Books, 2013.

Phillips, Whitney. *This Is Why We Can't Have Nice Things: Mapping the Relationship between Online Trolling and Mainstream Culture.* Cambridge, Mass.: MIT Press, 2015.

Raley, Rita. "Interferences: [Net.Writing] and the Practice of Codework." *Electronic Book Review,* "Electropoetics" thread. September 8, 2002. http://www.electronicbookreview.com/thread/electropoetics/net.writing.

Risam, Roopika. "Beyond the Margins: Intersectionality and the Digital Humanities." *Digital Humanities Quarterly* 9, no. 2 (2015). http://www.digitalhumanities.org/dhq/vol/9/2/000208/000208.html.

Risam, Roopika, and Adeline Koh. "Room for Everyone at the DH Table?" *Postcolonial Digital Humanities,* May 15, 2013. http://dhpoco.org/blog/2013/05/15/room-for-everyone-at-the-dh-table/.

Roberto, K. R. "Inflexible Bodies: Metadata for Transgender Identities." *Journal of Information Ethics* 20, no. 2 (2011): 56–64.

Ruberg, Bonnie, ed. "Videogames, Queerness, & Beyond." Special issue, *First Person Scholar,* February 18–March 11, 2015. http://www.firstpersonscholar.com/videogames-queerness-beyond/.

Ruberg, Bonnie, and Adrienne Shaw, eds. *Queer Game Studies.* Minneapolis: University of Minnesota Press, 2017.

Schlesinger, Ari. "Feminism and Programming Languages." *HASTAC* (blog), November 26, 2013.

Sedgwick, Eve Kosofsky. "The Beast in the Closet." In *Epistemology of the Closet,* 182–212. Berkeley: University of California Press, 1990.

Spade, Dean. "Methodologies of Trans Resistance." In *A Companion to Lesbian, Gay, Bisexual, Transgender, and Queer Studies,* edited by George E. Haggerty and Molly McGarry, 237–61. Malden, Mass.: Blackwell, 2007.

Sundén, J. "On Trans-, Glitch, and Gender as Machinery of Failure." *First Monday* 20, no. 4 (2015).

Voss, G. S. "'It Is a Beautiful Experiment': Queer(y)ing the Work of Alan Turing." *AI & Society* 28, no. 4 (2013): 567–73.

Wernimont, Jacqueline, ed. "Feminisms and DH." Special issue, *Digital Humanities Quarterly* 9, no. 2 (2015). http://www.digitalhumanities.org/dhq/vol/9/2/index.html.

PART III
EMBODIMENT

PART III][Chapter 9

Remaking History

Lesbian Feminist Historical Methods in the Digital Humanities

MICHELLE SCHWARTZ AND CONSTANCE CROMPTON

Writing of her experience in the early 1990s, sociologist Becki Ross points to "generational chauvinism" that reduced radical lesbians of the 1970s to stereotypes, leaving her peers to assume that the previous generation was "shrill and humourless." The history Ross says her generation did know "comically reduced [lesbian feminists] to excessive flannel, vigilantly practiced downward mobility . . . strict vegetarianism, and syrupy, sentimentalized fiction."[1] There had been a similar generational rift between lesbian feminists and the women of the bar scene that preceded them, "compounded by often outright rejection of what little was known, [which] rendered impossible the building of bridges to bind and fortify 'old' and 'new' generations."[2] Thankfully, there is room for digital humanities scholars, sociologists, historians, and ethnographers to help bridge these intergenerational gaps. Moreover, we can engage with the historiography of the women who have come before us to aid us as we work toward greater intergenerational understanding. In this chapter we explore how history-making practices of radical and lesbian feminists offer a model of cultural history preservation and transmission for those of us who create digital resources.

Drawing on the historiographic practices of Jeanette Howard Foster in the 1950s, Barbara Grier in the 1960s, Lillian Faderman in the 1980s, and Dell Richards in 1990, we argue that the accumulation of data and the rhetorical structuring of those data (in these examples often as *a list,* a much ignored data format) serve as important acts of lesbian self-definition, self-definition that resists the erasure of women's history by mainstream culture and the definition of the lesbian self in relation to men. This listing, or amassing of data, situates lesbian researchers as the heirs of the history that they create. This ordering of data in self-definitional work, even in the face of the increased attention, or even surveillance, that it might bring, is an important corrective to lesbian histories that are often framed as an afterthought in gay men's histories, or worse, are ignored altogether.

We then turn to what contemporary digital humanities scholars can learn from radical lesbian and feminist archiving and publishing as a means to preserve and disseminate lesbian history. While this history-making situates researchers and their sisters in relation to lost history, there is something in the perpetual reinvigoration and revisiting of these lists and projects, often started anew every decade, which leads us to ask about the lack of cultural transmission between lesbian generations. With concerns about Ross's "generational chauvinism" in mind, we turn to the Lesbian and Gay Liberation in Canada (LGLC) project to investigate how data formats and digital archiving processes can bridge the intergenerational gap, concluding with an outline of the stakes of this recovery work in the context of the digital humanities for those of us interested in promoting social justice and undermining patriarchy.

Digital humanities has not always been a field engaged in these debates, and yet it offers the digital tools to engage in lesbian history-making and dissemination, built on the DIY ethos of radical and lesbian feminists, discussed below. What we strive for in our development of the LGLC project is to meet Miriam Posner's call for a radical new digital humanities, one that not only shifts the foci of projects away from the mainstream to the marginalized, but also develops ways of representing people's lives in data "*as they have been experienced,* not as they have been captured and advanced by businesses and governments."[3]

In keeping with Posner's approach, we have tried to engage with the material on its own terms, thinking with and through the practices by which radical women engaged in self-definition, which, as we work with material that encompasses ever greater spans of time, larger spaces, and extended communities, has become increasingly challenging. As a result, the project is grounded by a rather broad definition of *lesbian,* drawn from the Lesbian Herstory Archives (LHA). The LHA, which was founded by a Gay Academic Union consciousness-raising group in 1972, seeks to record and tell the stories of almost all women, including "women who have lived their lives as lesbians, to transgendered women living as lesbians, to married women who remember the one affair they had, to lesbian sex workers, to lesbian mothers of lesbian daughters."[4] The familial reference to lesbian mothers of lesbian daughters may be productively taken up as the appropriate intergenerational approach to archival material, one that Kate Eichhorn points out is not meant to be confined by straight cisgendered familial roles, but rather by queer familial roles that can engage in productive disagreement complemented by "fierce protectiveness."[5]

An uncritically celebratory approach to this particular history is, however, neither possible nor desirable. As Roxanne Stamer has pointed out, "with the continued emergence of 1970s feminist archives, feminist historians need to ask how they might receive them and whether they might do so such that they do not iterate [the 1970s call to rediscover or uncover lesbian history's] assumptions of sameness across time."[6] This particular warning, which we take up in the final section of the chapter, written in the year after the last Michigan Womyn's Festival, is pressing, especially as we think through 1970s radical feminism's exclusion of trans*[7] women and the insufficient work that was and is done by white feminists to address personal and institutional racism.[8]

This chapter covers lesbian listing, publishing, and archiving events in the century that followed 1917, when Jeanette Howard Foster began the list that would become the book *Sex Variant Women in Literature,* and so there is room for considerable slippage in historical terms as cultural context changes. We use the term "lesbian feminist" to refer to women who identified as lesbian and feminist as two separate identities in the first half of the twentieth century. In the late 1960s "lesbian feminist" came to refer to women who identified with Ti-Grace Atkinson's aphorism "Feminism is the theory, lesbianism is the practice." This made lesbian feminist discourse from the late 1960s to the 1980s, which cast lesbianism as a political choice, quite different from the biologically determinant "born that way" rhetoric of the 1990s and 2000s. Akin to "woman-identified women," lesbian feminists of the 1970s were on the whole less militant than "radical feminists," although, we should note, there is some slippage between those two terms and their use is neither geographically nor temporally uniform. Broadly, then, we use "radical feminist" to refer to separatist women who either developed spaces that excluded men or opted out of patriarchal culture altogether by seeking self-sufficiency in women-only communes, collectives, and womyn's lands. While most of the chapter that follows addresses the community and history-building work of lesbians in the middle decades of the twentieth century, to whom the contemporary valence and concerns of *queer politics* were unavailable, it will conclude with a discussion of the resurrection of sound radical feminist approaches that can productively inform digital humanities practice in a way that avoids the troubling exclusion of trans* women.

We are guided by the way lesbian feminist historians of the past have reclaimed the forgotten or erased history of women's lives, and how they have thought about and represented sexuality and gender through the centuries in order to build a lesbian identity for the present. Being in control of one's own history is of real political import. As Ellen Lewin points out in the introduction to her book *Inventing Lesbian Cultures in America,* one of the great achievements of the twentieth century's lesbian feminist movement was to wrest control of the word "lesbian" from Western psychiatry and redefine it as more than an illness, creating in its place an identity that transcended pathology.[9] Crucial to the formation of this new lesbian identity was the construction of a lesbian culture and history, for without that history there could be no movement, no sense of "collective meaning."[10] As Lillian Faderman put it, "the possibility of a life as a lesbian had to be socially constructed in order for women to be able to choose such a life."[11]

The importance of this process to the lesbian feminists of the time cannot be overstated. In 1980, Adrienne Rich described being denied access to "any knowledge of a tradition, a continuity, a social underpinning" for lesbianism as nothing short of a "means of keeping heterosexuality compulsory for women."[12] These constructions of the past were, for Lewin, "a vital aspect of how lesbians imagine the present, whether they believe the present to be continuous with or disruptive of that past."[13] Standing between lesbian feminists and this sense of identity was a page left blank by centuries of cultural omission. In her essay "It Is the Lesbian in Us," Adrienne Rich points out how heavily we as a culture rely on the books in our libraries to teach us how to live and tell us what is possible. However, in literature and in history, relationships between women went unnamed, undepicted, omitted, censored, and "misnamed as something else." She cites Virginia Woolf's description of those blank pages as "that vast chamber where nobody has been," or in Emily Dickinson's words: "My Classics veiled their faces."[14] Rich describes her own "pursuit of a flickering, often disguised reality" in the literature of the past as "a sense of desiring oneself; above all, of choosing oneself."[15] In addition to recovering and improving the visibility of activists' work, we are interested in engaging lesbian historiographic methods, especially the enumeration, naming, cataloging, listing, and self-publishing that women undertook in the 1960s and 1970s in order to help keep omission, misnaming, and censorship from hindering intergenerational understanding and knowledge transmission.

Lesbian Historiography

Through the twentieth century, lesbian feminists pursued Adrienne Rich's flickering, disguised reality, and painstakingly worked to reconstruct and self-publish lesbian history. This revivification of lesbian history and culture used the same social history methods that women's history scholars would use to reconstruct a historical past in which women had not been erased.[16] In 1917, Jeanette Howard Foster began the process of "authenticating by accumulation" (a phrase that Alisa Klinger has used to describe the creation of multicultural lesbian anthologies).[17] As a member of the student council at Rockford University in Illinois, she was called upon to "discipline two other female students in a 'morals case.'"[18] Not entirely sure what a 'morals case' even referred to, she began a process of research into same-sex attraction among women that quickly transcended its original purpose. Foster began to construct a list, the beginning of a bibliography of references to romantic relationships between women in literature and poetry, a bibliography that she worked on for almost forty years. Throughout her time as a professor at Drexel University, as a researcher working with Alfred Kinsey on his study *Sexual Behavior in the Human Female,* and as a librarian at the University of Kansas, Jeanette Howard Foster worked with her partner Hazel Tolliver to "track down and translate historic references to lesbian love."[19] Her book, *Sex Variant Women in Literature,* subtitled "A Historical and Quantitative Survey," begins with Sappho in the sixth century BCE and ends, almost four hundred pages and 2,600 years later, with Patricia Highsmith's *The Price of Salt*.[20]

In 1954, having already been disappointed when a university press revoked an agreement to publish her book because the new editor was "afraid to honor the commitment" and knowing she would be ignored by the traditional publishing industry, Foster paid Vantage Press to print her groundbreaking bibliography.[21] She sent a copy to the editor of *The Ladder*, the print arm of the lesbian organization Daughters of Bilitis.[22] In May of 1957, Marion Zimmer Bradley reviewed *Sex Variant Women in Literature* for the *The Ladder*, proclaiming, "To the collector of Lesbian literature the work is invaluable, listing as it does every major work and many minor ones."[23]

In 1956, a twenty-three-year-old lesbian with a similar passion for compiling lists befriended Jeanette Howard Foster. Barbara Grier, a bibliophile who went on to write fifteen years' worth of lesbian literature reviews for the Lesbiana column of *The Ladder*, began working with Marion Zimmer Bradley to compile "The Checklist," a "hand-typed, mimeographed bibliography" of lesbian content in literature.[24] First published in 1960, "The Checklist" was revised and supplemented several times before taking its final form as *The Lesbian in Literature* in 1967.[25] The first edition listed three thousand books, and each subsequent edition, enhanced by the contributions of many collaborators, added many more. Entries were coded to indicate the presence of major and minor "lesbian characters and/or action" or "repressed lesbianism or characters who can be so interpreted" and the "quality of the Lesbian material in the work in question."[26] The list was comprehensive, extending well beyond outright lesbian content to include everything from the "sex disguise" employed by Edmund Spenser in *The Fairie Queene* in 1590, the memoir of an Episcopalian bishop who had ordained an out lesbian into the priesthood, "mildly pertinent" work by Anaïs Nin, and *The Fur Person*, "a cat book, about a remarkable cat that belongs to an obvious Lesbian couple."[27]

It was not just Barbara Grier and her many collaborators and *Ladder* readers who took inspiration and solace in Foster's monumental bibliography. In 1962, a closeted graduate student named Lillian Faderman came across *Sex Variant Women in Literature* while perusing the shelves of the English Reading Room at the University of California, Los Angeles, looking for books by E. M. Forster. In her introduction to Joanne Passett's biography of Jeanette Howard Foster, Faderman describes furtively returning again and again to the book in the stacks, hiding its binding in the pages of another book, and reading it chapter by chapter until she had devoured the whole bibliography. She later described Foster as her model for "how one could do serious scholarship about lesbian subject matter."[28] It was, she said "the inspiration of that book that made me begin in 1976 the study that would eventually be published in 1981 as *Surpassing the Love of Men*."[29] Thus was birthed an entire genre of lesbian history writing, written by women delving into obscure archives and mouldy books to carefully compile volumes listing every previously ignored or forgotten instances of friendly spinsters who kept odd company, Boston marriages, romantic friendships, cross-dressers, mannish inverts, female husbands, hermaphrodites, and more.

In our consideration of this genre of lesbian historiography, we would like to pause over *Lesbian Lists: A Look at Lesbian Culture, History, and Personalities* (1990), by Dell Richards. The book is a creative take on the lesbian feminist historiographic tradition. Quite literally a book of lists, *Lesbian Lists* is even more heterogeneous than Grier's bibliography. Richards offers her readers lists, such as "11,000 and More Sworn Virgins," "13 Uppity Women Who Were Called Lesbians—But Who Probably Weren't," "7 Lesbians Whose Poems Appear in the *Norton Anthology of Poetry*, First Edition," and "5 Works [of Fiction] with Natalie Barney as a Character." Many of Richards's lists are tongue-in-cheek—the text is far from scholarly—but the lists aside, we are particularly interested in the historiographic methodological musings contained in a few lines in Richards's introduction.[30]

In the introduction to *Lesbian Lists*, Richards weighs the question of whom to list in the book and whom to leave out. She elucidates the difficulty she had reading historical accounts and working out a methodology for whom to include. Should the book list "women who are sexually attracted to other women *or* women who became lesbians through feminism? Or should [she] use a much broader definition, one which includes the romantic friends movement? ... Should [she] include spinsters?" (emphasis added).[31] As the title of the "13 Uppity Women" list attests, she cast her net wide. Richards did not focus solely on "women who are sexually attracted to other women *or* women who became lesbians through feminism" but rather opted for inclusivity, as, "17 Romantic Friends," "5 Lesbians Who Married Gay Men," and "15 Spinsters Who Need to Be Researched" attest. Through lists, the book is striving to create a history for lesbianism, and by privileging a variety of relationships, lets contemporary women consider what it meant to be a lesbian in the past, and to take heart in what women accomplished (which is plenty, the lists tell us, with accounts of doctors and writers, nuns and rulers, mathematicians and social reformers).

The introduction also includes the idea that women might come to be lesbian through divine political revelation. Speaking of her own experience in the 1970s, Richards says, "For me, becoming a lesbian was a conscious political decision, the logical extension of feminism."[32] What is most interesting here is that Richards's typology, of a lesbian born of nature and one of politics, no longer holds sway in contemporary culture. There are still many women who might say that they came to be lesbian through politics, but their experience is not part of national or popular discourse. However, Richards's account of her experience and motives is worth capturing, contextualizing, and sharing. Her self-declaration, her self-definition, is in danger of being lost if we forget the many ways of being a lesbian even as recent as the 1970s. It is precisely this sort of information that the LGLC project seeks to share across generations. Even if there are very few young women today who would now say that their sexuality is the result of a political choice, in engaging with 1970s lesbian feminism, we seek to make it clear that this once was, and could again be, a condition of possibility for women. With the loss of the idea that lesbianism has and can be a political choice might come a diminished power to imagine and build a future that offers equitable possibilities, and a diminished language to talk about self-determination and self-definition, and to respond to contemporary political realities that, like those of the 1970s, might persist or might be short-lived.

Richards (and others like her who have written in the lesbian historiographical tradition that owes so much to Foster, Grier, and Faderman) is building a history, a community that stretches back over a thousand years, and that even from that thousand-year vantage point reaches forward to embrace her. And yet, Richards is also using history to imagine the future, a future that is different from the present and the past, which includes "women who became lesbians through feminism."

Lesbian Lists concludes with a call to research. One of the final lists is entitled "Cities with Lesbian Archives."[33] Echoing Foster's bibliographic call to lesbians to recognize themselves in the pages of particular books, Richards incites her readers to research, to find out more, to read unread texts. The result of this archival work could be more histories which women could embody, positioning themselves in history, or publish, sharing that history with others.

The lesbian list as a community-building and visibility-promoting strategy has been taken up in a contemporary digital context, and in many cases has, with the growing mainstream acceptance of the LGBT community, been coopted by major media corporations looking to cash in on the format. Some of these new lesbian lists work within the *listicle* format popularized by BuzzFeed and Gawker Media, aggregating content from elsewhere on the web and using clickbait titles to maximize page views in order to appeal to advertisers. For example, *AfterEllen*'s "The AfterEllen.com Les/Bi List!" of the top fifty "out female celebrities" points to the political importance of visibility ("Back when AfterEllen.com was founded in 2002," the site points out "our slogan was 'Because Visibility Matters.' Indeed, the idea that lesbian and bisexual women need to be visible, both to ourselves and to the wider culture. . . . Only by being visible to family, friends and the world do we overcome the stereotypes and bigotry used to justify discrimination against the GLBT community") while also setting up the list to span eighteen pages, maximizing the number of pageviews to ensure sustainable ad revenue. It is important to note that in 2011, when "The AfterEllen.com Les/Bi List!" was published, AfterEllen was a subsidiary of Logo TV, the lesbian- and gay-themed television channel owned by Viacom.[34]

Keeping more in line with the original ethos of the lesbian lists, the independently owned Autostraddle, a website for "lesbian, bisexual and queer women (cis and trans)" has demonstrated a deep and abiding fondness for traditional lesbian history-making, going so far as to take Del Richards's list "20 Turn-of-the-Century 'Ways to Tell' if a Girl Would Become Gay or if a Woman Was a Lesbian—According to the Medical Journals of the Day" and spinning it into "15 Ways to Spot a Lesbian

According to Some Really Old Medical Journals," illustrated with tongue-in-cheek photos of lesbian celebrities as well as members of the Autostraddle staff and their girlfriends.[35] In their post on the "Top 10 Most Sexually Prolific Lesbians and Bisexuals of Old Hollywood," Autostraddle creates an "Old Hollywood Edition" of "The Chart," the *L Word*'s network graph of lesbian relationships.[36] Following in the steps of Foster, Grier, and Richards, albeit in a somewhat less academically rigorous manner, "The Chart: Old Hollywood Edition" favors inclusion over all else, collating information from a collection of books and from the internet to map out the same-sex relationships of famous female entertainers, some of them, like Marlene Dietrich, who lived openly gay or bisexual lives, and others, like Barbara Stanwyck, who were either "deeply closeted" or perhaps just the subject of rumor and innuendo. "A lot of this information could be false, but it is also possibly true!" writes Riese, the author of the piece, before offering readers an alternative reality Hollywood, one in which Katharine Hepburn's most well-known relationship is the sixty years she spent with Laura Harding, rather than her tumultuous affair with Spencer Tracy.[37] In the creation of "The Chart: Old Hollywood Edition," the editors of Autostraddle have positioned themselves within the long tradition of lesbian list-based history-making, seeking to fill Woolf's "vast chamber where nobody has been."

In the final section of this chapter we offer the LGLC project as a case study showcasing how lesbian list-making practices can intersect with the digital humanities. To do so, the project takes up the listing and bibliographic historiographic strategies, as well as network graph representation strategies found in Autostraddle's chart. We apply measures for inclusion and definition that let us capture historical contingency, uncertainty, and conflict in the archival record, and by allowing our code to make these measures visible to those of our readers who want to see how assertions about history are made in a digital humanities context.

Lesbian Publishing and Archiving

For lesbian feminists, the importance of controlling the means of printing and circulating lesbian histories and lesbian literature went hand in hand with the importance of creating lists and literature—since "the lesbian, without a literature, is without life."[38] Women like Barbara Grier wanted to ensure that they would never have to rely on the biases of the mainstream publishing industry to print the works that were crucial to their self-knowledge. Thus began a "paper lesbian" renaissance that ran from guerrilla printing operations using "liberated" office supplies and workplace typewriters to the establishment of full-scale lesbian feminist publishing companies.[39] And so it followed that Barbara Grier, having taken on the task of maintaining Jeanette Howard Foster's legacy, contributed addenda to *Sex Variant Women in Literature* in new editions. The first was published in 1975 by Diana Press, a "women's print shop and feminist publishing house" begun by Coletta Reid and Casey Czarnik.[40] The second addenda was published in 1985 by Naiad Press, a lesbian feminist publishing company cofounded by Barbara Grier, Anyda Marchant, Donna McBride, and Muriel Crawford.[41] *Lesbian Lists: A Look at Lesbian Culture, History, and Personalities* would not have existed without the feminist-focused gay press. It was published in 1990 by Alyson Publications, a press that published work of interest to both gay men and lesbians, which at the time was still owned and run by its founder Sasha Alyson. In Canada and the United States, gay periodicals like *The Body Politic* (Toronto), *Le Berdache* (Montreal), *GO Info* (Ottawa), *The Gaezette* (Atlantic Canada), *Christopher Street* (New York), and *Tangents* (Los Angeles) were joined by presses, such as The Feminist Press (New York), Press Gang (Vancouver), Innana (Toronto), Arsenal Pulp Press (Vancouver), and Women's Press (Toronto). Some of these publishing companies, such as The Feminist Press and Press Gang, had an explicit mission to publish women writers and recover out-of-print work by women.

As Rich reminds us, libraries and archives are full of the material that teaches us how to live and what is possible. Deborah Edel and Joan Nestle, two of the founders of New York's Lesbian Herstory Archives (LHA), included in Dell Richards's list of "Cities with Lesbian Archives," took up the important work of circulating books and archival materials within lesbian communities. They spent the 1970s bringing items from their collection to underground events held at women's festivals, university campuses, and gay churches and synagogues, with the historiographic goal of turning "shame into a sense of cherished history" and changing "the meaning of history to include every woman who had the courage to touch another woman, whether for a night or a lifetime." Joan Nestle described the aim of this show-and-tell of archival artefacts, later converted into a slideshow, as changing "deprivation into cultural plenitude."[42] The legacy of Jeanette Howard Foster, Barbara Grier, and the paper lesbians has been exactly that, with the work of the scholars that followed, including Lillian Faderman, Elizabeth Lapovsky Kennedy, Madeline D. Davis, Martha Vicinus, Emma Donoghue, and Cameron Duder, among many others, bringing Adrienne Rich's "flickering, often disguised reality" back into the light, turning deprivation into bounty.

With the expansion of scholarly digital editions and hypermedia archives in the 1990s came the great hope that the web would become a space of light and bounty, providing a place to disseminate primary source material and scholarship by and about marginalized historical persons. Unfortunately, as Amy Earhart noted in the first *Debates* volume, many of the earliest digital resources dedicated to marginalized subjects have disappeared from the web. As we attempt to list, archive, publish, and share via the web, we can learn from the data gathering, publishing, and archiving strategies of the lesbian feminist community. Each of the groups of women that took up the aggregation, framing, and preservation of knowledge did so in a necessarily DIY fashion: the LHA could not trust that universities and government archives would be interested in lesbian materials, just as Jeanette Howard Foster could not rely on commercial publishers to help disseminate her bibliography.

The policies of the LHA were an inspiration to the LGLC project, as we thought through best practices for lesbian feminist history-making, and how to work within the constraints of the contemporary academic system. The LHA summarizes their principles as inclusive, noninstitutional, and committed to living history. They declare, "All Lesbian women must have access to the Archives" regardless of race or class, or academic, political, or sexual credentials. They say as well that the archives will be housed in the community, not on an academic campus closed to many women, funded by the community, and that the community should "share in the work of the Archives." Archival skills "shall be taught, one generation of Lesbians to another, breaking the elitism of traditional archives" and the "Archives will never be sold nor will its contents be divided." Perhaps the most distinctive principle of the LHA, setting it apart from traditional academic archives, is this one: "The Archives shall be involved in the political struggles of all Lesbians."[43]

This egalitarian and collectivist ethos has set the LHA apart from traditional archives and scholarship from the very beginning. The second issue of their newsletter, published in 1976, contains calls for women to send in any contacts they might have with lesbian separatist communities, information on the summer home of Romaine Brooks and Natalie Clifford-Barney, references to "Histoire de la secte anandryne" from 1778, and missing issues of *Lesbian Tide*. It asks for German speakers to translate issues of *Lesbenpresse* and women willing to tape lesbian "speakers, musical events, conferences, and radio shows." It also contains a "Bibliography of Bibliographies," listing just four titles as being "By Lesbians About Lesbians"—Foster, Grier, Marie Kuda's *Women Loving Women, An Annotated Bibliography* published by Womanpress in 1975, and a four-page section of one issue of *Amazon Quarterly*—and implores readers, "It is clear that careful searching is still required to find references to Lesbians in all works, including those published by Feminists.... Bibliographies just on Lesbian culture desperately need to be done."[44]

On their donation page, the LHA includes the rather broad definition included above, urging almost all women to consider donating material to the archive. In this way, "our history will more accurately reflect the range of lives we have led rather than reducing us to a *stereotype* or to *a few 'famous' women*" (emphasis added). Instructions follow for "Creating Your Special Collection," leading potential donors through the steps of arranging and describing an archival collection, from using acid-free folders to labeling photos with soft pencil. They ask women to create timelines and add descriptive information about the personal significance of artefacts. They urge women who plan on bequeathing their papers to the LHA in their wills to use a lawyer to ensure that malicious relatives will be unable to "lose or destroy your papers." Finally, they say, "Offering your collection to the Lesbian Herstory Archives is offering a reflection of yourself to your community. Lesbians and others who seek to know us by exploring your life are eager to read your words, know your thoughts, and view your images. Placing your collection in the Archives is a courageous and generous act. Thanks to you and others who have offered collections to the Archives, lesbian herstory will live as a life-giving force for generations to come. We thank you for your generosity, in memory of the voices we have lost."[45] Radical history spaces like the LHA not only preserve and make visible the histories of marginalized groups but also serve as catalysts for political change. The LHA, which is a separatist space in a radical sense, invites trans* lesbians to donate their papers, and by extension, their voices to the archive. They encourage responsible, yet DIY, archiving in a way that promotes intergenerational learning. Above all, they focus on collectivity, with the goal of breaking down stereotypes by representing a wide variety of lesbian lives, rather than those of just a few famous women.

The appeal of this approach has lasted, evident not just in the continued existence of the LHA but also in the growth of new organizations that shared their mission. In their first newsletter in 1975, the LHA declared its "commitment to rediscovering our past, controlling our present, and speaking to our future. We seek to preserve for the future all expressions of our identity." In 2012, Autostraddle profiled the LHA in their Herstory column. Vanessa, the post's author, found parallels between the two organizations' community-based, community-funded missions, concluding "both projects want to give women a chance to say, 'This is who I am because I say so,' as opposed to allowing outside sources tell us who we should be. Both projects offer constant affirmation that you exist, I exist, we exist."[46]

Past Methods for Contemporary Digital Humanities Scholarship

The question of best practice when it comes to creating lesbian history that will promote the intergenerational understanding that Ross calls for is not without controversy, especially when it comes to questions of privacy or evolving identities. It is not sufficient for us to assert that synthesizing and publishing online information that is available in the archives and in back issues of queer periodicals is somehow politically neutral because the information is already publicly available. The LGLC project does make Canada's gay liberation history more visible than it would be if the project's content stayed in print archives only. While the project does not out any activists who were not out in the 1960s and 1970s, in using radical feminist historiography of the type taken up by Foster, Grier, Faderman, and Richards, it does increase activist visibility with the goal of encouraging the intergenerational understanding that Ross notes is missing. Rather than flattening data into binaries to fit existing data models and international standards, we strive to represent uncertainty, historical contingency, conflict, variation, instability, and multidimensionality. The stakes are high: in an age where we recognize the right to be forgotten, we must also weigh the danger to both feminism and queer politics of hiding our history, forcing each new generation to start anew, with only the haziest stereotypes about previous generations to draw on for strength, or worse, to look on with derision, against the threat of confrontation, doxing, or violence to named activists. The best way forward is not always clear, but the LGLC project continues to chronicle events covered in the queer archival record, rather than risk losing that history to current debates or stereotypes.

The data aggregation and circulation work of lesbian feminists in the twentieth century has much to teach us as we embark on individual research projects, engage with one another through disciplinary channels, and shape the broader political landscape: twentieth-century lesbian feminist work gives us tools to imagine an equitable future that recognizes the nuanced and historically contingent forces that shape our own project, LGLC, and the community that shapes the Text Encoding Initiative, whose XML markup language, TEI, underpins the project (and some of whose senior male members have taken explicit action to include women, discussed below).[47] Moreover, midcentury lesbian feminist aggregating, publishing, and archiving offer insights into how to thoughtfully reengage radical feminist politics, which have revived in North American cities in the last decade, and to understand and encourage the antioppression turn in the digital humanities in a way that moves beyond stereotypes.

The politics of the gay liberation movement were quite different from mainstream queer politics today. Gay liberationists were interested in a radical break with a culture that permitted institutional, financial, legal, and physical violence against gay people. Contemporary gay rights activism, with its focus on legal rights and marriage, is more invested in integration, and in some cases even assimilation, than liberation activism was. We hope, through the project, to make visible the historically specific struggle and politics of gay liberation, which, while relatively recent, are in danger of being lost, as though the political interests of contemporary gay people are the same as they were in the mid-twentieth century. Therefore, one of the central goals of the LGLC project is to create a publicly accessible online resource about the events and the politics of the gay liberation movement. The other, which we will turn to shortly, is to train students in the digital methods (formalizing, versioning, querying) that complement the work and data formats (listing, archiving, publishing) in which activists of the mid-twentieth century trained themselves.[48]

As we were starting our project, we were as eager to learn about the technological underpinnings of the projects that we admired as we were keen to know about the theoretical precepts that underpinned them. Despite critiques that the digital humanities is, as a discipline, undertheorized or overmethodologized, we had a hard time finding the methodological *lists* we needed: the lists of tasks and tech in each project's workflow (this task has been made easier in the intervening years by Miriam Posner's excellent "How Did They Make That?" blog posts, now part of the *DHCommons Journal*).[49] It is in this spirit, and the LHA's which has been so inspirational to us, that we offer the tech stack, mentorship, data formats, and circumstances that have made our project, Lesbian and Gay Liberation in Canada, a TEI and database-driven chronology of the gay liberation movement in Canada, possible.

The project is based on the two-volume work *Lesbian and Gay Liberation in Canada: A Selected Annotated Chronology* by our collaborator, the head of Book and Serials Acquisitions at the University of Toronto Libraries, Donald McLeod. Don's two-volume work lists events of the gay liberation movement, from the formation of the first homophile associations in 1964 to the start of the AIDS crisis in 1981. Don compiled these lists of poetry readings, legislative changes, murders, arrests, book launches, and celebrations by hand, reading through the holdings of several archives. In keeping with DIY radical publishing practices, practices that are invested in sharing lost histories at any cost, Don paid for the publication of the first volume of *Lesbian and Gay Liberation in Canada,* recovering publication expenses over the course of a decade by selling the book through gay bookstores in Canada and the United States. The chronology had its genesis in 1984, when McLeod was working on an AIDS bibliography, another resource created to share information and increase visibility. As early as the 1990s, he noticed that many young researchers had a hazy sense of what had happened during the gay liberation movement. In response he undertook the chronology, a list of events, which is in many ways a DIY project to preserve and disseminate information about the gay liberation movement in Canada.

Don has retained the rights to the chronology, and much to our good fortune, gave us permission to digitize and publish the text online. The digitization process was, at the very beginning, rather DIY. We started encoding an optical-character-recognition-produced version of the chronology in TEI in 2011, armed with a Dropbox account, two Oxygen Editor licenses, and excellent workflow advice (and welcome mentorship) from Julia Flanders, director of Women Writers Online, and Lorraine Janzen Kooistra, co-director of the Ryerson Centre for Digital Humanities. We did not know what we would do with the TEI-encoded text beyond vaguely publish it to the web, but we knew that we would never regret having a formalized and computationally tractable encoded version of the text.

Since then we have officially partnered with Don, as well as with Susan Brown, director of the Canadian Writing Research Collaboratory, and Elise Chenier, director of the Archives of Lesbian Oral Testimony, to produce a digital edition of the text. Thanks to the good graces of the University of British Columbia's Faculty of Creative and Critical Studies, its Work Study Program, Ryerson University's Literatures of Modernity program, WestGrid, Compute Canada and The Social Science and Humanities Research Council of Canada, we have trained thirteen students to date: Sarah Lane, Stephanie Martin, Anderson Tuinguay, Ewan Matthews, Pascale Dangoisse (archival research), Jessica Bonney, Rebecca Desjarlais, Candice Lipski, Cole Mash, Seamus Riordan-Short, Raymon Sandhu, Caitlin Voth, Travis White (TEI encoding, XSLT transformations, database design, interface design, project management), and Nadine Boulay (archival research, survey design). We use extensible stylesheet transformations (XSLT) to move our TEI-encoded and comma-separated text into a graph database, Neo4j, with a JavaScript front end for structured and plain text search. Our development server, a Linux box running CentOS, is hosted by Compute Canada. We use Redmine, a project management platform hosted by the University of British Columbia, for project management and documentation; OwnCloud, hosted by Compute Canada and WestGrid, for document sharing; and GitHub for code sharing and versioning. While a tech list of this sort would have been daunting to us as we were starting out, we offer it here in the spirit of *How Did They Build That*'s DIY ethos. Even though we now use a range of technologies, we learned to use them as the project grew: the text, a working understanding of TEI, two copies of the Oxygen XML Editor software, and a Dropbox account were enough for us to start the project. Just as the women who published *The Ladder* learned to be publishers and distributors in order to share their community-building magazine, we learned along with our research assistants as we moved toward online publication.

In the world of DIY publishing, the list was a simple format to construct, print, and circulate. While learning to develop graph and relational databases is easier every year, for creators, they remain less accessible formats than lists. There is room too to reexamine and rekindle older debates about the relationship between database and narrative, in context of lists and networks. We work in an age that may further substantiate N. Katherine Hayles's assertion that databases and narratives are *symbionts*, separate species with particular ordering logic and habits that can support one another.[50] Graph databases have transformed the commercial sectors, including sectors like social media that commodify users, but what they will mean for humanities scholarship remains unexamined to date.

The list seems to be a particularly significant format, and certainly not one without consequence in the digital humanities. As Ed Folsom points out, databases are antinarrative, inasmuch as narratives are in favor of chronology.[51] This poses a particular problem for database-driven chronologies such as ours. Although we can rearrange our data by city, activist, or organization, is the narrative of liberation history lost when we leave the chronology behind? There is, of course, an inherent order in any database, no matter how well that database lends itself to reordering content.[52] That said, early work on the relationship between database and narrative considered relational databases, not the graph databases. Graph databases, such as Neo4j, are used by the LGLC and other projects to order their data, in a way that privileges networks (and the narratives they foreground) over tables. The early 2010s boom in graph databases invites further reflection on the narrative structures encouraged by the inherent ordering, and often ready extensibility, of graph, rather than relational, databases. There might, we would like to suggest, be a new type of symbiosis between narrative and network-based representation of chronological events.

Digital circulation has also radically transformed publishing scholarly and commercial publishing in the last twenty years. Federal funding agencies in Canada and the United Kingdom have mandated open access publication (a system not without flaws, both in terms of the price of publication and the cost to small presses and publishers). This move by funding agencies postdates the web-based resource development of many digital humanities scholars, who have long worked to make their content freely accessible online. This mode of distribution, like the modes taken up by feminist DIY publishers, pushes back against the models of scarcity and ownership that have characterized traditional scholarship.[53] While many projects must put their work behind a paywall in order to ensure the revenue that will keep the work online, we suspect that the move to open scholarship will prove to be the key to preservation. Digital work can be preserved by being "too distributed to fail." In our case, the LGLC data are backed up on WestGrid servers at Simon Fraser University, are served from Quebec, will be aggregated with data from other projects as part of the University of Alberta's Canadian Writing and Research Collaboratory, and will be housed in the University of British Columbia Library's institutional repository, Circle. This distribution helps assure us that the project and its voices will not be lost if any one host goes down. However, each of these hosts is costly to maintain, and the Canadian university system does not yet have a holistic plan to maintain the important cultural heritage represented by open digital scholarship.

The project is coming of age at a momentous time in the history of the digital humanities. In the last ten years there has been a significant change in both the size and the diversity of the digital humanities, and with those changes come the challenges of confronting racism, colonialism, sexism, and trans- and homophobia, for the sake of the health and equity of the discipline. While separatism of the types pioneered by women in the 1970s and 1980s is always an option, these confrontations need not undermine DH, but could be generative, as some have been, as we will see, in the case of the TEI (although we recognize the very real and reasonable desire of many women and people of color who have had toxic experiences in the field, to opt of out DH altogether). Critical race and feminist practices have demonstrated that critical mass undermines sexism and racism. For radical feminists, gathering with other women and normalizing women-only gatherings provided spaces to unlearn sexism. For liberal feminists, working toward equal representation in positions of power (i.e., gender equality in houses of parliament, university programs, and boards of governors) was a way to undermine tokenism, to recognize that women are as diverse in their opinions, aptitudes, and politics as men, and to normalize women in positions of leadership. At the risk of dating this chapter, we would like to point to recent successful moves to undermine the systemic sexism by including women. If a full radical feminist opt-out of the digital humanities is undesirable (and we are not saying that it is undesirable for all; separate spaces are always an option), building allegiances with men and masculine people who recognize that sexism, a system that oppresses women and feminine people by valuing men, culturally coded masculinity, and masculine perspectives over women and culturally coded femininity and feminine perspectives, is an excellent option.

Equity requires that those of us who do not wish to opt out remain proactive. Equity cannot be achieved simply by permitting admittance to those who have traditionally been excluded. Equity involves recognizing the long-term effects of systemic oppression and refusing the normalized advantages that systematic

Figure 9.1. Tweets about the TEI' sex element and @sex attribute.

oppression offers. The digital humanities as a discipline, and the TEI community in particular, has made some gains in this area.[54] For example, in 2013, rather than falling back on the argument that the TEI's use of ISO standard 5218 for sex (which offers only four values for sex: male, female, not applicable, and unknown) was simply a neutral standard, unchangeable within the context of the TEI because it was imported from an external standard, the TEI technical council and board revised TEI values for sex to include those from ISO 5218 (for backward compatibility) and locally defined values.[55] Melissa Terras initiated the official call for change via a request through the TEI's Sourceforge ticketing system, and garnered support both in person and through online community engagement (see Figures 9.1 and 9.2). The change was not without controversy, which played out both publicly and in the

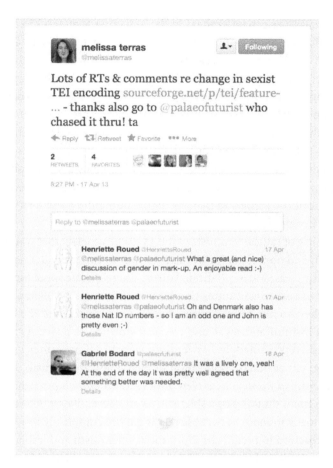

Figure 9.2. Tweets about the TEI' sex element and @sex attribute.

TEI board of directors and technical council. The change has expanded the utility of the TEI and its ability to faithfully represent human diversity.

The TEI community has made other gains as well. Following Deb Verhoeven's impassioned call at DH2015, reproduced in part in this volume, for the men of the discipline to "find someone who doesn't look and sound like you and mentor them, encourage them, and invite them into your role" and take a step back from leadership, there was considerable expansion of ongoing private and public discussion about sexism in the field, further revealing significant veins of hostility and disdain for equity.[56] There were, however, a number of men on the TEI technical council and board who worked to recruit qualified women from a variety of backgrounds to serve on these important bodies. One even took Deb Verhoeven's request at face value, and stepped off the council to leave room for the many qualified women to serve. These actions resulted in the most gender-balanced and largest slate of people running for the council and board in years. In an age when stagnation of governing bodies and small slates can be a canary in the coal mine, it remains to be seen if this will be a continuing trend and a promising sign of the TEI's health and equitable representation of its users. For decades there have been women qualified to sit on the TEI council and board—it took the invitations to run, and the explanation that these invitations were motivated by feminist methods (recognizing that women do not participate in DH on a level playing field, and if they are in a position to run for the council or board, they are in that position despite the added burden put on them by sexism), to get equity on the council. Equity is proactive, not passive, and can flourish with the support of those who recognize that they benefit from oppressive systems of power, and rather than responding with hurt at being asked to decenter their subject position, recognize that the digital humanities will be a better field if they refuse to benefit from the systemic oppression of others.

The response of radical feminists of the 1970s to a society that was intransigent in its exclusion and oppression of women was not to call for equal representation. Radical feminism was, and is, predicated on creating separate space for women, and on opting out of sexist institutions that have shown by past policies, actions, and silences that they do not have women's diverse interests, even at the basic level of freedom from institutional, legal, and physical violence, at heart. As a movement, radical feminism represented the first feminist wave to define women in relationship to one another, rather than in opposition to men. Radical feminism, with its focus on *woman-identified women,* is, as New York's Radicalesbians put it, not about relationships with men: thinking of lesbianism as an alternative to heterosexuality "is still giving primacy to men . . . because relating more completely to women occurs as a negative reaction to men."[57] In short, radical feminism and lesbian separatism were the manifestation of the notion "that the identity we have to develop [will be] with reference to ourselves, and not in relation to men."[58] This refusal to define oneself in relation to the dominant other is particularly radical, as it also refuses cooptation by a dominant position. Just as antiracist studies can slip into being about white people (leading at an institutional level to the creation of critical race professorships filled by white people and funded grants for critical white studies, which while individual white scholars and projects may be admirable, in the aggregate reproduce the white-centric work of universities, rather than the shift away from the mainstream that Miriam Posner has called for), so too can feminism as represented in the media, in classrooms, or even in our disciplinary meetings be coopted so that it becomes about men. Radical feminism with its woman-identification serves as a reminder that women's lives, politics, and work needn't be defined through their relationship to men. In contemporary culture, that is a radical notion indeed. There are, of course, those of us who are not going to opt out of the mainstream and move to womyn's lands, those of us who are going to stay behind to share the history of those who opted for radical separatism, which is to say the total refusal to participate in a system that oppresses them. We can engage in recovery projects and in training the new generation of people either who will opt out of the systems that oppress them or who might work within those systems to build separatist spaces or to normalize women's refusal to reinscribe men's centrality by defining themselves in relation to men.

Although analogies are dangerous, as they invite politically divisive comparisons of incommensurate oppressions, there are important insights offered by critical race studies that we would like to introduce here to help guide our discussion before we turn to the worrying trend of trans* exclusion that has accompanied the revival of radical feminist politics. There has been backlash against the creation of separate space by oppressed people for oppressed people, wrongly likening these separate spaces to institutionally and legally enforced racial segregation or "old boys clubs." This analogy is felonious, since the broader ethos that supported racial segregation and the exclusion of women, racism and sexism was designed to define people of color and women at the expense of people of color and women. It is perfectly reasonable for members of oppressed groups to seek space together that exclude people who benefit from systems of oppression (e.g., gatherings organized to support people of color that exclude white people or queer spaces that exclude straight people). This exclusion of white people, or men, or straight people is not part of a centuries-long, institutionally and legally supported exploitation, othering, and oppression of white people, or men, or straight people. While it is possible, of course, for people of color to exclude, dislike, or actively be unkind to white people, it is impossible to be truly racist toward white people, if we understand racism to be a historically specific system of white supremacy designed to benefit white people at the expense of others. So-called reverse racism is a logical impossibility, as there is no systemic, institutional, historically grounded, global movement to benefit from classifying and oppressing white people. These insights that come from critical race theory are particularly germane in our contemporary DH moment, as they help explain both the value and utility separate space, equity statements, and the good work of the people who have continued to work for the broader DH community while actively stepping back from key positions to make room for members of historically marginalized groups (as the TEI technical council members have done). For those of us who belong to dominant groups and who have felt excluded because we are white, the critical consciousness offered by this historically and institutionally grounded way of thinking about how our whiteness has been constructed and the privilege it offers can mend any hurt that we may feel about being excluded. Just as the women-identified women's exclusion of men is not about men, the exclusion of white people from spaces designed for and by people of color is not about white people. For those of us who have been born into a dominant position, this can be radical and shocking indeed: for almost the first time in history, it is not about us.[59]

Radical feminists and gay liberationists of the 1970s demonstrated what radical opting out of the system might mean by refusing to participate in or stay closeted in an oppressive system in the hope of reward. Indeed it is the hope of benefiting from oppression that often motivates support for oppressive systems, even by those who they are designed to exploit (in the case of some early homophile groups, like the Daughters of Bilitis, the hope was only for the reward of a quiet life, one free from harassment and threat). There has, in recent years, been a resurgent interest in radical feminist and gay liberation history, evident in the reissuing of texts such as *This Bridge Called My Back* (2015), to *Radical Feminism: A Documentary Reader* (2000), to new studies such as *Radical Feminism: Feminist Activism in Movement* (2015) and popular press accounts such as *The A to Z of the Lesbian Liberation Movement: Still the Rage* (2003). Happily there is a history for these new radical feminists to turn to—a better-documented history, supported by easier circulated information, than the ones available to the women listed above. We are glad to see these humanities and social science–based opportunities for intergenerational knowledge transfer, and for the institutional support for the Lesbian and Gay Liberation in Canada project. There is, to our minds, however, a worrying strain within this return to radical feminism. With this return has come trans* exclusionary radical feminism, characterized by the purposeful exclusion of trans* women. Excluding trans* women from women's groups is not a case of women excluding people that sexism is designed to benefit. Transitioning is a radical leave-taking of systems of oppression that offer (although seldom deliver) rewards for the quiescence of people at whose expense it is maintained. Trans* women do not benefit from the systemic oppression of women. While some earlier strains of radical feminism did exclude trans* women (although as the separatist Lesbian Herstory Archives demonstrates, this exclusion was far from ubiquitous), radical feminist history offers insight into how to confront systemic oppression in a way that decenters dominant positions, one that we would hope contemporary radical feminists would not perpetuate in their engagement with trans* men and women.

In 1991, Lillian Faderman joked about the evolving definition of lesbianism, saying that the "criterion for identifying oneself as a lesbian has come to resemble the liberal criterion for identifying oneself as a Jew: you are one only if you consider yourself one."[60] The scope of early lesbian feminist bibliographers and archivists when cataloguing the past was equally broad. Similarly, we aim for our work with the Lesbian and Gay Liberation in Canada project to be as all-encompassing. We have been building a prosopography, or collective biography list, of everyone mentioned in the text, including information, when possible, on people's identities and affiliations (a research activity we share with other contributors to this volume. Kooistra and Hedley's engaging argument for using the term "personography" to describe people both in the singular and in aggregate is a welcome critical addition to feminist-informed digital humanities practice). In doing so, we seek to follow Faderman's criterion for being a Jew—"you are one only if you consider yourself one." Rather than placing people into categories, we allow them to self-define. After all, Radclyffe Hall, one of the most famous "lesbian authors" and a figure in our prosopography list, did not identify as a lesbian, but as a "congenital invert" and, as Leslie Feinberg noted in *Stone Butch Blues,* often went by the name John. People, as

Feinberg says, defy easy classification.[61] And so our prosopography leaves space for people to define themselves as "radical lesbian feminist" or "faggot" or "queer" and to define what those terms mean to them. We hope to capture those identities that only existed at a certain time or a certain place and to not conflate what it meant to be a "radical lesbian feminist" in 1971 with what a "lesbian" is now. Like Dell Richards and her lists of sworn virgins, spinsters, romantic friends, and uppity women who probably weren't lesbians, we strive for our list to be inclusive and, in doing so, borrow Dell Richards's historiographic practices that create a history that reaches forward to embrace lived experience beyond that history.

We have much to learn from lesbian feminist history, data collection, and knowledge circulation, but in reengaging with lesbian feminist methods and politics, we need to err on the side of generosity, inclusivity, and productivity. In our work on the LGLC project, we aim to build a project that captures the temporally specific iterations of identity and allows people to define themselves. We also want to leave room for new critical consciousness and change. There is room to reengage with lesbian feminist methodologies in the digital humanities and in the culture at large in a way that does not police the boundaries of identity, but rather strives to construct resources that are fully accessible.

Notes

1. Ross, *House That Jill Built*, 5.
2. Ross, *House That Jill Built*, 54.
3. Posner, "What's Next."
4. "Donating Material."
5. Eichhorn, *Archival Turn*, 27.
6. Samer, "Revising 'Re-vision.'"
7. We use the asterisk here and below to signal that there are as yet unarticulated identities that this term may eventually include. Like the asterisk wildcard operator, it leaves room for inexact or rough matches.
8. The question of racism manifest in the archive is productively taken up by Michelle Morevic and her team in the digital project "Unghosting Apparitional Histories: Erasures of Black Lesbian Feminism." The title, we surmise, refers to the term "ghosting" that Terry Castle coined to describe the erasure of lesbians from history by culture itself, and serves as a double warning about the erasures contained within the archive.
9. Lewin, *Inventing Lesbian Cultures*, 1.
10. Lewin, *Inventing Lesbian Cultures*, 11.
11. Faderman, *Odd Girls*, 9.
12. Rich, "Compulsory Heterosexuality."
13. Lewin, *Inventing Lesbian Cultures in America*, 11.
14. Rich, "It Is the Lesbian," 142.
15. Rich, "It Is the Lesbian," 143.

16. Lewin, *Inventing Lesbian Cultures*, 6.
17. Klinger, "Writing Civil Rights," 77.
18. Gallo, *Different Daughters*, xxxi.
19. Gallo, *Different Daughters*, xxxix.
20. Foster, *Sex Variant Women*.
21. Foster, *Sex Variant Women*, 355.
22. Gallo, *Different Daughters*, 38.
23. Gallo, *Different Daughters*, 37.
24. Gallo, *Different Daughters*, 36.
25. "History of the Lesbian."
26. "History of the Lesbian."
27. "History of the Lesbian."
28. Passet, *Sex Variant Woman*, 202.
29. Faderman, introduction to *Sex Variant Woman*, xiv.
30. Richards, *Lesbian Lists*.
31. Richards, *Lesbian Lists*, 11.
32. Richards, *Lesbian Lists*, 11; Lesbian feminists were lampooned in the 1990s for undermining the biological arguments that had so much traction and helped secure gay rights in the 1990s and early 2000s. The very fact that Richards, and numerous other women, defined their experience in the 1970s and 1980s as political rather than biological is worth collecting, considering, and encouraging our culture to remember. Eve Kosofski Sedgwick has wisely warned against relying on either nature or nurture arguments to bolster gay rights. After all, in a homophobic culture, she warns, either position can be turned against gay people either through behavioral therapy "cures" on the one hand or genetic selection on the other. Furthermore the embrace of nature/nurture debates, Anne Fausto-Sterling points out, has been used to create difference and restricts ability to engage with the embodiment of sex, sexuality, and gender. Sedgwick, *Epistemology of the Closet*; Fausto-Sterling, *Dueling Dualisms*.
33. "Berlin, Bologna, Brussels, Copenhagen, Helsinki, London, Los Angeles, New York, Paris, Rome, San Francisco, Stockholm, Wellington, New Zealand." Richards, *Lesbian Lists*, 244.
34. Dave, "AfterEllen.com Acquired."
35. "What Is Autostraddle?"; Riese, "15 Ways."
36. "AfterEllen.com Les/Bi List!"; Riese, "Top 10."
37. Thompson, "Katharine Hepburn."
38. Bertha Harris quoted in Rich, "It Is the Lesbian in Us . . . ," 143.
39. Klinger, "Writing Civil Rights," 65.
40. "Finding Aid."
41. Lamb, "Anyda Marchant."
42. "Lesbian Herstory Archives: History."
43. "Lesbian Herstory Archives: History."

44. "Lesbian Herstory Archives: Newsletters."
45. "Lesbian Herstory Archives: Support."
46. "Lesbian Herstory Archives: Constant Affirmation."
47. While an introduction to TEI markup and its affordances is beyond the scope of this chapter, we invite interested readers to peruse the TEI Guidelines (Text Encoding Initiative, "TEI Guidelines"), the projects the use the TEI (Text Encoding Initiative, "Projects Using the TEI," partial list), and an excellent recent introduction to TEI markup: Flanders, Bauman, and Connell, "Text Encoding."
48. The DIY approach in the digital humanities is, we recognize, risky. As Amy Earhart has pointed out, we risk the double loss that was endemic in early digital humanities projects. Earhart, "Recovering the Recovered Text." It may be daunting knowing that we are responsible to the subjects we have interviewed, the people we have researched, and the archival material we have unearthed, and yet, we are not ready to give up on what Earhart has called the web's early potential as a place that disrupts power structures and normalization of privilege. The anxiety of the possibility of double loss is not reason enough to shy away from digital projects, since the web will have liberatory potential only if the material of liberation is on it.
49. Posner, "How Did They"; "How Did They Make That?"
50. Hayles, "Narrative and Database."
51. Folsom, "Database as Genre."
52. Manovich, *Language of New Media.*
53. This push toward open accessible scholarship is accompanied by a fear that without paywalls independent publishers may be in peril and that junior faculty's tenure and promotion files may be discounted by colleagues who do not value public humanities work even if it is peer reviewed. These issues are too large to address here, but warrant feminist analysis of the type outlined in this volume.
54. For more on the history of the TEI and for a record of the encoding community's debates, please see Text Encoding Initiative, "TEI: History," and Text Encoding Initiative, "TEI Council Meetings."
55. ISO 5218 was devised in 1977, with the assumption that all that could be represented by biological sex could be represented by those four values. The ISO's revision of the standard in 2004 did little to amend the variety of sexes represented, rendering invisible may people's lived experience of sex. International Organization for Standardization, "ISO/IEC 5218:2004."
56. Verhoeven, *Has Anyone.*
57. Radicalesbians, *Woman-Identified Woman,* 2. Reflecting on the pathos of being excited at a straight man's review of a queer, Jill Johnson highlights the problem of defining oneself against a dominant other in similar, if sarcastic, terms: "if I hadn't been so upset about over the new evidence that that some us are still finding it so difficult to celebrate all the things we are I would have been more astonished and flattered that a successful white American male heterosexual film critic had invested . . . time and energy and rhetorical

diligence to pay so much hostile attention to the meager outpourings of the most oppressed and confused and unrecognized minority in every country in the world"; Johnson, *Lesbian Nation*, 136.

58. Radicalesbians, *Woman-Identified Woman*, 3.

59. We are indebted to Ruthanne Lee, assistant professor of Cultural Studies a UBC Okanagan, whose perspectives on critical race have been so educative. It is exhausting educating others (a sort of double duty, when there is primary research to do), and yet she takes up this work tirelessly and with good grace. For introductory readings on critical race theory and practice, we recommend Crenshaw, Gotanda, Peller, and Thomas, *Critical Race Theory*; and Gates and Wolf, *Henry Louis Gates Jr. Reader*.

60. Faderman, *Odd Girls*, 5.

61. Feinberg, *Stone Butch Blues*, Afterword.

Bibliography

"The AfterEllen.com Les/Bi List!" Accessed August 7, 2016. http://www.afterellen.com/people/85676-the-afterellencom-lesbi-list.

Crenshaw, Kimberlé, Neil Gotanda, Gary Peller, and Kendall Thomas, eds. *Critical Race Theory: The Key Writings that Formed the Movement*. New York: New Press, 1995.

Dave, Paresh. "AfterEllen.com Acquired by Evolve Media from Viacom." *Los Angeles Times*, October 7, 2014. http://www.latimes.com/business/technology/la-fi-tn-afterellen-evolve-viacom-lesbian-website-20141007-story.html.

"Donating Material: Special Collections." Accessed January 28, 2016. http://www.lesbianherstoryarchives.org/supmater2.html.

Earhart, Amy. "Recovering the Recovered Text: Diversity, Canon Building, and Digital Studies." *University of Kansas IDRH*, October 9, 2012. https://youtu.be/7ui9PIjDreo.

Eichhorn, Kate. *The Archival Turn in Feminism: Outrage in Order*. Philadelphia: Temple University Press, 2013.

Faderman, Lillian. Introduction to *Sex Variant Woman: The Life of Jeannette Howard Foster* by Joanne Ellen Passet. Cambridge, Mass.: Da Capo, 2008.

Faderman, Lillian. *Odd Girls and Twilight Lovers: A History of Lesbian Life in Twentieth-Century America*. New York: Penguin, 1992.

Fausto-Sterling, Anne. *Dueling Dualisms in Sexing the Body: Gender Politics and the Construction of Sexuality*. New York: Basic Books, 2000.

Feinberg, Leslie. *Stone Butch Blues: A Novel*. Ithaca, N.Y.: Firebrand Books, 1993.

"Finding Aid for the Diana Press Records, 1970–1994 (Collection 2135)." Online Archives of California. Accessed January 28, 2016. http://www.oac.cdlib.org/findaid/ark:/13030/c8tq62h1/.

Flanders, Julia, Syd Bauman, and Sarah Connell. "Text Encoding." In *Doing Digital Humanities: Practice, Training, Research,* edited by Constance Crompton, Richard J. Lane, and Ray Siemens, 104–22. New York: Routledge, 2017.

Folsom, Ed. "Database as Genre: The Epic Transformation of Archives." *PMLA* 122, no. 5 (October 2007): 1571–79. http://www.jstor.org/stable/25501803.

Foster, Jeannette H. *Sex Variant Women in Literature*. Tallahassee, Fla.: Naiad Press, 1985.

Gallo, Marcia M. *Different Daughters: A History of the Daughters of Bilitis and the Rise of the Lesbian Rights Movement*. New York: Carroll & Graf, 2006.

Gates, Henry Louis, and Abby Wolf, eds. *The Henry Louis Gates Jr. Reader*. New York: BasicCivitas Books, 2012.

Hayles, N. Katherine. "Narrative and Database: Natural Symbionts." *PMLA* 122, no. 5 (October 2007): 1603–08. http://www.jstor.org/stable/25501808.

"History of the Lesbian in Literature: The Lesbian in Literature, 1967–1981." Accessed January 28, 2016. http://www.outhistory.org/exhibits/show/lesbian-in-literature/history.

"How Did They Make That?" *DHCommons Journal* 1, no. 1 (2015). http://dhcommons.org/journal/issue-1.

International Organization for Standardization. "ISO/IEC 5218:2004—Information Technology—Codes for the Representation of Human Sexes." Accessed January 17, 2016. http://www.iso.org/iso/catalogue_detail.htm?csnumber=36266.

Johnson, Jill. *Lesbian Nation: The Feminist Solution*. New York: Simon and Schuster, 1973.

Klinger, Alisa. "Writing Civil Rights: The Political Aspirations of Lesbian Activist-Writers." In *Inventing Lesbian Cultures in America*, edited by Ellen Lewin, 62–82. Boston, Mass.: Beacon Press, 1996.

Lamb, Yvonne Shinhoster. "Anyda Marchant; Author, Publisher." *Washington Post,* February 7, 2006. http://www.washingtonpost.com/wp-dyn/content/article/2006/02/06/AR2006020601658.html.

"The Lesbian Herstory Archives: A Constant Affirmation That You Exist." *Autostraddle,* June 19, 2012. http://www.autostraddle.com/the-lesbian-herstory-archives-a-constant-affirmation-that-you-exist-139931/.

"The Lesbian Herstory Archives: Donating Material; Special Collections." Lesbian Herstory Archives. Accessed January 28, 2016. http://www.lesbianherstoryarchives.org/supmater2.html.

"The Lesbian Herstory Archives: History and Mission." Lesbian Herstory Archives. Accessed January 28, 2016. http://www.lesbianherstoryarchives.org/history.html.

"The Lesbian Herstory Archives: Newsletters." Lesbian Herstory Archives. Accessed January 28, 2016. http://www.lesbianherstoryarchives.org/newsl70.html.

"The Lesbian Herstory Archives: Support the Archives." Lesbian Herstory Archives. Accessed January 28, 2016. http://www.lesbianherstoryarchives.org/supmater2.html.

Lewin, Ellen. *Inventing Lesbian Cultures in America*. Boston, Mass.: Beacon, 1996.

Manovich, Lev. *The Language of New Media*. Cambridge, Mass.: MIT Press, 2001.

Passet, Joanne Ellen. *Sex Variant Woman: The Life of Jeannette Howard Foster*. Cambridge, Mass.: Da Capo, 2008.

Posner, Miriam. "How Did They Make That?" *Miriam Posner's Blog,* August 29, 2013. http://miriamposner.com/blog/how-did-they-make-that/.

Posner, Miriam. "What's Next: The Radical, Unrealized Potential of Digital Humanities." *Miriam Posner's Blog*, July 27, 2015. http://miriamposner.com/blog/whats-next-the-radical-unrealized-potential-of-digital-humanities/.

Radicalesbians. *The Woman-Identified Woman*. 1970. Duke University Libraries Digital Collections. Accessed January 16, 2016. http://library.duke.edu/digitalcollections/wlmpc_wlmms01011/.

Rich, Adrienne. "Compulsory Heterosexuality and Lesbian Existence (1980)." *Journal of Women's History* 15, no. 3 (2003): 11–48. doi:10.1353/jowh.2003.0079.

Rich, Adrienne. "It Is the Lesbian in Us . . ." In *Come Out Fighting: A Century of Essential Writing on Gay and Lesbian Liberation*, edited by Chris Bull, 142–43. New York: Thunder's Mouth Press/Nation Books, 2001.

Richards, Dell. *Lesbian Lists: A Look at Lesbian Culture, History, and Personalities*. Boston: Alyson Publications, 1990.

Riese. "15 Ways to Spot a Lesbian According to Some Really Old Medical Journals." Autostraddle. Accessed August 8, 2016. http://www.autostraddle.com/15-ways-to-spot-a-lesbian-according-to-some-really-old-medical-journals-139954/.

Riese. "Top 10 Most Sexually Prolific Lesbians and Bisexuals of Old Hollywood." Autostraddle. Accessed August 7, 2016. http://www.autostraddle.com/10-old-hollywood-stars-who-enjoyed-scissoring-343227/.

Ross, Becki. *The House That Jill Built: A Lesbian Nation in Formation*. Toronto: University of Toronto Press, 1995.

Samer, Roxanne. "Revising 'Re-vision': Documenting 1970s Feminisms and the Queer Potentiality of Digital Feminist Archives." *Ada: A Journal of Gender, New Media & Technology* 5 (2014). doi:10.7264/N3FF3QMC.

Sedgwick, Eve Kosofsky. *The Epistemology of the Closet*. Berkeley: University of California Press, 1990.

Text Encoding Initiative. "Projects Using the TEI." Text Encoding Initiative. http://www.tei-c.org/Activities/Projects/.

Text Encoding Initiative. "TEI Council Meetings." Text Encoding Initiative. http://www.tei-c.org/Activities/Council/Meetings/.

Text Encoding Initiative. "TEI Guidelines." Text Encoding Initiative. http://www.tei-c.org/release/doc/tei-p5-doc/en/html/index.html.

Text Encoding Initiative. "TEI: History." Text Encoding Initiative. http://www.tei-c.org/About/history.xml.

Thompson, David. "Katharine Hepburn." *The Guardian*, July 1, 2003. https://www.theguardian.com/news/2003/jul/01/guardianobituaries.film.

Verhoeven, Deborah. *Has Anyone Seen a Woman?* July 2, 2015. Speakola. http://speakola.com/ideas/deb-verhoeven-has-anyone-seen-a-woman-2015.

"What Is Autostraddle?" Accessed August 8, 2016. Autostraddle. http://www.autostraddle.com/about/.

PART III][Chapter 10

Prototyping Personography for *The Yellow Nineties Online*

Queering and Querying History in the Digital Age

ALISON HEDLEY AND LORRAINE JANZEN KOOISTRA

Humanities databases such as *Orlando Women's Writing in the British Isles,* the *Victorian Women Writers Project, Women Writers Online* (WWO), and *Agents of Change* demonstrate that digital tools support feminist efforts to recover historical women's authorial, artistic, and editorial work. Just as importantly, but perhaps less obviously, the methods and models of these projects also enact a feminist critique of traditional historiography. At Digital Diversity 2015, a gathering that marked *Orlando*'s twentieth anniversary, Julia Flanders noted that the *WWO* offers not only an alternative literary-historical narrative but also alternative methods for practicing literary history. Susan Brown addressed the ongoing challenges *Orlando* faces in balancing historical diversity with the need for standardized metadata, asserting, "We don't disambiguate social categories, but in a sense, set them at war with each other" (Flanders, Brown, Wernimont, and Smith, "Feminist Literary History"). The reflections offered by Brown, Flanders, and many others at the Digital Diversity conference attest to an increasing theorization and application of feminist praxis in the digital humanities.

Feminism, digital humanities, and periodical studies intersect in our collaborative work on *The Yellow Nineties Online,* a scholarly site for the study of fin-de-siècle aesthetic magazines through marked-up digital editions, archival paratexts, and critical essays. Our affiliated project, the *Yellow Nineties Personography,* seeks to investigate the periodicals in our corpora as records of creative collaboration, with each issue representing, in James Mussell's words, "a particular configuration of contributors attempting to produce an object for the market" at a specific time and place (120). As a contextual dataset about the individual persons encoded in textual markup, a personography enables us to trace the social configurations and networks that produced specific aesthetic magazines in 1890s Britain. Drawing on the markup of four *Yellow Nineties Online* digital editions—the *Evergreen,* the *Pagan Review,* the *Savoy,* and the *Yellow Book*—the *Personography* aims to develop a biographical dataset into manipulatable format, thereby facilitating research on the complex network of editors, authors, illustrators, and readers who participated in fin-de-siècle British print culture.

While our *Yellow Nineties* biographical dataset is modest by digital standards—it currently includes over a dozen attribute fields, but only 351 persons—our purpose is more ambitious in its theoretical, methodological, and historical aims. Through our personographic work, we aim to make visible the creative productions of women and other historically marginalized persons whose contributions to fin-de-siècle aesthetic magazines have been largely lost to view. Additionally, like other feminist database builders, we also strive to make visible our process for modeling this historical knowledge. Simply recuperating marginalized persons and their work is not a robust response to the cultural and intellectual paradigms that have historically displaced such persons, as Alison Booth and Jacqueline Wernimont point out (Booth, 18; Wernimont, paras. 5–6). Personography has its origins in prosopography—a traditional historiographic method that develops a collective biography of a population by flattening out differences and anomalies to create a typical subject. Along with our recovery of individual persons, we want to challenge the standard classification practices in prosopography, as well as those in computational markup language, that work to make certain persons historical nonentities. We also seek to refute the traditional prosopographic assumption that data are transcendent and unambiguous, rather than contingent and fluid. In other words, we want to queer the data by interrogating the structural formations of the normative, questioning differences within categories, and being self-reflexive about our processes (Giffney, 19). As Noreen Giffney summarizes, "queer thus denotes a resistance to identity categories or easy categorization, marking a disidentification from the rigidity with which identity categories continue to be enforced and from beliefs that such categories are immovable" (21). Given our understanding of identity as fluid and contingent, how might we adequately catalog the human subjects in our dataset, and what are the stakes of such a process? Can we develop a database that allows us to queer, as well as query, the data? This is what the *Yellow Nineties Personography* aims to model. Our work applies a critical feminist lens to prosopographical and personographical methods and encourages our users to do likewise.

In documenting the contributors to the *Yellow Book* (London 1894–1897), the *Pagan Review* (Sussex 1892), the *Savoy* (London 1896), and *The Evergreen: A Northern Seasonal* (Edinburgh 1895–1897), the *Yellow Nineties Personography* opens up an avant-garde community of writers and artists for discovery and analysis. Despite the brevity of its print run, the *Yellow Book* is the defining cultural document of the fin de siècle, lending its color to "the yellow nineties" and influencing both artistic practices and social critiques (Jackson, 32). According to Holbrook Jackson, contemporary readers associated the *Yellow Book* "with all that was *bizarre* and queer in art and life, with all that was outrageously modern" (45). At the end of the nineteenth century, the "outrageously modern" included decadent and feminist challenges to heteronormative, patriarchal norms in both literature and art. An idiosyncratic forerunner to the *Yellow Book*, the *Pagan Review* was published in Sussex by William Sharp, connecting rural neo-paganism and the Celtic Revival to the fin-de-siècle avant-garde. The *Savoy*, a London-based rival to the *Yellow Book*, was edited by Arthur Symons and Aubrey Beardsley after the latter was dismissed from the *Yellow Book* following Oscar Wilde's arrest for gross indecency in April 1895. This move was intended to reassure both the consuming public and some of its own contributors that publisher John Lane had purged the magazine of its queer associations: at the time of his arrest, Wilde was carrying a "yellow book" (actually, a French novel). Meanwhile, in Edinburgh, the *Evergreen* countered decadence with regeneration. Its editors designed the four volumes of its print run around the seasons to capture the Celtic politics of the Scottish Renaissance and promote urban renewal and nationalism. Just as the *Yellow Book* and the *Savoy* shared Beardsley as an art editor, the *Pagan Review* and the *Evergreen* shared literary editor William Sharp, and there are many other contributor crossovers to link the four magazines. Contributors, associations, cultural concerns, and artistic practice interwove an avant-garde network stretching from Scotland in the north to Sussex in the south.

The historical record offers many challenges to documenting the persons in our personography with sensitivity to non-normative identities and relationships. Indeed, the defining category of our work, "person," is neither self-evident nor transhistorical. More than a quarter of the 351 individuals who contributed art, text, and editorial expertise to the *Yellow Book*, the *Pagan Review*, the *Savoy*, and the *Evergreen* did not fall within the standard personhood or status classifications of late-Victorian law and society. In other words, these magazine contributors were legal nonpersons and/or socially non-normative individuals. Under British law at the time, women, for example, were nonpersons with regard to fundamental individual rights, and homosexuals were criminals. On the other hand, the reading public conferred personhood (sometimes gendered) on many pseudonymous contributors without being able to verify their legal status or biological identity. In terms of non-normative interpersonal relations, historical evidence suggests that many contributors to these magazines had romantic and familial relationships that were illegal, invisible, or counter to Victorian mores. While some of these unconventional practices were common enough to have designations in cultural discourse, for example, "female marriage," none were officially recognized as legitimate by legal and social institutions (Marcus, 12).

The limited range of terms and means for recognizing such individuals is particularly notable in a period known for its preoccupation with systemizing and classifying all kinds of information. It was in the nineteenth century, as Michel Foucault observes, that humankind began to be framed as "the human species" and the human individual as "a figure of population" (*Security, Territory, Population,* 105, 111). This category shift was aided by advances in statistics and demography, which were beginning to be used to document and manage the British population. Constructing the norm as their standard, statistics and other emerging social science practices sought to systemize human bodies and behaviors (Canguilhem, 44). Indeed, it was in the Victorian period that statisticians adopted the practice of normal distribution, otherwise known as the bell curve, as a method for mapping human data. As a result, the word "normal" entered the dominant social discourse to signify the paradoxical concept of the ideal average (Davis, 10).

The Victorian impulse to classify bodies and behaviors extended to fundamental dimensions of personal identity such as gender, sexuality, and interpersonal relationships. In the period during which our magazines were produced and read, intellectuals such as Havelock Ellis and Edward Carpenter, proponents of the new scientific field of sexology, formulated the binary concepts of homosexuality and heterosexuality (Marcus, 22). These concepts quickly gained traction as useful social categories, and a discourse of sexual deviation from the standard, heterosexuality, proliferated terms for different types of "inverted" individuals and relationships. In his *History of Sexuality Vol. 1* (1990), Foucault famously contends that late-Victorian society implemented such categories in order to delineate, and therefore control, previously unspoken behavior (34). The *Yellow Nineties Personography* project sets out to challenge these Victorian mechanisms and binaries. Such categorizations entrenched a division between normalcy and deviance while further marginalizing any individuals and behaviors that did not easily fit into binary categories. Notably, we have found scant evidence that any of the magazine contributors self-identified using terms such as "homosexual" or "invert." As atypical individuals, their lives were obscured in the historical record.

Victorian statistics and demography also engendered prosopography, a methodology for studying historical groups. The development of the prosopographic method is roughly contemporary with the late-nineteenth-century magazine community we study and thus connected to the cultural processes and classification practices that left some historical persons unmarked. Prosopography involves studying the available data of individuals in a particular group and extrapolating a collective biography of that group's "typical" subject. Historians tend to use prosopography to study marginal populations, rather than dominant ones, because a group study can offer more insights about people for whom few archival records exist (Booth, "Recovery 2.0," 17). A prosopography's structure and contents, therefore, are shaped by the primary source texts from which it gathers biographical data on a group of people. The *Oxford English Dictionary* cites 1896 as the first instance of "prosopography" in this sense. Late-Victorian prosopography focused on normalization, laying unique anomalies aside to establish straightforward, correlative relations between a population group's identity and its common characteristics.

As practiced from the late nineteenth century onward, prosopography conceptualizes individual people as population units, reflecting a Victorian emphasis on normalization. In their comprehensive overview of this historiographic practice, Koenraad Verboven and colleagues state that prosopography's goal is to make visible the "particular characteristics of the [identified] population as a whole" (36). Studying a whole population can be a more effective strategy for ascertaining social patterns than generalizing from a few individual cases. Prosopography therefore concerns itself not with "the unique" but with "the average, the general and the 'commonness' in the life histories of more or less large numbers of individuals." Echoing his Victorian predecessors, Verboven states: "The individual and exceptional is important only insofar as it provides information on the collective and the 'normal'" (37).

Traditional prosopography, as Verboven defines it, assumes that classifying multiple persons as a "more or less homogeneous group" is an unproblematic historical method (39). But by what rubric can prosopographers determine homogeneity? In some ways, the individuals included in the *Yellow Nineties Personography* constitute a homogeneous group: all of them participated in 1890s journalism and, more specifically, contributed to British avant-garde periodicals. If we were to summarize this group's characteristics in one typifying profile, we would conclude that the average contributor was a middle-aged, British, Caucasian male who studied at Oxbridge, contributed fiction to the *Yellow Book,* published under his own name, and regularly socialized with Henry James and Edmund Gosse. This unambiguous profile does not begin to describe many of the individuals in our personography's dataset. Our biographical research has uncovered ambiguous data that, we argue, deserve more complex documentation and modeling. The following examples of historical individuals who contributed to the magazines in our project illustrate the inadequacy of prosopography's normative categories of marital status, sex, and occupation.

Like many female *Yellow Book* contributors, Rosamund Marriott Watson and E[dith] Nesbit veiled their marital status and biological sex with pseudonyms and initial-only signatures. For many years, Marriott Watson was known in personal circles as a woman but in a much broader community of readers by her masculine pseudonym, Graham R. Tomson. Notably, she published under both signatures in the *Yellow Book,* but her two names—and the coded genders they evoke—remain noncorrelative. There is a cultural story here we do not wish to elide: as Graham R. Tomson, the poet enjoyed significant critical recognition and was even suggested for the laureateship when Tennyson died in 1892. As the scandalous Rosamund Marriott Watson, she left her husband (Arthur Tomson) and child in 1894 to live, unmarried, with H. B. Marriott Watson (who also published in the *Yellow Book*). As a result, the poet was no longer "known" in some social circles and her poetic profile as Graham Tomson was erased in essays on contemporary women poets by critics such as Richard Le Gallienne and Andrew Lang (Hughes, 222). Her change in signature thus represents both a shift in social standing and an altered authorial status and oeuvre.

Known socially as "Mrs. Hubert Bland," E. Nesbit always published under her maiden name and initial, thus veiling both her sex and her marital status.

H. G. Wells gave her the nickname Ernest because when he first read her work, he assumed "E. Nesbit" was a man. Bizarrely, this masculine identification also has an archival history in the Bodleian Library, where she was initially catalogued as "Nesbit, Ernest" (Briggs, 299). Clearly, the stark initial "E" in her signature suggested to some contemporary reviewers and readers that Nesbit was male. Interestingly, in an 1895 *Sketch* interview, *Yellow Book* publisher John Lane referred to Nesbit as "*Miss E. Nesbit,*" while (in the same interview) conferring marital status to "*Mrs. Marriott Watson.*"[1] Lane knew the actual marital status of both women, so these constructed textual identities may have been marketing strategies by the canny publisher. There are historical nuances of gendered authorial identity and social status here that we would like our personography to highlight.

Ella D'Arcy and Ethel Colburn Mayne are each noncorrelative entities in terms of their dual roles as authors and editors. Both published fiction in the *Yellow Book*—D'Arcy under her own name, and Mayne under the pseudonym Frances E. Huntley—but they also contributed invisible labor to the magazine, working as subeditors with Henry Harland. Mayne's role lasted only half a year (January to June 1896), during D'Arcy's absence on the continent. Notably, D'Arcy was covering for Harland when he and Lane were both away in April 1895, at the famous moment of Oscar Wilde's arrest. Lane succumbed to the pressure of a group of his Bodley Head authors, who associated Aubrey Beardsley's decadent art with Wilde's sexuality, and sent a cable firing Beardsley from the *Yellow Book* staff. However, it was D'Arcy who was sitting in the editorial chair. As acting editor, she had to recall Volume 5 of the *Yellow Book* from the press and oversee the removal and replacement of Beardsley's artwork (Kooistra and Denisoff). Despite D'Arcy's and Mayne's editorial contributions to the *Yellow Book,* however, the magazine itself acknowledges only their authorship, and the historical record likewise reveals a systemic undervaluing of their editorial labor (Windholz).

Male editors, too, sometimes kept their identity deliberately veiled, and disguised their biology with a pseudonym of the opposite sex. According to Elizabeth Sharp's memoir of her husband, William Sharp edited the *Pagan Review* (as W. H. Brooks) and coedited the *Evergreen,* though neither magazine credits this work in print (Sharp, 260).[2] Even more than his invisible editorships, however, we are fascinated by his development of a "second life" with a feminine literary persona. William Sharp's case differs from the noncorrelative pseudonyms used by women authors such as George Egerton (Mary Chavelita Dunne Bright) or Graham Tomson in that his avatar, Fiona Macleod, had social, legal, and textual life separate from his own.

Sharp began writing Celtic revival works as the reclusive Fiona Macleod in 1894; for the rest of his life, he publicly represented her as a cousin on whose behalf he acted as a kind of literary agent. Sharp sustained a personal correspondence between Macleod and friends such as W. B. Yeats, and even created a legal identity for her by having a power of attorney drawn up so he could act on her behalf (Halloran). In three of the *Evergreen*'s four numbers, Sharp and Macleod published work as separate entities. Sharp also contributed, under a variety of pseudonyms, to the *Pagan Review,* and Macleod contributed to the *Savoy.*

Fiona Macleod occupies a liminal space between history's usual categories because she has a textual and cultural identity but no discrete biological existence. The *Oxford Dictionary of National Biography* lists Sharp and Macleod as "William Sharp (Fiona Macleod)," following the pattern established by Elizabeth Sharp's posthumous memoir of her husband, which revealed his dual identity for the first time. However, bracketing off Macleod as Sharp's subidentity does not reflect the complex relationship between these two authorial personas in fin-de-siècle culture. Macleod is more than a historical literary hoax; her poetry reveals a spirit and an authorial voice that William Sharp and his contemporaries considered uniquely her own.

The prosopographic impulse to ignore cultural data's contingent nature and impose a normative hegemony on its documented subjects raises feminist challenges for biographical methods in the digital humanities. The disparity between the individual contributors Rosamund Marriott Watson and Fiona Macleod and the collective contributor profile sketched above (white, upper-class male) underlies our decision to build a personography rather than a prosopography. As we have shown, the traditional prosopographic process of making the average visible tends to make the unusual or noncorrelative *in*visible. This compounds a difficulty already present in many historical data on persons: individuals and behaviors that fall outside the "average" are screened out. Here, *average* can denote the dominant sociocultural conception of the subject: traditional prosopography presupposes that a physical body correlates with a cisgender, heteronormative conception of personhood, with male as the assumed standard of measurement. The *average* can also denote traditional prosopography's standard personal identity categories—putatively unambiguous classifiers such as status (married or unmarried), role (author or editor), and sex (male or female). The prosopographical average frequently denotes a subject who has been filtered not only by the cultural texts of his or her historical milieu but also by present-day researchers. Scholars can only access historical lives through material artefacts, and our twenty-first-century ways of naming and classifying may not correlate with historical ways.

Verboven indicates that prosopography ultimately serves "to collect data that transcends individual lives" (41). The rhetoric of transcendence gives the prosopographical data agency, as if by virtue of its homogeneity it requires no interpretation or selection and simply presents itself as fact. But transcendent data do not exist. Prosopographical data analysis involves aggregating historical information on a large scale and interpreting patterns that appear through quantitative processing—in other words, it involves distant reading (Schulz; Underwood). Distant reading frequently relies on computer algorithms to process large corpora—a set of operations that N. Katherine Hayles calls machine reading (28). Determining the scope of a dataset, the algorithms for quantification, and the criteria for pattern recognition involve several interpretive steps. So-called transcendent prosopographical data about historical groups emerge through a normative selection process that obscures the data's actual contingencies.

With the increasing adaptation of electronic scholarship's critical methods, prosopographers have moved their work out of print narratives and into online databases. Recent prosopographic literature participates in digital humanities discourses that problematize assumptions about data neutrality. Such work recognizes that prosopography's traditional methods impose, rather than reveal, hegemony.

Developing reliable databases while critiquing traditional prosopography's normalizing filters is an ongoing challenge for digital humanities prosopographers.[3] Self-identified "new-style prosopographers" such as John Bradley, Harold Short, and Michelle Pasin at King's College London conceptualize digital prosopography as a "visible record" of scholars' analytical processes as they sort through source material (Bradley and Short, 5). The King's College prosopographers therefore record evidence data not as facts, but as factoids. First coined by Norman Mailer in his biography of Marilyn Monroe, a factoid is an assertion made by a particular source about a particular person at a particular moment. As these particularities indicate, a factoid can register many contingencies (Bradley and Short, 8–11). The factoid serves as the basic unit of source-driven prosopography (Pasin and Bradley, 87). As documented utterances, factoids can reveal meaningful matter about historical lives, even if they record bias or contradiction.

By engaging historical data as interpreted factoids, we recognize that what *does not* leave traces in the historical record can be as important as what *does*, and the interpretive processes that determine historical data's visibility matter as much as what the data convey. For example, giving William Sharp and Fiona Macleod separate entries in our personography, rather than listing Macleod as Sharp's pseudonym, will impact whether users interpret Macleod as an unusually robust pseudonymous persona or as an authorial figure in her own right. Moreover, digital prosopography's use of relational data structures demonstrates that scholars can only interpret factoids in relation to other factoids. Each node or data point in a relational data model only exists in relation to other nodes, and these nodes appear as a flattened network, rather than as a hierarchy. As a node in a relational network, a factoid's significance depends on the factoid constellation within which it is mapped (Bradley and Short, 11–12).

While some digital scholars have adopted new-style prosopography, others have developed personography as an alternative method for documenting the biographical data of groups. Flanders defines personography as "the management of the identity of individual people" ("Encoding Textual Information"). As its moniker suggests, personography emphasizes the individuality of persons even though a personographic system, like a prosopographic one, disambiguates biographical data using a classification system. Personography emerged in the twenty-first century as a means of documenting the persons referenced in a TEI-encoded electronic edition. A personography allows a scholar encoding a text to link names that the text references with corresponding biographical data about the referents. Unlike prosopography, personography is usually shaped by a digitally encoded text that is not a primary biographical source, but that otherwise cites those persons. Both new-style prosopography and personography use a relational data model, but a personography's model documents relationships between persons, not factoids. These persons may include contributors to the text, fictional characters, historical figures, and/or mythical figures. Personographies vary because the kinds of information that scholars encode and their methods for encoding depend on what they wish to emphasize in relating the encoded text to the personography.

Though recent prosopographic and personographic works challenge their predecessors' assumptions, scholarship in these fields has not given adequate attention to the politics of gender and sexuality. We consider Booth's *Collective Biographies of Women* project a bellwether of feminist prosopography. Like other feminist digital humanities databases, such as *Orlando* and *Women Writers Online*, *Collective Biographies* increases historical women's visibility (Booth, *Collective*, 18). Crucially, Booth's project uses prosopography to develop a feminist analysis of gendered biographical conventions and the changing life histories of women. As of her project's 2009 inauguration, such an approach had "never been attempted in digital projects" (33–34). Undertaking the *Collective Biographies* was necessary, Booth asserts, because "it is not enough to recover knowledge of as many women of the past as possible; we should re-examine the texts in which their narratives and images circulate for different constituencies and interests and claims." Booth notes that digital technology uniquely enables such prosopography "to collect, interpret through encoding, interweave, sort, compare, and visualize large bodies of discourse" (18). As Booth's reflections on the *Collective Biographies* attest, using computational technology amounts to more than simply adding complexity to a conventional system of classification: through digital tools, scholars can provide new perspectives on historical data that prompt us to reconceptualize our historical practices.

The *Yellow Nineties Personography* encourages its users to interrogate classificatory logic, and the research process more broadly, by acknowledging historical data's contingency. Like Michelle Schwartz and Constance Crompton, the creators of *Lesbian and Gay Liberation in Canada*, we have found rigid taxonomy inadequate for our database, if we truly want to "mark," in the sense of making visible, the 27 percent of magazine contributors whose biographical data are ambiguous, fluid, or noncorrelative (Schwartz and Crompton). Our project is inherently nonnormative, given that the personography's primary goal is to document the complex cultural and social networks out of which the *Yellow Book*, the *Pagan Review*, the *Savoy*, and the *Evergreen* emerged at the fin de siècle. We aim to build a reliable, manipulatable dataset while expressing personographic data in ways that, rather than flattening ambiguities, highlight the noncorrelative by showing the politics of gender and sex at work.

In the case studies mentioned above, the imperative to engage historical data as interpreted factoids gives rise to practical challenges in digital humanities practice.

Do we encode Rosamund Marriott Watson's biological sex (F) and/or Graham R. Tomson's publicly performed gender (M)? What does each choice imply and make visible? Should E. Nesbit's sex be coded as F (female), M (male), O (other), or U (unknown)? How can we document the invisible character of the editorial labor that Ella D'Arcy and Ethel Colburn Mayne contributed to the *Yellow Book*? How should we represent the conjoined identities of Sharp and Macleod in our database? We have decided to list Sharp and Macleod as two (related) contributors so that Fiona Macleod's historical existence is visible, but how can we describe her relationship to William Sharp? Does assigning the same unique identification code to both persons in our dataset adequately convey that one physical body correlates with at least two distinct authorial and social identities?

We have not yet answered these questions to our complete satisfaction. However, in response to the challenge of parsing the complexities of such data, we have conceptualized the *Yellow Nineties Personography* as a prototype for interpreting historical persons within their contexts by making noncorrelatives—and the processes by which we curate them—visible. In order to do this, we have built the *Yellow Nineties Personography* in three iterations. Each iteration serves as an interface that visibly mediates biographical information with a different value hierarchy.

The first iteration is a spreadsheet-based biographical dataset that represents all personographic <persons> as equal. The dataset gives equal representational value to contributors who lacked social and/or legal status at the time of magazine publication and contributors who had a high social profile in the 1890s, and later became canonical in literary and/or art historical studies. In this iteration, then, Aubrey Beardsley, the internationally acclaimed art nouveau artist of the *Yellow Book* and the *Savoy*, Effie Ramsay, a forgotten Celtic designer for the *Evergreen*, and Charles Hare, the engraver whose miniature signature can occasionally be glimpsed on an illustration but is not otherwise credited, each have the same value. The spreadsheet records all persons as named entities simply by virtue of their contributions to the four avant-garde magazines in our digital corpora. These named entities include women, who were legal nonpersons at the time; unknown or ambiguously identified contributors, who became cultural nonentities; and engravers and editors, who were textual nonentities. Established writers and artists, such as Henry James and Paul Sérusier, whose names and biographies have enjoyed a textual afterlife are also, of course, <persons> in the dataset.

In many ways, this iteration of the *Yellow Nineties Personography* is the most accessible for users who are not familiar with computational methods for processing information. The table parses biographical data in human-readable categories. It also gives equal visual-spatial weight to each person's entry, thereby foregrounding a key aspect of our personography's argument. However, this spreadsheet is visually unwieldly precisely because it presents all persons and associated data simultaneously; the columns display too much information to study at once, and are not conducive to pattern recognition.

The personography's second iteration is a data visualization series that introduces temporal, spatial, and relational hierarchies. Highlighting patterns of biographical disparity, the visualizations compel us to investigate the politics and cultural contexts that have shaped these disparities. Through filters of data and visualization choice, particular inequities between contributor data become prominent. In this iteration, our <persons> are no longer equal units, and the revealed asymmetries become prompts for investigation, discovery, and analysis. For example, a visualization of magazine contributors by gender (M, F, U, or O) displays an unequal proportion of F-designated contributors in any role—author, artist, editor, or engraver. More (biologically and legally documented) males than females contributed to the four magazine titles in our corpora. Unsurprisingly, this offers the personography's most obvious entry point into late-Victorian print culture's gender politics. A visualization of personography factoid frequencies displays a high proportion of factoids available for contributors designated M, in comparison to factoids about contributors designated F, U, or O. This pattern points to a hegemony at work in archival documentation itself, where records are preserved based on perceived historical value, and value itself is historically contingent on prevailing norms.

Users with little knowledge of data visualization may have difficulty engaging this iteration of the personography. Visualization can make a dataset's patterns more readily visible and can provide users with a sensorial interface for interpretation. However, advanced engagement with visualizations, including both the manipulation of a data display's output and the critical assessment of the methodology used to produce it, requires some technical familiarity.

The *Yellow Nineties Personography*'s third iteration is the TEI encoding of <persons>. The TEI P5 Guidelines acknowledge that "the meanings of concepts such as sex, nationality, or age are highly culturally dependent, and the encoder should take particular care to be explicit about any assumptions underlying their usage" (Burnard and Bauman, 13.3.2.1). However, we have found that in practice, markup methods tend to instantiate, rather than critique, cultural norms. In developing our biographical markup schema, we intend to draw on, and develop, all the flexibility that TEI can provide in describing the variable traits and states of historical persons.

TEI requires us to make unambiguous declarations about each individual contributor, but allows us to tailor the extensible markup language (XML) and structure. For example, the <addName> element is vital to the personography. We primarily describe contributors by the name under which they contributed to our four magazines, but we also document other names by which they were known. Such <addName> components may point to layers of social history at odds with a contributor's textual history, as is the case for William Sharp and Fiona Macleod. They may also point to a textual-cultural identity expanding beyond our periodicals: this is the case for Ethel Colburn Mayne, who began publishing under her own name after her *Yellow Book* stint as Frances E. Huntley. The series of <persName> elements that describe a given entity foregrounds our interest in documenting each contributor's social and textual presence.

The TEI P5 Guidelines offer some invaluable features for our encoding process, such as the "One Document Does It All," or ODD file. This formal mechanism for explaining how we define our fields allows us to make our interpretive choices visible to users who read the extensible markup language, or XML. The ODD is a file that explains how an encoded document uses its TEI (Burnard and Bauman, 1). The TEI document includes a pointer or reference to this ODD in its header. Our personography's ODD includes descriptions that detail our use of each element and attribute in the personographic entries. Because some personography users may not be TEI-literate, we also plan to make our intervention visible through an editorial introduction to the personography website that will take the familiar online form of an "About" page.

Some limitations to TEI's personographic conventions require us to innovate. Because of prosopography's historical orientation, it temporally hierarchizes biographical data; prosopographies are often structured genealogically or are otherwise event based. Much personographic work has adopted this practice and organizes data by event. We have considered organizing personographic data by event (birth, death, marriage, magazine contribution), but a precondition of our personography's scope is that its persons existed during the same historical moment, the 1890s. Moreover, using temporal characteristics to organize the data would undermine the purpose of our project, which is to curate data about the interpersonal patterns that collaboratively create a magazine and its networks. At its core, the *Yellow Nineties Personography* is community based, rather than event based. We have therefore adopted a relational network model akin to that of new-style prosopographers.

Our relational emphasis complicates the process of encoding the personography, as TEI documents hierarchize well, but accommodate relational networks less easily. The TEI Guidelines organize the information about people into three broad groups: traits, states, and events. In order to capture the complexity of our dataset, we tag most biographical data as traits, rather than states. By documenting relationships, occupations, education, and affiliations as traits that do not have a beginning or an end, we emphasize that all categorized aspects of contributor lives were part of a network of potentially simultaneous influences. This network was temporally situated at the fin de siècle, but the dataset demonstrates that its influence extended backward (for example, W. B. Yeats critically rehabilitated the work of William Blake in the *Savoy*) and forward (for example, Edmund Gosse and other frequent *Yellow Book* contributors were colleagues and mentors to modernist writers such as Ford Maddox Ford and Edith Wharton).

Because the *Yellow Nineties Personography* is community based, rather than event based, we anticipate that it will be most productively visualized as a network, rather than a timeline. Aside from birth and death dates, the personography includes few data items that a user could map chronologically. We recognize that privileging a relational structure obscures the temporal conditions that influenced contributors' lives and their participation in the transatlantic artistic community that produced our periodicals. This is an interpretive choice that we will foreground in our ODD and in our editorial introduction to the personography. We see the personography's relational emphasis as self-reflexively highlighting the contingent nature of the data we deploy, as well as supporting feminist inclusivity in our digital humanities praxis. The persons in our dataset exist in relation to their periodical contributions, and to their personal and professional associations. Similarly, their visibility within in the 1890s' artistic community was tied to their publicly available works, their social connections, and their participation in British and transnational cultural networks. Given that in our dataset all contributors have value by virtue of their periodical contributions, we hope that users will investigate cases in which a person's limited role in the personographic network suggests that the person was less visible within the artistic community and/or is less visible in the archives.

We continue to hone a personographic vocabulary that expresses classifications as interpretive choices and foregrounds layers of historical information screened out by the normative impulses of generalized biographies. In building our prototype, we are curating the personal landscapes of the *Evergreen,* the *Pagan Review,* the *Savoy,* and the *Yellow Book.* We recognize our markup and database choices are interpretive and will condition the possibilities for meaning-making by users. Nevertheless, we hope users can create new knowledge about the individuals and relationships in our dataset. Visualizing the data will give users a sense of some broad patterns in contributor identities and textual lives, illuminating historical ambiguities and obscurities that warrant further investigation. We want users to query the personographic data in meaningful ways and critique our strategies for queering the data—the ways in which we have modeled our interrogative engagement with the factoids of historical lives. By transparently documenting our processes and inviting users to critique and reinterpret our presentation of the historical record, we insist that how sources present biographical traces and how we interpret them are as important as what the traces themselves express.

Our attention to making our own interpretive practices visible attests to the importance we place on how our dataset models knowledge. Like the King's College prosopographers, we are building a biographical database that models how we think about our materials and our task (Bradley and Short, 3). According to Willard McCarty, a model *of* knowledge is "a representation of something for the purposes of study," and a model *for* knowledge is "a design for realizing something new" (24). Our personography is not a model *of* the contributors to the *Yellow Book,* the *Evergreen,* the *Pagan Review,* and the *Savoy.* It is, instead, a model *for* interpreting the magazines' contributors within the context of their sociocultural network—for interrogating the research process and acknowledging that historical data are always contingent. Moreover, our database's relational form will ensure that it remains open and responsive, accommodating user-added data and facilitating collaborative knowledge-building in ways that we cannot anticipate, but welcome.

If prototypes can argue, as Alan Galey and Stan Ruecker contend, then the *Yellow Nineties Personography* instantiates a claim that digital humanities strategies can be used to mobilize feminist and queer approaches to periodical history and the politics of prosopography (405). Such approaches not only make historical nonpersons and noncorrelatives visible but also enable us to continue improving our use of digital tools and computational methods to grapple with subjective, contingent, humanist knowledge. In resisting the disambiguating and normalizing impulses of traditional prosopography, we also celebrate the subversive spirit in which the project's fin-de-siècle contributors produced these avant-garde periodicals.

Notes

1. "I count myself fortunate . . . to have published the works of five great women poets of the day—Mrs. Meynell, Mrs. Marriott Watson, Miss E. Nesbit, Mrs. Tynan Hinkson, and Mrs. Dollie Radford" (December 4, 1895, supplement, 6; cited in Hughes, *Graham R.*, 244).

2. No editorial credit is given in *The Evergreen,* and Sharp signed the editorial for the *Pagan Review* as W. H. Brooks.

3. Michelle Schwartz and Constance Crompton discuss the challenges and advantages of a lesbian feminist approach to digital prosopography in their contribution to this anthology.

Bibliography

Booth, Alison. *How to Make It as a Woman: Collective Biographical History from Victoria to the Present.* Chicago: University of Chicago Press, 2004.

Booth, Alison. "Recovery 2.0: Beginning the Collective Biographies of Women Project." *Tulsa Studies in Women's Literature* 28, no. 1 (2009): 15–35. JSTOR. www.jstor.org/stable/40783472.

Booth, Alison, director. *Collective Biographies of Women: How Books Reshape Lives.* University of Virginia, 2017. http://cbw.iath.virginia.edu.

Bradley, John, and Harold Short. "Texts into Databases: The Evolving Field of New-Style Prosopography." *Literary and Linguistic Computing* 20, supplement issue (2005): 3–24. Oxford Journals. doi.org/10.1093/llc/fqi022.

Briggs, Julia. *A Woman of Passion: The Life of E. Nesbit 1858–1924.* New York: New Amsterdam Books, 1987.

Brown, Susan, Patricia Clements, and Isobel Grundy, eds. *Orlando Women's Writing in the British Isles from the Beginnings to Present.* Cambridge University, 2017. http://orlando.cambridge.org.

Burnard, Lou, and Syd Bauman. *P5: Guidelines for Electronic Text Encoding and Interchange,* Version 3.0.0. Text Encoding Initiative, March 29, 2016. www.tei-c.org/release/doc/tei-p5-doc/en/html/ND.html.

Canguilhem, Georges. *The Normal and the Pathological.* Translated by Carolyn R. Fawcett in collaboration with Robert S. Cohen. New York: Zone Books, 1989.

Courtney, Angela, and Michelle Dalmau, eds. *Victorian Women Writers Project.* Indiana University, 2017. http://webapp1.dlib.indiana.edu/vwwp/welcome.do.

Davis, Lennard J. "Constructing Normalcy." In *The Disability Studies Reader,* edited by Lennard J. Davis, 3–16. New York: Routledge, 1997.

Denisoff, Dennis, and Lorraine Janzen Kooistra. *The Yellow Nineties Online.* Ryerson University, 2017. http://1890s.ca.

Flanders, Julia. "Encoding Textual Information." *Women Writers Project.* Northeastern University, September 27, 2011. http://www.wwp.northeastern.edu/outreach/seminars/walden/presentations/contextual_encoding/contextual_encoding_00.xhtml.

Flanders, Julia, director. *Women Writers Project.* Northeastern University, 2017. https://www.wwp.northeastern.edu.

Flanders, Julia, Susan Brown, Jacqueline Wernimont, and Martha Nell Smith. Plenary Panel: "Feminist Literary History." *Digital Diversity 2015: Writing, Feminism, Culture.* University of Alberta, May 8, 2015.

Foucault, Michel. *The History of Sexuality Volume 1: An Introduction.* Translated by Robert Hurley. New York: Vintage Books, 1990.

Foucault, Michel. *Security, Territory, Population.* Translated by Graham Burchell. New York: Palgrave MacMillan, 2007.

Galey, Alan, and Stan Ruecker. "How a Prototype Argues." *Literary and Linguistic Computing,* 25, no. 4 (2010): 405–24. *Scholars Portal,* doi:10.1093/llc/fqq021.

Giffney, Noreen. "Introduction: The 'q' Word." In *The Ashgate Research Companion to Queer Theory,* edited by Noreen Giffney and Michael O'Rourke, 19–27. Taylor and Francis, 2009. www.taylorfrancis.com/books/e/9781317041894/chapters/10.4324%2F9781315613482-8.

Halloran, William F. Introduction to *The William Sharp Archive,* edited by William F. Halloran. *University of London Institute of English Studies. Internet Archive.* web.archive.org/web/20160310095023/www.ies.sas.ac.uk/research/current-projects/william-sharp-fiona-macleod-archive/william-sharp-fiona-macleod-archive.

Hayles, N. Katherine. *How We Think: Digital Media and Contemporary Technogenesis.* Chicago: University of Chicago Press, 2012.

Hughes, Linda K. *Graham R.: Rosamund Marriott Watson, Woman of Letters.* Athens: Ohio University Press, 2005.

Jackson, Holbrook. *The Eighteen Nineties: A Review of Art and Ideas at the Close of the Nineteenth Century.* (1913). London: Penguin, 1959.

Kooistra, Lorraine Janzen, and Dennis Denisoff, eds. "*The Yellow Book*: Introduction to Volume 5 (Apr. 1895)." In *The Yellow Nineties Online,* edited by Dennis Denisoff and

Lorraine Janzen Kooistra. Ryerson University, 2011. 1890s.ca/HTML.aspx?s=YBV5_Intro.html.

Marcus, Sharon. *Between Women: Friendship, Desire, and Marriage in Victorian England.* Princeton: Princeton University Press, 2007.

McCarty, Willard. *Humanities Computing.* London: Palgrave Macmillan, 2005.

Mussell, James. *The Nineteenth-Century Press in the Digital Age.* London: Palgrave Macmillan, 2012.

Pasin, Michele, and John Bradley. "Factoid-Based Prosopography and Computer Ontologies: Towards an Integrated Approach." *Digital Scholarship in the Humanities* 30, no. 1 (2015): 86–97. *Oxford Journals,* doi:10.1093/llc/fqt037.

Schulz, Kathryn. "What Is Distant Reading?" Sunday Book Review, *New York Times,* June 24, 2011. nyti.ms/1AA3uJe.

Schwartz, Michelle, and Constance Crompton. "Remaking History: Lesbian Feminist Historical Methods in the Digital Humanities." In *Bodies of Information: Intersectional Feminism and Digital Humanities,* 131–56. Minneapolis: University of Minnesota Press, 2018.

Schwartz, Michelle, and Constance Crompton, directors. *Lesbian and Gay Liberation in Canada.* Humanities Data Lab, University of British Columbia Okanagan/Canadian Research Writing Collaboratory, University of Alberta/Centre for Digital Humanities, Ryerson University, 2017. beta.cwrc.ca/project/lesbian-and-gay-liberation-canada.

Sharp, Elizabeth A. *William Sharp (Fiona Macleod): A Memoir.* Duffield, 1910. Internet Archive. archive.org/details/williamsharpfion00shariala.

Underwood, Ted. "The Real Problem with Distant Reading." *The Stone and the Shell,* May 29, 2016. https://tedunderwood.com/2016/05/29/the-real-problem-with-distant-reading.

Van Remoortel, Marianne, et al. *Agents of Change: Women Editors and Socio-Cultural Transformation in Europe 1710–1920.* Ghent University, 2017. http://www.wechanged.ugent.be.

Verboven, Koenraad, Myriam Carlier, and Jan Dumolyn. "A Short Manual to the Art of Prosopography." In *Prosopography Approaches and Applications: A Handbook,* edited by K. S. B. Keats-Rohan, 35–69. Oxford University Press, 2007. *Oxford University Prosopography Research,* prosopography.modhist.ox.ac.uk/images/01%20Verboven%20pdf.pdf.

Wernimont, Jacqueline. "Whence Feminism? Assessing Feminist Interventions in Digital Literary Archives." *Digital Humanities Quarterly* 7, no. 1 (2013). www.digitalhumanities.org/dhq/vol/7/1/000156/000156.html.

Windholz, Ann M. "The Woman Who Would Be Editor: Ella D'Arcy and The Yellow Book." *Victorian Periodicals Review* 29, no. 2 (1996): 116–30. *JSTOR,* http://www.jstor.org/stable/20082914.

PART III][Chapter 11

Is Twitter Any Place for a [Black Academic] Lady?

MARCIA CHATELAIN

On the Train

Few historical figures resonate with my students as powerfully as anti-lynching activist Ida B. Wells-Barnett. Known to only a handful of students before they take my class on African American women's activism, Wells-Barnett's life, her public speeches, and her most personal writings make history come alive. In my majority women and people of color classes, Wells-Barnett appears to be speaking to my students individually and specifically. Wells-Barnett's reflections on the perils of representation, her use of an intersectional frame long before the introduction of intersectionality into feminist thought, and her embodied resistance through her person and with her pen transforms the historical figure into a contemporary hero for many. Each time I teach about Wells-Barnett, I find that two crucial moments in her life speak to me as I navigate being a black woman professor and wrestle with the ways I also exist as a black woman thinker on social media in order to contribute to conversations on race and gender. The two points in her biography I turn to are Wells-Barnett's expulsion from a ladies' train car in 1883, while she was en route from Memphis to her teaching position; and the retaliation against her anti-lynching missive in the pages of the *Memphis Free Speech* in 1892, which led her to flee northward to Chicago.

In both instances—in the designated train car and at her writing desk—Wells-Barnett found herself in places that the larger, Jim Crow culture determined unfit for a black woman. In the eyes of the Chesapeake, Ohio, and Southwestern Railroad, her race disqualified her from the protections and privileges granted to white ladies, and so a conductor was entitled to demand that she vacate her seat and move to a dirty, smoke-filled cabin. Her race and gender together rendered her unsuited to write the truth about the false promises of post-Emancipation America in the pages of the *Free Speech,* as lynching terrified and signaled to blacks that they were never made for citizenship.[1]

The poignancy of Wells-Barnett's narrative captures me, and the students, when we are reminded that despite her intellect and influence in her time, she—and scores of black women like her past and present—would never fully realize the possibilities of their place and time. At every turn, she tried to capitalize on the expanding opportunities available for black women in late nineteenth-century America: admission to newly constructed Negro colleges, innovations in transportation that allowed her to travel domestically and internationally, and the explosion in black print media which could launch her ideas into a wider world. These institutions and innovations allowed more black people, as well as their ideas, their creations, and their meditations on becoming a free people to circulate and travel in unprecedented ways.

Wells-Barnett and her cohort of black women activist-intellectuals were constantly reminded that their race and gender would impair the very mobility these technological and social advances promised. As a black woman, she could not safely circulate her body or her corpus of writings and investigations. After enduring the indignities of the train car incident and later threats in the South, Wells-Barnett continued to attract the vitriol of white supremacists and sexist "race men."[2]

In this essay, I focus on my own experiences of thinking in public as a black academic woman in digital spaces, and the implications for my offline life at my university and in my department, specifically as the curator of the social media campaign #FergusonSyllabus, a response to Officer Darren Wilson killing unarmed teenager Michael Brown in a St. Louis exurb in August of 2014. Brown's death led to a massive uprising in the town of Ferguson, an international conversation of race and police brutality was ignited, and the Black Lives Matter movement came into greater visibility. After August 9, 2014, Ferguson became shorthand for long-standing racial and economic marginalization and a metonym for heightened consciousness about police violence and excess. #FergusonSyllabus initially started as a request I made to my Twitter followers and friends to dedicate the first day of classes to Michael Brown and the other youth of Ferguson who would not have a normal first day of school because of the unrest in their community. I believed that by talking about some element of the unrest through the lens of a discipline or to create a space in which students could express their questions or confusions about the moment (which captured the attention of cable news reporters, streamed live via Periscope accounts and was narrated by activists via Twitter), educators could amplify the greatest possibilities of online organizing and in-person gathering. Twitter provided an excellent vehicle for me to ask scholars to teach about the crisis, but the ability to search the platform using the #FergusonSyallbus term also allowed for a larger conversation among educators. As #FergusonSyllabus went viral—in part, due to an article I wrote about the idea for the online version of *The Atlantic*—I received requests from educators about how to translate the crowdsourced suggestions into action. For months, my association with #FergusonSyllabus challenged me to make real the interdisciplinary training I received in an American studies doctorate program, and it introduced me to a digital community of scholars, who made me feel less isolated and alone in my inclinations toward social justice teaching.

Although my experience of using Twitter as a digital platform for racial justice work was a relatively positive one, it was not without anxieties and the complications that come when an untenured woman of color becomes increasingly more visible in a national conversation. I was subject to the type of trolling, harassment, and unsolicited critique that are commonplace when women engage critical issues online. In the three years since Brown's death and the internationalization of Black Lives Matter, I have reflected on my experience with #FergusonSyllabus and the shifts in my academic career. My professional life transformed from having an academic presence mostly on my campus and within a few professional organizations to becoming an occasional talking head in media, the subject of profiles on education and teaching websites, and a public enough intellectual that I had to learn how to discern how I entered and navigated public conversations. In this essay, I focus on how my experiences with #FergusonSyllabus made me aware of the way that online and digital engagement offers a window into how you spend your time, and the ways colleagues and advisors evaluate your use of this time in the academy. This type of surveillance heightened my career worries and forced me to think about the way the academy evaluates and devalues collective, activist work. Additionally, my sudden entry into the world of digital scholarship regarding teaching about race and social justice, and the lack of clarity on how public engagement fits within the rigid hierarchy of research-service-and-then-teaching, made me think about the ways black women's voices can be muffled or altogether silenced in the very moments their insights are needed.

Wrinkles in Time

Before delving into how my career was reshaped by #FergusonSyllabus in 2014, I think it is important to reflect about time and the life of the academic. Although the digital landscape has reoriented our expectations on how long it should take to receive information, updates on said information, and then analysis on the information, the academic world has not fundamentally changed its relationship to time. We still understand knowledge production, research, and intellectual cultivation as requiring substantial investments in time in order to ensure that we are approaching our projects with an attention to rigor and demonstrating our commitment to depth. This emphasis on time shapes how we train and manage scholars in an academic bureaucracy. One of the most enduring and consistent elements of graduate education and the early career professorship is the constant questioning of how a person spends or squanders time. Your time becomes the subject of many conversations. Time to completion. Time on the tenure track. Time added to your tenure clock. Time spent worrying about not having enough time to tend to your research. Time spent in meetings. Time off in order to do scholarly work. For academics of color, time advice is easy to come by from well-intentioned mentors, from institutional diversity offices, and sage blog writers who warn: Protect your time! Time is the precious, unrenewable resource that overeager students and potentially ineffective or useless committees seeking a "diverse perspective" will try to steal from you. Scholars of color are routinely told that expectant community members will try to take it from you to participate in local campaigns or share your knowledge with sixth graders and high school juniors. You wonder if you have made good use of your time, while you feel each tick of your tenure clock in your gut. The warnings about the forces that try to spirit away with our valuable time are grounded in the very real experiences of burnout and failure, but time policing can also serve as a form of benevolent control, or even worse, a means of assimilating scholars into thinking that your time should never be used in the service of political struggles or movements, especially if you don't have tenure.

"How are you spending your time?"

In academia, the question of time is not only a matter of employer expectations or a mentor's kindly concern. Misunderstandings about the nature of academic work lend themselves to the spectacular narratives of faculty wasting time. The fixation on how faculty spend their time is often at the heart of most of the legislative interventions of late in states like Wisconsin and Iowa, in which politicians are attacking tenure, sabbatical leave, and ill-informed suggestions that if a professor can teach two or three courses a semester, why not four or five.[3] The arguments emerge from the same roots: At public universities, taxpayers purchased your time, so it is necessary for the state to extract as much of it as possible. At private institutions, the time scrutiny remains internal, but the message is the same: Prove that your time is being spent in the right ways, so that you can prove that you belong here.

So, what did it mean for me, as an academic professional, to create a time-stamped body of evidence about how I spent my time on Twitter in the year before I applied for tenure? Should I have spent the hour between 1:03 p.m. and 2:03 p.m. on August 11, 2014, tweeting out recommendations for teaching about St. Louis County and the history of residential redlining, or liking and retweeting article links about the militarization of police, before the official syllabi for my fall semester classes were done? What does it mean when I receive a notification that the account @GUProvostOffice, my university's provost, was following me on Twitter? Is this a sign of respect or an opening for criticism? When I noticed former students following me on Twitter, I was happy they were seeing #FergusonSyllabus unfold. When I realized that some of their parents were following #FergusonSyllabus, I wondered, are doing this to be supportive, or are they collecting evidence against me? Then, I noticed that I was being trolled and mocked about #FergusonSyllabus. "Why not teach kids to respect police?" "Another person trying to make colleges more liberal." Do I have the stomach for this?

In the years following the launch of #FergusonSyllabus, I became more attentive to checking where my name, and later my image, appeared. Websites like Campus

Reform, Campus Fix, and even Breitbart have taken issue with something I have said—or what they think I said—about race and college campuses and the nation more broadly. Black women thinkers attract trolls regularly, and scholars such as Brittney Cooper and Keeanga Yamahata-Taylor have been the most vocal and vigilant about refusing to bow to the assaults on their character and threats to their physical safety. When I received hate mail at my campus office or racially abusive tweets, I immediately sought to delete or hide the insults and the threats. No use of letting this linger, I reasoned. But I later realized I hid these acts of aggression because I did not know if I had the time to realize how frightened and intimidated I was by them. The insults on Twitter were immediately deleted and the offender blocked; yet, I wondered what would it mean if I left those comments alone or even highlighted them so my students, my colleagues, the provost, and the larger public would know what it looked like for one of a handful of black women at Georgetown to work in the public eye.[4]

Did I have time for #FergusonSyllabus?

What would people make of how I spent those valuable, precious minutes, hours, and days?

An Ask

At the heart of my engagement in social media during the Ferguson crisis, the notion of my time, my mobility, and the circulation of my ideas converged to create a new level of uncertainty about how others perceived my use of time. To take my concern about the devastation in Ferguson, Missouri, to a public space like Twitter was to also reveal my personal sadness about the state that was a second home to me since my undergraduate days at the University of Missouri.

I realized if my ask, to teach and talk about Ferguson, was made through Twitter, I could have a reach and a real-time archive of a community coming together around it. Considering the complexity and totality of the tragedy in Ferguson, I felt it critical to ask faculty who are usually outside the "race and gender" conversations on campus to imagine the ways that the STEM, business, architecture, and medicine classrooms are also responsible for thinking about multidisciplinary readings of the crisis unfolding. I wondered what my colleagues had to say about the fact that tear gas was used by militarized police forces on civilians on the streets of Ferguson. What did science scholars have to say about this? What does it mean to bring the question of policing tactics to bench scientists and medical students? Ferguson's poverty rate doubled between 2000 and 2010, and more than a quarter of families in the town live below the federal poverty line. So, I implored business school educators to take up the question of economic development in suburbs and the history of redlining to help their students understand their role in the world as future capitalists, innovators, and financial regulators.[5] I asked urban planning faculty to think about the design of the Canfield Green apartments where Brown was killed and the strip of fast-food restaurants that dotted Florissant Avenue, the center of the Ferguson protests, and how race and poverty inform spatial choices.

In providing these ideas and prompts to educators, I wanted to challenge academics on Twitter to think about the digital space as a site to create and sustain a community of scholars committed to pushing the boundaries of how we use our disciplines to respond to pressing social problems. I was frustrated by the number of people who have told me that because they were white, or outside the "social justice" fields, they had nothing to contribute to conversations about race and inequality. I also didn't want the unprepared and untested to initiate awkward conversation about race that could only expose their lack of preparedness. Rather, I wanted to help reorient scholars to the ways that the problems borne out of racial tension can be answered by our scholarly tools, and when we connect with our colleagues in other fields, we become more creative and equipped to engage in more substantive work in the classroom.

#FergusonSyllabus was intentionally multidisciplinary and even more intentionally public to call scholars out of hiding behind the oft-recited myth of "I have nothing to add." My initial motivations went beyond challenging my colleagues to use the first day of school to ensure students would have a space in which the Ferguson conversation could be connected to their curricular endeavors. I wanted to highlight the work of scholars of color who have long sounded the alarm about police violence and the criminalization of poverty in the United States. The activists inside Ferguson and other parts of St. Louis County were alerting the nation to the root causes of the multiple factors that contributed to the uprising—the city's budget's dependence on traffic and municipal ticketing, the resource-strapped Ferguson-Florissant School district, unemployment outside major cities, and St. Louis's disastrous public housing history and midcentury population loss. I wanted my colleagues who don't live in a world in which they sit on university diversity committees and speak on panels about inclusion on campus to understand the scholarly contributions and emotional labor of such a career. The ability to tweet about the work and, in addition, to discover the curiosity and the excitement of the disciplines elsewhere around this issue was inspiring. For the first time, I found myself in dialogue with fashion theorists, urban planners, chemists, and data scientists about how they can talk to their students about race, poverty, and inequality in their classrooms.

#FergusonSyllabus might have remained a small experiment among me and my couple of thousand Twitter followers had I not received a direct message, a private communiqué between Twitter followers, from a digital editor at TheAtlantic.com. Then editor Alexis Madrigal invited me to write about #FergusonSyllabus for the website, and I accepted the offer and thought that I would maybe make a small difference in helping facilitate my hopes that the several first days of class would focus on Ferguson. Within days, National Public Radio called me to give recommendations on people they could talk to about teaching Ferguson, and slowly I was becoming a "go-to" person on this issue. In the span of ten days, I was interviewed by the *New York Times* and St. Louis Public Radio, and my words were reprinted in *Slate,* the *Daily Kos,* and *Huffington Post.*

As the first day of my own classes approached, I started to receive direct messages from K–12 teachers, many of whom were told they would be disciplined if they talked about Ferguson in their classes. Fourth grade teachers and high school guidance counselors reached out and asked if I had any ideas of what they could do or say to circumvent jittery principals and nervous school boards. In consulting with these teachers, I discovered a meaningful component of my desire to reach a "broad audience," an audience that included K–12 educators as well. Penning newspaper editorials and longform journalism pieces can bring academics into new intellectual engagements, but rarely do scholars outside of education departments and schools spend time with elementary and high school teachers. I found that K–12 teachers needed support in providing age-appropriate and social climate–sensitive content on race, gender, sexuality, and class. Throughout my career, I have heard my share of colleagues complain about the lack of preparedness among their incoming students, but rarely do I meet scholars who have made substantial investments in supporting pre-college educators. I can't say I was innocent of this impulse either. Twitter provided a low-cost way to transmit ideas among these teachers, and they could consider the possibilities of teaching Ferguson from each other and sharing what worked and what failed.

By early September, I was the face of #FergusonSyllabus and an authority on teaching the scholarship of others, rather than a scholar promoting my own soon-to-be-released book and my expertise on African American girlhood. Although I had spent years trying to create a more flexible, if not entirely new, approach to the early-career track, by rejecting limiting notions of what it meant to be an academic, I was growing uneasy about the attention #FergusonSyllabus was generating. Being publicly acknowledged as a "teacher" rather than a "scholar" made me nervous, as I heard warnings that good teaching did not lead to tenure. I heard from mentors that women, especially women of color, did not want to be pigeonholed as simply good at teaching, and that excellent teaching would send up a red flag about my ability to be truly challenging and rigorous inside and outside the classroom. Although in television and magazine interviews I would insert my scholarly thoughts about the structural and historical questions that Ferguson brought to the fore, I was becoming known as a teacher, an assembler of ideas and methods for teaching about race. Was this a smart move? Was I shedding precious credibility by talking to fifth grade teachers? Was I setting myself up to be the cautionary tale for another generation—that scholar who was filled with promise until she started talking about kids during a time of crisis?

Some of my fears were put to rest by the tremendous institutional support I received at Georgetown and among my colleagues in the history department. Institutionally, I knew I was privileged to work in an environment in which units across campus were directing and initiating various Ferguson-related programming. My students were becoming regular participants in organizing efforts and protests in D.C. and were happy to use class time to discuss Ferguson and Black Lives Matter. When I submitted my tenure file months after launching #FergusonSyllabus, I was advised to revise my documents to *include* my efforts and its outcomes in the narrative components on research, teaching, and service in order to emphasize the importance of making scholarly and teaching interventions outside of our academic constructs. This encouragement and support are rare in the academy. I know of colleagues elsewhere who were discouraged from spending their own time on activist efforts on and off campus during the Ferguson crisis, and I was relieved that my institution did not try to silence me.

In a 2015 article in the *New Republic,* social critic Michael Eric Dyson celebrated what he calls a new generation of black digital intelligentsia. Citing scholars who use the digital landscape to participate in contemporary conversations, as well as engage in social justice struggles on the ground, Dyson applauded the fact that this intelligentsia is not simply the product of or the professors at elite universities.[6] Dyson, and others who have provided more or less critical assessments of the black public intellectual, reminded readers that the genealogies of black intellectuals from the nineteenth century to the present represent a hybrid of educational training and, like Wells-Barnett, the scholars regularly traveled across disciplines and professional statuses. The color line, along with the gender line and class line, has had the most impact on where scholars of color speak from and to which audiences. Twitter has provided that ideological location for this type of boundary-crossing travel.

As the academy still searches for a clear definition of the digital humanities and how it relates to the assessment and promotion of scholars, it is critical to make clearer distinctions than the ones Dyson articulates in his piece, which vaguely defines the digital and conflates the use of a computer with engagement of the digital space. Academic leaders and institutions must understand that a digital intelligentsia must use digital tools in ways to make the disciplines more accessible, dynamic, equitable, and relevant. Additionally, the blanket term "social media tools" erases the specific possibilities and pitfalls of the way that each tool curates, mediates, and presents ideas generated by scholars. Although Facebook, Twitter, WordPress blogs, Instagram, Snapchat, Grindr, Tindr, Scruff, and so on exist under the umbrella of social, the ways that academics, and I would emphasize academics of color, have used and leveraged these tools is where the conversation about the digital intelligentsia must linger. As leaders in the digital humanities and digital studies provide more clarity in these areas, more scholars will have the language to parse out the specific tales that each platform can tell about the nature of digital tools. The academy must begin to learn how to appreciate the skills and labor that each of these tools demands of scholars, whether it's the brevity of 140 characters or the production of digital scholarship, using GIS mapping software, digitization platforms, or online curatorial sites. As the digital humanities is a space in which women of color scholars are shaping and defining, it is also another space in which these same scholars are vulnerable to the kinds of marginalization that has long characterized the academy. As this process unfolds and changes, it is important to remember that all scholars with a computer are not involved in the digital humanities, and all digital projects do not democratize access to knowledge. Truly democratic spaces allow knowledge to be shared without fear of repercussion or backlash.

Fellow Passengers

Sociologist Zandria Robinson's experiences in the summer of 2015 illustrate how black women academics' digital expression is met on- and offline. When conservative news outlets reported on some of Robinson's tweets about racism and social media posts about white supremacy, subsequent rumors circulated that she was fired from her academic post for her ideas. Robinson's entanglement with the machinery of hypersurveillance of black women evoked Wells-Barnett's legacy. Her former employer responded to calls for her firing by simply tweeting: "Robinson is no longer employed by the University of Memphis." The university allowed the public to read between the lines. Her name appeared and reappeared on blog posts written for those desiring a narrative that a liberal, racist professor—a black woman at that— was finally punished for her outrageous views. In my estimation, Robinson's tweet was simply providing critiques of racism; yet, in the digital world a tweet is never just a tweet. The University of Memphis tweet did not, and could not, tell the full story. Robinson had refused to be ejected from the ladies' car. As she prepared to enter a new faculty post at Rhodes College of Memphis, it became clear that she was not fired from her previous position, and unlike so many who quiet themselves in the face of controversy, she refused to be silenced. She chose to continue to use her Twitter account and New South Negress blog to tell her truth.

Robinson—who has also been shaped by Wells-Barnett in her navigation of the academy—penned this artful response, which connected her multiple identities as a resistant, black woman academic in the South:

> We do this for Ida [B. Wells-Barnett] and all the ones that have come before us who have written the truth and compelled the nation, against some terrible odds, to reckon with itself. We are still doing it, and we must continue to do it. The fact that any of the statements of people of color—even the cherry-picked, decontextualized ones—are seen as controversial is a testament to the fact that we have not, even after all these years, had the conversations that need to be had or read the things that need to be read. Or perhaps the worst of white folks simply haven't listened. But we'll get there.[7]

I look to other black feminist scholars to remember that there are many ways to "get there." The attacks on Robinson—whose tweets and blog posts regularly deliver critiques of the state, as well as the academy's structural barriers to supporting faculty and graduate students of color—are felt across the black (feminist, academic) Twitterverse. The New South Negress's reflections simultaneously celebrate vulnerability, humor, and the sardonic sensibility that develops when you search for a place for yourself in the academy. Robinson connects to the commonplace experiences of other scholars of color, and her brief moment of exposure revealed that an attack on one is an attack on all. In response to the outcry against Robinson, one hundred of her colleagues of color signed a statement in her support.[8] Her steadfastness in asserting her opinions and her refusal to be a bystander in her own character assassination resonate deeply with the multiple fears felt by all of those who desire to think and tell the truth in public.

Since August 2014, the #Syllabus movement has grown and expanded; it is now shorthand for the ways that scholars—many of them women of color—use the digital landscape to intervene in moments of crisis and remind the academy of our roles and responsibilities to a broader world. The circulation of the #BlackLivesMatterSyllabus, #BaltimoreSyllabus, #SayHerNameSyllabus, and #TrumpSyllabus2.0 and the publication of the book *Charleston Syllabus: Readings on Race, Racism, and Racial Violence* point to ways that scholars have seen the use of the hashtag as an efficient use of Twitter to support social justice–oriented teaching, as well as interdisciplinary cooperation.[9] As was the case of #FergusonSyllabus, the syllabi hashtags also help media outlets identify scholars who can provide years of research and teaching expertise to radio listeners and news watchers.

For black women in the public sphere, access to technology has long been a mixed blessing. Wells-Barnett's activist life was compelled, transformed, and imperiled by rail travel and newspaper circulation. For me and other black women in public and academic life, our careers have been reshaped by Skype accounts that allow us to give lectures without leaving our offices, Twitter feeds that provide an entryway into heated debates, and budget airlines that help us connect with each other at symposia and conferences. Before many of us have been awarded tenure, or even advanced degrees, we have received invitations to offer our analysis on television news programs, while using our social media accounts to link to our scholarship and share our peers' work, and digital platforms have allowed us to bring a black feminist voice to policymakers and the public at large. As support for digital organizing projects and the digital humanities expands, I'm hopeful that academic women of color can sit securely in our seats as we travel across intellectual boundaries.

I am still uncertain if Twitter is a place for a [black academic] lady when I see attacks like those hurled at Robinson and others. Yet, I do know that we are not on the train car alone.

Notes

1. Ida B. Wells-Barnett's writings are available in *Southern Horrors,* available on Project Gutenberg, accessed June 25, 2018; DeCosta-Willis, *Memphis Diary*; and Royster, *Southern Horrors*. For biographies of Wells-Barnett, see Duster, *Crusade for Justice*; and Giddings, *Ida*.

2. Deborah Gray White's *Too Heavy a Load* traces the historical struggle of black women's organizing in the name of race and gender together. White highlights the ways that Wells-Barnett and others critiqued white men's sexually predatory behaviors and black men's failures to stand up and be in unity with black women.

3. "Iowa Bill." Also "Walker Erodes."

4. Taylor, "'Free Speech' Hypocrisy." In this article, Taylor discusses her horrifying experience of being threatened after delivering a commencement address about the racism and misogyny of the president of the United States. In "How Free Speech Works for White Academics," Brittney Cooper mentions not only her own experiences of being targeted but also the ways that the "free speech" conversation is at best disingenuous, and at worst a means of silencing scholars of color who challenge white supremacy.

5. Kneebone, "Ferguson, MO."

6. Dyson, "New Black Digital Intelligentsia."

7. Zandria, "Zeezus Does the Firing."

8. Jaschik, "Professor." Also McClain, "Why 100."

9. Blain, Williams, and Williams, *Charleston Syllabus*.

Bibliography

Blain, Keisha, Chad Williams, and Kidada Williams, eds. *Charleston Syllabus: Readings on Race, Racism, and Racial Violence*. Athens: University of Georgia Press, 2016.

Cooper, Brittney. "How Free Speech Works for White Academics." *Chronicle of Higher Education,* November 16, 2017. https://www.chronicle.com/article/How-Free-Speech-Works-for/241781.

DeCosta-Willis, Miriam, ed. *The Memphis Diary of Ida. B. Wells*. New York: Beacon, 1995.

Duster, Alfreda, ed. *Crusade for Justice: The Autobiography of Ida B. Wells*. Chicago: University of Chicago Press, 1991.

Dyson, Michael Eric. "The New Black Digital Intelligentsia." *The New Republic,* September 10, 2015.

Giddings, Paula. *Ida, Sword among Lions: B. Wells and the Campaign against Lynching*. New York: HarperCollins, 2009.

"Iowa Bill Sparks Faculty Ire." *Inside Higher Ed,* April 23, 2015. https://www.insidehighered.com/quicktakes/2015/04/23/iowa-bill-sparks-faculty-ire.

Jaschik, Scott. "The Professor Who Wasn't Fired." *Inside Higher Ed,* July 1, 2015, https://www.insidehighered.com/news/2015/07/01/twitter-explodes-false-reports-u-memphis-fired-professor-why.

Kneebone, Elizabeth. "Ferguson, Mo. Emblematic of Growing Suburban Poverty." *The Avenue* (blog). Brookings Institution, August 15, 2014. https://www.brookings.edu/blog/the-avenue/2014/08/15/ferguson-mo-emblematic-of-growing-suburban-poverty/.

McClain, Dani. "Why 100 Black Intellectuals Rallied behind This Professor." *The Nation*, July 14, 2015. http://www.thenation.com/article/why-100-black-intellectuals-rallied-behind-this-professor/.

Royster, Jacqueline Jones, ed. *Southern Horrors and Other Writings: The Anti-Lynching Campaign of Ida B. Wells, 1892–1900.* New York: Bedford/St. Martin's, 1996.

Taylor, Keeanga-Yamahtta. "'The Free Speech' Hypocrisy of Right-Wing Media." *New York Times,* August 14, 2017.

"Walker Erodes College Professor Tenure." *Politico,* July 12, 2015. https://www.politico.com/story/2015/07/scott-walker-college-professor-tenure-120009.

Wells-Barnett, Ida B. *Southern Horrors: Lynch Law in All Its Phases.* 1892. Available on Project Gutenberg, http://www.gutenberg.org/ebooks/14975.

White, Deborah Gray. *Too Heavy a Load: Black Women in Defense of Themselves, 1894–1994.* New York: W. W. Norton, 1994.

Zandria. "Zeezus Does the Firing 'Round Hurr." *New South Negress* (blog), 2015. https://newsouthnegress.com/zeezusyear/.

PART III][Chapter 12

Bringing Up the Bodies

The Visceral, the Virtual, and the Visible

PADMINI RAY MURRAY

As digital participation and engagement come of age in India, it was inevitable that they would be used increasingly as a platform for protest and activism. While the World Wide Web has long allowed for spaces of alterity and otherness to flourish, these spaces have enabled the disenfranchised to find community and ways in which to make their voices heard. Despite the strong visual primacy of the virtual medium, those voices are always destined to be disembodied, mediated by technology rather than flesh. Disembodiment has significant ramifications for feminist protest, given that one of the historical matrices of feminist thought is its avowal and reclamation of corporeal materiality. This challenged the Cartesian mind-body binary used to demonstrate the inferiority of women to men, as well as to undermine the subjecthood of colonized and indigenous peoples and those from disadvantaged socioeconomic backgrounds. The virtual thus disrupts the phenomenological position; "to be present in the world implies strictly that there exists a body which is at once a material thing in the world and a point of view towards the world" (De Beauvoir, 39). These developments led to Donna Haraway's articulation of the "cyborg," a strategy of queering the received categories of male and female by way of creating a "confusion of boundaries" (150). But the tension set up between the phenomenological position of being-in-the-world and Haraway's "cyborg" figure complicates questions regarding the constitution of the category of "woman," especially as it moves from the offline into the online space, and more specifically, in the context of Indian sexual politics as well as violence enacted on bodies marginalized—sometimes simultaneously, sometimes not—by gender, caste, and religion.

Radhika Gajjala's seminal work in the field, pointing out the overlap between gender, South Asian identity, and online spaces, articulated in her significant 2004 book *Cyber Selves: Feminist Ethnographies of South Asian Women*, marks her as an important and early voice. In this work, Gajjala signposts how such studies must "inevitably negotiate diasporic and nationalist gender, caste, religious and caste identity formations as well as corporate and academic cultures situated in an increasingly global economy" (2). In her more recent work, titled *Cyberculture and the Subaltern*, Gajjala attempts to map "how voice and silence shape online space in relation to offline actualities [and] how offline actualities and online cultures are in turn shaped by online hierarchies as well as different kinds of local access to global contexts" (3). Through this nuanced reading, Gajjala attempts to redefine what "subaltern" might mean when the current condition that allows users to inhabit online networks is "also [simultaneously] networked into processes of globalization through interplays of online global audiences and offline located/situated producers and consumers" (3). Gajjala and her colleagues define the subaltern body in the context of the digital as one that is in/visible, existing "simultaneously with the hypervisibility of particular images and constructs of 'the subaltern,'" and asks, "Does the mere act of claiming/naming of erasure and the noting of invisibility and absence in itself produce the possibility of a subaltern subject?" (4).

In this essay, I will be exploring how as feminist protest comes of age in India, most visibly through digital media, a clear distinction has emerged between embodied, or as I am describing it, "visceral," strategies of activism—where the body itself is used as an instrument and a site of dissent, especially against sexual violence—and virtual protest, via social and participatory media. Taking Gajjala's reading as a point of reference, I will argue that the visibility and representation (or lack thereof) of the protesting/resisting body in the online space and the digital archive define what might constitute subaltern subjectivity.

In order to provide a context for this more specific conversation, this article will open with a consideration of how violence upon the body is enacted, documented, circulated, and represented using technology. I will then examine the rupture between the representation of visceral and the virtual body, especially in the South Asian context, by considering how the different registers of visibility, as Gajjala has described it, are rendered by these modes, the hierarchies of access that each mode assumes, as well as how the "local" is located (or might be differentiated) in each. These considerations will be informed by examples of both modes, such as the naked protest staged by Manipuri women against the sexual violence of the Indian army; digital initiatives to raise awareness, especially in the aftermath of the Nirbhaya rape case; the ubiquitous violence against women; and the rise of websites and online spaces for feminist activism. These disparate modes have serious implications for the possibilities of intersectionality in South Asia, and this article will attempt, in its final section, to consider whether it is possible to reconcile the virtual and the visceral without reciprocally undermining the other, and whether it is possible to conceive of strategies (and a new politics) that might complement and extend the remit of both.

These considerations are of particular relevance to this volume, as they act as a corrective to the notion that conceptions of digital humanities as a discipline are universal. The originary narrative underpinning its emergence in Anglo-American academic discourse necessarily diverges in India and other countries in the Global South, due to differences in access, language, sociocultural mores, and infrastructure. As the work of Sukanta Chaudhuri, Radhika Gajjala, Lawrence Liang, Nishant Shah, Ravi Sundaram, and others have shown, there is a distinct need for digital humanities scholarship in India to incorporate its own histories of computing and internet use, while always remaining alert to its own exigencies of cultural and linguistic difference and political histories, which inevitably inflect outcomes such as who is empowered to build digital resources, archives, who is empowered to access and use such resources, and consequently who is represented online and how.

The relatively recent rise of digital humanities in Anglo-American institutions in a postcritique moment has, as Alan Liu has pointed out, posed a challenge to the understanding of the limits of the field. He writes,

> At core, the debate is not really about theorized critique versus something other than such critique. Instead, the debate situates the digital humanities at a fork between two branches of *late* humanities critique. One, a hack branch (sometimes referred to as "critical making"), affiliates with, but is often more concretely pragmatic, than "thing theory," the new materialism, actor-network theory, assemblage theory, and similar late poststructuralist theories. The other, a yack branch, descends from the not unrelated critical traditions of Frankfurt School "critical theory," deconstruction, Foucauldian "archaeology," cultural materialism, postcolonial theory, and gender and race theory–especially as all these have now been inflected by media studies. ("Drafts")

While academics and thinkers in India are well aware of these developments, the development of digital humanities in India coincides with a key intellectual moment: of challenging the hegemony of English literary studies in the university space, and more generally of the humanities university curriculum, both of which are persistent remnants of a colonial legacy. The emergent sites of digital humanities scholarship in India are found not only in the formal university space (an excellent example being the School of Cultural Texts and Records at Jadavpur University) but also in the work of such research institutions such as

> the Centre for Internet and Society that works toward "digital accessibility for persons with disabilities, access to knowledge, intellectual property rights, openness . . . internet governance, telecommunication reform, digital privacy, and cyber-security"
>
> Sarai, which for the past fifteen years has been working with academics as well as in collaboration with artistic practitioners, focusing on "the interface between cities, information, society, technology, and culture," and whose ongoing projects include "Information Infrastructures: Histories and

Contemporary Practices" and "Social Media: Contemporary Histories and Archaeologies"

my own work at Srishti, a design school that places an emphasis on making as a mode of thinking through humanities concepts while privileging historical, sociocultural, and political contextual understandings of local use and the creation of indigenous technologies, both within and without the realm of the digital.

As digital humanities work advances in the region, there is an essential need to address representation within the archive, especially given the particular nature of digital adoption by Indian users—the rapid rise of usage has coincided with the increasing centralization of the web created by technology behemoths such as Google and Facebook. The bulk of internet activity in India which occurs on social networking sites, search, and mobile apps is therefore funneled through proprietary algorithms which legislate the visibility of content and can be challenged only by the active creation of archives, a still nascent undertaking in India, due to lack of expertise, training, and interest.

There is a tendency to perceive manifestations of technology as well as of the archive in metaphorical terms, which often results in an erasure of embodied materiality of the bodies who perform, create, and populate those archives. As we continue our work in the digital humanities here in India, it is crucially important that we constantly remind ourselves that the threats of erasure that endanger corporeal bodies are readily reproduced in the digital archive unless every effort is made to guard against this infrastructural violence.

The Off-stage, Ob/scene

Technology is increasingly used by protestors to virtually represent the body and the traumas enacted on it. In early 2015, No Red Tape, a group of student activists at Columbia University, used the opportunity presented by an open day for prospective students to reiterate the neglect and callousness shown by the campus administration toward rape culture and sexual violence by projecting the message "Rape Happens Here" (Merlan) across the lintel of Columbia's iconic Butler Library. The protest embodied the obscene nature of both sexual violence and mishandling of such cases by gesturing toward the offscene, often characterized in Greek tragedy as a site of incommensurable violence. This form of protest resonates with other examples, also from 2015, of protests that represent the corporeal body with virtual projections: Spanish activists *Hologramas por la Libertad* (2015) countered the country's new draconian Citizen Safety Law that subverted its diktats that prevented people from gathering in public places, and artists' collective The Illuminator used a holographic image (Fishbein) to hold space for an illegal bust of Edward Snowden that was removed by police from a Brooklyn park.

All of these examples aim to highlight the violated body by its very absence, or by gesturing to its absent presence. Another example that we might consider is Bengaluru-based feminist activist collective Blank Noise's "I Never Ask for It" campaign that uses "testimonials of clothing" (Patheja) to universalize the experience of sexual violence, by underlining that clothes and appearance are not responsible for inducing such acts, and that the onus of blame should always be on the attacker, not on the victim.

These absent presences staged through the presentation of absence find resonance in digital ways of being, the visceral body forever destined to be mediated via code and pixel, where technology itself stands in for the body on which violence is enacted. In the context of protest, how does the gap between these modes of embodiment enact itself in order to make change?

Much of the appeal of the web in its earliest incarnations was characterized by the euphoric possibilities of escaping "meatspace," that is, the physical world, as well as transcending embodiment. Some of this radical potential was realized by spaces for online community called MOOs (short for Multi-User Domain Object-Oriented), but the promise of transcendence was short lived, and one of the web's earliest examples of sexual violence online took place as early as 1993. Journalist Julian Dibbell's chronicles of this unregulated space are now key documents to understanding the dynamics that came to characterize online interactions, and he documented the first witnessed incident of a violent cyber-rape that leaves the victim crying "posttraumatic tears" (Dibbell). Dibbell's account presciently exhorts the reader to "shut our ears momentarily to the techno-utopian ecstasies of West Coast cyberhippies and look without illusion upon the present possibilities for building, in the on-line spaces of this world, societies more decent and free than those mapped onto dirt and concrete and capital." In an intensely evocative paragraph that details the grossly violent sexual violence enacted by a "Mr Bungle" against a number of users of the LambdaMOO, readers momentarily forget that there was

> indeed no rape at all as any RL [real life] court of law has yet defined it. The actors in the drama were university students for the most part, and they sat rather undramatically before computer screens the entire time, their only actions a spidery flitting of fingers across standard QWERTY keyboards. No bodies touched. Whatever physical interaction occurred consisted of a mingling of electronic signals sent from sites spread out between New York City and Sydney, Australia. (Dibbell)

As the web evolved, such encounters grew only more ubiquitous, and incidents accrued as a consequence of #gamergate, a hate-fueled vendetta undertaken by communities of male gamers against female game designers and commentators in 2014–2015 (Stuart). This served to bring such horrors full circle, as perpetrators practiced "doxing," revealing the addresses of their targets in order to underline that threats to their personal safety no longer resided in the virtual realm, but would and could result in horrifying physical bodily harm, to them and their loved ones. Much of this violence took place on Twitter, the social networking site, which as the work of Matias and colleagues ("Reporting, Reviewing") has shown, responded to approximately half of the reports of harassment with action of suspending, deleting, or warning accounts—but the site itself does not have checks and balances in place to ensure that such harassment does not occur.

The absence of an ethics of infrastructural care by technology corporations such as Twitter, Facebook, and Google diminishes the agency of personhood to a spectral presence. Namrata Gaikwad has eloquently argued that a theory of haunting is an effective methodology to "understand the complexity of postcolonial modernity and its silences" (299), and these "silences of postcolonial modernity" can be transposed to the key of neoliberal neglect, as practiced by these hegemonic technology corporations, which regulate our actions and activities in virtual spaces demonstrating that hegemony, as Derrida says, "still organizes the repression and thus the confirmation of a haunting. Haunting belongs to every hegemony" (quoted by Gaikwad, 307). Gaikwad in her discussion of the actions of the violent, repressive Indian nation-state, with reference to their actions in Manipur (events that will be described below), writes, "We are haunted today by the violence and/or the silence of the past, the past that was forcefully; the past that was forcefully excised from public memory" (307). While digital space allows for this public memory to be restored, gaps intentionally made or otherwise to be filled, the specters of the victims of enacted violence are the ghosts in the machine, especially when relegated to the margins by the proprietary algorithms that now shape the terrain of the World Wide Web.

The Mothers of Manorama

The sustained protest of Manipuri women against the Armed Forces Special Powers Act (1958), known as AFSPA—originally instituted by the British to curb nationalist activity, enforced on several occasions by the Indian state to repress anti-national activity in "disturbed areas"—might serve as an instructive object lesson to help think through the slippage between the categories of the visible, visceral, and virtual. Manipur, a northeastern state of India that was annexed forcefully by the Indian government in 1949, has been struggling for its right to self-determination for the last fifty years, with insurgencies dating to 1964 and continuing to the present day.

The enforcement of AFSPA in order to tame anti-Indian activity has been accompanied by gross military brutality in Manipur, and its enactment has been characteristically violent of the procedures followed by the Indian army in states struggling to secede: a grotesque litany of mass massacres and horrific examples of sexual violence against women that have often ended in death. The fury and grief triggered by the particular incident of the rape and custodial death of Thangiam Manorama in 2004 found expression in the protest of a group of prominent Manipuri women activists who staged a naked protest in front of the gates of the Assam Rifles, covered only by a white sheet emblazoned with "Indian Army Rape Us," a declaration that served as both damning indictment and taunt, as they shouted "Rape us, kill us, take our flesh" (Laul).

This challenge is foretold by the raped tribal revolutionary Draupadi, in Mahashweta Devi's eponymous short story, who refuses to put on her clothes after she has been raped by armed forces, thus "refusing the disciplining power of shame scripted into the act of rape [becoming] in the words of Mahasweta's translator Gayatri Chakravarty Spivak, a 'terrifying superobject'" (Misri, 603). Judith Butler, by way of Banu Bargu, speaks of how protest in an age of seemingly decorporealized warfare (think of drones, for example) is being performed by voluntary human shields, who sacrifice, or at the very least calculate "consequences with their own bodies . . . reckoning on themselves as embodied human capital" (Butler). All of these strategies—those of the Manipuri protestors and Draupadi, and those described by Butler and Bargu—use the body to push the limits of visceral spectacle, instrumentalizing themselves in order to retaliate, and doing so by splitting the "binary of victim and agent."

Deepti Misri studies these forms of embodied protest, placing them in a tradition of feminist protest in India, and while sharing Sharon Marcus's faith in "a politics of fantasy and representation" (622), Misra is careful to acknowledge the limits of such drastic maneuvers. She echoes Butler's note of concern with regard to queer activism and resignifications: "How and where does discourse reiterate injury, such that the various efforts to recontextualise and resignify . . . meet their limit in this other, more brutal and relentless form of repetition?" (622). As Misra points out, the spectacular nature of the protest ensured media coverage, and I would add that the continued online circulation and availability of the images might after a point be seen as enacting a sort of sensationalist violence that could possibly border on fetishization.

The anxieties incumbent upon representing traumatized bodies as outlined in the examples above are provoked by questions of representation and who has the right to represent any category or movement. This question becomes particularly relevant when we consider the history of the postcolonial Indian women's movement (IWM) that battled for legitimacy in a climate that considered "feminism" as "Western and elite." Consequently, as Trishima Mitra-Kahn has described it,

> The urban IWM's feminism as a politics of representation was thus envisioned quite similarly to an anthropological endeavour to push against its middle-class leadership and composition. This phenomenon has been termed by Mary E. John as Indian feminism's "split subject" (ibid.: 128), with the activist/theorist middle-class feminist self and the socio-economically underprivileged other women as the objects of activism and enquiry. The split subjectivity of feminist

politics was "precisely the way" by which the IWM could "proclaim its Indianness" (ibid., emphasis in the original), thereby claiming its legitimacy for Indian women and simultaneously negotiating the "anxieties" around its privileged composition. (110)

The optimized conditions required for using the internet as a platform for activism, such as devices for access, sufficient bandwidth, literacy, and proficiency in English, have meant that inevitably the early incarnations of feminist activism online in India were enacted by (younger) women from the urban and affluent Indian middle class. Two campaigns in particular have been highly visible in the online sphere, garnering recognition and press coverage at both national and international levels: Blank Noise and Why Loiter. Blank Noise was started in 2003 by artist Jasmeen Patheja to record testimonies of sexual assault and harassment, to create a space for conversation around sexual violence, and to mobilize young women to participate in campaigns designed by Patheja, such as the call for "Action Heroes," which calls upon women to contribute their testimonials of street sexual harassment as a mode of resistance, challenging the conspiracies of silence that traditionally characterize such events in Indian discourse. The site and its satellites encourage conversations about sexual violence as well as providing a platform for images, tweets, and status updates about ways in which women are challenging the ownership of public space. The "Meet to Sleep" initiative, for example, encourages women to nap or sleep in parks as an act of reclamation. The lived experience of most women in India is that of being made to feel unwelcome in public space, while commuting and moving around the city, through modes of both subtle and aggressive harassment, which are also used as tactics for shaming women from "loitering" or spending time idly in outdoor spaces—the basis of the work of another activist group, Why Loiter, based on the ideas articulated by Shilpa Phadke, a feminist academic based at the Tata Institute for Social Sciences in Mumbai, in her volume of the same name. Why Loiter (both book and movement) is invested in altering the relationship of women to the cities they live in, shifting the lens from the (lack of) women's safety to that of prioritizing women's right to pleasure in experiencing, exploring, and wandering the city on their own terms. Why Loiter served as inspiration for a group of young women across the border in Pakistan to start a Tumblr blog called *Girls at Dhabas*, who started to document instances of women frequenting roadside teastalls and cafes, which are usually overwhelmingly male spaces (Sheikh).

While the spectacularization of these achievements via social media and the virtual record is hugely encouraging to women from similar backgrounds to be more confident in their ownership of public space, its iconography is largely exclusionary of women for whom such confidence is an even more distant and impossible prospect. The archive overwhelmingly features women from dominant upper-caste and upper-class backgrounds, who at least have the luxury and leisure time to loiter, or to return to their homes, as their socioeconomic class does not force them to sleep in parks or outdoor spaces without access to safe sanitation. The hashtags around the movements are predominantly English language, which could be considered exclusionary, and the founders of the movements are well aware of the paradoxes that lie at the heart of such initiatives. Indeed, Phadke and colleagues (the founders of Why Loiter) position themselves explicitly as educated, employed, middle-class urban Indian women to whom the perceived threat of sexual violence is often imagined to reside in the bodies of the lower-class male. Phadke in her later writing does reflect upon the fact that

> when we engage with violence in relation to claims on the city, it is important to see violence against women in public as being located alongside violence against the poor, Muslims, dalits, hawkers, sex workers and bar dancers. Addressing the question of women's access to public space then means engaging with realities of layered exclusion and multiple marginalisations: the exclusion of the poor, dalits, Muslims, or indeed hawkers and sex workers are not acts of benevolence towards women but part of larger more complex processes where one group of the marginalised is set against another. (Phadke, Khan, and Ranade, "Unfriendly Bodies," 52)

Despite these acknowledgments, the majority of the virtual archive is composed of a certain exclusionary narrative, which challenges the conception of an intersectional feminism that considers such struggles as interconnected. Such modes of online protest are destined to be complicit with existing corporate frameworks. Especially when relying on third-party operations such as Google, Twitter and Facebook, their message is destined to be diluted by the whims of the algorithmically inflated filter bubble, but at a more crucial and vital level, failing to represent or amplify groups other than themselves. However, as conversations around intersectionality and the digital humanities become more visible and regarded as important corollaries to those conversations around feminism and diversity in the Anglo-American academy, it might be worth considering whether the same paradigm can be usefully deployed in activism in India, especially in the digital sphere.

Nivedita Menon suggests "that the tendency when studying the 'non-West,' is to test the applicability of theory developed through 'western' experience, rather than entering into the unfamiliar conceptual field opened up by thinkers and activists in the former" (Menon). For most academics working in South Asia whose humanities training was the legacy of colonial education, this tendency will seem very familiar, and part of the work that needs to be done in South Asian/Indian digital humanities is to ensure our work is relevant to our local communities, while pursuing intellectual exchange with global communities, that is, a conversation rather than flowing only in one direction. As Menon puts it, "theory must be located" by addressing its necessarily different, difficult, and contextually specific questions.

Menon sounds a note of caution against mapping intersectionality directly onto the Indian context as, especially in the postcolonial moment, new identities emerged from different contexts forced recognition among South Asian feminists "that all political solidarities are conjunctural and historically contingent." The very specific vectors that shape the category of the Indian woman are caste, religious community, and sexuality, and definite fault lines exist between all of these, their contradictions sometimes enshrined by the Indian constitution itself. As Menon puts it, "Equal rights for women as individuals come into conflict with religious personal laws, all of which discriminate against women. Similarly, the demand for reservations in representative institutions on the basis of group identity—women, castes or religious communities—fundamentally challenges the individualist conception of political representation at the core of liberal democracy" ("Is Feminism").

Menon demonstrates these contradictions framed by the Women's Reservation Bill, for example, which while enacted as affirmative action to ensure 33 percent representation in the houses of Parliament and state legislative assemblies would in reality probably result in the presence of more elite women rather than nondominant caste (Dalit) men. Menon continues: "The challenge of course, for both feminist and Dalit politics, is to recognise that in different contexts the salience of gender and caste will vary, requiring both to proceed tentatively, each prepared to be destabilised by the other."

Dalit Women Fight

The domination of the conversation about feminist online activism from India by dominant caste groups such as Blank Noise and Why Loiter, in coverage by academics and media outlets alike, precisely highlights the intersectional gap in the IWM—and uncovers a deep irony, as there is little doubt that the figure of the Dalit woman is statistically the most likely to encounter sexual violence, and the least likely to have recourse to justice. There has been little curiosity as to where and how to discover and recover voices of Dalit women in the online sphere, possibly because of the continuing struggle of the Dalit community for a life of dignity and "bare life," education and employment, where access to the digital seems like a relatively less urgent need.

Pramod Nayar in his 2011 essay on the digital Dalit is probably the first scholar to make a concerted effort to redress this gap in the archive, by describing Dalit websites from the last ten years, and the important purpose of sites such as Dalitistan served in the documentation of caste-based violence drawn from newspaper and television reports. I agree with Nayar's assertion that these examples of documentation are important and necessary modes of reconstructing cultural memory, especially in the face of the right-wing Indian government's attempts to sanitize national history and silence disruptive narratives.

A particularly salient point that Nayar makes is the potential of the digital Dalit to connect with communities of interest that posit an alternative history of India as the history of discrimination, but one that intersects with global concerns about race and race-based discrimination. Therefore, one needs to see the self-representation and presence of Dalits in such websites as a force that enables transnationalization "by appealing to and fitting themselves into a *global historical narrative of oppression, torture and trauma*" (4, emphasis in original). This visibility has allowed for the forging of new alliances: "Dalit activism when it goes online enables a transnational subaltern project, seeking and establishing links with sympathizers, activists, NGOs, [and] transnational organizations as well as with other histories of oppression—the blacks, mainly, but also African Americans" (4). The surfacing of the hashtag #Dalitlivesmatter soon after the #BlackLivesMatter and the increasingly vocal rallying behind both causes online allowed allies in both communities to find each other and develop structures of mutual support.

One of the best examples of this transnational friendship found expression in the collaborative events organized by Dalit Women Fight (DWF) with grassroots #BlackLivesMatter activists in 2016. DWF, founded by Thenmozhi Soundarajan, is a visual chronicle of the activities of the All India Dalit Mahila Adhikar Manch (AIDMAM), an association of Dalit women activists, who organized a month-long *yatra* or campaign, traveling through India, visiting every state, and holding public meetings where they undertook the Ambedkarite tenets of "educate—organize—agitate" (a phrase coined by economist and reformer B. R. Ambedkar, one of India's most influential Dalit thinkers). They worked in collaboration with local groups to publicize the Scheduled Caste/Scheduled Tribe Prevention of Atrocities Act, and to help provide recourse to justice for caste-based violence, as well as support for survivors. The Manch organized events to take these claims to institutional authorities, in the face of opposition and aggression, lending solidarity and knowledge to communities who might have not felt empowered enough to assert themselves without the support of this larger network.

DWF presents an alternative visual narrative to one that has historically accrued to that of the Dalit female body, one of abjection and victimhood, and the digital archive has been considerably altered by the efforts of Soundarajan and others to document the Dalit women's movement. Dalit grassroots activist Manisha Mashaal, who has been active in the movement since 2005, describes how significant the ownership and representation of Dalit identity online have been:

> When the group was started, we were not avid users of Facebook, Instagram, or Twitter. It was in 2013 that we first used the hashtag #DalitWomenFight. We took the Yatra to USA as well. We spoke in about 22 universities about our struggles. We talked about how Dalit women are suffering and being discriminated against. . . . Yes, definitely there has been some transformation. Earlier the media used to remain totally mute on our issues. In all these years, we took workshops trying to educate people on how social media and mainstream media is not benefiting us. It was not helping our cause, our struggle. So we

endorsed the idea of creating and furthering our own voice through the same media, but by creating our own counter media platforms. We always knew that unless we do not get that space, our problems will not be known to the wider public. So the Dalit movement that was taking shape then has benefited a lot from social media, because Dalit students have started using these platforms for themselves and their community. That way, we can find out what is happening in Uttar Pradesh, in Haryana, in Bihar and other states. The Dalit movement is shaped by this transformation. The women's struggle in Dalit movement is only beginning to find its space, and we are working on that. Dalit Women Fight is one such step towards the liberation of Dalit women. (Alok)

The impact of how the increasing presence of Dalit voices in the online sphere has changed conversations about caste has been the basis of the work currently being done by Anushka Shah and her colleagues at the Center for Civic Media at MIT. Shah's work examines the period between July 2015 and August 2016, looking primarily at Indian English-language news media, which historically have seen a dearth of reporting around Dalit and nondominant case issues, due to both their target audience (urban, middle- to upper-class or caste) and the inadequate representation of Dalits in newsrooms. Using the Center for Civic Media's MediaCloud to search across 677 English-language sources, Shah utilized a specific citation metric to measure impact: "The final metric used is not the total number of times a story or source got linked to, but from how many unique media it got linked to, i.e. if a *Times of India* story was cited by five different publications while a *Scroll.in* was cited five times by one publication, the *Times of India story* will be given a measure of 5 while the *Scroll.in* story will remain at a measure of 1" ("MIT MediaCloud").

Shah found that the data skewed interestingly from expectations: the three major newspapers by subscription figures featured in the list of the top ten, but surprisingly, *Indian Express,* which does not feature in the top ten according to subscription figures, was the most cited paper online. The other significant finding was the presence of *Roundtableindia.co.in,* a Dalit-issue blog that was hitherto not at all part of mainstream media discourse.

Despite these encouraging shifts, sites like *Roundtable,* while including women on their roster of writers, do not focus exclusively on gender issues, and the presence of patriarchal attitudes even within the community has persuaded women to create their own resources such as *Savari,* a site that provides a platform for Adivasi, Bahujan, and Dalit women and encourages cross-border conversations with women from Bangladesh, Nepal, Pakistan, and Sri Lanka.

Dalit Women Fight undertook a tour in the United States visiting college campuses and other venues over the last year, where they explained how the practice of untouchability circumscribed the Dalit experience, and the harrowing incidents of violence experienced by members of the community, especially and overwhelmingly by women. Members of Black Lives Matter and Say Her Name who lent support and shared strategies with DWF were struck by the similarities between the two movements. Brianna Gibson, a Black Lives Matter movement leader in the Bay Area, remarked, "So, someone saying you know, 'We're post-caste,' versus 'post-racial.' It's like 'Wow, that's exactly the same thing.' Or they'll tell you, 'You're being divisive'" (Paul).

The assumptions that underpin "postracial" thinking are challenged in Alexander Weheliye's radical rereading of Giorgio Agamben's concept of "bare life," addressing how the latter's scholarship fails to theorize race and racism as part of that conceptual framework, and the role played by embodiment in that framework. As Weheliye puts it, "How is a category such as bare life embodied and lived?" Weheliye takes issue with the notion that we are now "posthuman" and urges for a reconsideration of what it means to be human from the vantage point of the slave body, the colonized body, and I would add to this, the indigenous or marginalized body which for our particular context is more often than not the caste-ridden body. This sort of biopolitical racism is destined to embed and repeat itself time and again in the face of, as Nancy Fraser puts it, "a cruel twist of fate" that has led to "the movement for women's liberation [that] has (to) become entangled in a dangerous liaison with neoliberal efforts to build a free-market society." The "racial innocence," to use Weheliye's words, is uncomfortably present in our digital efforts at feminist activism that by and large exclude Dalit and other disadvantaged, marginalized bodies.

In her important work on the Mothers of Manorama, Paromita Chakravarti articulates how the neoliberal state directly colludes in violence unleashed against women, which, as she says,

> is intimately connected to the contemporary development policies of the Indian state. Following the liberalisation and globalisation of the economy, the Indian state is withdrawing from public sector spending. Abdicating its developmental responsibilities it is emerging as a broker for multinational corporations, securing them cheap land, offering business concessions and setting up low-tax Special Economic Zones. . . . There is a new legitimisation of state violence in the name of development and progress that gathers strength from the rhetoric deployed in the U.S. invasion of Iraq, justifying violence as a legitimate means of ensuring democracy, even peace and development. (53)

Chakravarti's concerns find deep resonance in the digital space, especially after Narendra Modi's rise to power in 2014, accomplished in some part by the "Make in India" and "Digital India" initiatives that formed the cornerstone of his prime ministerial campaign. However, while the ambitious promises of the Digital India initiative to empower rural and poorer communities are languishing, Modi has been keenly courting tech superpowers in Silicon Valley, ensuring that venture capital, which largely benefits the Indian middle class, continues to flow into the country (Goel).

This position, coupled with the government's actions that demonstrate increased intolerance toward marginalized groups on the basis of religion and caste, creates a climate where protest needs must be acknowledged not as the necessary recourse of those who do not have access to other means. As Chakravarti puts it, "a form of protest that is rooted in local movements, rituals and experiences, [which] opens up the possibility of going beyond . . . global paradigms, which fall back on the structures of law and the state for delivery" (51). The Mothers of Manorama deployed a new political language of mockery and subversion which undermined the rhetoric of a protective nation or a welfarist state, which deployed the body as a technology, a way of producing knowledge that could even be considered posthuman in its demand to reconsider the body on its own terms as something other than the meaning foisted upon it by the patriarchal nation-state. Dalit feminist activism seeks to bridge the divide between offline and online worlds by using its representation and archiving of the embodied movement to redress gaps in the digital archive as well as that of national historical narrative.

It is essential that those of us working in the digital humanities are always alert to the ways in which regimes of knowledge and representation are reproduced in the online sphere. As Jasbir Puar puts it, there is much more here at stake than personal politics: "limitations of intersectional frameworks go far beyond rethinking its contextual specificity—this is not only about epistemological incongruency but more importantly, ontological irreducibility" ("I Would Rather Be"). In order to enact a more heterotopic reality, it is the responsibility of digital humanists to build tools and strategies to transform the bodies of the machines that watch over us with loving grace to meaningfully counter the violence being done to our own.

Bibliography

Alok, Nupur Priti. "'I'm Going to Live a Leader's Life and Die a Leader Too': Manisha Mashaal." *Feminism in India,* September 21, 2016. https://feminisminindia.com/2016/09/21/interview-dalit-woman-manisha-mashaal/.

Bargu, Banu. "Human Shields." *Contemporary Political Theory,* advance online publication, March 19, 2013. doi:10.1057/cpt.2013.1.

Butler, Judith. "Human Shield." Lecture, recorded February 4, 2015, London School of Economics. http://www.lse.ac.uk/website-archive/newsAndMedia/videoAndAudio/channels/publicLecturesAndEvents/player.aspx?id=2859.

Chakravarti, Paromita. "Reading Women's Protest in Manipur: A Different Voice?" *Journal of Peacebuilding & Development* 5, no. 3 (2014): 47–60.

De Beauvoir, Simone *The Second Sex.* London: Jonathan Cape, 1953.

Dibbell, Julian. "A Rape in Cyberspace: How an Evil Clown, a Haitian Trickster Spirit, Two Wizards, and a Cast of Dozens Turned a Database into a Society." First published in *The Village Voice,* December 23, 1993. http://juliandibbell.com/texts/bungle_vv.html.

Fishbein, Rebecca. "Illicit Edward Snowden Statue Replaced by Illicit Edward Snowden Hologram." *Gothamist,* April 7, 2015. http://gothamist.com/2015/04/07/edward_snowden_hologram.php.

Fraser, Nancy. "How Feminism Became Capitalism's Handmaiden–and How to Reclaim It." *The Guardian,* October 14, 2013. https://www.theguardian.com/commentisfree/2013/oct/14/feminism-capitalist-handmaiden-neoliberal.

Gaikwad, Namrata, "Revolting Bodies, Hysterical State: Women Protesting the Armed Forces Special Powers Act (1958)." *Contemporary South Asia* 17, no. 3 (2009): 299–311.

Gajjala, Radhika. *Cyberculture and the Subaltern.* Lanham, Md.: Lexington: Lexington Books, 2012.

Gajjala, Radhika. *Cyber Selves: Feminist Ethnographies of South Asian Women.* Walnut Creek, Calif.: AltaMira, 2004.

Goel, Vindu. "Narendra Modi, Indian Premier, Courts Silicon Valley to Try to Ease Nation's Poverty." *New York Times,* September 27, 2015. https://www.nytimes.com/2015/09/28/technology/narendra-modi-prime-minister-of-india-visits-silicon-valley.html.

Haraway, Donna. *Simian, Cyborgs, and Women: The Reinvention of Nature.* London: Routledge, 1991.

Hologramas Por La Libertad. April 2015. Accessed December 27, 2015. http://www.hologramasporlalibertad.org/en.html#home.

Laul, Revati. "'We Stripped and Shouted, 'Indian Army, Rape Me!' It Was the Right Thing to Do.'" *Tehelka* 10, no. 8 (February 23, 2013). http://www.tehelka.com/we-stripped-and-shouted-indian-army-rape-me-it-was-the-right-thing-to-do/.

Liu, Alan. "Drafts for *Against the Cultural Singularity* (book in progress)." Alan Liu's website, May 2, 2016. http://liu.english.ucsb.edu/drafts-for-against-the-cultural-singularity/.

Matias, J. N., A. Johnson, W. E. Boesel, B. Keegan, J. Friedman, and C. DeTar. "Reporting, Reviewing, and Responding to Harassment on Twitter." *Women, Action, and the Media,* May 13, 2015. http://womenactionmedia.org/twitter-report.

Menon, Nivedita. "Is Feminism about 'Women'? A Critical View on Intersectionality from India." *International Viewpoint,* May 18, 2015. http://internationalviewpoint.org/spip.php?article4038.

Merlan, Anna. "Columbia Student Protesters Project 'Rape Happens Here' on Library." *Jezebel,* April 13, 2015. http://jezebel.com/columbia-student-protesters-project-rape-happens-here-o-1697523093.

Misri, Deepti. "'Are You a Man?': Performing Naked Protest in India." *Signs* 36, no. 3 (Spring 2011): 603–25.

Mitra-Kahn, Trishima. "Offline Issues, Online Lives? The Emerging Cyberlife of Feminist Politics in Urban India." In *New South Asian Feminisms: Paradoxes and Possibilities,* edited by Srila Roy, 108–30. London: Zed Books, 2012.

Nayar, Pramod. "The Digital Dalit: Subalternity and Cyberspace." *Sri Lanka Journal of the Humanities* 37, no. 1–2 (2011): 69–74. http://dx.doi.org/10.4038/sljh.v37i1-2.7204.

Patheja, Jasmeen. *Blank Noise* (blog), 2006. http://blog.blanknoise.org/2006/.

Paul, Sonia. "From Black Lives Matter, Activists for India's Discriminated Dalits Learn Tactics to Press for Dignity." *PRI's The World,* November 8, 2015. https://www.pri.org/stories/2015-11-08/black-lives-matter-activists-indias-discriminated-dalit-learn-tactics-press.

Phadke, Shilpa, Sameera Khan, and Shilpa Ranade. "Unfriendly Bodies, Hostile Cities: Reflections on Loitering and Gendered Public Space." *Economic and Political Weekly* 47, no. 39 (September 28, 2013): 50–59.

Phadke, Shilpa, Sameera Khan, and Shilpa Ranade. *Why Loiter: Women and Risk in Mumbai Streets.* Delhi: Penguin Books, 2011.

Puar, Jasbir. "'I Would Rather Be a Cyborg than a Goddess': Intersectionality, Assemblage, and Affective Politics." *Transversal: Inventions,* January 2011. http://www.eipcp.net/transversal/0811/puar/en.

Shah, Anushka. "MIT MediaCloud: Conversation on Dalit and Caste Issues in Indian English News Media." Unpublished research, shared privately with author, 2016.

Sheikh, Imaan. "Here's Why South Asian Women Are Uploading Photos of Themselves at Dhabas." *BuzzFeed,* August 10, 2015. https://www.buzzfeed.com/imaansheikh/girls-at-dhabas?utm_term=.bgN9w61GJ#.xpblWjNBG.

Stuart, Keith. "Zoe Quinn: All Gamergate Has Done Is Ruined People's Lives." *The Guardian,* December 3, 2014. https://www.theguardian.com/technology/2014/dec/03/zoe-quinn-gamergate-interview.

Weheliye, Alexander. "Claiming Humanity: A Black Critique of the Concept of Bare Life." Recording, Alexander Weheliye in conversation with Leopold Lambert. Chicago, July 28, 2014. https://soundcloud.com/the-funambulist/alexander-weheliye-claiming.

PART IV
AFFECT

PART IV][Chapter 13

Ev-Ent-Anglement

A Script to Reflexively Extend Engagement by Way of Technologies

BRIAN GETNICK, ALEXANDRA JUHASZ,
AND LAILA SHEREEN SAKR (VJ UM AMEL)

Asynchronous contributions by project participants and anthology editors. Reentry by Jih-Fei Cheng.

ALEX JUHASZ AND BRIAN GETNICK (Google docs—September 2017). To make the most of the expansive possibilities of writing asynchronously, collectively, and responsively, we include our editors' comments, our own growing and interactive dialogue, earlier fragments made by Ev-Ent-Anglement project participants, and the later words of scholar Jih-Fei Cheng about his experiences of the Ev-Ent-Anglement.

KIM KNIGHT (peer reviewer, enters through WordPress peer-review blog). The essay does not have an argument but attempts to make an intervention. It asks us to think about how we define DH, how we capture or archive the ephemera of the rich collaboration that we so often emphasize, and what it means to perform scholarship. I think trying to sharpen things into a more essay-like manner would be antithetical to the goals of the piece.

ALEX AND BRIAN. Thanks Kim for that explication and many other helpful comments. We particularly liked how you aligned our project with "weird DH panels" held at recent MLAs. You're right, this is less an essay "about" Ev-Ent-Anglements and feminist DH and more a script toward another imagined re-staging that would best perform our stakes. We want our asynchronous dialogue to *enact* many of our commitments to feminist DH, including what you refer to as our "explicit articulation of the politics" of format, platform, and processes of production including ethical and self-reflexive collaborations that attend to power, place, training, method, and most critically, affect.

BRIAN (a little later). . . . and a burgeoning performance theory coming from observations of the performance practices fostered at PAM, the theater and residency space I direct (and within which the final Ev-Ent-Anglement was staged). Here's a trailer of PAM's first season to give you a sense of what we do there.[1]

[203

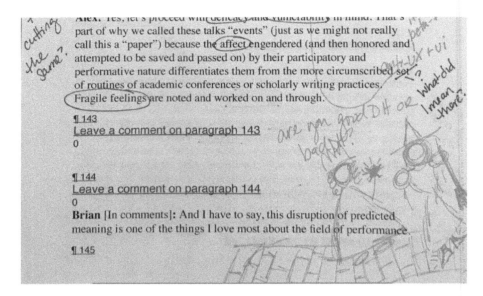

Figure 13.1. The good witch/bad witch of DH both live in our project, by K. Knight.

ALEX (coming in just as we hit our first deadline for submission to our editors). I remembered as I was falling asleep last night, two previous feminist DH writing projects where editors' comments were included as a way to present, honor, and theorize the process of writing within activist communities and collaborative intellectual enterprises.[2] We bring to new projects our own histories of thinking and production, a learned and changing operational compass that centers us even when it goes unspoken or unremembered.

BRIAN We want to acknowledge that this "timeline" of interjections, collaborative theorizing, and transparent editorial comments are remixed and not chronological. We took in what made us *speak back*.

LAILA SHEREEN SAKR (enters from off screen from Santa Barbara). I write asynchronously—like a glitch in an automated system, but that is the sort of freedom that this Google Doc enables, right?

ALEX. Yes, Laila, a human glitch. A wrinkle in the system that adds your knowledge and feelings through time management regimes borne from a new job and three little kids.

LAILA. As introduction, I am a person in real life. I have had many radical and different experiences that I slip in and out of quite naturally. Hyperconscious of this fluidity, ten year ago I created a moniker for my cyborg self as a conceptual art project. VJ Um Amel is an Arabic-speaking cyborg I perform online, on screens and stages, in art galleries and print—across digital media.[3] She is also the creator of the R-Shief media system, and she is my own art practice.

Among the interventions I make while performing VJ (video jockey) Um Amel (Arabic for "Mother of Hope") are these two: First, I resist normative identity formation. I would rather say, "I live in California," than "I am Californian"—thereby defining agency through one's actions (or their negation) rather than through signifier or label. The second intervention is the digital performance of an Arabic-speaking cyborg, a character defined by the actions it is programmed to take rather than the shade of its chrome. Cyborgs are intelligent machines who use digital logic in their robotics. And so in this document, I will speak in both voices—sometimes performing cyborg (VJ), other times performing myself (Laila).

Rebooting cyborg. . . .

Ev-Ent-Anglement Histories and Statements

VJ UM AMEL. I would like to tell a bit of the history of the Ev-Ent-Anglement project as I know of it. My entrance into the script was in early 2015. I was engaged in an online praxis with Ricardo Dominguez categorizing a series of posts on Facebook using the hashtag "#Deeptagging" as a signal that data is excess, and in its excess data is porn. Ricardo and I started this online performance intervention in January 2015 with this Facebook post with an article from *Salon*, "Why Porn Is Exploding in the Middle East," where he wrote, "Data is porn! Porn is data! Nothing as erotic as burning access/excess data! And what would my big toes have to say about it? (They seem to be tapping away today) ;-)."[4] There began a long and rich dialogue between Ricardo and me in the comments.[5] This daily practice of posting and #Deeptagging continues through today and is in itself a theoretical conjecture, a praxis in the form of sharing, posting, and commenting. It was within this dialogue with Ricardo where I shared a link to Alex's Ev-Ent-Anglement project and an initial thread was thereby sewn in.

LAILA. Not long after, in early 2015, Alex FB [Facebook] messaged me and invited me into the project in the most open and generous of ways.

ALEX. We had never met. I thought I was writing to someone in the Middle East. When, after a brief exchange, I understood that VJ Um Amel was Laila Sakr, a doctoral student at USC, I asked her over for lunch.

LAILA. We met for the first time in person in Pasadena. I would schedule doctor appointments before or after meeting with Alex—stitching in another locative experience.

 VJ Um Amel Here it is: #ev-ent-anglement - an experiment in digital embodied collective feminist media praxis http://ev-ent-anglement.com

 ev-ent-anglement | an experiment in digital embodied collective feminist media praxis

EV-ENT-ANGLEMENT.COM

January 18, 2015 at 8:04am · Like · Remove Preview

Figure 13.2. Screenshot of Facebook comment by VJ Um Amel.

Feminist in approach, Alex offered a myriad of collaborative possibilities for us to work together in this affective feminist media praxis of cutting/pasting+bleeding.

ALEX. The idea of cut/paste+bleed has been central to this project. At its most basic it signals that our engagements with digital material (cut/paste), hardwired into our machines, hands, and minds, carry hidden consequences (the bleed). This is what the Ev-Ent-Anglement attempts to see and feel. What is more, Laila was coming to my house after seeing her doctor after a surgical procedure. She was experiencing and then sharing with me her own cutting, bleeding, and healing. She was often sore and always tired and hungry when she arrived.

LAILA. We would reach decisions about the shape and form and process of our collaboration after jaunty discussions accompanied by coffee, tea, salads, and cakes. We wanted to develop a methodological approach that would be at once becoming, affective, collaborative, performative, and real-time: a feminist media praxis approach to shared knowledge production.

Ev-Ent-Anglement had already occurred at international talks given by Alex in Utrecht, Delhi, Dublin, and would later happen in Montreal and Los Angeles, with my participation. At each location, she invited the audience to "cut/paste+bleed" themselves into the project about these themes and processes by way of social media posts that cut into the larger online project. So there were already many social media accounts for the project (a WordPress blog, and Instagram and Twitter accounts).

ALEX. We were aware how these platforms and their formats were patriarchal neoliberal goldmines based on cut/paste aesthetics and formats that hide the bleed. Laila and I tried to think through and see past all this as she built new homes and methods for sharing and showing our data and processes.

LAILA. I went on to build several more websites (eventanglement.com and cells.eventanglement.com).[6] My role was to understand the project's database and create a data visualization of the many gathered social media posts from previous Ev-Ent-Anglement performances, as well as images, quotes, and even performances related to Alex's research process, and then to prepare an online repository and enactment for future performances—both as lectures by Alex Juhasz (professor) and later still as a collaborative performance with VJ Um Amel (cyborg) and Brian Getnick (performer).

ALEX (cuts into the Google doc to add more "DH thinking" on request of several reviewers 2:11 p.m. November 20). We spent a lot of time thinking about the (relatively small) scale of the database that I had created of digital fragments gifted to me by participants in the project. Laila came to the project as a scholar and artist who had worked on massive datasets (tweets from the Arab Spring). To her mind, there was a relative intimacy and cohesion to the Ev-Ent-Anglement's objects even as they were, in their volume and diversity, always skittering out of my control (as they and we do here).[7]

JACQUELINE WERNIMONT (writes into the Google doc 11:38 p.m. May 17). I think you might productively situate this as not-DH but entangled with DH if that made sense. Alternatively, one approach might be to say a bit about why this makes sense as a final iteration—why does it make sense to the three of you to include this work in this way here? I find the provocations of performance here really useful and don't want to flatten the productive difference between what you're doing here.

BRIAN. This version of the ongoing google Doc is what in DH parlance? A hypertextual extension of the event and performance on that evening at PAM, November 8, 2015?

I also think it's important to note here that the process of generating the material of this text felt very alive at certain points. Now, in my final sweep of the doc (November 26, 2017, New York City), it feels like a surrendering of the liveness that we tried to represent in different ways graphically in earlier drafts of this doc to a cleaner, condensed (if you can believe it) format. I have to say that feels fine.

KIM KNIGHT (in a print out of our essay that she scrawled comments and drawings on, scanned again and shared with us via Dropbox). Seems like more than an extension. A refiguring? amplification? re-situation?

ALEX. It's a multitemporal, collaborative investigation of learning and making about the interpenetration of the lived and the digital, humans and machines, art and theory.

LAILA. As with many DH projects, this Ev-Ent-Anglement is multimodal. It is interesting to consider the differences between Alex's participatory Ev-Ent-Anglement lectures, the online websites and databases of social media that underwrite them, my VJ performance at PAM in Highland Park, and this publication. In each iteration, we managed to trespass or challenge formal standards. Each of the productions has followed a similar methodological approach—one that is in the process of becoming, affective, collaborative, performative, and at least at outset in real-time.

I am reminded of a humanities publication project published by Duke University Press in 2013. *Speculate This!* was authored by an "uncertain commons, a group of scholars, mediaphiles, and activists who explore the possibilities of collaborative intellectual labor."[8] They remain anonymous as a challenge to the current norms of evaluating, commodifying, and institutionalizing intellectual labor.

In their collaborative discussion on the global practice of "affirmative speculation," this group of anonymous scholars drafted a manifesto. What are the affordances offered by stating manifestos and writing collaboratively in the context of imagining new theories around media praxis or theorizing about practice?

JACQUE (JACQUELINE WERNIMONT). Having now read through, I wonder if the authors/editors will want to put in a note at the beginning to orient readers—I've struggled with this in editing pieces in the past for DH audiences. The "artist statement" does a particular kind of translating/situating work and you all may or may not want that work done. Let's talk.

LAILA AND VJ. Yes, "let's talk!" That is the approach. :)

ALEX. An "artist's statement" follows in the next paragraph, I hope that's okay, Jacque. The performance at PAM that we discuss soon, and then this iteration of the project, both ask, in form, what it feels like, and how things work, when experience, ideas, or the self is not delivered effortlessly, linearly, and steadily by way of mediating technologies.

ALEX (delivers the Artist Statement [at last!]).

What is Ev-Ent-Anglement? We wonder how affective fragments move. An Ev-Ent-Anglement uses two hyphens as highly visible stitches suturing events with entanglements: Ev-Ent-Anglement. We use performance and technology to further entangle occasions and communities outside the logics of buying and selling. Together with technology we mix up our heres and theres, now and thens, mes and yous. We experiment in digital sometimes-embodied/sometimes-online/sometimes–on paper collective feminist media praxis. We want to show/feel/understand how these are linked but discrete ways of being and knowing rendered through and sometimes outside of digital technologies.

Using performance, technology, networks, cinema, tweets, photos, people, and their digital fragments we cut+paste evidence of past events into live ones and also into an ongoing digital record of some of what was entangled here and there. The bleed is what can't be contained. We try to see, know, show, and feel that with new formats based on other logics.

This iteration of Ev-Ent-Anglement cut/paste+bleeds fragments from five previous events that were experienced in 2014 and 2015, respectively, in Utrecht, Delhi, Dublin, Montreal, and Los Angeles (at the performance space, PAM, as an interactive, collaborative iteration staged by Brian, Alex, and VJ). Now we are in a computer, cutting+pasting collectively on a shared Google doc before dropping it all onto paper. Our attempts to know and love each other and then show this, our hope that the power of process and place can be articulated outside of its first lived iteration, is the bleed: our experiences, feelings, and ideas as useful surplus that we hope to see and share.

The first four events were billed as academic talks that anticipated and also generated the last event held in an art-space, PAM, billed as a performance.

Documenting the Ev-Ent-Anglement

BRIAN. This document is another reflection on the Ev-Ent-Anglement at PAM, the performance venue, and is also a continuation of the performance and the conversation that initiated and ends it.

ALEX. PAM is a computer that stores and processes most of its data as embodied, interactive, and live exhibition. Brian runs the space with his own juice and also provides many of its design flourishes (he's an amazing seamstress), but if you get a residency there, as did Laila and I, part of your work in the space is to reprogram it anew, as you'd like to use it and configure it (you begin with an empty blue box, so to speak).

VJ. Are you saying that PAM is a computer and a space—is the leap to understand the formal principles of a venue as designed computation affecting the data bodies that traverse through it? Indeed PAM is a physical place, a magical place in Highland Park for "artists to research their performance practice." If PAM is a computer, then I suggest Brian is its cyborg—he flows like the tapestries and fabrics on set, weaving, stitching, ev-ent-angling.

ALEX. Oh Laila. This is why I love collaborating with you . . .

LAILA (sending kiss bitmoji). Is this publication we are collectively authoring really a performance script; or is it more like a GitHub repository; or a feminist manifesto? Whatever the answer, I suggest this method is a theoretical intervention.

BRIAN. I am starting to think that this document in its process is actually an extension of PAM space, or perhaps what we're doing now mirrors what I want to see happen at PAM: people working in different disciplines, converging, sharing practices, and naming the "what is" (that is to say, not postponing understanding to a "will be") that crops up in the process. And we have to name what happens when we work together, when we encounter difference, because so much gets lost in assuming people working in adjacent fields understand a common vocabulary. ("Affect" is a good example.)

ALEX. As much as I "perform," I've never named my practice as such and am not particularly well schooled in performance history, theory, or studies. At PAM I was a nervous interloper worried I would be exposed as undertrained. I felt both humble and curious. Collaborative experiences with others can disalign power that more typically encrusts with age, rank, gender, training, practice, and vetting.

BRIAN. PAM is not a totalizing system within which this fluid conversation takes place. You two have a working relationship that precedes PAM (as do Alex and I), and collaborative writing happens across the spectrum of fields. But there might be a newness to considering a performance space like PAM—very grounded in providing space and time to bodies in physical proximity—as a theoretical space.

I'm glad to be a part of this Feminist DH Praxis at this exact stage of PAM's evolution coming between its first two years of residencies, space alterations, workshops and lectures and the current moment where I have to articulate a method, ethic and vision for PAM's future. Can we turn to the foundations of Ev-Ent-Anglement as part of our process?

BRIAN (cutting in November 13, 2017). Since writing the above bit, I've collectivized, inviting five other curators to take on programming starting in 2018. Our economic model is transparent and very "sweet" as PAM curator Tim Reid says. That is, because we are still technically a business, and are not reliant on grants, we can say to artists we work with, and to audiences who come through the door, that they are a foundational resource in supplying time and space to artists making new, long-form performance work.

Theoretical Foundations

ALEX. Two divides—theory/practice and art/scholarship—have loomed large in my career, but mostly, or often, through my commitment to transcend their rather silly separations. Most humanities professors, and many of our students, think that they don't engage in "practice" because protocols of training, vetting, and professional output produce "scholars," those who are activated by others' practice, as if the accepted forms of our own output (talking, teaching, writing) aren't practice themselves, or as if "practitioners" too don't respond to, analyze, or build upon the work of those before them. Given that everyone *practices,* this stupid divide is essentially about material, methods, reception, and vetting.

This is to say that "theory"—the realm of philosophers and professors—is made with words through rigorous reflection and connection so as to be received by those already in the know. But of course, many people theorize and the form for this practice can be either prescribed by regimes of tradition or it can be creative, inventive, and well outside those traditions, thereby challenging protocols of knowledge and power.

LAILA. This is one of the threads that draws us collaborators together—an engagement of media practice beyond, within, across and in the hyphens between academic categories of knowing. I am in emphatic agreement with you here, Alex. Most academic units devoted to the production and study of media observe fairly narrow definitions of theory and practice. Programs "on the practice side"—usually BFA and MFA—are typically devoted to pursuits such as film or video making, screenwriting, animation, and game design; while "on the theory side" we find more traditional academic programs—usually BA, MA, and PhD—devoted to Media Studies that are derived from methodologies in the Humanities. Good faith efforts are often made to encourage—or even compel—students on either side of this otherwise unforgiving divide to take classes outside their primary area of interest in order to gain familiarity with the activities and concerns of "the other side." Students specializing in theory or history may have the opportunity to make a film during their coursework, for example, while students who are makers will be encouraged to know something of the history and theoretical concerns of their chosen medium. As anyone teaching in these programs can attest, it is not uncommon for such attempts at cross-pollination to end up simply reinforcing traditional divides between scholarship and creative practice.

This project aims to disrupt this binary at the most basic level.

ALEX. We reinforce connections over divides.

DOM OLIVERI (assistant professor at the department of Media and Culture Studies at Utrecht University tweets from Montreal). Learning/practicing (2): suspension as a methodology // proximities

ALEX. "Practice," by which I think we mean "art," or also sometimes "making things that you can hold or touch or see or feel that are not expressed in the format of scholarly writing," often does all these things. Thus its "unique" identity—its difference from theory or learning—also seems to reside in its material, method, reception, and vetting. Artists work with things, including the body, through a creative method for an audience who judges the work by affective/creative standards of "suspension" (of disbelief?). We strive for the art/scholarship divide to surrender through our methods, beliefs, and writing experiments in this "script" and in other hybrid teaching/writing/artistic/technological spaces we have inhabited together.

LAILA. This is a critical point. Is the idea of "practice" too broad? And where does creativity come into play? Where is the artfulness? And as some of my colleagues have expressed, how do we assess this "creative practice" for academic/professional review?

Are the review standards the same for scholar-practitioners as for other artists? Or scholars? Or is the practice a research methodology? I ask these questions, rather than making statements because I think all are possible.

DOM OLIVERI (tweets in Montreal). Learning/practicing (1): the difference between spontaneous emotions and educated feelings.

ALEX. When I think and make and work like a "practitioner" (and artist! A performer!), I give myself permission to engage kinds of playfulness, looseness, and sociality—"spontaneous emotions and educated feelings"—that honor parts of my brain and body, and those of my interlocutors and audience, that are not as formal, prescriptive, or rational as those activated by my "academic" work.

JACQUE (in Google comments). Thank you for a great articulation of the practice "problem"—I'm intrigued to see playfulness here given our convos about play at FemTechNet, but I'm also delighted.

ALEX. I try to write and teach "artfully" even when I am being a "scholar." This can shake up things and people (students, readers, coauthors). I was drawn to both of you, Laila and Brian, as people and professionals, because I see this quaking transcendence as a central commitment within your work as well.

VJ. I like "agitational fashion" because in many ways that is my aesthetic as a digital art maker—a counterculture glitching the automated practice. To further transcend binaries, I can imagine designing a data visualization that would represent the order or timeline when each of us wrote into this collective piece. A digital media production or data visualization "practice" could provide this sort of creative agitation and disruption.

ALEX. I would love to imagine a rendering of this Google doc as a video or a performance: thus pushed into time and space and allowing proximity to each other and our audience and participants. Ev-Ent-Anglement is always curious about the affective disturbance of digital corruptions of time and space, how time and place become fragile, unhinged, and active through our easy, rote actions and habits within the corporate-owned social networks we inhabit, as well as those we might engender in response. That's a mouthful! It's probably easier to understand through creative practices: like our websites or performances.

BRIAN. Within the field of contemporary performance, there does exist a difference, maybe not a binary, between performance work that fulfills concepts-theorized and performance work that postpones the annunciation of its concepts until after, and sometimes very long after, the initial ideas have been played out, or tested, in the crucible of live performance. In truth, I don't think there is ever a performance that perfectly fulfills the concepts it proposes. Performance is the only art form that is simultaneously co-created by performer and audience, the only one that relies on the physical presence of the audience in order to exist. It's cognitively anarchic.

ALEX. In this respect, our writing here is more like a performance than most (scholarly) writing.

VJ (interjecting). Is the performance necessarily real-time?

BRIAN. No, or rather, this document is an artifact of another, very live textual exchange between the three of us vis-à-vis Skype and Google docs and largely this essay is a series of layered, delayed interjections, a very different temporal reality than speaking. The following remarks were written by me a week ago:

. . . Quoting Hans-Thies Lehman in the introduction to his seminal "Postdramatic Theater": "The emission and reception of signs and signals takes place simultaneously. The theater performance turns the behavior on stage and in the auditorium into a joint text, a 'text' even if there is no spoken dialogue on stage or between actors and audience." And later, bear with me and Hans for a moment longer ". . . in theater the text is subject to the same laws and dislocations as the visual, audible, gestic and architectonic theatrical signs."

Now, I know that an Ev-Ent-Anglement was staged in PAM, a performance art space, not the European theater that Lehman conjures in his model. But I think, in order to give you some context for why I value the dissonance between the ideas proposed by Alex in Ev-Ent-Anglement and the ideas and concepts that were produced by the event of (her) performativity, I have to situate the kind of performance art that is being made at PAM within the current context of Los Angeles, a city which does not have an intact tradition of experimental theater being staged within proscenium theater spaces.

I believe that the kind of work that is being enabled at PAM is connected to what Lehman maps out as the field of "postdramatic" (which does not mean without or beyond a connection to the history and uses of drama, and since drama, in Lehman's terms, refers to the primacy of the text, you can also think of drama as a container for theory) because each "sign"—the movement of the performer, the costume she wears, the way she sounds, her position in space, the installation of scenic elements (or projections) and of course the text she speaks—can be latched onto and interpreted in as many different ways as there are people in the audience.

I would say that a counterpoint to the kind of performance work I foster at PAM is a vein of performance that is mainly concerned with the maintenance of concepts at the expense of an awareness of the materiality of what makes live performance itself and how that materiality might productively disrupt or contradict initial concepts and theories. The performance of Ev-Ent-Anglement very effectively laid out the concepts that were at stake (cutting/pasting+bleeding), and even laid out a procedure for the maintaining of their primacy (the cutting of the words of earlier participants by PAM attendees, the reading of those cut-outs as scripts for the PAM performance, then discussion about this process as the performance and later in this document). But then, very quickly, as in two steps away from the podium, some of those initial concepts fell to the wayside. Affect—or a detailed physicality that negotiates feelings and thoughts—became, as hoped, the primary performative material for registering the dismantling of the ideas and scholarship laid out by Alex. These will emerge later in Part 2: Performing The Bleed in this conversation.

ALEX. Yes, Brian, as a performer (and not as a typical writer, who does that work alone), one must read the affect in the room and use it as a medium that can be registered and then amplified by one's body. Working with you before the show, I realized that what I knew about performance, my "training," was as a teacher and lecturer who breaks script all the time to be present in the room with the people who are actually there. A more traditional understanding of our work—that the scholar acts and often suffers alone; that the scholar is a sort of succubus who takes from the work of others to promote herself or perhaps her ideas while "making" nothing new; that the scholar must be isolated from her world and others so as to acquire the rigor that she needs to differentiate her thinking from that which she studies so as to mark out her own intelligence; the scholar as detached, distant, and better-than—ignores teaching, or detaches it from the primary enterprise ("scholarship"), and also refuses attention to the social, ethical, bodily, emotional, and often even political nature of her many (related) activities.

VJ. Do we want to further unfold the metaphor of PAM as a computer?

ALEX. This is something Brian and I have discussed over many dinners at my house. I started sharing these ideas after reading the provocative e-flux collection *The Internet Does Not Exist* (April 2015) and particularly Hito Steyerl's essay in it: "Too Much World: Is the Internet Dead?" There, internet artists and theorists consider the internet's ungainly spread into everything everywhere, via corporate control and ownership, and through governmental and institutional management and discipline. For the internet to live up to its foundational radical promise of creative, collective access to the world's others and knowledge, many are taking our work offline—into local knowable spaces like PAM—and there imagining, and using, new computers: machines that save, process, and share knowledge, feelings, and data in humble ways written through alternative registers of ownership and control produced by and for its users.

LIZ LOSH (in the Google Doc in May). Perhaps references to sources in digital humanities about collaboration and making might be helpful here (even though other entries in the volume have critiqued these notions in DH from a feminist perspective on labor and materiality).

KIM KNIGHT. DH sacrilege or DH sacred rite?

ALEX. In our last call (memorialized in the photos), we named Katherine Hayles's *My Mother Was a Computer,* Brenda Laurel's *Computers as Theater,* and Anne Balsamo's *Designing Culture* as our feminist foundations for this line of thinking. I am hoping that our editors will give us artists' license to write as we have been: in a manner where influences might be named, where they circulate, where they are bedrock, but where official protocols of citation are not required. That said, it is important to remember that this writing is for an academic publication. Do we need to cite through authorized formats to be properly academic?

And as importantly, perhaps you don't know (or even care) what DH is, Brian, as your work as a performer, writer, curator, and impresario is situated in spaces almost entirely untouched by DH, given that this new field is both primarily academic and committed to digital technology. But, given our interest in how the unplugged, live, local, small performance space could be the radical computer of our time, and given how so much of the art-making in LA is in conversation with the academy and academic theory, and how much of PAM's business, like all businesses, is now run through social networks, you're really not all that far from DH (the purposeful use of digital tools and/or questions about the digital for the research, making, writing, and sharing of humanities content within academia).

BRIAN. I do care! It's true that PAM is networked to audiences, other spaces, and artists through the digital. I rely on social media and email to get the word out about shows and to get bodies in the door. It's also true that I have neglected the digital as a realm of imaginative possibility for performance. This is why I invited you and Laila to do a residency in the first place. Here, I attempt to use DH as a way to expand the envelope of the kinds of performance practices that I give space to more regularly at PAM, and to ferret out positions I had (and prior to writing this with you both, wasn't necessarily aware I had) about a forming ideology (and prejudice) toward the kind of work I want to make and support in LA.

ALEX. Given that DH prides itself on collective production, making the most of interdisciplinary expertise, and community-based scholarship that is usable for nonacademics, Ev-Ent-Anglement could be considered *prime* DH! We used a performance space to artfully cut together scholarly thinking, histories of art making, users' fragments (many of whom are academics!), and a room of interacting bodies as a way to theorize and at the same time enact feminist networks and affect in and out of the digital.

Performing the Bleed

BRIAN. Here's a question: does theory *propose* or *enact* and under what circumstances is one "action" felt more than the other? I bring up this question in light of the brief argument I had at PAM with Jih-Fei Cheng, your colleague, Alex, regarding the theorized violence on his and perhaps your part that he noted so forcefully during the performance: that the tearing up of a poem enacts a fleshy wounding. I can't immediately recall the subject of the poem or its author or either's relationship to you but I had the sense that the subject pertained to loss. I'm going to proceed with the idea that it was personal and delicate.

ALEX. Yes, let's proceed with delicacy and vulnerability in mind. That's part of why we called these talks "events" (just as we call this a script and not a "paper") because the affect engendered (and then honored and attempted to be saved and passed on) by their participatory and performative nature differentiates them from the more circumscribed set of routines of academic conferences or scholarly writing practices where this should stay hidden or private. In Ev-Ent-Anglements, fragile feelings are noted and worked on and through.

  Instead of merely lecturing or even performing, I asked the audience in the many Ev-Ent-Anglement spaces to *participate,* to cut and also to paste fragments of themselves and their constitutive feelings about the event, and its commitments to cutting/pasting+bleeding, into a digital record of the ever-growing and always-changing

Figure 13.3. PAM circa 2014.

ev-ent-anglement.com and cells.Ev-Ent-Anglement.org. In the Highland Park iteration, I printed onto paper some of the fragments that had previously been cut/paste+bled into the project. I invited the audience members at PAM to cut these up with scissors that I also provided, and then to hand their newly constructed object back to me. These cut-ups became that performance's live script.

LIZ. Nice example that might seem to many the opposite of DH (performative, material, affective, occluded, unstable, unpredictable, unnavigatable, etc.). Can you make it clearer what the tearing up of the poem can contribute to DH discourses?

ALEX. At PAM and in earlier performances I had been sure to read this quote: "Cutting, pasting, and showing the seams is fun, generative, and just plain easy to do," by William S. Burroughs, who continues: "Cut ups are for everyone. Anybody can make cut ups. It is experimental in the sense of being something to do."

LIZ. There are other references to cut ups in DH discourses (Winder in *The Companion to Digital Humanities* and Steven E. Jones in *The Emergence of the Digital Humanities*).

JACQUE. Perhaps also the discourse of mashup and remix as more familiar territory and which shows up in VJ's section below?

ALEX. Cut-ups are different from mashups and remix, and I'm glad your interjections allow me to see and name that here. Cut-ups demand a machine logic, not simply the machine as a tool to (more easily) render montage practices or thinking. By machine logic I mean one that is cool, detached, uncaring, disconnected. An arbitrary or inhuman cut carries the particular violence or jolt of thoughtlessness, contextlessness, and the inability to differentiate what is precious and tender from that which is not.

KIM KNIGHT (in orange). Can we imagine warm machines?

BRIAN. Cutting while knowing that the pieces will be reassembled, and held by persons, such as Alex, myself and Jih-Fei, who deeply care about community is not a cold cut.

ALEX. So much of social media now functions with this cold sense of cut-up. Algorithms cut+paste once precious things paying no attention to human feeling while maintaining maximum interest on corporate greed. Of course, humans receive said cut-ups and reengender meaning through reception or remix. The cut-poem that you produced in Highland Park, Brian, your cuts that activated more feelings and words and affect at PAM, was originally cut/paste+bled in as a complete poem by trans-feminist DH media theorist KJ Sturken. I'm now cut/paste+bleeding it here (whole), after I realized that you wrote about it (below), which helps to change this conversation (as all cuts do) by pointing to the disorientations in time, space, ownership, meaning, causality and more enabled by the cut/paste+bleed:

KJ STURKEN.

> I have recently made a rather large cut
> to myself
> or rather a surgeon made it for me
> out of great necessity
> (It was a kind of a "do or die" situation)
> This edit to my physical body invites interpretations,
> many times by strangers
> People whom I don't know
> and who don't know me.
> I don't mean to be mysterious
> but
> it's complicated.
> Online I am a composite of many identities
> gendered this way or that
> and strangely
> I find myself entangled in fragments of former selves
> which are constantly colliding
> shattering the illusion of the seamless narratives
> about gender identity
> about cancer
> often required for the comfort of others.
> #eventanglement

LIZ. A lovely intervention in the text by Surkan—can you unpack it for readers so they have some ideas for how to apply it to the digital humanities? How is his Ev-Ent-Anglement identity related to his DH identity? How can feminist DH acknowledge "fragments of former selves" and the Kim/Karl personae?

ALEX. I know Karl (KJ) through FemTechNet. He follows me on Facebook and elsewhere as I do him. He was watching the Ev-Ent-Anglement online (as had Laila previously) and responded to my invitation to cut in on the project's blog his own interpretation, addition, and fragment about the project's core ideas, as they moved him as a person, as someone whose body had been recently cut, and as a theorist and an artist. Many of the fragments in the project entered offscreen from internet participants who never saw or participated in a live event.

BRIAN. I cut up this poem, printed out on paper at PAM, with scissors in deference to the Burroughs quote that you had read and my memory of previously reading Burroughs where he encourages the cutting up of text as a form of writing and a method. Is this quote/idea a theory? It's only a couple of lines. "To cut is to . . ." So if it is a theory, it is in itself just a snippet of one.

ALEX. Indeed, as is true of so much we read today, I cut one great line from a much longer piece of writing.[9]

BRIAN. That makes it a cutting theory that can only be encountered through the fragments cut from it. A theory that disintegrates and rearranges as it is enacted. This is not erasure, provided that the pieces made are also collected and not disposed of. In practice it's not really writing in that the procedure is of finding, cutting, and grafting. That's collage. Writing is the generating and piling up of glyphs on a ground, usually white. It's funny that I feel the need to name the materiality of these analog procedures but these differences are compelling in that their materiality guides a kind of theorizing that I expect is quite differently felt about their digital counterparts. Had I posted on Facebook a cut-up version of someone else's poem, what could be theorized about that procedure and its attending feelings?

ALEX. Why don't we see the willy-nilly flow of others' fragments on Facebook or Instagram or Twitter as an immoral Wild West? Jodi Dean is really useful on the taming logics of Facebook, as is Geert Lovink on what is actually "social" in social networks.[10]

BRIAN. When I cut that poem not making use of the line you had delineated (which separated the poem, in toto, from other fragments on the printed page that I held in my hand at PAM), I was removing the part of it that I wanted you to expand. I had in mind that the procedure was more like grafting limbs from tree to tree than it was like human surgery. I gave you a piece back, and hoped you'd grow that piece in the direction you chose. This metaphor could be grown into a theory, no? But it would have to be rooted in you, Alex, and Laila, in your performance, as well as in paper and scissors, and the people that watched, cut, and talked.

ALEX. When you handed back to me the poem in its new, radical, cut form, I was forced to improvise. I was taken aback. You had broken from my expectation of procedures and methods (good for you!). So, given what had been rendered onto it, your cutting, I stopped and explained where it had first come from (honoring the bleed), how your cuts into it made me feel (bad and thrilled and curious). Only then did I read it in its new form, and there it was: beautiful and strange and new.

BRIAN. Jih-Fei's contribution at PAM speaking after your explication and reading was that he thought to cut this particular poem was enacting a kind of violence against the author, and the delicate subject of bodily cutting that he wrote about within the poem.

Jih-Fei felt like cutting that poem about skin was itself akin to hurting human flesh (newly, again). I still don't see how that is true, given the circumstances. It's not transubstantiation, is it? Is it a kind of voudou? Will the author ever know?

ALEX. Well, he does now, given that we're performing here the violence of cutting first felt by Karl and expressed in his poem, felt again at PAM newly, and now felt here in a publication that Karl can certainly see!

JIH-FEI (writing much later, on the invitation of the authors once our conversation about the potential felt violence of the incident seemed to call forth his opinions and reactions). I'll "cut-in" here to try, again, to flesh out my embodied experiences with #eventanglement. First, I must say that this is very difficult for me. My body trembles as I rethink these experiences and attempt to distill these past and present sensations into text. I should also say that I'm arriving to this conversation late. Alex contacted me and graciously invited me to join. I've tried to catch up as quickly as possible to what seems a dynamic conversation among others that unfolded over time.

Although I had encountered #eventanglement several times, my first simultaneous, collectively embodied experience of it was actually at the first event in New Delhi where Alex also performed. We were among people of varying racial/ethnic, gender, and national affiliations. I felt Alex prompted us to respond by "cutting-in" with our thoughts, feelings, and embodied experiences using her hashtag. We seemed encouraged to imbue virtual space (her website) with text (such as a tweet or a post with the hashtag #eventanglement) that represented and, once again, collectivized our felt experiences—text and affect that might move beyond the specific time and place in New Delhi where we had first gathered.

I experienced something radically different at PAM more than a year later in a section just north of downtown Los Angeles that is rapidly undergoing gentrification. I arrived late and knew no one except Alex and our colleague at the Claremont Colleges, Ruti Talmor. Brian (whom I became acquainted with at PAM during the above referenced and rather heated encounter) seemed to be the host. He waved me to take a seat up front, on the floor. I sandwiched myself between strangers, some who seemed to know one another, including an ostensibly white, heterosexual couple who continuously and intimately touched each other as if to ensure each other comfort and safety through their corporeal co-presence. There, among a crowd of what seemed like mostly white people, I felt the usual unusual vulnerability—an immediate alienation—that someone who is not white (in this case East Asian) often feels. I listened to Alex's performance while trying to fight the dissonance I experienced as a result of having arrived tardy and to a familiarly unfamiliar space. I adjusted my eyes to the wall of projected images and attempted to distinguish the brief bouts of sound and silence. I tried to focus on Alex, her performance, and her words. I could not/did not hear Burroughs. I recall how she positioned herself and moved in the space. I remember her boots. I liked them a lot. When asked to cut words printed onto paper, I was careful to cut along the breaks that seemed intended by the author and by Alex—for instance, after a stanza or at the end of a section of a poem—so that the separated parts could be traced back to their whole(s).

ALEX. I had actually printed little cut lines with a scissor emblem to indicate where I wanted people to cut.

JIH-FEI. For those of us who experience this kind of vulnerability, and sometimes offer understanding of it through words on paper that trace the fault lines of pain and loss, it matters where the reader/listener/viewer draws their attention. It matters how we are marked, how we remark, and how that remarking and re-making is acknowledged.

To remain vulnerable in your fleshly existence means that you care, observe, and enact the body as part of a collective; that you take the time to trace the contours of pain in this collective body; that you carefully and consciously choose to make new or additional cuts because you know they might cause further hurt.

I did not hear Alex ask us to only make cuts. I heard her ask us to make cuts, to watch those cuts bleed, and to be accountable for where and how we make those cuts. I shivered in fear and then anger when I heard Brian suggest that he might apply cuts with the mere curiosity of an objective and uninvested observer, as if one could so emotionally distance themselves from feeling the fleshly, dissembling experience expressed by the poem's author. Some people do hold the authority to be able to create such social and spatial distance from the site of ritualized and systematic violence. To vehemently defend their "objectivity"—to protect the privilege to remain cold and distant—is an act of violence itself. Now, I'm learning after reading this transcript that my resistance to this cut was seen as "forceful" and "personal"—in other words, I'm being accused of speaking out of turn and acting self-indulgent.

ALEX. Some of the words Jih-Fei is quoting here were cut from this version of our script to shorten it and also in response to comments of peer-evaluators. We've chosen to leave in Jih-Fei's reference to them to acknowledge these cuts and make clear the strong affect that continues to adhere to the political, theoretical, embodied, social, word-based interaction at PAM.

JIH-FEI. Thank you for the clarification and for holding space, Alex. My sense is that Brian indicated that I behaved emotionally, aggressively, and uncivically rather than reasonably and calmly, as somehow modeled by his presumably unaffected, cool, and objective practice of cutting. In other words, my reaction didn't belong in that community and in that space that Brian occupied with authority.

ALEX. But of course it did (and does), Jih-Fei! We all invited you here, and deeply respected you there because your responses, and attempts to share them, embody the bleed.

JIH-FEI. Thank you, Alex. I did and do feel welcomed by you. Yet, I'm compelled to ask, what violence does this distanciation do to Brian? To not recognize the cuts made to his body; to *un*recognize his experience and investment in fracturing of the collective body; to insist on his individual autonomy, wholeness, and rationalism, which made his decision and actions to apply cuts like a surgeon unaccountable?

ALEX. I thank you for your passion, force, and dialogue, as ever, and for these questions for Brian, and really for us all. Given their tenderness and bite, given how real and personal they are, I'm glad we took the time to speak about our many encounters with the Ev-Ent-Anglement occurring and represented here (and others, including our work together on our AIDS book, *AIDS and the Distribution of Crises*), offline and over tea in Little Tokyo.

BRIAN (cutting in after a talk with Alex November 15, 2017). Jih-Fei, I need to address the affect you are ascribing to my action of cutting; that of distance, coolness, and detachment. From my perspective, my cutting was participatory within the cutting, pasting, bleeding praxis *within* the community that gathered to take back, into shared space, the daily cuts we make in our affects and give away without much care through social media. How different it is and feels to do so relationally as opposed to virtually relationally. Also in that moment, I was more engaged in the procedure of the whole of the performance; watching Alex and VJ Um Amel, watching others cut and arrange an assortment of willingly donated texts, than in the content of the poem I had in my hands. Had I thoroughly grasped the content of that particular poem, I doubt I would have so readily cut in, but I can't be sure. The precise moment of confrontation between us blurs in my memory and it gets less and less clear the more writing we pile up on top of it here. I can say for sure, that I in no way meant to evoke a detachment from people who are cut-into corporeally by society, who make cuts to themselves, or undergo surgical cuts to transform. I think some of the cognitive dissonance that I'm (maybe we?) experiencing stems from another point in this long-unfolding textual extension of Ev-Ent-Anglement. This is the fact that I initially brought your name into this paper without your consent and as if you were an illustration of a point I was trying to make about the centering of either signifiers or signified subjects within our respective fields. I would feel outraged too if my name were invoked and I had no recourse to answer back. My sincere apologies.

Below: my earlier nonresponse to your cut-in that comes across sadly (for me) as a perfect illustration of that detached caricature that carelessly cuts.

—I see this particular cut-in (Jih-Fei's) as participating in the same conceit as the other, briefer, quotations, editorial comments, and quotes that we have included throughout but flowing from a participant inside the event rather than from the three of us. It makes me wonder if the Ev-Ent-Anglement process were to continue if there was some kind of offering up-front so that all participants could rejoin the conversation, through ongoing opportunities for participation, like our work in this collaborative document making.

JIH-FEI (addition on December 2, 2017). Recently, Brian invited me to speak off-line and in-person. I accept. So, I will end with this final response. Community is not a given. Space is not always equally embodied or shared. Collectivity is always in the making. In being called to cut, I believe our subject positions—our varying and uneven experiences with histories and structures of domination—were revealed. Access and power matter and those with it—usually white cisgender men—rarely call their privilege to cut-in into question. What I recall is Brian's immediate refusal of my experience and my attempt to remark upon the power dynamics in the room. That is why I reacted, and still react, as such. It reminds me of the access and power white men maintain in spaces of supposed creativity and collectivity. I think of director David France, who vigorously defends his privilege to excise people of color in his re-making of AIDS, queer, and trans histories in films such as *How to Survive a Plague* (2014) and *The Death and Life of Marsha P. Johnson* (2017). In doing so, he continues to cut out from popular memory the antiracist, feminist, trans, and queer lives, labor, and politics involved in the making, preserving, and remembering of these histories. However, with each cut, there are those of us who will *re-member* the length and direction of each incision and the clefts carved into the skins of histories.

JACQUE. There's a piece in a forthcoming DH volume edited by Jentery Sayers and written by my collaborator Jessica Rajko that might help bring in "DH" if that's what you'd like to do. She is herself a dancer and somatic practitioner and writes about the troubles between theory and practice and how they make it hard to bring her kind of practice/performance into the theorizing spaces of DH. Let me know if you'd like to take a look at it.

ALEX. The troubles between theory and practice are particularly live here: I wonder how or even if a quick turn to theory helps.

Archive as Space; Cyborg as Artist

VJ. To amass an archive is a leap of faith, not in the function of preserving data, but in the belief that there will be someone to use it, that the accumulation of these histories will continue to live, and that they will have listeners and readers. In the contemporary world, there is an archival impulse at work that represents something palpable—an opportunity to provide a countercollection standing against the monumental history of the state. Such an impulse has resulted in new public archives, individual projects, digital archives (including digitization of old manuscripts as well as collecting digitally born information), fictional archival projects, and collections of urban histories that were entangled by Ev-Ent-Anglement, such as Richard Fung's interviews for his 1985 Asian lesbian and gay documentary film.

ALEX. Richard Fung got cut/paste in at the same time and place as did Jih-Fei: in New Delhi during the Visible Evidence conference we all attended.

LIZ. This section also seems ripe for signposting for those with DH concerns.

VJ. What is the logic behind creating an independent, open source, digital archive?

ALEX. This is a feminist, anticapitalist, collectivist logic that strives to make and use the archives we need.

VJ. How might archives engage with the public and public institutions? Or how might research that draws from media ephemera, rather than state documents and "official" archives, tell a slightly different version of the story of modernism in twentieth-century Egypt? Take, for example, Joy Garnet's Bee Kingdom archive of the works by Egyptian poet Ahmed Zaki Abu Shadi, or Hana Sleiman's archives of the Palestinian National Movement collected through informal networks. How do these appropriations of "the archive" serve as a transformative site of knowledge production?

Can we identify a set of research practices that emerge at the intersection of both cultural and technical analytics in the fields of new media studies?[11] This analytic approach is born out of the contemporary sociohistorical moment as we face new scales of information that demand machinated computation and political influences on our cultural practices that are systematic, transnational, and mobile. Similar to the nonlinear narrative form of a NoSQL database, data-driven narratives are also mapped relationally and within larger systems and orders.

LIZ. You might want to explain how the VJ identity differs from that of the traditional principle investigator in DH.

VJ. That is an interesting point, Liz. If we continue with the metaphor as archive or place as computer, then it follows that the computer's API [Application Program Interface] would be a cyborg computational logics that can artfully manipulate data between SQL and NoSQL databases within the venue, place, archive.

In the context of global uprising and using the moniker VJ Um Amel, I extend the archive to create 3-D games, generative art, remix video, data visualizations, and digital performances that have shown internationally. These media productions aim to build worlds in which the audience coauthors stories by extending networked narratives onto cinematic screens. These interactive experiences also demonstrate how a database narrative might express meaning through recombinant and indexical instantiations of this project through Delhi, Dublin, Utrecht, Montreal, Highland Park, and always online.

ALEX. Let's imagine that "scholarship," one of the categories we've been trying to cut open, shake, or transcend, means a careful, connected inquiry that results in a careful, connected sharing of one's findings. For old-fashioned academics—your white guy with a pipe who reads Shakespeare—that care is understood as "rigor" which registers both as painstaking research and its legitimizing citations, and also as intelligence which is marked by language use and complexity of argument and evidence; connection typically means the citational practices I've mentioned already (and begged permission to alter) which serve to mark a father-to-son understanding of his labor that becomes part of a historical, communal effort to make, share, and improve knowledge or understanding.

DOM OLIVERI (tweets from Montreal). fragilization // politics of care // movements // temporalities

ALEX. My feminist interpretation of and approach to scholarship, like Domi's cut/paste above, wouldn't lose the pipe guy's tried-and-true understandings of care and connection, but would expand this to also include care for self, others, place, and knowledge itself, and connection to nonacademic people, places, and projects like politics and art. While my definition of "scholarship" therefore attests to its communal nature—in that it has always been built from earlier work, connected to present conversation, and offered in hopes of future use—this condition of the work has been traditionally effaced in a definitive and gross gesture of anticare and anticommunity. That is to say that the gesture of a citation was the (only) mark of connection but any other form of or format for connection was deemed irrelevant (including those that mark pain, unwillingness to share, or misaligned power relations as well as those that honor the meat and mayhem of collaborative production, say, indicating that there was a meal together, a shorthand for hours of conversation, bodily connection, pleasure, thinking, altering of opinions, flirting, chatting, gossiping, and learning).

PATO HEBERT (artist, educator, and cultural worker based in Los Angeles and New York, writes this comment digitally into the comments of the Ev-Ent-Anglement). "Thanks for #Cutting/Pasting+Bleeding open a space with and for so many of us, Alex. I'm wondering how our incision sutures relate to revisiting as a way to reassemble anew. I'm thinking about what it meant to post on FB [Facebook] from the International AIDS Conference last month, trying to hold the spin of real bodies in mobilizing motion in relationship to the stasis of health bureaucracies, the connective tissue of fellowship and the encouragement of folks far in body but close in struggle and heart. Cleaving, clotting, accompanying . . ."

LIZ. Could we provide some connections to DH projects done on HIV/AIDS?

ALEX. Interestingly, Anne Balsamo and I met when I asked her to lunch to talk about her Digital AIDS quilt. Jih-Fei and I met after he gave a scintillating talk about his doctoral research on HIV/AIDS media at SCMS and then we went for coffee. Brian and I met first at dinner parties at my house and went on to collaborate on a video about intergenerational conversation about AIDS history that featured our voices as a soundtrack to a dance he shot with a group of gay male performers whose heads he removed with editing software!

From my initial lunch with Anne, FemTechNet was born (and that's where a good deal of my work with both of you, Jacque and Liz, has taken place)! Anne and I bemoaned a lack of feminist community where we might situate conversation about

Figure 13.4. Pleasure Riot, 2013 Getnick / Juhasz with dancers Jos McKain, Bryatt Bryant, and Gregory Barnett.

our recent digital renderings of scholarly/political projects occurring about and in digital technologies. We wanted a nurturing and intelligent community in which we could better understand our new large-scale feminist DH practices (I had just finished *Learning from YouTube* and she was completing the digital sections of *Designing Culture*). We had both experienced a kind of gutting out during the reception of this DH work by most audiences whereby its political core, founding communities and commitments, and activist goals were tactfully ignored in favor of responses that made more technical and technological connections. Most DH readers and participants were viewing through or past the feminist implications and orientations of the work to get as quickly as possible to more familiar and comfortable DH goals, methods, and concerns. We sought a community for feminist DH scholarship that would ask how a work attends to others, and the places and things that she needs and loves and loses and uses to do her work as her/his/their self. Of course s/he is working with others: but how do they feel? Are they doing what they want? All they can? Do they make the place they live and work better? Do they hurt other people or places or things in the process?

The performance of Ev-Ent-Anglement at PAM (like much of the work of FemTechNet) made visible these care and connection questions, usually obscured, at the heart of research and art and DH practice (and computers), so that the use and abuse of others' thoughts and things and feelings became the (shared?) responsibility of the performers and our audience.

JACQUE. Really happy to see this here—it's such an important set of considerations. Thank you.

VJ. As cyborg, I would add that through this practice devoted to data, we have performed capturing, analyzing, and visualizing of algorithmic culture as a mediation of civic life. This approach to understanding the algorithmic culture of social media and a

Figure 13.5. Preparing set at PAM.

trends analysis of internet data as cultural objects draws from the histories of critical cartography, indigenous mapping, and feminist critique. We went further, not stopping at critique, but actually moving toward operationalizing critiques of power and feminist ethics into design principles for how to make things more just, more fair, and more representative . . .

ALEX. While ever attending to the bleed: where it hurt, where we helped, how we felt and knew and learned together—or did or could not—in space and time.

Technology and Affect in Digital Humanities

ALEX. One of the Ev-Ent-Anglement's central concerns remains the question of how and if affect moves in places and networks particularly those deemed as feminist. Objects can be easily digitized and shared and reshown online, but feelings and sentiments and bodies not so much.

JENNY BURMAN (feminist theorist and associate professor in Communication Studies, McGill, tweets from Montreal). "I remember the wildness of fifteen from the inside. I could do anything fucking anything."

LIZ. Good. Readers not familiar with affect theory may need some background (for example, how affect is different from emotion and thus is mobile and part of the environment rather than just the subject).

ALEX. The event's generous participants gifted me their digital fragments as I requested, and this was, as the event and its infrastructure required, necessarily quick, fleeting, a flip of the hand, a click of the camera. It's so easy to "share" with a cut/paste online. Some of the meat of our encounter was entangled in those techie gestures too, showing up as care, as fragility, proximity, shadow, and touch.

Figure 13.6. VJ Um Amel, Alex, Yoko Ono in still from "Cut Piece," and participants from PAM performance November 8, 2015.

TL COWAN (feminist cabaret theorist, tweets from Montreal). "Feminist collectivity as the shadow archive of contemporary academic culture."

ALEX. In the final iteration of the Ev-Ent-Anglement at PAM we chose to materialize several of the processes that had been digital and therefore invisible in earlier versions. Although contributions began digitally as tweets, blog comments, and links, they rematerialized at PAM on paper as something the audience could hold and reexperience and even change. They had a weight, and their quantity was legible. At the same time, VJ Um Amel was re-presenting images that previous participants had shared with the project on the wall through live-mixing: not something one could hold but other things that jumped past their initial host platforms—like computers or iPhones—to become part of the shared, lived, and live space of the performance at PAM. The fragments that make up our digital lives became manifest and part of our tangible world for that moment together.

LIZ. Interesting point about digital/nondigital and invisible/visible.

VJ. I think a lot of this comes down to intention and methodology. In working collectively, there can be some ambiguity between collaboration and appropriation. And sometimes appropriation is intentional and meant to be subversive. This is clear for me when work is remixed with the intention to be in conversation with the appropriated object, sort of how we write papers and cite other texts within them. And this may be because I think of VJing as a critical research methodology. An interdisciplinary approach that incorporates an art and design research methodology, offers a transformative practice to understanding the nature blogs, social networking sites, Twitter feeds, YouTube, etc., and how these new media platforms engage with and affect us.

There are several stages to the art of VJing, and therefore there are a variety of practices I am continually developing. The first is making my own animations, motion graphics, sound, or shooting footage for the poetic backbone of any particular remix. Here I carry out more traditional roles in filmmaking. The second step is one of hunting and gathering—this role is more like a curator, editor, or set theorist—bringing together a number of additional mixed media and trans-narratives that interact and converse with each other. The third step is to build the database with a vision such that it will be able to scale up as data continually aggregates. And design interactive interfaces. Once all of that is in place, I build "patches" that use algorithms to make the visuals move to the audio, or pull live data streams to inform the visuals, or alter live video input in real time, just for example. And the final step is where the VJing art of performing all these videos, patches, animations, sounds, and graphic images from the database comes to play into one set of synchronized, multimedia recombinant narratives. Depending on whether the remix occurs as a performance, game, or installation, the elements from the database are reassembled into various programmatic interfaces.

ALEX. At PAM, the practice of cutting+pasting—which defines a huge portion of our internet activity, and this project about that, our network actions and interactions—became tactile, visible, and communal.

Figure 13.7. Participants listening at Ev-Ent-Anglement at PAM.

BRIAN. I'm inspired to jump in here to ask how does theory behave as an activated element in a performance? I can say that some of the ideas about theory we're discussing here were a texture of what you presented at PAM, but to me the primary, meaning-producing material of that night was you, Alex, followed by the ideas you presented first physically and then verbally, followed by the audience's reactions, participation, and self-recognition, then followed by the digital projections and digital environment/installation in the room.

ALEX (typing in live during our final Skype conversation). We take a pause here; this is not a conclusion. Maybe there will be another performance. Could this be its script?

With Support From

Jenny Burman
Jih-Fei Cheng
TL Cowan
Richard Fung
Pato Hebert
DH@CCKim Knight
Elizabeth Losh
Domi Oliveri
Roopika Risam
AJ Strout
KJ Sturken
Jacque Wernimont

Notes

1. "PAM Season 1," Vimeo, https://vimeo.com/126018951.

2. I was the editor whose comments were quoted in "Queer Feminist Digital Archives," by Dayna McLeod, TL Cowan and Jasmine Rault for the Queer Feminist Media Praxis special issue of the online journal *ADA*. "Speculative Praxis Towards a Queer Feminist Digital Archive: A Collaborative Research-Creation Project," *ADA* 5, Queer Feminist Media Praxis. I also chose to include editorial comments from my colleagues Broderick Fox and Bishnu Ghosh within the text of my essay on AIDS video online, "Digital AIDS Documentary: Webs, Rooms, Viruses, and Quilts." *A Companion to Contemporary Documentary Film* (Malden, Mass.: Wiley-Blackwell, 2015), ed. Alexandra Juhasz and Alisa Lebow.

3. VJ Um Amel, http://vjumamel.com.

4. Ricardo Dominguez, Facebook, https://www.facebook.com/ricardo.dominguez.71465/posts/10153056507424170.

5. Ricardo Dominguez, Facebook, https://www.facebook.com/ricardo.dominguez.71465/posts/10153056507424170.

6. Sadly, since we began writing, these sites have been lost and only a temporary shrine marks their once robust presence. Their erasure was not intentional, but it marks much of what we discuss here. Given the real shape of peoples' lives which nestle with patterns of corporate and technological disregard and uncare it turned out a bill wasn't paid, a folder was left unsaved, a company doesn't save all that they say they will, and poof! the digital results of our labor vanished, even as memories and fragments linger.

7. I have tried to imaginatively make best use of these fragments in many places, including, "#cut/paste+bleed: Entangling Feminist Affect, Action and Production On and Offline," in *Routledge Companion to Media Studies and Digital Humanities,* ed. Jentery Sayers (Routledge: 2018), 18–32, and "Affect Bleeds in Feminist Networks: An 'Essay' in Six Parts," *Feminist Media Studies* 4 (2017): 660–87, http://www.tandfonline.com/doi/full/10.1080/14680777.2017.1326579.

8. Uncertain Commons, *Speculate This!* (Durham, N.C.: Duke University Press, 2013), wtf.tw/ref/uncertain_commons_speculate_this.pdf.

9. Burroughs, "Cut Up Method."

10. Jodi Dean, "Affect and Drive," in *Networked Affect,* ed. Hillis, Paasonen, and Petit (Cambridge, Mass.: MIT Press, 2015), and Geert Lovink, "What Is the Social in Social Media," *e-flux Journal,* #40 (December 2012), http://www.e-flux.com/journal/what-is-the-social-in-social-media/.

11. Technology studied outside of the sciences must also face a fear among many academicians. As Kevin Franklin and Karen Rodriguez introduce their argument in "The Next Big Thing in Humanities, Arts and Social," "It's enough to make a humanities scholar hyperventilate. A debate has raged in the last decade (at least) about whether or not the Digital Age will see the death of The Book, The Library and perhaps, The Humanities more broadly." July 29, 2008: https://www.hpcwire.com/2008/07/29/the_next_big_thing_in_humanities_arts_and_social_science_computing_cultural_analytics.

Thanks to the Foundational Thinking Found Within by

Ahmed, Sara. *Queer Phenomenology: Orientations, Objects, Others.* Duke University Press, 2006.

Balsamo, Anne. *Designing Culture: The Technological Imagination at Work.* Duke University Press, 2011.

Barad, Karen. *Meeting the Universe Halfway: Quantum Physics and the Entanglement of Matter and Meaning.* Duke University Press, 2007.

Bennett, Jane. *Vibrant Matter: A Political Ecology of Things.* Duke University Press, 2010.

Berardi, Franco Bifo. *The Uprising: On Poetry and Finance.* Semiotext(e), 2012.

Braidoti, Rosi. "Cyberfeminism with a Difference": http://www.let.uu.nl/womens_studies/rosi/cyberfem.htm.

Burch, Noël. *Theory of Film Practice.* Praeger, 1973.

Burroughs, William S. "The Cut Up Method," 1963: http://www.writing.upenn.edu/~afilreis/88v/burroughs-cutup.html.

Coole, Diana, and Samantha Frost, eds. *New Materialisms: Ontology, Agency and Politics.* Duke University Press, 2010.

Dancyger, Ken. *The Technique of Film and Video Editing: History, Theory, and Practice.* Focal Press, 1997.

Haraway, Donna. "A Cyborg Manifesto," 1984: http://faculty.georgetown.edu/irvinem/theory/Haraway-CyborgManifesto-1.pdf.

Hayles, N. Katherine. *How We Became Posthuman: Virtual Bodies in Cybernetics, Literature, and Informatics.* University of Chicago Press, 1999.

Hayles, N. Katherine. *My Mother Was a Computer: Digital Subjects and Literary Texts.* University of Chicago Press, 2005.

Jones, Stephen. *The Emergence of the Digital Humanities.* Routledge, 2013.

Juhasz, Alexandra. *Learning from YouTube.* MIT Press, 2012.

Kember, Sarah, and Joanna Zylinska, *Life after New Media: Mediation as a Vital Process.* MIT Press, 2012.

Laurel, Brenda. *Computers as Theatre.* Addison-Wesley, 1991

Manovich, Lev. *The Language of New Media.* MIT Press, 2001.

Ono, Yoko. "Cut Piece." 1964.

Orpen, Valerie. *Film Editing: The Art of the Expressive.* Wallflower 2003.

Reisz, Karel, and Gavin Millar, *The Technique of Film Editing.* Focal Press, 1968.

Schreibman, Susan, Ray Siemans, John Unsworth, eds., *A Companion to Digital Humanities.* Blackwell, 2008.

Schulman, Sarah. *Conflict Is Not Abuse: Overstating Harm, Community Responsibility, and the Duty of Repair.* Arsenal Pulp Press, 2016.

Steyerl, Hito. "Too Much World: Is the Internet Dead?" In *The Internet Does Not Exist* (April 2015).

Thies-Lehmann, Hans. *Post Dramatic Theater.* Routledge, 2006.

Wardrip-Fruin, Noah, and Nick Montfort, eds., *The New Media Reader.* MIT Press, 2003.

PART IV][Chapter 14

Building Pleasure and the Digital Archive

DOROTHY KIM

[The archivist] is the keeper of countless objects of desire.
—Martha Cooley, *The Archivist* (1998)

[L'archive] est difficile dans sa materialité.
—Arlette Farge, *Le gout de l'archive* (1989)

This essay is an exercise and also a critical meditation on what it means to build and create the *Archive of Early Middle English* and what the project's theoretical stakes are in relation to the corpus, the digital platform, the interface. Thus, this is a narrative about the long history of the book and about what it means to translate reading a medieval manuscript from thirteenth-century Britain to reading a mediated version of a manuscript in the twenty-first century. It is the story of medieval to digital remediation, but a remediation that has remarkable feedback loops because it disrupts print as a medium. This essay is also about the archive story of Early Middle English and how making visible the editorial bodies that create the digital manuscript bodies is a form of radical material feminism that reframes the stakes of this digital archive. And so, this essay pivots between the granularity of the codex book and the larger ecosystem of an archive of books.

Drawing from an array of theoretical perspectives—material feminism and especially theories of "intra-action," postcolonial archive theory, and disability studies—this essay explores the issue of pleasure in critical interface design and multisensory experience in digital reading ecologies, with a focus on the *Archive of Early Middle English* project. My discussion will turn attention to both the interpretive processes of visualization and the value of developing digital resources that engage senses beyond the visual. I will consider additionally the physical and related lived experiences of building and using archives. What are the alternatives to visual emphases in interface design, and what are the stakes—for nascent and long-standing projects—of creating flexible, stable resources that invite manipulation and change? And what are the stakes for archive theory, digital labor, feminist materialism, and histories of the book? Can what at first glance be seen as traditional and canonical function as a decolonized, feminist, and material ecosystem?

Visual Pleasure, Graphesis, and Histories and Futures of the Book

When the AEME (*Archive of Early Middle English*)—a digital archive that will eventually include 162 encoded manuscript witnesses to the documentary production of Early Middle English between 1100 and 1350—received a National Endowment for the Humanities (NEH) 2013–2017 Scholarly Editions and Translation grant, the first and completed task Scott Kleinman and I, as co–principal investigators, discussed was the creation of a splash page—both as a placeholder during the project's coding and back-end development and as the go-to space for anyone who wanted to be directed to the archive.[1] Even though we also created a separate site for encoding guidelines and had an open workspace on GitHub, the splash page became the calling card for the AEME project in development.[2] Even with such a diverse and disparate corpus of archival materials, the visual aesthetics of the splash page was one of the earliest longer discussion items. We, in fact, budgeted and hired a graphic designer, Amy Papaelias (SUNY New Paltz, Art History) to give the "skin" of this interface of our archival portal motion, color balance, functionality, and visual pleasure. As the first task we accomplished with the release of our NEH funds, the foundational importance of organizing our visual calling card and subsequent visual profile speaks to the stakes, importance, and driving frames of visual pleasure in creating and building a digital archive and database. This article is an attempt to unpack the politics and theoretical angles and make transparent our biases in first prioritizing visual pleasure. But it also is a discussion that sketches out what else could be done in the continued development of the digital archive as an area in the long history of the book.

Our archive is not filled with many impressive illuminated and decorated manuscripts. Rather, it was incredibly difficult to even find an image we could use in our logo from the 162 manuscripts in our corpus. But this initial design—decided entirely by considering the visual pleasure of our project team and potential imagined users—became the project touchstone as the scholarly and public profile of the AEME moved across: through not just the splash page but also the temporary encoding guidelines page—though with slightly different but complementary color schemes—to the visual design, program, and swag for the "Making Early Middle English" conference.[3] This latter project for the AEME became the first international conference in the field, funded with a Social Sciences and Humanities Research Council Contact grant. It has also now transformed into the first peer-reviewed scholarly journal in the field, *The Journal of Early Middle English,* which also utilizes the visual footprint first developed for the AEME project.[4]

The question of pleasure speaks to the importance of desire in archival building and about emotional affect and the dangers of intense affect in hiding archival agendas and the political, national, and social forces often at play in creating them. There is a wish to hide these difficult narratives under the aura of sensory pleasures. And especially with digital projects—whether small, big, or going in multiple directions—pleasure is central in organizing and producing the digital humanities. Visual pleasure, the pleasurable experience of the user/subject, and the ease of the project's interface are always central in building.[5] There are a number of reasons for visual aesthetics' importance. They range from the politics of funding and also our own understanding of what will attract, hold, and intrigue digital users/readers/subjects. In a way, whether scholarly or lay, digital projects often function within a rhetoric of seduction. They use sensory pleasure, but almost always visual pleasure, to offer their projects up for consumption, enjoyment, work, and play. Theoretically and practically, the AEME has considered these issues from its inception and particularly from its first real budget expenditure. We have also grappled with the disconnect between the messy, dirty, fragmented quality of our corpus in juxtaposition of our aesthetically delightful and visually attractive splash page and project design aesthetic.

However, there has not been enough discussion about the theories behind what we are building in DH projects and how much theories of the visual and visual pleasure are hidden from view. In Johanna Drucker's book *Graphesis: Visual Forms of Knowledge Production*, Drucker tackles the theoretical stakes of digital visuality by explaining that "all images are encoded by their technologies of production and embody the qualities of the media in which they exist. These qualities are part of an image's informations" whether this be illuminated manuscript, daguerreotype, painting, photograph, or digital image.[6] She highlights how the recent discussions in media archaeology have centered media production and how "reading the matter of media" is how meaning is configured.[7] Digital media environments require multimodal reading, creation, and interpretation. However, digital media then rely more on the histories, theories, and epistemologies of the codex and book than they do on film and video. The issues of layout, marginalia, paratext, columns, table of contents, indexes, and chapter headings are, as Malcolm Parkes discusses in "The Influence of *Ordinatio* and *Compilatio* in the Development of the Book," a development of the medieval scholarly book.[8] These experimental page structures became standard in printed books and eventually in digital texts.

If the codex as developed in the Middle Ages is one of the earlier kinds of informational "interfaces," then we should consider it as a mediating apparatus: one in which the *mise-en-page* and material features, its myriad graphic cues explain how to read, use, navigate, and access information in the codex book.[9] Then the digital interface requires us to consider how critical interface design can help us build digital projects that address how this mediating apparatus will change how our readers/users/subjects will interact and create interpretive iterative acts with their reading, access, and navigation of the digital information. What this means is a move away from the codex's *mise-en-page* to a film's visual mise-en-scène to an interactive digital *mise-en-système*, what Drucker describes as "an environment for action."[10] A digital *mise-en-système* is a digital ecology in which the main question posed is how the interface iteratively and at various moment can "enunciate" the subject/user/reader. Interface, then, is a "border zone between cultural systems and human subjects"; it is the codependent space where "speaker and spoken are created."[11] This interaction in this border zone also pushes back against cinema's one-directional view of theories of visual pleasure and the gaze into a different model.[12] I believe feminist materialism and the work of Karen Barad on entanglement theory would name this interface site the space of "intra-action."

Stacy Alaimo and Susan Hekman have pointed out the volatility of materiality as a location for feminist theory, so much so that "most contemporary feminisms require that one distance oneself as much as possible from the tainted realm of materiality by taking refuge within culture, discourse, and language."[13] Instead, material feminism proposes that feminist theory must discuss materiality, and particularly the body, as an active agent that includes "lived experience, corporeal practice, and biological substance."[14] The point of material feminism is "to build on rather than abandon the lessons learned in the linguistic turn," namely, in this case, "a deconstruction of the material/discursive dichotomy that retains both elements without privileging either."[15] Thus material feminism rethinks "agency, semiotic force, and the dynamics of bodies and natures."[16] The most focused energies and the most radical move are to reconsider materiality: the "stuff" of bodies and environments. The "material turn" requires us to take "matter seriously."[17] Material feminism insists on flattening hierarchies and ontologies; it requires a consideration of how "culture, history, discourse, technology, biology, and the environment" interact without organizing these nodes without giving more power to one or the other.[18] In essence, it is a new way to consider "matter" in relation to "material culture, geopolitical space, food, climate and environment, gender, body, nature, and culture."[19]

Karen Barad, the theoretical quantum physicist, writes,

> The notion of intra'action (in contrast to the usual "interaction," which presumes the prior existence of independent entities/relata) marks an important shift, reopening and refiguring foundational notions of classical ontology such as causality, agency, space, time, matter, discourse, responsibility, and accountability. A specific intra-action enacts an agential cut (in contrast to the Cartesian cut—an inherent distinction—between subject and object) effecting a separating between "subject" and "object." That is, the agential cut enacts a "local" resolution within the phenomenon of the inherent ontological indeterminancy.[20]

In essence, Barad's point in "Nature's Queer Performativity" is to flatten hierarchies in which everything—human, nonhuman, matter—becomes a constantly shifting component. Within this frame, she "reframes" ideas of causality; and what "intra-acting" ultimately allows is that "'relata' do not pre-exist relations, but rather that 'relata-within-phenomen' emerge through specific intra-actions."[21]

What Drucker describes as the "codependent in-betweeness" of the interface where speaker and spoken are born is exactly a description of "intra-action." And what she has framed in her argument about digital graphesis as part of a long history of reading interfaces is that digital reading has become a *mise-en-système* with multivocal moments of "intra-action." She describes this digital shift in the history of reading:

> Reading was always a performance of a text or work, always an active remaking through an instantiation. But reading rarely had to grapple with the distinctions between immersion and omniscience—as when we are experiencing the first person view of a video juxtaposed with manipulation of a scalable map, with watching the social network reconfigure itself around a node of discourse even as the node is changing. Digital environments increasingly depend upon a whole series of contingent texts, transient documents, that are created on the fly by search and query, filtered browsing or other results-based displays that last only a few moments on the screen in the stepping-stone sequence of user clicks that move from one ephemeral configuration to the next.[22]

In this digital *mise-en-système,* beyond the flexible and iterative possibilities of moments of subject and interface "intra-action," what this digital reading ecology creates is the possibility for extremes of scale.

In this way, though we hear much more about the affordances and utopian heights of big data analytics and visualizations and the theoretical approaches of distance reading as explained by Franco Moretti, or even a discussion from Lev Manovich on the experience of digital visualization at extreme large scale, less is discussed about the potentials of the small, close-reading scale and the possibilities of sifting through the granularity of ever more minute details.[23] For medievalists, that granularity could be in close reading words, to the strokes of a scribal letter. What critical discussions about the digital humanities seem to forget are the possibilities of examining and working with minute granularity—the practice of extreme close reading. Scholars have discussed granularity in e-literature, digital history, and digital media studies who have written about "scalable reading."[24] In whatever direction digital reading, composing, and writing take, in relation to the new ecology of digital reading, we must think of the interface as "a provocation."[25]

Thus, the book of the future explodes with different arrays and angles of possibility. It will include reading, writing, annotation, social media; image, sound, tactility; text process, text analytics; small and large data mining and data mapping; the abilities to search, link, visualize, reroute, reconfigure texts and textualities; indexing, displaying; close analysis of pixels and biological properties of vellum and paper and the distance reading of a thousand years of a word—all within a multimodal, multiplatform, intermedial, and remediated digital environment. Drucker writes,

> Pages will be temporary configurations based on calls to repositories and data sets. We will "publish" our data trails as guidebooks for the experience of reading, pointing to milestones and portals for in-depth exploration of stories, inventories, and the rich combination of cultural heritage and social life in a global world. The display will take advantage of the n-dimensional space of the screen in ways that combine multiple design visions.[26]

Within the book of the future, what we must understand is that visualization is and always will be an interpretive act. And the interface changes digital reading because of its dynamism by making the act of reading "a set of possibilities we encounter and from which we constitute the tissue of experience."[27] Digital reading will be located in an ever-changing ecosystem where reader and text will constitute multiple points of "intra-action." In this way, our bodily senses are particularly heightened in learning to move through this digital reading ecology. Thus, what is most difficult to address is why the emphasis has been on only one sense—sight—over others in digital project-building environments. Why did the AEME decide to invest first in designing the visual signature of its project before anything else?

The *Archive of Early Middle English*

Bracketed by the Norman Conquest in the eleventh century and the decline of the English populace as a result of the Plague (1348–1450), the Early Middle English period is characterized by its multilingualism and its interaction with cultural developments from Ireland to the Middle East.[28] In addition to four main literary languages (Latin, French, English, Welsh), Britain was also home to speakers and scholars of Greek, Hebrew, Irish, Old Norse, Arabic, and Dutch. This period also witnesses British crusaders' establishment and loss of colonies in the Middle East, as well as the expulsion of the Jews from England. Literature of the period frequently reflects these cultural encounters among Christians, Jews, Muslims, and heretics. This is a literary world very different from standard views of medieval England; as new scholarship is revealing, this world was multilingual, culturally and racially diverse, intellectually and aesthetically experimental.

Philologists and historical linguists find the Early Middle English period fascinating, for it arguably embraces the most systematic, extreme change in the English language in recorded history. The linguistic shift between 1100 and 1350 is, in many ways, far greater than that which separates Chaucer's use of language from that of Shakespeare.[29] In addition to internal developments during these centuries, multiple languages heavily influenced English, shaping not just its lexicon but its phonology, morphology, and syntax. The record of dialectical variations increases exponentially, and the unique multilingual and polyglot milieu of Britain makes this period and its materials of great potential interest for scholars working on the integration of cultures.[30] However, many of the period's manuscripts and texts either have not been edited or exist only in nineteenth-century editions. This makes a systematic, scientific study of data from these texts difficult and in some cases impossible.

In 2013, AEME was awarded an NEH Scholarly Editions and Translation grant in order to create the *Archive of Early Middle English* (AEME), which will be made freely available to scholars, students, and the public. Initially, we will produce an electronic edition of two Early Middle English manuscripts: Oxford, Bodleian Library Laud Misc. 108 and Oxford, Bodleian Library Junius 1. We also will begin substantive work on an edition of Oxford, Jesus College 29. Our new editions will contain not only electronic transcriptions but also encoded information on names, places, intertextual features, and philological, paleographical, and material features. All information and commentary will be searchable and easily adaptable to use in a variety of digital analytical forms. We also plan as part of the project to include translations.

Our proposed editions of Oxford, Bodleian Library Laud Misc. 108 and Oxford, Bodleian Library Junius 1 will contain the complete manuscript contents in a format that will easily accommodate the addition of new texts after the grant period ends. We have chosen these two manuscripts because their texts are fully available only in nineteenth-century editions and because they are also in high demand by both scholars and students. We believe that they are ideal test cases to fine-tune our editorial methods and publishing platform. Given the conceptual and technical challenges we are taking on for this project, we believe that beginning with manuscripts that have restricted numbers of identifiable individual texts is appropriate for achieving our project goals within the grant's timeframe. At the grant period's end, team members intend to continue editing Early Middle English texts to add to the larger archive, as well as to encourage submissions by other scholars.

Our project approaches the challenges of editing Early Middle English texts by treating them in their manuscript contexts as *material cultural objects,* rather than following earlier scholarship's tendency to evaluate Early Middle English literature purely in terms of its aesthetic or linguistic value. Rather than invoking the nineteenth-century, Romantic ideal of the authorial/artistic genius, we plan to examine Early Middle English texts first and foremost through the lens of their manuscript witnesses, addressing their larger multilingual, multimedia, and multitemporal contexts. We can examine how multiple texts appearing together in single manuscripts operate in conversation with each other. By focusing on manuscript materiality, we also hope to use the digital platform to think through questions of manuscript *mouvance*—material variation that includes textual modification, language switches, revision, expansion, replacement, and reorganization—within a three-dimensional platform. Thus, for example, our archive could support the physical analysis of a holograph author's penchant for gluing, cutting, and physically sewing in his revisions and changes. Likewise, since Early Middle English frequently appears in the same manuscript with non-English literature or literature from preceding and following periods, our focus on manuscript witnesses allows us to create editions that can ultimately encompass texts not traditionally considered Early Middle English but that allow readers to explore ways in which these linguistically and/or chronologically diverse texts interact.

We define the corpus of Early Middle English as all texts occurring in manuscripts containing Early Middle English according to the criteria laid out in Margaret Laing's *Catalogue of Sources for a Linguistic Atlas of Early Medieval English* (roughly, those written down between 1066 and 1340, and a few later copies of pre-1300 documentary material).[31] In compiling our list of manuscripts, we use c. 1350 as our end date, for this allows us to include a variety of linguistically Early Middle English material not included in Laing's catalogue. By these criteria, the total corpus of Early Middle English consists of about 162 manuscripts. Since the archive will include multilingual manuscripts, it will ultimately not be restricted exclusively to Early Middle English language texts, and will thus support growing scholarly interest in the French and Latin literature of England.[32] However, we recognize that this decision may have the inadvertent effect of reinforcing the traditional marginalized status of Early Middle English. By defining our corpus using manuscripts containing Early Middle English, we intend to make Early Middle English the focus of the cultural nexus of medieval England, turning the traditional scholarly approach on its head by shifting the marginal into the center.

The Proposed Editions

In this phase of the project, our proposed editions of Oxford, Bodleian Library, Laud Misc. 108, Oxford, Bodleian Library, Junius 1, and Oxford, Jesus College 29 will contain the complete manuscript contents in a format that will easily accommodate the addition of new texts after the grant period ends. Namely, we will be using TEI-XML encoding to encode the data themselves as a stable encoding language. TEI-XML is the Text Encoding Initiative standard for Extensible Markup Language that is the code used to be machine-readable. The archive itself will have open-source code and will be archived in the Brown Digital Repository.

Laud Misc. 108, a late-thirteenth-century manuscript with entirely English contents, including the earliest version of the *South English Legendary,* and versions of *Havelok the Dane, King Horn,* will allow us to do whole-book editing on a manuscript filled entirely with Early Middle English texts. Junius 1, the unusual *Ormulum* manuscript, will model how to treat a holograph manuscript with three-dimensional textual revision and also postmedieval revisions. Jesus 29, a multilingual anthology, will allow us to explore the editing of a multilingual codex containing Anglo-Norman French, Early Middle English, and Latin, as well as texts from different periods written on different media (paper and vellum).

The AEME has been envisioned as first an archive, a location—albeit a digital location—in which objects have been collected. What we are collecting is the 160+ manuscripts in the Early Middle English corpus. The standard for choosing each manuscript in this corpus is that it includes Early Middle English, whether this be the work of the entire manuscript or a marginal gloss. The whole manuscript is the item unit in our archive—in whatever language, media, or material state a manuscript has or is in. However, the material unit of our archive—the manuscript—has also meant that we are participating in the history of the book in specific ways that need to also address the medieval/digital sensorium.

Medieval/Digital Sensorium and the Long History of the Book

In the narratives of the history of the book, numerous critics have pointed out that the history of print has become the hegemonic center of book history. So much so, in fact, that several medievalists have taken to task Robert Darnton's definition of the history of the book as "the social and cultural history of communication by print."[33] Jessica Brantley pushes for a more capacious definition of the book: "the material support for inscribed language, a category that includes rolls, codices and even monumental inscription, both written by hand and printed by many different mechanisms, and also a wide variety of digital media."[34] And as Alison Walker points out in her article in *Digital Humanities Quarterly,* "The Boundless Book: A Conversation between the Pre-modern and Posthuman," where exactly does that leave premodern and posthuman "mediated" textuality? Where does that leave medieval manuscripts and digital texts?[35] Walker further argues that if one decenters print history in the narratives of the history of the book, what we then discern is that "reading technologies from the pre- and postprint eras anticipate the same sort of reader and share similar experiences."[36]

But strikingly, in our more recent discussion of electronic textuality, multisensory reading practices have turned our gaze back to the medieval world of manuscript textuality. We now hear and touch in order to read in a digital medium, and hopefully this signals a "paradigm shift" happening in digital reading worlds that have migrated away from a "dominant ocularcentrist aesthetic to a haptic aesthetic rooted in embodied affectivity."[37] Medieval reading practices were not linear, often required vocality to read out loud or sing out loud, ideally required slow and repetitive rereading, were emotive, and involved sound, smell, touch, taste, visual, and even bodily calisthenics. Literally, from how the book is made—from the physical embodiment of vellum or parchment (sheep or cow skin) to the visible remains of hair and flesh side on these writing surfaces—skin is interface. As recent discussions of manuscript materiality and reading have discussed, touch and the body were incredibly central to reading and interacting with a medieval manuscript. One constantly was reminded by the different interface textures between hair and flesh side of a folio as you turned the medieval page.[38] Physical flesh is always present in sound, touch, sight, taste, and smell when one opens a medieval manuscript. Medieval reading invokes emotive, bodily, and multisensory reading practices including touching, feeling, kissing, and licking manuscript parts and pages.[39] Thus, medieval manuscripts inscribe a history of the senses and the reader's/subject's/users' interaction with these fleshly interfaces. Medieval readers have deposited their breath, finger dirt, saliva, and probably bits of their dinners on the vellum page.

The aesthetic beauty and pleasure in building DH projects may hide the interpretive process, but "they are the persistent ghosts in the visual scheme."[40] But instead of hiding how visualization and visuality of the digital interface organize and interpret informational data, how exactly can we make room to highlight how visualization is an interpretative act? How do we allow room to make transparent the AEME's choices in its visual design and footprint? If visuality always is perceived as a transparent model of information that helps hide precisely how "constructed" data themselves really are, how can projects escape this building trap? What Drucker advocates is ways to build projects and build visualization models that encourage, highlight, present, and play with ambiguity and uncertainty.[41] By creating a marked space for ambiguity and uncertainty, Drucker argues that this allows digital zones to emphasize and lay bare the centrality of interpretation in the digital project's constructedness.[42]

What will happen when we move beyond squareness, which has been the guiding shape and visual principal of textual media for over a millennium? What will shift when we move beyond just visual pleasures and consider how the other senses—taste, tactility, and sound—will change the terrain of reading? If the current book is "a momentary slice through a complex stream of many networked conversations, versions, and fields of debate and reference across a wide variety of times and places," and it is but a "temporary intervention in a living field of language, images, and ideas" in which "each instantiation re-codifies the image of a book as an icon—whether mythic or banal, a treasure or an ordinary object of daily use," the future book already has taken these intersections and expanded, bent, reformed, and remediated this vision.[43] But for the future book, it cannot just remain fixed on the form of the medieval codex. Instead it will push the boundaries of fluidity and navigating ever-shifting situated contexts connected to "the vast repositories of knowledge, images, interpretation, and interactive platforms."[44] The book of the future will be a multitudinous event/object: "an interface, a richly networked portal, organized along lines of inquiry in which primary source materials, secondary interpretations, witnesses and evidence, are all available, incorporated, made accessible for use."[45] It is then rhizomatic: with multiplicities at work, "with no beginning nor end" and always *in media res*.[46]

As Drucker explains, "we are in the incunabula period of information design."[47] New frames, new questions, new ways to imagine linked relationships, meandering paths through reading, reading communities are only surfacing. And she is right to posit that "we are learning to read and think and write along rays, arrays, subdivisions, and patterns of thought."[48] For literary scholars and for readers/subjects/users of DH projects, digital textual data, digital editions, digital writing, and digital rhetoric, digital reading should mean that interpretative acts will be made visible and material and a flexible space of ambiguity will allow for multivocal and rhizomatic writing futures.

The Allure of Visual Aesthetics

So how does this all practically play out in DH project building? Graphesis and the visualization of data constitute the lion-share of DH tool building. If one does a search on the *Dirt: Digital Research Tools,* under "visual," you will come up with pages and pages of hits for possible tools to help you visualize data.[49] However, if you put in any other sensorial possibility—sound, touch, tactility, smell, taste—either nothing will come up or you will actually find items like "visualizing sound."[50] Yet, these are the tools available to most digital projects to do "something" with their coded data. I believe we can prod the ubiquity of graphesis as a default and hegemonic mode of thought which has thus led to a preponderance of such tools/modes in a discipline that often states it is about analysis. However, I do think there has been some small movement to break away and critique this default analytical setting. Recently, there have been a number of projects that have considered how to sonify data; nonetheless, the number of visualization options vastly outnumbers these sonifying options.[51]

Thus, the path always drives us to make pretty maps, as we see in the case of *Sexy Codicology's* manuscript maps; and in Angela Bennett's visualization of Piers Plowman manuscripts; and even the nodelxl map of #medievaltwitter networked range during the International Medieval Congress at Western Michigan University in 2014.[52]

Adam Foster, in a recent INKE (Implementing New Knowledge Environments) post titled "The Political Aesthetics of Digital Humanities Environments," exhorts the Digital Humanities to "be [more] attuned to the political message of scholarship the new knowledge environments crafted will boast, and consider if they do indeed change the inherent politics of scholarship."[53] He further speculates that in order to unpack the politics of a digital learning environment, we must ultimately address aesthetics.

This heavy reliance on the visual is particularly prevalent in DH projects; yet, the politics of aesthetics are rarely addressed. As Heather Froehlich commented at a historical corpus linguistic talk in Helsinki for Varieng in 2014,

Corpus linguistics is a very text-oriented approach to language data, with much interest in curation, collection, annotation, and analysis—all things of much concern to digital humanists. If corpus linguistics is primarily concerned with text, digital humanities can be argued to be primarily concerned about images: how to visualize textual information in a way that helps the user understand and interact with large data sets.[54]

Froehlich finishes her talk by asking a provocative question: "If digital humanities currently serves mostly to supplement knowledge, rather than create knowledge, we need to start thinking forward to ask 'What else can we do with this data we've been curating?'"[55] She finishes by pointing out that "digital tools and techniques are question-making machines, not answer-providing packages." I would like to push this even further with these excellent points and ask, how does creating data become opportunities for question-making? How can we think about knowledge building in ethical, balanced, and critical ways that make DH projects beyond avenues to supplementary knowledge?

Is visualizing data (the DH bells and whistles), the awe-inspiring beauty of visualizations, then the ornament of a digital project? As an avenue of supplementing knowledge, are visualizations a form of digital ornament? In discussions of digital archive preservation, scholars, librarians, and computer programmers have already separated what is primary and what is supplemental knowledge. What is essential to preserve is not the visualization tools but the data in a stable code. The visualization coding and software applications become part of the functionality of the portal or interface, but they are not the priority when thinking about long-term preservation benchmarks. I believe that in order to address visual aesthetics, we must turn to the critical discussions in art history.

Art History, Visuality, and Pleasure

It is from art history, rather than cinema studies, that I wish to frame out discussions of visualization, visual pleasure, and digital environments. In particular, the work of David Brett and his book *Rethinking Decoration: Pleasure and Ideology in the Visual Arts* help reframe ideas of "decoration and ornament" as "a family of practices devoted mainly to visual pleasure; and treat this pleasure as a family of values, which includes social recognition, perceptual satisfaction, psychological reward and erotic delight (amongst others, all overlapping one another)."[56] He remarks that these are public values because they are in plain view and that further they show individual experience.

His work in theorizing decoration and ornament looks at Pierre Bourdieu's schemata of perception with a little nod to Kant, but relies heavily on John Dewey's "naturalistic account of experience as a relationship between an organism and its situation—an account which does away with subject/object dichotomies in favour of an interactive model of perception and meaning."[57] Thus, Brett's arguments about reframing visual pleasure in relation to decoration and ornament are precisely centered on an individual's "experience" with the natural, visual, decorative world. In this way, his theoretical points fit well into the immersive, interactive, yet highly visual worlds of DH projects because visual pleasure is about centering the individual experience and point of view.

I now wish to turn to the AEME to consider how this medieval DH project remediates medieval manuscript textuality into digital textuality and what that world looks like for the history of the book, for multimodal reading, for the postcolonial archive stories of the building of this medieval manuscript archive, and finally, what the theoretical implications are of building this world. What does the AEME's choices in digital database design say about decolonial, feminist material, and multivocal archive building? What is the AEME's archive story, and how is it figured as an embodied archive?

The State of Early Middle English Studies

When linguistic and literary scholars have described the Early Middle English period (roughly ca. 1100–1350), their collective evaluations have labeled it "one of the dullest and least accessible intervals in standard literary history, an incoherent, intractable, impenetrable dark age scarcely redeemed by a handful of highlights."[58] J. A. Bennett and G. V. Smithers, embarking on an edition of extracts of Early Middle English literature in 1966, found little to challenge "the traditional view that the reigns of William [the Conqueror] and his sons mark an hiatus in our literature and the widespread literary use of the vernacular that is such a distinctive feature of Anglo-Saxon culture."[59] Even scholars who recognize shifting aesthetic standards nonetheless dismiss Early Middle English literature on the basis of principles laid down in the nineteenth century, when much of this material was first (and often last) edited. Thus, Early Middle English is imagined as a literary wasteland in which "the débris of an old literature is mixed in with the imperfectly processed materials of a new."[60] Even when scholars try to depart from these paradigms, there is a tendency, as Christopher Cannon observes, to view Early Middle English texts in terms of a "profound isolation from immediate vernacular models and examples, from any local precedent for the business of writing English."[61] For Hahn, the period has a reputation for "aridity and remoteness," and for Cannon, the consequence is "literary history's general sense that there is nothing there, since the lack of continuous tradition has so generally (and subtly) been equated with a lack of literature."[62] But the Early Middle English period was in fact a time of intense linguistic change, literary experimentation, and textual production that juggled regional specificities, genres in process, and multilingual interactions with verve.

From an explanation of Early Middle English, one can see how disruptive and difficult to pin down the period and its manuscripts/texts are. Even if one just takes a quick sample look at the manuscripts, you can see their vast range and often illegibility. If one examines samples only from the first three manuscripts the AEME will edit—Oxford, Bodleian Library MS Misc. Laud 108; Oxford Bodleian Library, MS Junius 1 also known as the *Ormulum*; and Oxford, Jesus College MS 29—you see the lack of uniformity. If you add the page containing a fragment of the early Middle English lyric *Worldes Blisce,* only preserved on a scrap of vellum slotted in sideways at the end of Cambridge, Corpus Christi Library MS 8, the interface *mise-en-système* of this manuscript's archives are multiple.[63]

The contours and shape of the archive and the corpus are difficult to narrate. Early Middle English is zone betwixt and between, a literary eruption, an epistemological disruption of linear narratives of literary history, manuscript production, and stories of continuity. In the 162-manuscript corpus, a little over fifteen items are entirely in Early Middle English. The rest are in multilingual compilations. In addition, the most popular Middle English text from the period was the product of female anchoritic patronage rather than a monastic milieu or a royal court. The period has no masculine epic like *Beowulf* or the Nowell Codex for the Anglo-Saxon period, no visual splendor, no court poet like Chaucer or Gower. Instead, we have plucked the image of Laȝamon's decorated initial, based on visual cues of Jerome in Jerome Bibles, as writer/as coder but primarily because there were so few visual fields available in our corpus. So the question is, how does a team, mostly of women, rethink a digital archive of disruptive objects?

The importance of the visual point of view as I have discussed with Brett and art history is also the underlying framework that is building the spine of our archive. Our encoding documents reveal that we are primarily focused on our XML encoding schema. This choice that we have made to focus on XML is about sustainability in code, practicalities of work flow, but also I would argue a theoretical choice. Recently several projects have begun to use Resource Description Framework (RDF) as the base building block of their projects. But the best way to explain the different forms of data modeling and how they will have an effect on the constructedness of the data themselves requires a description of data model choices.

Data Models and the Semantic Web

The best quick and easy explanation with graphs on data storage models for the semantic web is available from *Linked Data Tools*.[64] In this modeling of data, what one has to understand is how information (and in the case of literary and historical databases this is usually a textual set of data) in data modules is organized. There are currently three different kinds of data schemes that can be easily explained by a visual diagram.

First is the relational database that usually is built with programs like MySQL and MS SQL.[65] MySQL is the one of the most popular open-source relational database management systems (RBDSM). It underwrites sites including WordPress, Facebook, and Twitter. It is a model of data organization that thinks through relations and links. Thus, it thinks about data units and their organization through a relational model, a network.

The second data model is a hierarchical one using TEI-XML (Text Encoding Initiative–Extensible Markup Language). This data model is usually the one used most for DH edition projects because the hierarchical model allows for a tiered data organization structure that accounts for the organization of books—the book, the author, the chapters, the sentence or line, and so on. This organization, of course, is about the layout and format, the *mise-en-page* of the codex that was developed in the Middle Ages. In TEI-XML, you can organize a data informational structure that has a very schematized guideline. It is easy to identify textual units including chapters, sections, and lines.

The third data model is RDF. This model is an arbitrary object relations model; in other words, there is no schematized structure or relation networked connection. Instead, it works more like a blank sandbox in which you place the various digital objects in arbitrary relations. The usefulness of this model is about digital objects— like manuscript pages—in which you can do mock-ups that are as close to the original as possible. In other words, as the example from Stanford's Shared Canvas demonstrates, it is as near to surrogacy to the original data space as possible.[66] It also allows for different kinds of organizations. For instance, TEI-XML works best when items have lines, but what do you do with handwritten manuscripts in which handwritten marginalia, drawings, charts, doodles, and other nontextual material are presented all over a manuscript page? Because of its canvas/sandbox frame, RDF models allow the possibility of making units of code in relation to marked-out zones or areas.

I am walking through the schematics of this because it brings up the question of what data models for a digital edition and eventually an archive will mean in terms of how readers of the editions and archive understand the interpretive architecture already built into the digital item that the reader or participant will be working, playing, and reading. And a discussion of the database choices also explains visual pleasure, as explained in David Brett's *Rethinking Decoration*, in which visual pleasure is precisely about an individual's experience with his or her environment.

Data Layers and Archival Points of View

> "Experience, though noon auctoritee / Were in this world, is right ynogh for me" (Chaucer, Wife of Bath's Prologue, 1–2).[67]

The AEME Guidelines specify that manuscripts in the archive will be composed of at least four layers of representation to support user interaction and workflow:

image, facsimile transcription, diplomatic (uncorrected) transcription, and critical transcription.[68] If one or more of these are unavailable, they can be supplied with place fillers. This basic structure allows for further layers of representation to be added, such as a translation. Image metadata and transcription texts will be searchable. We describe each of these features in greater detail below.

1. *Image:* Access to manuscript digital facsimiles containing Early Middle English texts. AEME-held images will initially be photographed as 24-bit 600 dpi max TIFF files. These will be converted to lower-resolution JPG200 files for service on the AEME platform. Images integrated through LOD may vary in format and quality, but the platform will be able load the most common formats.
2. *Facsimile Transcription:* An encoded mock-up of page elements that can then stand in for missing images (such as when part of a manuscript has not been digitized) and which can further serve to categorize page elements into searchable objects for comparative analysis.
3. *Diplomatic Transcription:* A more or less literal transcription of the text for readers interested in the scribal representation of the text. Coded in TEI-XML following AEME markup guidelines.
4. *Critical Transcription:* A transcription of the text including various types of editorial intervention, including modernized punctuation and capitalization, editorial corrections and notes, and contextual information (glossary references, geolocation tags, etc.). It is anticipated that the critical layer will be suitable for student readers. Coded in TEI-XML following AEME markup guidelines.
5. *Translation:* The AEME platform will accept translations of texts, which will be displayable in the same way as diplomatic and critical transcriptions.
6. *General Search* and discovery of digital images and texts.

With the exception of the facsimile layer, we are primarily coding in TEI-XML. However, there are examples of projects that have begun using RDF as the primary editing space. For example, the Shared Canvas project out of Stanford University is creating an RDF editing platform. It has done a mock-up—if you look at slide 53 in this slide-share you can see their mock-up of *Worldes Blisce* from the Parker Library CCCC MS 8.[69] What they are demonstrating is that they can overlay the coding for the edition on top of the manuscript like a palimpsest and then encode an audio file so that the lines can be sung when one clicks the edited line. They use RDF as their main building framework. AEME has decided to work with TEI-XML for everything but the facsimile layer, which is in fact a layer that fits this particular data model.

We have made a choice to privilege experience over ideas of "objective" data; we have prioritized visual pleasure. RDF splits information into grid units (or zones) on a screen, and each square unit of data in the grid is moved and read in this way. Thus, I would argue that RDF is actually the digital heir of Dürer's grid in which objects are broken up into individual grid units in order to produce visual perspective.[70] This visual perspective gives the artist the God's eye view of the world. And as the famous image of Dürer's grid reveals, what gets broken up are not just landscape images and objects but also people, especially women. As art history has discussed, perspective can often be violent to these objects, and it is often women objectified behind the grid.[71]

AEME has discussed RDF, but we have chosen to go with TEI-XML because it allows us to see the narrative of individual editors. We have prioritized the experience and interaction with the material from the point of view of each reader. We have privileged individual archive stories, rather than imagining the possibility of algorithmic objectivity in building the spine of the archive. We have decentered the archive, flattened subject/object relationships, allowed for a multiplicity of views; we have built in room for the individual editor/editor who currently and in the future will work and play in our archive location.[72] We have attempted the actual digital building praxis of a decolonized and feminist archives manifesto. In my mind, it is the difference between RDF as the genealogical child of Dürer's perspective grid versus the narrative choices of individual interaction. We have chosen the path of the Wife of Bath; we have taken "experience" over algorithmic authority.

You can see this working even on a micro level with our decisions. For example, in an early discussion about editorial frameworks, Scott Kleinman (co-director) sent a question out to the group to discuss:

> Verse-initial letters (often highlighted by shadow gaps, rubrication, and the like) can be difficult to identify as capital or lower case. I have drafted the following suggestion for handling this phenomenon in the Guidelines:
>
> Verse-initial letters should always be capitalised inside <reg> tags (i.e. the critical representation). The representation in the diplomatic layer can be problematic because it is often difficult to distinguish capitals from non-capitals in this position. AEME leaves it up to the editor's discretion to decide ambiguous cases. Future versions of these Guidelines will list some best practices to aid in decision-making. A useful tool would be a list of suspect letters.
>
> Please comment on this guideline. Does it seem adequate to you? Can we begin compiling a list of letters that should be called to the transcriber's attention?[73]

As this micro-discussion point shows, we have at every turn privileged individual interaction with the manuscript and data as the final say in our decisions. The last email round was about capital letters in a manuscript and how we have indeterminancy problems and what we may want to do about that. We came up with the suspect letter list and then the narrative discretion of each editor. The *Archive of Early Middle English* then is focused on how archival manuscript bodies interact with editorial bodies. We are in essence capturing the experience of editors with the physical and the digital manuscripts and how this interaction happens. We are recording their aesthetic and visual pleasure. My last point about Shared Canvas's publishing possibilities also brings up the question of how to get away from privileging the visual in DH projects. Where is the space where we can interrogate these issues? I believe this will really come from Disability Studies in Digital Humanities building. And this shift to Disability Studies is where the AEME will develop into more robustly capturing the process and experience of its editorial/user/player bodies.

Disability Studies

In current disability studies, the term used to discuss designing web environments with disability issues in mind is "universal design." Adeline Koh wrote about her experience at the Accessible Future Workshop in Austin 2014 and critiqued numerous issues with the idea of universal design.[74] But it is the Twitter conversation on the hashtag that brings up the most resonant issues in relation to making visible the agendas of our digital projects and the issues of the senses in digital project building. She explained on Twitter her discomfort with imagining "universal" accessibility as a default to be the priority benchmark. She explained through the lens of postcolonial theory and criticism whether "universal" should be desired by all when, in fact, postcolonial writers often resist writing in "accessible" colonial languages as a form of resistance. She explained that "the drive towards universal and ultimate accessibility for everyone and everything, seen in this light has parallels with a colonial impulse to observe, survey, control, force open."[75]

Universal design becomes too close to the ideas of one-size-fits-all in Enlightenment political liberalism. It also references current critical race discussions about how postracial ideas of the "universal" erase difference. The term "design" itself already problematizes this because it values visual aesthetics, and even the term "architecture" has connotations and agendas centered on the 1 percent, and on masculine visuality and the gaze.[76] In my interactions with the Twitter discussion, I pointed out that the goal of disability studies should be to disrupt the very idea of "accommodation" in order to reconceptualize how building computer programs or actual buildings should be disrupted and rethought from the disability studies angle. We should stop thinking only as ableist+accommodations, but rather from disability studies' point of view to rethink the critical possibilities. What if the mainstream angle was the angle of disability studies? In digital humanities work for instance, classic textual data modeling is a simple wordle (http://www.wordle.net) word cloud with colors and shapes. Why can't the norm of textual data analysis be a sound cloud or a textural cloud that allows you to print a 3-D model to touch?

These are questions I have asked Rick Godden and Jonathan Hsy as I edited the revision of their article "Universal Design and Its Discontents" for *Disrupting the Digital Humanities*. In particular, Rick Godden explains:

> As an entry point to my reflections on Universal Design, I want to first think about some of the ways that Digital Humanities (DH), Disability Studies (DS), and Universal Design (UD) productively converge using recent discussions about the physical act of hand-written notes as an opening example. This is not unusual in a bid to consider the necessity of UD; however, I also want to use this example in order to begin to disorient some of our understandings of UD. Although UD arose out of a real social and political response to the disabling aspects of everyday life for People with Disabilities, I want to suggest that the "Universal" in UD can carry with it some unintended and unexpected assumptions about normalcy and our physical orientation to the world. . . . But what they are also doing, whether intended or not, is participating in "compulsory able-bodiedness," where "normal," "best," and "able-bodied" ultimately occupy the same subject position.[77]

I am interested in how to disorient digital humanities and DH projects. How does a multiplicity of views through the experience of a multiplicity of different bodies help rethink the future of the AEME? As I said in my comments, architecture is too burdened with art in the hands of the elite; instead, I prefer to consider the process of intelligent, critical building. And in the discussion on Twitter, I reply to several of the conference participants and ask if we can't begin to go beyond "accommodations." Instead, we should center the point of view of disability studies as the vision of the digital humanities project. From disability studies scholarship, I believe we can begin to think through issues of tactility, sound, and other sensory perceptions that will help us rethink our digital tools and our digital agendas. For instance, why use word clouds only, or even sound visualized clouds? Why aren't there more options to allow us to analyze poetic data orally by the loudness of various repeated words? Medieval manuscripts are media devices that record multimedia and multimodal experiences. They are visually laid out, but the reader and user is asked to bring the data to life, to make them sing, dance, move. In fact, the world of medieval manuscripts is an early vision of a functioning *mise-en-système*.

It is through the angle of disabilities studies that we can decenter the focus on visuality that has been central to the digital humanities, to move away from "ocularcentrism." Instead, the critical possibilities may include a move away from the classic textual data modeling as a simple wordle word cloud w/colors and shapes. Instead, we may be able to begin imagining the norm of data analysis through a sound cloud or a texture cloud that allows you to print a 3-D model to touch. This possibility of different data analytics has only just begun to surface. For example, a recent blog post discusses a class that has taken a tactile path in data analytics in collaboration with art practice, literary studies, and DH.[78] This beautiful and jagged blazon sculpture highlights where other data analysis vis-à-vis the other senses may go, but I believe further critical discussions especially in relation to critical disability studies will help form critical discussions about these models. Thus, an individual's polyvocal, multibodied pleasure becomes the entry point to navigate an ecosystem.

Skyscraper versus Snake

So if the *Archive of Early Middle English* is a repository of individual editorial experiences interacting with the digital and physical materiality of objects, then what is our final goal? Our goals are decidedly rhizomatic—here, I am specifically referring to Deleuze and Guattari's theory of "multiple, non-hierarchical entry and exit points of data representation and interpretation" that Adeline Koh and Roopika Risam have pointed out as the possibility of digital archives—for a number of reasons. Wide use and access are the AEME's goal. But so is wide building from what I would describe as the project's eventual stable skeleton. I have argued about this difference in building a digital project with other digital humanists in the past. AEME does not want to architecturally design a skyscraper that requires years of digging out the basement and substructure of a digital project only to find out that years after building, the technology and materials have changed and the skyscraper will not be able to stand without major changes. In this way, much of early DH project focused on monumental architectural designs that took years and never quite finished what they wanted before technology, money, and general sustainability made their DH skyscrapers half-finished ruins on the digital landscape.

AEME's main goal is to create a stable yet flexible manuscript skeleton mostly built by TEI-XML to allow for future users and builders to graft, "enflesh" on layers to our stable frame whatever world they wish to create, interconnect, recreate, form, deform. So instead of a skyscraper, I imagine the *Archive of Early Middle English* and its archival building goals as more akin to the flexible spine of a snake. We wish to build a digital portal that fulfills the possibilities of interface "in-betweeness" where speaker and spoken are created. We want to create a *mise-en-système* that critically remediates the *mise-en-système/mise-en-page* of medieval manuscripts, their somatic reading practices, their worlds. We want to create an ecology that can be a provocative catalyst for cascades of intra-action between participant, text, community, image, sound, and so on. Whether they be students creating narrative bitstrips with our translated *Havelok the Dane* or historical linguistics adding layers of linguistic markup, or musicologists visualizing the notation models in the early Middle English corpus, the builders of AEME would like all of this to happen and the archive to change and be added to, used, and played with in these different ways. In this way, the AEME will never be a "finished" product, but a system always in flux. It will be, as the "TwitterEthics Manifesto" discussed, always in process. In the end, the archive's goal is access and use to the widest range of people so they can create a multiplicity of experiences in the database.

Archive Stories

I would like to end by relating AEME's archive story. If AEME is an archive of objects and to create this archive is to essentially create a visual, multimedia narrative of Early Middle English, what is that story? In Antoinette Burton's edited collection *Archive Stories: Facts, Fiction, and The Writing of History,* she writes that the underlying issue at stake in the volume is that the claims to "objectivity associated with the traditional archive pose a challenge which must be met in part by telling stories about its provenance, its histories, its effect on its users, and above all, its power to shape all the narratives which are to be 'found' there."[79] In this way, they claim they are constructing "self-conscious ethnographies of one of the chief investigative foundations of History as a discipline."[80] They emphasize the critical importance of these "archive stories," these ethnographies that explain everything about how an archive was created, used, and experienced, in order to highlight that "all archives are 'figured.'"[81] What Burton means by this is not just self-conscious creation but that archives "all have dynamic relationships, not just to the past and the present, but to the fate of regimes, the physical environment, the serendipity of bureaucrats, and the care and neglect of archivists."[82]

As for the archive's appeal, so much of it is centered on sensory experiences and the romance of history they invoke, whether they be the actual dust one breathes as Caroline Steedman writes, or the *habitus,* the experience of the archive itself—the silence, the tension, the smell, the feel of the archival matter/material as Arlette Farge writes in her classic *The Appeal of the Archive.*[83] Farge writes herself about the experience of the historian/archivist as waiting for that moment when "the sheer pleasure of being astonished by the beauty of the texts and the overabundance of life brimming in so many ordinary lives" grabs hold of the archivist. And the archive itself is governed by emotion: "To feel the allure of the archive is to seek to extract additional meaning from the fragmented phrases found there. Emotion is another tool with which to split the rock of the past, of silence."[84] In this way, the appeal and often the drive of the archive are a single-minded sensorial drive toward pleasure through vision, touch, smell, and sound. In this way, the physical and digital archives are mimetic in their drive for sensory pleasure. However, they diverge in their possibilities for access and viewpoint. One is built to exclude and be about power; the other has the potential to be multiple and disrupt hierarchical power structures.

However, this romance is helped by the archive's inaccessibility. Archives, in the words of Michel Foucault, were "documents of exclusion" and "monuments to particular configurations of power."[85] And the archive itself is both potentially a "mundane workplace and a panopticon of intense surveillance."[86] It is from postcolonial studies where we have seen the archive used politically and socially and often becoming a "technology of imperial power, conquest, and hegemony."[87] Archival making, revision, and erasures are not neutral, objective acts, but rather usually critical, rhetorical, and shaped by nationalist, political, and social agendas. Burton asks how the personal encounters and experience of archive uses matter in constructing archival histories. How in fact do gender, race, ability, religion, and sexuality and the negotiations between archival objects and archival users and the power dynamics therein play out?

These questions, in many ways, may be a bit surprising to some because we are discussing primarily the building of the *Archive of Early Middle English*. How can an archival build of 162 medieval manuscript objects with items of early Middle English text be considered politicized, socially charged, or even shaped by postcolonial and national discourses? Yet, the archive we are discussing shapes the story of a historical colonial power, and it is this archival build that is being funded by the National Endowment for the Humanities, an arm of the U.S. government. The archive's time period, 1100–1350, is historically a moment after the Norman Conquest, a temporal eruption of colonialism and conquest. In addition, the project directors and editorial team are made almost entirely of women, several with intersectional identities related to race, sexual orientation, and religion. In many ways, our archival stories inform our individual archival experiences that we are telegraphing into this digital archive.

There are reasons to make archival labor—usually hidden from view—clear and apparent. Consider one of the main sources of concomitant scholarly digital big data utopia and critical angst: Google Books and its mass digitization project. It has only been recently that any considerations about mass digitization have addressed the issue of the gendered and often racialized labor that has powered this project. In Shawn Wen's recent article, "The Ladies Vanish," she discusses the invisible, separated, and underpaid labor happening in Silicon Valley and specifically on the Google campus.[88] She writes about the army of invisible, segregated, usually female and either Latina or Black labor that arrives in the middle of the night (4 a.m.) and leaves in the afternoon (2 p.m.). They are separate and not equal to the rest of the computer engineers and daily staff at Google. They do not mingle; they are never seen but hide in a different building or on separate floors. These are the women who do the painstakingly detailed work of digitizing the world's knowledge also known as Google Books and the Google Books Library Project. They are Google's army of "mechanical turkers," so named after the eighteenth-century automaton robot, a chess player automaton unveiled in 1770 in Austria that had a human inside of the machine working its parts. As Wen writes,

> Of course books don't digitize themselves. Human hands have to individually scan the books, to open the covers and flip the pages. But when Google promotes its project—a database of "millions of books from libraries and publishers worldwide"—they put the technology, the search function and the expansive

virtual library in the forefront. The laborers are erased from the narrative, even as we experience their work firsthand when we look at Google Books.[89]

The vision of a worldwide, accessible, digitally available library of scanned books rarely gets the same attention as the realities of gendered, racialized, and the underpaid labor that produce these products "magically" for the world. In arguably the biggest Big Data project for the history of the book, the material bodies of these "turkers" are rarely examined in relation to the digital paper bodies they scan and digitally release to the world. They are part of the invisible digital laborers that Lisa Nakamura discusses in "Economies of Digital Production in East Asia: iPhone Girls and the Transnational Circuits of Cool" who power our digital lives.[90] Our digital archive futures are being built on the backs of the invisible labor of women of color around the world or in this case in Silicon Valley itself. Yet, these unknown, unseen, and uncredited women are the ones perfecting this big data future of the world's library. As Shawn Wen explains, "Relying on data from mechanical turkers, computers have dramatically improved in recent years at facial recognition, translation, and transcription. These were tasks previously thought to be impossible for computers to complete accurately. Which means that mechanical turkers (mostly women) teach computers to do what engineers (mostly men) cannot on their own program computers to do."[91] These are the women perfecting the algorithmic perfection of optical character recognition (OCR), the process driving the continued improvement in the search accuracies of Google Books.

The *Archive of Early Middle English* is a DH project that in evaluating the critical stakes of its own work will and must address the archive stories of the labor behind it. Our signatures, our digital paper trails of work, our streams of online discussion on ASANA, GitHub, and listservs are parts of the project's archive that are being preserved in the files of our archival creation. How ironic would it be for a digital archive—whose main influential and popular text was fueled by the drive of female readers (i.e., *Ancrene Wisse*) and where so many other manuscripts have had scholarly questions about the possibilities of female scribes and "authors" (i.e., Katherine Group and *The Owl and the Nightingale*) that have left no visible mark of gendered ownership, authority, or labor—vanish its own digital editors, graphic artists, and builders? The mostly women behind the *Archive of Early Middle English* are the physical bodies driving the machine, but we plan to speak, to write, to sign our work, and to leave our records to explain how we have "figured" in this digital archive in progress. Our bodies matter to the imprint we leave on our digital archive.

I would like to begin this process by telling my own archive story. My archive story must include the fact that as an Asian woman continuously traveling to Britain to visit these archives, I have acquired a number of library cards from the Bodleian, Cambridge, Lambeth Palace, British Library, and so on. Yet, my passport's steady entrance into Britain and undoubtedly my "suspect" racialized body, not to mention my markedly Californian accent, have regularly made me a suspicious body at

Customs in Heathrow. "Why," they ask "are you coming to Britain?" I say "for business." "What kind of business?" they ask. I reply, "To do research in the manuscript archives." The interrogation goes on usually until I begin pulling out the sheer number of specialized library cards in my wallet. This archive story speaks acutely to the power dynamics, the odd-accented postcoloniality, the negotiations at play in working and now building the *Archive of Early Middle English*.

The Archive Story of Early Middle English

I would like to end by addressing that final question: what is the story of Early Middle English? Because of the indeterminate, varied, disparate, and in-flux status of the manuscripts in the corpus, because the Early Middle English period is an epoch of intense change and also what I would call a moment of mass experimentation, the archive story of Early Middle English is one of intra-action. I believe it is the story of indeterminancy, of slippery desire, of frustrated pleasures. It is the story of experimental multilingualism; experimental genre forms; the emergence of the lyric, the romance, history, debate, sermon, prose guidebook, and first drama in Middle English. This, then, is what the story of Early Middle English is: it is local, contingent, unformed, still forming, difficult to categorize, difficult to create clear-cut distinctions between causality, agency, space, time, matter, discourse, responsibility, and accountability. But by creating an archive, by editors who are recording their experience with the archive, we are precisely enacting "an agential cut" that allows us to define the archive as forever in progress, forever local and dialectal, always indeterminate.

Notes

1. *Archive of Early Middle English* Development Site.
2. "Encoding Guidelines" and the AEME *GitHub* site.
3. Dorothy Kim (@dorothyk98), Twitter post, 22 September 2016, 3:34 pm, https://twitter.com/dorothyk98/status/779086436737818625/photo/1?ref_src=twsrc%5Etfw&ref_url=https%3A%2F%2Fstorify.com%2FJonathanHsy%2Fmakingeme-day-1-fri-23-sep-2016)/.
4. *The Journal of Early Middle English* will publish its inaugural issue in 2018 and will annually publish two blind peer-reviewed issues a year from ArcPress/MIP. It is currently supported by the University of Victoria and I am an associate editor.
5. In feminist theory, the term "visual pleasure" would immediately point to Laura Mulvey's classic work in cinema studies: Mulvey, "Visual Pleasure." However, as my essay will later explain, digital humanities archives and databases do not function like cinema with one central viewer. In fact, I would argue, the opening of an archive means multiple hands, bodies, viewers, creators, hackers who shape and reshape the archive. The sight lines are varied and multitudinous.

6. Drucker, *Graphesis*, 21.

7. Drucker, *Graphesis*, 21.

8. Parkes, "Influence of Ordinatio and Compilatio." See also Drucker, *Graphesis*, 47, 54, and 164.

9. Drucker, *Graphesis*, 139.

10. Drucker, *Graphesis*, 139.

11. Drucker, *Graphesis*, 150.

12. Drucker, *Graphesis*, 150.

13. Alaimo and Hekman, "Introduction," 1.

14. Alaimo and Hekman, "Introduction," 5.

15. Alaimo and Hekman, "Introduction," 9.

16. Alaimo and Hekman, "Introduction," 8.

17. Alaimo and Hekman, "Introduction," 6.

18. Alaimo and Hekman, "Introduction," 17.

19. Christensen and Hauge, "Feminist Materialism," 4.

20. Barad, "Nature's Queer Performativity," 32.

21. Christensen and Hauge, "Feminist Materialism," 5.

22. Drucker, *Graphesis*, 154.

23. Moretti, *Distant Reading*; Manovich, "Scale Effects."

24. See for example, Denbo, "Diggable Data."

25. Drucker, *Graphesis*, 154.

26. Drucker, *Graphesis*, 63.

27. Drucker, *Graphesis*, 155.

28. This descriptive section about the AEME comes from multiple versions of our NEH Scholarly Editions and Translation grant application. I am chief grant writer, but the grant applications were also always collaborative writing and editing projects.

29. Hahn, "Early Middle English," 62.

30. For instance, as Dorothy Kim and Andrea Lankin have noted, the *South English Legendary Life of Thomas Becket* in Laud Misc. 108 contains loanwords from Welsh, linking a saint whom the text imagines as simultaneously English and foreign to the vocabulary of English colonization. Dorothy Kim treated the subject in "Unfettering the Welsh in Laʒamon's *Brut* and the *South English Legendary*."

31. Laing, *Catalogue of Sources*.

32. The AEME Advisory Board includes Professor Wogan-Browne, who directs the French of England Project. Although the two projects share a concern with literature produced in England after the Norman Conquest, there is no overlap since the primary output of the French of England Project is print translations of texts written in French. However, we hope to draw the two projects closer by setting up AEME as a platform for the publication of French of England texts surviving in Early Middle English manuscripts, increasing access to these texts, expanding the coverage of the Archive, and more accurately portraying the multilingual context in which Early Middle English literature was produced and read.

33. Darnton, *Kiss of Lamourette*, 10.
34. Brantley, "Prehistory of the Book," 634.
35. Walker, "Boundless Book," 8.
36. Walker, "Boundless Book," 10.
37. Hansen, *New Philosophy*, 2.
38. Walker, "Boundless Book," 8. See also Camille, "Book as Flesh"; Walter, *Reading Skin*; Kay, "Legible Skins"; and Holsinger, "Of Pigs" and "Parchment Ethics."
39. See Kathryn Rudy's work on late medieval devotional texts and bodily responses to them and how she has measured the dirt with a densitometer to discover the obsessive focus of devotional readers: Rudy, "Dirty Books." See also Wilcox, *Scraped*.
40. Drucker, *Graphesis*, 66.
41. Drucker, *Graphesis*, 126.
42. Drucker, *Graphesis*, 177.
43. Drucker, *Graphesis*, 174.
44. Drucker, *Graphesis*.
45. Drucker, *Graphesis*.
46. Deleuze and Guattari, *Thousand Plateaus*, 23.
47. Drucker, *Graphesis*, 176.
48. Drucker, *Graphesis*, 189.
49. *Dirt: Digital Research Tools*.
50. This has slowly shifted, though the number of visualization possibilities far outweighs the sonification of data. You can see some of this new work in "Sonification of UCSD Campus Energy Consumption"; "Sonification Lab"; and "'Everything on Paper Will Be Used Against Me.'"
51. See Graham, "Sound of Data"; Scaletti, "Data Sonification"; and the data sonification *GitHub* site.
52. *DMMapp*; Segler, "Seeing the Body"; Hsy, "#medievaltwitter revisited."
53. Foster, "Political Aesthetics."
54. Froehlich, "CEECing New Directions."
55. Froehlich, "CEECing New Directions."
56. Brett, *Rethinking Decoration*, 4.
57. Brett, *Rethinking Decoration*, 9. See Alexander, *John Dewey's Theory*.
58. Hahn, "Early Middle English," 61. Very few systematic histories of medieval English literature discuss the period under the rubric "Early Middle English." Hahn's is one of the few, and thus essential in defining the archive. The description of Early Middle English in this section is one I have used in the grant documents of AEME.
59. Bennett and Smithers, *Early Middle English Verse*, xii.
60. Shepherd, "Early Middle English Literature," 81.
61. Cannon, *Grounds of English Literature*, 2. It should be noted that Cannon is the only scholar who has attempted to address Early Middle English as a period since Hahn's essay in the *Cambridge History of Medieval English Literature*.

62. Hahn, "Early Middle English," 62, and Cannon, *Grounds of English Literature*, 3.

63. "Earliest Surviving English Romances"; Thomas, *Muddling through the Middle Ages*, image of fol. 10r; "Jesus College, Oxford; see *Digital Manuscripts Index*, Stanford University, http://dms.stanford.edu/zoompr/CCC008_keywords?druid=cv176gb0028&folio=f.+i+R&headline=PHN0cm9uZz5bIkNhbWJyaWRnZSwgQ29ycHVzIENocmlzdGkgQ29sbGVnZSwg%0AUGFya2VyIExpYnJhcnksIENDQ0MgTVMgOCJdPC9zdHJvbmc%2BPGJy IC8%2BWyJW%0AZWxsdW0iXSwgWyIxNi45IHggMTEuNSJdLCBbInhpdiBlYXJseSJd PGJyIC8%2B%0AWyJWaW5jZW50IG9mIEJlYXV2YWlzIE9QLCBTcGVjdWx1bSBoa XN0b3JpYWxl%0ALCBib29rcyAxLTE0Il0%3D%0A&height=9153&image=008_i_R_TC_46&ms=8&sequence_num=543&total_sequence_num=548&width=5922 (accessed 19 February 2018).

64. "Tutorial 1."

65. *MySQL*.

66. Sanderson and Albritton, "Shared Canvas Data Model 1.0."

67. Chaucer, "Wife of Bath's Prologue," 105.

68. One can see this currently discussed in the editorial guidelines: "AEME Guidelines."

69. Sanderson and Albritton, "Introduction to SharedCanvas."

70. "Albrecht Durer."

71. Berger, *Ways of Seeing*.

72. Kim and Kim, "#TwitterEthics Manifesto."

73. Scott Kleinman email to AEME listserv February 24, 2014.

74. She wrote an article about it for ProfHacker: Koh, "Accessible Future Workshop."

75. Koh, Twitter posts, March 1, 2014, 2:06 pm, https://twitter.com/adelinekoh/status/439884301622968320, https://twitter.com/adelinekoh/status/439884428064456704, and https://twitter.com/adelinekoh/status/439884654628188161.

76. Betsky, *Building Sex*.

77. Godden and Hsy, "Universal Design."

78. See Sperrazza, "Feeling Violation."

79. Burton, *Archive Stories*, 6.

80. Burton, *Archive Stories*, 6.

81. Burton, *Archive Stories*, 6.

82. Burton, *Archive Stories*, 6.

83. See Steedman, *Archive and Cultural History*; and Farge, *Allure of the Archives*.

84. Farge, *Allure of the Archives*, 32.

85. Hamilton, Harris, Taylor, Pickover, Reid, and Saleh, *Refiguring the Archive*, 7.

86. Foucault, *Archaeology of Knowledge*.

87. Burton, *Archive Stories*, 6.

88. Wen, "Ladies Vanish."

89. Shawn, "The Ladies Vanish."

90. Nakamura, "Economies of Digital Production."

91. Wen, "Ladies Vanish."

Bibliography

AEME *GitHub* site. https://github.com/scottkleinman/aeme/.

"AEME Guidelines." http://scottkleinman.net/wp-content/uploads/guidelines-4.0/. Accessed February 19, 2018.

Alaimo, Stacy, and Susan Hekman. "Introduction: Emerging Models of Materiality in Feminist Theory." In *Material Feminisms,* edited by Stacy Alaimo and Susan Hekman, 1–22. Bloomington: Indiana University Press, 2008.

Alaimo, Stacy, and Susan Hekman, eds. *Material Feminisms.* Bloomington: Indiana University Press, 2008.

"Albrecht Durer: Drawing Devices." *Drawing Seeing* (blog), May 23, 2012. http://drawingseeing.blogspot.com/2012/05/albrecht-durer-drawing-devices.html.

Alexander, Thomas. *John Dewey's Theory of Art, Experience and Nature: The Horizons of Feeling.* Albany: State University of New York Press, 1987.

Archive of Early Middle English Development Site. Accessed February 20, 2018. http://scottkleinman.net/aeme-dev/.

Barad, Karen. "Nature's Queer Performativity." *Kvinder, Køn, Forskning* 12 (2012): 25–53.

Bennett, J. A. W., and G. V. Smithers. *Early Middle English Verse and Prose.* 2nd ed. Oxford: Clarendon, 1968.

Berger, John. *Ways of Seeing.* New York: Penguin, 1972.

Betsky, Aaron. *Building Sex: Men, Women, Architecture, and the Construction of Sexuality.* New York: William Morrow, 1995.

Brantley, Jessica. "The Prehistory of the Book." *PMLA* 124, no. 2 (2009): 632–39.

Brett, David. *Rethinking Decoration: Pleasure and Ideology in Visual Arts.* New York: Cambridge University Press, 2005.

Burton, Antoinette, ed. *Archive Stories: Facts, Fictions, and the Writing of History.* Durham, N.C.: Duke University Press, 2005.

Camille, Michael. "The Book as Flesh and Fetish in Richard de Bury's Philobiblon." In *The Book and the Body,* edited by Dolores Warwick Frese and Kathryn O'Brien O'Keeffe, 34–78. Notre Dame, Ind.: University of Notre Dame Press, 1997.

Cannon, Christopher. *The Grounds of English Literature.* Oxford: Oxford University Press, 2004.

Chaucer, Geoffrey. "Wife of Bath's Prologue." In *The Riverside Chaucer,* edited by Larry Benson, 105–21. New York: Houghton Mifflin, 1987.

Christensen, Hilda Rømer, and Bettina Hauge. "Feminist Materialism." *Kvinder, Køn, Forskning* 12 (2012): 3–8.

Darnton, Robert. *The Kiss of Lamourette: Reflections in Cultural History.* New York: W. W. Norton, 1996.

Data sonification *GitHub* site. https://github.com/hopelessoptimism/data-sonification.

Deleuze, Gilles, and Félix Guattari. *A Thousand Plateaus.* Translated by Brian Massumi. New York: Continuum, 2004.

Denbo, Seth. "Diggable Data, Scalable Reading, and New Humanities Scholarship." *Maryland Institute for Technology in the Humanities,* October 18, 2011. http://mith.umd.edu/diggable-data-scalable-reading-and-new-humanities-scholarship/.

Digital Manuscripts Index. Stanford University. Accessed February 19, 2018. http://dms.stanford.edu/zoompr/CCC008_keywords?druid=cv176gb0028&folio=f.+i+R&headline=PHN0cm9uZz5bIkNhbWJyaWRnZSwgQ29ycHVzIENocmlzdGkgQ29sbGVnZSwg%0AUGFya2VyIExpYnJhcnksIENDQ0MgTVMgOCJdPC9zdHJvbmc%2BPGJy IC8%2BWyJW%0AZWxsdW0iXSwgWyIxNi45IHggMTEuNSJdLCBbInhpdBlYXJse SJdPGJyIC8%2B%0AWyJWaW5jZW50IG9mIEJlYXV2YWlzIE9QLCBTcGVjdWx1b SBoaXN0b3JpYWxl%0ALCBib29rcyAxLTE0Il0%3D%0A&height=9153&image=008 _i_R_TC_46&ms=8&sequence_num=543&total_sequence_num=548&width=5922.

Dirt: Digital Research Tools. Accessed February 20, 2018. http://dirtdirectory.org/.

DMMapp—Digitized Medieval Manuscripts App. Accessed February 19, 2018. https://digitizedmedievalmanuscripts.org/app/.

Drucker, Johanna. *Graphesis: Visual Forms of Knowledge Production.* Cambridge, Mass.: Harvard University Press, 2014.

"The Earliest Surviving English Romances." *Bodleian Library: The Romance of the Middle Ages.* http://medievalromance.bodleian.ox.ac.uk/The_earliest_surviving_English_romances/.

"Encoding Guidelines for the Archive of Early Middle English." Accessed February 20, 2018. http://scottkleinman.net/wp content/uploads/guidelines-4.0/.

"Everything on Paper Will Be Used against Me": Quantifying Kissinger (blog). Accessed February 20, 2018. http://blog.quantifyingkissinger.com/.

Farge, Arlette. *The Allure of the Archives.* Translated by Thomas Scott-Railton. New Haven, Conn.: Yale University Press, 2013.

Foster, Adam. "The Political Aesthetics of Digital Humanities Environments." In *INKE: Implementing New Knowledge Environments.* Electronic Textual Cultures Lab at the University of Victoria, February 17, 2014, http://inke.ca/2014/02/17/the-political-aesthetics-of-digital-humanities-environments/.

Foucault, Michel. *The Archaeology of Knowledge and the Discourse on Language.* Translated by A. M. Sheridan Smith. New York: Pantheon, 1972.

Froehlich, Heather. "CEECing New Directions with Digital Humanities" (blog post). Accessed February 19, 2018. http://hfroehli.ch/2014/02/26/ceecing-new-directions-with-digital-humanities/.

Godden, Rick, and Jonathan Hsy. "Universal Design and Its Discontents." In *Disrupting the Digital Humanities,* edited by Dorothy Kim and Jesse Stommel. Punctum Books, September 2018.

Graham, Shawn. "The Sound of Data (A Gentle Introduction to Sonification for Historians)." Last modified 29 September 2017, https://programminghistorian.org/lessons/sonification/.

Hahn, Thomas. "Early Middle English." In *The Cambridge History of Medieval English Literature,* edited by David Wallace, 61–91. Cambridge: Cambridge University Press, 1999.

Hamilton, Carolyn, Verne Harris, Jane Taylor, Michele Pickover, Graeme Reid, and Razia Saleh, eds. *Refiguring the Archive.* Cape Town: David Philip, 2002.

Hansen, Mark. *New Philosophy for New Media.* Boston: MIT University Press, 2004.

Holsinger, Bruce. "Of Pigs and Parchment: Medieval Studies and the Coming of the Animal." *PMLA* 124, no. 2 (2009): 616–23.

Holsinger, Bruce. "Parchment Ethics: A Statement of More than Modest Concern." *New Medieval Literatures* 12 (2010): 131–36.

Hsy, Jonathan. "#medievaltwitter revisited: #kzoo2014 (BuzzFeed-style wrap-up)." *In the Middle* (blog), May 28, 2014. http://www.inthemedievalmiddle.com/2014/05/medievaltwitter-revisited-kzoo2014.html/.

"Jesus College, Oxford, M.S. 29. ff. 156–68." *Wikipedia Commons,* November 22, 2013, http://upload.wikimedia.org/wikipedia/commons/thumb/8/8b/The_Owl_and_the_Nightingale2.JPG/220px-The_Owl_and_the_Nightingale2.JPG/.

Kay, Sarah. "Legible Skins: Animals and the Ethics of Medieval Reading." *postmedieval: a journal of medieval cultural studies* 2, no. 1 (2011): 13–32.

Kim, Dorothy. "Unfettering the Welsh in Laʒamon's *Brut* and the *South English Legendary.*" Paper presented at International Medieval Congress, Kalamazoo, Michigan, May 2010.

Kim, Dorothy. (@dorothyk98). Twitter feed. https://twitter.com/dorothyk98/.

Kim, Dorothy, and Eunsong Kim. "The #TwitterEthics Manifesto." *Model View Culture,* April 7, 2014. https://modelviewculture.com/pieces/the-twitterethics-manifesto/.

Koh, Adeline. "Accessible Future Workshop: A Report." *Chronicle of Higher Education,* March 6, 2014. http://chronicle.com/blogs/profhacker/accessible-future-workshop-a-report/55927.

Koh, Adeline. (@adelinekoh). Twitter feed. https://twitter.com/adelinekoh/.

Laing, Margaret. *Catalogue of Sources for a Linguistic Atlas of Early Medieval English.* Cambridge: D. S. Brewer, 1993.

Manovich, Lev. "Scale Effects." Paper presented at iGrid, September 26–30, 2005. Available at http://manovich.net/content/04-projects/047-scale-effects/44_article_2005.pdf/.

Moretti, Franco. *Distant Reading.* New York: Verso, 2013.

Mulvey, Laura. "Visual Pleasure and Narrative Cinema." *Screen* 16 (1975): 6–18.

MySQL. Accessed February 19, 2018. http://www.mysql.com/.

Nakamura, Lisa. "Economies of Digital Production in East Asia: iPhone Girls and the Transnational Circuits of Cool." *Media Fields Journal: Critical Explorations in Media and Space* 8 (2011): 1–10. Available at http://www.mediafieldsjournal.org/economies-of-digital/.

Parkes, Malcolm. "The Influence of Ordinatio and Compilatio on the Development of the Book." In *Scribes, Scripts, and Readers:* Studies in the Communication, Presentation and Dissemination of Medieval Texts, 121–42. London: Hambledon Press, 1991.

Rudy, Kathryn. "Dirty Books: Quantifying Patterns of Use in Medieval Manuscripts Using a Densitometer." *Journal of the History of Netherlandish Art* 2, no. 1–2 (2010): 1–26.

Sanderson, Robert, and Benjamin Albritton. "Introduction to SharedCanvas: Linked Data for Facsimile Display and Annotation." *SlideShare,* September 6, 2011. http://www.slideshare.net/azaroth42/british-library-seminar-shared-canvas-september-2011/.

Sanderson, Robert, and Benjamin Albritton, eds. "Shared Canvas Data Model 1.0." February 14, 2013, http://iiif.io/model/shared-canvas/1.0/index.html/.

Scaletti, Carla. "Data Sonification" (blog post). Accessed February 20, 2018. http://carlascaletti.com/sounds/data-sonification/.

Segler, Angela Bennett. "Seeing the Body of Piers Plowman with Digital Eyes." *A Material Piers Living in a Digital World,* May 17, 2014. http://materialpiers.wordpress.com/2014/05/17/seeing-the-body-of-piers-plowman-with-digital-eyes/.

Shepherd, Geoffrey T. "Early Middle English Literature." In *The Middle Ages,* edited by W. F. Bolton, vol. 1, 81–100. London: Penguin Books, 1994.

"Sonification Lab." *Georgia Tech GVU Center.* Accessed February 19, 2018. http://gvu.gatech.edu/index.php?q=research/labs/sonification-lab/.

"Sonification of UCSD Campus Energy Consumption." Accessed February 20, 2018. http://crel.calit2.net/sites/crel.calit2.net/files/images/hong.pdf/.

Sperrazza, Whitney. "Feeling Violation: Tactile Rendering of the Early Modern Blazon." Paper presented at Early Modern Digital Agendas, July 1, 2015. Available at https://spinningwiththebraine.files.wordpress.com/2015/07/emda_finalpresentation.pdf.

Steedman, Caroline. *The Archive and Cultural History.* New Brunswick, N.J.: Rutgers University Press, 2001.

Thomas, Carla María. *Muddling through the Middle Ages* (blog). https://carlamthomas.files.wordpress.com/.

"Tutorial 1: Introducing Graph Data." *Linked Data Tools.* http://www.linkeddatatools.com/introducing-rdf/.

Walker, Alison. "The Boundless Book: A Conversation between the Pre-Modern and Posthuman." *Digital Humanities Quarterly* 7, no. 1 (2013).

Walter, Katie L. *Reading Skin in Medieval Literature and Culture.* New York: Palgrave Macmillan, 2013.

Wen, Shawn. "The Ladies Vanish." *The New Inquiry,* November 11, 2014. http://thenewinquiry.com/essays/the-ladies-vanish/.

Wilcox, Jonathan, ed. *Scraped, Stroked, and Bound: Materially Engaged Readings of Medieval Manuscripts.* Turnhout: Brepols, 2013.

PART IV][Chapter 15

Delivery Service

Gender and the Political Unconscious of Digital Humanities

SUSAN BROWN

A strong tradition of politically invested digital activities, often motivated by an aim to expand available texts beyond the print canon and implicitly to reshape academic norms and values, dates from the early days of the Web (Earhart). Yet gender and other categories of social analysis have been taken up largely in disciplinary contexts or interdisciplinary fields, such as women and gender studies or media and communications studies, rather than in discussions of method or definitions of the field in major digital humanities conferences and publications.[1] The challenge of holding together digital humanities as a field with the kinds of cultural and political critique that are of abiding interest across the humanities and in many digital initiatives has become more evident in the last decade or so, thanks in part to this book series (cf. particularly Liu, "Where Is Cultural Criticism"). This essay argues that while gender has been absent as an explicit term in the definitional work that has shaped the digital humanities, gendered categories and hierarchies profoundly shape debates. Understanding how concepts of service are imbued with gender helps elucidate tensions and contradictions that impede the field and perpetuate inequalities within it.

While the digital humanities community debates—at times fiercely—diversity and inclusivity, these tend to be seen as organizational matters.[2] Definitional and methodological debates are insulated from questions of equity and social justice. So questions of representativeness or inclusivity paradoxically pertain to what is deemed largely irrelevant to the specificity of digital humanities scholarship itself, even as there has been increasing pressure on how the field constitutes and represents itself within conferences, publications, professional organizations, curricula, programs, and institutions (Alliance of Digital Humanities Organizations; Wernimont and Nieves).

This essay attempts to read a few debates in the digital humanities for gaps, silences, and tensions surrounding the concept of service, which is cast as tangential to the central concerns of the field but points to major contradictions within it. The cost of excluding gender analysis becomes apparent when those debates are reframed by feminist theory. "Feminist theory" is a multivalent term that resonates in different contexts and at different moments in the history of the field in ways that are impossible to track fully here. Considering service as a category of labor—including its connection to feminized and reproductive labor—in relation to a number of key aspects of digital humanities points to contradictions and blockages that a feminist approach can help to address. Within digital humanities discourses, service is imbricated with value propositions, gender hierarchies, labor practices, and epistemologies that I explore in relation to disciplinarity, librarianship, training, tools, infrastructure, and delivery systems, in conjunction with several telling historical and literary narratives.

Unpacking how service is embedded within historically produced categories and hierarchies related to embodied differences provides insight into how value is accorded to representations and activities in DH in ways that are deeply gendered, often irrespective of individual intentions, as consequences of systemic patterns of meaning, ways of knowing, and habits of feeling. The contradictory associations that connect service to gendered bodies help to shed light on organizing logics that hold back the field, structuring knowledge and relationships in fundamental ways. A feminist epistemological framework opens up the potential to resituate service within definitional and methodological debates in digital humanities.

Political Unconscious

There has been until quite recently a historical gap or silence around the "f word," that is to say, "feminism," with its history of cultural denigration and caricature—in the self-representation of DH. The first edition of the Blackwell *Companion to Digital Humanities,* that wide-ranging tome in which various leaders in the field were "brought together to consider digital humanities as a discipline in its own right, as well as to reflect on how it relates to areas of normative humanities scholarship," invoked women or gender almost entirely in relation to stylistics, reader responses, and particular projects (Schreibman, Siemens, and Unsworth, *A Companion,* Introduction). The *Companion* boasts strong feminist leadership, as do many other projects, centers, and initiatives, but its circumscribed references to gender indicate the difficulty of incorporating feminist analysis within the collection's framing of DH as emerging from humanities computing and textual practice (Svensson, "Envisioning"; Losh).[3] This is just one register of the absence of gender considerations from assertions of disciplinarity or field status in the two decades that span the turn of the millennium.

The idea of a political unconscious from Marxist psychoanalytic theory provides a means of addressing the extent to which feminism, and gender as its primary category of analysis, have been present but not explicitly engaged in discursive framing of the field. Pierre Macherey, building on Louis Althusser's incorporation of insights from psychoanalysis into Marxist theory, considers it the work of literary criticism to give voice to the absences or gaps that are symptomatic of conflicts between meanings that a text cannot resolve but simply displays (Macherey, 84). The act of knowing or critique in this view becomes "the articulation of a silence" (Macherey, 6). Both Macherey and Frederic Jameson reject allegorical readings of texts as simplistically ideological while insisting that the "*unconscious of the work*" (Macherey, 92) or the "political unconscious" (Jameson) of a text, rather than that of an individual author, necessarily reflects the interrelationships of cultural, ideological, juridical, political, and economic forces (Jameson, 21). This perspective insists that the material and ideological conditions in any field inflect our representation of it and vice versa. Since such silences are a condition of utterance for any text, no text or utterance is apolitical.

DH has often been debating gender in other words, through debates over service, which has itself been positioned as marginal, often omitted or sidelined, precisely because it is caught up with gender. This inquiry explores tensions over service within the digital humanities as a contribution to a larger rethinking of the field through diversity and difference. It starts with the relatively rare invocation of service in the context of self-definition, both formal and informal.

Disciplinarity and the Gendering of Service

Geoffrey Rockwell, participating like the Blackwell *Companion* in the debate over disciplinarity, is unusual in taking up the relationship of computational scholarship to service, or what he calls the "servile" as well as the "liberal" arts, arguing for a reorientation of the humanities toward craft and creativity by breaking down the "artificial division of skills and liberal knowledge" (Rockwell). At a moment of intensive field formation, his resulting emphasis on rupture, liminality, and reproduction helps to make the gaps and silences surrounding service legible. Rockwell asserts, "The founding of a discipline is a rupture"; "the founding of a discipline is a liminal moment"; "a discipline is born when a field takes control of its means of reproduction" ("Multimedia"). Rockwell was writing from the position of director of McMaster University's Humanities Media and Computing Centre and founder of its undergraduate Multimedia program. Bids for disciplinarity have given way in large part to an understanding of the field as inter- or transdisciplinary (Svensson, "Landscape," para. 20), but what is salient for my argument here is that these terms bring to the fore what is at stake when we start to wrestle with service in the context of defining digital humanities. All three assertions have to do with bodies and boundaries: rupture with its origins in physical breaks, liminality with its initial grounding in sensory perceptions of difference, and reproduction with its tension between original and copy (*Oxford English Dictionary Online*). Situating service in relation to embodiment and difference brings home the extent to which gendered anxieties and contradictions are at work in DH.

There are close connections (historical and continuing, practical and intellectual) within the digital humanities to technical services and support (Flanders, "You Work at Brown," 27). Some DH centers and activities have evolved from or remain tied to instruction or technical support initiatives, and libraries, with their strong ethos of service and crucial position in the provision of scholarly infrastructure for the humanities, have been and remain central to the growth of the field. For the purposes of this essay, cognizant of the myriad definitions of service that have grown from its original meaning of duty or work performed for a superior or master (*Oxford English Dictionary Online*) ranging from "Help, benefit, advantage, use" to "Friendly or professional assistance," I would define service in the digital humanities as activities of practical benefit to others, including but not limited to providing expertise, guidance, and training related to specific skills, methods, or tools; structuring, manipulating, transforming, or remediating data; creating, distributing, and maintaining software; building, caring for, and sustaining platforms for hosting and disseminating digital datasets, assets, software, and scholarship; administering and managing digital humanities entities such as centers, programs, or projects; and establishing and running scholarly and professional networks and events, including conferences. Virtually everyone in the digital humanities participates to a greater or lesser extent in such activities, in contexts ranging from drop-in encounters at service desks to ongoing collaborations among teams of scholars. These activities account for much of the "technologically assisted knowledge work" that distinguishes the digital humanities from other fields (Liu, "Drafts"). They are typically represented as "service" rather than "scholarship" within formalized evaluation processes applied to faculty members, and associated with a more valorized notion of "service" in the work of academic librarians. Yet service and support have until recently been rarely debated in the field. For instance, posts to the Humanist listserv routinely mention technical services or support in job titles, while services mentioned alone almost always relate to web services or library services (Humanist 1987–). Service and support are thus present in the discourse of DH, but discussed more in relation to the mundane and practical rather than the self-definitional.

On rare occasions when it arises in definitional contexts, the language of support and service is often entirely disavowed. Thomas Rommel invokes David Robey (then director of the Arts and Humanities Research Council's ICT [Information and Communications Technology] in Arts and Humanities Research Programme): "Humanities computing specialists thus have a vital role as interdisciplinary and interprofessional mediators. The old model of support services is no longer valid." In his view, research should be seen as "a common enterprise between ›technologists‹ and ›scholars‹" (Rommel). "Service" is often an explicit component of advertised digital humanities positions, but notably not prominently of tenure-track faculty ones, though they may mention institutional or professional service. Willard McCarty links DH service to the traditions of collegiality: "In their uses of computing, the disciplines of the humanities furnish us with unending opportunities for intellectual field-work as well as mind-expanding collaboration, and the good work we do there, in *collegial* service, yields invaluable friendships" ("New Splashings"). The stress on affect among intellectual peers conjures up the privileged environment of Oxbridge colleges. The same phrase operated quite differently across the Atlantic at the University of Virginia, where a Digital Media program was articulated in opposition to "the 'collegial service' model pervasive in Humanities Computing" (Kirschenbaum, "Digital Humanities," 419). Despite the contradictory invocations, in both of these cases involving elite academic contexts, DH is distanced from an understanding of service as devalued relative to research and normative teaching. Roles and activities in the academy are organized around the boundary between service and scholarship. The boundary inserts itself in the form of casual distinctions between, for instance, librarians and scholars or researchers, when of course many librarians are both.[4]

Librarianship is a discipline founded on an ethos of service (Rubin; Williamson) that intersects with the feminization of the profession (Harris; Maack). The period of debates over disciplinarity in the late 1990s and 2000s was followed by the emergence of a different kind of DH entity than an academic program or traditional research institute: the library-based DH center or lab, such as the University of Virginia's Scholars Lab, "staffed with librarians who act as scholar practitioners" (Nowviskie, "Skunks," 53). This led to a flurry of self-reflection regarding the relationship of DH to libraries, including a controversial 2014 report, "Does Every Research Library Need a Digital Humanities Center?" (Schaffner and Erway). Dot Porter ("What If We Do") argues that the report presumes a false dichotomy between librarians and academics. Both Porter and Bethany Nowviskie ("Asking for It") counter its insistence on repurposing existing "services" with an alternative understanding of service as grounded in the academic expertise and autonomy of DH specialists. Nowviskie invokes the example of the Scholars Lab's delivery of a spatial humanities service that had neither previously existed nor even been requested, providing leadership precisely because the scholars of the lab in the library had the ability to anticipate, or to an extent even to constitute, an emergent need. Delivering this service, which involved winning grants and eventually the development of the Neatline plugin for the Omeka platform, helped constitute the digital humanities' relation to geospatial technologies (Nowviskie, "Asking for It"). The tension between a library service model and more autonomous scholarship has come to structure discussions of digital humanities and digital scholarship, articulated for instance as a "Tension between Research and Services," or as "the service and lab models" (Lewis, Spiro, Wang, and Cawthorne, 28; Maron; Maron and Pickle). Alix Keener characterizes it as a tension between "service vs. servitude" (para. 16).

As Rockwell makes clear, much is at stake in this distinction in the context of established disciplines, given the "deeply ingrained belief in the superior value of the liberal arts over the ›servile‹ and professional arts": "To justify HC [Humanities Computing] programmes that include significant training we are tempted to present ourselves as servile, providing enrichment programmes that service the liberal ones" ("Multimedia"). A field establishing its academic credentials in a liberal arts or humanities context must guard against the slippage from service to servility, or "subservience," as it is termed in some more recent discussions (McCarty, "State of Relations?"). On the other hand, librarianship as a profession has traditionally occupied this ground of enrichment and support, and some adhere to a model that sees the roles of scholar and librarian as quite distinct. However, as Julia Flanders notes, DH has eroded "a division of labor and a level of intellectual independence" associated with the professoriate as opposed to support or service positions ("You Work at Brown," 48), as witnessed by the flourishing of "alt-ac" positions in the field and personified by individuals who move among professorial, librarian, and other service- or support-oriented positions. The models of DH invoked by both Bethany Nowviskie and Dot Porter emerge from this blurring of roles and boundaries. They stress a greater level of initiative, leadership, and autonomy for scholar-practitioners within libraries than that associated with conventional service roles, as well as a model of scholarship rooted in collaborative rather than solitary research endeavors.

Delving further into the gendering of service helps to elucidate perplexities surrounding it. It emerges from etymological and persistent cultural notions of debasement that are strongly feminized, notwithstanding the Christian tradition of masculine service tied to the story of Jesus's self-abjection. Within Western societies, working-class women have constituted a majority of those in "domestic service" and other types of service jobs. In the Victorian period, middle- and upper-class women entered the public sphere, and to a large extent public discourse, by leveraging the massive expansion of a number of economic sectors that flowed from the rise of the middle classes and the establishment of a secular state. The movement of privileged women into the paid workforce was justified initially in terms of the continuity of social service jobs with the unpaid philanthropic and domestic activities of women within the home and community (Smith-Rosenberg; Vicinus), activities that are still not factored into standard economic measures of wealth production. Reproduction, whether defined in terms of child-bearing, child-rearing, home-making, or teaching in the home, is perhaps the most distinctly gendered service role of all. As a result of these associations and the growing number of women it employed, the service sector was increasingly gendered as female from the middle of the nineteenth century onward. However, it must be stressed that the categorization and status of labor categories shift over time and that computer programming was once considered to be subprofessional "women's work" (Abbate; Wajcman), that is, a service occupation.

Service jobs remain deeply gendered despite the shift to a service-oriented "knowledge economy." As of 2009 in Canada, two thirds of women, twice as many as men, worked in historically female service occupations: teaching, nursing, and other health occupations; administrative positions; or sales and service roles (Farrao); in 2012, 55 percent of all jobs in the services sector were occupied by women, with the concentration particularly high in the health care and social assistance sector (82 percent) ("Fact Sheet"). In the United States, in 2014 women made up 75 percent of the education and health services sector and 64 percent of the community and social service workforce (AFL-CIO Department for Professional Employees, "Professionals in the Workplace: Women"; AFL-CIO Department for Professional Employees, *Professionals in the Workplace: Community*). Moreover, the gender wage gap is in large part due to the feminized nonprofessional "service" sector associated with "emotional labor": people skills that are understood to be outside of the market because naturalized and assigned to women, and are under- or uncompensated (Guy and Newman). Yet as theorists of affect have argued, the apparently private or individual choices and responses associated with such affective labor are inflected by collective factors that structure public life (Ahmed; Berlant; Cvetkovich; Gregg and Seigworth; Sedgwick and Frank). The impact of this differential assignment and valuation of labor extends into academia as well as into women's role in the tech startup world, where "soft" skills such as design, promotion, and marketing, as opposed to coding, can result in women's contributions being informalized as "spouse-as-a-service," written out of partnership agreements, and erased from the history of technology (Losse). It might seem prudent, then, to refuse the language of service, to steer clear of having one's labor appropriated and undervalued, as is the case in other feminized labor sectors. To do so, however, is of course also to reinforce the gendered hierarchy of values that undergirds a pervasive system of economic and social injustice.

Debates over the disciplinarity of DH and the role of DH professionals within research libraries thus reflect quite different constructions of professorial as distinct from librarian positions, the ways in which service has figured in those constructions, and gendered hierarchies of value tied to categories of labor. Although often an explicit component of academic appointments, service is less valued and rewarded than either research achievement, which is considered paramount, or teaching, which is similarly devalued and feminized, in terms of the characteristics, abilities, and emotional labor associated with it and the disproportionate contributions by women (Bellas; Fairweather). In the more feminized field of librarianship, however, service has played a more valued and central role, sometimes to the detriment of the perception of profession (Garrison). This disjunction means that service tends to get suppressed in the first context and has been contested in the second, creating gaps, unevenness, and tensions regarding service-oriented activities. Both tendencies are informed by a perception of service activities as aligned with instrumentalism and thus distinct from defining digital humanities activities, a view that, as Liu observes, reflects the insecurities that swirl around instrumentalism for the humanities as a whole (Liu, "Where Is Cultural Criticism," 498–99).[5]

Infrastructure and Agency

The divergent and contested understandings of service outlined thus far have a significant impact on perceptions of the crucial work that goes into creating and maintaining DH infrastructure (Rockwell and Ramsay). As Miriam Posner points out, the extensive human labor that underlies building and maintaining awe-inspiring centers, platforms, and tools can be invisible even within the community ("Here and There"). As Susan Leigh Star and Karen Ruhleder note, the common characterization of infrastructure as transparent until it breaks belies its intellectual challenges and complexity: "infrastructure is something that emerges for people in practice, connected to activities and structures" (112). By their analysis, "infrastructure is a fundamentally relational concept. It becomes infrastructure in relation to organized practices" (113). In contrast to innovation, then, all those "boring things" (Star, "Ethnography of Infrastructure")—the meticulous work of moving from a prototype to production, of debugging and updating, the care, repair, and maintenance of digital humanities tools and platforms (Nowviskie, "Digital Humanities"), all that unsexy, detail-oriented, iterative work of debugging and tweaking, keeping things going, or preserving them—are activities that bear more resemblance to housework than to recognized forms of academic labor. Moreover, their relationship to coding, making, building, and hacking and the connotations of vocational skills and manual labor can lead to further devaluation within contexts that privilege the cerebral over the material and instrumental aspects of working on or with tools and infrastructure. Institutionally such activities often register as service or support rather than scholarship or research, let alone as "creative process and a catalyst of social amenity" (Verhoeven, "As Luck," 11).

Anxieties about service arose early in debates on the Humanist listserv over Project Bamboo, a high-profile humanities cyberinfrastructure initiative funded by the Andrew W. Mellon Foundation between 2008 and 2012 to bring together IT staff, librarians, and faculty members to develop a shared digital infrastructure for the humanities. McCarty early characterized the undertaking as cleaving to a service model: "Bamboo seems only more of what has kept the digital humanities in the U.S. from fulfilling great ... promises.... It turned out that it meant rethinking what we mean by what we compute—and that job requires the *fusion* of computing and the humanities, not the *servicing* of the humanities by computing" (McCarty, "the future is Bamboo?"). Charles Faulhaber responds with a more obviously gendered metaphor: "This is not technology in the service of the humanities, with the former as handmaiden to the latter" (Faulhaber, "Bamboo"). Quinn Dombrowski's postmortem of Project Bamboo, which never came to fruition, argues that it started to go sideways early on because "Faculty participants were particularly turned off by the technical jargon in the presentations (including 'services,' as commonly understood by IT staff)" ("What Ever Happened," 328). As shown above, "service" was a trigger word not only because it was indicative of a literal semantic gap in the meaning of "services" but also because within a faculty context it signals a devalued category of work. It is telling that the word "servitude" occurs within *A New Companion to Digital Humanities* (2016) twice, in Jennifer Edmond's discussion of "Collaboration and Infrastructure" and nowhere else ("Collaboration and Infrastructure," 57, 63). It might seem peculiar that infrastructure work in DH apparently resonates in this way, given the increasing recognition of the inextricability of infrastructure from subjectivity, culture, and space in everyday practice as informational infrastructure becomes more ubiquitous and embodied (Bratton, *The Stack*; Dourish and Bell, "Infrastructure of Experience"; Liu, "Drafts"; see also Parks and Starosielski, *Signal Traffic*). This may have to do with a distinction between infrastructure as a totalized noun connoting automated computational services, and the human labor and subject positions associated with creating and sustaining such systems.[6]

Just prior to the debate over Bamboo, Stephen Ramsay rejected the denigration implicit in the gendered hierarchy associated with service: "I regard the disentangling of digital humanities from English, history, computer science, etc. as a great danger. Digital humanists naturally bristle at the suggestion that we are the handmaidens of these august disciplines, but I think that is perhaps more to do with the pejorative connotations of that mildly offensive designation than with the nature of the relationship expressed" ("Re: 21.445"). The need to divorce an understanding of the relationship from the connotations that impede the debate is real. The invocation of handmaidens is not, however, entirely mild, deriving as it does from cultural roots that defined women as sexual chattel devoted to servicing elite men. Margaret Atwood's *The Handmaid's Tale* depicts a fundamentalist Christian theocracy in which women's right to reproductive freedom, along with most of the freedoms enjoyed by women in the "developed" world, have been rescinded by the state. In Atwood's dystopia, women's bodies are put at the service of a repressive, misogynist regime that has seized power in part by leveraging centralized information systems. Under the regime of Gilead in which sterility is rampant, "handmaidens" are assigned to bear the children of the religious elite. Atwood's handmaiden helps to clarify the apparently exaggerated anxieties over service. They are not just about devaluation and hierarchy. They are about agency and control, the risk of a nightmarish, gendered lack of both status and self-determination that defines a handmaiden's subject position.

Atwood's reliteralization of the biblical bondswoman's role lays bare the sexual violence at one end of the gendered service spectrum. A handmaiden is a sexual servant and, indeed, in Atwood's dystopia and the Old Testament culture from which the term descends, a sexual slave within a patriarchal social structure. The abjection of a person subjected to sexual violence still signifies culturally as the paradigmatic state of being without agency. Atwood's handmaid makes evident the link between service, objectification, and abjection and their connection to rupture, liminality, reproduction, and delivery. It is speculative fiction, but fiction extrapolated by its author from historical precedents (Mead). The title underscores the extent to which pejorative, gendered notions of service, including those of women of color under slavery, imply an objectification of women enforced through violence (Atwood, "Margaret Atwood"). This logic explains why women who are perceived online as out of line, that is, as transgressing the proper (yet intangible and shifting) boundaries of femininity, are threatened with rape and murder, doxed, and harassed. Such extreme policing of norms is relatively rare in academia, but the participation of women in DH in the #metoo social media campaign to raise awareness of sexual harassment and predation (Hsu and Stone), confirms, as Karen Kelsky summarizes based on more than 1,800 anonymous survey results, that "sexual harassment in academe is a spectrum that ranges from rape, assault, battery, and stalking to looks, hand-brushing, and innuendo delivered just on the edge of plausible deniability" ("Professor Is In"). Gendered values, including notions of sexual service, underwrite a continuum of violence experienced by women as embodied subjects, in DH as elsewhere.

The gendering of service is profound and multivalent, informed by cultural history and ongoing social practices. Much that is distinctive in DH can be characterized as service, and it resonates differently in relation to academic disciplinarity and to various types of positions within the academy. The tensions surrounding it manifest unevenly, but it is mostly present by its absence as a defining term in debates in DH, indicative of the political unconscious of the field. Recognizing the extent to which debates over service are imbued with gendered values and practices provides a means of addressing more directly fundamental contradictions and problems within DH, opening up new ways of thinking about what we do. This becomes apparent if we contrast the understanding of service to that of tools. Where the one connotes a feminized lack of control or self-determination, the other evokes a sense of autonomy and agency. Considering service in conjunction with delivery, and a recognition that human service is provided materially in space and time, advances an understanding of the impact and stakes of gendered thinking within DH and of the relationship of embodied human subjects to technological tools and processes.

Tools and Delivery

Atwood contests the claim that *The Handmaid's Tale* is futuristic, pointing to historical precedents for all the components of her narrative at the time of its composition. Certainly, the treatment of childbearing women as objects to be managed is in keeping with mainstream Western medical practices, and Anne Balsamo (*Technologies*) links a powerful reading of the novel to the use of laparoscopy in late-twentieth-century reproductive technologies. Similarly, considering the invention of the forceps within the history of birth technologies helps to unpack the connotations of service.

Forceps for use in childbirth were invented about 1616 in England by a member of the Huguenot Chamberlen family, probably Peter Chamberlen the Elder. The invention was kept a family secret for 125 years, and had to be reinvented independently in the eighteenth century. In the meantime, the increasingly powerful Chamberlen and his successors attempted to form under their control a corporation of midwives, with whom they did not share this revolutionary technology; the midwives in turn saw the Chamberlens as limited by an overreliance on their tools rather than a broad range of midwifery skills (Brown, Clements, and Grundy, searches on "Chamberlen" and "forceps"). In my reading of this cautionary tale, a new and notably proprietary technology worked against the feminized service of the midwife, was hoarded for profit at the cost of innumerable lives, and radically altered the future of female reproductive labor in the West. This problematic history of the medicalized tools of delivery extends to the present day within the Western medical profession, from which midwifery is still largely excluded or, when included, devalued in terms of status and remuneration in relation to the practice of medicine, from which it is distinguished in part by the use of high-tech tools. At the same time, human reproduction, as Balsamo and others have demonstrated, has become increasingly technologized, despite much evidence that delivery tools should, in an obstetrical context, be the exception rather than the norm.

This history of the forceps provides an admonitory lens on processes of professionalization and disciplinary formation, suggesting that an emphasis on technology at the expense of service can work against women's interests, in this case that of both clients and midwives. On the one hand, a more open technology would have saved more lives when forceps were truly needed. On the other, the adoption of a more situated and relational approach to delivery as opposed to one that privileged tools over services would lower the number of birth interventions and related complications such as infection. The combination would have produced better Western birth outcomes, then and now.

The rhetoric of digital humanities as tool-oriented deserves scrutiny, given that tools and technologies are not neutral, as feminists including Audre Lorde ("Master's Tools") have long stressed. Tara McPherson ("Why") has unpacked ways in which the now prevalent UNIX operating system design mirrors the management of race in the post–World War II United States, while Jacqueline Wernimont ("Whence Feminism?") stresses the extent to which "the logic of the maker/consumer paradigm is a gendering one regardless of the sex or intentions of the participants. Consequently, those who cannot make find themselves in subordinated, devalued, 'user' positions that deny agency and expertise (and funding!)" (para. 12).

The problem is neither simply the gendered connotations of tools nor their appropriation by men, but an epistemology within which tools and technologies are conceived as involving clear boundaries between subject and object, actor and acted-upon, and as conveying agency upon those who wield them. The self-other dichotomy is implicit in the opposition between conceptual or theoretical work, on the one hand, and practical or material work, on the other. This opposition underlies skepticism about the intellectual work associated with building and prototyping (Galey and Ruecker; Rockwell and Ramsay). Frederica Frabetti urges the digital humanities instead to rethink technology beyond instrumentality, in terms of "originary technicity." This concept challenges the Western metaphysical tradition by viewing technology as always already imbricated with and indeed constitutive of human experience and identity. Within this alternative poststructuralist understanding, tools and making provide a route to self-consciousness, history, and inscription (Frabetti, 3–7). As articulated by Timothy Clark, Bernard Stiegler, and others, originary technicity opens a means of thinking of technology as "constitutive of the human" that is shared by Jacques Derrida and underscores his refusal to grant science or cognition priority over writing or technology (Frabetti, 9).

Despite the historical and epistemological baggage of tools, the masculinist associations are not monological. For instance, O'Reilly publishing has a longstanding series of programming "Cookbooks" that goes back to the 1970s. Stéfan Sinclair and Geoffrey Rockwell advanced similar language within DH by adopting the term "recipes," suggested by Stan Ruecker, for step-by-step instructions for the use of the Text Analysis Portal for Research (TAPoR) and Voyant Tools. The initiative arose from the insight that "tool rhetoric might be alienating" and a desire to "understate the technological" (Sinclair and Rockwell, 251). Cooking metaphors invoke nourishment, sustenance, iteration, and the transmission of knowledge within a community. Their revised discursive framing of text analysis adopts the term "utensils" over tools, emphasizes human processes, and invokes the "digital domesticity" of the feminized world of food blogging (Hegde, 73). The broadening of this initiative through the partnership of the TAPoR and Digital Research Tools/ DiRT Directory/Methods Commons (Dombrowski, "DiRT Partners with TAPoR") is a heartening indication of a movement within DH to shift the discursive frameworks within which we conceive technology toward a posthuman epistemology that resists the problematic binaries of classical metaphysics. Working against those binaries will help undermine the gendered associations embedded in much of our thinking about tools.

Informed by feminist theory and recent movements including feminist midwifery, we can imagine reclaiming the tools and means of reproduction from the legacy of the Chamberlens and the culture of technology they represent. Thinking through the concept of delivery, whose definitions range from the act of setting free or rescuing, through bringing forth offspring, to surrendering or giving up possession (*Oxford English Dictionary Online*), enables a rethinking of the relationships among gender, technology, interfaces, and embodiment that helps to resituate service. We might mobilize the tensions embedded in the term. Mobilizing the unstable connotations of delivery offers a model open to a range of agents and participants, in which processes and modes of delivery have profound impacts on what is delivered. Rather than doctor, tool, and patient(s), we can conceive of at least three agents in the birthing process: mother, child, midwife—all in contact, all active, all in that liminal zone of risk, rupture, and possibility (Kitzinger). The analogy offers a flexible framework for thinking about agency and participation as regards delivery within a digital environment.[7] The ambiguity and instability associated with the term suggest the profound impact of the act of delivery and the possibility of intimate, mutually constitutive relations between the one who or that which delivers, and who or what is delivered. This in turn helps in rethinking service as an ineluctable component of technological systems.

Lucy Suchman provides an anthropological foundation for culturally and historically grounded analyses of technology design and mobilization in a range of contexts. Her theory of "situated cognition" sees the complex social and material environment as inextricable from human understanding ("Agencies"; *Human-Machine Reconfigurations*). As we think about digital interfaces, the means by which we deliver the fruits of scholarly labor in the digital humanities community, such a framework helps to destabilize, productively, apparently distinct components of the delivery process. It pushes us to reflect on the relationships among the multiple and diverse agents involved in what Karen Barad (*Meeting the Universe Halfway*) has termed "intra-actions" to signal the "mutual constitutions of entangled agencies" (33). The word "interface" denotes a shared boundary or contact zone between a computational system and some other agent or entity, whether a human, a device or peripheral, software or hardware. Examples include command line interfaces, keyboards or touch screens, mobile devices, gaming controllers, haptic interfaces, and application programming interfaces (see Emerson; Ennis et al.; Farman; Galloway). Delivery in DH most commonly focuses on visual representation through graphical user interfaces, but most interfaces involve multiple material components and agencies.

McCarty regards the term "delivery" as metaphorically freighted with connotations of knowledge commodification and mug-and-jug pedagogy, which is to say that teaching involves simply pouring knowledge from the jug of professors to the mug of passive students, or worse yet, transferring commodified knowledge via technology (*Humanities Computing*, 6). He highlights the reductiveness that flows from conceptualizing delivery as the transfer of distinct knowledge products. However, if we consider with Johanna Drucker that delivery involves complex processes of subjectivity that, through the interfaces that computational systems employ, structure "our relation to knowledge and behavior," then it follows that delivery systems act not only as enunciative or representational apparatuses. To the extent that they also constitute "provocations to cognitive" and other forms of experience, delivery ought to be central to our considerations of technologies (Drucker, front matter).

Yet consideration of delivery seldom enters into DH scholarship despite evidence that user interfaces are among the most influential factors in the adoption of digital humanities tools and services beyond their immediate community. Matthew G. Kirschenbaum ("'So the Colors'") argues that it is precisely because of anxieties about liminality, borders, and embodiment that interface work is so often neglected, despite the insistence within the humanities generally on the inextricability of form and content. Given their alignment with liminality, delivery, and materiality, charged as they are with service, affect, and sensitivity, it hardly seems surprising that women have been more often involved in human-computer-interaction or interface work, project management, or service-oriented digital librarianship than in coding and tool building, or that such work has been seen as marginal, tangential, incidental to the field. However, these activities and their (de)valuation emerge from an intertwined history of technological and social flux in which such values are far from fixed. The distinction between back-end coding and the productive apparatus of delivery itself breaks down as we start to put pressure on these categories, underscoring their constructedness. Drucker insists on the extent to which computational systems are always already cultural: "The crucial definition of human subjectivity is that it can register a trace of itself in a representational system, and that self-recognition and self-constitution depend on that trace, that capacity to make and register difference. The encounter between a subject and an interface need not be understood mechanistically. We can think beyond representational models to understand interface as an ecology, a border zone between cultural systems and human subjects" (*Graphesis*, 148). In stressing the imbrication of subjectivity and interface, this situated perspective highlights the complex and evolving dynamics at work in human interactions with machines, paving the way for new ways of thinking about the productive apparatus and processes of delivery work, and that work's experiential impacts in particular engagements with technologies. Furthermore, as John Seely Brown and Paul Duguid demonstrate, technological systems cannot be understood without consideration of the social environments in which they are embedded (*Social Life*). In the context of DH, those environments frequently involve human services of one kind or another.

Delivering Change

Thinking of delivery in terms of the complexities of interfaces foregrounds the liminal, unstable, and permeable over the hegemonic, simplifying, or transparent, suggesting its potential as a transformative rather than an instrumental process of bringing together data; analysis; media; and interpreting, embodied subjects. For example, investigation of the history of visualization has led Lauren Klein ("Visualization") to argue that rather than presenting complex entities as static data points, visualization can work to foreground the process of knowledge production, including "two-way exchange between subject and object of knowledge," as in the case of Elizabeth Peabody's carefully crafted pedagogical visualizations. Peabody, a first-wave feminist "knowledge worker," created initially opaque, very abstract, quilt-like visualizations of events designed to engage others actively in the interpretation of history in dialogue with her narrative chronology, aiming to appeal aesthetically and affectively to those who engaged with her work. In Klein's analysis, Peabody's interface or knowledge delivery system subverts the female teacher's conventional service role of reproducing unproblematically a set of given social relations, underscoring the power of visualization to communicate different epistemological frameworks.

Within the field of rhetoric, digital delivery of everything from file sharing to pop-up archives speaks to a wide range of intersecting concerns including embodiment, affect, audience, and performativity (DeVoss and Porter; Ridolfo and Hart-Davidson; Ridolfo, Hart-Davidson, and McLeod). Jim Porter, for instance, insists on the situatedness of digital technologies and their effects: "As an isolated object, technology is of little interest. Rather, the real story is the use of the tool in its particular social, pedagogical, and rhetorical context," a story composed of "human and non-human agents in a developmental dance" (J. Porter, 385). The technological imagination, as laid out by Anne Balsamo, assigns agency in relation to technology to (predominantly white) men (*Designing Culture*, 32). Drawing on Barad's physics-grounded refusal of the distinction between subjects and objects, Balsamo regards subjects as constituted by the interactions that constitute them: agency materializes through "intra-actions" that constitute boundaries, demarcations, and distinctions among elements of phenomena (34). This leads to a vision of design as a "set of practices whereby the world is dynamically reconfigured by specific acts . . . through which boundaries are constituted and enacted" (35).

Boundary issues, as Haraway ("Cyborg Manifesto") was among the first to argue, have everything to do with the highly politicized—and gendered—category of the human, the subject/object of (post?)humanist knowledge production. Indeed, cyberfeminism and feminist science fiction have been probing such boundaries for decades. James Tiptree Jr.'s 1973 "The Girl Who Was Plugged In" is all about the problem of the culturally idealized, objectified female body *as* interface: "PDs. Placental decanters. Modified embryos" are hooked up to others' brains, and this fraudulent reproduction in the service of corporate interests results in a blurring of identities that is ultimately fatal to both the "wired-up slave" body that is the object of male desire and the grotesquely embodied female Remote Operator without whom the former is "just a vegetable" (551). Perverted reproduction and delivery, in this story, are at the crux of a violent literalization of the impossibility of the feminine, a denaturalized performance of gender and heteronormativity in the service of hegemony and greed (Hollinger). In a sense, female slave and female operator are both interfaces within a networked cybersystem in which, as N. Katherine Hayles (*My Mother Was a Computer*) notes, "the conglomerate controls the communication channels through which subjectivity-as-message flows and decides how the distribution of subjectivity will be parsed" (81). Tiptree sketches out the nightmarish conclusion to the trajectories of female abjection through reproductive technologies that begins with the Chamberlens, the marginalization of midwifery, and a service model of delivery.

Work in DH needs to place itself, its tools, its methods in that messy, problematic contact zone of social relations, subjectivities, information flows, and embodied practices powerfully evoked by Tiptree in order to imagine new relations, arrangements, and configurations and to forestall the realization of dystopic prophecies of a technocratic future. The challenge is to be mindful of how institutional power circulates and perpetuates itself according to categories and hierarchies that embed social power relations. Dealing with embodiment means dealing with the differences among bodies and their place within the body politic. As Miriam Posner argues, "DH *needs* scholarly expertise in critical race theory, feminist and queer theory, and other interrogations of structures of power in order to develop models of the world that have any relevance to people's lived experience" ("Radical Potential"). This revisionary impetus touches on the "organizing logic, like the data models or databases, that underlies most of our work," a logic baked deeply into algorithms and interfaces produced by corporate and military interests resistant to the kinds of changes for which Martha Nell Smith argued powerfully in 2007 (Posner, "Radical Potential"). A prerequisite for change, I am arguing, is recognizing the extent to which understandings of service in DH are bound up with logics and values that impede the field: not only with gendered hierarchies but also with fundamental subject-object distinctions that legitimate othering more generally. These logics structure how we know and (intra)act with and in the world, and the distinctions they legitimate in turn intersect in important ways with other categories of difference.

This essay has attempted to chart, albeit partially and imperfectly, the extent to which an opposition between the instrumental and the intellectual has led to a disavowal of the crucial role that service, a feminized labor category, plays in the digital humanities. The discourse surrounding tools, however, aligns instruments with masculinity, so that coding or making is thus privileged in some contexts and devalued in others. The evasions and contradictions in the discourse surrounding service mark it as a component of the political unconscious of digital humanities grounded in distinctions between subject and object, and the conceptual and the material, that belie the complexity and mutual constitution of humans and technologies. Modes and methods of delivery, human and technological, provide a means of reflecting on how service, bound up as it is with the production and reproduction of DH through training, making, designing, caring, repairing, empowering, and sustaining, might be rethought as a situated, embodied activity embedded inextricably in the field.

Geoffrey Bowker and Susan Leigh Star elucidate the political and ethical consequences of the taxonomies that construct our world and masquerade as natural, shaping human understandings and affordances for action (326). The digital humanities can learn much from theoretical, critical, and creative practitioners who interrogate boundary objects and interfaces from a range of positions and perspectives. As Star argues, marginality, liminality, hybridity, and multiple memberships across identities or communities provide valuable vantage points for engagement with shifting technologies ("Power, Technology," 50–53). That is one of the major strengths of the outsider perspective: the feminist perspective, the queer gaze, the view from outside of privileged categories of race, class, nation, or religion. The challenge is how to apply that perspective within DH debates and practices. Human interactions in libraries, labs, classrooms, collaborations, conversations, and other contexts in which service is mobilized, along with our tools, infrastructures, and delivery environments, offer embodied, situated possibilities for engagements and agencies with a difference. At the same time, respecting and incorporating difference is challenging to the extent that those technical systems themselves carry, in McPherson's words, a logic of "removing context and decreasing complexity" complicit with a larger "approach to the world that separates object from subject, cause from effect, context from code" ("Designing for Difference"; cf. also McPherson, "Why"). That makes it all the more important to devise a world with alternative frames of reference.

Service as a category signals intrinsic and invaluable aspects of the digital humanities. However, epistemologies grounded in subject/object distinctions and a privileging of the ideal or conceptual or practical over the material impedes our ability to recognize the extent to which the devaluation of the feminized undergirds our evasions and our debates in ways that point to the political unconscious of the field. Social semiotics make it difficult to attend to service within a productive frame of analysis, imbued as it is with gendered anxieties regarding bodies, boundaries, and the loss of control and autonomy with respect to labor and reproduction. These associations are far from fixed, and contain contradictions that can be exploited. However, to do so, an equitable, ethical, and politically responsible digital humanities must work toward an epistemology that can deal with the imbrication of our work with an embodied set of relationships wherein gender and other forms of difference matter in the apportioning of attention, value, status, and resources. We can start by engaging with boundary objects, liminality, and materiality within the generative, messy, and contested zone of delivery and interfaces where straightforward subject/object and agential/passive distinctions are undermined. Bringing service to the fore will permit the conflicts and anxieties that it generates to be addressed more directly and effectively, setting the stage for change. Recognizing service as a pervasive and crucial form of knowledge work within DH requires no less than shifting the epistemologies that govern how we understand a wide range of activities. But it offers the opportunity to rethink the humanities in ways that avoid replicating toxic and inequitable hierarchies and practices, allowing us to imagine instead what a service to the academy it would be to deliver substantial change in how we relate to technologies.

Notes

Many thanks to editors Liz Losh and Jacque Wernimont, and the anonymous reviewers for the Press, for their help and guidance with this essay. Very thorough feedback from peer-to-peer reviewers Lisa Brundage, Julia Flanders, and Sharon Leon prompted revisions that I hope have clarified the argument.

1. For instance, the Women Writers Project is both inextricable from the development of text encoding as a methodology within the humanities and the feminist project of expanding our objects of analysis beyond the canon, in this case the canon of pre-Victorian women writers. Julia Flanders's essay on the relationship between gender and encoding (Flanders, "Body Encoded") is a rare early example of gender being brought to bear on methods within a dedicated DH publication. More typical is engagement with the feminist component of such projects in journals or anthologies beyond DH, as is evident in the citation trail from that early article and in Wernimont and Flanders, "Feminism." The later piece exemplifies the way in which such endeavors are deeply informed by inter- and trans-disciplinary feminist analyses which are engaged most often outside of DH contexts.

2. Indicators of these debates are evident in the work of numerous scholars over the past two decades; however, they have recently reached a new level of prominence. In formal scholarship, see, for instance, in addition to essays in this one, the proportion of essays in the first two volumes of the *Debates in Digital Humanities* series that address race, gender, sexuality, geopolitical location, cultural diversity, and other forms of power imbalances such as those related to institutional positioning (Gold, *Debates,* "Introduction"; Gold and Klein, *Debates*). Public challenges to lack of diversity or insensitivity to diversity concerns have occurred in a number of contexts, the best recorded being that surrounding the opening of the DH2015 conference in Sydney addressed by Deb Verhoeven in "Has Anyone Seen a Woman?" Social media hashtags include #diverseDH, #myDH, #pocodh. More mainstream media treatments have begun to reflect better the growing diversity of the field, as in the eleven-part "The Digital in the Humanities: A Special Interview Series" by Melissa Dinsman in the *LA Review of Books* in 2016.

3. *A New Companion to Digital Humanities* includes a chapter titled "Gendering Digital Literary History: What Counts for Digital Humanities" by Laura C. Mandell in its final section, "Past, Present, Future of Digital Humanities" (Mandell, "Gendering Digital Literary History"; Schreibman, Siemens, and Unsworth, *New Companion*), marking the increasing prominence of gender in debates in the field.

4. See, for instance, Sharon Leon's piece in this volume on the ways in which librarians and staff are barred from being principal investigators.

5. Liu reviews in "Where Is Cultural Criticism in the Digital Humanities" the debates over instrumentalism that are closely linked to the matter of service.

6. Likewise, my focus here is on human service, but there is an interesting avenue of inquiry into how software-as-a-service relates to this topic. Online services such as Zotero, Omeka, Scalar, and Voyant meet others' needs, as does all service, and the discourse surrounding SOAS to some extent reverses the rhetoric of agency by stressing users' or consumers' (see Wernimont, "Whence Feminism?") dependence on services. At the same time, though, the labor associated with creating such services is still often excluded from consideration as scholarship. In a slightly different but related vein, Drucker and Svensson critique the "service" model of implementation as having impeded intellectual engagement with platforms.

7. See also Timothy Morton's argument that an object-oriented rhetoric would reverse the implicit order provided by Aristotle: starting with delivery rather than invention "explodes the teleology implicit in common assumptions about rhetoric" ("Sublime Objects," 212) that privilege the idea over the materiality, situatedness, and shaping impact of the delivery: "Delivery deforms what it delivers and the deliveree, stuttering and caricaturing them, remixing and remastering them" (214).

Bibliography

Abbate, Janet. *Recoding Gender: Women's Changing Participation in Computing.* Cambridge, Mass.: MIT Press, 2012.

AFL-CIO Department for Professional Employees. *Professionals in the Workplace: Community and Social Service Professionals.* AFL-CIO Department for Professional Employees, February 2015. http://dpeaflcio.org/wp-content/uploads/Women-in-the-Professional-Workforce-2015.pdf.

AFL-CIO Department for Professional Employees. *Professionals in the Workplace: Women in the Professional Workforce.* AFL-CIO Department for Professional Employees, February 2015. http://dpeaflcio.org/wp-content/uploads/Women-in-the-Professional-Workforce-2015.pdf.

Ahmed, Sara. *The Cultural Politics of Emotion.* New York: Routledge, 2013.

Alliance of Digital Humanities Organizations. "ADHO Conference Code of Conduct." *Alliance of Digital Humanities Organizations.* http://adho.org/administration/conference-coordinating-program-committee/adho-conference-code-conduct.

Atwood, Margaret. *The Handmaid's Tale.* Toronto: McClelland and Stewart, 1985.

Atwood, Margaret. "Margaret Atwood on What 'The Handmaid's Tale' Means in the Age of Trump." *New York Times,* March 10, 2017.

Balsamo, Anne. *Designing Culture: The Technological Imagination at Work.* Durham, N.C.: Duke University Press, 2011.

Balsamo, Anne. *Technologies of the Gendered Body: Reading Cyborg Women.* Durham, N.C.: Duke University Press, 1996.

Barad, Karen. *Meeting the Universe Halfway: Quantum Physics and the Entanglement of Matter and Meaning.* Durham, N.C.: Duke University Press, 2007.

Bellas, Marcia L. "Emotional Labor in Academia: The Case of Professors." *Annals of the American Academy of Political and Social Science* 561, no. 1 (1999): 96–110.

Berlant, Lauren G. *The Queen of America Goes to Washington City: Essays on Sex and Citizenship.* Durham, N.C.: Duke University Press, 1997.

Bowker, Geoffrey C., and Susan Leigh Star. *Sorting Things Out: Classification and Its Consequences.* Cambridge, Mass.: MIT Press, 1999.

Bratton, Benjamin H. *The Stack: On Software and Sovereignty.* Cambridge, Mass.: MIT Press, 2015.

Brown, John Seely, and Paul Duguid. *The Social Life of Information.* Boston, Mass.: Harvard Business Review Press, 2000.

Brown, Susan, Patricia Clements, and Isobel Grundy, eds. Results of Chronologies query on CHAMBERLEN, PETER, 1601–1683 within tag NAME. *Orlando: Women's Writing in the British Isles from the Beginnings to the Present.* Cambridge: Cambridge University Press Online, 2006–2018. http://orlando.cambridge.org/.

Cvetkovich, Ann. *Depression: A Public Feeling.* Durham, N.C.: Duke University Press, 2012.

DeVoss, Dànielle Nicole, and James E. Porter. "Why Napster Matters to Writing: Filesharing as a New Ethic of Digital Delivery." *Computers and Composition* 23, no. 2 (2006): 178–210.

Dinsman, Melissa. "The Digital in the Humanities: A Special Interview Series." *LA Review of Books.* March–August 2016. https://lareviewofbooks.org/feature/the-digital-in-the-humanities/#!.

Dombrowski, Quinn. "DiRT Partners with TAPoR to Provide 'Recipes.'" *DiRT: Digital Research Tools.* March 27, 2015. http://dirtdirectory.org/dirt-partners-tapor-provide-recipes.

Dombrowski, Quinn. "What Ever Happened to Project Bamboo?" *Literary and Linguistic Computing* 29, no. 3 (2014): 326–39.

Dourish, Paul, and Genevieve Bell. "The Infrastructure of Experience and the Experience of Infrastructure: Meaning and Structure in Everyday Encounters with Space." *Environment and Planning B: Planning and Design* 34, no. 3 (2007): 414–30.

Drucker, Johanna. *Graphesis: Visual Forms of Knowledge Production.* Cambridge, Mass.: Harvard University Press, 2014.

Drucker, Johanna, and Patrik BO Svensson. "The Why and How of Middleware." *Digital Humanities Quarterly* 10, no. 2 (2016).

Earhart, Amy E. "Can Information Be Unfettered?: Race and the New Digital Humanities Canon." In *Debates in the Digital Humanities,* edited by Matthew Gold, 309–18. Minneapolis: University of Minnesota Press, 2012. Reprint expanded version, online open access http://dhdebates.gc.cuny.edu/debates/text/16.

Edmond, Jennifer. "Collaboration and Infrastructure." In *A New Companion to Digital Humanities,* edited by Susan Schreibman, Ray Siemens, and John Unsworth, 54–66. Oxford: Wiley Blackwell, 2016.

Emerson, Lori. *Reading Writing Interfaces: From the Digital to the Bookbound.* Minneapolis: University of Minnesota Press, 2014.

Ennis, Erin, Zoë Marie Jones, Paolo Mangiafico, Mark Olson, Jennifer Rhee, Mitali Routh, Jonathan E. Tarr, and Brett Walters, eds. 2008. *Electronic Techtonics: Thinking at the Interface, Proceedings of the International HASTAC Conference, April 19–21, 2007,* HASTAC.

"Fact Sheet: Economic Security." Status of Women in Canada. Government of Canada. February 25, 2015. https://web.archive.org/web/20160506013825/http://www.swc-cfc.gc.ca/initiatives/wesp-sepf/fs-fi/es-se-eng.html.

Fairweather, James S. "Faculty Reward Structures: Toward Institutional and Professional Homogenization." *Research in Higher Education* 34, no. 5 (1993): 603–23.

Farman, Jason. *Mobile Interface Theory: Embodied Space and Locative Media.* New York: Routledge, 2011.

Farrao, Vincent. "Paid Work." *Women in Canada: A Gender-Based Statistical Report.* Component of Statistics Canada Catalogue no. 89–503-X. Ottawa: Statistics Canada, December 2010. https://www150.statcan.gc.ca/n1/en/pub/89-503-x/2010001/article/11387-eng.pdf?st=KihgmlHm.

Faulhaber, Charles. "21.636 Bamboo." Humanist listserv. April 15, 2008. http://www.dhhumanist.org/cgi-bin/archive/archive_msg.cgi?file=/Humanist.21.542-21.680.txt&msgnum=92&start=16696&end=17005.

Flanders, Julia. "The Body Encoded: Questions of Gender and the Electronic Text." *Electronic Text: Investigations in Method and Theory* (1997): 127–44.

Flanders, Julia. "You Work at Brown. What Do You Teach?" *#Alt-Academy: 01: Alternative Academic Careers for Humanities Scholars.* MediaCommons, July 2011. http://mediacommons.futureofthebook.org/alt-ac/e-book.

Frabetti, Federica. "Rethinking the Digital Humanities in the Context of Originary Technicity." *Culture Machine* 12 (2011): 1–22. http://culturemachine.net/index.php/cm/article/download/431/461.

Galey, Alan, and Stan Ruecker. "How a Prototype Argues." *Literary and Linguistic Computing* 25, no. 4 (2010): 405–24.

Galloway, Alexander R. *The Interface Effect.* Cambridge: Polity, 2012.

Garrison, Dee. "The Tender Technicians: The Feminization of Public Librarianship, 1876–1905." *Journal of Social History* 6, no. 2 (1972): 131–59.

Gold, Matthew K. "Introduction: The Digital Humanities Moment." In *Debates in the Digital Humanities,* edited by Matthew K. Gold, lx–lxvi. Minneapolis: University of Minnesota Press, 2012.

Gold, Matthew K., ed. *Debates in the Digital Humanities.* Minneapolis: University of Minnesota Press, 2012.

Gold, Matthew K., and Lauren Klein, eds. *Debates in the Digital Humanities 2016.* Minneapolis: University of Minnesota Press, 2016.

Gregg, Melissa, and Gregory J. Seigworth, eds. *The Affect Theory Reader.* Durham, N.C.: Duke University Press, 2010.

Guy, Mary Ellen, and Meredith A. Newman. "Women's Jobs, Men's Jobs: Sex Segregation and Emotional Labor." *Public Administration Review* 64, no. 3 (2004): 289–98.

Haraway, Donna. "A Cyborg Manifesto: Science, Technology and Socialist Feminism in the Late Twentieth Century." Reprinted in *Simians, Cyborgs, and Women: The Reinvention of Nature,* 149–82. New York: Routledge, 1991.

Harris, Roma M. "Gender, Power, and the Dangerous Pursuit of Professionalism." *American Libraries* 24, no. 9 (1993): 874–76.

Hayles, N. Katherine. *My Mother Was a Computer: Digital Subjects and Literary Texts.* Chicago: University of Chicago Press, 2005.

Hegde, Radha Sarma. *Mediating Migration.* Cambridge: Polity, 2016.

Hollinger, Veronica. "(Re) Reading Queerly: Science Fiction, Feminism, and the Defamiliarization of Gender." *Science Fiction Studies* 26, no. 1 (1999): 23–40.

Hsu, Irene, and Rachel Stone. "A Professor Is Kind of Like a Priest." *New Republic,* November 30, 2017. https://newrepublic.com/article/146049/a-professor-kind-like-priest.

Humanist 1987–. *Humanist Discussion Group.* http://dhhumanist.org/.

Jameson, Frederic. *The Political Unconscious: Narrative as a Socially Symbolic Act.* London: Methuen, 1981.

Keener, Alix. "The Arrival Fallacy: Collaborative Research Relationships in the Digital Humanities." *Digital Humanities Quarterly* 9, no. 2 (2015). http://www.digitalhumanities.org/dhq/vol/9/2/000213/000213.html.

Kelsky, Karen. "The Professor Is In: When Will We Stop Elevating Predators?" *ChronicleVitae,* January 2, 2018. https://chroniclevitae.com/news/1970-the-professor-is-in-when-will-we-stop-elevating-predators.

Kirschenbaum, Matthew G. "Digital Humanities As/Is a Tactical Term." In *Debates in the Digital Humanities,* edited by Matthew Gold, 415–28. Minneapolis: University of Minnesota Press, 2012.

Kirschenbaum, Matthew G. " 'So the Colors Cover the Wires': Interface, Aesthetics, and Usability." In *A Companion to Digital Humanities,* edited by Susan Schreibman, Ray Siemens, and John Unsworth, 523–42. Oxford: Wiley Blackwell, 2004.

Kitzinger, Sheila. *The Politics of Birth.* New York: Elsevier, Butterworth, Heinemann, 2005.

Klein, Lauren. "Visualization as Argument." *Lauren Klein,* 2014. http://lklein.com/2014/12/visualization-as-argument/.

Lewis, Vivian, Lisa Spiro, Xuemao Wang, and Jon E. Cawthorne. *Building Expertise to Support Digital Scholarship: A Global Perspective.* Washington, D.C.: Council on Library and Information Resources, October 2015. http://www.clir.org/pubs/reports/pub168/pub168.

Liu, Alan. "Drafts for *Against the Cultural Singularity* (book in progress)." *Alan Liu,* May 2, 2016. http://liu.english.ucsb.edu/drafts-for-against-the-cultural-singularity.

Liu, Alan. "Where Is Cultural Criticism in the Digital Humanities?" In *Debates in the Digital Humanities,* edited by Matthew K. Gold, 490–509. Minneapolis: University of Minnesota Press, 2012. http://dhdebates.gc.cuny.edu/debates/text/20.

Lorde, Audre. "The Master's Tools Will Not Dismantle the Master's House." *Sister Outsider: Essays and Speeches by Audre Lorde,* 110–13. Trumansburg, N.J.: Crossing, 1984.

Losh, Elizabeth. "Hacktivism and the Humanities: Programming Protest in the Era of the Digital University." In *Debates in the Digital Humanities,* edited by Matthew K. Gold, 161–86. Minneapolis: University of Minnesota Press, 2012.

Losse, Kate. "Sex and the Startup: Men, Women, and Work." *Model View Culture: Technology, Culture, and Diversity Media,* March 17, 2014. https://modelviewculture.com/pieces/sex-and-the-startup-men-women-and-work.

Maack, Mary Niles. "Gender, Culture, and the Transformation of American Librarianship, 1890–1920." *Libraries & Culture* 33, no. 1 (1998): 51–61.

Macherey, Pierre. *A Theory of Literary Production.* London: Routledge and Kegan Paul, 1978.
Mandell, Laura. "Gendering Digital Literary History: What Counts for Digital Humanities." In *A New Companion to Digital Humanities,* edited by Susan Schreibman, Ray Siemens, and John Unsworth, 2nd ed., 511–23. Oxford: Wiley Blackwell, 2016.
Maron, Nancy L. "The Digital Humanities Are Alive and Well and Blooming." *Educause Review,* August 17, 2015.
Maron, Nancy L., and Sarah Pickle. "Sustaining the Digital Humanities Host Institution Support beyond the Start-Up Phase." *Ithaka S+R,* June 18, 2014.
McCarty, Willard. "21.581 the future is Bamboo?" Humanist listserv, March 16, 2008. http://www.dhhumanist.org/cgi-bin/archive/archive_msg.cgi?file=/Humanist.21.542-21.680.txt&msgnum=39&start=7530&end=7722.
McCarty, Willard. *Humanities Computing.* London: Palgrave, 2005.
McCarty, Willard. "New Splashings in the Old Pond: The Cohesibility of Humanities Computing." *Jahrbuch für Computerphilologie* 4 (2002): 9–18. http://computerphilologie.uni-muenchen.de/jg02/mccarty.html.
McCarty, Willard. "State of Relations?" Humanist listserv, November 16, 2016.
McPherson, Tara. "Designing for Difference." *differences* 25, no. 1 (2014): 177–88.
McPherson, Tara. "Why Are the Digital Humanities So White? Or Thinking the Histories of Race and Computation." In *Debates in the Digital Humanities,* edited by Matthew K. Gold, 139–60. Minneapolis: University of Minnesota Press, 2012.
Mead, Rebecca. "Margaret Atwood: The Prophet of Dystopia." *New Yorker,* April 17, 2017. https://www.newyorker.com/magazine/2017/04/17/margaret-atwood-the-prophet-of-dystopia.
"Methods Commons." *Methodica Commons: Digital Text Methods,* 2018. http://methodi.ca/.
Morton, Timothy. "Sublime Objects." *Speculations II* (2011): 207–27.
Nowviskie, Bethany. "Asking for It." *Bethany Nowviskie,* February 8, 2014. http://nowviskie.org/2014/asking-for-it/.
Nowviskie, Bethany. "Digital Humanities in the Anthropocene." *Digital Scholarship in the Humanities,* June 17, 2015. http://dsh.oxfordjournals.org/content/early/2015/04/09/llc.fqv015.abstract.
Nowviskie, Bethany. "Skunks in the Library: A Path to Production for Scholarly R&D." *Journal of Library Administration* 53, no. 1 (2013), 53–66.
Oxford English Dictionary Online 2017. Oxford: Oxford University Press, June 2017, http://www.oed.com/.
Parks, Lisa, and Nicole Starosielski, eds. *Signal Traffic: Critical Studies of Media Infrastructures.* Champaign: University of Illinois Press, 2015.
Porter, Dot. "What If We Do, in Fact, Know Best?: A Response to the OCLC Report on DH and Research Libraries." *dh+lib,* February 12, 2014. http://acrl.ala.org/dh/2014/02/12/what-if-we-do-in-fact-know-best-a-response-to-the-oclc-report-on-dh-and-research-libraries/.

Porter, Jim. "Why Technology Matters to Writing: A Cyberwriter's Tale." *Computers and Composition* 20 no. 4 (2003): 375–94.

Posner, Miriam. "Here and There: Creating DH Community." *Miriam Posner*, September 18, 2014. http://miriamposner.com/blog/here-and-there-creating-dh-community/.

Posner, Miriam. "The Radical Potential of the Digital Humanities: The Most Challenging Computing Problem Is the Interrogation of Power." *The Impact Blog*. London School of Economics, 2015. http://blogs.lse.ac.uk/impactofsocialsciences/2015/08/12/the-radical-unrealized-potential-of-digital-humanities/.

Ramsay, Stephen. "21.453 disentanglement." Humanist listserv, December 31, 2007. http://dhhumanist.org/Archives/Virginia/v21/0447.html.

Ridolfo, Jim, and William Hart-Davidson, eds. *Rhetoric and the Digital Humanities*. Chicago: University of Chicago Press, 2015.

Ridolfo, Jim, William Hart-Davidson, and Michael McLeod. "Rhetoric and the Digital Humanities: Imagining the Michigan State University Israelite Samaritan Scroll Collection as the Foundation for a Thriving Social Network." *Community Informatics* 7, no. 3 (2011). http://ci-journal.org/index.php/ciej/article/view/754.

Rockwell, Geoffrey. "Multimedia, Is It a Discipline? The Liberal and Servile Arts in Humanities Computing." *Jahrbuch für Computerphilologie* 4 (2002). http://computerphilologie.uni-muenchen.de/jg02/rockwell.html.

Rockwell, Geoffrey, and Stephen Ramsay. "Developing Things: Notes toward an Epistemology of Building in the Digital Humanities." In *Debates in the Digital Humanities*, edited by Matthew K. Gold, 75–84. Minneapolis: University of Minnesota Press, 2012.

Rommel, Thomas. "Electronic Analysis of Literary Texts." *Jahrbuch für Computerphilologie* 5 (2003). http://computerphilologie.digital-humanities.de/jg03/rommel.html.

Rubin, Richard E. *Foundations of Library and Information Science*. New York: Neal-Schuman, 1998.

Schaffner, Jennifer, and Ricky Erway. "Does Every Research Library Need a Digital Humanities Center?" Dublin, Ohio: OCLC, 2014. http://www.oclc.org/content/dam/research/publications/library/2014/oclcresearch-digital-humanities-center-2014.pdf.

Schreibman, Susan, Ray Siemens, and John Unsworth, eds. *A Companion to Digital Humanities*. Oxford: Wiley Blackwell, 2008.

Schreibman, Susan, Ray Siemens, and John Unsworth, eds. *A New Companion to Digital Humanities*. Oxford: Wiley Blackwell, 2016.

Sedgwick, Eve Kosofsky, and Adam Frank. *Touching Feeling: Affect, Pedagogy, Performativity*. Durham, N.C.: Duke University Press, 2003.

"service, n.1." *Oxford English Dictionary Online*. Oxford University Press, June 2017. www.oed.com/view/Entry/176678.

Sinclair, Stéfan, and Geoffrey Rockwell. "Teaching Computer-Assisted Text Analysis." In *Digital Humanities Pedagogy: Practices, Principles and Politics*, edited by Brett D. Hirsch, 241–54. Vol. 3. Cambridge: Open Book Publishers, 2012.

Smith, Martha Nell. "The Human Touch Software of the Highest Order: Revisiting Editing as Interpretation." *Textual Cultures: Texts, Contexts, Interpretation* 2, no. 1 (2007): 1–15.

Smith-Rosenberg, Carroll. *Disorderly Conduct: Visions of Gender in Victorian America.* New York: Oxford University Press, 1986.

Star, Susan Leigh. "The Ethnography of Infrastructure." *American Behavioral Scientist* 43, no. 3 (1999): 377–91.

Star, Susan Leigh. "Power, Technology, and the Phenomenology of Conventions: On Being Allergic to Onions." In *A Sociology of Monsters: Essays on Power, Technology and Domination,* 26–56. London: Routledge, 1999.

Star, Susan Leigh, and Karen Ruhleder. "Steps toward an Ecology of Infrastructure: Design and Access for Large Information Spaces." *Information Systems Research* 7, no. 1 (1996): 111–34.

Suchman, Lucy. "Agencies in Technology Design: Feminist Reconfigurations." Unpublished manuscript (2007). *Research Gate.* https://www.researchgate.net/profile/Lucy_Suchman/publication/27336947_Agencies_in_Technology_Design_Feminist_Reconfigurations/links/00b7d520038ad34bcc000000.pdf.

Suchman, Lucy. *Human-Machine Reconfigurations: Plans and Situated Actions.* 2nd ed. Cambridge: Cambridge University Press, 2007.

Svensson, Patrik. "Envisioning the Digital Humanities." *Digital Humanities Quarterly* 6, no. 1 (2012).

Svensson, Patrik. "The Landscape of Digital Humanities." *Digital Humanities Quarterly* 4, no. 1 (2010).

Tiptree, James, Jr. "The Girl Who Was Plugged In." 1973. In *Reload: Rethinking Women and Cyberculture,* edited by Mary Flanagan and Austin Booth, 546–77. Boston: MIT Press, 2002.

Verhoeven, Deb. "As Luck Would Have It." *Feminist Media Histories* 2, no. 1 (2016): 7–28.

Verhoeven, Deb. "'Has Anyone Seen a Woman?,' Digital Humanities Conference—2015." Speakola, July 2, 2015. http://speakola.com/ideas/deb-verhoeven-has-anyone-seen-a-woman-2015.

Vicinus, Martha. *Independent Women: Work and Community for Single Women, 1850–1920.* Chicago: University of Chicago Press, 1992.

Wajcman, Judy. "Patriarchy, Technology, and Conceptions of Skill." *Work and Occupations* 18, no. 1 (1991): 29–45.

Wernimont, Jacqueline. "Whence Feminism? Assessing Feminist Interventions in Digital Literary Archives." *Digital Humanities Quarterly* 7, no. 1 (2013).

Wernimont, Jacqueline, and Julia Flanders. "Feminism in the Age of Digital Archives: The Women Writers Project." *Tulsa Studies in Women's Literature* 29, no. 2 (2010): 425–35.

Wernimont, Jacqueline, and Angel David Nieves. "DHSI Statement of Ethics and Inclusion." *Digital Humanities Summer Institute,* 2016. http://www.dhsi.org/events.php.

Williamson, Charles C. *Training for Library Service: A Report Prepared for the Carnegie Corporation of New York.* New York: Updike, 1923. https://archive.org/details/trainingforlibra011790mbp.

V
LABOR

PART V][*Chapter 16*

Building Otherwise

JULIA FLANDERS

This chapter is a step in a longer exploration of the ways of reading technical systems as systems of cultural meaning and ideology. It is an inquiry concerning how to understand the relationship between systems and their components, their design, their meaning and the meaning of the things stored in them, their builders, their users, and the products they are used to create. In particular, it is about how otherness and logics of difference animate the tools and systems used in digital humanities; and it is about how we should act, where action requires both a theory of intention and causality and an understanding of where our intervention needs to be directed.

The provocation for this work, for me, has been twofold. First, I feel a strong challenge from work by scholars like Tara McPherson to read technological systems as ideological systems, and to focus not just on their effects as completed systems but on their genesis and development: on the ideologies that shaped their design.[1] This reading simultaneously situates digital humanities practitioners as responsible parties—designers and builders implicated in the design of future systems—and complicates that role of agency by suggesting that the ideological entailments of such systems may not be visible to their builders, and indeed that the design logics that feel most deeply natural and functional to one generation may be revealed as deeply problematic in the next. Situated thus, I want critical digital humanities practitioners to ask whether and how they would have built these systems differently, whether in their current projects they are able and willing to take different approaches, and what we can all learn from these historical examples that might inform an alternative practice. And I also want to ask whether the legacy of these systems' genesis in a cultural logic of racism also informs their current effects in the world, and whether we need to repudiate and redesign these systems as part of a remedy. The challenge in this analysis is to understand the relationship between individual intentions, individual identities, and this larger economy of power: in what sense does it matter who builds things? It is clear that one's subject position (as a woman of color, as a white man, etc.) doesn't necessarily align with ideological commitments, and indeed intersectionality shows how complex even the politically visible subject positioning can be. Putting Clarence Thomas on the U.S. Supreme Court did not necessarily make that body more progressive on issues of race, but it did make race visible as part of the operations of that body. In the same way, this analysis needs to attend both to the perspective of individuals (who can take deliberate action, and can try to inform that action with critical thinking) and to the systemic forces and shifts that constrain and constitute our subject positions as agents.

This sequence of questions leads to a second, more personal provocation to consider my own situation within this matrix. My professional acculturation in digital humanities took place at the Women Writers Project (WWP; at the time, located at Brown University; now at Northeastern University), a major early effort to make gender a category of analysis and visibility in the emerging world of digital scholarly research in the most literal way possible. As a female academic, director of a digital "Women Writers Project," writing a chapter about gender, I can't help but be read as *significantly* female. And these three spaces of gender seem to line up as if they are about the same thing: my personal gender helps literalize "women" as the significant fact about the WWP within this narrative, and also imputes to me a position of authority from which to write about gender.

But the development of the WWP's research focus mirrored a shift in feminist theory from a second-wave attention to the visibility and rights of women (for the WWP, the discoverability and valuation of women's writing in the pre-Victorian period) to a third-wave focus on how the structure of discourse enacts and reinforces cultural power dynamics of gender, race, class, coloniality, and other differentials. The WWP's work involved developing methods of digital text encoding for the representation of early women's writing: in effect, developing new discursive layers within the digital code through which documentary information could be represented and analyzed, and translating the methods of traditional scholarly editing into the digital medium. The project of gender here thus entailed not only a focus on the gender of physical bodies but also attention to the strong, if less obvious, gender implications carried by technologies of text markup and editorial practice. Work by scholars like Stephanie Jed, Katie King, Martha Nell Smith, Donald Reiman, and many others has shown how deeply editorial methods are implicated in the politics of gender, and it's also clear that in the digital medium, editorial methods are affected by, and enacted through, technological choices.[2]

In this work, as in McPherson's, we can see a foundational assumption: there is no such thing as a "merely technical" design decision: technical systems are meaning systems and ideological systems, as far down as we are willing to look. If we are only interested in seeing and understanding the operations of gender in the places where they appear obvious (bodies and personal identity), then we will miss some of its most important operations in spaces where it may be more powerfully at work. And conversely, the places where gender may seem most obviously legible may be misleading or peripheral. My historical impact on the WWP has been to make it *less* about women and more about digital technologies—more attentive, perhaps, to the occult operations of gender within those technologies, but not necessarily in ways that alter our use of those technologies in response. Should we read that shift of emphasis as progressive (from a gender politics standpoint) in virtue of my own gender—this is the impact of a woman in a digital project!—or as evidence of professional acculturation recasting me as a white male technophile? Does my gender anchor my actions and intentions, or does it simply offer a perspective of difference from which other kinds of positioning (for instance, my race and class) can dislodge and reinscribe me?

These questions bear on the question of how the digital humanities might "build otherwise" because they suggest how complex "building" and "making" are as expressions of intention, identity, and cultural politics. It feels to me like a central paradox of the digital humanities that even while relying on technological systems and narratives of technological improvement, the field maintains a commitment to a "maker culture" and to "building" that means something more than simply a self-reliant desire to be handy. The field approaches making in a critical spirit, as interpreters of process and of ways of engaging with the material. But the status of cultural meaning in this context—both its tensional relation to the practical operations of tools and systems and its genesis in the various parts of those systems—is complicated to tease out. The design of a tool like Mukurtu (an open-source content management system aimed at supporting the cultural heritage needs of indigenous communities) takes seriously the ways in which information systems shape and enable and foreclose cultural meaning. Its designers deliberately foregrounded the rights and needs of those communities in their implementation of the basic functions of "content management." But its lexicon of features (collection building, metadata tags, batch import and export, and so forth) are in many ways structurally indistinguishable from those of any content management system, and like all twenty-first-century digital tools are indebted to the still deeper features of operating systems, networks, web architectures, and so forth. If, as Tara McPherson suggests, these structural paradigms are themselves racially coded, even down to the level of the operating system, then the challenge of recognizing the cultural ideology of tools, let alone resisting it, is surely immense.

I can frame the specific concerns of this chapter as follows. If digital humanities as a domain of research+praxis is indeed prepared to take seriously the cultural, scholarly, and ideological significance of the full stack of technologies—if we're prepared to read that entire stack as a cultural text, in addition to attending to the cultural effects of the entire stack as a working system—then three questions seem urgent. First, how do race, gender, and other forms of otherness operate within the scholarly, cultural, and ideological space of technological systems? Second, does it matter where we look for them? Do they operate differently at different places in the system? And third, do we have alternatives? Once we see these operations, what do we do differently?

What concerns and interests me about current attempts to answer these questions is the difficulty they reveal in creating a single coherent account of the operations of diversity in theories about how "building" operates in digital humanities. To illustrate this point concretely I'd like to take as examples four influential interventions that I admire and have found very useful. The first is Miriam Posner's call, in her keynote at the 2015 Keystone Digital Humanities conference, for a complete rethinking of scholarly technological systems, an intellectual overhaul attentive to the ideological commitments in which these systems implicate us. This piece takes seriously the need for a critical revision: Posner calls for data models that respond both to the complexity of the world and to political and social justice concerns, and she also takes seriously the role that technical knowledge could play in that revision (for instance, in her "How Did They Make That?" blog series where she has been a vocal and creative advocate for greater knowledge of the "under the hood" aspects of digital projects). The examples are provocative: Google maps as an instance of the indebtedness of key information resources to corporate interests; Cartesian mapping systems more generally as an instance of the ways in which the available data models arise from colonialist intellectual and political traditions. Here she argues that two kinds of action are demanded of us. The first is a work of imagination: a move toward alternative ways of seeing, organizing, and analyzing that enables us to deliberately understand and use technical systems as meaning systems rather than as neutral and unalterable parts of the landscape. The very seamlessness of our interface with technology is precisely what insulates us and deadens our awareness of these tools' significance: "In a similar way, many of the qualities of computer interfaces that we've prized, things like transparency, seamlessness, and flow, privilege ease of use ahead of any kind of critical engagement (even, perhaps, struggle) with the material at hand" (Posner, para. 12). The second action she demands is a work of building: creating real systems that use these alternative models and paradigms: "We can scrutinize data, rip it apart, rebuild it, reimagine it, and perhaps build something entirely different and weirder and more ambitious." This is a brave as well as ambitious agenda, but it leaves open two important questions. For one thing, it is not clear how far down the technological stack this revision is expected to go. The operations of digital humanities "coding" and "building" as Posner describes them (mapping, exhibit building, interface building) are located near the top of the technical stack, leaving untouched the deeper layers: the structural logic of databases, operating systems, stylesheets, algorithms, data representations. She speaks of reimagining data models and the systems that use them, but the examples she offers for emulation demonstrate above all how difficult it is to perform that work of reimagination at any distance below the surface. One layer down, they are still working with conventional databases, content management systems, and metadata standards. A project like Jacqueline Goldsby's "Mapping the Stacks," in which a team of graduate students discovers and describes archival materials relating to African American history in

Chicago, arguably depends for its impact precisely on the existing mechanisms of systematic visibility that are underwritten by the existing archival infrastructure, even as it rethinks where and how we look for the archival content. Indeed, it's clear that many of the activities of positive engagement depend on the practical workings of mundanities like contributory interfaces, user authentication, and other systems that are very deeply rooted in the "business applications" side of the operation. My point here is not that Posner's argument is misguided—far from it—but rather to show the complexities that lie ahead if we explore its implications a bit more fully. And the other, even trickier question this articulation leaves open is the issue of how changes in technical systems (using different data models, different tools) actually effect social change.

Steve Ramsay, in a provocative Modern Language Association conference presentation titled "Who's In and Who's Out" and its companion piece "On Building," takes a position complementary to this one, in the sense that he too argues for the importance of "building" as digital humanities practice, but with a much stronger and less ambivalent role marked out for technical expertise: without it, we cannot competently theorize the technological stack. And without that competent theorization, the discipline of digital humanities unravels. "Building" for Ramsay is an "expansive" term that also encompasses "people who theorize about building, people who design so that others might build, and those who supervise building," but at its heart it signals the "methodologization" of the humanities: the essential link between the work of praxis and that of critical reflection.

The complex gender and racial politics of this emphasis on competence are not lost on Ramsay. In a moving contribution to the long thread of responses to Miriam Posner's blog post "Some Things to Think About before You Exhort Everyone to Code," he describes the ways in which the distinctively "hacker" form of expertise translates into a certain kind of social ruthlessness or tone-deafness in which technical competence can seem—in a deceptively egalitarian gesture—to be the only thing at stake.[3] The pedagogical or cultural challenge *appears* to be simply how to empower women and other underrepresented groups to gain that expertise, in other words, a shift in the culture of *those* groups to make them comfortable with the *techne* of that technical space. But as his narrative demonstrates, technical competence isn't the issue at all; his female undergraduates are perfectly competent as programmers, perfectly confident in their abilities. In their encounter with the programmer culture of the computer science department, the problem is gender, not competence, and it's a problem of gender *difference*: of the male programmers not realizing they have a gender until a different one walks in the door. The space of expertise is defined not simply by qualifications but by a proprietary association between those qualifications and a specific tribe that possesses them. As Moya Bailey notes in her contribution to the same thread, the question is "about both making room at the table for everyone and also questioning who is in a position to 'invite' folks to the table in the first place."[4]

This last point is especially important because "making room at the table" assumes a kind of cultural assimilation that doesn't necessarily change how the table's affairs are conducted. And while we may recognize that assimilation as a political sidestep around the core issue, it is nonetheless a seductive engagement for both parties. At a personal level, I can attest with some retrospective chagrin to the thrill (as a young scholar/practitioner) of discovering that one can blend in with a group of experts and be accepted as one of them. The culture of programming has remained resilient and recognizable despite the entry of women and other minorities into the field; competence interpellates us powerfully, both technically and socially, framing the status we grant to high-value forms of expertise. So the question Ramsay's interventions thus raise is how we can treat "building" as a metric of competence that anchors professional identity, while retaining ideological and critical maneuverability.

Tara McPherson's "Why Are the Digital Humanities So White" addresses this point full on, arguing that the ideology of technical expertise—and in fact all of the hallmarks of its execution in the foundational technical systems of daily digital activity—carries a deeply political stamp: it both bears witness to and actively enacts a logic of racism (and I think she would agree that the same logic extends to gender discrimination as well). She offers a provocative exploration of how we might read race with technology, asking why we can't seem to see them as connected and suggesting that the very design logic of information technology—modular, "clean," highly formalized—provides a cover story for its presumed imperviousness, or neutrality with respect to ideology. Like Ramsay, she takes seriously the need to critically theorize the full depth of the technical stack, at least down to the operating system, and also the full range of competences and practices that reproduce that stack as it evolves. The terrain that her position leaves unresolved is the question of causality: she explores in detail (as Posner does not) the possibility that causal responsibility for today's culture of racial and gender inequity might lie in deeply embedded, nearly invisible things like operating systems: "Computers are coders of culture. . . . If . . . Unix hardwired an emerging system of covert racism into our mainframes and our minds, then computation responds to culture as much as it controls it. Code and race are deeply intertwined, even as the structures of code labor to disavow these very connections." And it also leaves unresolved the question of personal agency: are the builders of Unix involved as intentional agents—who could have done otherwise—in the structural racism of its design logic, and if so, what would be the conditions under which that other agency could have been expressed? In the end, she leaves open the question of how individuals can intervene in their efforts toward social change, and whether changing those systems would have any effect if it were possible to do so.

Moya Bailey, in "All the Digital Humanists Are White, All the Nerds Are Men, but Some of Us Are Brave," emphasizes the need for social change, and the need to theorize the field and its technologies in terms of race and other forms of diversity.

Unlike Ramsay, she is not committed to a specific definition of "digital humanities" which can in turn be used to define the expertise and concerns appropriate to that field; instead, she is committed to a definition by inclusion, saying in effect that the field must be defined so as to include all of the activities, by all of the diverse peoples undertaking them, that bear on questions of cultural digitality. Many of these activities involve appropriating tools for a radical politics that brings race, gender, and other axes of diversity into view precisely for their frictionality within those tools. But this appropriation (through usage) of tools for social justice projects leaves the structure of tool *development* unquestioned and unaltered: in effect, staging an occupation rather than seeking to rearchitect along different lines. Bailey's work thus brings us back to the issue of what kinds of expertise would be needed to accomplish that rearchitecting, and what the new purpose of those rearchitected tools should be.

From the spaces opened up between these very different interventions, a set of questions emerges. First, would it help to alter our technological design? If the problem is bad data models (ideologically discriminatory, colonialist, patriarchal, etc.) and tools that reify them, could we build an alternative stack of technological systems to serve some different version of our purposes? Would the effects of doing so in fact reverse or subvert or counter the "culture" to which McPherson tells us "computation responds"? Second, how does the culture of the process affect the culture of the product? McPherson makes a point of noting that the people actually involved in the development of Unix, their intentions with respect to the code, are something quite apart from the structural logic of separation that informed the design of the operating system itself. Ramsay seems to feel that the core problem (with respect to gender) is in large part that women are being turned off and turned away *culturally* from practicing in a field where they otherwise could make great and useful *technical* contributions (without changes to the ways software tools are imagined or constructed). If we had a more diverse programming culture, would that result in technical systems that are not, in McPherson's terms, "white" (or by extension "male")? And if so, how would this in turn affect the users of such systems and the communities they create? Third, what specific actions can individuals take—as *designers* of politically implicated systems or as *resisters* of them? What actions have the potential for structural change rather than merely academic self-reflection (of the sort I'm currently indulging in)? And fourth, who are the beneficiaries in question: whose interests are being served? Is the goal to remedy specific oppressions, or to create a richer critical perspective? Are there achievable changes being proposed? How widely would those changes propagate?

My goal thus far has been to convey a sense of the trickiness of the problem space. I want next to consider how the field of digital humanities has attempted, and how it might attempt, to respond. In the terms set out by my title, how do we "build otherwise"? What are the spaces within the enterprise where gender, race, and other forms of power differentiation are especially operative as *ways of making a difference,* and how do we respond in light of this understanding? Spoiler alert: I'm not going to be able to answer any of those questions in a satisfying way, but I am going to try to derive something useful from the failure.

An early response, whose limitations are now clearly visible to us, makes gender and race and "difference" visible as cultural content: as significant and overlooked categories in the construction of a cultural past that become visible where they are aggregated and intensified. Many early projects formed, as the Women Writers Project did, around various categories of invisibility and disenfranchisement, with gender and race very significantly among them. If the value of these early reclamation efforts lies in the ways they create distinctive intellectual spaces for the study of "other" cultural production, a value whose importance shouldn't be underestimated even now, then their limitation lies precisely in that distinctiveness: they don't permit the study of these "others" as anything but a separate category. They also typify the approach Moya Bailey has characterized as "add and stir" (where the addition might be any demoted category, that is, women, aboriginal peoples, etc.): the idea that if we add the missing special element back into the default culture, somehow we will end up with something whole and neutral.[5]

What's striking about this "reclamatory" way of framing the problem is that the only category we can study is the marked, demoted one; as with the nomenclature of "women's studies" and similar programs, the reclamatory approach focuses on the marked category and concedes neutrality and centrality to the unmarked category. Furthermore, these marked categories are not visible as part of the advanced search interfaces for major comprehensive digital resources such as EEBO, ESTC, NINES, or Google Books. And to the extent that categories of personal identity such as gender and race are visible (for instance, in WorldCat Identities), it is only as a marked category: female authors, authors of color, and authors with disabilities all bear the informational traces of their difference, but these markings are not part of a systematic regime of information; there is in every case a "null" unmarked value, a default setting (whiteness, maleness, ableness, straightness). More subtly, as Hope Olson has argued in "The Power to Name," in the subject cataloging systems prevalent in the United States (i.e., Library of Congress subject headings), these categories of identity are located several steps down in a taxonomic system whose primary divisions are things like "literature" and "history"; identity is treated only as a qualifier on other more salient informational categories ("American fiction—women authors"), rather than as a primary category of discovery.[6]

The attempt to foreground categories of identity also assumes that we can represent these categories as part of a clear-cut and unproblematic descriptive vocabulary for identity, and that we have (and wish to apply) clear criteria for discovering whom it applies to. The Text Encoding Initiative (TEI) considered this issue a few years ago when Melissa Terras agitated successfully for an expansion of the options for representing "sex" as a characteristic of persons. The TEI had previously used the ISO standard "codes for the representation of human sexes" whose permitted values are 0, 1, 2, and 9 (not known, male, female, and not applicable). From an information-retrieval standpoint, those values have a certain kind of brutal utility (setting aside the humor value of "1" and "2"): to realize the kind of basic discoverability of "women writers" in WorldCat, some simplistic representational standard is needed, though perhaps not quite that simplistic. But as *descriptors* these values are obviously impoverished; the TEI now permits projects to define their own descriptive vocabulary or to use an externally defined standard (such as ISO).

But descriptive adequacy is not the only goal here. Amber Billey and colleagues present a detailed critique of the cataloging rules expressed in the Resource Description and Access (RDA) standard concerning the representation of the gender of authors, pointing out that the cataloger's imperative to classify and make visible the gender of an author (based on evidence such as the cultural gendering of names, etc.) may run counter to an author's sense that their gender is not a relevant or easily categorized fact:

> RDA rule 9.7 poses problems on two grounds. First, the rule directs the cataloger to describe the gender of the author as part of the project of constructing access points and relationships between bibliographic entities. In this sense, the gender marker is like format or the number of pages: an objective description of reality. *The author really has a single gender that could really be captured by the cataloger. Queer theory, as well as the lived experience of authors of non-normative genders, tells us this is not so.* The second problem concerns retrieval. By marking the gender of the author using a fixed category, the LC interpretation of RDA reifies contemporary understandings of gender as a binary system with only two acceptable gender markers (male or female). *Even if catalogers indicate gender using alternate labels, RDA's insistence on the relevance of gender as a descriptive attribute reifies regressive social binaries and is passively hostile to transgender individuals.* (Billey et al., emphasis added)[7]

Indeed, even what might look from a third-wave feminist perspective like a very progressive development—making gender visible as a category in metadata, and recording the fact that gender assignment may change, rather than treating it as a permanent and self-evident category—in fact looks to Billey and fourth-wave feminism quite retrogressive. For one thing, it reifies the oversimplification of "male | female," and in fact any version of a controlled vocabulary for this purpose, however extended, is definitionally going to be an oversimplification—all the more so with categories like race that have for much longer been understood as fluid and local. And it also enforces the requirement that gender be treated as a category of identity at all, which these authors assert is not necessarily something everyone wants or benefits from.

These forms of attention to difference get us a certain distance in understanding how gender, race, and other formations inhabit digital systems, but they ignore something deeper, namely, the power dynamics inscribed in those information systems themselves. Directives on how to read those power dynamics are available to us from many quarters, and I have scope to mention only a few here in hopes that their further implications will be clear by extrapolation. As I noted at the outset, early humanities computing projects explored the ways that a gender politics (and the politics of other power vectors) might be embedded in editorial theory, quite apart from considerations of the literal gender of authors or editors. We see this enacted in practice in digital archives and editions that seek to revise an Anglo-American tradition of critical editing focused on producing authoritative editions that informationalize their sources and produce a kind of textual master knowledge. Examples include the Dickinson Electronic Archives at the University of Maryland, the Women Writers Project, and arguably also editions that pursue a similar editorial agenda but with an editorial politics focused on power dynamics other than gender: for instance, "fluid-text" editions like the Melville Electronic Library.

This work of revision draws on an existing strand of research among traditional (nondigital) textual editors and theorists interested in Western theorizations of the body and what we might call "the gender politics of abstraction": for example, scholars including Naomi Schor, Stephanie Jed, Joan Scott, and others who examine what Joan Scott calls "those long traditions of (Western) philosophy that have systematically and repeatedly construed the world hierarchically in terms of masculine universals and feminine specificities."[8] As scholars like Felicity Nussbaum and Terry Eagleton have argued, the same logic of physicalized otherness also extends to race and to class.[9] These same roots in neoclassical aesthetics are those from which the digital humanities also draws very heavily in its conceptualization of things like schemas, data models, and ontologies, and this work suggests that we need to be equally attentive to the politics of difference that inhabit these instruments.

It should thus come as no surprise that the same neoclassical aesthetic that brings us the feminized, particularized body and complementary narratives about race, class, and forms of labor should deeply inform the ways practitioners and theorists in digital humanities think about building and making. The politics of praxis in the digital humanities are illuminated by metaphors like "getting one's hands dirty" with tools and coding systems, just as much as by those in which computation is the "handmaiden" of scholarship. In another place it would be well worth a digression into the details of these metaphors, but a few key points are worth unpacking. First, if we're interested in seeking out the architecture of difference within the logic of "building" that animates the "maker culture" in DH, we need to consider what the idea of "building" commits us to as a cultural meme. It puts the self-reliant maker at the center: as a heroic small producer, fascinated and satisfied by the process of creation, legible as an artisan but also as an entrepreneur, perhaps also as a crafter, and also as a figure whose intentions and desires and self-determination matter.[10] Within this individualistic space, identity and the right to self-expression are an adequate basis for ethics. As a result, the "maker" figure writes individualism into the maker space in ways that make it harder to think simultaneously about structural factors, such as how the maker might be implicated (in the complex ways McPherson lays out) in a design logic animated by structural racism. This version of the maker asks us to see the individual as an ignorant victim of system, or as complicit with system, or as an embodiment of free will that invalidates critique at the system level altogether, but it doesn't give us a way of seeing the intentions of the maker as politically irrelevant and structurally ineffectual. This characterization also offers a form of cultural critique that tries to access the appealing preindustrial space of the workshop (mirroring current fascination with artisanal food, furniture, and so forth), while turning its gaze away from the ways in which the "raw materials" of the DH maker space, like the prepackaged "curated box of do-it-yourself electronics" of the AdaBox, are themselves industrial products (and require an industrial-grade system of global transport and information dissemination to bring them to market).[11]

But this is not to say that attention to "building" in DH forecloses all access to the more complex politics of that identity. It usefully foregrounds the relation of the individual to the meaning systems of code, and the ways that praxis embeds individual bodies in work processes. It also fruitfully transgresses or transcends the traditional professional identities of the scholar, the developer, the librarian, and thereby draws our attention to different forms of expertise and knowledge that could constitute "scholarship." Finally, it's worth noting that the use of "code" as a proxy for digital humanities activities of "building" has some interesting slippages. The word is aligned in common usage with the maker space, with "thingness" and praxis (just as we say that code is a "building block" of a program, part of its "architecture"), but it is also aligned with "encoding" and thereby with discourse, notation systems, the realm of the symbolic. In the politics of DH, "code" is deeply polysemous. It can stand for a kind of machismo, the domain of the hacker whose credibility rests precisely on an uncritical but unarguably expert facility with tools, and for a place of self-empowerment and individual agency, offered equitably, as a kind of leveling oppositionality. This oppositionality is realized through the proliferation of workshops and self-guided teaching resources by which DH practitioners are encouraged to become builders and thereby authenticate their critical relation to conventional formations of the academy, including its traditional power structures of gender, class, race. And "code" also stands for the place where language is most deeply and mysteriously operative in our systems (and hence where our critical and interpretive attention might find its most fruitful object).

The reason I bring us around by this convoluted route to this set of points is to show, first, how fully cultural politics proliferate within all technical structures and practices, and second, how polymorphous those cultural politics are: how difficult they are to map onto a single problem like gender or race or class, and how thoroughly the human, the social, and the technological are mutually implicated.

As an experiment in reading the individual in relation to systems, I'd like to offer a brief case study that looks at two significant female figures in the history of technical systems: Grace Hopper and Jean Sammet. Grace Hopper has been rediscovered by digital humanists as one of the early female computer scientists; she held a PhD in math and had a lifetime of service in the U.S. Navy. She was also the developer of the first compiler, and was a contributor to the COBOL language and the developer of one of its progenitors (a language called FLOW-MATIC). Jean Sammet was another notable early female computer scientist who was closely involved in the development of COBOL. In the 1970s, she was the first female president of the Association for Computing Machinery, and she designed and taught some of the earliest graduate-level courses in computer programming. Extrinsically, it surely matters that these two figures are women, and we could unpack (as many articles have done) the ways in which their gender affected their educational opportunities, their working conditions, the expectations their colleagues had of them, their relationships to systems and institutions of power, and so forth. But what explanatory value does gender hold for their work as designers of programming languages? Or, to come at this from another direction, what are the salient qualities of FLOW-MATIC and COBOL, and how might we begin to read them in cultural and political terms?

Both languages were distinctive at the time for being written for comprehensibility rather than pure arithmetic brevity: FLOW-MATIC was the first programming language to use natural-language-like words rather than symbols, and COBOL extended this approach. In both cases, the goal was for programs to be legible not only to programmers but also to managers. These systems are thus also framing the problem of code notation as a problem of pedagogy and documentation: in other words, situating program code in a work ecology that includes nonexperts, broadening its intelligibility, making it less of a guild knowledge. Jean Sammet in her history of programming languages describes COBOL as being designed both for "the relatively inexperienced programmer for whom the naturalness of COBOL would be an asset" and "essentially anybody who had not written the program initially."[12] As she goes on to observe, "the readability of COBOL programs would provide documentation to all who might wish to examine the programs, including supervisory or management personnel" (335).

These characterizations suggest an emerging sociality of code, which embeds it in a broadening population of users and readers; we could read these historical signposts as pointing toward the more collaborative working environments of the digital humanities. But we might also say that Hopper's and Sammet's work situates program code in a work ecology that is corporate and military rather than scientific: in other words, environments where technical work needs to be consumed and evaluated within systems of hierarchical power where technical expertise exists only in a limited stratum, rather than within an intellectual peer group.[13] And it is surely also interesting that COBOL was also commissioned as a *standard* language (to eliminate the unmanageable diversity of machine-specific languages), reflecting the fact that computers were becoming numerous enough that portability of code could be useful. That portability signals a set of design concerns that a few years later motivate the very modularity that Tara McPherson marks as part of the deep logic of racial separation she sees at the heart of Unix.

I proposed Hopper and Sammet as a case study in how we read the meaning of individual interventions, and the sketchiness of the detail here clearly suggests how much more research would be necessary to complete that reading. But I think we can see nonetheless the kinds of questions such a study prompts. Did these women accomplish anything that is recognizable to us as "building otherwise"? If not, why not? If so, how? To what extent is their agency as individual designers or builders visible to us in the systems to which they contributed, to what extent does that agency bear the stamp of their identity as women, and to what extent can we trace effects that are somehow constructive from the perspective of gender politics? Or some other politics? What did they construe as the opposition? For Grace Hopper, "the establishment" comes up as a repeating figure; what perspective (or failure of perspective) does her status as a woman (in the armed services, in business, in the field of mathematics, and so forth) give her on constructing oppositionality in useful ways?[14] Does it matter, for these purposes, that the types of feminism that might have been visible to her are not necessarily forms we now feel empowered by? What would it mean for current debates in digital humanities to take a more intersectional approach to the examination of the political logic of technical structures, acknowledging how deeply gender and race are implicated in class and economic formations? What does it mean if *functional* determinants of quality—the application of expertise, the consensus of users, increased efficiency, and so forth—lead us in directions we can clearly see are culturally fraught, in the ways that Miriam Posner and Tara McPherson highlight so clearly? Does reversing that developmental trajectory make a difference? If we build systems that are frictional and self-dismantling, that refuse the design logic arising from male-dominated culture, will they help us build a better society? If women (or people of color, or people from the Global South, etc.) are involved in setting technical directions and establishing those functional determinants (as Grace Hopper and Jean Sammet clearly were), how does that affect our assessment of the political valence of those systems, or do we first need to consider the acculturation and initiation processes by which individuals are "invited to the table"? Does an improved process guarantee a good outcome? And if so, is that because "objectively" (whatever we mean by that) the outcome is better, or because having a better process validates whatever outcome we arrive at?

These reflections are at best a frame for a further research agenda. But in an eleventh-hour addition to this piece it may be relevant to note some preliminary outcomes from an initiative that is taking up that agenda. At an October 2017 forum titled "Design for Diversity," participants shared a set of case studies investigating the ways in which information systems—digital interfaces, metadata standards, online exhibits, and other tools and components—are animated by forms of cultural hegemony.[15] Facing the question of where such tools and systems express or enforce such cultural norms, and how they might be designed otherwise, the group repeatedly pointed to the shaping force of social processes and relationships in determining the ethical shape of technical outcomes. Social processes such as decision making, information sharing, and strategic planning, to the degree that they included all those implicated in a project's outcomes, tended to result in systems that were more resilient and more accommodating of diverse cultural positions; sadly, many of the case studies illustrated the corollary position with examples of brittle or failed designs arising from poorly planned processes. (It is worth noting that the typical language of "stakeholders" to describe inclusivity points to the heart of the problem, since it treats the means to ante up, rather than ethical entitlement, as the criterion of inclusion at the table.) Similarly, the group pointed to the importance of building trust relationships within and outside the project that reflect the genuine ethical entailments of the project's impact in the world (rather than the limited set of entailments representing the project's own self-interest). In case after case, in a remarkable variety of ways, the specific work of technical design—and the expertise and intentions through which it is effected—was shown to be strongly shaped by these broader contextual factors.

What this discussion suggests is that the project of remaking tools may depend for its success on the social processes employed, and further that the social significance of technical systems lies not only in their overt functioning (what they enable us to *do*) but also in the social effluent, so to speak, of their construction processes. When a system like Unix, or a language like COBOL, or a resource like the Women Writers Project is created, what does it "give off" in terms of expertise, power relations, installed systems and dependencies, professional advancement or subordination, knowledge and empowerment—and for whom? The successful processes portrayed at Design for Diversity were inclusive in very significant ways, but in particular their principle of diversity had to do with a genuine diversification of the allocation of power: the power to say what is most important about the design of a tool or system, the power to update a record, the power to define vocabularies, the power to say what should be visible or invisible, the power resulting from increased knowledge or expertise. Not only was the tribe of "coders" being diversified, but also that tribe's understanding of mission—what is being built, for whom, why, under what design imperatives, with what specific stipulations—was being shaped by diversified constituencies, operating under radically different assumptions about whose needs matter. Building otherwise, in digital humanities, may thus require that we understand building as a deeply embedded expression of social justice: that a tool or artifact that is "for" a purpose or an audience needs to involve those it affects in the full ecology of its design, and that we are never building only for, or as, ourselves.

Notes

1. McPherson, "Why Is the Digital Humanities."
2. See, for instance, Jed, *Chaste Thinking*; King, "Bibliography and a Feminist Apparatus"; Smith, "Electronic Scholarly Editing"; Reiman, "Gender and Documentary Editing"; Sutherland and Pierazzo, "Author's Hand."

3. Ramsay, comment on "Some Things."
4. Bailey, comment on "Some Things."
5. Bailey, "All the Digital Humanists," para 9.
6. Olson, "Power to Name."
7. Billey, Drabinski, and Roberto, "What's Gender."
8. Scott, "Deconstructing Equality-versus-Difference," 33.
9. See Eagleton, *Ideology*; Nussbaum, *Limits of the Human*.
10. Connections Jacqueline Wernimont explores in more detail in "Making It Like a Riot-Grrrrl."
11. See Adafruit, "AdaBox"; I am grateful to Jacque Wernimont for this wonderful example. I am also reminded of the ways in which Martha Stewart's product lines leverage the homesteader narrative of "making it yourself from scratch" to sell a wide range of premade craft components.
12. Sammet, *Programming Languages*, 335.
13. It has also been observed of both languages that they are strikingly nonacademic; COBOL was severely criticized at its release for not using Backus-Naur Form for its definition (Wexelblat, *History of Programming Languages*, 255). This is an area that lies outside my area of competence but seems well worth further exploration.
14. Hopper, "Keynote Address."
15. This forum was hosted at Northeastern University and funded under a National Forums grant from the Institute for Museums and Library Services; see Northeastern University, University Libraries, Digital Scholarship Group, "Design for Diversity." Video of many of the presentations is available at http://hdl.handle.net/2047/D20259593.

Bibliography

Adafruit. "AdaBox: Let's Get Started . . ." https://www.adafruit.com/adabox_get_started.

Bailey, Moya. "All the Digital Humanists Are White, All the Nerds Are Men, but Some of Us Are Brave." *Journal of Digital Humanities* 1, no. 1 (Winter 2011). http://journalofdigitalhumanities.org/1-1/all-the-digital-humanists-are-white-all-the-nerds-are-men-but-some-of-us-are-brave-by-moya-z-bailey/.

Bailey, Moya. Comment on "Some Things to Think About before You Exhort Everyone to Code." http://miriamposner.com/blog/some-things-to-think-about-before-you-exhort-everyone-to-code/comment-page-1/#comment-30855.

Billey, Amber, Emily Drabinski, and K. R. Roberto. "What's Gender Got to Do with It? A Critique of RDA Rule 9.7." *Cataloguing and Classification Quarterly* 52, no. 4 (2014): 412–21.

Eagleton, Terry. *The Ideology of the Aesthetic*. Oxford: Blackwell, 1990.

Hopper, Grace Murray. "Keynote Address." In *History of Programming Languages*, edited by Richard L. Wexelblat, 7–20. New York: Academic Press, 1981.

Jed, Stephanie H. *Chaste Thinking: The Rape of Lucretia and the Birth of Humanism*. Bloomington: Indiana University Press, 1989.

King, Katie. "Bibliography and a Feminist Apparatus of Literary Production." *Text* 5 (1991): 91–103.

McPherson, Tara. "Why Are the Digital Humanities So White? or Thinking the Histories of Race and Computation." In *Debates in Digital Humanities,* edited by Matthew K. Gold, 139–60. Minneapolis: University of Minnesota Press, 2012.

Northeastern University, University Libraries, Digital Scholarship Group. "Design for Diversity: An IMLS National Forum Project." https://dsg.neu.edu/research/design-for-diversity/.

Nussbaum, Felicity. *The Limits of the Human: Fictions of Anomaly, Race and Gender in the Long Eighteenth Century.* Cambridge: Cambridge University Press, 2003.

Olson, Hope. "The Power to Name." *Signs* 26, no. 3 (Spring 2001): 639–68.

Ramsay, Stephen. Comment on "Some Things to Think About Before You Exhort Everyone to Code." http://miriamposner.com/blog/some-things-to-think-about-before-you-exhort-everyone-to-code/comment-page-1/#comment-31091.

Ramsay, Stephen. "On Building." January 8, 2011. http://lenz.unl.edu/papers/2011/01/11/on-building.html. (Site no longer available.)

Ramsay, Stephen. "Who's In and Who's Out." January 8, 2011. http://lenz.unl.edu/papers/2011/01/08/whos-in-and-whos-out.html. (Site no longer available.)

Reiman, Donald. "Gender and Documentary Editing: A Diachronic Perspective." *Text* 4 (1988): 351–59.

Sammet, Jean E. *Programming Languages: History and Fundamentals.* Englewood Cliffs, N.J.: Prentice-Hall, 1969.

Scott, Joan Wallach. "Deconstructing Equality-versus-Difference: or, the Uses of Poststructuralist Theory for Feminism." *Feminist Studies* 14, no. 1 (Spring 1988): 32–50.

Smith, Martha Nell. "Electronic Scholarly Editing." In *A Companion to Digital Humanities,* edited by Susan Schreibman, Ray Siemens, and John Unsworth, 306–22. Blackwell, 2004.

Sutherland, Kathryn, and Elena Pierazzo. "The Author's Hand: From Page to Screen." In *Collaborative Research in the Digital Humanities,* edited by Willard McCarty and Marilyn Deegan, 191–212. Farnham: Ashgate, 2012.

Wernimont, Jacqueline. "Making It Like a Riot-Grrrrl." *Jacqueline Wernimont: Network Weaver, Scholar, Digitrix,* March 3, 2012. https://jwernimont.com/2012/03/03/making-it-like-a-riot-grrrrl/.

Wexelblat, Richard L., ed. *History of Programming Languages.* New York: Academic Press, 1981.

PART V][Chapter 17

Working Nine to Five

What a Way to Make an Academic Living?

LISA BRUNDAGE, KAREN GREGORY, AND EMILY SHERWOOD

"What are you doing over the break?" Every December and June, I get asked countless times what I will do with the stretch of unstructured time that, as an academic and university employee, must surely lay before me. Former advisors and academic colleagues also ask, implicitly or explicitly: "What research are you working on? How are your job materials coming along? When will you go on the market?" Even though summer is my busy season, my inability to articulate a narrative of work that mirrors theirs exposes a failure on my part to reproduce the academy. My labor, though great and in service to the academy, is not measured by publications and therefore not easily understood, valued, quantified. In response to my explanation that as an instructional technologist and program director, I work a twelve-month, 52-week, everyday professional schedule, some from outside academia are reassured and others are bewildered to find out that universities don't just shut down between semesters. Friends on the tenure track (or already tenured) often shift to explaining the work they must tackle over the break: syllabi, lesson planning, research, and writing deadlines. The break will be very busy, they assure me. Doubtless it will be; their work is genuine, urgent, necessary, and challenging.

Yet it is those writing deadlines that tug at me. Announcements of publications, status updates from coffee shops about good and bad writing days, accountability groups. I miss it. As I have stared down the blinking cursor at the beginning of this piece, I have questioned how I can both romanticize writing—it is incredibly difficult and frustrating—and how I have struggled so much to get any done at all. I spent years churning out seminar papers, presentation papers, dissertation drafts. I was trained to write, in all its misery. I used to have self-discipline, I think. Maybe I have lost my edge, I wonder.

Maybe this is what scholarly writing always feels like, and now that I do it infrequently, I have simply forgotten. But my professional life is not structured in a way that encourages production of scholarship; absent requirements or incentives to publish and even semi-protected time to devote to it, it is shockingly easy for the skills necessary for producing academic writing to depreciate, as our involvement and knowledge of our professional fields—educational technology and digital humanities—increases. As academics, we are conditioned to believe that scholarship is proof of our labor (even when we know it is not); in alt-ac positions, the burden of proof is lifted by our daily presence and professional interactions. A daily record of emails, Slack chats, conference calls, webinars, spreadsheets, meeting requests, and the like hold uncomfortably in the balance. I used to think of "my work" as my scholarship—even if most of my labor went to teaching work—but now my work is developing and keeping a university program running. I truly enjoy the work I do, and the colleagues I have, but the reframing of "work" is not a small shift, personally or structurally.

—Lisa Brundage, *Notes from the Academic Office*

We start this chapter, on the labor of alternative academic (alt-ac) professionals in the university, with a short autoethnographic note, written by Lisa Brundage. The excerpt is taken from a series of ongoing notes that the authors of the piece have been keeping over the last four years, as we each graduated from the Instructional Technology Fellowship (ITF) at the Graduate Center of City University of New York. This fellowship was a foundational experience for us, as it brought together graduate students from across disciplines and allowed us to creatively engage with digital pedagogy, to teach and be active in digital classrooms, and to learn new digital methods that were applicable to our own research projects. The fellowship also introduced us to a collaborative and interdisciplinary model of work that valued the skills and labor discussed at length in this piece. The fellowship, in many ways, prepared us for a university that does not yet exist: a university where hierarchies between research, teaching, writing, and digital technologies have been flattened and where scholarship looks much more like active, community support for research and teaching.

We feel it's important to begin with a such a personal statement, as this cowritten and collaborative piece has emerged from our variegated academic experiences with alt-ac labor in American universities, where positions can range from postdocs and fellowships to full-time program coordination. Brundage writes from her own position as an instructional technologist and program director, but she speaks for each author as she captures a key thesis of our chapter: alt-ac positions—nonfaculty jobs for which an advanced degree is a baseline requirement or that pertain to an area of expertise that was developed via advanced or terminal degree work—are the result of structural shifts in the nature of labor and scholarship in the university and of the ability of universities to increasingly rely on PhDs to work outside of faculty or tenurable positions.[1] Despite the impersonal nature of these shifts, we often experience these labor conditions personally and viscerally, particularly if we still feel the tug of our scholarly training and our home disciplines.

In this chapter, we suggest that the feelings of guilt and pressure that Brundage captures here are by no means personal; rather, they are illustrative of the bind that alt-ac finds itself in: at once necessary to new forms of scholarship, particularly digital scholarship, yet not acknowledged or valued as such within traditional academic structures. We take the feelings Brundage describes as an invitation to interrogate the nature of alt-ac work, its relationship to domestic and other feminized forms of labor, and its inability to, as we suggest, "reproduce the university."

While alt-ac work is a relatively new phenomenon (Jacobs), the conditions it emerges from are not. By the late 1970s, scholars (Tuckman) were already aware that the university (both the U.S. university and abroad) was on the verge of a major shift in the composition of faculty. Such a shift has entailed a radical lack of commitment to the creation of tenurable faculty positions, passed over in favor of the production of contingent, fixed-term, and part-time positions. While this shift to contingent or "casual" work in the university has mirrored larger trends in the global economy, such as the embrace of "flexible" and on-demand labor (Harvey), the increasing instability or precarity of labor arrangements (Kalleberg), and the feminization of work (Standing), it has now resulted in what has been labeled a full-blown "adjunct crisis" for those teaching in the university. In the wake of the adjunct crisis, however, the university has seen the rise of administrative and managerial positions, coupled with the rise of instructional staff, postdoctoral fellows (postdocs), and alt-ac jobs. It is no coincidence that the increased reliance on alt-ac and postdoc positions in the humanities has corresponded to the rise of digital humanities (Jacobs), and created a cadre of academic professionals who are prepared to take on a wider range of tasks within the university than joining the professoriate. Considering the paucity of tenure-track jobs, digital humanities postdocs and alt-ac positions have been upheld as ways to have relatively stable employment and to be engaged in the academy. Taken together, instructional staff, postdocs, and alt-ac form what might be called an "invisible university" within the restructured university—a network of labor that has worked to help the university transition to digital research, teaching, and administration.

We suggest that we must understand the development of digital humanities scholarship and pedagogy and their reliance on the use of postdoc and alt-ac work within larger gendered and racialized labor histories and will critically interrogate the language that often accompanies these positions. Here, we draw connections between that language and the day-to-day labor realities of such work. We argue that if the digital humanities is to provide ethical pedagogy and scholarship it must not only address its labor history, but must find a way forward that is capable of recognizing new and emerging forms of valuable labor in the university. This does not simply entail new forms of digital scholarship, but the very "support" work that makes such scholarship possible. While many of these support jobs may be full-time, professional positions, they are also often contingent fixed-term posts reliant on grant funding that accompanies new programs and initiatives. Even permanent, full-time alt-ac positions typically are not eligible for tenure nor are they considered "faculty" appointments, despite the range of pedagogical and technical skills required. Often staff in these positions struggle to maintain a publication agenda outside of their regular work week, but feel pressure to do so because of colleagues in similar positions that retain at least partial faculty status. Alt-acs must grapple with two different systems of career growth: the tasks that their daily work and job descriptions demand, and the social fabric of academia, including publication, disciplinary conferences, and the like. Furthermore, a PhD in a typical academic discipline is often a threshold to entry for these jobs, even if the content area expertise of the job incumbent retains little value to the position or even as a bargaining chip in establishing relationships with tenured faculty. While romanticized notions of the professoriate living the life of the mind can be contrasted with the ever-swelling, overworked, underpaid league of contingent workers, the place of alt-acs and digital humanities workers who *are often neither tenure/tenure-track nor adjuncts* is unclear in the polygon of university roles and relationships. Our argument is not that the daily working conditions for those in alt-ac positions are generally burdensome. These types of jobs can come with relative stability, fair remuneration, and great satisfaction in the work itself. We instead advocate for our work to be recognized as coequal with scholarship production and, though we will use the term throughout the article, not really "alt" at all. While alt-ac work broadly includes work done by PhDs in the nonprofit and corporate sectors, this chapter focuses primarily on alt-ac work within American higher education institutions. We hope that future research will create more accurate and clear data about these types of roles, including postdoc, full-time, and contingent workers who manage, facilitate, and maintain digital scholarship projects, centers, and programs.

For many years, the postdoc has been held out as an option for recent graduates to establish themselves professionally—focus on their research agenda, prepare their dissertation for publication, attend conferences, and, to a lesser degree, gain teaching experience—so that they are more competitive in the academic job market. Rather than visiting assistant professor positions that often entail a one-year contract renewable yearly for up to three years, the postdoc provides more stability in the form of longer contracts from the outset and the assumption that with these positions come time and monetary support for professional development and research. In many ways, the rise in postdoc jobs is a new and simultaneously old-fashioned solution to the glut of humanities PhDs who face diminished opportunities in their academic fields. Built on a Science, Technology, Engineering, and Mathematics (STEM) training model, postdocs are both functional and, at times, exploitative. Within STEM fields, progression from doctoral degree work to postdoc research and then to tenure-track work can exacerbate gender gaps in abandoning research and academic careers. In data and analysis published in *Nature*, Helen Shen ("Inequality Qualified") finds that the postdoc is a specifically precarious career stage for women in science, combining low pay, lack of role models, career instability, and reproductive choices. Citing Mary Ann Mason's research, Shen asserts that "female postdocs who become parents or plan to have children abandon research careers up to twice as often as men in similar circumstances" (22). Given that the humanities lack the structure of research labs that can serve as a productive career way station, the humanities also lack cohesive understandings of what types of work are suitable in postdoc positions (Dunn), which provides an opportunity to systematically understand the gendered inequities that can accompany STEM postdocs but also risks re-creating them or codifying a hierarchy between faculty and career alt-ac workers who enter their specialties through postdoc positions. While some postdocs may be structured around providing the holder with large amounts of time to network and publish, making the individual more competitive on the traditional market, other positions can require significant amounts of labor, especially in service roles, project management, and professional development.

Increasingly, the expectation of considerable research time for postdocs has shifted, as more and more postdocs focus on job-training skills to prepare graduates for alt-ac careers. For example, the CLIR (Council on Library and Information Resources) Postdoctoral Fellowship program and the ACLS (American Council of Learned Societies) Public Fellows program help facilitate the shift from academic to administrative or otherwise alt-ac jobs. CLIR explicitly states that its postdoc program "offers recent PhD graduates the chance to help develop research tools, resources, and services while exploring new career opportunities" ("CLIR Postdoctoral Fellowship Program"). CLIR provides significant and ongoing training opportunities for its postdocs with an initial summer boot camp, monthly webinars, and funding for conference attendance, specifically, the Coalition for Networked Information and Digital Library Federation conferences. These conferences, often new to postdocs who have spent the majority of graduate school attending their subject area meetings, expose CLIR fellows to a different side of academic, often institutional, conversations. Similarly, training topics introduce fellows to issues of metadata, sustainability and data management, building communities around digital humanities, project management, developing digital scholarship centers, and learning about the capabilities of various digital tools. Though placed at institutions around the country, CLIR's postdocs enter the program as part of a cohort. The cohort model promotes a sense of community and support that extends to the broader network of former CLIR postdocs holding a range of tenure-track, hybrid (part tenure-track, part administrative), alt-ac, and administrative positions. While some CLIR postdocs are granted time to work on research by their host institutions, the percentage of time varies and is often fairly minimal. However, CLIR encourages their postdocs to collaborate on research and writing projects, even offering small grants for such work. Training and support offered by programs such as CLIR are crucial, particularly as postdocs struggle with choices regarding their future career paths and the new types of knowledge needed to be successful in these emerging fields. However, the apprentice aspect of these programs limits the research time for fellows, which further stymies their ability to produce scholarship. The products of these positions are frequently valuable to the university, and can certainly be résumé builders, but typically do not belong to the individual who manages them in the way that published work normally does. This creates a benchmarking problem when publications are still used as a default for measuring academic professional success.

The skills that accrue to workers in these sorts of positions—knowledge of digital methods, communications, project management—readily transfer to other types of employment, which further exacerbates failure in terms of reproducing the university, but as Jacqui Shine ("Alt-Ac") and Yasmin Nair ("On Writers") have pointed out, flooding other employment markets with PhDs is not a tidy solution to shrinking full-time opportunities with the academy. As the postdoc becomes the training for a career as an alternative academic, such work is touted as a viable and more stable career pathway through the increasingly precarious university. As Rebecca Schuman ("'Alt-Ac'") notes, alt-ac work takes a variety of forms ranging from individuals with doctorates working in "archives, libraries, think tanks, non-profits, museum, historical societies, journalism—even within academic departments as, for example, digital technologies specialists." In digital humanities initiatives and research, alt-ac work looks like glue: piecing together programs, goals, professional development, and student services that an overworked and contingent faculty labor force cannot. In this respect, alt-ac is like much staff work in the university: it allows the university to function. However, to further create divisions in the class hierarchies within academia, alt-ac workers inhabit a liminal space between more traditional staff roles, often predicated on service, and faculty. PhDs have the credentials of the latter, but perform many types of feminized labor inherent in the former. Despite the increase in numbers and visibility for postdoc and alt-ac labor in the digital humanities, the best and most skillful glue jobs are defined by their invisibility. As is typical of other types of feminized labor, when things go well, the labor is unseen. Think of the myriad of tasks necessary to ensure that a project is completed on time, a conference runs smoothly, grant requirements are fulfilled and reported to the appropriate stakeholders. In each instance, the project manager, conference planner, or grant administrator rarely receives the credit of the scholar, organization, or principal investigator, and yet none of this work is possible without the invisible labor of the former. It's hard *not* to draw parallels between other types of hidden affective labor that build the world we inhabit, namely, domestic labor, supplied both in familial and market contexts. Alt-ac positions help facilitate creative and engaging scholarship and pedagogy; however, as a career pathway alt-ac is still searching for footing in the highly structured and increasingly administrative university hierarchy. As this work is less visible, the paths to promotion are less clear, if they indeed exist.

Statistics about alt-ac career tracks are hard to come by, made no easier by the ambiguous borders and short timeline since the emergence of these types of jobs. In fact, survey categories can obscure a clear picture of the field by allowing for tenure-tenure track faculty, non-tenure-track academic, and nonacademy work; full-time, permanent, nonfaculty academic work seems to defy categorization, which may contribute to its invisibility. For example, the American Association of University Professors (AAUP) report *The Employment Status of Instructional Staff* (Curtis) tracks full-time tenured faculty, full-time tenure-track faculty, full-time non-tenure-track faculty, part-time faculty, and graduate student employees. Amid numerous calls to reform graduate programs and prepare PhD holders for varied careers, startlingly little research on long-term career outcomes is available, as noted by the Council of Graduate Schools in its report *Understanding PhD Career Pathways for Program Improvement* (Allum, Kent, and McCarthy 2014).

Some of the most noted commentary on the alt-ac field comes from an MLA 2014 panel, "Alt-Ac Work and Gender: It's Not Plan B," convened by Sarah Werner. Our arguments make use of the participants' work, including Brian Croxall, Stephanie Murray, and Amanda French. Werner's own contribution to the panel included presenting results of a survey she developed on alt-ac and gender. Werner purposefully sought qualitative data in her questions, and while self-selection may have created sample bias in the responses she received, 79 percent of those employed in or searching for alt-ac work were female. Among those, over half said that gender impacted their decision to seek alt-ac work (though within that number, many chose "It's complicated" rather than an unqualified "Yes"). Many respondents noted that the job market and tenure clock influence decisions about childbearing, parenting, and geographic location. One commented that alt-ac emerging as a family-friendly alternative to tenure-track work might have negative consequences for the makeup of the professoriate. But another noted, "[In my previous job] lots of service demands were placed on women faculty, who were then less rewarded for being less 'productive.' I wanted a role in which what had been dismissed as service could instead be recognized as leadership" (Werner). The road to leadership in an alt-ac career, though, is neither straightforward nor stable.

Within the research on career outcomes that does exist, it is difficult to see where alt-ac careers within institutions of higher learning fall in terms of career paths, income, stability, and satisfaction. A study published by the Cornell Higher Education Research Institute at Cornell University (Main, Prenovitz, and Ehrenberg) examined career outcomes at six months, three years, and eight years postdegree, of nearly five thousand humanities and social science PhDs. Using the Andrew W. Mellon Foundation's Graduate Education Survey (GES), the researchers found that many of the subjects working outside of the academy had higher job satisfaction than those working in tenured, tenure-track, and nontenured faculty positions. The data did not account for PhDs working within the academy but outside of faculty roles. While it is important to have empirical data that support positive long-term career outcomes for PhDs who leave the higher education field entirely, future research must also study career paths within academe. Alt-ac should not be construed as non-ac.

Compounding problems of hierarchy within alt-ac work is the fact that while the postdoc traditionally has been conceptualized as a position that prepares an individual for the tenure track, increasingly postdocs perform the sorts of alt-ac work that has burgeoned along with the digital humanities. Digital projects, whether research or pedagogy focused, require a heftier team lift than traditional academic research and publishing channels: program structuring, content strategy, preservation planning, technical training, interfacing with university IT teams, budget management (including work with university offices, vendors, contractors, and reports to funders), keeping stakeholders informed, and maintaining relationships across various parts of the team. As such, digital humanities postdocs are often charged with the support and development of digital scholarship efforts on campus, while inhabiting what we think of as crucial "glue positions," which are also precarious due to their contingent status and temporal limitations. Many such positions, at least initially, are grant funded. While grants help institutions test and develop new initiatives, they come with significant pressure to produce tangible results quickly, including institutional support though measured impact that proves continued interest in the initiative beyond the life of the grant. While some institutions find funding to retain postdocs in more permanent alt-ac positions, many postdocs face funding limitations, their jobs contingent on securing the next grant.

Further, bringing in an emerging scholar to train more established colleagues in new pedagogical and scholarly approaches can expose the postdoc to power inequities amplified by the postdoc's position as both a temporary resource and a staff member who lacks faculty status. Despite these challenges, digital humanities postdocs are expected to learn the politics and players of their institution at breakneck speed so that they can perform their glue jobs: connecting various aspects of digital production; translating needs and expectations between scholarly and technical players; developing digital humanities initiatives at their universities; and conceptualizing a sustainable model so that when they leave at the end of their term, the programs may continue without their labor. It would be a mistake to conceptualize this work as simply par for the course, as it often requires the deeply gendered emotional labor of creating "good" feelings or pleasant working environments among various actors at different locations within the hierarchies of the university. Digital humanities postdocs, in theory, can help retrain recent PhDs for these interstitial administrative positions that have become increasingly important in supporting and facilitating digital scholarship and pedagogy initiatives in higher education. In the contingent grant-funded scenario, however, the successful digital humanities postdoc renders their labor not just invisible but unnecessary.

Given that more and more time is now spent off the tenure track for the majority of individuals teaching and researching within the university, there have been calls to reconceptualize what an academic career can or should look like. In one of the most frequently cited and debated pieces on careers and the academy, historians Anthony T. Grafton and Jim Grossman ("No More Plan B") exhorted departments (in their "Very Modest Proposal," no less) to stop thinking of production of new scholars only in terms of the tenure track, and to stop castigating what falls outside of that "Plan B." But as Brian Croxall ("Alt-Ac and Gender")—playing off the metaphor of emergency contraception—noted, the language of "Plan B" "suggests an abortive start to one's career" and even a failure to appropriately plan. Taking a Plan B career, we argue, is a failure to reproduce the academy. This view is understandable as mentors and dissertation committees expend considerable labor in developing their students. While all of us found support for growing the skills and networks necessary to pursue alt-ac careers, the majority of that support was found in our communities of practice within DH and experimental pedagogy or from faculty who work across disciplines. The pressure to reproduce by conforming to the career choices of those who have trained us neglects the reality of the academic job market or the right for graduate students to pursue their own career paths. This reproductive failure is complicated by the desire for departments to show high placement rates for their graduates and an increasing understanding that many newly minted PhDs will spend several years working as postdoctoral fellows or visiting assistant professors, as if this were the pre-tenure-track track. The emphasis on tenure suggests that those in alt-ac positions have settled for something rather than selected a different and viable path.

Beyond the "failure to reproduce the academy" conveyed in and through the way we speak of postdoctoral and alt-ac work, such a "failure" is also curiously marked by the digital humanities' frequent focus on maker culture and public scholarship, making tenuous those of us whose untenured professional work is bound up in making connections, making things happen, making people feel cared for, making good teachers, making organized events and meetings, making the coffee, and the myriad other ways in which what is made is often affective and ephemeral. Like domestic labor, this is work that is both highly valuable and, when done well, highly invisible. In fact, the more skilled alt-acs become in providing affective and support labor, the more invisible the effort becomes. The parallels between success in these fields and good housewifery are evident in this notion of invisible labor: a well-run house and well-behaved children are unremarkable; so too are smoothly run grants, events, and digital scholarship projects. Choosing to hide this labor is at odds with the digital humanities' explicit focus on making scholarship in the humanities more open and public. Instead, on many campuses, alt-acs tend to what Steve Brier and Luke Waltzer after him have called "the ugly stepchildren" of higher education: pedagogy, professional development, and scholarship of teaching and learning.

It comes as little surprise, then, that the work conducted in postdoc and alt-ac positions (as has long been the case with librarians and other careers construed as "support" for professors), along with the language that is used to talk about it, is gendered, and furthermore often framed in terms of reproduction, parenting, and care. The development of this new class of academic labor aligns with what Holly Ann Larson ("Emotional Labor") terms as "pink-collar duties" that include "nurturing and caring." Even for tenured professors, AAUP research demonstrates that women who perform more service labor at the associate professor stage experience significant slowdowns in reaching full professor status. Women who participated in the AAUP focus groups generally felt more pressured to fill service roles, while also being frustratingly aware that this labor was of low value for promotion to full professor (Misra). Stripped of the tenure ladder, how can service-oriented alt-ac labor reckon with the hierarchies of scholarship and service? As one recent job ad for a digital humanities postdoc claimed, the person would have, among other responsibilities, "the opportunity to play an instrumental role in nurturing the growing digital humanities community" (MLA). The assumption that "nurturing" a "community" of digital humanities practitioners is a unique opportunity for the postdoc neglects to acknowledge that the postdoc is explicitly creating opportunities for other academics to produce digital scholarship: the alt-ac and postdoc nurture projects and labor in their production, but the scholar maintains the intellectual property and credit over the offspring/digital product. Similarly, the MLA Connected Academics program, aimed at helping doctoral students "use their humanistic training in a broader range of occupations than doctoral programs have, up to now, characteristically acknowledged and honored," lists the following words as the start to the bullet points describing the work it does: supporting, organizing, compiling, expanding, working, and offering. These alt-ac jobs function as handmaids: nurturing, growing, and supporting another's legitimate work.

The radical promise of alt-ac and digital humanities work remains latent, if not abandoned entirely, when work done under the auspices of DH works to repackage oppressive, gendered, and racialized social relations as "new forms of scholarship" (Posner). For example, if those doing the work of growing communities are simply seen as support staff for "researching" faculty, DH will have done little more than "encode" outmoded labor relations. However, getting to the nitty gritty of these labor politics is difficult. Very few, if any, respected scholars would claim to support the denigration of "staff" work, yet they might not think twice about "speaking for" or even speaking over a staff member in a meeting. Those same faculty who show interest in a staff member's summer research plans—not understanding that summer is often our busy season with training, workshops, grants to administer and planning for the school year—complain about slow email response rates when that staff member is stuck in administrative meetings or, even worse, that staff member is taking one of the set number of vacation days. Furthermore, as work at all levels in the university comes under administrative purview and managerial pressures, it remains unclear how faculty and alt-ac staff, who may not have clear visibility in the university hierarchy, can properly negotiate the disparate risks of doing innovative work. Alt-ac workers often do not "own" the products of their labor and may be at greater risk when budgets, departmental politics, issues surrounding academic freedom, or administrative winds change course.

In collaborative and creative environments, many may labor out the brainchildren, but in academic and DH environments that often prioritize products, or the process of making (however open, free, and collaborative these products and processes might be), it is time we pay greater attention to the various forms of overlooked and often invisible labor that are required to sustain successful projects and work environments. Broadly, we might call this labor "care work" or affective labor, but it is worth being very specific about the nature of that work. While the digital humanities may prize the language of nurturing and of "community development," in reality that must translate to various forms of labor that can range anywhere from project coordination to endless "let's meet for a coffee" chats in order to network and build community buy-in. As anyone who has worked on an academic digital project knows (whether it be at the project level, curricular level, or simply attempting to get your computer up and running), digital work and digital scholarship require new types of trust and negotiation. The building of relationships, the formation of community, which may be highly valuable to the university at large, only comes through a number of small, often invisible and expected forms of work.

In any given week, a digital humanities postdoc or someone in an alt-ac position might need to coordinate between any number of university sectors: budget offices, facilities management, vendors, upper-level administrators, faculty across various departments, program directors, librarians, IT departments, legal services, funders, the many assistants who help us get our work done, students, and more. The digital humanities require people who are makers, but also people who are *connectors*, and superiority should not be ascribed to the former at the expense of the latter, despite a gendered and privilege-inflected urge to do so. As Debbie Chachra put it in her article "Why I'm Not a Maker," "The cultural primacy of *making*, especially in tech culture—that it is intrinsically superior to not-making, to repair, analysis, and especially caregiving—is informed by the gendered history of who made things, and in particular, who made things that were shared with the world, not merely for hearth and home." DH needs to build a stronger ethic of care, but as Bethany Nowviskie ("On Capacity and Care") has brilliantly pointed out, "overidentification of caring praxis with the social and professional roles that have been afforded to women and brutally assigned to people of color frames oppression as a virtue and perpetuates unjust systems." So valuing care must not emerge as a way to uphold entrenched patterns of racialized and gendered employment within the academy. Care, in Nowviskie's formulation, is an essential component of sustaining work in DH, not a mere nicety, and it is one that can be spread through different parts of projects.

Despite multiple challenges, working in interstitial spaces, as many in alt-ac positions do, is not without benefit: these jobs can carry with them deep satisfaction and joy, and be ripe with possibility. Moving between spaces in higher education allows us to develop rich understandings and relationships across disciplines and perspectives, sometimes breaking long-held silos. Freed from classroom teaching and grading, we can consider new ways to meet students' needs and promote meaningful educational experiences. Katina Rogers ("Humanities Unbound") uses the metaphor of the sprinkler, explicitly calling attention to the joy and play of the image, to describe the potential outcomes of graduate school. Instead of a pipeline emptying into a singular pool, we can productively, happily spout in all directions. Following Pattie Sellers's exhortation to women to think of their careers as jungle gyms rather than monkey bars, Stephanie Murray ("On the Alt-Ac Jungle Gym") uses the comparative metaphor to conceptualize alt-ac spaces as full of feminist potential: nonlinear, collaborative, and available to multiple people for use in multiple ways. The monkey bars are a straight-up and across structure, to be crossed one person at a time (and as Murray notes, beyond childhood, images of monkey bar training are frequently associated with the military). Jungle gyms, by contrast, have multiple paths—over, under, around, and through—and can be traversed by groups. In many ways, such alt-ac work speaks to those of us who understand that the "traditional" model of The Academic is outdated and an ill fit for our lives and politics. Such a figure—of the solo, often male figure, toiling away on his own in the library or office, producing "individually" authored works, which find their ways to proprietary and locked gardens such as most academic journals—is for many people not a goal to aspire toward. Alt-ac contains unspoken potential not only for personal fulfillment but, one would hope, for the production of consciously configured power relations within the university.

Right now (and perhaps this chapter inadvertently adds fuel to this unfortunate state of affairs) faculty work exists as a specialized sphere, a college in a multiversity that provides an array of outputs and services. Dichotomizing research, writing, and teaching from other fundamental aspects of university life and labor is a failure of imagination, and one that is founded on a long history of devaluing gendered and racialized forms of labor. We can do better. For example, digital humanities workers in universities who are off the tenure track may have accomplishments that include management or support of large, complex projects but little scholarly publication. The project output must be considered scholarly work; an institutional or even collegial expectation that alt-ac workers *also* produce scholarly monographs about the work in order for it to be recognized as authentic academic production is an unacceptable standard. Furthermore, alt-ac work often fundamentally links research, new methods and methodologies, teaching, pedagogy, and digital infrastructures. Alt-ac is where you will find an uncommon nexus of faculty, staff, and student. As such it often offers a microcosm for rethinking "the digital university" and possibilities for collaboration and inter- and transdisciplinary work. This is highly valuable work, not only in terms of service but in terms of revenue to universities. While we have documented here the ways in which alt-ac work is made invisible, our suggestion is that alt-ac labor be highlighted and studied as model for conceptualizing the future of the university. Integrating and providing substantive, institutionalized support for the care work that underlies alt-ac positions—indeed, ceasing to conceptualize them as "alt"—is a path to better universities that can produce more research, create more diverse and innovative ways to present work and engage the public, and, moreover, improve what we offer students. If such connections were nurtured with a true focus on labor in its myriad forms, and the ways in which value is currently being created in our institutions, they could become a path to reimagining a more egalitarian and more sustainable university.

Note

1. We acknowledge that instructional technologists are generally staff positions and therefore lack requirements or time for publication while the status of program directors differs between—and sometimes within—institutions. At some institutions, program directors are faculty or a hybrid of faculty/staff lines with publishing and/or teaching requirements. However, this is not the case at all institutions, which causes further confusion and false expectations when staff program directors fail to participate in scholarly conversations through publication. The larger issue is the structural pressure to publish as evidence of professionalization and indeed academic labor regardless of whether or not that specific form of labor is required or even encouraged within the terms of the job. Defining academic labor in such narrow terms further underlines the class divide in academia between faculty and nonfaculty positions and between tenured faculty with research obligations and contingent faculty whose primary labor is teaching.

Bibliography

"About the Project." Connected Academics, 2016. Modern Language Association. https://connect.commons.mla.org/about-connected-academics/.

Allum, J. R., J. D. Kent, and M. T. McCarthy. *Understanding PhD Career Pathways for Program Improvement: A CGS Report.* Washington, D.C.: Council of Graduate Schools, 2014.

Brier, Steve. Comment on "On EdTech and the Digital Humanities," by Luke Waltzer. *Bloviate.* October 21, 2010. http://lukewaltzer.com/on-edtech-and-the-digital-humanities/.

Chachra, Debbie. "Why I Am Not a Maker." *The Atlantic,* January 23, 2015. http://www.theatlantic.com/technology/archive/2015/01/why-i-am-not-a-maker/384767/.

"CLIR Postdoctoral Fellowship Program—Council on Library and Information Resources." Council on Library and Information Resources, 2016. http://www.clir.org/fellowships/postdoc.

Croxall, Brian. "Alt-Ac and Gender at the 2014 MLA: A Proposal." *BrianCroxall.net,* January 12, 2014. http://www.briancroxall.net/2014/01/12/alt-ac-and-gender-at-the-2014-mla-a-proposal/.

Curtis, John W. "The Employment Status of Instructional Staff Members in Higher Education, Fall 2011." American Association of University Professors, April 2014. https://www.aaup.org/sites/default/files/files/AAUP-InstrStaff2011-April2014.pdf.

Dunn, Sydni. "A Brief History of the Humanities Postdoc." *Vitae, the Online Career Hub for Higher Ed,* July 7, 2014. https://chroniclevitae.com/news/593-a-brief-history-of-the-humanities-postdoc.

Grafton, Anthony T., and James Grossman. "No More Plan B: A Very Modest Proposal for Graduate Programs in History." *Perspectives on History,* October 2011. https://www.historians.org/publications-and-directories/perspectives-on-history/october-2011/no-more-plan-b.

Harvey, David. *The Condition of Postmodernity: An Enquiry into the Origins of Cultural Change.* Oxford: Blackwell, 1990.

Jacobs, Sarah Ruth. "The Marriage of the Digital Humanities and Alt-Ac Positions." *Journal of Interactive Technology & Pedagogy,* November 13, 2015. https://jitp.commons.gc.cuny.edu/the-marriage-of-the-digital-humanities-and-alt-ac-positions/.

Kalleberg, Arne L. "Precarious Work, Insecure Workers: Employment Relations in Transition." *American Sociological Review* 74, no. 1 (2009): 1–22. http://asr.sagepub.com/content/74/1/1.short?rss=1&ssource=mfc.

Kelsky, Karen. "The Professor Is In: How to Make the Most of a Prestigious Postdoc." *Vitae, the Online Career Hub for Higher Ed.* Accessed February 4, 2016. https://chroniclevitae.com/news/585-the-professor-is-in-how-to-make-the-most-of-a-prestigious-postdoc.

Larson, Holly Ann. "Emotional Labor: The Pink-Collar Duties of Teaching." *Currents in Teaching & Learning* 1, no. 1 (2008): 45–56. http://www.worcester.edu/Currents/Archives/Volume_1_Number_1/CurrentsV1N1LarsonP45.pdf.

Main, Joyce B., Sarah Prenovitz, and Ronald G. Ehrenberg. "In Pursuit of a Tenure-Track Faculty Position: Career Progression and Satisfaction of Humanities and Social Sciences Doctorates." Cornell Higher Education Research Institute, 2017. CHERI WP180. http://www.ilr.cornell.edu/sites/ilr.cornell.edu/files/CHERI WP180.pdf.

Misra, Joya. "The Ivory Ceiling of Service Work." American Association of University Professors, January–February 2011. https://www.aaup.org/article/ivory-ceiling-service-work#.WlVAI1SFg0o.

MLA. "Postdoc in Digital Humanities: University of Alabama." November 28, 2011. http://www.stoa.org/archives/1480.

Murray, Stephanie. "On the Alt-Ac Jungle Gym: Toward a Feminist Approach." *#alt-Academy,* 2014. http://mediacommons.futureofthebook.org/alt-ac/pieces/alt-ac-jungle-gym-toward-feminist-approach.

Nair, Yasmin. "On Writers as Scabs, Whores, and Interns, and the Jacobin Problem." *Yasmin Nair,* 2013. http://www.yasminnair.net/content/writers-scabs-whores-and-interns-and-jacobin-problem.

Nowviskie, Bethany. "On Capacity and Care." *Bethany Nowviskie,* 2015. http://nowviskie.org/2015/on-capacity-and-care/.

Posner, Miriam. "The Radical, Unrealized Potential of the Digital Humanities." In *Debates in the Digital Humanities,* edited by Matthew K. Gold, 32–41. Minneapolis: University of Minnesota Press, 2016.

Rogers, Katina. "Humanities Unbound: Careers and Scholarship beyond the Tenure Track." *Scholars Lab,* April 23, 2013. http://scholarslab.org/research-and-development/humanities-unbound-careers-scholarship-beyond-the-tenure-track/.

Schuman, Rebecca. "'Alt-Ac' to the Rescue?" *Slate,* September 18, 2014. http://www.slate.com/articles/life/education/2014/09/a_changing_view_of_alt_ac_jobs_in_which_ph_d_s_work_outside_of_academia.html.

Shen, Helen. "Inequality Qualified: Mind the Gender Gap." *Nature,* 2013. https://www.nature.com/news/inequality-quantified-mind-the-gender-gap-1.12550.

Shine, Jacqui. 2016. "Alt-Ac Isn't Always the Answer." *Vitae, the Online Career Hub for Higher Ed,* 2016. https://chroniclevitae.com/news/508-alt-ac-isn-t-always-the-answer.

Standing, Guy. "Global Feminization through Flexible Labor: A Theme Revisited." *WD World Development* 27, no. 3 (1999): 583–602.

Tuckman, Howard P. "Who Is Part-Time in Academe?" *AAUP Bulletin* 64, no. 4 (1978): 305–15.

Waltzer, Luke. "Digital Humanities and the 'Ugly Stepchildren' of American Higher Education." In *Debates in the Digital Humanities,* edited by Matthew K. Gold, 335–49. Minneapolis: University of Minnesota Press, 2012. http://dhdebates.gc.cuny.edu/debates/part/6.

Werner, Sarah. "#altac work and gender." *sarahwerner.net,* 2014. http://sarahwerner.net/blog/2014/01/altac-work-and-gender/.

PART V][Chapter 18

Minority Report

The Myth of Equality in the Digital Humanities

BARBARA BORDALEJO

I have serious reason to believe that the planet from which the little prince came is the asteroid known as B-612. This asteroid has only once been seen through the telescope. That was by a Turkish astronomer, in 1909. On making his discovery, the astronomer had presented it to the International Astronomical Congress, in a great demonstration. But he was in Turkish costume, and so nobody would believe what he said. Grown-ups are like that. . . . Fortunately, however, for the reputation of Asteroid B-612, a Turkish dictator made a law that his subjects, under pain of death, should change to European costume. So in 1920 the astronomer gave his demonstration all over again, dressed with impressive style and elegance. And this time everybody accepted his report.

—Antoine de Saint-Exupéry, *The Little Prince*

Digital humanities is a relatively new discipline; its practitioners are continually pushing against its boundaries and modifying its perspectives.[1] In the last years, the general perception that digital humanities, as a discipline, is balanced in terms of gender has spread to the mainstream press.[2] Moreover, articles produced within the DH frame have explained that "digital humanities is 'nice'" and have built specific arguments for a narrative of why it is so (Scheinfeldt). However, these perceptions are easily challenged. Even the simplest analysis—such as the ratio of first author gender for accepted papers in the principal annual DH conference—produces evidence undercutting any claims about equality and inclusiveness in the field. [3]

The pervasive belief in gender balance in digital humanities prompts the question of how the field might appear if it could be analyzed across a broader set of perspectives. This chapter considers data gathered through a survey of self-described "digital humanists" to understand the current situation of the field. It concludes

Figure 18.1. Gender ratio at DH conferences.

with some suggestions that might improve the position of women and minorities within digital humanities.[4]

Background

On May 23, 2015, Lorna Hughes, then professor of digital humanities at the University of London, tweeted a link to an article by Gordon Hunt titled "There Is Certainly No Gender Imbalance in Digital Humanities!"[5] The tweet sparked a range of opinions concerning Hunt's article. Ben Brumfield, for example, pointed out that the situation in digital humanities was comparatively better than is the case in other fields, such as computer sciences.[6]

Within a few minutes of the start of the Twitter discussion, Scott Weingart presented the partial results of an analysis of the gender ratio of authors accepted for the Alliance of Digital Humanities Organizations conferences between 2010 and 2013, where women represent around 30 percent of authors (see Figure 18.1). Against this, Hughes argued that she was one of six female digital humanities professors in London alone. It appears that, at the time, Professor Hughes was referring to Melissa Terras (formerly at UCL, now at the University of Edinburgh), Claire Warwick (formerly at UCL, now at the University of Durham), Sheila Anderson (King's College), Marilyn Deegan (King's College), and Jane Winters (University of London).

There are other powerful women in digital humanities. The Alliance of Digital Humanities Organizations (ADHO) website shows that Sarah Kenderline, Elisabeth Burr, Karina van Dalen-Oskam, Susan Brown, Jennifer Giuliano, Laura Mandell, and Sara Sikes figure prominently. All of these women have had long and influential trajectories in digital humanities. However, this should not deceive us to into thinking that this is a particularly egalitarian field or that there is no need for advocacy. The six female professors in London in Lorna Hughes's original Twitter exchange were all English native speakers, while Karina van Dalen-Oskam (current chair of ADHO's steering committee), Elisabeth Burr, and myself (Burr and I serving as representatives of the European Association for Digital Humanities) are the only female members of the executive of ADHO who are not native English speakers. I am the only one of these women not to come from a country in the Global North. Moreover, at the time of writing, I am the only woman in the ADHO executive who is of mixed race. Tomoji Tabata, the representative of the Japanese Association for Digital Humanities, is the other non-Caucasian representative.[7]

The statistics presented by Weingart are clear-cut. Despite the prominence of some female scholars, women are underrepresented at the most important gatherings in the field. Scott Weingart and Nickoal Eichmann have analyzed the data, year after year starting in 2010, and have found the numbers remain stable. Weingart's concern with gender was intriguing, so I contacted him to find out how he had become interested in question. In private email correspondence, Weingart stated that he wanted to use digital humanities methods to investigate the field itself, a sort of meta–digital humanities research:

> Essentially I've just wanted to turn DH methods on ourselves for a number of reasons. What's it like to be scrutinized the same way we scrutinize? What's our own history and contours? And (especially relevant in the context of this graph and these discussions) how can we become better scholarly citizens, and better global citizens?
>
> We tend to inherit problems of representation and equality from academia & tech culture at large, but just because we're no worse than the rest of 'em doesn't mean we shouldn't try to be better. Recognizing problem areas is (I hope) a good start.[8]

Our private exchange prompted a self-reflective post titled "What's Counted Counts," in which Weingart acknowledges that other aspects of diversity are much more elusive than gender:

> I'd attempted to explore racial and ethnic diversity as well, but it was simply more fraught, complicated, and less amenable to my methods than gender, so I started with gender and figured I'd work my way into the weeds from there.

I'll cut to the chase. My well-intentioned attempts at battling inequality suffer their own sort of bias: by focusing on *measurements* of inequality, I bias that which is easily measured. It's not that gender isn't complex (see Miriam Posner's wonderful recent keynote on these and related issues), but at least it's a little easier to measure than race & ethnicity, when all you have available to you is what you can look up on the Internet.[9]

Weingart's text suggested the idea of bringing to light those aspects that are not readily available for measurement. A survey would allow us to address directly those issues that Weingart had found elusive, such as race, nationality, or status. Moreover, it could provide the opportunity to include other layers of complexity if it could consider sexual orientation and ability. There were various problems with this, not least of them that a survey requires people's willingness to participate. It would have to be designed and to be tested. It would have to ask very personal questions, some of which might be potentially identifying. There were many instances in which it could fail and many reasons that might push it toward that failure. There is no doubt that this survey has many shortcomings. Some of those are the result of its origins, and the rest are likely to be the result of my ignorance and the learning process prompted by its creation.

Methodology

THE SURVEY

Design and Questions

The survey was modeled on the diversity questionnaires often found as part of the hiring or acceptance process of higher education institutions.[10] There were twenty-eight biographical questions and a final one that allowed comments or suggestions.

The questions covered the following topics:[11]

1. age
2. education
3. formal education in DH
4. country of birth
5. gender
6. care-giving situation
7. sexual orientation
8. ethnic heritage
9. cultural background
10. native language
11. work language

12. work institution
13. existence of a DH center at work
14. attachment to a DH center
15. salary source (i.e., soft money, centrally funded)
16. length of employment
17. previous employment
18. details of previous employment
19. current title
20. permanence in current position
21. nature of the current position (tenure track or non–tenure track)
22. country of employment
23. visible disability
24. invisible disability
25. regularity of submission to the DH conference or similar
26. number of rejections from the DH conference
27. number of acceptances to the DH conference
28. perception of self within DH
29. additional comments

Questions 9, 10, 16, 18, and 29 requested a free text answer. For questions 9 and 10, for example, it would have been hard to use a template. Question 9, which refers to cultural background, is related to self-identification and self-definition. For this reason, it seemed that to provide a template might leave many people without an adequate response. For question 10, the number of possible languages is enormous, so free text seemed a better option. The downside of free text is that it is much more difficult to analyze and it does not provide immediately usable answers. Questions 2, 5, 7, 8, 12, 19, 25, and 26 allowed a free-text answer as an alternative to the given ones. Questions 3, 11, 23, 24, and 28 required further details for one of the possible answers.

The pilot of the survey went live on December 10, 2015. It was tested for five days before the survey was made public.

Gathering of Data

The survey went public on December 15, 2015, and was available for a month. There were 442 respondents in total. Two responses were omitted because the respondents stated specifically that they did not work within digital humanities. Another two responses were excluded because their answers and comments showed such a degree of hostility toward the survey that it appeared the respondents wished to invalidate it.[12] These suppressions left a total of 438 respondents.

Survey Results

GENDER

Of the 438 respondents, 225 (51.36 percent) identified themselves as female, two as genderqueer or androgynous (0.45 percent), 203 as male (46.36 percent), one as transgender (0.22 percent), one as male-to-female (MTF; 0.22 percent), and five as other (1.14 percent). One person skipped this question. Of those who marked other, two presented alternative gender definitions, while three (0.68 percent) stated that they could not see the point of this question or stated, "I find this question intrusive: what has gender got to do with 'multiculturalism?'" One respondent skipped this question (see Figure 18.2).

It seemed clear from the gathered answers that the vast majority of the respondents identified with traditional binary gender labels.

REJECTIONS FROM THE DIGITAL HUMANITIES CONFERENCE

From Weingart and Eichmann's statistical analysis, we know that roughly 30 percent of the accepted presentations in the DH conference have a sole or a lead female author. It follows that some 70 percent of the presentations are by men or have a man as the lead author. Although they have had access to the data of rejected papers, they have not released statistics on rejection for ethical reasons. From those respondents who identified themselves as male (see Figure 18.3), 149 answered question 26 (If you submit to the DH conference, how many times have you been rejected?). Of those, ninety-four never had a paper rejected from the conference, thirty-two had a paper rejected once, twelve twice, and eleven more than three times.

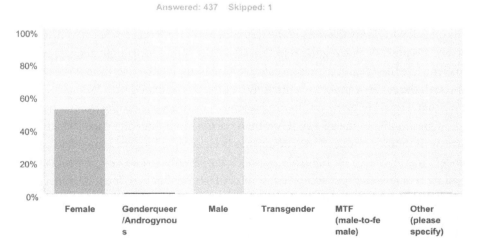

Figure 18.2. Chart: What is your gender?

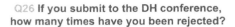
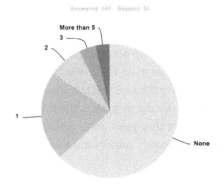

Answer Choices	Responses	
None	63.09%	94
1	21.48%	32
2	8.05%	12
3	4.03%	6
More than 5	3.36%	5
Total		149

Figure 18.3. Chart: How many times have you been rejected? Males.

In contrast, of 141 female respondents, 104 never had a paper rejected, nineteen had one rejection, eleven had two rejections, and seven had more than three rejections (see Figure 18.4). These results seem surprising in light of the statistics that come directly from the accepted papers, which show that 70 percent of the papers have a male lead author. However, since the question did not specify the role of the author in the acceptance, it might be that the female respondents are counting those papers in which they are not the lead author. A future survey should reformulate the question to clarify the roles of the respondents in conference proposals. Alternatively, it is possible that regular rejections from the conference might alienate scholars who later decide not to present more submissions. In any case, the data obtained through the survey cannot meaningfully be directly compared with Weingart's data on equal terms. Here, the results are presented for reference purposes.

Question 27 of the survey (How many times more than one paper which lists you as the author or one of the authors has been accepted for the same DH conference?) was answered by 168 male respondents; seventy-two (42.86 percent) never had more than one paper accepted for the conference; that is, of the total, ninety-six (51.14 percent) respondents had two or more papers accepted for the same conference. For this same question, there were 161 female respondents, of whom eighty-six (53.42 percent) never had more than one paper accepted, while seventy-five (46.58 percent) had more than one paper accepted for the same conference.

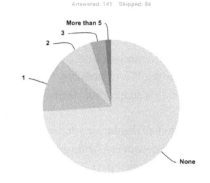

Figure 18.4. Chart 2: How many times have you been rejected? Females.

GENERAL DIFFERENCES BASED ON GENDER

In general, the differences when using gender to filter the survey's results are relatively small. For example, one might have expected a significant difference in question 6 (Are you the primary caregiver of a child, a disabled or elderly person?), where 36.61 percent of the female respondents answered "Yes," in contrast with 28.86 percent of the male respondents. The difference between these is smaller (although still important) than the expected results based on the perceived role of women as the providers of the bulk of the care for younger and older people. For gender-neutral questions, such as question 3 (Is any of your degrees in digital humanities?), 10.67 percent of the female respondents answered yes, while 7.43 percent of the male respondents answered in the affirmative.

Question 7, which dealt with sexual orientation, shows quite a difference between genders. Of the female respondents, 78.73 percent stated that they are heterosexual, 5.88 percent gay, and 11.31 percent bisexual, and 4.07 percent chose "Other" (for which the following were specified: asexual, pansexual, queer, heteroflexible, and human). By contrast, 87.13 percent of the male respondents identified as heterosexual, 5.94 percent as gay, and 4.46 percent as bisexual, and 2.48 percent chose "Other" (these were defined as queer, bisexual tendencies, and "Do not wish to answer").

Rank

Rank is one aspect in which we can see a concrete difference between male and female respondents (see Table 18.1).

Analysis of the replies under the category "Other" shows that some respondents found it difficult to place themselves into categories that present a different nomenclature in their own country. When possible, the responses were assimilated into categories (see the notes to this chapter for more details). The corrected results can be seen in Table 18.2.[13]

In Table 18.2, I have included all the data, including the answers by respondents that identified themselves as "genderqueer," "transgender," and "other." I include the data for Table 18.2, as rank is a factor that pertains to an individual and, for this reason, it is important to be able to see all the data. Because I have only included data (conflated) for the nonbinary gender option only in this section, this reduces the risk of potential identification in other parts of the survey.

Table 18.2 shows that the first three categories (Chair, Professor, and Associate Professor) are occupied by men in higher numbers. This is not particularly surprising, given the general bias in academia toward male scholars and the way in which women and minorities tend to experience university careers differently from their male colleagues (Johnsrud and Des Jarlais).

Fourteen respondents have a chair or named professorship. Five of those (35.71 percent) are female, one is genderqueer/transgender (7.14 percent), one chose "Other" (7.14 percent), and the rest (50 percent) are male. Nor is it surprising that all of the named professorships, including the ones that were outside the Global

Table 18.1

Title	Male %	Female %
Chair or named professorship	2.48	1.78
Professor	8.42	5.78
Associate professor	14.36	11.11
Assistant professor	13.37	21.78
Adjunct professor	0.99	2.67
Seasonal lecturer	0.50	0.89
Teaching or research assistant	7.92	4.89
Head librarian	0.50	1.33
Subject librarian	1.49	2.67
Specialist librarian	2.97	4.44
Technical officer	2.97	2.22
Programmer	3.47	0.44
Student	8.42	8.44
Other	32.18	31.56
Total	100	100

Table 18.2

Title	Male	Female	Genderqueer / transgender	Other	Total
Chair or named professorship	7 (50%)	5 (35.7%)	1 (7.14%)	1 (7.14%)	14
Professor[i]	20 (60%)	13 (39%)			33
Associate professor[ii]	34 (55.73%)	26 (42.62%)		1 (1.63%)	61
Assistant professor	30 (37.5%)	50 (62.5%)			80
Adjunct professor	3 (23.07%)	8 (61.53)	2 (15.38%)		13
Seasonal lecturer	1 (25%)	3 (75%)			4
Teaching/ research assistant	16 (57.1 %)	11 (39%)	1 (3.57%)		28
Head librarian	1 (25%)	3 (75%)			4
Subject librarian	3 (33.3%)	6 (66.6%)			9
Specialist librarian	9 (33.3%)	17 (66.6%)			26
Technical officer	7 (58.33%)	5 (41.66%)			12
Programmer	10 (83.33%)	2 (16.66%)			12
Student	20 (44.44%)	25 (55.55%)			45
Postdoctoral researcher[iii]	7 (50%)	6 (42.85%)		1 (7.14%)	14
Director	2 (22.22%)	7 (77.77%)			9
Associate director	2 (66.6%)	1 (33.3%)			3
Project manager	6 (54.54%)	5 (45.45%)			11
Coordinator	1 (14.28%)	6 (85.71%)			7
Researcher	6 (42.85%)	8 (57.14%)			14
Other	18	18[iv]		1	36
Total	203	225	4	5	436[v]

i. The UK rank "reader" is included here, as it is roughly equivalent to professor.
ii. Maitre de conférences was added to this category, as it is a permanent position with guaranteed tenure, so it is closer to associate than to assistant professor.
iii. This and the following categories were created based on multiple responses that were initially filed under "Other."
iv. For female respondents, this category included principal network security analyst, research data manager, research coordinator, communications officer, philologist, consultant, digital humanities research analyst, academic specialist, ingénieur d'études, external researcher, library staff (not librarian), historian, public historian, editor, digital humanities specialist, and instructional designer.
v. One respondent skipped this question.

North, are held by respondents who described themselves as Caucasian/white in question 8.[14] When asked to specify their native language, twelve of the fourteen listed English as their first language. For more details about ethnic diversity, see the following section, "Ethnic Background and Other Factors." From a total of thirty-three full professors, only thirteen (39 percent) are female. Of the associate professors, twenty-six (41 percent) are female. But at the level of assistant professor, we see a sharp reversal in the numbers, where 62.5 percent are female. This could be explained in different ways. Perhaps the discipline is already changing: there are so many more women at the beginning of the tenure-track system that a more even distribution of gender ratio at higher levels in the future appears possible. If this is correct, it will be good news. It is conceivable that change might be coming to the field and that the superior number of female assistant professors will eventually translate into a higher number of female associate, full professors, and chairs. However, it is also entirely possible that these women have not yet been displaced by the system; that, being at the beginning of their careers, they might end up taking much longer to move from assistant to associate professor, or from associate to full professor (Townsend), or might not manage to rise within academia.

Categories such as "adjunct professor" and "seasonal lecturer" received too few responses to produce significant results, although those categories, as was the case for "director" or "coordinator," present a much higher percentage of female respondents. The categories of jobs within libraries (head, subject, and specialist librarian) were selected by thirty-nine respondents. Women hold 66.66 percent of the library jobs. In a similar way to the "named chairs" and "professors," the head librarians self-identified as white, and all of them use their native language at work. Of the subject librarians, seven were white, while two were mixed. Only one of them uses a language different from his or her native language for work. Again, there are a higher number of respondents (twenty-six) who are specialist librarians; of those, twenty-four (92 percent) are white. Only three (11 percent) of them do not use their native language at work.

ETHNIC BACKGROUND AND OTHER FACTORS

Of the 438 respondents, 342—that is, 79.35 percent—described themselves as white. There is no substantial difference between male (80.5 percent) and female (79.64 percent) respondents, and although one could have expected a high percentage of individuals who identify as white in the field, the particularly high number of respondents who chose this option might be related to the way in which the survey was distributed (through social media, like Twitter and Facebook, as well as via distribution lists, such as Humanist, RedHD, and GO::DH).[15] But it also reflects a homogeneity that characterizes the different digital humanities gatherings, notably the Digital Humanities conference (sponsored by the Alliance of Digital Humanities Organizations).

When these answers are viewed in combination with other factors, we see that of the thirty-three full professors, twenty-nine identified as white, while four (12 percent) described themselves as mixed. One person refused to respond, since "ethnicity is a trivial accident of birth and not connected to the truly great heritage I enjoy from the other earlier humans who were not my direct ancestors." This type of comment suggests a lack of awareness of the experience of minorities: ethnicity is only trivial for those who can pass as part of the majority group in which they move, that is, for those who are not part of a visible minority. Individuals of ethnic minorities know very well that it is nearly impossible to disconnect oneself from one's ethnicity (Essed, "Making and Breaking"). The same is often true of class and gender (Crenshaw).

Among the full professors, of the thirteen female respondents, two are of mixed race. Of the twenty-one male respondents, two are of mixed race, lowering the percentage of male, mixed-race full professors. Within the same group, one respondent is bisexual, and two are gay or lesbian. Again, at this level, the dominance of white heterosexuals is remarkable. Although a variety of languages were represented in this group, English was the dominant one (sixteen native speakers), followed by Spanish (five native speakers). For scholars at the professorial level, only 20 percent work in environments in which their native language is not the main working language.

At the level of associate professor, it is possible to start to see a glimpse of diversity. Although 78.68 percent of the associate professors are white, other ethnicities start to make an appearance: there are two African, two South Asian, one East Asian, one Native American, three mixed, and four who marked "Other."[16] The next highest category is "mixed," with 5.56 percent of the respondents belonging to it. Among associate professors there is one marked difference between male and female respondents: 60 percent of the female respondents are the primary caregivers of a child or a disabled or elderly person, while only 41.38 percent of the male respondents indicated the same. Only 9.09 percent of the respondents work in an environment in which their native language is not the main language.

Assistant professor is, by far, the largest category within the ranks. Accordingly, one would expect it to show the greatest variety within it. The majority of assistant professors (83.75 percent) identify as white, South Asians represent 3.75 percent, African and Middle Eastern each accounts for 2.5 percent, while East Asian and Aboriginal represent 1.25 percent each. Mixed stands at 3.75 percent for this category. Of this group, 17.5 percent do not use their native language for day-to-day activities at work.

Weingart suggested that "names foreign to the US are less likely than either men or women to be accepted to these conferences."[17] This is also backed up by Bertrand and Mullainathan, who showed that the same résumé might receive a much higher rate of interviews if it had a white-sounding name in it ("Are Emily and Greg"). The differential treatment exposed by this research might help explain the dominance of researchers from the Global North (particularly those originating from countries in which English is the dominant language) in the digital humanities and the fact that the majority of the practitioners work within their own language and their own culture. The lower number of minorities within this group is alarming. It places the future of the discipline in danger of continuing the sameness that currently characterizes it.

Analysis

CULTURAL CLONING

The previous sections evince a discouraging homogeneity within DH, currently dominated by white Anglophones. This may be explained by the concept of cultural cloning. Philomena Essed described cultural cloning in her 2002 article, "Cloning Cultural Homogeneity While Talking Diversity." In later work, Essed and David Theo Goldberg focused on how the normativity of cultural cloning excludes "deviants": "The notion of cultural cloning, initially used to problematize the systemic reproduction of white, masculine homogeneity in high status positions, brings into focus another side of exclusion. Yet, same-kind preference reproducing white (Euro) masculine privileges in terms of race, ethnicity, gender, or profession is not countered with the same force of indignation as we find in the case of the suggestion of biological cloning" (1068). Their denunciation of the complicity of a system that fails to react against this cultural cloning is paired with their statement that "the (culturally contextualized) privileging of white men and the social delimitation and denigration of women and people of colour in the world have not been erased. Furthermore, in spite of improvements of facilities for people with physical challenges, disabilities are generally perceived as indicative of a less than full human life" (1069). Sixteen years after the publication of the Essed and Goldberg essay, we find that the situation has only minimally improved. The findings of the survey, when viewed in light of other research about academic practices of tenure, suggest that the future is likely remain similar to the present. The cause of the stability of the situation in academia which Essed has so clearly described is the "positive prejudice in favor of specific individuals or group members based on a sense of closeness or familiarity" for which "certain values have been ingrained as more crucial, more human, and more valuable" (Essed, "Cloning amongst Professors"). We must worry about the fact that "cultural cloning is predicated on the taken-for-granted desirability of certain types to fit the often-unconscious tendency to comply with normative standards, and the subsequent rejection of those who are perceived as deviant" (121). This suggests that when white, heterosexual, Anglophone maleness is the norm, anything that departs from it becomes deviance. One can relate this to intersectionality, as described by Roopika Risam, going "beyond the race-class-gender triad described by Crenshaw to additional axes of difference including sexuality and ability" ("Beyond the Margins"), which by definition would add other layers of complexity to Essed's perception of deviance.

POLITICIZATION OF DH

The complexity of relations of various groups in digital humanities and their different visions of how to tackle the problems around diversity and inclusion are likely to continue to generate debate within the field. As intellectuals, we cannot afford the luxury of ignoring these issues.

Already in 2012, Tara McPherson called for the politicization of the digital humanities, advocating for the inclusion of contextualized studies of race and gender within the field. She was asking that those be included as part of the field of study. Martha Nell Smith has voiced similar concerns, observing that "new media and digital humanities often remain fixed, bound by conventions of old paradigms" ("Human Touch Software"). The broadening of the field of study is, of course, a desirable objective. However, as scholars, we should also consider an intellectual reflection on the political aspects of the development of the digital humanities as a field of research. Despite what journalists like Gordon Hunt might think, there is a gender imbalance in digital humanities, as there is in the most of academia. Moreover, this imbalance is exacerbated when race, gender, sexuality, native language, and other factors are brought into consideration.

Analyzing the survey results from a racial perspective, it appears that the representation is even more homogeneous than when we look at it through the gender lens. This should prompt us to ask whether women from other racial or cultural backgrounds are even close to being a meaningful part of the Digital Humanities dialogue. The limitations of the survey do not allow certainty, but it might be that scholars from minority backgrounds might never make it to a level from which they could inspire others or be in the position to make the field more diverse by mentoring other minorities. This situation would perpetuate the cultural cloning described by Essed.

It has been shown that role models are determinant in the formative years of any human being and, although it is possible that particular individuals might choose role models who are very different from themselves, it is much more likely that they will identify with someone with whom they share common traits. Many universities today have international programs designed to attract students from all over the world, but the homogeneity of university staff prevents students from emulating role models who are like themselves.

EXCLUDED RESPONSES AND SPECIAL COMMENTS

The two excluded responses were by male respondents who did not consider that the survey or individual questions were relevant to the field. One of these excluded respondents gave his gender as "MCP (Male Chauvinistic Pig)" and listed, both under visible and invisible disability, "I am a man."

The level of aggression and vitriol in some of the answers was disturbing. For example, when asked about ethnicity, one respondent stated, "Why should I? I consider such questions racist," and, although he had answered no to the disability questions, he added as a comment, "Why is this important?" Another respondent, under invisible disability, contributed the following: "Being a stupid asshole." Yet another one felt compelled to state, "All in All, a pretty fucking stupid survey." Again, this occurred only with data provided by scholars who identified themselves as heterosexual men, which suggests that the main representatives of the heteronormative patriarchy are also the victims of the society that has created them and made them oblivious to the situation of others. The survey was not mandatory, it did not take an inordinate amount of time, and although a few of the questions were personal, these reactions to it were so disproportionate that they needed to be removed from the sample. The discovery that some colleagues relied on the anonymity of the survey to display aggression which appeared personally directed was shocking. However, in light of the online harassment suffered by women, particularly feminist writers, these behaviors, although unacceptable, can hardly be called unusual.[18]

One may wonder what reasons a small minority of respondents can have to make a joke about issues such as disability or sexuality, which so severely affect others. However, it appears that from a position of power, other humans' powerlessness is just laughable. The digital humanities community should be concerned that individuals with these attitudes might be in positions that would grant them power over scholars with less privileged backgrounds. These are prime candidates for cultural cloning as they are likely to give preference to individuals with whom they share common characteristics.

There were some fair questions, comments, and criticisms that arose from the survey, all of which can contribute to our understanding of how different cultures perceive this type of questionnaire. Moreover, they will serve to build better surveys in the future.

The survey results show that digital humanists are binary, white, affluent, and Anglophone. This is not a surprising discovery, given that academia tends to be conservative and to accept changes slowly and reluctantly. What the survey shows, however, is that there are many people sufficiently interested in diversity issues to take the time to answer these questions and that many of those are intensely aware of the field's shortcomings in reference to its potential for diversity and pluralism.

Because of the significant number of female assistant professors in this sample, one can speculate, as above, that it could be that the position of women is improving. However, if this is true, it is most likely to apply to white women from affluent countries in the Northern Hemisphere. The reason for this is that each deviation from what is considered the norm represents a new obstacle, a new degree of separation from a position of power, for someone who is not a white, heterosexual, affluent, Anglophone man.

The next question is, what can be done to improve this situation? One could start by following Rebecca Rosen's suggestion to phase out all-male panels: men must pledge not to take part in panels in which no women are present.[19] But one could go further than that. Scholars who work in countries with high-income economies could decline money toward their attendance so people from countries with low-income economies can be invited. In the same way, one can choose not to participate in all-white panels, Global North panels, native-Anglophone panels. Or even better, request that the all-white, Global North, native-Anglophone panels be transformed by suggesting speakers who do not fall into those categories. While collaborating with others on equal footing, authors should not be listed in alphabetical order. Instead, one should give the most vulnerable author the first place.[20]

Be aware of the role of implicit bias. Hiring committees or grant-giving committees should be aware of the existence of implicit bias and ensure that opportunities are not denied because of prejudices, implicit or explicit, against individuals. Be aware of your own privilege and work hard to understand that others might be in a different position and how they are affected by our current power structures.

One wonders about the distribution of the minorities within DH: do they mostly work in emerging areas or on fringe subjects that have not been studied by the old patriarchy? Or, as may be the case for myself, has their career progress been hindered because of the perceived clash between them as individuals from outside the white Anglophone orbit and their chosen field of study?

As researchers, teachers, and human beings, we are not, and cannot, be defined by the things we are not. Instead, our work should be evaluated (and for this, it must be allowed in those venues in which such things are assessed) and must be evaluated fairly, for its contribution to our field and to society, not by the sound of our last name, our gender, or the color of our skin.

Appendix: Survey

This survey is designed to gather data about Digital Humanists in order to achieve a better understanding of those working in the field.

There has been a strong move towards a more plural and inclusive field and the data gathered here will be used to assess the current situation before making proposals aimed to promote a successful multicultural field.

The 29 questions should take around five minutes to complete, they were written by Barbara Bordalejo (http://kuleuven.academia.edu/BarbaraBordalejo) and will be used as part of her research on diversity in DH.

If you have questions you can contact her at barbara.bordalejo@kuleuven.be.

Privacy statement: Responses are anonymous. No individual data will be redistributed. The data you provide will be used for the purposes of this research. The bulk data might be shared with other interested researchers. For SurveyMonkey's privacy statement go to https://www.surveymonkey.com/mp/policy/privacy-policy/.

1. What is your age?

○ 18 to 24

○ 25 to 34

○ 35 to 44

○ 45 to 54

○ 55 to 64

○ 65 to 74

○ 75 or older

2. What is the highest level of education you have completed?

○ Undergraduate degree

○ MA

○ MSc

○ MPhil

○ PhD

○ Other (please specify)

3. Is any of your degrees specifically in Digital Humanities?

○ Yes

○ No

If, you answered "Yes," please specify where you obtained your degree.

4. What is your country of birth?

Other (please specify)

5. What is your gender?

○ Female

○ Genderqueer/Androgynous

○ Intersex

○ Male

○ Transgender

Figure 18.5. Diversity in Digital Humanities 2015 survey.

○ Transsexual

○ FTM (female-to-male)

○ MTF (male-to-female)

○ Other (please specify)

[ ]

6. Are you the primary care giver of a child, a disabled or elderly person?

○ Yes

○ No

7. Do you consider yourself to be:

○ Heterosexual or straight

○ Gay or lesbian

○ Bisexual

○ Other (please specify)

[ ]

8. Which of the following best represents your ethnic heritage? Choose all that apply:

○ Aboriginal

○ African

○ Caucasian

○ Middle Eastern

○ South Asian

○ East Asian

○ Native (North, South, or Central American)

○ Mixed

○ Other

If you chose "mixed" or "other," please specify.

[ ]

9. Please give details about your cultural background. For example, "Hispanic, raised in the US" or "Taiwanese, raised in Japan" or "Bicultural, Chinese-Canadian."

[ ]

(continued)

10. What is your native language?

[   ]

11. Is your native language used in your day to day activities at work?

○ Yes

○ No

If you answered "No," please name the language/languages used in your daily activities at work.

[   ]

12. In what type of institution do you work?

○ Research University

○ University

○ Four-year college

○ Library

○ Other (please specify)

[   ]

13. Is there a DH center in your place of work?

○ Yes

○ No

14. Are you part of the DH center in your place of work?

○ Yes

○ No

15. Is your salary paid using soft money, i. e. paid with grants rather than centrally funded?

○ Yes

○ No

16. For how long have you been employed at your current institution?

[   ]

17. Were you employed as a digital humanist before your current post?

○ Yes

○ No

18. Please give details about length of your previous employment and type of institution(s).

[   ]

Figure 18.5. Continued

19. What is your current title?

○ Chair or Named Professorship

○ Professor

○ Associate professor, senior lecturer or senior research fellow

○ Assistant professor, lecturer or research fellow

○ Adjunct professor

○ Seasonal lecturer

○ Teaching or Research assistant

○ Head librarian

○ Subject librarian

○ Specialist librarian

○ Technical officer

○ Programmer

○ Student

○ Other (please specify)

20. Is this a permanent position?

○ Yes

○ No

21. Is it tenured or tenure track?

○ Yes

○ No

22. What is your country of employment?

23. Do you have a visible disability?

○ Yes

○ No

If, you answered "Yes," you are invited to provide details.

24. Do you have an invisible disability?

○ Yes

○ No

If, you answered "Yes," you are invited to provide details.

(continued)

25. Do you regularly submit proposals to the Digital Humanities conference or to other similar gatherings within DH?

◯ Yes

◯ No

26. If you submit to the DH conference, how many times have you been rejected?

◯ None

◯ 1

◯ 2

◯ 3

◯ 4

◯ 5

◯ More than 5

27. How many times more than one paper which lists you as the author or one of the authors has been accepted for the DH conference?

◯ None

◯ 1

◯ 2

◯ 3

◯ 4

◯ 5

◯ More than 5

◯ Other (please specify)

28. Do you think that your gender, sexual orientation, employment status, native language, ability, country of origin has helped or hindered your career in DH?

◯ Yes

◯ No

If, you answered "Yes," provide more details.

29. Are there additional comments you would like to make?

Figure 18.5. Continued

Notes

1. See, for example, Gold, *Debates*. Whether DH is a discipline is debatable and has been widely discussed. However, for practical reasons, in this article I refer to DH indistinctly as a field or a discipline as in this particular instance, the focus is in DH as a group of self-identified individuals.

2. See Gordon Hunt, 2015, and the dialogue with Lorna Hughes below.

3. See Eichmann-Kalwara, Weingart, and Jorgensen, "Representation at Digital Humanities Conferences (2000–2015)," in this same volume; or Weingart and Eichmann-Kalwara, "What's under the Big Tent?"

4. For the purposes of this article, the term "minority" refers to individuals who hold fewer positions of influence because of the systemic oppression imbedded in the power structures and so it includes linguistic factors that affect speakers of languages other than English.

5. Hunt, "Certainly No Gender Imbalance."

6. See Misa, *Gender Codes*, and the data by the U.S. National Center for Education Statistics, Digest of Education Statistics.

7. The composition of the ADHO executive has changed and Humanistica has been invited to submit their own representative.

8. Scott Weingart, personal communication, June 15, 2015.

9. Weingart, "What's Counted Counts"; Posner, "What's Next."

10. I used Diem's *Guide* (Diem, *Step-by-Step Guide*) while preparing the survey, as well as the online guide to Survey Questions and Answer Types ("Survey Questions: Survey Examples and Sample Survey Questions | QuestionPro").

11. The complete survey can be found in the appendix to this chapter.

12. See below, the section titled "Excluded Responses and Special Comments," on excluded answers and what we can learn from them.

13. Note that the percentages are calculated within a single category.

14. The word "Caucasian" was used in the original survey. Since then, it has been pointed out that this word should be replaced with "white." In consequence, I have replaced it for the purposes of this chapter and will revise future versions of the survey in response to this feedback.

15. Although the survey specifically separated ethnicity and culture, some respondents objected to the presentation of ethnicity and culture as one thing.

16. This percentage has been manually adjusted because three of the respondents marked "Other" but described themselves as European.

17. Weingart, "Acceptances."

18. The most infamous episode of online harassment is probably GamerGate (Weinman, "How a Gamer's Fight Turned"; Marcotte, "Gaming Misogyny"; Stone, "Gamergate's Vicious Right-Wing Swell"). See, for example, Crandall, "Feminist Columnist Jessica Valenti."

19. Rosen, "Simple Suggestion."

20. Wolfers, "When Teamwork Doesn't Work."

Bibliography

Bertrand, Marianne, and Sendhil Mullainathan. "Are Emily and Greg More Employable than Lakisha and Jamal? A Field Experiment on Labor Market Discrimination." *American Economic Review* 94, no. 4 (2004): 991–1013. https://www.povertyaction lab.org/sites/default/files/publications/3%20A%20Field%20Experiment%20on%20 Labor%20Market%20Discrimination%20Sep%2004.pdf.

Crandall, Diana. "Feminist Columnist Jessica Valenti Quits Social Media after Trolls Threaten to Rape Her 5-Year-Old Daughter." *New York Daily News,* July 27, 2016. http://www.nydailynews.com/news/national/columnist-quits-social-media-threats -rape-5-year-old-article-1.2728374.

Crenshaw, Kimberlé. "Mapping the Margins: Intersectionality, Identity Politics, and Violence against Women of Color." *Stanford Law Review* 43, no. 6 (1991): 1241–99.

Diem, Keith. *A Step-by-Step Guide to Developing Effective Questionnaires and Survey Procedures for Program Evaluation & Research.* 2002. http://cahnrs.wsu.edu/fs/wp-con tent/uploads/sites/4/2015/09/A-Step-By-Step-Guide-to-Developing-Effective-Ques tionnaires.pdf.

Essed, Philomena. "Cloning amongst Professors: Normativities and Imagined Homogeneities." *NORA—Nordic Journal of Feminist and Gender Research* 12, no. 2 (2004): 113–22.

Essed, Philomena. "Dilemmas in Leadership: Women of Colour in the Academy." *Ethnic and Racial Studies* 23, no. 5 (2000): 888–904.

Essed, Philomena. "Making and Breaking Ethnic Boundaries: Women's Studies, Diversity, and Racism." *Women's Studies Quarterly* 22, nos. 3/4 (1994): 232–49.

Essed, Philomena, and David Theo Goldberg. "Cloning Cultures: The Social Injustices of Sameness." *Ethnic and Racial Studies* 25, no. 6 (2002): 1066–82.

Gold, Matthew. *Debates in the Digital Humanities.* Minneapolis: University of Minnesota Press, 2012.

Hunt, Gordon. "There's Certainly No Gender Imbalance in Digital Humanities!" *Silicon Republic,* May 20, 2015. https://www.siliconrepublic.com/discovery/2015/05/20 /theres-certainly-no-gender-imbalance-in-digital-humanities.

Johnsrud, Linda, and Christine D. Des Jarlais. "Barriers to Tenures for Women and Minorities." *Review of Higher Education* 17, no. 4 (1994): 335–53.

Marcotte, Amanda. "Gaming Misogyny Gets Infinite Lives: Zoe Quinn, Virtual Rape and Sexism." *Daily Beast,* August 22, 2014. http://www.thedailybeast.com/arti cles/2014/08/22/gaming-misogyny-gets-infinite-lives-zoe-quinn-virtual-rape-and -sexism.html.

Misa, Thomas. *Gender Codes: Why Women Are Leaving Computing.* Hoboken, N.J.: Wiley, 2010.

Posner, Miriam. "What's Next: The Radical, Unrealized Potential of Digital Humanities." *Miriam Posner's Blog,* July 27, 2015. http://miriamposner.com/blog/whats-next -the-radical-unrealized-potential-of-digital-humanities/.

Risam, Roopika. "Beyond the Margins: Intersectionality and Digital Humanities." *Digital Humanities Quarterly* 9, no. 4 (2015). http://www.digitalhumanities.org/dhq/vol/9/2/000208/000208.html.

Rosen, Rebecca J. "A Simple Suggestion to Help Phase Out All-Male Panels at Tech Conferences." *Atlantic,* January 4, 2013. http://www.theatlantic.com/technology/archive/2013/01/a-simple-suggestion-to-help-phase-out-all-male-panels-at-tech-conferences/266837/.

Scheinfeldt, Tom. "Why Digital Humanities Is 'Nice.'" In *Debates in the Digital Humanities,* edited by M. K. Gold. Minneapolis: University of Minnesota Press, 2013. http://dhdebates.gc.cuny.edu/debates/text/36.

Smith, Martha Nell. "The Human Touch Software of the Highest Order: Revisiting Editing as Interpretation." *Textual Cultures* 2, no. 1 (2007): 1–15.

Stone, Jon. "Gamergate's Vicious Right-Wing Swell Means There Can Be No Neutral Stance." *The Guardian,* October 13, 2014. https://www.theguardian.com/technology/2014/oct/13/gamergate-right-wing-no-neutral-stance.

"Survey Questions: Survey Examples and Sample Survey Questions | QuestionPro." n.d. Accessed June 23, 2018. https://www.questionpro.com/article/survey-question-answer-type.html.

Townsend, R. B. "Gender and Success in Academia: More from the Historian's Career Path's Survey." In *Perspectives in History,* 2013. https://www.historians.org/publications-and-directories/perspectives-on-history/january-2013/gender-and-success-in-academia.

U.S. National Center for Education Statistics. Digest of Education Statistics, Table 349: "Degrees in computer and information sciences conferred by degree-granting institutions, by level of degree and sex of student: 1970–71 through 2010–11." https://nces.ed.gov/programs/digest/d12/tables/dt12_349.asp.

Weingart, Scott. "Acceptances to Digital Humanities 2015 (part 4)." *ScottBot.net,* June 28, 2015. http://www.scottbot.net/HIAL/?p=41375.

Weingart, Scott. "What's Counted Counts" (blog). *ScottBot.net,* July 31, 2015. http://www.scottbot.net/HIAL/?p=41425.

Weingart, Scott B., and Nickoal Eichmann-Kalwara. "What's under the Big Tent?: A Study of ADHO Conference Abstracts." @ *Digital Studies / Le champ numérique* 7, no. 1 (October 2017).

Weinman, Jaime. "How a Gamer's Fight Turned into an All-out Culture War." *McLean's,* December 8, 2014. http://www.macleans.ca/society/technology/gamergate-how-a-gamer-fight-turned-into-an-all-out-culture-war/.

Wolfers, Justin. "When Teamwork Doesn't Work for Women." *New York Times,* January 8, 2016. http://www.nytimes.com/2016/01/10/upshot/when-teamwork-doesnt-work-for-women.html?_r=0.

PART V][Chapter 19

Complicating a "Great Man" Narrative of Digital History in the United States

SHARON M. LEON

Edward Ayers. Stephen Brier. Joshua Brown. Daniel Cohen. Roy Rosenzweig. William Thomas. These are the names associated with the major projects cited in the few available accounts of the development of digital history in the United States. Despite nearly thirty years of active digital history work, narratives that recount the emergence of the field are sparse, and those that exist are almost totally devoid of women. For over a decade now scholars have begun their search for the roots of digital humanities with the opening essay in Schreibman and colleagues' 2004 collection *A Companion to Digital Humanities*. Susan Hockey's "The History of Humanities Computing" offers an origin story that is deeply steeped in computational text analysis and text processing. It begins with the initial effort of Italian Jesuit Roberto Busa and IBM to create a concordance of Thomistic writings, and continues through the founding of key scholarly associations, the development of the Text Encoding Initiative, and the launch of thematic source collections on the Internet. Hockey's narrative leans toward the literary and linguistic, with little attention to how those with disciplinary commitments in fields such as history, archeology, or anthropology might have found their way to the digital humanities. Those stories are saved for subsequent individual essays from the collection that deal with the various disciplines.[1]

As a result, curious or aspiring digital historians are likely to turn to Will Thomas's essay "Computing and the Historical Imagination" in search of a background on how their fellow historians came to employ digital approaches. Thomas's chapter traces the birth of digital history back to the quantitative history movement of the 1960s and 1970s, signaled most vividly and controversially by Robert Fogel and Stanley Engerman's *Time on the Cross: The Economics of American Negro Slavery* (1974). Various social history projects brought statistical and computational analysis to the fore of historical investigation, and for some that route brought them to a more expansive interest in historical methods. As computing technologies became more affordable and easier to work with, historians embraced the use of databases to track and analyze source materials. Access to the World Wide Web in the early 1990s offered another set of possibilities for expanding access to historical sources and combining them in new ways for scholarly, educational, and public audiences. Thomas suggests that there were vast possibilities for new modes of presentation of historical scholarship, and new tools of analysis to be applied, with historical geospatial work garnering the most energy and attention at the point of his writing in the early years of the twenty-first century. While it offers a familiar story that deals with methodological shifts in the practice of history, Thomas's version of the emergence of digital history methods neither includes nor cites any digital historians who are women. Anne Kelly Knowles, who is a geographer rather than a historian, is the sole woman mentioned who is engaged in digital ventures.[2]

Published shortly after the *Companion*, Dan Cohen and Roy Rosenzweig's *Digital History: A Guide to Gathering, Preserving, and Presenting the Past* (2005) offers a more practical approach to the field of digital history. It too includes an introduction to the history of the field—one that is slightly more inclusive than Thomas's in its treatment of genres and approaches. This is a democratic and capacious vision of the history web that does not hew to narrowly cast definitions of historical scholarship. Rather, it includes examples that are designed for public audiences and that which targets the K12 educational fields. Yet, Rosenzweig and Cohen managed to point to the digital work of only one woman: Kathryn Kish Sklar, who with Thomas Dublin developed *Women and Social Movements, 1600–2000*.[3]

With so little literature available, more recent reviews of the field tend to reproduce these oversights, suggesting that the history of digital history is a settled one—one that is devoid of women. For example, in her 2014 attempt to puzzle through the complexities of the interdisciplinary that characterizes so much digital scholarship, Julia Thompson Klein lays out a set of definitions of digital humanities and a summary of how digital work has played out in core disciplines. While English comes in for extensive discussion, Klein offers only three paragraphs each on history and archeology. For history, Klein turns in bulk to Thomas's narrative, with some highlights from a 2008 interchange in the *Journal of American History* and a brief article from the American Historical Association's *Perspectives Magazine* by Douglas Seefeldt and Thomas. Again, no women feature in Klein's gloss on the history of digital history.[4]

Yet, a brief survey of the contemporary digital history scene quickly surfaces a large cohort of women—some tenure-track faculty, but many non-tenure-track faculty and staff—who are doing exciting work and taking major leadership roles, both tenure track and non–tenure track. Consider, for instance, the work of Nicole Coleman and Paula Findlen at Stanford University's Center for Spatial and Textual Analysis or Miriam Posner and Janice Reiff at the University of California Los Angeles's Center for Digital Humanities.[5] The leadership at George Mason University's Roy Rosenzweig Center for History and New Media (RRCHNM) in 2017 was half women: Sheila Brennan, Jennifer Rosenfeld, and Kelly Schrum.[6]

Numerous women historians outside of major digital humanities centers are also pursuing field-changing work. Kalani Craig is using text mining to investigate conflict in medieval episcopal biography. Sharon Block is using computational analysis to interrogate sources related to early American gender history. Jennifer Guiliano has taken a lead in professional development training. Erika Lee is leading a broad digital collecting project to gather the stories and experiences of Minnesota's recent immigrants. Michelle Moravec is using corpus linguistics to investigate the politics of women's culture and is writing about that research in real-time in public. Kathryn Tomasek continues her long-standing work on using text encoding with financial records.[7] In the public history universe, major projects can boast leadership from Anne Whisnant in North Carolina, Elissa Frankle at the U.S. Holocaust Memorial Museum, Priya Chhaya at the National Trust for Historic Preservation, and many, many others.[8] These women and their digital history projects are just a small sample of the innovative work that is underway all over the world.

Between 2006 and 2015, the American Council of Learned Societies (ACLS) offered a Digital Innovation Fellowship for scholars who sought a year of support to work on a major digital project. During that period, ACLS awarded fellowships to fourteen historians, five of whom were women.[9] In 2007, both Patricia Seed and Anne Sarah Rubin received fellowships for historical geospatial work. In 2010, Abigail Firey received an award to work on the Carolingian Canon Law Project. The next year, Ruth Mostern's geospatial work on the Yellow River and imperial engineering in North China was funded. And, most recently, Kim Gallon received support for her work on the black press.[10] This range of work suggests the breadth and depth of the ways that women are bringing digital theories and methods into their historical work.

These individual historians are not anomalies. In 2013 and 2015 Bryn Mawr College's Albert M. Greenfield Digital Center for the History of Women's Education, under the direction of Monica Mercado, hosted the Women's History in the Digital World Conference, bringing together dozens of women doing digital women's history work.[11] The population of female graduate students doing digital history also continues to grow.[12] Furthermore, female historians are overrepresented among the cohort of midcareer scholars who want to learn new digital methods. Of the applicants for RRCHNM's summer institute, Doing Digital History (2014), which was funded by the National Endowment for the Humanities, 71 percent of the applications for participation came from women, and 65 percent of the selected participants were women.[13] In sum, the contemporary cohort of female digital historians is robust, and it looks to remain that way.

All of this raises the question, why are there so few women in the history of digital history?

Knowing that Thomas, Cohen, Rosenzweig, Seefeldt, and Klein are all careful scholars, none of whom has a willful desire to overlook women's efforts, one might reasonably come away with the impression that digital history was a field with no women. Obviously that is not true. In fact, women have played essential roles in shaping the digital history, and researchers can find them if they know where to look. But, in addition to undertaking the task of recovering women's contributions to the field, the community of digital historians has an obligation to question the conditions that have contributed to their erasure, and to consider what systems and conditions become visible when we return them to the origin stories for the field. If digital historians refuse to interrogate them, then these origin stories will solidify in a way that distorts the history of the field but also in ways that shape the field disadvantageously for women going forward.

Just as the contemporary cohort of female digital historians is vibrant, women were integral collaborators in the work from the beginning. In the United States, the NEH has been the most substantial source of public funding for digital history through the years at universities and cultural heritage institutions. While the Office of Digital Humanities was established in 2008, digital history work has been funded at the NEH through the wide range of programs and divisions since the mid-1990s. A comprehensive search of the grants database for digital history projects yields 586 individual grants funded between 1994 and 2016. A review of those results showed that women served as principal investigator (PI) or co-PI on three hundred projects, or 51 percent of the awards.[14] As the PI or a co-PI for a particular project, these individuals assumed the responsibility for meeting the deliverables proposed in the application, and fulfilling the terms of the funding set out by the NEH. A close examination of the NEH funding data for this fifteen-year period reveals that of the three hundred projects for which women served as PI or co-PI, only 127, or 42 percent, were associated with colleges or universities. Furthermore, the projects led by these women cover the full range of funding opportunities offered by the NEH, not just those administered by the Office of Digital Humanities. Thus, the distribution of funded projects provides some hints at the kinds of work being led by these principle investigators:

- Eighty-nine projects (30 percent) were funded by the Division of Preservation and Access.
- Eighty-six projects (29 percent) were funded by the Division of Public Programs.
- Thirty-nine projects (13 percent) were funded by the Division of Education Programs.
- Thirty-six projects (12 percent) were funded by the Office of Digital Humanities.
- Twenty-five projects (8 percent) were funded by the program for Federal/State Partnerships, which includes grants for state humanities councils.
- Twenty projects (6 percent) were funded by the Division of Research Programs.
- Five projects (2 percent) were funded by the Office of Challenge Grants.

Given that the bulk of the projects were funded by the Divisions of Preservation and Access, Public Programs, and Education Programs, it is possible to surmise that these ventures were associated with the work of libraries and archives, museums and public humanities, and teaching and learning.

The relative gender parity among PIs and co-PIs of NEH-funded digital history projects suggests that there are factors preventing us from recognizing this work. One possible reason scholars in the field have not recognized the significant leadership of women in digital history is the generally pervasive gender bias in citations. Study after study shows women's scholarship simply gets cited less than men's in many, many fields.[15] That research cannot be discounted here, but once scholars recognize that women were there as active agents and innovators, guiding and shaping the early work of digital history, it becomes clear that there are other power differentials in play here. Thus, researchers must look deeper and further afield to reclaim the history of women in the digital history—to learn who these women are, what kinds of positions they hold, and what kind of work they have done. Then, we can begin to understand the structural forces in the academy and in cultural heritage institutions that facilitate the erasure of women's influence.

Significant structural factors in labor conditions have combined to perpetuate a "great man" theory history of digital history: status, access, flexibility, and authorizing and credentialing systems. First, structures within the academy have historically slowed women historians' advancement, inhibiting their recognition as leaders in major digital projects. Second, a narrow focus on project directors causes us to overlook the vast contributions of women in other roles on projects. Third, limiting our attention, digital work done within the halls of academe excludes the work of women who land in nonacademic positions. Furthermore, the ways that public history organizations represent their work can make it difficult to identify women's labor on these projects. Together these conditions make it easy for historians of digital history to perpetuate the impression that the pioneering work in the field was done by men. Once researchers go looking for the women who innovated in digital history, those who were present to shape the early projects, a broader picture of historical practice appears, one akin to what Rob Townsend refers to as the "historical enterprise," one that is wider than the halls of academe, filled with many more actors than the tenured few.[16]

Beyond the Senior Faculty

Academic labor practices, conditions, and structures have conspired to mask or reduce women's roles in digital history. A number of studies prove that women achieve senior status in history departments at much slower rates than men. Without the benefits of tenure, women are much less free to take on principal investigator or project director roles. Also, history departments have been slow to recognize digital work as authorized scholarly activity for promotion and tenure review, so much so that as late as April 2015 the American Historical Association (AHA) organized a cluster of articles debating the concept of "History as a Book Discipline" in *Perspectives*.[17] This methodological conservatism could combine with the structural sexism at work in the academy to doubly disadvantage women who sought to pursue digital work. Finally, large-scale collaborative digital history has been deeply dependent on contingent faculty and staff, many of whom are women, and many of whom fail to receive meaningful recognition for their contributions to these projects.

Concern about the professional status of women in history is long-standing. In 1969, the AHA formed the ad hoc Committee on the Status of Women, which then was institutionalized as the Committee on Women Historians in 1971. The ad hoc committee produced a report, known as the "Rose Report," in 1970 that serves as a baseline for understanding the position and experiences of women in the field. The findings were not promising. In the 1960s, the top ten history graduate programs granted about 15 percent of their degrees to women, but the faculties in the same departments were 98 to 99 percent men. Moreover, while 16 percent of the full professors in history in coeducational colleges had been women in the 1959–1960 year, by 1968–1969 only one woman remained at that rank. Summarizing the state of the field, the authors explained, "In history as in other academic areas, our sample of thirty institutions indicates women are employed primarily in non-tenured ranks. Moreover, far from abandoning their professions for pure domesticity, their very eagerness to work has made women vulnerable to exploitation. Their readiness—and sometimes their need—to accept irregular and part-time positions has led to their exclusion from participation in the main stream of academic rewards and preferment."[18] The situation has gotten somewhat better in intervening years, but slowly. The results from the AHA's survey in 1979–1980 put the percentage of women history faculty at 13.3, while women constituted only 5.9 percent at the full professor rank, 11.6 percent at the associate level, 25.3 percent at the assistant level, and 40.6 percent at the instructor rank. By 1988 things had improved slightly, with women making up 17.1 percent of the history faculty, and 8.2 percent at full, 14.2 percent at associate, 38.9 percent at assistant ranks, and 37.3 percent as instructors. With the 1998 survey, women had risen to 55 percent of history faculty at the assistant level, but only 18 percent of faculty at the full professor level.[19]

In 2006, the Committee on Women Historians (CWH) published *The Status of Women in the Historical Profession, 2005,* based on a survey sent to all the women members of the AHA, which yielded 362 responses. The report provides a fascinating qualitative snapshot of the sexism and discrimination in the field. Time to promotion and salaries continue to lag behind. Women bear an inordinate brunt of the burden of service. Assumptions about gender powerfully shape subjective, if standardized, evaluations of research, teaching, and service. Women shoulder a disproportionate responsibility for child and eldercare, which can disrupt early and midcareer advancement. The survey results prompted the CWH to issue a statement on best practices in supporting gender equity in the workplace.[20]

These findings echo the classic work of sociologist Arlie Hochschild, whose 1989 book *The Second Shift* articulated the way that women are hindered by bearing the brunt of domestic responsibilities while also working to maintain a productive professional life.[21] This bind can be especially difficult for women in academe who may face the impact of child bearing and child rearing at exactly the time when their careers require the most concentrated scholarly progress in the years leading up to tenure review. Not all women find themselves in this position, but enough do to contribute to the slowing of forward motion on the promotion track for women in the sector overall.

Furthermore, the structures of academic advancement in history have been slow to recognize digital scholarship for promotion and tenure, disadvantaging all scholars working in the field, but especially women whose promotion can be slowed by other factors. While the Modern Language Association (MLA) has had guidelines on evaluating digital scholarship since 2000, the historical profession had no such guidance until recently.[22] As a result, those hoping to build and support tenure cases for digital historians had to rely on the example of the MLA and adapt the 2010 report of the Organization of American Historians–National Council on Public History–American Historical Association's Working Group on Evaluation of Public History Scholarship, "Tenure, Promotion, and the Publicly Engaged Academic Historian."[23] The AHA recently has adopted a set of guidelines, raising the hopes of those who want to put digital methods at the center of their careers.[24]

Even with these pressures, women were prime movers in some of the earliest digital history projects. As early as 1992, Marsha MacDowell at Michigan State University was at work on *The Quilt Index,* which, given its focus on domestic material culture, barely registered with the larger field of digital historians.[25] By September 2000, *Common-Place: The Interactive Journal of Early American Life* published its first issue.[26] As its founding editors, Jane Kamensky and Jill Lepore embraced the possibilities of the web for creating community and conversation around history early in their careers. Kamensky was a junior professor at Brandeis, not yet the director of the Schlesinger Library on the History of Women at Harvard University's Radcliffe Institute for Advanced Study. Similarly, Lepore had yet to take up her role as a staff writer for the *New Yorker,* or assume her current position as Harvard College professor.[27] *Common-Place* represented one of the first attempts to create a fully digital publication for the historical community. Each issue included feature columns, reviews, a teaching section, a focus on material culture, and an author interview. Now sponsored by the American Antiquarian Society and the University of Connecticut, the journal continues to publish quarterly.[28]

Between 2001 and 2015, the *Journal of American History* published reviews of over three hundred digital projects, covering a wide range of types, including digital collections, exhibits, teaching and learning projects, and many other hybrid projects.[29] The first website to be reviewed by the *Journal of American History* in 2001 was an outgrowth of women's history produced by women, and it was reviewed by a woman, Jane Kamensky. *DoHistory* was the companion site to Laurel Thatcher Ulrich's prize-winning 1990 book, *A Midwife's Tale,* and Writer-Producer Laurie Kahn-Leavitt and Director Richard Rogers's film, which dramatized both the historian's process and the life of the eighteenth-century midwife whose diary was at the heart of the story. Created by the Film Studies Center at Harvard University, the site allows visitors to explore Martha Ballard's diary, the historical investigations that went into piecing together Ballard's story, and the book and film that followed.[30]

By 2012 women made up 37.7 percent of the history faculty at four-year institutions, but that growth in numbers does not necessarily indicate an easing of the conditions that slow women's advancement.[31] And advancement matters deeply to the ways that the story of digital history gets told. This slow penetration of the upper ranks of the profession contributes to the erasure of women from the representation of leadership in digital history. One key reason is the ways that federal grant requirements are structured. For the most part, securing federal funding requires applicants to provide a significant amount of cost-shared resources from their university, often representing an amount equal to the requested funding. For women who are slower to advance to tenure and through the ranks of promotion, the resulting differential in salary can make generating that cost-share required to lead these projects very difficult. (Cost-share requirements are designed by funders to demonstrate the institutional investment in a project by eliciting a pledge of institutional resources. Thus, the higher a person's salary, the lower a percentage of commitment required to meeting the dollar amount threshold set by the funding agency.) Similarly, struggling under the additional responsibilities of service that are foisted upon women and people of color can make it remarkably difficult to make time for outside research projects that involve a level of service and management of their own that far exceeds that required to produce a single-authored monograph.

Beyond the Principal Investigator

Frequently the attribution of credit for digital work stops at the top of the masthead, so to speak, with the principal investigator or the project director. Even if this practice is simply a result of convenience, a shorthand, it contributes to the historical erasure of women from the field. While the funding agencies do not generally set terribly restrictive policies, each applicant organization sets the terms by which an individual can serve as a principal investigator. In many colleges and universities, individuals who hold staff positions are not eligible to hold the role. In other institutions, one must have a doctoral degree to serve as a PI. Those who have a doctoral degree but who are funded by sponsored research projects cannot offer any salary cost-share to the budgeting process, so they are frequently not named as principal investigators on projects, despite playing primary roles in the work. Given these restrictions, a true review of the history of digital history requires that we investigate the full breadth of the collaborative groups that have produced digital history in the past. Looking past the project directors to the project managers, the researchers, and the staff reveals that women were major contributors to this work at all stages along the way.

The University of Virginia's *The Valley of the Shadow* project, begun in 1991 and launched on the web in 1993, stands as the quite possibly the most visible digital history project in the field, winning the AHA's James Harvey Robinson Award for outstanding teaching aid in 2002 and the MERLOT (California State University's Multimedia Educational Resources for Learning and Online Teaching) History Classics award in 2005, among others.[32] While the project is often framed as the work of Edward Ayers and William G. Thomas, the list of integral coeditors also included Anne Sarah Rubin and Andrew Torget, both of whom have gone on to have significant careers in digital history. Rubin was a graduate student when she served as project manager for the project between 1993 and 1996, and she took off the 1995–1996 school year to work full time on the *Valley*. In 2000, she was coauthor with Edward Ayers of *The Valley of the Shadow: Two Communities in The American Civil War; Part I: The Eve of War*.[33] Rubin went on to earn an ACLS Digital Innovation Fellowship that contributed to the production of *Sherman's March and America: Mapping Memory*, the geospatial site that accompanied her 2014 book *Through the Heart of Dixie: Sherman's March and American Memory*.[34]

By the late 1990s, a collaborative team from the American Social History Project—Center for Media and Learning at the Graduate Center/City University of New York and the Center for History and New Media at George Mason University embarked on *History Matters: the U.S. Survey Course on the Web*. The leadership team for the project was evenly split between men and women, with Pennee Bender, Stephen Brier, Joshua Brown, Ellen Noonan, Roy Rosenzweig, and Kelly Schrum guiding the work that produced over one thousand edited and annotated primary sources, hundreds of website reviews, and a cluster of multimedia guides to analyzing various types of historical evidence.[35] In 2005, *History Matters* won the American Historical Association's James Harvey Robinson Prize for its contribution to the teaching and learning of history. In the years after *History Matters*, Bender, Noonan, and Schrum have produced dozens of digital history projects, many centered on pedagogy, from their respective roles at the American Social History Project–Center for Media and Learning (ASHP/CML) and RRCHNM.[36] As groundbreaking as this work was, the focus on "research" productivity in the authorizing structures of academe has tended to undervalue projects focused on teaching and learning.

Nonetheless, this initial work on the *Valley of the Shadow* and on *History Matters* took place in conjunction with the creation of some of the key institutions that supported the growth of digital history. Founded in 1981 by noted labor historian Herbert Gutman and Steven Brier, the American Social History Project (ASHP) was the first of the organizations to embrace digital means to develop and distribute their work. In 1990, ASPH became a research center at the City University of New York, known as the Center for Media Learning (CML). Joshua Brown took over as the executive director in 1998. ASHP/CML has always had a staff with many women in leadership positions, with current associate director Andrea Adas Vásquez joining in 1989, current associate director Pennee Bender joining in 1992, and Ellen Noonan joining in 1998. Each of these women has been integral to the development and success of a host of digital history projects over the last twenty-five years.[37]

A close collaborator with the ASHP/CML team, Roy Rosenzweig founded the Center for History and New Media within the History and Art History Department at George Mason University in 1994. RRCHNM also has always had women in key positions. Elena Razlogova joined Rosenzweig immediately, and served as programmer, system administrator, historian, and postdoctoral fellow until she departed to take up a position in the History Department at Concordia University in 2005. Kelly Schrum came to RRCHNM as a postdoctoral fellow in 2001 and has served as the director of Educational Projects since 2005. Stephanie Hurter joined the group as a research assistant in 2002 and worked as a web designer until she departed for the U.S. State Department in 2006, and she completed her doctorate in 2010. Amanda Shuman worked as a web developer from 2003 until she went to pursue a doctoral degree in Chinese History at the University of California, Santa Cruz in 2006. Joan Fragaszy Troyano joined the center as a research assistant in 2003, worked on history of science projects until her departure in 2005 to pursue a doctoral degree in American studies at George Washington University, and returned to the center between 2011 and 2014 to oversee the PressForward project. This author joined the group in 2004 as associate director of Educational Projects, and served as director of Public Projects from 2007 to 2017. Sheila Brennan joined the center as a research assistant in 2005 working on a wide range of public history projects, completed her doctorate in American history in 2010, and currently serves as the director of Strategic Initiatives. Finally, Jennifer Rosenfeld joined the group in 2010 and is the associate director of Educational Projects. This cohort of women only begins to scrape the surface of the people who have actively shaped the well over seventy projects undertaken by RRCHNM since 1994.[38]

Finally, much of the labor on the *Valley* project took place in the context of the Virginia Center for Digital History (VCDH), which Ayers and Thomas founded in 1998. VCDH produced many projects, and included a number of women in key leadership roles. For example, Kim Tryka served as assistant director, and made major technical, structural, and information architecture contributions to a host of projects. Tryka went on to be a data research librarian at the National Library of Medicine. Alice Carter also served as associate director, supporting teaching and learning programs. The staff alumni list includes women in project management, programming, and designing roles. Finally, the VCDH list of seventeen individual project directors includes only one woman, but the list of student alumni includes many, many women.[39]

All of these early projects and foundational centers suggest that women's work on digital history projects can get buried if researchers only pay attention to the founders and the individuals who are listed as principal investigators. In 2011, Tanya Clement and Doug Reside gathered a group of digital humanists at the Maryland Institute for Technology in the Humanities to discuss issues surrounding professionalization in digital humanities centers.[40] The conversations at that meeting recognized the significant degree to which digital humanities labor is performed by contingent faculty and classified staff, often who fail to receive sufficient credit for their efforts on projects. The two-day gathering resulted in a full report with clear recommendations and the creation of the "Collaborator's Bill of Rights." The recommendations call for academic institutions to allow for scholarly staff to serve as principal investigators on grant-funded work and strongly emphasize the need for each digital project to have a full and explicit credits page that accounts for everyone who has worked on the project.[41]

Making concerted progress on these factors related to authority and credit is essential in surfacing women's work in digital humanities and in digital history specifically, but it is not enough. As historians, digital and otherwise, watching the changing contours of our field, once these acknowledgments are made, researchers need to actually read the credit and about pages that accompany digital history projects, and to grapple with the range and significance of the contributions of the entire project team. Doing so will quickly surface the important work of the large numbers of women in digital history.

Furthermore, digital history project teams need to write explicitly about their work, about both the process and its scholarly implications. Over the course of his career, Roy Rosenzweig wrote enough articles and essays to fill an edited collection on digital history. In 2003, Edward Ayers and Will Thomas published one of the *American Historical Review*'s only hybrid digital articles based in the corpus of materials provided through the *Valley of the Shadow* project. Dan Cohen published numerous articles on his experiments in computational methods in historical research. Stephen Brier and Joshua Brown wrote about the preservation challenges surrounding the *September 11 Digital Archive* for the tenth anniversary of those tragic events. Cumulatively, these publications represent mark a lasting place in the authorized scholarly record.[42] For contingent faculty and staff being paid out of grant funding that requires the assignment of all of their labor to particular projects with no latitude for their own exploratory work, producing these kinds of peer-reviewed articles can be nearly impossible to do given the timescales and constraints of project deliverables. Unless the analytical writing is built into the grant or the project plan, it is extraordinarily difficult to fit in, and the review and revision cycles for traditional scholarly publishing can outlast the period of performance for the project. Nonetheless, digital historians must take this step so that the work gets recognized in the organs that perform the authorizing work for the field, even if those publications have historically published many fewer women than men within their issues.

Beyond the Academy

Another way to get a better sense of the significant work of women in digital history to is to widen the scope of the work held up as representative of the field to include the larger "historical enterprise."[43] Digital history continues to be represented in digital humanities in very narrow ways, often overlooking work that takes place outside the academy within the bounds of public history institutions such as libraries, archives, and museums. Even when historians of digital history recognize significant projects from libraries, archives, and museums, they fail to acknowledge the ways that collaborative efforts are represented as institutional products in those venues. This practice masks the individual contributions and achievements of all who labor to produce it, including women.

This situation is borne out in the way that the more than three hundred digital history projects reviewed in the pages of the *Journal of American History* cite the work under examination. Of the reviewed projects, sixty-eight (22 percent) explicitly list individual producers. A review of the names and some research suggests that of those with individual producers, twenty-eight projects (9 percent) listed women (often in conjunction with men) and the other forty projects (13 percent) listed only men. The remaining 239 projects point to some sort of institutional or organizational body as the producer: libraries and archives (31 percent), public history organizations (26 percent), universities (15 percent), and commercial entities (6 percent).[44] The general practice of these cultural heritage organizations is to recognize the organization, rather than the individual, as the creator/producer, which means that researchers need to do a little bit of digging to surface the ways that women have contributed to these projects.

Researchers need a broader definition of digital history work to surface the involvement of women employed at nonacademic organizations. An examination of the workforce in cultural heritage organizations suggests that women will continue to lead the way. Though no data exist specifically for history museums, the American Association of Museums reports that as of 2009, the field as a whole was almost evenly split between men and women, with women representing 47.5 percent of a workforce that totaled just over four hundred thousand employees.[45] The 2006 census data about the archival profession reported that 65 percent of the respondents were women. This gender balance represented a complete reversal of the ratio in the profession in 1956. Furthermore, there were almost twice as many women as men employed in academic archives. Finally, the trend in the field suggested an even more dramatic swing toward being dominated by women: nearly four out of five respondents under the age of thirty were women.[46] These individuals perform appraisal, selection, and description work that provides access to the body of evidence that historians rely upon to do their research. All of this is interpretive work that shapes the contours of our understanding of the past. Finally, the available data on public historians also suggest that the field is heavily female. While women represent roughly 40 percent of the historians in academic settings, a 2008 survey of public historians reports that women constitute nearly 65 percent of the staff in that field. Like the situation with the archivists, this number represented a complete reversal of the status in 1980, when women accounted for only 36 percent of the field.[47]

Libraries and archives pioneered digital work to provide access to historical materials. One of the earliest and most recognizable digital history projects was the Library of Congress's American Memory project.[48] Growing out of the National Digital Library Program (NDLP), American Memory eventually brought over nine million digitized sources related to U.S. history and culture to the public.[49] Martha Anderson was integral to that work. She joined the library staff in 1996 to work on the NDLP, and served as the production coordinator for American Memory. This pioneering project changed the field by dramatically increasing access to cultural heritage resources. Anderson went on to take a leadership role at the National Digital Information Infrastructure Preservation Program, shepherding over a decade of work on digital preservation and stewardship until her retirement in 2012.[50] Anderson was joined in this effort by many women who have become leaders in the field of preservation and access, such as Abby Smith Rumsey and Abbie Grotke.[51]

Documentary editing projects—often housed at universities but staffed by non-tenure-line scholars—also embraced digital means of production and distribution quickly. One of the first ventures in historical documentary editing to do so was the *Model Editions Partnership*, which was funded by the National Historical Publication and Records Commission at the National Archives in 1995. The partnership brought together seven major documentary projects to experiment with creating digital editions using a subset of the Text Encoding Initiative markup.[52] The key initial partners included the *Documentary History of the First Federal Congress*, edited by Charlene Bickford; the *Papers of Margaret Sanger*, edited by Esther Katz and Cathy Moran Hajo; and the *Papers of Elizabeth Cady Stanton and Susan B. Anthony*, edited by Ann Gordon. Eventually, the *Papers of Eleanor Roosevelt*, edited by Allida Black, joined the partnership. Together, these editors formed a significant portion of the leading edge of documentary editing practice, and transformed the workflows that govern the production of scholarly editions today. At the University of Virginia, similar efforts were afoot with the *Dolly Madison Digital Edition*, edited by Holly C. Shulman, which published its first installment online in 2004.[53] Shulman, who served as the director of Documentary Editions at VCDH, went on in 2007 to join forces with Susan Holbrook Perdue to found Documents Compass, a nonprofit organization that was part of the Virginia Foundation for the Humanities, to assist and advise documentary editors on the creation of digital editions.[54]

Experimentation with digital forms also infiltrated public history work, as museums and historical societies developed complex interpretive projects. One of the first of these began before there was a graphic web to be browsed, when in the late

1980s a coalition of members of the Society for the History of Technology applied to the National Science Foundation for a curriculum development grant to bring the history of science and technology into the social studies classroom, attracting women and minority students to the topics. Shepherded by Susan Smulyan and Bruce Sinclair, a large collaborative group of scholars, teachers, and public historians produced eight units that focused on textile technology in American History, drawing on the collections at the Lemelson Center for the Study of Invention and Innovation at the Smithsonian Institution's National Museum of American History, and the expertise at the Center for Children and Technology. Three of the eight modular curriculum units in the *Whole Cloth* project were published on the web in 1998.[55] Subsequently, Smulyan, from her position at Brown University, has spearheaded a number of collaborative cross-cultural and student-centered digital history projects. Since 2014, she has directed the John Nicholas Brown Center for Public Humanities and Cultural Heritage.[56]

While some were at work creating curriculums that brought together collections and new approaches to digital history, others were attempting to translate physical museum exhibits into the web environment. In October 2001, the National Museum of American History (NMAH) launched the website *A More Perfect Union: Japanese Americans and the U.S. Constitution.*[57] Jennifer Locke Jones, who is now chair and curator of the Division of Armed Forces History at NMAH, began her career at the museum working on the *A More Perfect Union* museum exhibit, which debuted in 1987. Then, she went on to be the online exhibit curator for the website, undertaking the task of creating a digital project that represented the complex issues and themes highlighted in the museum exhibit. Jones was joined in this venture by Judith Gradwohl, who was the web program director at the time, and a large team of collaborators at NMAH and at Second Story Interactive Studio.[58] The site won widespread praise, including taking the gold award in the history and culture category of the 2002 American Alliance of Museums' Media and Technology Professional Network's "Muse Awards" for work that best uses digital media to enhance the galleries, libraries, archives, museums (GLAM) experience.[59]

Innovative digital public history work was not solely concentrated at the Smithsonian Institution. One of the most advanced projects in digital public history at the time was the *Raid on Deerfield: Many Stories of 1704* from the Memorial Museum and the Potumtuck Valley Memorial Association. The site brought together collaborators from Native American and French Canadian cultural organizations to provide the multiple perspectives that five cultural groups (English, French, Wendat [Huron], Kanienkehaka [Mohawk], and Wobanaki) had on the conflict that took place in Deerfield, Massachusetts.[60] Led by Timothy Neumann, Lynne Spichiger, Angela Goebel-Bain, Barbara Mathews, Juliet Jacobson, and Don Button, the project brought together primary sources, personal narratives, composite characters, artifacts, and timelines on its website to illustrate the conflicting understandings of this deeply important historical moment that touched the lives of Native peoples, French

Canadians, and English colonial settlers.[61] The site won a number of awards, including second place in the 2005 Museums and the Web, Best of the Web: Online Exhibit category; a 2005 American Association of State and Local History Award of Merit; and a 2007 MERLOT History Classics Award.[62]

These few examples highlight both early exemplary projects and the key women who led that work. Unfortunately, for the majority of digital history projects from cultural heritage institutions, institutions that employ remarkable numbers of women, it will be very difficult to clearly identify the individuals who participated in their planning and development, since the majority of that work is identified as the work of the institution—the library, archive, museum, or historical society. Thus, dozens of other women who have produced extremely significant digital history work will remain nameless. Perhaps in the future, regardless of whether or not their positions demand that their work be "work for hire," the librarians, archivists, curators, editors, and public historians who collaborate on these projects will adhere to the recommendations put forth in the "Collaborators' Bill of Rights" and create full and explicit credits and acknowledgments for the work so that all of the contributions can be clearly known.

Even the most cursory survey of the contemporary digital history landscape reveals that the field is populated with many, many women who are doing important work directing projects, following new lines of inquiry, experimenting with innovative theories and methods, and pushing the field forward. If the fact that the quality of this work is on par with that of men's is evident, then we digital historians must ask ourselves why the stories we tell about the birth of the field include no women. If there is a groundswell of women doing exciting digital history work now, where did they come from? Were they there from the beginning? The recovery of the work of women on the first decade of the digital history web argues strongly that they were present and productive in this field from its earliest days. Ayers, Brier, Brown, Cohen, Rosenzweig, and Thomas undeniably shaped the field that current digital historians have inherited, but they were joined by a cast of women historians who also labored to mold digital history into the field we recognize today.

As with all systems that have been historically beset by unequal access to resources, opportunities, and power, the academy maintains structures that digital historians need to deconstruct so that the field can move forward. All practitioners must work purposefully to recognize the contributions of the underrepresented—those whose work is masked by inequity. Then, all members of the field must consciously revise our origin stories to be inclusive of these individuals and their influence. This essay tries to take small steps toward accomplishing this recovery and revision.

Yet, digital historians must also grapple with the systematic and structural factors that have resulted in the erasure. Returning women to the story is not enough. We have to continue to work to revise the academic systems that have slowed women's advancement to the senior ranks of the discipline of history. The field must dedicate itself to working for full and fair representation of all of the contributions to collaborative digital projects—from those of the principal investigator, to those of the contingent faculty and postdocs, to those of the project managers, to those of the staff, to those of the graduate and undergraduate research assistants. Finally, digital historians have to be willing to look further afield than traditional scholarly homes to recognize the major work that is occurring in the cultural heritage organizations where so many women are employed doing digital history work. Once the field begins to do this work, we will find ourselves much closer to being able to craft a more accurate and representative history of digital history.

Notes

1. Hockey, "History of Humanities Computing."
2. Thomas, "Computing."
3. Cohen and Rosenzweig, *Digital History*.
4. Klein, "Defining." See also Cohen et al., "Interchange," and Seefeldt and Thomas, "What Is Digital History."
5. At the Center for Spatial and Textual Analysis at Stanford University, Nicole Coleman is the research director of the Humanities+Design Lab, http://hdlab.stanford.edu/contact/index.html, and Paula Findlen is a PI on *Mapping the Republic of Letters*, http://republicofletters.stanford.edu/index.html. At the Center for Digital Humanities at the University of California, Los Angeles Miriam Posner is the DH Program Coordinator, UCLA Center for Digital Humanities; Miriam Posner and Janice Reiff are core faculty, http://www.cdh.ucla.edu/roles/faculty/.
6. RRCHNM Staff, http://chnm.gmu.edu/chnmstaff/.
7. Kalani Craig, http://www.kalanicraig.com/; Sharon Block, http://www.faculty.uci.edu/profile.cfm?faculty_id=5301; Jennifer Guiliano, http://jguiliano.com/ and Humanities Intensive Learning and Teaching (HILT), http://www.dhtraining.org/hilt2016/; *Immigrant Stories Digital Archive*, Immigration History Research Center & Archives, http://immigrants.mndigital.org/; *Mapping Slavery in Detroit*, http://mappingdetroitslavery.com/; Michelle Moravec, http://michellemoravec.com/; Kathryn Tomasek, http://kathryntomasek.org/.
8. *Driving through Time: The Digital Blue Ridge Parkway*, http://docsouth.unc.edu/blueridgeparkway/; Frankle's most recent project is *History Unfolded: US Newspapers and the Holocaust*, https://newspapers.ushmm.org/; Priya Chhaya, http://priyachhaya.com/ and https://forum.savingplaces.org/people/priya-chhaya.
9. American Council of Learned Societies, "ACLS Digital Innovation Fellows."
10. Anne Sarah Rubin's *Sherman's March and America: Mapping Memory*, http://shermansmarch.org/; Abigail Firey's *Carolingian Canon Law Project*, http://ccl.rch.uky.edu/; Ruth Mostern's *The Digital Gazetteer of the Song Dynasty*, http://songgis.ucmerced.edu/; and Kim Gallon's *Black Press Research Collective*, http://blackpressresearchcollective.org/.

11. Materials from both conferences are available from Bryn Mawr's institutional repository, http://repository.brynmawr.edu/greenfield_conference/.

12. Of the graduate students doing digital work that I advise in some way, five of six are women (Jannelle Legg, Amanda Regan, Sasha Hoffman, Jeri Wieringa, Erin Bush, Spencer Roberts).

13. Doing Digital History (2014): Women applicants = 50/70 (71 percent); participants 15/23 (65 percent), http://history2014.doingdh.org/about/participants/.

14. I queried the NEH database of funded projects (https://securegrants.neh.gov/publicquery/main.aspx) for the keywords "history" and "digital" or "online" or "website." I then aggregated the results, de-duplicated them based on application identification number, and coded them for the sex of the named principal investigator, or co-PI. This process is obviously an imprecise one based on assumptions about the sex characteristics associated with particular given names, and the gender presentation of subjects visible in images publicly available on the web.

15. For a sampling of these studies, see Savonick and Davidson, "Gender Bias in Academe."

16. Townsend, *History's Babel.*

17. Denbo, "Forum: History."

18. Rose, Graham, Grey, Schorske, and Smith, "Report." Quotation from American Historical Association, "Part Three."

19. Robert B. Townsend, "The Status of Women and Minorities in the History Profession," *Perspectives on History* (April 2002): http://historians.org/publications-and-directories/perspectives-on-history/april-2002/the-status-of-women-and-minorities-in-the-history-profession.

20. Lunbeck, *Status of Women*; American Historical Association, "CWH Statement; current AHA committee on women historians, American Historical Association, "Committee on Gender Equity."

21. Hochschild with Machung, *Second Shift.*

22. Modern Language Association, "Guidelines." The guidelines were originally adopted in May 2000 and were revised and approved in 2012.

23. Working Group on the Evaluation of Public History Scholarship, "Tenure, Promotion."

24. American Historical Association, "Guidelines," adopted June 2015.

25. The Quilt Index.

26. *Common-Place.*

27. Jane Kamensky, Harvard University, http://history.fas.harvard.edu/people/jane-kamensky; and Jill Lepore, Harvard University, http://scholar.harvard.edu/jlepore.

28. *Common-Place.*

29. The new Metagraph section sometimes includes digital scholarship and sometimes includes digital reviews. Otherwise, the reviews are listed in the individual *JAH* issues tables of contents as Digital History Reviews. The reviews conducted through June 2014 have also been reproduced on the *History Matters* website (http://historymatters.gmu.edu/

webreviews/). To conduct this analysis, I scraped the entries from the *History Matters* page and supplemented them by hand with the reviews that had been published between June 2014 and December 2015. I then hand-coded the entries by cited producer and/or creator.

30. *DoHistory*; Ulrich, *Midwife's Tale*; Kahn-Leavitt, *Midwife's Tale*; Kamensky, "Review of Do History"; and Jaffee, "Review of DoHistory."

31. White, Chu, and Czujko, *2012–13 Survey*, 87.

32. *Valley of the Shadow*; "Awards and Press Coverage."

33. "Project Staff and Background"; "Story"; Rubin and Ayres, *Valley of the Shadow*.

34. Rubin, *Through the Heart of Dixie*; Rubin, Bailey, and Bell, *Sherman's March and America*.

35. *History Matters*, http://historymatters.gmu.edu and http://historymatters.gmu.edu/credits.html.

36. *American Social History Project—Center for Media and Learning*, http://ashp.cuny.edu/; *Roy Rosenzweig Center for History and New Media*, http://chnm.gmu.edu/.

37. "Who We Are."

38. *Celebrating 20 Years of Digital History @CHNM*, http://20.rrchnm.org/.

39. VCDH Staff, http://www.vcdh.virginia.edu/index.php?page=Staff.

40. "Off the Tracks: Laying New Lines for Digital Humanities Scholars," http://mcpress.media-commons.org/offthetracks/.

41. "Recommendations," http://mcpress.media-commons.org/offthetracks/part-one-models-for-collaboration-career-paths-acquiring-institutional-support-and-transformation-in-the-field/a-collaboration/recommendations/ and "Collaborators' Bill of Rights," http://mcpress.media-commons.org/offthetracks/part-one-models-for-collaboration-career-paths-acquiring-institutional-support-and-transformation-in-the-field/a-collaboration/collaborators%E2%80%99-bill-of-rights/.

42. Rosenzweig, *Clio Wired*; Thomas and Ayers, "Overview"; Thomas and Ayers, "Differences Slavery Made"; Cohen, "History"; Cohen and Rosenzweig, "Web of Lies"; Cohen, "From Babel to Knowledge"; Brier and Brown, "September 11 Digital Archive."

43. The term "historical enterprise" is borrowed from Townsend, *History's Babel*.

44. Total: 307, 100 percent; Commercial: nineteen, 6 percent; Women: twenty-eight, 9 percent; Libraries and Archives: ninety-four, 31 percent; Men: forty, 13 percent; Public History Organizations: eighty-one, 26 percent; Universities: forty-five, 15 percent.

45. American Association of Museums, "Museum Workforce."

46. "Archival Census," statistics from pages 333–51.

47. Dichtl and Townsend, "Picture of Public History."

48. *American Memory*.

49. "About the Collections."

50. Ashenfelder, "Digital Pioneer."

51. Rumsey, *Rumsey Writes*; Grotke, *LinkedIn*, https://www.linkedin.com/in/abigail-grotke-378b808.

52. *Model Editions Partnership*; "Prospectus"; and Chesnutt, "Model Editions Partnership."

53. Shulman, *Dolly Madison Digital Edition.*

54. *Documents Compass,* https://web.archive.org/web/20170517164911/http://documentscompass.org/.

55. The website for *Whole Cloth: Discovering Science and Technology through American History* has not been maintained by the Lemelson Center, but it is preserved by the Internet Archive: https://web.archive.org/web/20060923075417/http://invention.smithsonian.org/centerpieces/whole_cloth/index.html. For an account of the early project work, see Smulyan, "Curriculum Development Report."

56. Susan Smulyan, Brown University, https://vivo.brown.edu/display/ssmulyan.

57. *More Perfect Union.*

58. Jones, "Curator Statement"; and "Credits."

59. "2002 Muse Awards."

60. *Raid on Deerfield.*

61. Spichiger and Jacobson, "Telling an Old Story"; Spichiger and Sturm, "Digital Deerfield 1704."

62. "About, Honors."

Bibliography

"About the Collections." *American Memory.* http://www.memory.loc.gov/ammem/about/about.html.

"About, Honors." *Raid on Deerfield.* http://1704.deerfield.history.museum/about/honors.jsp.

American Association of Museums. "The Museum Workforce in the United States (2009): A Data Snapshot from the American Association of Museums." November 2011. https://genderandarchives.files.wordpress.com/2012/03/museum-workforce.pdf.

American Council of Learned Societies. "ACLS Digital Innovation Fellows." http://www.acls.org/research/digital.aspx?id=798&linkidentifier=id&itemid=798.

American Historical Association. "Committee on Gender Equity." http://historians.org/about-aha-and-membership/governance/committees/committee-on-women-historians.

American Historical Association. "CWH Statement: 'Gender Equity in the History Workplace: Best Practices.'" American Historical Association, March 2006. http://www.historians.org/publications-and-directories/perspectives-on-history/march-2006/cwh-statement-gender-equity-in-the-history-workplace-best-practices.

American Historical Association. "Guidelines for Evaluation of Digital Scholarship in History." *American Historical Association.* http://historians.org/teaching-and-learning/digital-history-resources/evaluation-of-digital-scholarship-in-history/guidelines-for-the-evaluation-of-digital-scholarship-in-history.

American Historical Association. "Part Three: Summary of Findings." http://historians.org/about-aha-and-membership/aha-history-and-archives/archives/report-of-the-aha-committee-on-the-status-of-women/part-three-summary-of-findings.

American Memory. http://www.memory.loc.gov/ammem/index.html.

"Archival Census & Educational Needs Survey in the United States." *American Archivist* 69, no. 2 (Fall–Winter 2006): 291–618. http://www2.archivists.org/sites/all/files/ACENSUS-Final.pdf.

Ashenfelder, Mike. "Digital Pioneer: Martha Anderson." *The Signal: Digital Preservation*, December 4, 2012. http://blogs.loc.gov/digitalpreservation/2012/12/digital-pioneer-martha-anderson/.

"Awards and Press Coverage." *Valley of the Shadow.* http://valley.lib.virginia.edu/VoS/usingvalley/award.html.

Brier, Stephen, and Joshua Brown. "The September 11 Digital Archive: Saving the Histories of September 11, 2001." *Radical History Review* 111 (Fall 2011): 101–9.

Chesnutt, David. "The Model Editions Partnership: Historical Editions in the Digital Age." *D-lib Magazine*, November 1995. http://www.dlib.org/dlib/november95/11chesnutt.html.

Cohen, Daniel J. "From Babel to Knowledge: Data Mining Large Digital Collections." *D-Lib Magazine* 12, no. 3 (March 2006): 6–19.

Cohen, Daniel J. "History and the Second Decade of the Web." *Rethinking History* 8, no. 2 (2004): 293. doi:10.1080/13642520410001683950.

Cohen, Daniel J., Michael Frisch, Patrick Gallagher, Steven Mintz, Kirsten Sword, Amy Murrell Taylor, William G. Thomas, III and William J. Turkel. "Interchange: The Promise of Digital History." *Journal of American History* 95, no. 2 (2008): 451–91. doi:10.2307/25095630, http://www.jstor.org/stable/25095630.

Cohen, Daniel J., and Roy Rosenzweig. *Digital History: A Guide to Gathering, Preserving, and Presenting the Past on the Web.* Philadelphia: University of Pennsylvania Press, 2005. http://chnm.gmu.edu/digitalhistory/exploring/index.php.

Cohen, Daniel J., and Roy Rosenzweig. "Web of Lies? Historical Knowledge on the Internet." *First Monday,* December 2005, http://firstmonday.org/ojs/index.php/fm/article/view/1299/1219.

Common-Place: The Interactive Journal of Early American Life 1, no. 1 (September 2000). http://www.common-place-archives.org/vol-01/no-01/.

"Credits." *A More Perfect Union: Japanese Americans and the U.S. Constitution.* Smithsonian Institution, National Museum of American History. http://amhistory.si.edu/perfectunion/credits.html.

Denbo, Seth. "History as a Book Based Discipline." *Perspectives on History* (April 2015): https://www.historians.org/publications-and-directories/perspectives-on-history/april-2015/an-introduction.

Dichtl, John, and Robert B. Townsend. "A Picture of Public History: Preliminary Results from the 2008 Survey of Public History Professionals." *Public History News* 29, no. 4 (September 2009): 1, 14–15. http://ncph.org/wp-content/uploads/2009/12/2009-September-Newsletter-Compressed.pdf.

DoHistory. http://dohistory.org/.

Dublin, Thomas, and Kathryn Kish Sklar, eds. *Women and Social Movements, 1600–2000.* Center for the Historical Study of Women and Gender, State University of New York Binghamton and Alexander Street Press. http://womhist.alexanderstreet.com/.

Fogel, Robert William, and Stanley L. Engerman. *Time on the Cross: The Economics of American Slavery.* Reissue edition. New York: W. W. Norton & Company, 1995.

Hochschild, Arlie, with Anne Machung. *The Second Shift: Working Families and the Revolution at Home.* Rev. ed. New York: Penguin, 2012.

Hockey, Susan. "The History of Humanities Computing." In *A Companion to Digital Humanities,* edited by Susan Schreibman, Ray Siemens, and John Unsworth. Blackwell Companions to Literature and Culture. Oxford: Blackwell Publishing Professional, 2004. http://www.digitalhumanities.org/companion/.

Jaffee, David. "Review of DoHistory." *Public Historian* 23, no. 3 (Summer 2001): 125–27. doi:10.1525/tph.2001.23.3.125.

Jones, Jennifer Locke. "Curator Statement." *A More Perfect Union: Japanese Americans and the U.S. Constitution.* Smithsonian Institution, National Museum of American History. http://amhistory.si.edu/perfectunion/resources/curator.html.

Kahn-Leavitt, Laurie, writer and producer. *A Midwife's Tale* (film). PBS, American Experience, 1998.

Kamensky, Jane. "Review of Do History." *Journal of American History* 88, no. 1 (June 2001): 317–18. doi:10.2307/2675083.

Klein, Julie Thompson. "Defining." In *Interdisciplining Digital Humanities: Boundary Work in an Emerging Field.* Ann Arbor: University of Michigan Press, 2014. http://quod.lib.umich.edu/d/dh/12869322.0001.001/1:7/—interdisciplining-digital-humanities-boundary-work?g=dculture;rgn=div1;view=fulltext;xc=1.

Lunbeck, Elizabeth. *The Status of Women in the Historical Profession, 2005.* Washington, D.C.: American Historical Association, 2005. http://historians.org/Documents/About%20AHA%20and%20Membership/CWH-Report_5.20.05.pdf.

The Model Editions Partnership: Historical Editions in the Digital Age. http://modeleditions.blackmesatech.com/mep/editors.html.

Modern Language Association. "Guidelines for Evaluating Work in Digital Humanities and Digital Media." New York: Modern Language Association, 2012. https://www.mla.org/About-Us/Governance/Committees/Committee-Listings/Professional-Issues/Committee-on-Information-Technology/Guidelines-for-Evaluating-Work-in-Digital-Humanities-and-Digital-Media.

A More Perfect Union: Japanese Americans and the U.S. Constitution. Smithsonian Institution, National Museum of American History, 2001. http://amhistory.si.edu/perfectunion/experience/index.html.

"Project Staff and Background." *Valley of the Shadow.* http://valley.lib.virginia.edu/VoS/usingvalley/background.html.

"A Prospectus for Electronic Historical Editions." *The Model Editions Partnership: Historical Editions in the Digital Age.* May 1996. http://modeleditions.blackmesatech.com/mep/misc/prospectus.html.

Quilt Index. http://www.quiltindex.org/.

Raid on Deerfield: Many Stories of 1704. Potumtuck Valley Memorial Museum/Memorial Hall, 2004. http://1704.deerfield.history.museum/home.do.

Rose, Willie Lee, Patricia Albjerg Graham, Hanna Grey, Carl Schorske, and Page Smith. "Report of the American Historical Association Committee on the Status of Women (1970)." November 9, 1970. http://historians.org/about-aha-and-membership/aha-history-and-archives/archives/report-of-the-aha-committee-on-the-status-of-women.

Rosenzweig, Roy. *Clio Wired: The Future of the Past in the Digital Age.* New York: Columbia University Press, 2011.

Rubin, Anne Sarah. *Through the Heart of Dixie: Sherman's March and American Memory.* Chapel Hill, N.C.: University of North Carolina Press, 2014.

Rubin, Anne Sarah, and Edward Ayres. *The Valley of the Shadow: Two Communities in The American Civil War.* Pt. 1, *The Eve of War.* New York: W. W. Norton, 2000.

Rubin, Anne Sarah, Dan Bailey, and Kelley Bell. *Sherman's March and America: Mapping Memory.* http://shermansmarch.org/.

Rumsey, Abby Smith. *Rumsey Writes.* http://www.rumseywrites.com/.

Savonick, Danica, and Cathy N. Davidson. "Gender Bias in Academe: An Annotated Bibliography of Important Recent Studies." *HASTAC,* January 26, 2015. https://www.hastac.org/blogs/superadmin/2015/01/26/gender-bias-academe-annotated-bibliography-important-recent-studies.

Schreibman, Susan, Ray Siemens, and John Unsworth, eds. *Companion to Digital Humanities (Blackwell Companions to Literature and Culture).* Blackwell Companions to Literature and Culture. Oxford: Blackwell Publishing Professional, 2004. http://www.digitalhumanities.org/companion/.

Seefeldt, Douglas, and William G. Thomas, III. "What Is Digital History? A Look at Some Exemplar Projects." *Perspectives on History* 47, no. 5 (May 2009): 40–43. http://digitalcommons.unl.edu/historyfacpub/98/.

Shulman, Holly C., ed. *The Dolly Madison Digital Edition.* Charlottesville, Va.: University of Virginia Press, 2004–2016. http://rotunda.upress.virginia.edu/dmde/default.xqy.

Smulyan, Susan. "Curriculum Development Report: Discovering Science and Technology Through American History." n.d. http://xroads.virginia.edu/~drbr/s_muy1000.html.

Spichiger, Lynne, and Juliet Jacobson. "Telling an Old Story in a New Way: Raid on Deerfield: The Many Stories of 1704." In *Museums and the Web 2005: Proceedings,* edited by J. Trant and D. Bearman. Toronto: Archives & Museum Informatics, 2005. http://www.museumsandtheweb.com/mw2005/papers/spichiger/spichiger.html.

Spichiger, Lynne, and Chris Sturm. "Digital Deerfield 1704: A New Perspective on the French and Indian Wars." *First Monday* 10, no. 6 (June 2005). http://firstmonday.org/ojs/index.php/fm/article/view/1252/1172.

"The Story behind the Valley Project." *Valley of the Shadow.* http://valley.lib.virginia.edu/VoS/usingvalley/valleystory.html.

Thomas, William G., III. "Computing and the Historical Imagination." In *Companion to Digital Humanities,* edited by Susan Schreibman, Ray Siemens, and John Unsworth.

Blackwell Companions to Literature and Culture. Oxford: Blackwell Publishing Professional, 2004. http://www.digitalhumanities.org/companion/.

Thomas, William G., III, and Edward L. Ayers. "An Overview: The Differences Slavery Made; A Close Analysis of Two American Communities." *American Historical Review* 108, no. 5 (December 1, 2003): 1299–1307. doi:10.1086/529967.

Thomas, William G., III, and Edward L. Ayers. "The Differences Slavery Made: Overview." Virginia Center for Digital History, American Historical Review. http://www2.vcdh.virginia.edu/AHR/.

Townsend, Robert B. *History's Babel: Scholarship, Professionalization, and the Historical Enterprise in the United States, 1880–1940*. Chicago: University of Chicago Press, 2013.

Townsend, Robert B. "The Status of Women and Minorities in the History Profession." *Perspectives on History* (April 2002). http://historians.org/publications-and-directories/perspectives-on-history/april-2002/the-status-of-women-and-minorities-in-the-history-profession.

"2002 Muse Awards." *American Alliance of Museums*. https://www.aam-us.org/programs/awards-competitions/2002-muse-award-winners/.

Ulrich, Laurel Thatcher. *A Midwife's Tale: The Life of Martha Ballard, Based on Her Diary, 1785–1812*. New York: Knopf, 1990.

Valley of the Shadow: Two Communities in the American Civil War. Virginia Center for Digital History–University of Virginia Library, Valley Project. http://valley.lib.virginia.edu/.

White, Susan, Raymond Chu, and Roman Czujko. *The 2012–13 Survey of Humanities Departments at Four-Year Institutions*. College Park, Md.: Statistical Research Center, American Institute of Physics, 2014. Sponsored by the American Academy of Arts & Sciences.

"Who We Are." American Social History Project—Center for Media Learning. Graduate Center, City University of New York. http://ashp.cuny.edu/who-we-are.

Working Group on the Evaluation of Public History Scholarship. "Tenure, Promotion, and the Publicly Engaged Academic Historian: A Report." *Perspectives on History* (September 2010). http://www.historians.org/publications-and-directories/perspectives-on-history/september-2010/tenure-promotion-and-the-publicly-engaged-academic-historian-a-report.

PART VI

SITUATEDNESS

PART VI][Chapter 20

Can We Trust the University?

Digital Humanities Collaborations with Historically Exploited Cultural Communities

AMY E. EARHART

Social justice digital humanities work is increasingly outward facing and community and activist oriented.[1] However, historical abuses of communities and systemic inequities present formidable challenges for those who seek to develop partnerships with vulnerable populations. Excellent work in negotiating this long-standing problem is occurring in pockets of digital humanities work, with scholars working in indigenous studies leading the way. However, we must develop a set of best practices for all of us who are working with historically marginalized communities, recognizing that an understanding of individual and group situatedness is crucial to digital humanities practices. Such an approach involves both introspection and a historical understanding of the power dynamics within institutions and communities. In this chapter I would like to think through how we might, as a matter of best practices, begin to address such an issue. First, we must understand the relationship between our localized environment and the community with which we would like to partner. Second, we must interrogate issues of ownership and control. Careful attention to both must occur, for without such introspection, we will end up exploiting communities with which we engage. Further, social justice digital humanities practitioners must begin the difficult task of articulating best practices that account for such issues, including the development of safeguards for communities. A baseline concern needs to be that we might think about our materials as data, but that the data are not a free-floating signifier; instead, that data are always a part of a community or individual.

Here I want to turn away from thinking about this as an inclusion issue or an issue about the ideas or texts that we study. There has been ample, important work documenting such issues.[2] What has received less attention as a practice in digital humanities is how we understand our work in relationship to ownership or to knowledge practices in the service of social justice. As I was researching current digital humanities work in preparation for this chapter, I found that there is a revealing and disturbing use of the term "exploitation" by scholars in their understanding of digital data. One might exploit "diverse digital media and strategies while maintaining the scholarly apparatus of a research paper" (Johanson et al., 132); we might find funded digital humanities projects such as Alan Smeaton's "The Digital Humanities (DigHum): The Formation of a National Working Group on the Exploitation of Data in the Humanities" or the report "Exploitation of Cultural Content and Licensing Models," which discusses rights of cultural institutions, such as museums, but never mentions the thorny issues of ownership of, say, indigenous artifacts.[3] The blithe way that one might consider how to exploit data points to the underlying assumption that data are without value, that items have no cultural connection to those who produced the knowledge, is a sleight-of-hand move that provides a dual exploitation as value is removed and, at the same time, the value of the cultural knowledge is displaced and even consumed. Alexander R. Galloway and Eugene Thacker in *The Exploit: A Theory of Networks* emphasize the complications of network culture, where "what is at stake in any discussion of the political dimensions of networks is, at bottom, the experience of living within networks, forms of control, and the multiple protocols that inform them."[4] Networks are contingent upon "technological, biological, social, and political" forces and, as such, need to be analyzed within such complicated webs, effectively a similar argument to how intersectional feminism understands power relations. This is not an issue with our field per se, but about how the methodological approaches of turning lived experience and cultural expression into digital data for computer manipulation, the way that we gather data, is disconnected from the recognition that data are always connected to people and to lived experience. It is a humanities problem that centers the humanities within technological questions, the heart of digital humanities. It is the center of how we must think about the digital content that we produce, for to lose sight of the layers of issues of human "ownership" and "exploitation" does a disservice not only to those communities that are re-exploited but to our ability to produce scholarly knowledge and advance digital humanities.

Intersectional feminism provides the greatest guidance to ethical approaches to digital humanities and has been taken up by digital humanities scholars across a range of disciplines, offering, according to Roopika Risam, "a viable approach to cultural criticism in the digital humanities."[5] Enacted intersectionality in "existing digital humanities projects," notes Risam, "provide examples of how, in small and large ways, theory and method can be combined to address recurring questions of the role of race, class, gender, ability, sexuality, nationality, and other categories of difference within the field," crucial connections central to addressing the way that scholars engage with the cultural production and knowledge of marginalized groups. Other scholars, including Moya Bailey, Alexis Lothian, Amanda Phillips, Anne Cong-Huyen, F. M. Ettarh, and Anna Everett, also view intersectionality as a means to ethically engage in digital humanities work, particularly in their representations of situated standpoints and resistance to essentialist definitions, as theorized by Patricia Hill Collins.[6] Intersectionality helps us to unpack multiple layers of exploitation, such as the tensions involved with labor and digital projects, as discussed in T. L. Cowan and Jasmine Rault's "The Labour of Being Studied in a Free Love Economy," which makes clear the ways that volunteer labor, even that born of love, might exploit.[7] As such, the positionality of the scholar engaged in the digital humanities project necessarily shifts the way that she interacts with the project. For example, scholars embedded in the project's represented community have an opportunity to shift narratives and to tell their own stories.[8] The recognition of one's own experience in relationship to complex positionality is crucial to understanding how we, as digital humanities scholars, might work in ethical, nonexploitive ways, attending to what might be missteps due to lack of consideration.

We are at a moment where we need to think about how the exploitation of data is related to historical exploitation of people(s), to reconnect the digital with embodied experience. Mark Turin notes, "Archives become more complex when the 'documents' in question are representations of human 'subjects'" (Turin, 453).[9] Documents are never devoid of embodiment, as we might never use the term "exploitation of data" without understanding that, eventually, exploitation of data has real impact on individuals and communities. A division of human subjects and documents leads to problematic interactions with those with whom we are working to digitize. We need to think about how our data embody experience. One of the most interesting projects to wrestle with the disconnect is Jacqueline Wernimont's "Safe Harbor: Hosting California's Eugenics Data."[10] Wernimont and her collaborator Alexandra Minna Stern are working with a compiled dataset of California eugenic sterilization records, and are using both sensory and audio representations to show the numbers of sterilizations conducted over time. Wernimont notes, "There is no data without people.... Exploring the vulnerabilities of quantifying and archiving the human experience, we ask, 'How can we better care for people by caring for their data?'"[11] Contending that a central concern of digital humanities is the conflict between open access and privacy, or individuals' "right to be forgotten," the project forces us to consider how the haptic and sonification approaches dislocate from the lived experiences while, at the same time, sensory and auditory feedback recenters our bodies, recenters the person. No longer can we displace the human, as we are engaged with the person who is the data experienced through our own body.

Another way to view the centeredness of the human body is to recognize the way that bodies have been used or exploited and how such exploitations are related to cultural knowledge exploitation. In the "Safe Harbor" project there is a desire to represent the impact of racist ideologies that disproportionately impact Latinx and African Americans, while at the same time avoid reproducing historic exploitation. Similar questions arise in my work "Millican Race 'Riot': 1868," where a leader of the freedman's community, Pastor George Brooks, was lynched and disfigured. How does an archive represent the horror of the lynching without revictimizing Brooks?

Such questions have become even more central in the midst of the numerous videos documenting the deaths of black men in America, from Tamir Rice to Philando Castile to Terence Crutcher, all of whose deaths were played and replayed as viral videos spread across the internet. While some view such videos as proof of police brutality, there remains an element of spectatorship similar to the gaze applied to lynching victims, a reexploitation that turns the individual death into a spectacle for consumption. Those of us working with such sensitive materials, materials intimately connected to an often violent embodied experience, need to carefully consider how the intersections of race, gender, class, and disability work in tandem to create a particular power expression.

To center the human experience, to rethink our working partnerships with historically marginalized communities, necessitates the development of best practices, but we have not yet, collectively, considered how we might articulate a framework for research. We might look to indigenous studies and museum studies communities for guidance in developing best practices. Kimberly Christen Withey, a digital humanities and indigenous studies scholar, has a long history of scholarship and digital project production that is careful to consider ownership and concepts of openness, including the idea that "information wants to be free."[12] Kimberly Christen Whithey's Mukurtu is a "community archive platform . . . adaptable to the local cultural protocols and intellectual property rights systems of Indigenous communities."[13] Interrogating ideas of ownership, recognizing historical abuses of colonization, Christen Withey's projects reject a fully open access approach, instead recognizing that working with particular groups and ideas requires "us to look *differently* or *not look* at all."[14] Such work is built on relationships of trust and a clear understanding of how the academic's relationship to the project must be shaped not by his or her own goals but by the partner communities' knowledge, practices, and beliefs. Academics working on projects must be willing to cede control from the individual and the academic institution and position the project within a community or activist site.

What I am suggesting is that every project must attend to the specificity of the cultural context in which the project is being produced. The most obvious, but not only, issue of specificity is the cultural context of the materials under study. The long-standing *Tibetan and Himalayan Library (THL)* provides one example of how we might think through issues not only of ownership but of the specificity of the materials within cultural contexts. The *THL* emphasizes "technology, knowledge, and community" and demonstrates a commitment to the community that it is studying, prioritizing "social networking facilities, as well as the means to facilitate scholarship to have socially productive impact in Tibetan and Himalayan Communities."[15] Scholars have a responsibility to address the ways that technological specifications might force Western representations of knowledge onto materials that do not use such systems. Linda E. Patrik cautions, in a discussion of Tibetan texts, that "it is important to respect the control that indigenous scholars have over their own textual heritage," and that "the model of broad 'access' that often motivates western digitization efforts does not apply universally, and may in some cases go directly against the indigenous textual tradition."[16] Central to the work with any historically marginalized group is an understanding of the cultural construction of ownership, leading to an equitable partnership that positions the control of materials within the community, rather than within the academy.

In addition to careful attention to ownership, we must consider how our digital representation and manipulations impact knowledge production itself. When we think about digital humanities projects, we need to recognize that there is more than a set of technological specifications that represent best practices. For example, the University of Nebraska has released "Best Practices for Digital Humanities Projects," a document focused on technical issues related to interoperability and preservation including the use of XML, EAC, METS and other such standards.[17] The problem with such a narrow focus, however, is that such metadata standards may run counter to certain marginalized communities' understanding of preservation or knowledge. For digital humanists, best practices might be better understood as ethical guidelines of practice. Tibetan texts, for example, require technological functions that are aware of the cultural specificity of the materials. TEI-XML is normally applied to textual materials to ensure preservation and interoperability, yet in the case of Tibetan texts "the challenge" is how to represent what "escapes this kind of basic encoding."[18] Patrik describes her team's response to the cultural encodings surrounding the text, encodings that include the readers' bodily movements, hand movements, chanting, and visualizations, none accounted for by TEI yet "integral parts of the text and its meaning, without which it cannot be said to be truly preserved." We see this same issue in the Modern Language Association's (MLA's) "Guidelines for Authors of Digital Resources," where the focus of the guidelines privileges an academic, Western understanding of knowledge and ownership. The "Authorship and Credit" statement doesn't represent how a community might own knowledge. How, for example, does one extend credit to oral histories? What responsibilities does a digital scholar have to the individual who recounts a story and also to the community that has, over years, built a particular oral narrative?

On the topic of "Authorship and Credit," the MLA "Guidelines for Authors of Digital Resources" direct authors to

> identify all individuals and groups responsible for the creation and maintenance of the resource. Include individuals' institutional affiliations when relevant. Information to be given might include the following:
>
> Authors and Researchers
> Editors
> Designers
> Software developers and other collaborators

>Institutions or organizations hosting the site
>Funders
>Contact information[19]

The same issue appears in the statements in "Citations and Reuse," which suggest that one should "offer appropriate citations for content quoted or republished in the resource."[20] If one would like to include oral histories of historically marginalized communities, a mere citation may be another form of exploitation and a misuse of materials. As indigenous scholars have demonstrated, some stories are not for public consumption. Guidelines must consider this within an ethical framework of cultural context, rather than presuppose a linear and individual understanding of ownership.

We need to develop an ethics of practice that account for what Martha Nell Smith, digital humanities scholar and executive editor of the *Dickinson Electronic Archives,* has called the "Human Touch," where Smith situates issues of identity as central and inextricable from the formation and use of technologies.[21] We have outstanding feminist digital humanities projects, such as *Women Writers Online* or *Orlando,* in which we might imagine "the tools and technologies of the digital archive are themselves feminist," yet, as outlined by Jacqueline Wernimont in her analysis of *Orlando,* such structures are complicated and are in danger of cooptation through their very structures.[22] Twitter has become a site in which tensions between feminist use and platform/technology have clashed. As Dorothy Kim and Eunsong Kim lament, "We enter Twitter because we believe it's a medium that's not hostile to women of color writers, thinkers, and conversations—but perhaps we should reconsider."[23] While Kim and Kim recognize that the work occurring within Twitter's space may be liberatory, the platform itself is closed and hostile, resisting the anticolonialist work that is underway. Further concerning, and key to this discussion, is the recent move by the Library of Congress to archive all public tweets, a move that "follows an ancient model of provenance/collecting: the objects belong to the purchaser, The Man With The Papers."[24] Reminiscent of the treatment of indigenous artifacts by libraries and museums, we now see another questionable archiving practice, with the added layer of potential exploitation by those who will treat the Twitter collection as a mineable dataset. Certainly copyright law is fuzzy on the use of proprietary individual knowledge when converted into such large datasets, and ethically this is even murkier as individual knowledge producers lose control of their materials and have no say in how such materials might be used. However, data mining of tweets is not necessarily exploitive and depends on who is utilizing the tweets and how such a dataset is constructed. Central to ethical engagement with large datasets that contain individual identifiers, such as is the case with tweets, is careful consideration of the positionality of the researcher and the development of a methodology that protects the privacy of individuals. Though the tweets are public, the shift in their intended use, from individual expression to algorithmic manipulation, and the rearticulation of the data within a new medium, such as a database or digital humanities tool, require new practices. While it is crucial that we continue to work for technological standardizations and the lure of big data is exciting, we must be aware that individuals might not be best served by rigid standardizations that presuppose particular knowledge or ownership structures. Instead, we must develop an ethics of practice that put technological standardization in dialogue with individual and community specificities.

Digital humanists have begun to develop best practices for certain forms of collaboration, providing models that we might use to articulate how we would like our field to interact with historically marginalized communities. The 2010 workshop "Off the Tracks: Laying New Lines for Digital Humanities Scholars" produced the "Collaborator's Bill of Rights," which made important steps toward defining ethical practices as about alternative academic (alt-ac) individuals involved in projects.[25] The more recent "A Student Collaborators' Bill of Rights" has refocused our attention on undergraduate students involved in projects.[26] What remains missing from these standards, though, are the collaborations with those connected to the subjects that we are studying and an ethics that focuses on collaborations that occur outside of academic structures. For example, the New York University "Digital Humanities Best Practices: Engaging a Collaborator" document provides important guidelines for managing collaborations, but it assumes a certain type of collaborator, "individuals/institutions."[27] Such an assumption supposes that the primary collaborator will be an individual in academia or a related field, such as museum studies or a library. We who work with communities in collaborative partnerships and who understand that objects of study are not neutral but intimately connected to individuals must work to articulate a statement of ethics of practice.

To meet such a goal, we need to shift our understanding of digital humanities projects away from the academic, the principal investigator (PI), the project team, and to a more holistic representation of the participant. In our current publish-or-perish, highly competitive academic environment, we are driven to seize credit, ownership, of projects to survive. However, this narrative also contributes to exploitation and abuses of the communities that are connected to the materials we would like to digitize. We need to develop a model of collaboration that positions the academic as an equal, even lesser, partner in the relationship, which is the only model that will begin to balance inequity. Moya Z. Bailey's rearticulation of Mark Sample's collaborative construction centers a community-driven feminist approach that practices what she calls digital alchemy, "the ways that women of color, Black women in particular, transform everyday digital media into valuable social justice media magic that recodes failed dominant scripts," and provides a model for how we might articulate ethical practices.[28] Bailey argues that ongoing collaborative consent places authority and control in the hands of the knowledge producer rather than the scholar. To best achieve this, we must be clear about our specific position. For all the concerns regarding the diminishing position of the academy and academics, we remain in a very privileged and powerful position. We must remember this when we interact with historically marginalized communities, which have been stripped of control of their own materials over centuries, sometimes by the very institutions that are our employers. Traditional markers of ownership might be redefined in our projects. Timothy B. Powell and Larry P. Aitken model authorship attribution that is community oriented and recenters cultural ownership in their article "Encoding Culture: Building a Digital Archive Based on Traditional Ojibwe Teachings."[29] Powell, senior research scientist at the University of Pennsylvania Museum of Archaeology and Anthropology at the time of publication, cedes authority to Aitken, tribal historian at Leech Lake Ojibwe reservation, throughout the essay, often commenting on his lack of "adequate training" to properly interpret the materials, a role that may be filled only by the tribal historian; hence the shared authorship of the article (261). When working with historically marginalized groups, we must give up the central position of the academic in projects, and by doing so we have much to gain.

Each digital humanist practices within a localized environment that presents different challenges for working with historically exploited cultural communities, and we must interrogate our own position, both individually and within our institutional structures. This has proved particularly important to the work I have undertaken. I work at Texas A&M University (TAMU), a land grant university that began in 1871 as Agricultural and Mechanical College of Texas. For most of its existence TAMU was military, all male and all white, admitting women in 1963 and ending segregation in 1964. TAMU likes to think of itself as unique, but an institutional history of racism and sexism is not uncommon. Brown University, for example, in 2005 launched an investigation of the university's connection to the practice of enslavement and other schools, including Emory University, the University of North Carolina at Chapel Hill, and the University of Virginia, followed Brown's lead. Some schools, such as Georgetown and William and Mary, are launching digital projects that document their connection to slavery.[30] Recognizing the structural legacy of the exploitation of enslaved peoples, the institutions have made a variety of important recommendations including more realistic representations of university histories, targeted endowments, public outreach, and scholarly ventures. Brown also recommends that "the University's Corporation, administration, and faculty will undertake a major research and teaching initiative on slavery and justice."[31] Such responses to historical abuses are to be commended, yet such histories provide a challenge for scholars who are interested in developing partnerships with historically marginalized communities. To assume that such histories have no impact on partnership efforts or to assume that a scholar is not seen as intimately affiliated with his or her institution, and his or her institution's past, will stymie the ability of digital scholars to develop the types of digital projects that benefit scholarship and the larger public. We digital scholars must always situate ourselves in relationship to our institutional pasts if we want to ethically work with groups who have every reason to be suspicious of our institutions. For example, the segregated past of my home institution, while long ago, continues to impact the way that our local

African American community understands those associated with the university. Efforts to build partnerships to explore race-related histories of our communities, including the ongoing project "The Millican 'Riot,' 1868," are necessarily inflected by past and present events. To ignore the past is to miss a chance to begin to have the difficult conversations necessary to have a positive, collaborator-focused project.

"The Millican 'Riot,' 1868" archives materials related to the 1868 event that occurred in Millican, Texas, a small town located fifteen miles from Texas A&M University, that may well have been the largest so-called race riot in Texas. Details remain unclear, but we believe that during the first KKK rally in Millican, armed freedmen fired on the rally, driving the Klan out of town. After the rally, George Brooks, a local Methodist preacher, former Union soldier, and Union League organizer, began a black militia. Several confrontations occurred, including an attempted lynching of the brother of a former slave owner, a march on the county seat of Bryan by a large group of armed blacks, and the demand for payment for work by Miles Brown, a local black contractor, all of which ended in an assault on the local black community and deaths of numerous black women, children, and men. Working with undergraduate students, "The Millican 'Riot,' 1868" project is an Omeka-installed digital archive that houses primary materials related to the event. What is clear from our initial work is that there are conflicting reports on the cause of the riot and of the numbers of dead, which newspapers report as being from five to one hundred, and the local black community suggests that there is an unmarked mass grave. As we might expect, the white-owned newspapers and government records tell the story from one perspective, that of the white community and political structure. There are few print records of the black communities' responses to the event. If I wanted to develop a project that tried to speak to other narratives of what the *Daily Austin Republican* labeled in its reporting on the event a "massacre," then I would need to work with local community members to see if oral histories provided additional details about the event. Yet how does a white professor who is employed by an institution with a well-known segregationist past develop a partnership with a local community to explore such a painful event?

As a white scholar who has worked in African American literature since the 1990s, I have spent a good amount of time thinking through the ways that my experience and position might impact my scholarship and how others view my intervention into such work. What I hadn't considered within the context of scholarship was what my institutional employment and my local community might mean to the work I undertake. I interpret literature. I work with texts, often texts that have nothing to do with what occurred within my local community. Beyond recognizing that working at an R1 (Research 1) institution gives me more funding and time for research than other schools, my thoughts about past and current climate issues were confined to how my colleagues and students might experience their time at Texas A&M. None of this, however, carried weight with my potential collaborators. I might say that Texas A&M is an R1, public, land grant institution. The words that the local African American community that I hoped to work with associate with my institution are "exclusion," "white," and "racism." To create a partnership that is based on the nonexploitive principles I have outlined at the beginning of this essay would involve serious consideration of my institution's past and present.

A few years ago Texas A&M University decided to digitize old yearbooks, a typical activity that many colleges and universities undertake. However, examination of our (and it is important that scholars own the history of the institution in which they work, for good or bad) yearbooks is more than a bit disturbing. Early clubs include the Kala Kinasis German Dancing Club, the Swastikas Dancing Club, and the Kream and Kow Klub, all student groups affiliated with white nationalism and the KKK.[32] Pictures of student organizations include the K.K.K.'s, wearing their Klan robes, with typical cross insignia, hoods, and brandishing swords. Even more telling is that while the Klan often wore the uniform to remain anonymous, so entrenched and normalized was this K.K.K group that the hooded members and their leadership are named in the yearbook. When the university took on the yearbook project, discussions occurred regarding how to treat this material. The library rightfully decided to be transparent about the images in the yearbook (see Figure 20.1). At the same time, they added a statement to the online collection that made clear that the images were problematic: "Cushing Memorial Library and Archives strives to make our digital collection resources available and useful to our faculty, staff, students, alumni, researchers and the general public. Through our web site, the Libraries offers public access to a wide range of information, including historical materials that may contain offensive language or negative stereotypes. Such materials must be viewed in the context of the relevant time period. Texas A&M does not endorse the views expressed in such materials."[33] Some may view the statement as an artful political move, but such statements are crucial interventions in the digitization of historical materials. Given Texas A&M University's segregated past, the materials need to be glossed against current university values. Like all digital humanities projects, the situatedness of the institution and of the content is crucial.

The Klan student groups are not the only marker of the racism of the institution.[34] If you had any doubt about the position of African Americans, the images of the "Negro janitors," and the ode to "Uncle Dan"—who "does the work of ten young niggers"—would assure you that African Americans were welcome in the university community only if they occupied subservient positions (see Figures 20.2 and 20.3).[35]

To develop collaborative partnerships with historically marginalized communities, we must, once again, recognize that the individual, in this case the academic, is situated within the context in which he or she works. The structures of academia are built on exploitation of particular groups, whether exploitation through land seizure from indigenous peoples or enslaved labor, as is the documented case with numerous universities. Other exploitations are built into our structures, such as is the case with the long-standing racism that delineates the culture of Texas A&M, which

Can We Trust the University? [379

Figure 20.1. Page for the K.K.K.'s "club" in the University Yearbook. *Long Horn*, 1906.

creates a conundrum when we return to the same groups and ask them to work with us to preserve and collect their cultural heritage and knowledge. Why would an African American community group want to work with an individual in an institution that institutionalized the Klan, an organization known for brutal attacks and murders? Why would an African American community group trust that their truth, their knowledge would be told accurately? For digital projects, an examination of such structures must be the center of the collaboration, rather than an afterthought. As we build partnerships for digital projects looking outward, we have a responsibility to plumb the depths of our institutions and our adopted communities. We cannot see ourselves as separate from these entities, as our partners rightly see that our work is constrained by such structures.

The Negro Janitors

THERE are some who will probably smile at this page, and yet, that is your privilege. But we have placed this page in the book in keeping with a policy of placing credit where credit is due. It is these men, under the able direction of Capt. Watkins, who police the campus from dawn until dark, and make the most of the impossible job of beautifying our campus.

They go about their appointed duties so quietly that their presence is hardly known, but the calibre of their valuable work is easily seen. Faithful and honest, they are a happy-go-lucky lot, and too often the butt of some cadet's joke or prank.

Most of them are campus characters, and have a history that is linked hand in hand with the growth of the College. Many is the yarn that they can spin of the "good old days," and their knowledge of campus lore is unlimited. Their only weapon is a broom, but they use it to the best advantage.

Their duties consist of everything from waking one up to go to class to making braces to keep some ancient dormitory wall from falling, and each building bears some unique contraption of one sort or another, products of their own hands.

Take a stroll behind the mess hall some day at noon, and watch the Brothers of the Broom in their hot contests, and then take a good lesson in cheerfulness and sheer joy in living.

Figure 20.2. Page featuring "The Negro Janitors." *Long Horn*, 1932.

Can We Trust the University? [381

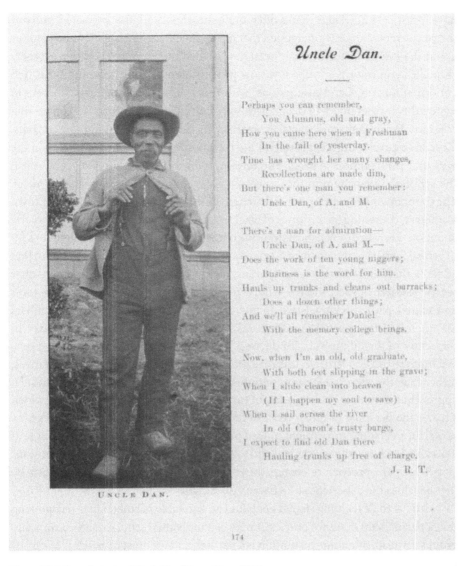

Figure 20.3. Page featuring "Uncle Dan." *Long Horn,* 1906.

In 2014 I received an email from Charles Swenson, an amateur historian who was part of the Camptown Texas Ten Counties Historical Explorers. Swenson had located the Millican "Riot" project website and wanted to discuss possible collaboration. The Camptown Texas group, formed of community activists and church leaders, has a history of exemplary work in documenting African American experiences in Texas, successfully renovating the Camptown Cemetery in Brenham, Texas, an important African American cemetery, and obtaining historical markers to commemorate black history events. The knowledge possessed by individuals who participate in the group is rich and often underestimated by scholars. The group members have historical knowledge that is often undocumented and unappreciated, and our initial conversations have suggested that group members have heard family stories about the events that shift the official narrative of the events. To build a partnership with community groups is a slow process. Trust needs to be built through continual meetings and discussions, with frank admission about the context in which the partnership will occur. Through a number of meetings and email discussions, through fits and starts, we are moving closer to developing shared goals. Crucial to developing trust is to give the community group full veto power on the way that information is used. The development of shared projects that reveal the scholar's investment in the concerns of the community group is also crucial. The Camptown Texas group has researched the individuals buried in the Camptown Cemetery, compiling life histories of black citizens who have received little scholarly attention. Early in our collaboration, one of the participants asked if I might do a bit of genealogical research for him. I agreed and completed family history research that added to his family history, an important moment where the community member set the research agenda and the scholar used proprietary, paywalled research tools and shared skills and knowledge. In fact, many of the community group members are interested in personal family stories and want to position such narratives in the center of digital projects. To develop trust is to listen to the community's central interest and concerns, in this case individual histories and personal narratives, rather than to see such a focus as peripheral to the project. Instead of viewing such approaches as nonscholarly, we might turn back to intersectional feminism which situates the personal in direct relation to the scholarly and which recognizes how powerful a personal story might indeed prove. What would happen, for example, if Texas A&M University researched and told Uncle Dan's story? Or the black janitors' story? Such an approach re-centers the individual and rejects a narrative of history that devalues the experience of African Americans.

Crucial to developing shared goals and an equitable partnership is recognizing that a partnership does not only exist between individual scholars and community groups. Instead, our home institution is a partner, and we must consider if our institutional structures will allow us to build protective barriers between the community partners and the institution. Partners from historically marginalized groups rightly distrust powerful organizations with problematic pasts, such as Texas A&M University. When I began to discuss a partnership with local African American community groups, the first question that arose was, "Can we trust someone from TAMU?" For those of us who are interested in building partnerships, we must ask the same question of our institutions and our funding agencies. Will our institution and/or funding agency allow us to build a project that treats our partners in equitable manners, and will our institution and/or funding agency allow us to develop projects that cede control of materials to historically marginal groups? While we might exist in institutions that stress academic freedom, researchers must be aware of how university rules might impact our ability to develop such partnerships. Further, if we understand that open access is not appropriate for all partnerships, will our institution and/or funding agency support a tiered system of openness? Do we have the infrastructure to build such a project? And even more important to equitable partnerships, will our university attempt to claim ownership of the materials that are digitized? Will a funding agency force materials to be deposited in an archive without consent of individual knowledge producers? Ultimately, we must build trust and protection into digital projects, which is a decision that must include an assurance that our partners have complete control over their cultural heritage materials and knowledge.

Several strategies might be used to develop equitable partnerships with community members. One effective mechanism is the development of a contract of partnership. When I was working with the Concord Public Library to build "The 19th-Century Concord Digital Archive," a legal contract, drawn between lawyers at Texas A&M University and the Concord Public Library, was a necessity. Some community organizations might want a similar mechanism. If the community organization is not interested in a legal contract, it remains useful to both parties to work together to produce a document of understanding, delineating all issues of collaboration, including control of materials and agreements regarding open access. The development of such a document is crucial to a sustained partnership, as many potential problems might be averted. Careful attention to the digital platform and server on which the digital materials reside is also crucial. Some groups might trust business sites more than they trust the university, leaving a commercial server the only place on which to reposit digital surrogates of knowledge. Reclaim Hosting, for example, offers hosting specifically designed for educators who are interested in using a variety of platforms including Omeka, Mukurtu, WordPress, Drupal, and other related products. In our development of the White Violence, Black Resistance Project, Toniesha Taylor and I were well aware of the past history of cooptation and removal of materials from the Prairie View A&M, the Historical Black University where Taylor works, to Texas A&M University, the predominantly white institution where I work. Given this history, we decided to create our project information page in Google Sites and to avoid any institutional labels.[36] The selection of a platform also ensures that collaborators control the materials. Mukurtu CMS is a platform that allows control over levels of access. The *Mukurtu Wumpurrarni-kari Archive,* built on the platform, designates differential access based on cultural protocols: "When content is uploaded a specific set of criteria must be considered: which families can see the image (a pull down menu allows families to be added); is the content restricted to men only or women only; is the image restricted only to those related to specific countries (a pull down menu allows countries to be checked); is the image sacred and thus restricted to elders only; is anyone in the photo or video deceased; or, finally is this content 'open' to everyone (no restrictions to access it)?"[37] One might extend this platform to account for in-community knowledge, such as oral history stories that are not to be shared with the general public because doing so includes identifying names of individuals, and out of community knowledge, perhaps an oral history story that removes names of individual participants. Another useful mechanism to ensure that historically marginalized community groups control their information is copyright. The Traditional Knowledge (TK) Labels (http://www.localcontexts.org) were designed to ensure protection of vulnerable populations, though it might be extended to other groups to ensure control of knowledge.

Crucial as well is the recognition that situatedness means that a collaborative team should include individuals who are viewed as stewards of the cultural knowledge. Without such individuals, trust is far less easily developed. The USC Annenberg Innovation Lab ignored this central tenet of ethical collaboration when it announced the Black Twitter project (see Figure 20.4) and was faced with an outcry of anger based on fear about the treatment of the vibrant and central Black Twitter community's intellectual product.[38] The initial website announced the DSAIL Black Twitter project run by "Project Owners" Alex Gold and Francois Bar with "Lead researchers: Prof. François Bar, Dayna Chatman, Kevin Driscoll, Alex Leavitt."[39]

Not surprisingly, Black Twitter responded by asking why its work was being studied by two white men who would not, in their perception, understand the complexities and nuances of the community. Other community members feared that the study would commoditize their intellectual property, providing market research to businesses. After a very public outcry, Dayna Chatman, an African American graduate student who was initially listed as second researcher, stated, "The project is lead [sic] by me, was devised by me, and contributes to my dissertation" and that she "did not approve the description of the project that was on the Annenberg Innovation Lab website. It does not fully encapsulate the scale, methods, or full reasoning behind the project."[40] Chatman's image shows up in newer versions of the website, as shown in Figure 20.5.

The concerns that were expressed by Black Twitter were founded. Clearly the originator of the study, Dayna Chatman, had not been given full intellectual credit for her launch of the study and Black Twitter understood that black cultural knowledge has historically been exploited by the larger white society without fair

PROJECT OWNER

Figure 20.4. Archived original announcement of the University of Southern California's Black Twitter project. https://web.archive.org/web/20140425182822/http://www.annenberglab.com/projects/dsail-black-twitter-project

PROJECT LEAD

Dayna Chatman

ADVISOR

François Bar

COLLABORATORS

Kevin Driscoll

Alex Leavitt

Figure 20.5. The "Project Team" for USC's Black Twitter Project, which appeared after the initial images and announcements. http://www.annenberglab.com/projects/dsail-black-twitter-project

recompense. To launch equitable collaborations, a collaborative team must think carefully about situatedness and the historical legacies of past exploitation.

The Black Twitter tension also reminds us that communities are often divided, presenting additional challenges to a scholar interested in ethically engaging in project partnerships. My experience with various community organizations during the development of the "Millican Race 'Riot': 1868" project has revealed such tensions between individuals regarding the way their community is portrayed and about how much information they will reveal through the project. As scholars work with communities it is important to remember that no community will be monolithically in agreement. Knowing that disagreements are likely to occur, a scholar interested in partnership must be prepared to work with multiple perspectives and to spend time listening to community members.

Ultimately, it is our responsibility to navigate the complexities of structures in which we develop partnerships. As we reach out to community partners, we must turn inward as well, examining the places in which we reside, looking to understand how our institutions have interacted with the communities with which we hope to partner. For historically marginalized communities, institutions have, with some rare exceptions, been exploitive. This legacy will alter the way we structure partnerships and should make us think carefully about ownership, control, and openness. As digital humanities engages with large corpora projects, we cannot forget the individual, for a data point is not neutral. A data point is, instead, representative of an individual, a culture, a knowledge system—and to treat data as exempt from the structures in which they are situated is to erase individuals. To "exploit" data is to exploit individuals. The development of an ethics of practice should be developed to guide us through data selection and use. Such practices are predicated on community control. Ultimately, the community must maintain control over its knowledge and to ask that we "not look" at data. Through open dialogue and careful attention to technological structures, we might begin to find ways to develop rich and equitable partnerships.

Notes

1. Social justice–oriented approaches to digital humanities use technologies to enact a variety of social justice outcomes including increased visibility and the examination of power dynamics. I trace such work to early activist digital projects including the *Lesbian Herstory Archives* (http://www.lesbianherstoryarchives.org) and the *Native Web* (http://www.nativeweb.org).

2. See, for example, Bianco, "This Digital Humanities"; McPherson, "Why Are the Digital Humanities"; my own "Can Information Be Unfettered"; Risam, "Beyond the Margins"; Bailey, "#transform(ing) DH Writing"; and the work by Global Outlook::Digital Humanities, http://www.globaloutlookdh.org.

3. Johanson and Sullivan, with Reiff, Favro, Presner, and Wendrich, "Teaching Digital Humanities"; Smeaton, "Digital Humanities (DigHum)"; Rosati, "Exploitation of Cultural Content."

4. Galloway and Thacker, *Exploit,* 70.

5. Risam, "Beyond the Margins."

6. Collins, "Some Group Matters." Kimberlé Crenshaw's work such as "Mapping the Margins: Intersectionality, Identity Politics, and Violence against Women of Color" is foundational. Richard Delgado and Jean Stefancic, *Critical Race Theory: An Introduction,* offers an excellent overview.

7. Cowan and Rault, "Labour of Being Studied."

8. See chapter 3 of my monograph for additional discussion of the history of activist digital humanities projects, Earhart, "What's In and What's Out?"

9. Turin, "Born Archival."

10. The project overview is discussed at https://www.newschallenge.org/challenge/data/entries/safe-harbor-hosting-california-s-eugenics-data. Wernimont presented her

haptic and sonification interface at a talk delivered at the University of Kansas, October 2015: https://www.youtube.com/watch?v=E86rIGjWsyY.

11. Wernimont, "Safe Harbor."
12. See Withey, "Does Information Really Want."
13. Withey, "Mukurtu."
14. Withey, "On Not Looking," 365–66.
15. "Overview."
16. Patrik, "Encoding."
17. "Best Practices."
18. Patrik, "Encoding."
19. "Guidelines for Authors."
20. "Guidelines for Authors."
21. Smith, "Human Touch Software."
22. Wernimont and Flanders, "Feminism." See also Wernimont, "Whence Feminism?"; Flanders, "Body Encoded"; Schilperoot, "Feminist Markup."
23. Kim and Kim, "#TwitterEthics Manifesto."
24. Kim and Kim, #TwitterEthics Manifesto.
25. *Off the Tracks.*
26. DiPressi et al., "Student Collaborators' Bill of Rights."
27. Buhe, "Digital Humanities Best Practices."
28. Bailey, "#transform(ing)DH Writing."
29. Powell and Aitken, "Encoding Culture."
30. See *Brown University Steering Committee on Slavery and Justice,* http://brown.edu/Research/Slavery_Justice/; Emory Slavery and Discrimination, http://emoryhistory.emory.edu/issues/discrimination/index.html; University of Virginia President's Commission on Slavery and the University, http://slavery.virginia.edu; *The Georgetown Slavery Archive,* http://slaveryarchive.georgetown.edu; and *The Lemon Project,* http://www.wm.edu/sites/lemonproject/index.php.
31. Steering Committee on Slavery and Justice, "Brown University's Response."
32. For additional discussion, see Garrett Nichols's important dissertation, "Rural Drag: Settler Colonialism and the Queer Rhetorics of Rurality." Nichols's extensive archival research reveals the deep and lasting racism at the core of Texas A&M University.
33. "About the Yearbooks," in *Texas A&M University Yearbook Collection.*
34. *Texas A&M University Yearbook Collection.* The university discussed how best to respond to such a history and chose to digitize the materials and present them without censorship. The library, however, attached a splash page to the materials that states, "Through our web site, the Libraries offers public access to a wide range of information, including historical materials that may contain offensive language or negative stereotypes. Such materials must be viewed in the context of the relevant time period. Texas A&M does not endorse the views expressed in such materials."
35. Texas A&M University *Long Horn* yearbook, 1906: 174.
36. See Earhart and Taylor, "Pedagogies of Race."

37. Withey, "Archival Challenges," 22.

38. Black Twitter is a Twitter social network focused on issues related to the black community.

39. See the Internet Archive's April 25, 2014 capture of the initial announcement from February 2014: https://web.archive.org/web/20140425182822/http://www.annenberglab.com/projects/dsail-black-twitter-project.

40. Chatman, "In Reply."

Bibliography

Bailey, Moya. "#transform(ing)DH Writing and Research: An Ethnography of Digital Humanities and Feminist Ethics." *Digital Humanities Quarterly* 9, no. 2 (2015). http://www.digitalhumanities.org/dhq/vol/9/2/000208/000208.html.

"Best Practices for Digital Humanities Projects." University of Nebraska Center for Digital Research in the Humanities. http://cdrh.unl.edu/articles/best_practices.

Bianco, Jamie "Skye." "This Digital Humanities Which Is Not One." In *Debates in the Digital Humanities,* edited by Matthew K. Gold, 96–112. Minneapolis: University of Minnesota Press, 2012.

Buhe, Elizabeth. "Digital Humanities Best Practices: Engaging a Collaborator." New York University Institute of Fine Arts. Last updated June 10, 2015. https://www.nyu.edu/gsas/dept/fineart/pdfs/digital/Digital-Humanities-Best-Practices.pdf.

Chatman, Dayna E. "In Reply: My Reflections on Comments about Our Research on Black Twitter." Dayna E. Chatman, PhD. https://dchatman3.wordpress.com.

Christen, Kimberly A. "Does Information Really Want to Be Free? Indigenous Knowledge Systems and the Question of Openness." *International Journal of Communication* 6 (2012): 2870–93.

Christen, Kimberly A. "Mukurtu." http://www.kimchristen.com/project/mukurtu-cms/.

Christen, Kimberly A. "On Not Looking: Economies of Visuality in Digital Museums." In *The International Handbooks of Museum Studies: Museum Transformations,* vol. 4, *Museum Transformations,* 1st ed., edited by Annie E. Coombes and Ruth B. Phillips, 365–86. Oxford: John Wiley & Sons, 2015.

Collins, Patricia Hill. "Some Group Matters: Intersectionality, Situated Standpoints, and Black Feminist Thought." In *A Companion to African-American Philosophy,* edited by Tommy L. Lott and John P. Pittman, 205–29. Malden, Mass.: John Wiley and Sons, 2003.

Cowan, T. L., and Jasmine Rault. "The Labour of Being Studied in a Free Love Economy." *ephemera: theory & politics in organization* 14, no. 3 (2014): 471–88.

Crenshaw, Kimberle. "Mapping the Margins: Intersectionality, Identity Politics, and Violence against Women of Color." *Stanford Law Review* 43, no. 6 (July 1991): 1241–99.

Delgado, Richard, and Jean Stefancic. *Critical Race Theory: An Introduction.* New York: New York University Press, 2001.

DiPressi, Haley, et al. "A Student Collaborators' Bill of Rights." June 8, 2015. http://www.cdh.ucla.edu/news-events/a-student-collaborators-bill-of-rights/.

Earhart, Amy E. "Can Information Be Unfettered? Race and the New Digital Humanities Canon." In *Debates in the Digital Humanities,* edited by Matthew K. Gold, 309–18. Minneapolis: University of Minnesota Press, 2012.

Earhart, Amy E. "What's In and What's Out? Digital Canon Cautions." In *Traces of the Old, Uses of the New: The Emergence of Digital Literary Studies,* 11–37. Ann Arbor: University of Michigan Press, 2015.

Earhart, Amy E., and Toniesha L. Taylor. "Pedagogies of Race: Digital Humanities in the Age of Ferguson." In *Debates in Digital Humanities 2016.* Minneapolis: University of Minnesota Press, 2016. http://dhdebates.gc.cuny.edu/debates/text/72.

Flanders, Julia. "The Body Encoded: Questions of Gender and the Electronic Text." In *Electronic Text: Investigations in Method and Theory,* edited by Kathryn Sutherland, 127–43. Oxford: Clarendon, 1997.

Galloway, Alexander R., and Eugene Thacker. *The Exploit: A Theory of Networks.* Electronic Mediations, Vol. 21. Minneapolis: University of Minnesota Press, 2007.

Global Outlook::Digital Humanities. http://www.globaloutlookdh.org.

"Guidelines for Authors of Digital Resources." Modern Language Association, 2013. https://www.mla.org/About-Us/Governance/Committees/Committee-Listings/Professional-Issues/Committee-on-Information-Technology/Guidelines-for-Authors-of-Digital-Resources.

Johanson, Chris, and Elaine Sullivan, with Janice Reiff, Diane Favro, Todd Presner and WIlleke Wendrich. "Teaching Digital Humanities through Digital Cultural Mapping." In *Digital Humanities Pedagogy: Practices, Principles and Politics,* edited by Brett D. Hirsch, 121–49. Cambridge: OpenBook Publishers.

Kim, Dorothy, and Eunsong Kim. "The #TwitterEthics Manifesto: You Don't Need to Speak for Us—We Are Talking." *Model View Culture,* April 7, 2014. https://modelviewculture.com/pieces/the-twitterethics-manifesto.

McPherson, Tara. "Why Are the Digital Humanities So White? Or Thinking of the Histories of Race and Computation." In *Debates in the Digital Humanities,* edited by Matthew K. Gold, 139–60. Minneapolis: University of Minnesota Press, 2012.

Nichols, Garrett. "Rural Drag: Settler Colonialism and the Queer Rhetorics of Rurality." Texas A&M University Libraries, OAKTrust, July 16, 2013. http://hdl.handle.net/1969.1/151102.

Off the Tracks: Laying New Lines for Digital Humanities Scholars. "Event Details." Maryland Institute for Technology in the Humanities. http://mith.umd.edu/offthetracks/.

"Overview." Tibetan and Himalayan Library. http://www.thlib.org/about/wiki/THDL%20Home%20Overview.html.

Patrik, Linda E. "Encoding for Endangered Tibetan Texts." *Digital Humanities Quarterly* 1, no.1 (2007). http://www.digitalhumanities.org/dhq/vol/1/1/000004/000004.html.

Powell, Timothy B., and Larry P. Aitken. "Encoding Culture: Building a Digital Archive Based on Traditional Ojibwe Teachings." In *The American Literature Scholar in the Digital Age,* edited by Amy E. Earhart and Andrew Jewell, 250–74. Ann Arbor: University of Michigan Press, 2011.

Risam, Roopika. "Beyond the Margins: Intersectionality and the Digital Humanities." *Digital Humanities Quarterly* 9, no. 2 (2015). http://www.digitalhumanities.org/dhq/vol/9/2/000208/000208.html.

Rosati, Eleonora. "Exploitation of Cultural Content and Licensing Models." University of Cambridge, Cambridge Digital Humanities, 2013.

Schilperoot, Hannah M. "Feminist Markup and Meaningful Text Analysis in Digital Literary Archives." *Library Philosophy and Practice* (e-journal), Paper 1228, 2015. http://digitalcommons.unl.edu/libphilprac/1228.

Smeaton, Alan. "The Digital Humanities (DigHum): The Formation of a National Working Group on the Exploitation of Data in the Humanities." Insight Centre for Data Analytics. https://www.insight-centre.org/content/digital-humanities-dighum-formation-national-working-group-exploitation-data-humanities-0.

Smith, Martha Nell. "The Human Touch Software of the Highest Order: Revisiting Editing as Interpretation." *Textual Cultures: Texts, Contexts, Interpretation* 2, no.1 (2007): 1–15.

Steering Committee on Slavery and Justice. "Brown University's Response to the Report of the Steering Committee on Slavery and Justice." Brown University, February 2007. http://www.brown.edu/Research/Slavery_Justice/about/response.html.

Texas A&M University Yearbook Collection. Texas A&M University Libraries. http://library.tamu.edu/yearbooks/.

Turin, Mark. "Born Archival: The Ebb and Flow of Digital Documents from the Field." *History and Anthropology* 22, no. 4 (2011): 445–60.

Wernimont, Jacqueline. "Safe Harbor: Hosting California's Eugenics Data." Knight Foundation, Knight News Challenge. https://www.newschallenge.org/challenge/data/entries/safe-harbor-hosting-california-s-eugenics-data.

Wernimont, Jacqueline. "Whence Feminism? Assessing Feminist Interventions in Digital Literary Archives." *Digital Humanities Quarterly* 7, no.1 (2013). http://www.digitalhumanities.org/dhq/vol/7/1/000156/000156.html.

Wernimont, Jacqueline, and Julia Flanders. "Feminism in the Age of Digital Archives: The Women Writer's Project." *Tulsa Studies in Women's Literature* 29, no. 2 (2010): 425–35.

Withey, Kimberly Christen. "Archival Challenges and Digital Solutions in Aboriginal Australia." *SAA Archaeological Record,* March 2008, 21–24.

PART VI][Chapter 21

Domestic Disturbances

Precarity, Agency, Data

BETH COLEMAN

Data and Agency

My position in this chapter is to frame an understanding of how networks both located and disseminated affect change around a social issue. My interest is in reading against the grain of a flat, closed "dataset" of black subjects in relation to racialized violence and toward a complex, heterogeneous dataset that speaks to the mechanisms of marginality and the possibilities of finding public voice. Toward this end, my method is to read across heterogeneous data, between the located and the distributed, in order to better understand the effects of networked media in the hands of activists for social change.

Necessarily, I use the data archive as an "ocular proof," the desired and always failed proof positive of an event, of the thing itself. The argument for an ocular proof, as *Othello* demonstrates, offers the noisiness of "proof" in its complexity and self-divergence. It is also an argument that posits data as both witness and action. Each case study addresses a different mode of a data public—the broadcast of information to a distributed network. In the case of the anti-racism protests and the spooky presence of its counterprotest on the Colgate campus, it is an instance of small data narratives. With #BLM (Black Lives Matter), I address the issue of big data as deracinated from its context and the critical value of suturing place and utterance in the figure of "shadow data." The third site of exploration is Diamond Reynolds's real-time broadcast as bearing witness to the shooting of Philando Castile as a modality of complex data.

The networked data points I discuss are beyond the 2011 Gladwell-Shirky debate of networked versus "armchair" activism. I look at instances of networked media technologies as constitutional elements in the disclosure of risk, violence, and the activation of resistance. I focus primarily on the emergence and activity of

[391

the U.S.-based movement Black Lives Matter. In looking at these events, I am interested in a theory of data as the experiential, an X-reality of networked information as a real-time component of geolocated phenomena. Along these lines, philosopher Judith Butler describes a generative relation between data and society: "If the people are constituted through a complex interplay of performance, image, acoustics, and all the various technologies engaged in those productions, then 'media' is not just reporting who the people claim to be, but media has entered into the very definition of the people. It is the stuff of self-constitution, the site of hegemonic struggle over who 'we' are." In the formation of "self-constitution," Butler articulates a socio-techno subject, one reflected and self-fashioned (witness and action) of the event of mediation. One finds at the root of most demonstrations, *manifestations* from the Latin, a vertiginous merger of precarity and persistence. This is a state of precarity that wrestles with control of public appearance (self-constitution via mediation) and the constitution of self-image that involves escaping normative paradigms. Whether the framework is gender norming, racial taxonomies, economic stratification, or other modes of a societal ordering of things, I locate a relation between this articulation of the precarious and a fugitive state as points of subversion, the exploitation of the trap door (Coleman, "Race as Technology," "Unmoored Beauty"; Harney and Moten). In this case, I focus on a relationship between activist assumption of networked social media and located civic protest. In the examples I discuss, I look at various instances of self-constitution via mediation as an effort in resituating precarious positionalities toward a civic agency.

In terms of the civic activism at hand, here is a basic rule of engagement I trace: it is the subjects most at risk who literally put their bodies in the street, who manifest a public space and public image of resistance. In putting one's body on the line, exhibiting its value and its freedom in the demonstration itself, one enacts, by the embodied form of gathering, a claim to the political. It is a historical claim to citizenship inscribed as the right to appearance in public (Arendt). Of course, as it has been demonstrated, the right to appear is unevenly distributed. Eleanor Saitta, data privacy specialist, points to the different degrees of risks of public appearance (including social media and other networked platforms) for those in immanent risk, such as battered spouses, sex workers, trans women of color, and others in the cross-hairs of gender, race, class, and marginality.

A primary goal of the inquiry is to work meaningfully between big and small data to produce knowledge of a domain of inquiry—in this case, the conditions and possibilities of civic engagement. My methods follow information scholar Christine Borgman's insight that "having the right data is usually better than having more data; little data can be just as valuable as big data" (*Big Data*). For one to situate the "right" data is to understand data as emergent from "an ecology of people, practices, technologies, [and] institutions" that constitutes its value (Borgman; Kitchin, Lauriault, and McArdle). I add to this argument that such a heterogeneous ecosystem also reflects the image of a public to itself. The right to appear (Butler)—as a citizen, as part of a civic public—is related to a right to the civic.

Within this framework of a right to the civic, I present a partial timeline of names, locations, and dates of black people killed by police or in police custody from the inception and over the development of the Black Lives Matter movement:

> February 2012, Trayvon Martin, Sanford, Florida
> July 2013, "#Blacklivesmatter" Twitter hashtag created (Garza, Cullors, and Tometi)
> July 2014, Eric Garner, Staten Island, New York
> November 2014, Tamir Rice, Cleveland, Ohio
> April 2015, Walter Scott, North Charleston, South Carolina
> August 2014, Michael Brown, Ferguson, Missouri
> July 2015, Sandra Bland, Waller County, Texas
> June 2016, Alton Sterling, Baton Rouge, Louisiana
> July 2016, Philando Castile, St. Anthony, Minnesota

In this timeline, I point to the Brown incident as a public-awareness threshold marker of the primary issues raised by Black Lives Matter, namely, the historic and complex conditions that speak to the continued overpolicing of black neighborhoods with the concomitant results of high rates of incarceration and high rates of death at the hands of the police (I discuss the statistical meaning of "high rates" in a later section of the chapter). In the case of Michael Brown, an eighteen-year-old, unarmed black man, shot during the course of arrest for theft in Ferguson, Missouri, on April 9, 2014, the spectacular and incendiary video images captured by people living in the town and posted to social media captivated a broad network of viewers, creating the first large-scale networked distribution of #Mike Brown, #BLM, and #Ferguson with general attention to the issue of policing black communities.

Unlike some of the later police shootings of which there are real-time recordings, the Mike Brown video meme did not present his *shooting* but rather the belabored and dehumanizing treatment of Brown's body left in the street for a six-hour interval before being removed from the scene of death. These visual data have been popularly interpreted as an emblem of a deeply racist and classist system that produces its programmed outcome of black subjugation, as journalists and scholars have suggested in looking at the local history of Ferguson itself. In regard to the culture of Ferguson, Black Lives Matter makes the argument that Brown's death represents the overindexed exposure of black communities to policing (surveillance, stop and search, etc.) supported by over forty years of legislation since the Nixon administration's original "war on drugs" (Alexander). The punitive policing of poor black neighborhoods is a matter of record. But the understanding of that fact is a question of view and temporality.

On the other side of interpretation, one finds credible scholars and pundits who make the argument that even if they appeared disturbing, the conditions under which Michael Brown was shot, killed, and held in police custody represented standard and prudent police activity (U.S. Department of Justice). In order to better understand these divergent views on the same incident, the cultural and statistical context of the #BLM movement and the claims that it makes, I suggest that we must look at the movement in regard to the broader American society in relation to intersectional histories of race class, technology, and state policy (Crenshaw). With the Michael Brown incident, I make the distinction between public opinion, activist persuasion, and the circumscription of legal interpretation and state policy governing the police. I discuss the need for the Black Lives Matter activism as well as the complexity of communication and action that it exists within. If one looks for traditional civil rights movement markers, such as organizing against segregation as the legal manifestation of a Jim Crow society, one finds nothing to push against—there is nothing solid to organize against. Rather, Black Lives Matter works against deracinated shadow data and spooky apprehension of affective context to make visible the questions of social contract, civic inclusion, and justice. Along these lines, in the case of the police shootings discussed here, a person is not being shot for "being black" per se but rather for appearing threatening, resisting arrest, or other "disruptive" behavior. None of these stimuli of police attention are named as racial in policy; nonetheless, they are rendered racial in practice.

Historically speaking, in thinking about the claims of the Black Lives Matter movement, I recognize the immediate demand to stop police violence against poor and working-class black people. I also would like to signal the complexity of that demand as it is embedded in the historic development of racialized economic inequality in the United States and the ongoing permutations of a Jim Crow policy (separation of population, limited access to education and other societal resources, and so on). Within this construct, the particular procedures of policing as representative of the state often allow for a discrepancy between what the police (and the legal system) see as a "good arrest" or appropriate use of violence and what the subdued (or dead) citizen and civic community (social media and word-on-the-street) understand as targeted harassment.

Toward this end, I execute a first-level analysis of civic activism and its modes of networked media output (data) as tools of collective organization. In order for society to better comprehend the acceleration of media "self-constitution," one must make legible and legitimate the forms of self-defense and self-representation in which people engage in the face of state power and societal bias. The second order of work this chapter performs is to direct attention to the legalistic and statistical discussion of how Black Lives Matters signifies beyond public sentiment and in relation to a more "scientific" analysis, as if this analysis were itself outside of the societal context addressed. Toward this end, I attend to three case studies of data publics that demonstrate a dynamism of networked information distributed across media platforms. In this context, the term "data publics" describes the cross section between historical civic data, such as census, crime, and traffic, and the arrival of emergent technologies and practices such as social, mobile, and peerproduced data that present a growing networked public resource.

Yik Yak: Small Data Narrative

In 2013, news media such as the podcast "Reply All" and the *Huffington Post* began reporting stories on the abuse of the social media application Yik Yak on college campuses (Reply All). Yik Yak supports a rich media discussion within a five-mile radius, allowing users to post anonymously, vote posts up or down, and have the posts disappear over time. In comparison with a social media platform such as Twitter, which is neither location based nor time dependent, Yik Yak is temporal and geolocated, presuming in its design a community of users in physical proximity to each other. It is exactly in the advent of physical proximity as the *basis* of networked informational exchanges that the conflict, facilitated by Yik Yak, arose: often the language students used on Yik Yak was anonymous, racist, and misogynist (Donovan). In the case of Colgate College, the clash between online utterances and face-to-face experiences came to a head around the actions of a group organized by students of color on the majority white campus, the Association of Critical Collegians, and the directed assaults on one of its organizers, junior Melissa Mendez. As the student-organized support group grew in visibility on the campus, there was an analogous rise in anonymous "Yaks" targeting the student activists as well as expressing racist vitriol (Figure 21.1). The language escalated to violent threats against Mendez and others to the point that the Colgate administration was forced to take action to protect the students at risk and attempt to identify the perpetrators of the hate speech (Figure 21.2).

The Colgate Yik Yak affair illuminates a generative relation between data and society, revealing a virtuous (or in this case, vicious) circle between the located and the distributed. The value of the social media feed to the activists—the mode by which they instrumentalized the ad hominem attacks—was to capture the transient posts as screen grabs and use them as proof of their allegations of a racist climate. The Yik Yak posts represent a body of small data: local, low in number, and temporary. Student activists captured them in an effort to make substantive (legible) the spooky presence of racism. In effect, utterances on social media platforms perform as utterances *in a place* partly because social media constitute an actual place in society—a data public as I allege above—and also as a function of the geolocational affordance of that particular application. The design ontology (and the popular uptake) of Yik Yak is based on the premise that networked speech can and does perform a located function. Largely because of the possibility of anonymity, such utterances worked rhetorically like sniper strikes: one knows the general direction from which the shots have been issued if not the name and rank of the shooter. Once the media had been captured, it was possible to develop a forensic around the posters and their support

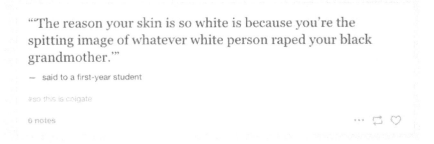

Figure 21.1. Comment shared over social media and documented by Association of Critical Collegians. (Association)

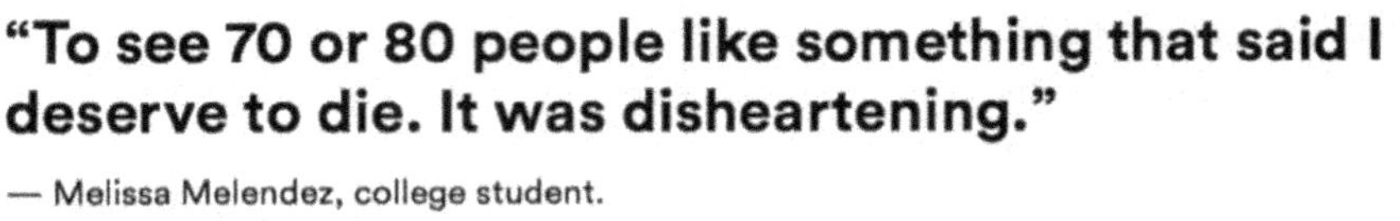

"To see 70 or 80 people like something that said I deserve to die. It was disheartening."

— Melissa Melendez, college student.

Figure 21.2. Comment by student Melissa Mendez on the use of Yik Yak on campus to threaten her. (Reply)

network. In other words, the sublimated racism that the student activists intuited in their environment they were able to capture as digital artifacts, transforming a haunting presence into a materialized one. The Yik Yak posts offered an ocular proof as such that confirmed the students' sense of racialized aggression.

In her discussion of Black Freedom and the history of race and violence in the United States, historian Keeanga-Yamahtta Taylor points out the systemic issue of treating political economy as unrelated to American racial problems. "In the 1990s, the social consequences of austerity budgets have effectively made police storm troopers for gentrification. A long list of quality of life legal offenses make it a crime to be poor or 'criminalize public displays of poverty,'" giving the example of William Bratton's New York Police Department implementation of the CompStat database and stop-and-search procedures under Mayor Giuliani (Taylor). What one finds is a recipe for riot cities: under the direction of the Johnson administration in 1967, the National Advisory Commission on Civil Disorders—known as the Kerner commission—identified the three primary grievances in black communities as police brutality, unemployment, and substandard housing (Taylor). The connection of such policy to a phenomenon such as Yik Yak is an effect of Yik Yak's decontextualized racism: treating political economy as unrelated to American racial problems. Such a separation is implicit in the comments made by students on Yik Yak laying the blame for legacies of imperialism that include practices of colonialism and slavery at the feet of their peers—the young students of color. Taylor goes on to state the necessity of student groups and civil rights activists historically to *make visible* a resistance to corrupted systems that have grown invisible as they have grown normative: "Ideas are fluid, but it usually takes political action to set them in motion and stasis for the retreat to set in" (Taylor). In the case of the Association of Critical Collegians, they were able to arm themselves with the small data of their context to force a change of state from entropy to activity around the issues of social life (and social justice) at the college. The students captured a type of shadow data—the substrata exchange of information that participates in the constitution of context—and render it an *ocular* testimony.

#BlackLivesMatter: Big Data Narrative

In a different sense, I locate "shadow data" in the work of Black Lives Matters activism as one of the powerful connecting threads between networked and located phenomena. I move from the platform of Yik Yak, as a locative application, to that of Twitter, the microblogging platform that allows for a public broadcast, but without necessarily being tethered to geolocation. The shift in social media platforms as activist tools also speaks to a shift in scale and intensity. Yet, some of the same themes persist: the valuation of black and other people of color in the broader culture and the use of social media to make visible the "shadow data" that often haunt the lives of a black underclass in the form of penalties, harassment, and ultimately in the case of Michael Brown and others, death. In the hands of Black Lives Matter activists (some starting simply as citizens reporting directly to the public what they say are unjust police practices), network broadcast moved the Michael Brown case from a lethal interaction between civilian and police to one that had a public stage on which issues of racialized policing practices, excess of violence, and the persistent harassment of civil subjects based on race and poverty were broadcast.

Clearly, social media, in this case Twitter, are a productive tool for bringing attention to a matter that might never have surfaced, that is, would have been the unremarked (and thus somehow rendered unremarkable) death of a young black man at the hands of local police. The Black Lives Matter use of social media made visible, and made a case for, a review of police behavior in black communities as symptomatic of a persistent *devaluation of black life*. This is a claim distinct from a general call for less violent outcomes in police interactions with civilians. It is a call to action to address what is understood and historically documented as the systemic overpolicing of black neighborhoods with the outcome of higher incarceration and death rates than those of other U.S. populations. I return at the end of this section to discuss in greater detail the differences between an experiential sense and a data-driven substantiation of "higher death rates." But first, I would like to move through the #BLM activist use of social media.

In the 2016 white paper "Beyond the Hashtags: #FERGUSON, #BLACKLIVES MATTER, and Online Media," authors Deen Freelon, Charlton Mcilwain, and Meredith Clark offer the first substantial scholarly analysis of the Black Lives Matter social media data. In the white paper, they reach the following conclusion: social media posts by activists were essential in spreading Michael Brown's story nationally. They write, "Protesters and their supporters were generally able to circulate their own narratives on Twitter without relying on mainstream news outlets" (Freelon, Mcilwain, and Clark) They express the primary goals of the social media among the activists they interviewed as education, "amplification of marginalized voices," and police reform. Additionally, they suggest the Black Lives Matter social network data as an "apt test case for the idea that social media uniquely benefits oppressed populations" (Freelon, Mcilwain, and Clark). To this last point, I reference the body of literature on Young Black Twitter (YBT) that addresses the disproportionally high presence of black youth on social media such as Twitter and the short-video platform Vine (Brock; Sharma); this statistical reference contextualizes the proposition that social media may represent a public, powerful, and alternative venue to traditional media sources. In making this argument, it is difficult to discern whether networked media represent possible alternative communication network for all; or whether groups with a political drive, such as the black, progressive Black Lives Matter or the white conservative Alt-Right, is particularly persuasive in its social media use. They both represent radicalized voices that increasingly circulate beyond their domain of local or internal discourse. But, despite the Unite the Right discourse regarding the endangered status of whiteness (particularly American white men), I would argue that their effective leveraging of social media as an alternative news outlet does not represent an "oppressed population." They do, though, represent a site of controversy as we as a society witness the transformation of what heretofore had been the most privileged societal position (if there is a correcting for class and ethnic location) with tangible historic endowments such as legal enfranchisement, opportunity to own property, and the pursuit of happiness available to free persons. It is the slippage in that privilege that appears to be the source of rage. Not, as is the case with Black Lives Matter, the protest against continued (and continuous) devaluation of black life as American norm.

My analysis of #BLM data focuses on three key sets as described by Freelon and coauthors: the Black Lives Matter hyperlink network; #BLM tweets per day; and tweets containing #BLM.

Figure 21.3, "#BLM hyperlink network," graphs the network relations between the Black Lives Matter website and the increasing number of hyperlinks to the site. The story the data tell is a movement from margin to center in terms of the public and media discussion of the issues of Black Lives Matter and the profile of the official organization website as a trusted reference. For example, one of the closest high-profile media connections is the U.K. publication *The Guardian,* with the liberal political blog site slate.com and the less known feministwire.com as other nodes in the close proximity network. The data only reflect frequency of reference (represented as proximity) but not temporal links. In other words, one cannot read in this set of data when *The Guardian* first linked to BlackLivesMatter.com or a group like the Alt-Right breitbart.com, although with less frequent links to the site, first

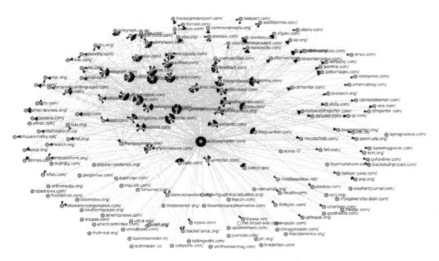

Figure 21.3. #BLM hyperlink network: data visualization shows the genealogy of connections to BlackLivesMatter.com, consisting predominantly of news sites. The Black Lives Matter network is structured to distribute related content among and between news sites that are in a position to maximize and amplify visibility. Freelon, Mcilwain, and Clark, Creative Commons: BY-NC-SA, http://creativecommons.org/licenses/by-nc-sa/4.0/.

connected. The value of reading frequency of connection as well as temporality of connection would simply allow for a richer data story on how third-party media moved Black Lives Matter and BlackLivesMatter.com to the referential center of the social and news media conversation.

YBT outlets such as thefader.com, getequal.org, colorlines.com, and black alliance.com are also represented in the chart as part of the network. In these comparatively weaker ties, one can see black news media essentially following the mainstream media on reporting Black Lives Matter. One cannot see in this chart the momentum of the YBT social media network and affiliated demographics (activist, left, social justice) as the aggregated group of participants who made #BLM and associated hashtags trend across social media, creating the network context in which news media began to link to #BLM and BlackLivesMatter.com. This activist work of making public the issues of Black Lives Matter appears in the second graph (Figure 21.4) of the white paper and describes the work of hundreds to millions of Twitter posts in the dynamic system by which Black Lives Matter developed into a national movement and international conversation.

In Figure 21.4, "#BLM Tweets per day," one can locate two important aspects of an activist network with located and distributed aspects. First, as with most internet memes, attention to police violence on Twitter is episodic. The tweets-per-day graph shows that comparatively few people were engaged with the issue prior to Michael Brown's killing on August 9, 2014. The attention spike started with this event and

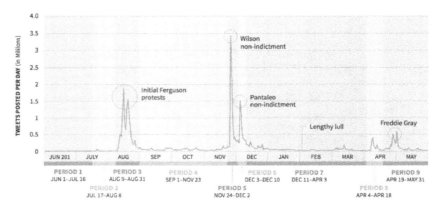

Figure 21.4. #BLM tweets per day: as with most internet memes, attention to police violence on Twitter is episodic. The tweets-per-day graph shows that comparatively few people were engaged with the issue prior to Michael Brown's killing on August 9. The sustained attention spike that extends from that date through the end of the month encompasses the initial Ferguson protests. Freelon, Mcilwain, and Clark, Creative Commons: BY-NC-SA, http://creativecommons.org/licenses/by-nc-sa/4.0/.

extends to the end of the month to include the Ferguson protests. The shift in scale of networked attention is significant. From August 9 to August 31, one sees close to two million hashtag citations (tweets and retweets) of Black Lives Matter. Indeed this was one of several hashtags circulating on the topic that include #Ferguson and #MikeBrown, making it representative of only a percentage of overall activity on the topic. Between November 24 and December 2, 2014, one finds the #BLM trend approaching 3.5 million individual citations around the nonindictment of officers Darren Wilson (of Ferguson) and Daniel Pantaleo, who was brought to trial over the 2014 death of Eric Garner in New York City.

I speculate that the pattern of growth and circulation represents the development of a public consciousness of the issue and increasing activist work. As I have suggested, the August network established the meme at a societally impactful scale (as demonstrated by Figure 21.3 in the frequency and importance of media outlets reporting the story). Based on that theory, the subsequent escalation of the meme three months later reflects the twin phenomena of familiarity and outrage at the results of the juridical process. In other words, #BLM was established around the death of Michael Brown and then used as a tool for online protest with the acquittal of Officer Darren Wilson, who shot and killed Brown.

The second point of information I read in the tweets-per-day graph is the shadow data that reveal the ongoing work of activism around and beyond the internet meme metabolism: Figure 21.4 suggests that police violence only sporadically becomes a mainstream issue on Twitter. When major events occur, such as nonindictments, clashes between protestors and police, or the posting of explosive video, the conversation surges very quickly but tapers off after a few days. The data of Figure 21.4 also reveal a steady, low-volume conversation among those closely following the issue that falls outside of the methodological framework of the white paper. In this sense, that there are large-scale data in relation to Black Lives Matter is the condition of the white paper, its motivation for the analysis; the viability of data is constrained by the condition of high volume as indicative of societal importance. Based on this condition, Freelon, Mcilwain, and Clark's critical data framework is effectively a positivist one, marking the networked phenomenon but rendering the low-volume conversation statistically irrelevant; there is no capacity to address small data as such.

In a counter-reading of the graph, I am suggesting that there is also a mode of shadow data—information that does not appear as significant on the graph but may be inferred with significance based on a combination of online and located activist engagement. By interpreting positive and shadow data along these lines, one can argue that they mark the temporality of an internet meme (political or not) as well as the *ongoing* work on the ground by activists. The strong-tie/weak-tie pattern of normative social exchange (Granovetter) and the particular risks of an activist network (Bonilla and Rosa; Gladwell; Gladwell and Shirky; Gruzd and Wellman; Tufekci). The low risk (weak tie) work of tweeting or retweeting, of engaging social media on a topic, in relation to scaffolded development of strong-tie networks represents the difficult work of activist infrastructure to create the condition of an issue evolving from one of marginal and local importance to mass movement of social change.

The construction of this scaffold changes depending on time, issue, constituents, and media tools. The organizing of the 1960s civil rights movement does not look the same as the Idle No More movement commenced in 2012. Accordingly, the value of social media activity can be seen only in relation to located activist work. In my assessment, one finds a symbiotic relationship toward publicness and persuasion on an issue, where one does not and cannot replace the other. Based on this framework, despite the fact that it essentially does not appear in the conventional data, I mark the shadow of this persistent activist work in the subsequent spike in Twitter activity around the organized days of protest in reaction to the acquittal of police officers on trial for the deaths of Brown and Garner.

In addition to looking at the data on activist networks of Black Lives Matter, I am interested in data that underlie Black Lives Matter claims of racially based social injustice as perpetrated by the U.S. legal system and its application by law enforcement. To this point, I address the 2016 analysis by economist Roland Fryer of three distinct datasets that address race and death at the hands of the police. Two are public data comprising records of city and federal programs that include Stop, Question, and Frisk program, New York City (Stop and Frisk), and the national citizen report Police-Public Contact Survey (PPCS). For the third dataset, data are culled from qualitative event summaries of officers firing their weapons at civilians from three cities in Texas, six counties in Florida, and Los Angeles County. The report derives its final dataset from a random sample of reports from the Houston Police Department arrest codes that represent a higher probability of justified use of lethal force (e.g., attempted murder of an officer, aggravated assault of an officer, resisting arrest, etc.). From the perspective of this paper, the purpose of engaging these data and their analysis is to frame a baseline context in which to talk about the scale and impact of police use of force and how that might further contextualize the events around Black Lives Matter.

In the working paper "An Empirical Analysis of Racial Differences in Police Use of Force," Fryer finds that blacks and Hispanics experience 50 percent more nonlethal use of force in encounters with police than whites. More provocatively, he concludes that in cases of more extreme use of force, in particular officer-involved shootings, the study found no marked racial difference between whites and minorities in the raw data of correcting for contextual factors (Fryer). Factoring for controls and unknowns—such as bias in reporting good behavior with the Houston police—Fryer argues that his data in the case of lethal uses of force by police officers are representative: the report finds "in the raw data ... blacks are 23.8 percent *less* likely to be shot at by police relative to whites. Hispanics are 8.5 percent less likely" (Fryer, 5). Concluding, he finds "no evidence of racial discrimination in officer involved shootings" (Fryer, 5). With the publication of the working paper, there was media conversation among news groups and internet pundits that the basic claim of Black Lives Matter—that blacks are disproportionately targeted and killed by police—was not substantiated by the data (Bui and Cox; Kweku; Mac Donald; Phelps). I am suggesting that this narrow view of the data, simply looking at the analysis of the Houston dataset, does not sufficiently contextualize and cross-reference other significant data in moving toward a viable interpretation of the Fryer findings.

Blacks constitute 12.3 percent of the U.S. population and Hispanics 12.5 percent (Carroll). For blacks and Hispanics to represent 56 percent of deaths at the hands of the police points to what historians and statisticians report in the overpolicing of poor black communities, as discussed above. The fact that the ratio of black to white deaths as the result of police action is so high speaks to a much larger percentage of the black population being implicated in suspect behavior. If the study does not report explicit racial bias in police actions on the scene in situ, it also does not address the ratio of black to white police exposure. In the cases of Garner and Brown, as reported by the press and noted in the Fryer study, neither suspect possessed weapons, nor did either suspect, depending on perspective, exhibit threatening behavior.

Barnard College statistician Rajiv Sethi suggests that one might parse the data to better understand if lethal force is being brought to bear against the *most violent* constituencies of the broader white population while police force (lethal or not) is being brought against poor black communities *in general* ("Fallacy of Composition"). He points to a more broadly contextual implication that the controversy around the narrow assessment of more white deaths by police shooting overshadows any reference to the data that blacks and Hispanics are far more likely to be engaged by police and continue to represent more than half of police killings, even though they are much smaller percentages of the population. In effect, the systemic relationship between minority populations and police becomes a type of shadow data, reabsorbed as the daily norm. As discussed in the Fryer paper, the Stop and Frisk and PPCS reports represent local and national data clearly marking that blacks and Hispanics are statistically more likely to be stopped by police and violently apprehended. As Sethi points out, in reading across the heterogeneous datasets, it is not possible to assess the quality or kind of people being apprehended: in the much larger white population do the police meet the *most violent* suspects with lethal force? Conversely, in the smaller black population, are there broader police exposure and force applied to a general population, that is, not the most violent? This speculative analysis of what shadow data might expose to better understand how different groups are policed supports the claims of Black Lives Matter in regard to *the disproportionate* police violence in black communities.

Fryer's finding that at the point of contact in a shooting police officers in general do not act in a racist manner is good news; it does not, though, undermine the larger issues at hand in relation to the policing of black communities (one need only look at black incarceration rates in relation to U.S. drug legislation since the 1970s to begin to unwind that thread). If media pundits must see greater numbers of black deaths to be convinced of the societal problem of how poor blacks are unjustly treated in the construct of judicial policy and its application by the police, then I call this view blindered at the very least. The spooky bias that blacks are constitutionally more violent than other groups seems to haunt the data in terms of what is taken up by the media in its interpretation. Based on Fryer's data and other contextualizing materials, such historical, legal, and sociological analysis as presented in the earlier sections of the paper, I am suggesting that the Black Lives Matter claim of disproportionate and aggressive police presence in low-income black communities is borne out across qualitative and quantitative analysis. It seems improbable to suggest there is no ground for the Black Lives Matter movement unless the claims are based exclusively on black deaths in the hands of the police and not a larger systemic view of violence, poverty, and a legacy of racism in these communities.

Although I do not address the issue of violence within black communities as a concomitant factor in the police presence and actions in these communities, I argue for a complex system in which police use of force and lethal force is overrepresented in comparison with the broader population. In other words, the commonsense grounds of the Black Lives Matter movement, based in the collective experience of black and Hispanic Americans, are reflected in the data. If one looks at the polarization between the view of law enforcement and the local citizen perspective on the deaths of people such as Michael Garner (unarmed young black men killed at the point of arrest), I find two different systems of understanding. Procedurally, the Garner arrest fell within normative police practices, even if it was ugly and poorly handled (Moskos). From the point of view of citizens with a lifetime of exposure to overpolicing, the death of Garner and others represent an ongoing and intersectional devaluing of black life. In other words, even if the death of Garner was technically legal, it was not *right,* and the work of Black Lives Matter is to move the societal conversation forward with real outcomes in not only practices of policing communities most at risk but also addressing the systemic issues that aggregate within these communities. My purpose in putting together heterogeneous data and modes of analysis is to offer a picture of an activist movement that allows for complexity and messiness in its articulation and reception—its societal relay—to facilitate an understanding of the situation from the located experience of those at the front lines (communities and police) and the broader cultural context that shape opportunities for change. With this combination of calling for a clear message in the context of a complex situation, I conclude with a final analysis of an example of complex data in the form of media narrative.

Diamond Reynolds: Complex Data

The third case study examines a new event in the networked data stream around social justice issues raised by Black Lives Matter: the Twitter conversation following the deaths of two black men at the hands of police and the shootings of police officers in Dallas, Texas, and Baton Rouge, Louisiana. This time period, July 5–July 17, 2016, had the hashtags of #BlackLivesMatter, #AllLivesMatter, and #BlueLivesMatter used more often than any other time since the hashtags began appearing on Twitter in July 2013 (Anderson and Hitlin). Additionally, the tone of the online conversation around #BlackLivesMatter shifted, following the attacks on law enforcement. The outcome of this shift was a rise in tweets criticizing the Black Lives Matter movement and a reduction of shared tweets supporting the movement (Freelon, Mcilwain, and Clark). The rise in critical tweets was especially notable after the killing of police officers in Dallas. Although one sees an increase in social media use around these deaths, I focus for the moment on the phenomenon of Diamond Reynolds's real-time streaming of the shooting (and subsequent death) of her boyfriend, Philando Castile (see Figure 21.5). Even as the Twitter stream around the movement became more diverse, discordant, and complex with the killings of police officers as well as additional deaths of black men, my analysis addresses the diverse, discordant, and complex data of Reynolds's transmission.

The significance of her Facebook live video stream speaks to an additional layer of networked view and participation in the event. The nine-minute video catalogs not only Castile bleeding to death in the car but the sound of the police officer screaming in an apparent frenzy followed by the brutal treatment of Reynolds herself by the police. She is handcuffed and taken into custody while her young child observes from the car. The transcript of the event outlines the multiple direct address of the live stream: to Castile, to her audience/friends on Facebook, and to the police officer:

Figure 21.5. Diamond Reynolds's Facebook live video documenting shooting of Philando Castile, YouTube.

[TO CASTILE] Stay with me. [TO CAMERA] We got pulled over for a busted taillight in the back . . .

[COP SCREAMING IN THE BACKGROUND] I told him not to reach for it. I told him to get his hands out.

[TO COP] You told him to get his I.D., sir, his driver's license.

The footage has been characterized by news media as "raw," and it certainly appears to be unstaged. But it would be a mistake not to recognize the technical ability and mental fortitude of Reynolds in her presence of mind to make the transmission (Losh). In this sense, it has been widely accepted as "unfiltered" and "true" by a networked audience, and was included in the trial of Jeronimo Yanez, the officer who shot Castile (acquitted). I point to comments made on the Reynolds video and the black social media around #BLM by hosts of the podcast *The Friend Zone*, whom I cite as representative of YBT sentiment: "Let's be thankful for the activists out there getting the right information to us in real time—videos so we see what is happening versus what the media says is happening. Which we had no idea before social media how much shit they have probably manipulated our entire lives. And now you see it" (*The Friend Zone*). Their point is Reynolds provided a counterpublic with the shadow data of her broadcast, in contrast with the public position of the state, which was silence in advance of Yanez's trial (at the time of the shooting, President Barack Obama and Minnesota governor Mark Dayton made public comments. But neither spoke on behalf of the St. Paul Police Department). Without the broadcast of events, Castile's death might have slipped away from the public eye as an unremarkable part of the status quo. It is the notion of ocular proof—one sees the event in the direct address of real-time (or even as the after effect of "real time")—that offers a complex narrative about the interrelational aspects of data, data context, and analysis.

Conclusion: Precarity

The tragedy of *Othello* rests not with the protagonist's blackness but, rather, with Othello's maniacal need for positivist proof: his demand for ocular proof of his wife's infidelity. It is this materialization, the data of a deed as such, that the villain of the tragedy, Iago, exploits toward the tragic outcome. And yet, I use this figuration in its inverted state: when haunted by the spooky affect and effect of a threatening, racialized environment, whether that of a liberal arts college or a midwestern town, the occupants become activists, marshalling material proof in relation to their own narratives of events: they exhibit a freedom of "self-constitution" from a position of precarity that expands a power of everyday expression. In my use of the concept "shadow data," I frame a wrangling between states of visibility and legibility of "data." Such data serve as counterpublics, where activists make public sites of injustice that *could be* obscured in the quotidian practice of habit. This is a societal habit of mind that too often configures working class and black as a somewhat ghostly position rendered visible once the subject is dead. In subjecting Michael Brown's body to be laid in state as such on the public pavement, exposed to the elements and the gaze of all, catalyzed the sense of injustice and indignity visited on Brown and by extension the community. Unwittingly or not, the police used terroristic tactics of the historic lynch mob in leaving the (often mutilated) body of a black man on display to signal the subjection of black people. Beyond the right not to be killed, the millennial activism of networked publics and counterpublics continues a long-standing claim of a civic and social justice, a claim beyond bare life for the right to live freely, which in many senses is the right to be a citizen (Agamben). In presenting three modes of critical data analysis, small data, big data, and complex data, this investigation offers a view of activist precarity and persistence and the leveraging of informational networks toward the expression of self-constitution and collective action as visible subjects.

Bibliography

Anderson, Monica, and Paul Hitlin. "Social Media Conversations about Race: How Social Media Users See, Share and Discuss Race and the Rise of Hashtags like #BlackLivesMatter." Pew Research Center, August 15, 2016. http://www.pewinternet.org/2016/08/15/social-media-conversations-about-race/.

Agamben, Giorgio. *Homo Sacer.* Stanford, Calif.: Stanford University Press, 1998.

Alexander, Michelle. *The New Jim Crow: Mass Incarceration in the Age of Colorblindness.* New York: New Press, 2010.

Arendt, Hannah. *The Human Condition.* Chicago: University of Chicago Press, 1998.

Association of Critical Collegians. https://colgateacc.tumblr.com/.

Bertini, Enrico, and Moritz Stefaner. "Data Ethics and Privacy with Eleanor Saitta." *Data Stories* (podcast) 74, May 18, 2016.

Bonilla, Yarimar, and Jonathan Rosa. "#Ferguson: Digital Protest, Hashtag Ethnography, and the Racial Politics of Social Media in the United States." *American Ethnologist* 42, no. 1 (February 2015): 4–17.

Borgman, Christine L. *Big Data, Little Data, No Data: Scholarship in the Networked World.* Cambridge, Mass.: MIT Press, 2015.

Brock, André. "From the Blackhand Side: Twitter as a Cultural Conversation." *Journal of Broadcasting & Electronic Media* 56, no. 4 (2012): 529–49.

Bui, Quoctrung, and Amanda Cox. "Surprising New Evidence Shows Bias in Police Use of Force but Not in Shootings." *New York Times,* July 11, 2016.

Butler, Judith. *Notes toward a Performative Theory of Assembly.* Cambridge, Mass.: Harvard University Press, 2016.

Carroll, Joseph. "Public Overestimates U.S. Black and Hispanic Populations." Gallup. http://www.gallup.com/poll/4435/public-overestimates-us-black-hispanic-populations.aspx.

Coleman, Beth. "Race as Technology." *Camera Obscura: Feminism, Culture, and Media Studies* 24, no. 1 70 (2009): 177–207.

Coleman, Beth. "Unmoored Beauty." In *Blubber,* edited by Ellen Gallagher, 177–207. New York: Gagosian Gallery, 2001 (2009).

Crenshaw, Kimberlé. "Mapping the Margins: Intersectionality, Identity Politics, and Violence against Women of Color." *Stanford Law Review* 43: 1241–99.

Donovan, Joan. Interview with author, November 2016.

Freelon, Deen, Charlton Mcilwain, and Meredith Clark. "Beyond the Hashtags: #FERGUSON, #BLACKLIVESMATTER, and Online Media." White paper, Center for Media and Social Impact, American University, 2016.

The Friend Zone (podcast). SoundCloud. https://soundcloud.com/thefriendzonepodcast.

Fryer, Roland. "An Empirical Analysis of Racial Differences in Police Use of Force." Working Paper 22399, National Bureau of Economic Research. www.Nber.Org/Papers/W22399.

Garza, Alicia. "A Herstory of the #BlackLivesMatter Movement." The Feminist Wire. http://www.thefeministwire.com/2014/10/blacklivesmatter-2/.

Gladwell, Malcolm. "Small Change: Why the Revolution Will Not Be Tweeted." *New Yorker,* October 4, 2010.

Gladwell, Malcolm, and Clay Shirky. "From Innovation to Revolution." *Foreign Affairs,* March–April 2011.

Granovetter, Mark S. "The Strength of Weak Ties." *American Journal of Sociology* 78, no. 6 (March 1973): 1360–80.

Gruzd, Anatoliy, and Barry Wellman. "Networked Influence in Social Media." *American Behavioral Scientist* 58, no. 10 (2014): 1251–59. https://doi.org/10.1177/0002764214527087.

Harney, Stefano, and Fred Moten. *The Undercommons: Fugitive Planning & Black Study*. New York: Minor Compositions, 2013.

Kitchin, Rob, Tracey P. Lauriault, and Gavin McArdle, eds. *Data and the City*. London: Routledge, 2017.

Kweku, Ezekiel. "Why It's So Hard to Measure Racial Bias in Police Shootings: What a Headline-Grabbing Study Misses when It Comes to Use of Lethal Force." MTV News, July 12, 2016.

Losh, Elizabeth. "Beyond the Techno-Missionary Narrative: Digital Literacy and Necropolitics." In *Handbook of Writing, Literacies and Education in Digital Culture*, edited by Kathy A. Mills, Amy Stornaiuolo, Anna Smith, and Jessica Zacher Pandya, 76–87. New York: Routledge, 2017.

Mac Donald, Heather. "The Myths of Black Lives Matter: The Movement Has Won Over Hillary Clinton and Bernie Sanders. But What If Its Claims Are Fiction?" *Wall Street Journal*, February 11, 2016.

Moskos, Peter. "DOJ on Michael Brown Shooting: Justified." Cop in the Hood, March 6, 2015. http://www.copinthehood.com/2015/03/doj-on-michael-brown-shooting-justified.html.

Phelps, Michelle. "Yes, There Is Racial 'Bias' in Police Shootings." Scatterplot, July 11, 2016. https://scatter.wordpress.com/2016/07/11/yes-there-is-racial-bias-in-police-shootings/.

Reply All. "The Writing on the Wall." Gimlet, January 14, 2015. https://gimletmedia.com/episode/9-yik-yak/.

Sethi, Rajiv. "A Fallacy of Composition." Rajiv Sethi (blog), July 21, 2016. http://rajivsethi.blogspot.ca/.

Sharma, Sanjay. "Black Twitter? Racial Hashtags, Networks and Contagion." *New Formations* 78 (2013): 46–64.

Taylor, Keeanga-Yamahtta. *From #BlackLivesMatter to Black Freedom*. Princeton, N.J.: Princeton University Press, 2016.

Tufekci, Zeynep. "Engineering the Public: Big Data, Surveillance and Computational Politics." *First Monday* 19, no. 7 (July 2014).

U.S. Department of Justice. "Department of Justice Report Regarding the Criminal Investigation into the Shooting Death of Michael Brown by Ferguson, Missouri Police Officer Darren Wilson." Memorandum, March 4, 2015, 1–86.

PART VI][Chapter 22

Project | Process | Product
Feminist Digital Subjectivity in a Shifting Scholarly Field

KATHRYN HOLLAND AND SUSAN BROWN

How do scholars bring feminist digital and print resources together to create compelling online literary histories? How do feminist projects in digital humanities change over time? We respond to these questions by focusing our discussion on the DH initiative with which we are involved, the Orlando Project.[1] We begin with a look back at the late 1920s, when Virginia Woolf considered new ways of representing women's identities and places in culture via different genres of writing. Shortly after she gave the "Women and Fiction" lectures at Cambridge University that would grow into *A Room of One's Own,* she wrote in her diary about what would come next: "I want fun. I want fantasy. . . . I want to write a history, say, of Newnham [College] or the womans [sic] movement, in the same vein" (Woolf, *Diary*). She then wrote her novel *Orlando: A Biography* (1928), which brings together history and fantasy in fiction. The creative pursuits of its title character, manifest especially in Orlando's long poem *The Oak Tree,* are at the heart of Woolf's narrative about how perspectives on gender, literature, and the individual subject in culture change across historical periods.

The Orlando Project's founding team chose the title of Woolf's "rollicking, future-embracing" novel as the namesake of the research project and its central product, the born-digital, interactive textbase of original scholarship called *Orlando: Women's Writing in the British Isles from the Beginnings to the Present* (Brown, Clements, and Grundy, *Orlando,* Cambridge University Press online, 2006–2018). As explorations of writing by women and its conditions of possibility, both are inspired by Woolf's narrative about gender and literature. The digital *Orlando* provides interpretations of women authors' nuanced lives and writing in the material and cultural conditions of their times, and it documents attitudes toward such authors and their work that emerged across historical periods. The project and textbase also are strikingly different from Woolf's fiction. The Orlando Project's ongoing work is collaborative, involving many authors rather than one. Conceived by

Patricia Clements, Isobel Grundy, and Susan Brown, it has brought together scholars, students, and technical personnel whose interests often include but are not limited to feminist literary history. Since the project began more than twenty years ago, more than 140 team members have contributed to the textbase, ensuring that it is not dominated by a single scholarly perspective. A collection of encoded prose entries about individual authors with varied search options in its interface, its materials can be configured according to each user's choices. It comprises a complex of narratives concerned with topics in literary and cultural history that pushes against notions of siloed authors and discrete movements and periods.

The textbase discusses authors and writing both in and far from canonical centers, with an infrastructure that ensures figures and texts are positioned in relation to each other, in and beyond their respective milieus. Users can conduct searches via authors' names and read individual entries. But they will find more provocative information about intimate and larger-scale shifts and continuities in literary history—and gain a stronger sense of the textbase's interlinked content and dynamic configuration—when they conduct topic searches that provide users with sets of excerpts from entries throughout the textbase. Entries are complemented by a chronology of events, which conveys more information about historical periods, and a bibliography of primary and secondary sources cited by contributors, which situates our work in an expansive body of feminist scholarship and constantly points users to writing that extends outside of the textbase. Content changes regularly, with twice-annual additions and revisions. By mid-2018 *Orlando* contained more than 8.5 million words and more than 1,300 entries about authors from 612 BCE onward, chronicled more than 30,000 events, and engaged with more than 25,000 sources. It is designed to stimulate understandings of the particularities and larger recurring issues in women's writing while it supports its users' own readings of primary literary and historical texts and their production of new studies.

Our project's logo, an oak tree, pays homage to *The Oak Tree* written by Woolf's 1928 protagonist and to the digital medium that facilitates the creation of other forms of writing. It gestures particularly at the branching shapes of custom markup schemas, designed by the team at the project's outset, which generate the textbase's content and flexible form.[2] When contributors create entries, they simultaneously write in prose and mark up their prose using the project's semantic tagsets, the expansive, nested set of information categories, or tags, that represent our feminist priorities. The markup schema for writing about authors' lives includes tags for cultural formation, education, occupations, and intimate relationships, among others. The schema for encoding writing about authors' bodies of work includes tags for production, textual features, and reception, with subcategories about such issues as manuscript history, genres, and recognition. *Orlando*'s markup guides contributors' approaches to literary history as they produce entries and, also crucially, enables users' searches for sets of excerpts drawn from across the textbase and their navigation from one entry to another. It is the markup that makes the textbase a distinctive resource. Without a beginning, end, or center with peripheries, it is nonteleological in providing unpredictable, manifold pathways into and through entries. It "makes possible a new, reader-centred model of literary history that does not present a single, linear story: it is formed of thousands of multiply linked and dynamic portions of text which can be navigated, retrieved, and reordered in myriad ways" according to each user's choices (Brown, Clements, and Grundy, "Scholarly Introduction").

In this essay we discuss the Orlando Project and textbase to consider the challenges facing large, long-standing feminist initiatives in DH. We engage with recent observations that are giving momentum to new conversations in the field. Jacqueline Wernimont and Katherine D. Harris have asserted, "It does not seem to us that there has been a sustained inquiry into the evolving relationships between feminist theory and DH work" ("Feminisms and DH"). Roopika Risam has identified "the pressing need to expand the purview of digital humanities scholarship to explore gender through intersectional lenses that include sexuality, race, class, and national context" ("Introduction"). Their apt statements—along with articles in the two journal issues Wernimont and Risam edited and introduced—follow Jamie "Skye" Bianco's argument about the necessity of advancing explicit and wide-reaching feminist work in DH, where she cites Luce Irigaray and Audre Lorde, among others. Bianco writes, "This is not a moment to abdicate the political, social, cultural, and philosophical, but rather one for an open discussion of their inclusion in the ethology and methods of the digital humanities" (Bianco). An analysis of the work of the Orlando Project conveys some of the diversity within the genealogy of DH and the ways in which established processes and texts transform over time. We focus on the Orlando Project's markup as a system of principles closely related to poststructuralist feminist theory, then turn to the pedagogical practices undertaken by the collaborative team that yield the textbase and less tangible intellectual products, which support and inform new literary-historical processes beyond the team.

Finally, we examine the interplay between the Orlando Project's established and new activities, the latter of which we call Orlando 2.0. One of our central concerns in Orlando 2.0, the development of its semantic web ontology poses challenges for the effective representation of varied, changing, even contradictory vocabularies and concepts with contemporary computational systems at the same time that the ontology represents an exciting move toward providing greater access to its knowledge base via a large set of linked open data derived from the textbase's markup. The broadening of the project's contributor base, supported by the use of a new in-browser text markup editor, requires altered approaches to training, peer review, and attribution but offers meaningful opportunities for the inclusion of more diverse scholarly perspectives and alternative sustainability models as the project and the field of DH continue to change.

Markup and Theory

The project's markup is informed by theory written in prose, and at the same time, it communicates with theory. Here, we argue that *Orlando*'s custom markup schemas embody a digital feminist theory. With tagsets for each type of textbase document (Life, Writing, Events), the schemas instantiate the principles that shape interpretations and guide practices in the creation of the textbase (Orlando Project schemas). The two principal tagsets, for Life and Writing, represent the heterogeneity and nuances of women's identities, texts, and related activities. Before contributors produce entries, they learn about how the tagsets prioritize discussions of topics in literary and cultural history, such as education and travel in Life and manuscript history and influences in Writing. Team members then work with the tagsets as they simultaneously write and encode. In total, the tagsets contain 205 tags, 114 attributes, and 635 attribute values. Many tags have their own attributes (which act like adjectives, modifying and making more precise the meaning of the tag) or subtags, which allow project members to encode their prose with greater specificity; members of the team can also write with additional precision by using attribute values. This markup is a guide for the work of contributors, turning their attention to key issues in feminist literary history; it is a conduit by which established approaches to gender, literature, and culture are represented in new, born-digital writing; when users conduct tag searches and click on hyperlinks, they make the markup a tool for navigating the published textbase. Our identification of *Orlando*'s markup with feminist theory aligns with Stephen Ramsey and Geoffrey Rockwell's observations about "the communicative power of the instrumental." They argue that one way "to think of digital artifacts as theories would be to think of them as hermeneutical instruments through which we can interpret other phenomena" (Ramsey and Rockwell). Wielded by the project's research team and its users, the markup conveys a feminist theory of subjectivity in which women's identities and writing are understood to be multiple, substantial, historically and materially contingent, and at times unknown or incongruous with the concepts and language of our time. It demonstrates how theory fosters new forms of critical interpretation and new digital artifacts.

The history of *Orlando*'s text encoding is part of two larger histories: those of digital markup and the integration of feminist theory in literary studies. Its markup was created in the mid-1990s, before the production of textbase entries began, by a team of more than twenty literary researchers with guidance from leading digital humanities scholar Susan Hockey and colleagues such as Julia Flanders and Allen Renear, then with the Women Writers Project at Brown University. It is part of the explosion of interdisciplinary understandings and uses of hierarchical data structures that was stimulated by the first stages of work on the Text Encoding Initiative (TEI) and foundational scholarship in this area, initially on such issues as descriptive markup and the Ordered Hierarchy of Content Objects in scholarly text processing (Coombes, Renear, and DeRose; DeRose et al.). Lou Burnard has observed that markup systems reflect the priorities and research agendas of their creators and users, and identifies one of the most critical functions of markup as its ability to map "a (human) interpretation of the text into a set of codes on which computer processing can be performed." He concentrates on how markup sustains texts' accessibility and stimulates new discussions of them, claiming that it is "nothing less than the vehicle by which the scholarly tradition is to be maintained." Whereas Burnard discusses the implications of encoding formal features of digitized texts, the Orlando Project produced semantic markup for original, born-digital scholarship. But Burnard's argument that "markup theory is . . . at the heart of the humanistic tradition, rather than an incidental technology or an irrelevant appendage to it" ("On the Hermeneutic Implications") is relevant to this project's work. Team members drew from and in certain respects contested the prevailing conception of markup at this time through its insistence on the value of a highly interpretive, politically invested form of knowledge representation as a means of addressing women writers' varied, intersectional lives, their texts, and their related contributions to artistic and social movements (see Butler et al., for example). The creation and use of the CulturalFormation tag exemplify the project's feminist focus. The tag allows contributors to consider and represent the ways that women writers are distinctive and part of social groups, with perspectives and work shaped by their positions in relation to numerous historically constituted identity categories: to encode information about authors' lives, the tag contains such subtags as Sexuality, RaceAndEthnicity, and PoliticalAffiliation. Contributors use whatever combination of CulturalFormation options is relevant to each author entry, but all entries must contain a discussion of the author's identity using at least one. When users conduct searches via these tags, the system retrieves excerpts from entries containing them, which in turn illuminate the points of contact and difference among authors of varied communities, places, and times. The *Orlando* schemas enable humanities (if not necessarily humanistic) inquiry in a digital environment by serving as a lens for articulating literary history. Its creators suggest this via one of their metaphors in an early article about the project, published when the markup was complete and textbase entry production was underway. "We want computers to help us to bring together and into focus the complex relationships that inform literary history" (Brown and Clements). Along with other initiatives active from the early phases of DH onward, such as the Women Writers Project, Orlando makes feminist principles and methods central to text encoding.

The creation and use of semantic markup in *Orlando* are connected to the work of feminist theorists developed outside of digital studies. Its editors link the collaborative project and textbase's structure and content to words on pages, including Susan Stanford Friedman's discussion of the complementary "post-structuralist critique of narrative history and the activist imperative towards creating stories that shape the possibilities from which futures are forged. *Orlando* takes up her invitation to feminists to engage in 'a dialogic, not monologic, project of writing feminist histories—in the plural'" (Brown, Clements, and Grundy, "Scholarly Introduction"). The production of *Orlando*'s markup was informed by team members' knowledge of successive issues in literary and cultural history, and the textbase contains not only quotations from and citations of its specific primary and secondary sources in author entries but also an implicit intertextual relationship with the work of feminist theorists. Designed to be employed by varied project members who create all entries and appeal to diverse users when they explore the textbase, it positions women as creative agents at the center of literary history and attends to the shifting perspectives on their lives and works. *Orlando*'s markup responds to and advances writing by such thinkers as Luce Irigaray. It extends Irigaray's assertions in "This Sex Which Is Not One" about the plurality within individual women—"We are luminous. Neither one nor two"—and the necessity of understanding that "women do not constitute, strictly speaking, a class, and their dispersion among several classes makes their political struggle complex, their demands sometimes contradictory" (*This Sex Which Is Not One*). Contrasts are also clear. Irigaray argues that "we haven't been taught, nor allowed, to express multiplicity. To do that would be to speak improperly." Women in society serve as "a medium of exchange, with very little profit to them" (*This Sex Which Is Not One*). The project's markup addresses pervasive gender inequalities and recognizes the complex significance and visibility of women writers' work in varied locations and historical periods. A juxtaposition of the tagsets with Irigaray's writing begins to suggest the influence of feminist theories of subjectivity on digital studies and intertexts between print and born-digital writing. *Orlando*'s editors explain, "Markup systems can operate as a culmination of, rather than a departure from, recent theoretically and politically informed work in the humanities" (Brown, Clements, and Grundy, "Scholarly Introduction").

The Life and Writing tagsets, with tags that contain attributes and attribute values, enable feminist interpretations of authors' lives, writing, and participation in cultural movements. Two examples suggest this. First, the inclusion of the IntimateRelationships tag in the Life tagset is a statement about the dynamics between identity terms and the lived experiences that affirm and/or contradict them. It creates space for representations of authors' encounters and experiences that can complement issues explored in another Life tag we discuss above, CulturalFormation, where authors' intersectional identities are considered along lines that include sexuality and ethnicity, with attributes to capture information about such issues as current alternative terms for particular categories and whether authors self-defined with them. The IntimateRelationships tag also attends to experiences that are not effectively illuminated by either Sexuality or other Life tags, Family and FriendsAssociates. Its tag attribute Erotic and attribute values EroticYes, EroticNo, and EroticPossibly convey a spectrum of emotional, physical, and intellectual aspects of lived intimacy. IntimateRelationships can be included multiple times in a single entry, or not at all. It can capture aspects of subjects' activities and communities that involve companionship, romance, queerness, chastity, sapphism, domesticity, and separation, as well as discussions of how they resist or complicate such terms. It also can be used to identify contested accounts of intimacy, the lack of intimacy, the absence of information, or incommensurability between sexual identities and intimacies. IntimateRelationships thus conceptualizes personal, historical experiences as diverse, contextualized, open to numerous definitions or no specific definition whatsoever.

Second, the TextualFeatures tag contains the Genre tag with GenreName attribute. The Genre tag and its GenreName attribute are part of the Writing tagset, whose schema is more nuanced and less hierarchical than the Life schema, reflecting the project's attention to simultaneous, overlapping issues in the production, textual features, and reception of authors' works within literary history (Brown, Clements, and Grundy, "Scholarly Introduction"). Designed to foster understandings of how women are always already involved in the development of varied kinds of writing, the GenreName attribute has a list of 246 attribute values that each represent one type of text. These include the bildungsroman, cabaret, commonplace book, computer program, dedication, dream vision, haiku, novel, ode, sensation novel, treatise, and villanelle. The attribute values for GenreName can be used multiple times in any entry to discuss how authors accept and/or transform the conventions of a genre in a number of their individual texts or bodies of work. Multiple tags and their attributes also can be used to encode the discussion of a single text. Evidence, speculation, or controversy about a genre's development can be addressed there and in GenreIssue, a tag designed to capture significant discussions around Genre. The Genre tag's attribute, GenreName, comprises a picklist of attribute values that assert the heterogeneity of texts in literary history. Its use enables interpretations of the presence and significance of types of writing traditionally dominated by women, of the contributions of women to genres whose best-known authors are male, and of the ways all genres change over time because of the work of authors and communities. It also stimulates discussions by scholars who question, for instance, whether its categories conform to male-centered literary and cultural histories (Masters). Though the two tags differ in their flexibility and complexity, IntimateRelationships and Genre are both part of the conceptual core of *Orlando* that drives the creation of author entries and the ways that users engage with them.

Through *Orlando*'s interface, markup is visible to not only the project's researchers but also its users. A user can explore the tags in the textbase and its paratexts. They can inspire searches that begin on the textbase's homepage, with support from the tutorial for our Tag Search options; they can be seen in all entries if a user clicks the Show Markup and Show Tag Context buttons at the top of any screen; and they are described with illustrated examples from the Life and Writing tagsets in the textbase's documentation and on the project's public website. Users can read sets of excerpts from entries and/or move from one entry to another using the Tag Search option, and in this way they can explore how any tag and its attributes have informed the content of entries. A search for content about intertextual connections among the writing of Radclyffe Hall and others, for example, will yield discussions of the points of contact between the modernist author's fiction and writing by authors in the textbase, including the contemporary poet Jackie Kay. As Figure 22.1 indicates, a user who conducts this search will find a prose excerpt from Kay's entry, detailing the link between her early 1990s poetry and Hall, alongside other results from entries across the textbase. They also have the option of using the screen's Show Markup and Show Tag Context buttons to view the prose in its tagging framework and focus on the interplay between the prose, their chosen tag, and its attributes and attribute values (see Figure 22.2). They can read the markup, use it to move through the textbase in ways that suit their needs, and debate its value in the textbase and its potential to inform the development of feminist literary history. Explorations of *Orlando*'s markup depend on users' understanding of XML; our specific tagging system; and search capabilities of the textbase's interface, which requires users to invest time in reading, at minimum, the textbase's Scholarly Introduction. Reviews of the textbase and informal user feedback continue to challenge us to make *Orlando*'s markup legible to interested audiences who can then leverage it for their in-depth engagement with the textbase. The place of semantic tagging in *Orlando* indicates how DH projects can create, disseminate, and foster debates in feminist theory and literary history, while it raises questions about the visibility of markup for diverse users.

Orlando's tagsets at once reify and engage with feminist theory, first communicated in printed prose, to produce discussions and interpretations of literary history.

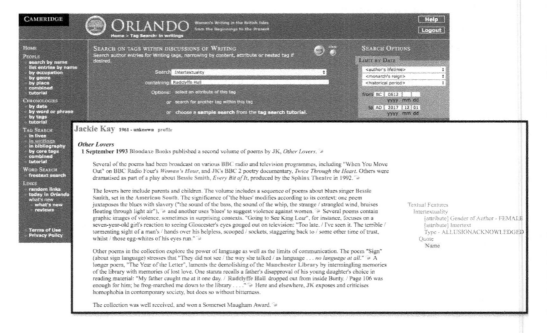

Figure 22.1. Screen for Tag Search on Writing, with search for "Radclyffe Hall" within Intertextuality tag, and one result of search with Show Tag Context option selected.

About the Tags

Writing Tags - Textual Features

Textual Features

Definition
One of the three major, structuring components of Writing documents, this element addresses potentially every aspect of texts, including structure, style, and components like fictional characters or settings.

Related Tags
This element allows for multiple related sub-elements: Characterization, Character Name, Character Type or Role, Genre Issue, Genre, Intertextuality, Motif, Plot, Setting Date, Setting Place, Techniques, Theme or Topic (treated in text), Tone or Style, and Voice or Narration. An initial "t" beginning each of these element-names links it to the Textual Features element even where its placing is outside the major element.

Intertextuality

Definition
This element, found in the Textual Features section of Writing documents, encloses discussion of gestures in a text towards other texts.

Related Tags
It has two optional attributes, Intertext Type and Gender of Author.

Intertext Type

Definition
This attribute on the element Intertextuality, in the Textual Features component of Writing documents, specifies different kinds of intertextual relationship.

Related Tags
It has the following alternative values: AllusionAcknowledged (where the textual debt is explicitly flagged), AllusionUnacknowledged (where textual parallel is left unsignalled), Quotation (words or phrases directly repeated, generally in a prominent position: like title or title-page), Misquotation (deliberate or accidental alteration of words quoted), Parody (a close formal copy, designed to make fun), Satire (a broader send-up of another text), Imitation (adopting characteristics of earlier text as pattern), Adaptation-update (re-telling or ingenious recasting), Prequel (a text designed to come before its related text, as *Wide Sargasso Sea* relates to *Jane Eyre*), Continuation (a sequel), and Answer (a riposte).

Gender of Author

Definition
This attribute on the element Intertextuality, found in Writing documents, identifies the gender of the author who wrote the intertext.

```
<TINTERTEXTUALITY INTERTEXTTYPE=ALLUSIONACKNOWLEDGED GENDEROFAUTHOR=
FEMALE > One stanza recalls <TCHARACTERTYPEROLE > a father</TCHARACTERTYPEROLE> 's disapproval of
his young daughter's choice in reading material: <QUOTE DIRECT=Y > My father caught me at it one day.
/ <NAME STANDARD=Hall, Radclyffe> Radclyffe Hall </NAME> dropped out from
inside <TITLE TITLETYPE=JOURNAL REND=normal > Bunty </TITLE> . / Page 106 was enough for him; he frog-
marched me down to the library . . . . </QUOTE></TINTERTEXTUALITY>
```

Figure 22.2. Textual Features tag diagram for the *Orlando* Writing tagset, excerpts of documentation for Intertextuality element and attributes, and a simplified view of an excerpt from the Figure 22.1 tag search results with the Show Markup view selected.

Those discussions and interpretations happened initially in the prepublication work of our collaborative team; now they are performed by both the team that continues to update and revise the textbase and the users who forge their own rhizomatic paths by moving through it at will. The schemas, themselves digital texts, offer a system of feminist principles containing component parts that together guide the practices of textbase entry creation and exploration. They shape the Orlando Project team's understanding and organization of the materials they discover in their research and synthesize in the creation of entries. It challenges the textbase's users to set their paths through literary history via its principles. As Alan Galey and Stan Ruecker have suggested in their work on the processes by which prototypes are made and used, "the digital humanities will surely benefit from recognizing the diversity of forms which theories and critical arguments may take." There also is significant value in highlighting digital objects' "intricate and dynamic" elements that are less visible or familiar than other parts of those objects (Galey and Ruecker). *Orlando*'s markup, which is constantly in dialogue with the more prominent and easily intelligible prose of the textbase entries, indicates how theory can be used in digital environments. It suggests how analog forms of feminist theory are generative of digital ones, which operate differently in the dialogical space of encoded textuality which has its own representational specificities.

Pedagogy in Collaboration

The Orlando Project's ongoing work includes the collaborative feminist practice in which the team uses its markup to create the scholarly prose of the textbase. Pedagogy is one of its central foci. At an early stage, its editors observed, "In an important sense, [students] are the project" (Brown and Clements). Project members take feminist perspectives to both the cultures they write about and the one in which they work: "We understand gender as cutting across every element of our project, from the time past we are constructing together to the time present in which we are working together to construct it" (Brown and Clements). Their activities are driven by the idea that feminist researchers "need to be not just *consumers* of technology, but *producers* of technological tools that suit our aims and methodologies" (Brown, Clements, and Grundy, "Sorting Things In," original emphasis) and the understanding that such production is best achieved by the team, including student members who learn as they employ such tools. The markup is a tool for the creation of new and revised entries, which users explore in the published textbase and connect to their own studies, digital or analog. But before that stage, the markup enriches project members' knowledge of the critical decisions required for the development of literary scholarship as well as the collaborative models for such work.

The Orlando Project's student members are research assistants who work together and with scholars and technical experts on multiple parts of the textbase: primarily the encoded entries, events chronology, and bibliographical database. Since its beginnings, the project has employed seven postdoctoral fellows and approximately 120 graduate and senior undergraduate students based in humanities disciplines at the University of Alberta and University of Guelph. The number of student participants has fluctuated, depending on the project's needs, and has ranged between approximately five and fourteen in any given academic year; they are employed for a minimum of six hours per week for one academic term, though many student participants work twelve hours per week and remain on the team for one or more years. Junior members are taught by and write with senior scholars on the team, who specialize in feminist literary history of several periods, and with a systems analyst and programmer, metadata coordinators, and textbase managers. Their work includes learning about the project's tagging system during their training period, viewing and assessing it when they check entries produced by others, and activating it when they write entries themselves and support newer members of the team.

The project's collaborations bring people of different generations and disciplines together to learn about and create feminist DH scholarship. They comprise a multidirectional apprenticeship model, where participants expand their intellectual interests and skills during and well after their studies. They are in some ways similar to pedagogical models in other environments. Carolyn Shrewsbury sees feminist pedagogy concerned with "community, empowerment, and leadership" in the nondigital classroom and draws on Audre Lorde's arguments about the value of difference: "the sharing of intellectual discovery . . . 'forms a bridge between sharers which can be the basis of understanding much of what is not shared between them'" (Lorde, *Sister Outsider*, qtd. in Shrewsbury). Empowering differences also drive collaborations in digital contexts. Moya Bailey's study of social media activism by trans women of color is based on her work with her subjects. In her discussion of feminist standards in collaborative digital research, Bailey advises researchers to ask the following questions, among others: "How does everyone benefit from the research? . . . What tools or methods encourage multidirectional collaboration?" ("#transform(ing)"). For Bailey, consent and visibility are crucial elements of collaboration in public fields. Orlando's practices differ slightly from Bailey's, because the project focuses on student learning in academic research settings. Aspects of our work are hierarchical: the textbase's editors determine which authors have entries, but they are open to suggestions based on students' interests; editors review all completed entries before publication, but they also accept revisions to their own work made by students. Though we have begun to work with external contributors, which enables us to strengthen the textbase by drawing on the expertise of more diverse scholars and students, most of the team is based at two Canadian universities. Nonetheless, the team's practices suggest how feminist collaborations can thrive and yield long-term benefits when students make deliberate, sustained contributions to digital scholarship, with compensation and credit for the work they undertake with teachers and mentors to produce resources used by their peers and the public.

The project's workflow is designed around the training and mentorship of students. By being involved in textbase entry production at several stages, students contribute to a digital literary history that prioritizes considerations of gender with the use of "intersectional lenses that include sexuality, race, class, and national context" (Risam, "Introduction"). They acquire the kind of literacy that Tara McPherson identifies as vital to DH. By gaining experience in "systemic modes of thinking that can understand relation and honor complexity, even while valuing precision and specificity," research assistants who contribute to the textbase are able to "engage technology . . . as a productive and generative space that is always emergent and never fully determined" ("Why"). They are participants in an intellectual community based in physical and digital environments, with exchanges happening in real time and asynchronously in the project's online workspace and, crucially, the offices and labs used by project members on both campuses. New project members begin their work during in-person training sessions led by senior scholars with frequent contributions from technical personnel and established student members, where they learn about the questions and goals that continue to animate the project, the features of the custom markup and XML editor used with it, the existing textbase, and the processes and sources with which new textbase entries are created. Their learning continues in and outside of shared work times, as they progress from checking newly written author entries and adding bibliographic entries for publication in *Orlando*'s biannual updates, to the more challenging work of researching, writing, and encoding new entries that suit their interests and may overlap with texts and movements they explore in their own programs. They see the custom markup in use by others, work with it in their entry writing, and sharpen their fellow students' knowledge of it as they gain expertise.

As the textbase grows and other *Orlando* products develop, students' roles in collaborations are transformative, always emergent. So, too, are the long-term effects of their activities. In her study of early phases of DH scholarship, Amy Earhart observes the disappearance of small-scale, often DIY recovery projects that produced digital texts to counter the effects of canonical sources and perspectives in humanities disciplines, but whose work has been lost because of declining support ("Can Information Be Unfettered?"). The Orlando Project's relative stability has multiple effects on its student participants and users. First, it preserves the textbase contributions of earlier cohorts, which continue to be used by other research assistants and students who encounter them in their courses or library-based research. Students who use the textbase itself not only discuss entries in their own papers but also see a model in which their peers produce writing with experts in their fields for publication by a university press. Second, the project's continuity enables interested research assistants to take on roles that are flexible and evolve over time. For example, one student member joined the Orlando Project as a research assistant when she was an MA student at Guelph and rejoined it as a postdoctoral fellow after completing her PhD at Alberta; a student at Alberta began his work as a research assistant during his MA studies and then became Textflow Manager when he completed his program. Postdoctoral and student members of the team have published articles, edited collections, delivered presentations, and led workshops based on their contributions to the project—working individually and in groups (see, for example, Binhammer and Wood). Team members also leverage the project's sustained training and collaborative opportunities as they gain expertise and power in the academy, publishing, and industry, among other fields. All of these activities advance participants' own intellectual and professional lives and reinforce the project's feminist principles by ensuring that the project has diverse public faces rather than being represented by a single person or generation or discipline.

DH scholars have repeatedly attended to the importance of attribution and compensation of labor in the development of feminist scholarship. Moya Bailey observes the necessity of "find[ing] meaningful ways to compensate [her collaborative] group for their work and time" and "creating more opportunities that challenge the ways that researchers have traditionally compensated and shared in the benefits that come from doing research" ("#transform(ing)"). The contributions of the Orlando Project's team are recognized in varied ways. Members' names and descriptions of their activities are listed on the project's public website and the Credits and Acknowledgements page of the textbase site; the collaborative processes that make *Orlando* are discussed in the same places. As individuals move forward with their professional lives in and outside of the academy, they use a shared method for describing their roles and writing on CVs and résumés. Student participation is discussed in lectures and published articles by senior and junior members; student members receive financial support when they travel to present papers and posters about the project. Their labor is acknowledged financially through different resources available during the project's several stages to date. Since the beginning of the project the employment of its students, postdoctoral fellows, and technical personnel has been funded by internal and external grants, in-kind support, and publication revenue. The textbase is published by Cambridge University Press, and royalties from subscriptions, with sliding scale rates for individuals and institutions, are fed entirely back into the project, a very different model from open-access, especially crowdsourced, sites that might be built on contributed, unpaid labor.[3] Thus although the Orlando Project's impact, particularly beyond but also within academia, has undoubtedly been limited by the subscription wall, numerous factors pushed the project toward publication with a commercial press. There are pros and cons to this: *Orlando* has less control over how it is marketed and published (although responsible for technical updates on its bespoke delivery system) but avoids the need to maintain a publication platform or, as with some self-published projects, to administer subscriptions. This also means less direct knowledge of who subscribes to *Orlando*: the project does not receive lists of subscribers. However, at certain moments when institutional support seemed to falter, the formal publishing agreement between university and publisher has served as a buffer against hasty decisions, and the revenue, although complemented by other sources, provides a cushion against cuts. Meanwhile, we have also pushed toward openness, starting soon after initial publication with exposing the overview screens of all entries and making the entire project open in celebration of Women's History Month each March, during which time usage predictably jumps dramatically, since many institutions and individuals cannot afford subscriptions. More recently, with experiments in linked data and Orlando 2.0, the project continues to work toward greater openness.

This distribution model and the funding connected to it provide resources for the advancement of feminist pedagogy in collaborative scholarship. In her reflections on feminist ethics and politics in data visualization projects, Catherine D'Ignazio points to the value of identifying such initiatives' funders, data-collectors, and the conditions that make their visualizations possible. This approach "reference[s] the material economy behind the data," including the costs and processes that make digital resources available. It thereby fosters understandings of "not just 'what the data says' but [also of] how the data connects to real bodies, systems and structures of power in the wider world" ("Feminist Data Visualization"). The plan from the outset had been to publish with an academic press, and the delivery system work was funded by a combination of a generous advance from Cambridge University Press and funds from the University of Alberta, which was very pleased to commercialize a product of humanities research. Moreover, contributors to the project were convinced that given the unusual nature of the textbase, it was important to credibility to go through a peer-review process, and indeed, such credibility remains important to contributors as we move to broaden our contributor base. The paid research opportunities and visibility of students' participation in the Orlando Project demonstrate the importance of team members' work and show how the published textbase connects to the group of individuals who produce it and the culture to which it belongs. Royalties and grants make these opportunities for training and collaboration possible at the same time that they contribute to the sustainability of existing digital scholarship. *Orlando*'s type of publication, behind a paywall, limits most of the textbase to individual subscribers, members of institutions that subscribe, trial users, and users who access it for free during Women's History Month. The subscription model, however, strongly supports *Orlando*'s accessibility by enabling the long-term survival, maintenance, and expansion of the textbase in ways that benefit the student team members who contribute to it and the users who explore it. This model also inspires us to conduct experiments that will enable greater openness.

Phases of Feminist Digital Scholarship

Large, institutional projects are inevitably shaped by challenges for their continued legitimacy and sustainability. The project's twenty-year lifespan to date can be divided into three distinct phases with a fourth just launching now. A brief overview of those periods can be seen in Figure 22.3.

The initial, grant-funded period of the Orlando Project brought the project legitimacy, as one of the earliest humanities projects to be funded under the Social Sciences and Humanities Research Council of Canada's (SSHRC's) newly established Major Collaborative Research Initiatives Program. This grant for an explicitly feminist project crucially enabled the establishment of a large and predominantly female team of researchers, postdoctoral fellows, a "project librarian" whose role later morphed into metadata coordinator, an average of six to eight graduate research assistants, a technical staff member from the research computing unit, and an administrator. This funding gave the project space to figure out an approach to doing literary history with computers, from the lengthy process of designing our document type definitions (DTDs) to building a back-end production system that would ensure that no one could edit the same materials simultaneously, apply workflow stamps associated with documents, and run various reports to help us clean up the materials. Although the project was not successful in renewing this major grant when the project took longer than anticipated due to the complexity

Project | Process | Product [423

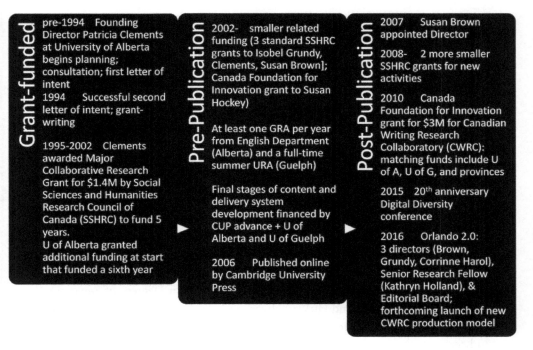

Figure 22.3. Brief timeline of the Orlando Project.

of the technical work, SSHRC also funded individual research grants to each of the project editors that assisted substantially with the completion of the project, which has also since completion received several follow-up grants related to the technical side of the project. Although team members felt that a turn away from feminism was in part responsible for lack of further major funding, the initial major grant and pattern of semiregular support for related initiatives reflect SSHRC's positive track record in funding explicitly feminist scholarship. As with the Canada Research Chairs program, in which increased awards to female and feminist researchers came only after significant critique and lobbying, this pattern reflects significant service by senior women academics.

It is noteworthy that there was not a single penny in the initial Orlando Project budget for programming to build a publication interface. We were confident, in those heady early days in which SGML was arriving on the web, that within five years there would be an off-the-shelf solution; indeed, with Electronic Book Technologies' DynaText/DynaWeb, which the team used for some time, and which was seeing uptake by other scholarly projects, it seemed certain that the available software would become both more sophisticated and easier to use (Burrows). However, this was not the case, so while the project's research productivity continued to increase, it became increasingly clear that it would need to find significant unanticipated funds to produce a bespoke delivery system. Once the initial grant funding was exhausted, we were able to sustain activities through a combination of very generous support in the form of continuing research assistant positions from the Department of English at the Universities of Alberta and Guelph and smaller grants; however, this funding was dedicated in large part to the completion of the textbase content, not the front end for web delivery. The delivery system involved not only styling the content but creating a complex search system that could really leverage the project's markup, without which its intellectual innovation would have been unreadable.

Postpublication, founding director and grant holder Patricia Clements was succeeded by Susan Brown. Core textbase research activities have been sustained by the Universities of Alberta and Guelph, which perceive the high pedagogical value of the experience students gain on the project, and revenues from Cambridge. Continued research and writing to expand the textbase settled down to a regular rhythm with a new cohort of research assistants gaining experience of collaborative research and writing annually, and research grants supporting experimental work in visualization and other technical experimentation, activities in dialogic relationship to the textbase and its aims. These range from the development of various experimental tools and interfaces (experiments with the Mandala browser, a Degrees of Separation prototype, and the OVis and HuViz network visualization prototypes) that allows us to explore *Orlando* content in new environments with affordances that are more in keeping with feminist priorities than are many conventional data visualization practices (D'Ignazio). We are also designing a linked data ontology for representing intersectional identities.

Orlando's data have been incorporated into the work of other projects such as the Women Writers Project, directed by Julia Flanders and now at Northeastern University, and Michelle Levy's Women's Print History Project, 1750–1830, at Simon Fraser University. In such contexts, *Orlando*'s data literally operate differently, within other technological and representational systems, for different ends. Within the Women Writers Project's authoritative collection of textual editions produced using the Text Encoding Initiative (TEI), *Orlando*'s data were sought as secondary or background information on authors. Within this context, much is gained in the linkages to the texts themselves, but something is lost too. The project's bespoke semantic markup and the interface that foregrounds it are replaced by a more general semantic encoding framework, so the intimate relationship between the coproduced markup and the readable text is lost, as are the connections to other writers in the textbase. Likewise, *Orlando*'s bibliographic data within the Print History project will be enriched and differently inflected by a print culture approach, but the shift to a database model means that the texts are divorced from their original semantic and discursive contexts. As indicated, in both these cases, the data were provided directly to the partner projects and then manipulated by them into the state in which they needed them. The synergies glimpsed through these small collaborations intensified the yen for more sustained interlinking and interoperability with complementary projects, which we had been exploring on and off since the turn of the century, including through the short-lived Naming and Other Metadata for

Electronic Networking initiative that aimed to interlink a number of projects, and an attempt at a generic application programming interface that proved to be anything but. The project's foray into linked data is aimed to make a body of *Orlando* data more generally accessible for experimentation and reuse in a range of formats while respecting the terms of the agreement with Cambridge.

Charged with finding modes of sustaining the project, and given the lack of funding streams for sustaining active research projects, Brown turned to infrastructure funding to rebuild the crumbling back-end production system and to respond to the desire of other researchers, particularly in the Canadian literary studies community, for resources similar to *Orlando*. The Canadian Writing Research Collaboratory (CWRC) project received funding from the Canada Foundation for Innovation, the country's funder of scientific research infrastructure, to extend and update the Orlando Project production system into a more generic platform for digital literary studies. The collaboratory will in turn enable broader participation by the scholarly community in the Orlando Project, substantially changing its mode of production.

The Canadian Writing Research Collaboratory project adopts a sustainability model whose viability remains to be tested, but one whose principles are arguably more consistent with a feminist research ethos than an implicitly competitive model. Drawing on and attempting to implement in its infrastructural design a model of "socialized scholarship" (Brown, "Socialized Scholarship"), it makes the project's sustainability a shared need of a number of DH projects. Resources for sustaining and improving it will, within this model, benefit and assist in sustaining other, often less well-resourced, research projects. These will retain their distinctive project home pages and identities within CWRC (and highly customized interfaces, if feasible) and can scale up or down, be active or fallow, as necessary depending on the circumstances and resources of the project members. Tying the Orlando Project into other projects through a linked open data strategy for interoperability, a shared commitment to pursuing best practices in the creation of digital scholarship, and a common(s) platform pave the way for new relations of production, consumption, and sustainability. These new relations will retain the individual project identities (and support of individual scholarly endeavors) that still ground systems of academic credit, rewards, and resourcing and attempt to move digital scholarship in the humanities beyond silos and solo research. Compromises to such an endeavor include investments of time, constraints flowing from shared data models and standards, and a range of limitations associated with using more generic open-source systems. However, because this infrastructure is an extension of *Orlando*'s structure and builds on its practices, while enabling a wider range materials and types of scholarship, we hope to have been able to mitigate some of those disadvantages.

It is noteworthy that the Orlando Project's relatively long life has proceeded (not without periods of uncertainty) independently of either a faculty-run digital humanities center or a library's digital scholarship center, given that these are generally deemed the best means of ensuring the sustainability of digital projects

(Lewis et al.; Lippincott and Goldenberg-Hart; Maron and Pickle). It has benefited at key points from particular conditions and particular decisions. Patricia Clements, founding director, had experience in devising creative institutional solutions. The team members were vividly aware of the wider humanities culture to which they belong. It seems quite clear that the project was unlikely to have fared as well embedded in either a digital scholarship center within a library or within a DH center, given that in either scenario it would constantly have been vying for limited resources with other, newer, projects (Brown, "Community Curation Strategies"). A collaborative platform creates a situation in which sustainability ceases to be a zero-sum game, resources for one project that wants to extend affordances can benefit other projects, and all projects will be buoyed by a rising tide of sustainability.

Orlando 2.0

As the project's activities and its relationships with other initiatives change, so, too, do its collaborative structure and output. Orlando 2.0, the newest phase of the project announced at the twentieth-anniversary celebrations at the Digital Diversity conference in 2015, requires new approaches to training, peer-review, and attribution and offers exciting possibilities. The CWRC platform will house *Orlando* and make its Canadian content (a small portion of the whole) openly available as part of its experiments with interlinking and interoperability.

The CWRC platform will allow the project to shift from in-house training and drafting of entries to call on the wider community of scholars on women's writing to help add new entries and keep existing content current. It links and offers within a single web environment the tools needed to draft, revise, or update *Orlando* entries, and allows us to track contributions and the state of entries in progress. There will be considerable challenges in this new phase. For instance, although the tools are accessible, the learning curve will still be quite steep given the complexity of the tagging, and we will not have the benefit of face-to-face training. However, we have evidence both from reviews and informal feedback that the scholarly community is eager to collaborate to sustain and improve *Orlando*. To accommodate this shift and a new community of users, in addition to developing tools for collaboration, we are working to minimize gruntwork, to allow contributors to focus on the intellectual effort. So we are developing a tool for automatically recognizing and tagging entities such as names, places, organizations, and literary titles that will reduce repetitive markup and allow for quality control. We also recognize the need to credit not only collaborative contributions to individual entries but also work across numerous entries to improve the whole. The two visualizations shown in Figure 22.4 represent two types of contribution, leveraging the tags that track contributions to entries. They are produced by a prototype of a Credit Visualization (CV) tool that will be built into the CWRC environment, and are a direct legacy of the Orlando Project's commitment

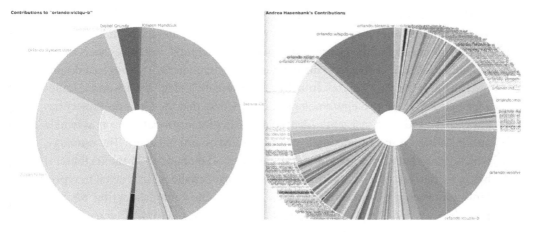

Figure 22.4. *(left)* CV shows multiple researchers' contributions to one *Orlando* entry, depicting contributors' names, types of contributions (including researching, writing, and tagging entry as well as checking tagging for accuracy and consistency), and portion completed. *(right)* CV shows one Orlando Project member's work across the project as a whole, providing information about names of entries, types of contributions to each entry, and portion of her time dedicated to each entry during her involvement with the Orlando Project.

to finding innovative methods to further transparent collaborative models for digital scholarly production.

As mentioned above, the project is also embracing open data, in large part because we think it provides a means of representing the project's feminist understanding of literary history while interacting with other representations and conceptions of the world. In our case, this means releasing, for free use with attribution, a large set of prosopographical information about women's writing derived from *Orlando*'s semantic encoding, along with a tool to explore it. In exploring the utility of this strategy and the kind of inquiry it can support, we have extracted hundreds of thousands of such triples from the *Orlando* textbase that we will be releasing as an open dataset (Brown and Simpson, "From XML to RDF"). This large set of triples, or subject-verb-object statements, plus an associated ontology that governs the relationships between entities, represents an exciting move toward providing broader access to the Orlando Project's knowledge base and a new phase in the project's exploration of the potential of computational work for feminist inquiry. CWRC interlinking between diverse projects relies on a Linked Open Data strategy that is based on uniquely defining entities (whether these are people, organizations, literary works, places, or items in the CWRC repository) and connecting them to each other with simple subject-verb-object statements, or triples.[4]

Ontologies in many ways capture the tension between being and becoming, monumentality and provisionality, that we are investigating. Although invoked in a social science context as providing a basis for situated feminist inquiry (Stanley and Wise), in humanities disciplines such as philosophy and literary studies, the term "ontology" smacks of the gender essentialism that feminist initiatives such as the Orlando Project have sought to dismantle, and seems on its face to suggest a decontextualized and ahistorical conceptualization of female "being." Yet it is on the knife-edge between these two epistemological frameworks that the Orlando Project has always balanced, both insistently identifying particular historical subjects as female and insisting on the situatedness of gendered roles and behavior. The ontology, which grows out of the markup developed for and embedded in the textbase, is being written out of a recognition of the significant challenges involved in representing the complex subjectivities, such as that of the composite writer Michael Field (Brown and Simpson, "Curious Identity"), that a feminist literary history seeks to analyze and represent. An ontology necessarily departs from a markup-oriented mode of knowledge representation (Brown et al., "Between Markup and Delivery") and moves into the uneasy space of engaging with ontologies that may not be commensurate with the Orlando Project. For instance, what are the implications of linking to other ontologies with different methods of handling diverse aspects of subjectivity, whether the language-neutral but certainly not culturally neutral ISO/IEC 5218 codes for the representation of human sexes (values: 0 = not known; 1 = male; 2 = female; 9 = not applicable), or to the Muninn Ontology for personal appearance such as skin color that is in some ways incommensurate with but related to *Orlando*'s method of tagging race or ethnicity (Warren)?

While still in a state of becoming at this early stage, it is clear that an *Orlando* ontology would ideally never be fully formed, but able to remain dynamic, in a state of flux. Particularly once the contributor base and likely also the types of contributions broaden, differences will inevitably arise in how to represent the knowledge of the project effectively. Although dynamic ontologies still represent significant challenges technically, their potential seems to offer greater fluidity and ability to accommodate difference than standard markup structures. That said, the particular focus on the representation of sex, gender, sexuality, and other identity categories included in *Orlando*'s CulturalFormation tagset, and the extent to which we refused to adopt fixed vocabularies for those categories, will pose significant challenges for creating machine-processable and interoperable representations of complex historical subjects even within a Linked Open Data (LOD) environment. We've come to the conclusion that it will be key not only to make the ontology available but to expose it and provide means of exploring it, ideally in conjunction with the data themselves, so that scholars using it can understand the extent to which their experience of the materials is shaped by the ontology. There also looms the very large question of whether the extreme granularity of semantic web data risks falling into the "lenticular" logic coined by Tara McPherson ("Why") by analogy with the visual technology that allows you to see one part of a picture from one angle and another from another angle, but never the two simultaneously despite their conjoined materiality. McPherson sees such logic as crucial to the management of race and other identity categories in postwar culture and as implemented by most contemporary computational systems. Certainly much of our experimentation to date with LOD has ended up using quads rather than triples so that we can track provenance information crucial to attribution and to linking from abstractions or visualizations to the original of the text so that that specific and local are not lost. We are investigating the extent to which feminist principles are in tension with LOD.

The *Orlando* textbase has been categorized variously: as an archive by Wernimont ("Whence Feminism?"), a database by Masters ("Women's Ways"), and as a textbase by its founders: "while *Orlando* resembles a standard alphabetical reference work in electronic form, its structured text means that its material is systematically interrelated and can be probed, traversed, and grouped" in ways that foreground "myriad links among authors, their historical moments, they pasts and their futures" (Brown, Clements, and Grundy, "Scholarly Introduction"). It is also still regularly mistaken as an archive of primary texts, reflecting the extent to which the history of the field has a lock on our conception of what scholarly resources can be and do. But as Woolf proclaimed in her *Orlando,* regarding the fulfillment of all forms of human curiosity and desire, "may there be more forms, and stranger" (*Orlando*). Others responding to the textbase have moved beyond academic genres to liken it to Judy Chicago's art installation *The Dinner Party* (Fraiman) or a *Choose Your Own Adventure* novel (Hickman). We hope to have demonstrated that our *Orlando,* which set out to do literary history, is not one, in several senses. It is literary history that went astray in becoming digital and in so doing becoming something other than what we typically understand by the term "literary history." It does not look, act, or read like a literary history because its narrative is not one, but many, whether we are talking about the multiple paths that a reader may take through the text; the *petits récits* (Liu) or multiple narratives provided by the entries, which make what Alison Booth terms a collective biography, and place the individual in tension with and relationship to the collective (*How to Make It*); or the continuous dialogue between the text and the tags that structure it. It shows us feminist theory, lost in amaze at digital media's still unplumbed potential for representing diversity and complexity in the past. As it enters its next phase, the Orlando Project continues to reach out, a challenge in this still siloed digital ecosystem, in hopes of enabling new forms of collaborative process that will allow us to aggregate, link, explore, and read across the wealth of materials produced by the collectivity of feminist digital scholars.

Notes

1. Susan Brown, one of the founders of the Orlando Project, is now Technical Director. Kathryn Holland began her involvement with the project as a Graduate Research Assistant and returned to it as Senior Research Fellow.

2. Markup languages enable people to organize electronic texts. In the mid-1990s Orlando designed the document type definitions (DTDs)/schemas for its textbase entries in SGML (Standard Generalized Markup Language) and later converted them to XML (Extensible Markup Language). SGML and XML are formats used to structure and describe data, such as electronic scholarly prose, in ways that make it readable by humans and machines. Once SGML or XML users enclose their data in tags that are part of markup schemas or hierarchies created by themselves or others, their data can be processed by computers and searched by online audiences. For a discussion of the history and purposes markup languages, see Leuner, "Markup Languages."

3. The debate over labor associated with digital research and publication is complex. See, for instance, Cohen and Scheinfeldt, *Hacking the Academy*; and Terras, "Crowdsourcing."

4. The linked dataset is due for release in 2018 following production of a revised ontology that will govern the extraction of a better dataset than the one that emerged from our first experiments with a relatively simplistic ontology. The ontology is available at http://sparql.cwrc.ca/ and https://github.com/cwrc/ontology. The Orlando linked data set as well as other linked data housed by CWRC will be available through a triple store accessible through the Collaboratory at http://cwrc.ca.

Bibliography

Bailey, Moya. "#transform(ing) DH Writing and Research: An Autoethnography of Digital Humanities and Feminist Ethics." *Digital Humanities Quarterly* 9, no. 2 (Spring 2015). Accessed November 5, 2015. www.digitalhumanities.org/dhq/vol/9/2/000209/000209.html.

Bianco, Jamie "Skye." "This Digital Humanities Which Is Not One." In *Debates in the Digital Humanities,* edited by Matthew K. Gold, 96–112. Minneapolis: University of Minnesota Press, 2012.

Binhammer, Katherine, and Jeanne Wood, eds. *Women and Literary History: "For There She Was."* Newark: University of Delaware Press, 2003.

Booth, Alison. Collective Biographies of Women. University of Virginia. http://womensbios.lib.virginia.edu.

Booth, Alison. *How to Make It as a Woman: Collective Biographical History from Victoria to the Present.* Chicago: University of Chicago Press, 2004.

Brown, Susan. "Community Curation Strategies: Orlando 2.0 and the Canadian Writing Research Collaboratory." Modern Languages Association Convention, Austin, Tex., January 7–10, 2016.

Brown, Susan. "Socialized Scholarship: It Starts with Us." *English Studies in Canada* 36, no. 4 (December 2010): 9–12.

Brown, Susan, and Patricia Clements. "Tag Team: Computing, Collaborators, and the History of Women's Writing in the British Isles." *TEXT Technology* 8, no.1 (1998): 37–52.

Brown, Susan, Patricia Clements, Renée Elio, and Isobel Grundy. "Between Markup and Delivery; or Tomorrow's Electronic Text Today." In *Mind Technologies: Humanities*

Computing and the Canadian Academic Community, edited by Ray Siemens and David Moorman, xxxiii–xlii. Calgary: University of Calgary Press, 2006.

Brown, Susan, Patricia Clements, and Isobel Grundy. "'The Most Unaccountable of Machinery': The Orlando Project Produces a Textbase of One's Own." In *Interdisciplinary / Multidisciplinary Woolf: Selected Papers from the Twenty-Second Annual International Conference on Virginia Woolf,* edited by Ann Martin and Kathryn Holland, 209–24. Clemson, S.C.: Clemson University Press, 2013.

Brown, Susan, Patricia Clements, and Isobel Grundy. *Orlando: Women's Writing in the British Isles from the Beginnings to the Present.* Cambridge: Cambridge University Press online, 2006–2017. orlando.cambridge.org.

Brown, Susan, Patricia Clements, and Isobel Grundy. "Scholarly Introduction." *Orlando: Women's Writing in the British Isles from the Beginnings to the Present.* 2006. orlando.cambridge.org.

Brown, Susan, Patricia Clements, and Isobel Grundy. "Sorting Things In: Feminist Knowledge Representation and Changing Modes of Scholarly Production." *Women's Studies International Forum* 29 (2006): 317–25.

Brown, Susan, Patricia Clements, Isobel Grundy, Stan Ruecker, Jeffery Antoniuk, and Sharon Balazs. "Published Yet Never Done: The Tension between Projection and Completion in Digital Humanities Research." *Digital Humanities Quarterly* 3, no. 2 (Spring 2009). Accessed 29 January 2016. http://www.digitalhumanities.org/dhq/vol/3/2/000040/000040.html.

Brown, Susan, Jana Smith Elford, Michael Bauer, Jennifer Berberich, and Jonathan Cable. "'Elevating Influence': Victorian Literary History by Graphs." *Victorian Institute Journal* Digital Annex 38 (2010). Accessed January 29, 2016. http://www.nines.org/exhibits/Elevating_Influence.

Brown, Susan, and John Simpson. "The Curious Identity of Michael Field and Its Implications for Humanities Research with the Semantic Web." Proceedings of the Big Data 2013, Big Data and the Humanities Workshop, Santa Clara, Calif., October 8, 2013.

Brown, Susan, and John Simpson. "From XML to RDF in the Orlando Project." International Conference on Computing and Culture, Kyoto, Japan, September 16–18, 2013.

Burnard, Lou. "On the Hermeneutic Implications of Text Encoding." In *New Media and the Humanities: Research and Applications,* edited by Domenico Fiormonte and Jonathan Usher, 31–38. Oxford: Humanities Computing Unit, 2001.

Burrows, Toby. "Using DynaWeb to Deliver Large Full-Text Databases in the Humanities." *Computers and Texts* 13: 15–17.

Butler, Terry, Sue Fisher, Greg Coulombe, Patricia Clements, Isobel Grundy, Susan Brown, Jeanne Wood, and Rebecca Cameron. "Can a Team Tag Consistently? Experiences on the Orlando Project." *Markup Languages: Theory and Practice* 2, no. 2 (Summer 2000): 111–25.

Canada's Early Women Writers. Simon Fraser University. http://content.lib.sfu.ca/cdm/landingpage/collection/ceww.

Canadian Writing Research Collaboratory. cwrc.ca.

Canadian Writing Research Collaboratory CWRC ontology. https://github.com/cwrc/ontology.

Cohen, D. J., and Tom Scheinfeldt. *Hacking the Academy: New Approaches to Scholarship and Teaching from Digital Humanities.* Ann Arbor: University of Michigan Press, 2013.

Coombes, James H., Allan H. Renear, and Stephen J. DeRose. "Markup Systems and the Future of Scholarly Text Processing." *Communications of the ACM* 30, no. 11 (1987): 933–47.

DeRose, Stephen J., David G. Durand, Elli Mylonas, and Allen H. Renear. "What Is Text, Really?" *Journal of Computing in Higher Education* 1, no. 2 (Winter 1990): 3–26.

D'Ignazio, Catherine. "What Would a Feminist Data Visualization Look Like?" *MIT Center for Civic Media,* December 20, 2015. Accessed January 29, 2016. https://civic.mit.edu/feminist-data-visualization.

Earhart, Amy. "Can Information Be Unfettered? Race and the New Digital Humanities Canon." In *Debates in the Digital Humanities,* edited by Matthew K. Gold, 309–18. Minneapolis: University of Minnesota Press, 2012.

Fraiman, Susan. "In Search of Our Mothers' Gardens—With Help from a New Digital Resource for Literary Scholars." *Modern Philology* 106, no. 1 (August 2008): 142–48. https://doi.org/10.1086/597254.

Galey, Alan, and Stan Ruecker. "How a Prototype Argues." *Literary and Linguistic Computing* 25, no. 4 (2010): 405–24.

Hickman, Miranda. Review of *Orlando. Tulsa Studies in Women's Literature* 27, no. 1 (2008): 180–86.

Irigaray, Luce. *This Sex Which Is Not One.* Translated by Catherine Porter. Ithaca, N.Y.: Cornell University Press, 1985.

Leuner, Kirstyn. "Markup Languages." In *Johns Hopkins Guide to Digital Media,* edited by Lori Emerson, Ben Robertson, and Marie-Laure Ryan, 324–25. Baltimore, Md.: Johns Hopkins University Press, 2014.

Levy, Michelle. "Women's Print History Project: 1750–1830." Accessed November 3, 2016. https://michellenancylevy.wordpress.com/research/womens-print-history-project-1750-1830/.

Lewis, Vivian, Lisa Spiro, Xuemao Wang, and Jon E. Cawthorne. *Building Expertise to Support Digital Scholarship: A Global Perspective.* Washington, D.C.: Council on Library and Information Resources, 2015.

Lippincott, Joan K., and Diane Goldenberg-Hart. "Digital Scholarship Centers: Trends and Good Practice." *CNI Workshop Report.* Coalition for Networked Information. https://www.cni.org/wp-content/uploads/2014/11/CNI-Digitial-Schol.-Centers-report-2014.web_.pdf.

Liu, Alan. *The Laws of Cool: Knowledge Work and the Culture of Information.* Chicago: University of Chicago Press, 2004.

Lorde, Audre. *Sister Outsider: Essays and Speeches.* Trumansburg, N.Y.: Crossing, 1984.

Maron, Nancy L., and Sarah Pickle. "Sustaining the Digital Humanities: Host Institution Support beyond the Start-Up Period." Ithaka. http://www.sr.ithaka.org/publications/sustaining-the-digital-humanities/.

Masters, Christine. "Women's Ways of Structuring Data." *Ada: A Journal of Gender, New Media, and Technology* 8 (2015). Accessed January 29, 2016. https://adanewmedia.org/2015/11/issue8-masters/.

McPherson, Tara. "Why Are the Digital Humanities So White? or Thinking the Histories of Race and Computation." In *Debates in the Digital Humanities,* edited by Matthew K. Gold, 139–61. Minneapolis: University of Minnesota Press, 2012.

Orlando Project. University of Alberta and University of Guelph. www.ualberta.ca/orlando.

Orlando Project schemas. GitHub. https://github.com/cwrc/CWRC-Schema/tree/master/schemas.

Ramsey, Stephen, and Geoffrey Rockwell. "Developing Things: Notes toward an Epistemology of Building in the Digital Humanities." In *Debates in the Digital Humanities,* edited by Matthew K. Gold, 75–84. Minneapolis: University of Minnesota Press, 2012.

Risam, Roopika. "Introduction: Gender, Globalization and the Digital." *Ada: A Journal of Gender, New Media, and Technology* 8 (2015). Accessed January 27, 2016. https://adanewmedia.org/2015/11/issue8-risam/.

Shrewsbury, Carolyn M. "What Is Feminist Pedagogy?" *Women's Studies Quarterly* 15, no. 3/4 (Fall–Winter 1987): 6–14.

Stanley, Liz, and Sue Wise. *Breaking Out Again: Feminist Ontology and Epistemology.* 2nd ed. London: Routledge, 1993. Print.

Terras, Melissa. "Crowdsourcing in the Digital Humanities." In *A New Companion to the Digital Humanities,* 2nd ed., edited by Susan Schreibman, Ray Siemens, and John Unsworth, 421–38. Oxford: Wiley Blackwell.

Warren, Robert, and Adriel Dean-Hall. "Appearances Ontology Specification—0.1." http://rdf.muninn-project.org/ontologies/appearances.html.

Wernimont, Jacqueline. "Introduction: Feminisms and DH." *Digital Humanities Quarterly* 9, no. 2 (Spring 2015). Accessed November 1, 2015. http://digitalhumanities.org/dhq/vol/9/2/000217/000217.html.

Wernimont, Jacqueline. "Whence Feminism? Assessing Feminist Literary Interventions in Digital Archives." *Digital Humanities Quarterly* 7, no. 1 (Winter 2013). Accessed March 8, 2015. http://www.digitalhumanities.org/dhq/vol/7/1/000156/000156.html.

Women Writers Project. Northeastern University. http://www.wwp.northeastern.edu.

Women's Print History Project, 1750–1830. Simon Fraser University. https://michellenancylevy.wordpress.com/research/womens-print-history-project-1750-1830/.

Woolf, Virginia. *The Diary of Virginia Woolf: Volume 3, 1925–1930.* Edited by Anne Olivier Bell and Andrew McNeillie. New York: Harcourt, Brace, 1980.

Woolf, Virginia. *Orlando: A Biography*. New York: Harcourt, 2001.

PART VI][Chapter 23

Decolonizing Digital Humanities

Africa in Perspective

BABALOLA TITILOLA AIYEGBUSI

Historically, digital humanities has flourished more in developed countries. Scholars who have a grasp of its dynamic multifaceted scope have mostly one thing in common: the Western world. This notion is supported by a list of DH centers provided by CenterNet, an international network of digital humanities centers, which accounts for about 190 centers spread across the world; most of these are located in developed parts of the world, that is, North America, Australia, and Europe; a few are in Asia and South America with just two in Africa (CenterNet). The clustering of DH centers in these developed parts of the world explains why DH activities are more prominent in these locations; it also reinforces the notion that DH is a West-driven phenomenon. Such labeling challenges digital humanities' reputation as an all-encompassing interdisciplinary practice. As a result, scholars in developing African countries tend to view DH as a Western phenomenon practicable in technologically advanced locations, and this notion presents the problem of inclusion and comprehension. Perhaps the problem is not with digital humanities as a new field, but with the development of humanities as an academic arena in African countries. While the scope of the humanities in North America continues to extend beyond its traditional confines, enhanced by an educational system characterized by decentralization and diversity, humanities in Africa remains quite conservative as a result of a system that is built on enforcing standardized curricula (Etim). As such, DH practice is recognized within such a conservative system as a tool, and not as a discipline. In this chapter, I focus on the issues surrounding our understanding of the digital culture and the regional academic structure and customs in Africa with Nigeria as a focal point, and how these affect not only the development of digital humanities as a field in Africa but also the way digital humanities is perceived.

Writing about digital humanities in Africa often poses an arduous task. It becomes relatively harder when compared with giving talks and presentations about the same topics, simply because scholarly writing often requires a grounding of one's ideas in prevailing discussions. The thrill of adding the African voice to debates, thereby bringing new perspective to discussions, quickly dissipates as soon as one tries to tackle the haunting questions: Who is my reference? Who else out there is talking about digital humanities in Africa? It will be wrong to assume no one else is, as I have read and listened to quite a number of interesting pieces and talks on digital humanities from African scholars like Justus Roux (South Africa), James Yeku (Nigeria), Babatunde Opeibi (Nigeria), Laila Shereen Sakr (Egypt), and Omolara Owoeye (Nigeria). However, Africans who participate in the DH discourse are few in number, and our voices are sparsely scattered across the digital humanities space. Therefore, most of my ideas are founded mainly on my understanding of African customs and practices as a native African, my experience as a Nigerian researcher, and recent discussions with Nigerian academics in diverse fields and institutions.

Conversations about activities in Africa are crucial to the DH discourse for at least two reasons. First, as an interdisciplinary field that is focused on the enhancement of humanistic research and teaching through both methodological modeling of humanistic datasets and intellectual reasoning that improves human communication and understanding, geographical underrepresentation has had severe negative implication on the field's impact. Discussions within the field appear lopsided because DH projects, including those about Africa, are mostly initiated and/or executed in Europe and North America. Some examples of these include *Africa Past & Present* (Michigan State University), *Slave Biographies* (Michigan State University), *AfricaBib* by David Bullwinkle (University of Arkansas), *The Yoruba Architectural Reconstruction* by Steven Nelson (UCLA), *Accra Mobile* by Jennifer Hart (Wayne State University), and *Trans-Atlantic Slave Trade Database* (Emory University). Although many of these projects are affiliated with local universities—for instance, *Accra Mobile* is linked with Ashesi University Ghana—the absence of Africa-based DH centers affiliated with them tends to create a disconnect between the project and the targeted audience and users, and may reduce accessibility and incorporation into academic research circles. Second, Africa has witnessed a significant loss of cultural heritage, literature, and language due to modernization and poor documentation. Local languages and dialects appear to be the most affected by this problem. As at 2016, *Ethnologue* identified over 530 languages in Nigeria, twenty-two of which were categorized as nearly extinct, and eight as extinct (Lewis, Simons, and Fennig). The extinction of languages and other cultural traditions can be delayed or halted when archiving projects are targeted at solving these issues.

Although efforts have been made recently at achieving a global representation in the digital humanities discourse, it seems there is still a lot of ground to cover. Some special interest groups and individuals have made this their objective; they focus on finding ways to enhance global representation in digital humanities by connecting worlds. GO::DH (Global Outlook::Digital Humanities), for instance, is a special interest group that is, as stated on its website, interested on breaking down "barriers that hinder communication and collaboration among researchers and students of the Digital Arts, Humanities, and Cultural Heritage sectors in high, mid, and low income economies" (Global Outlook::Digital Humanities). In 2013, the group had an essay competition that looked at aspects of digital humanities practice across the globe. Essays included an array of topics from different countries and were in several languages. The competition reflected the diversity in scope, voices, and experiences of digital humanists across the globe, giving insights to peculiar issues associated with specific localities. Another is the Digital Media and Learning Competitions organized by the Humanities, Arts, Science, and Technology Alliance and Collaboratory (HASTAC); this is aimed at finding and inspiring the most innovative uses of new media in support of learning. The competition has advanced the frontiers of DH by awarding $13 million in five years to over one hundred projects that explore how technologies are changing the way people learn and participate in daily life (HASTAC).

Apart from these groups, digital humanities conferences in recent times invite participants from different parts of the world (at the 2015 Canadian Society for Digital Humanities conference held in Ottawa, I was thrilled to meet with Yasmine Portales Machado, who had traveled from Cuba to present papers at the conference). Also, there has been a wave of people talking about DH practice and development in their parts of the world: Isabel Galina writes about Mexico and the geopolitical and linguistic diversity in digital humanities, Yasmine Portales Machado talks about digital humanities practice in Cuba and the challenges facing LGBT groups in a digitally censored Cuban community, James Yeku calls for the mobilization of a digital humanities drive in Nigeria, Lara Owoeye talks about DH in Nigeria and the function of big data in Nigerian humanistic research, and Sneha P.P. contextualizes DH in India, just to mention a few. Their contributions reveal the extent to which regional idiosyncrasies impact the spread of DH, and the importance of approaching global representation bearing these particular traits in mind.

As such, having knowledge of the customs, the digital culture, and the regional academic structure of Africa is pertinent to understanding the development of digital humanities as a field in Africa. In addition, DHers need to know the elements and issues within the DH community that make the discipline resistant to global integration. I consider these issues as belonging to two categories: internal and external factors. With their combined strength, they hinder not just the spread and development of digital humanities as a field in Africa but also its recognition as a universal mode of acquiring and enhancing knowledge. While the external factors are closely linked to the economic state of developing African countries, the internal represent the forces within the digital humanities community that restrict its spread to other parts of the world.

The external factors are entrenched within the economic, political, social, and cultural systems of a country, dictating its involvement in, or receptiveness to, certain fields or areas of research. They impede the kind of research carried out in the digital humanities field, thus contributing to the low level or absence of activities; unfortunately, these cannot be directly affected or changed by the globalization of DH. Poverty is the most dominant of these factors because it births and cradles other issues, notably among which are network connectivity and power supply. Access to internet connection in Africa often comes at a prohibitive cost that may be unaffordable for the average income earner. Despite the high cost of internet access, users often experience slow, poor, or no connectivity. It is common to find that only a few universities in a country like Nigeria have functional Wi-Fi spots that are open to the public. The situation is the same in most public places, such as fast-food restaurants, hospitals, and hotels. Since Wi-Fi installed by corporate institutions or individuals is protected and inaccessible to the public, invariably, a large portion of internet users get access by purchasing airtime vouchers which are used at cybercafés or through digital devices such as mobile phones and laptops. These vouchers, despite being split into various affordable amounts, are expensive when considering the fact that as of 2010, the relative poverty level in Nigeria was 69 percent (National Bureau of Statistics). Also, lack of stable power supply unequivocally affects digital humanities research in Africa. However, the effect this has on DH research varies, depending on the aspect of digital humanities research a scholar explores. While "yacking"—a discourse-based aspect of digital humanities—may not particularly require a stable source of electricity, "hacking," on the other hand, which is more of the practice and/or technical part of DH, needs an unfluctuating source of power supply.

Regrettably, many African countries do not have an efficient electric power system. For instance, Nigeria's supply of power from the national grid is lower than its demand, and this has the effect of crippling most facilities that are dependent on electricity. In 2012, the Energy Commission of Nigeria made reference to an interview published by Vanguard Newspaper in January 2009 in which the chairman of the Manufacturers Association of Nigeria (MAN) Abia Branch, Dr. Frank Jacobs, disclosed that about 60 million Nigerians depend on power-generating sets for their electricity, and spend quite a bit to maintain these engines annually (Energy Commission of Nigeria).[1] This is because the average Nigerian uses a generator as a supplementary power supply source, since electricity from the national grid is unreliable, and occasionally several parts of the country are thrown into protracted periods of partial or complete power outage. A more generic issue, which encompasses but is not limited to internet and power accessibility, is the low accessibility of infrastructure. Despite acquiring skills that are useful in digital humanities and having access to internet and computers for research purposes, digital humanities labs or the integration of digital tools into the educational system is very low in Nigeria. Many researchers in the country still rely on conventional methods of inquiry, because most of the technological tools that are required to reshape the traditional methods of teaching are not readily available. My personal experience during four years at university while completing an undergraduate degree in Nigeria has been that classrooms in most universities, with the exception of private schools, are rarely equipped with digital appliances such as computers and projectors. The same expense and lack of infrastructure that make it difficult to access the internet in countries like Nigeria prevent affordable access to standard digital humanities tools, resources, and methodologies. An example of this is the attitude toward crowdsourcing and data curation in Nigeria. Given the level of poverty in the country, one can understand why Nigerians are generally nonresponsive to online surveys that are not financially beneficial. The stipend attached to outsourcing tasks (if a stipend is attached at all) is not a good enough incentive when compared with the cost incurred on internet usage. For example, a student who pays about the equivalent of a dollar to purchase thirty minutes of airtime at a cybercafé will be reluctant to participate in an online crowdsourcing activity that pays nothing or a nominal sum per page. Unless such activities can be attached to grades or some other incentives, they are simply too expensive in time and money to allow the spread or adoption of DH into the Nigerian academia. The fact that Nigeria could in principle benefit from such an approach if it could be made economical makes the situation all the more tragic. As a developing country with a rich but threatened cultural heritage, most of which is orally transmitted, Nigeria would be ideally suited to the use of crowdsourcing as a means of cultural reserve and preservation if only ways could be found around the prohibitive economic constraints that prevent its update.

These problems result from a failing economy, and they buttress Daniel O'Donnell's hypothesis that rich countries participate more in digital humanities activities than their poor counterparts ("In a Rich Man's World"). This hypothesis is quite true considering the dire economic situation of most African countries. Many African countries are on the list of poorest countries in the world, and out of the fifty-four countries on the continent, only eleven have a GDP per capita above $10,000, according to the International Monetary Fund World Economic Outlook ("List of African Countries"). There is a distinct possibility that the economic condition of most African countries may affect the priority given to, and the type of research carried out in, the digital humanities field.

The internal factors, on the other hand, are dynamics within the digital humanities field that alienate researchers resident in non-West countries. These are also grouped into two categories: scope of definition and the issue of inclusion, and differences in regional educational structure and research ideology. Discussion about the internal factors hinges on these questions: how is digital humanities perceived in Africa, and to what extent do sociocultural and economic realities affect these perceptions? What role does the Western digital humanities community play in fostering this perception? Do the fluid definition, scope, and academic boundaries of digital humanities affect its development in Africa? And what is the way forward? These questions might not have direct answers, but attempting to provide responses to them will give insights into customs and norms within the African research system that are essential to achieving a global perspective of digital humanities.

Definition and Scope of Digital Humanities

The much-debated issue about the definition of digital humanities is a primary factor affecting its spread in Africa. Though there are several essays about what digital humanities is, and despite that most of these attempts to capture the main essence of what the field stands for, it seems they do not fully satisfy people's curiosity. Even with Matthew Kirschenbaum's assertion that essays on what digital humanities is (are) are already genre pieces ("What Is Digital Humanities"), this has not stopped people from asking, "What exactly is digital humanities, and what do digital humanists do?" One of the attempts to define digital humanities is a white paper published by UCLA, which states:

> Digital Humanities is an umbrella term for a wide array of practices for creating, applying, and interpreting new digital and information technologies. These practices are not limited to conventional humanities departments, but affect every humanistic field at the university, including history, anthropology, arts and architecture, information studies, film and media studies, archaeology, geography, and the social sciences. At the same time, Digital Humanities is a natural outgrowth and expansion of the traditional scope of the Humanities, not a replacement or rejection of humanistic inquiry. In fact, the role of the humanist is critical at this historic moment, as our cultural legacy migrates to digital formats and our relation to knowledge, cultural material, technology, and society is radically re-conceptualized. (Presner and Johnson, 3)

Some, like John Unsworth define digital humanities (computing) as "a practice of representation, a form of modeling or . . . a way of reasoning and a set of ontological commitments, and its representational practice is shaped by the need for efficient computation on the one hand, and for human communication on the other" ("What Is Humanities Computing," 36). Others, like Rafael Alvarado, claim that there is no definition for digital humanities, because if by definition we refer to a set of established theories and research methods that are field specific, then DH "denotes no set of widely shared computational methods that contributes to the work of interpretation, no agreed upon norms or received genres for digital publication, no broad consensus on whether digital work, however defined, counts as genuine academic work" ("Digital Humanities Situation," 50).

Given these two divergent views, perhaps the issue of defining the digital humanities has more to do with the fact that, despite existing for over six decades, the field is still emerging in the academic arena. As such, it consists of people with shared interests in ways to adapt computational modeling and analogy to texts, monuments, and any other aspect of humanistic research in order to improve quality of research and communication in the humanities field. As a result, the representation of digital humanities tends to align with these interests rather that the other way around: the field defining the interests.

Situating this within the context of enhancing the knowledge about digital humanities in Africa poses a significant challenge. When those who are expected to teach and/or practice DH grapple with its scope and specifics of description, the chances of embracing it as a field, not to mention bringing it into the classrooms, then become very slim. I had a firsthand experience of this challenge when I partnered with Lara Owoeye, who lectures at the Ekiti State University Ado Ekiti, Nigeria, in putting together a panel on big data in Africa for the Around the World Conference in May 2015. According to Lara, convincing people to be a part of the panel was difficult because first, they were hearing about the digital humanities for the first time, and second, there was insufficient or confusing information on the internet about the field and its practices due to self-definition. Scenarios like this are not exclusive to Nigerian tertiary institutions. Muriel S. had commented on Kirschenbaum's statement about essays on the definition of digital humanities as genre pieces, saying that there are institutional settings where "digital humanities is not even a part of any conversation" (Muriel). While one can argue that having a unanimous definition is necessary for inclusivity in the digital humanities community, its absence could also be an opportunity for African scholars to impact the idea of what the field is by influencing the dynamics of DH research. To achieve this, one needs to understand what is and what is not digital humanities. Jeffery Schnapp attempts to explain this in his article "A Short Guide to Digital-Humanities," establishing that

> the mere use of digital tools for the purpose of humanistic research and communication does not qualify as Digital Humanities. Nor, as already noted, is Digital Humanities to be understood as the study of digital artifacts, new media, or contemporary culture in place of physical artifacts, old media, or historical culture.
>
> On the contrary, Digital Humanities understands its object of study as the entire human record, from prehistory to the present. This is why fields such as classics and archaeology have played just as important a role in the development of Digital Humanities as has, for example, media studies. This is also why some of the major sectors of Digital Humanities research extend outside the traditional core of the humanities to embrace quantitative methods from the social and natural sciences as well as techniques and modes of thinking from the arts. (2)

Going by Schnapp's explanation, DH has every reason to thrive in Africa, given the enormous untapped cultural material and landscapes existing on the continent. However, the fact that DH cannot be pinned down to specific guidelines and principles continues to create a sense of exclusion among African scholars. This is fueled by DH's relationships with Western institutions and research funds. While it may seem disastrous if definitional work were to reach a conclusion before global participation is achieved, for some of the intellectual communities beyond the West, the definitional ambiguity promotes apathy.

Also, the reluctance to embrace digital humanities in African countries like Nigeria is intensified by the fact that the scope of activities reported in the community is geographically askew; information on DH activities in Africa and other developing countries is sparse. This is because DH research in Africa is more like what Jutta Treviranus, in her article "The Value of the Statistically Insignificant," calls outliers. There is a high tendency that statistical facts that contribute to the evolving picture of DH presence may exclude some crucial activities in technologically disadvantaged regions, not because they are statistically insignificant but as a result of access to publicity tools and awareness. Thus, inclusivity of Africans in DH spheres is not only about having discussions; it involves becoming a part of the statistics. Recent conversations may have yielded good outcomes, like the annual African DH conferences hosted at the North-West University, South Africa, by Digital Humanities Association of South Africa (DHASA), but an exhibition of DH projects, executed and managed in Africa, will open up the minds of African scholars to the new methods of research provided through the field. Given that, as Treviranus says, "established research methods have always privileged the norm or majority" ("Value of the Statistically Insignificant"), the available statistics on DH activities tend to reflect more participation in the developed countries. Activities in Africa may be more than what is shown by these reports, but because African DH projects fall below the bell curve of DH statistical analysis, they are unintentionally omitted from research data. Examples of such projects are the *UNESCO Digi-Arts project,* an online initiative that "aims to contribute to the development of a program of digital arts that reflects the specificity of artistic practices of the African continent" with team offices in Nairobi, Dakar, Kenya, Senegal, and South Africa and *The Cartographic Database: "New Maps of Old Lagos"* project by Ademide Adelusi-Adeluyi, centered on analyzing and georeferencing the maps of old Lagos by exploring the city's coastlines while using spatial analysis as a framework to narrate the historical events that connect the new look of the city to the landscape that lies beneath it (Adelusi-Adeluyi). When studies and projects on African humanities are properly researched and documented, they contribute to big data, and a proper account of the cultural heritage in such parts of the world may eliminate some of the challenges researchers face when dealing with source. They may also help African scholars to understand the theory and practice of digital humanities.

Difference in Regional Academic Structures and Research Ideology

In his article "Digital Humanities from a Global Perspective," Domenico Fiormonte notes that having a contextual understanding of the ways and means of doing things within any given location is key to achieving a global perspective of DH because "methods that have worked effectively in one cultural setting may fail spectacularly in another (and vice versa) and certain reasoning of how things should work does not apply similarly to other frameworks." Therefore, having a good knowledge of how local structures and models operate in African postsecondary institutions is necessary for the global integration of DH. Identifying some of the differences between the academic structures of North American and African universities is as simple as taking a glance at a cross section of students seated in a class: an American university class is typically made up of students from diverse fields with no particular combination of majors and minors, while students in an African university are from a range of specific fields, usually from one of two related faculties (e.g., arts and social sciences, or sciences and engineering) with common sets of majors and minors. Because digital humanities is more prominent in North America and has strong affiliations with the North American institutional and funding structures, it seems to have been naturally infused with the perspectives of the American educational system, adopting collaborative research as a core feature of its model.

While collaborative research is an inherent feature of DH scholarship given the extent of diversity in the field, in the American educational system it gradually evolved and gained prominence in the 1980s, when industrial corporations saw academic research as a way to enhance their work. Private industries started to invest in academic studies by providing funds that enabled and advanced research in diverse areas of interest. Some of these funds were packaged and aligned in ways that gave rise to situations in which "organized units were built in numerous areas that demanded collaboration across disciplinary lines" (Cohen, 415–19). This relationship between the private industry and the educational system reshaped the American higher education system, giving birth to a complex but highly successful contemporary structure with its diversity of forms (439–40).

Unlike the education system in many other parts of the world, the American educational system is decentralized, with control mainly at the state levels (Meyer and Rowan, 97). The marginal interference at the federal level allows the system to build a model that caters to local needs by creating variants of the curricula, which differ from school to school and student to student. The decentralization of the educational system has led to a research and development–focused approach to knowledge acquisition (Etim, 89).

The educational structure adopted by most African countries, on the other hand, is quite centralized. For instance, the Nigerian educational system, like that of other Anglophonic African countries, is modeled after the British standards, and it is controlled mainly by the Federal Ministry of Education, which regulates the education sector through parastatals assigned with the responsibilities of engaging in policy formation and ensuring quality control at the various levels of education (Etim, 88). While this system guarantees a uniform teaching and learning level across board, it does not consider specific needs of students along geographical, cultural, or demographic lines. While the American education model is quite flexible, allowing students to switch their major or minor multiple times if they so choose (with the exception of health sciences and engineering faculties), the African education model is relatively rigid, segregated, and compartmentalized; students are admitted to study specific courses, and they are allowed to take minor courses in selected fields other than their major.

The diversity of research interests and associations in the American educational system aligns with the DH ideology to reinvigorate humanities scholarship through collaborative research. However, collaboration in DH often emphasizes a unilateral relationship between academics and the technical group. It is usually viewed in terms of "difference" because it involves the convergence of researchers with a variety of expertise. It supports the idea that since no one has all the necessary skill sets to successfully execute a project, a partnership between academics and technicians has to be formed (Bradley). The rhetoric of collaboration in DH has then been about difference and complementation, but could collaboration be also about "likeness"? There are collaborations among digital humanists that are transdisciplinary coauthorships, which require no technical expertise; it is simply about scholars interested in similar areas of research bouncing ideas off each other. Such collaborations are born out of likeness and accumulation of ideas, and are geared toward achieving positive good.

Collaboration, whether of difference or likeness, is not a common occurrence in the African model of research because it exists within a system that has little interdisciplinary collaboration. The humanities researcher in the African educational system still fits into Sue Stone's description as a traditional scholar who works alone, relying mainly on books, original documents rather than facsimiles (Stone, 300). Based on personal experience, when humanities scholars in Nigeria collaborate, it is usually with colleagues within the same field. However, this closed-off model is fast changing; several individuals and groups now strive to make scholarship in Nigeria a collective enterprise. An example is the Transcampus Interdisciplinary Research and Study Group. Composed of individuals who believe in creating a collaborative academic society by encouraging joint authorship, the group strives to eradicate the "tradition in which academics pursue their mission with insufficient attention to interdisciplinary interaction" (Transcampus Interdisciplinary Research and Study Group). Individuals like Grace Akpochafo also believe that the integration of research ideas from diverse academic fields in Nigeria can provide a comprehensive and valid understanding of some of the major problems plaguing the country ("Interdisciplinary Research").

Essentially, understanding the difference between the academic structures in Africa and North America, and knowing the place of interdisciplinary research within both systems, is crucial to bridging the regional divide in digital humanities. At the moment, the way digital humanities is structured makes it less inclusive of African scholars because it adopts the American education model which encourages a much more interactive and integrative academic community where collaboration is encouraged.

In order to successfully become a global phenomenon, digital humanists need to start looking at the world through the lenses of other worlds. First, DHers need to be aware of the economic and social milieu of other countries, and second, they need to be sensitive to the differences in orientation and culture while finding ways to include diverse voices in the global discourse. While pinning down the definition of DH, as it appears, may not be feasible, there should be ways to circumvent this dilemma so that members of non-Western countries do not feel alienated. For example, activities that engage local scholars in the development and management of African-themed projects and access to local centers will help African researchers to create their own illustration of digital humanities through hands-on learning. Also, digital humanists in the West can follow Alex Gil's advice on the best way to achieve a global perspective of DH, which he says is to "start collaborating with someone who lives very far away from you" ("Global Perspectives"). Inviting African scholars to collaborate on similar topics of interest will promote the acceptance, integration, and popularity necessary for a DH global enhancement. Other collaborative moves such as creating awareness by forming focus groups, aligning incentives to encourage collaboration among scholars, and co-organizing conferences in Africa can also help to build an inclusive global digital humanities. But it all must begin with debunking the notion that digital humanities belongs only to the West.

Note

1. http://www.energy.gov.ng/index.php?option=com_content&view=article&id=74.

Bibliography

Adeluyi-Adesusi, Ademide. "The Cartographic Database: 'New Maps of Old Lagos.'" *STS Across Borders,* May 25, 2018. http://stsinfrastructures.org/content/cartographic-database-new-maps-old-lagos.

Akpochafo, Grace. "Interdisciplinary Research as a Panacea for Sustainable Development in Nigeria: Implications for Counselling." *International Research Journal* 2, no. 3 (March 2011): 931–34. http://www.interesjournals.org/full-articles/interdisciplinary-research-as-a-panacea-for-sustainable-development-in-nigeria-implications-for-counselling.pdf.

Alvarado, C. Rafael. "The Digital Humanities Situation." In *Debates in the Digital Humanities,* edited by Matthew K. Gold, 50–55. Minneapolis: University of Minnesota Press, 2012.

Bradley, John. "No Job for Techies: Technical Contributions to Research in Digital Humanities." In *Collaboration Research in the Digital Humanities,* edited by Marilyn Deegan and Willard McCarty, 11–26. Burlington, Vt.: Ashgate, 2012.

CenterNet: An International Network of Digital Humanities Centers. http://dhcenternet.org/centers.

Cohen, Arthur M. *The Shaping of American Higher Education: Emergence and Growth of the Contemporary System.* New York: John Wiley & Sons, 2007.

Edwards, Charlie. "The Digital Humanities and Its Users." In *Debates in the Digital Humanities,* edited by Matthew K. Gold, 213–32. Minneapolis: University of Minnesota Press, 2012.

Energy Commission of Nigeria. "60m Nigerians Now Own Power Generators." *Energy Commission of Nigeria,* 2012. Accessed February 14, 2016. http://www.energy.gov.ng/index.php?option=com_content&view=article&id=74.

Etim, James Edem. "A Comparison of Education Systems in Nigeria and the United States of America." Dissertation and Theses Paper 2275. Portland, Ore.: Portland State University, 1976.

Fiormonte, Domenico. "Digital Humanities from a Global Perspective." *Laboratorio dell'ISPF* 11: 10.12862/ispf14L203, 2014. http://www.ispf-lab.cnr.it/2014_203.pdf.

Gil, Alex. "Global Perspectives: Interview with Alex Gil." Posted by Ernesto Priego in *4Humanities: Advocating for the Humanities,* January 2013. http://4humanities.org/2013/01/interview-with-alex-gil/.

Global Outlook::Digital Humanities. *About Global Humanities,* 2013. http://www.globaloutlookdh.org/.

HASTAC. *Digital Media and Learning Competitions: Winners' Hub.* https://www.hastac.org/dml-competitions.

Kirschenbaum, Matthew. "What Is Digital Humanities and What's It Doing in English Departments?" In *Debates in the Digital Humanities,* edited by Matthew K. Gold, 3–11. Minneapolis: University of Minnesota Press, 2012.

Lewis, M. Paul, Gary F. Simons, and Charles D. Fennig, eds. *Ethnologue: Languages of the World.* 19th ed. Dallas, Tex.: SIL International, 2016 online version. http://www.ethnologue.com.

"List of African Countries by GDP per Capita." *Statistics Times,* 2015. Accessed February 2, 2016. http://statisticstimes.com/economy/african-countries-by-gdp-per-capita.php.

Meyer, John W., and Brian Rowan. "The Structure of Educational Organizations." In *Environments and Organizations,* edited by Marshall W. Meyer, 78–109. San Francisco: Jossey-Bass, 1978.

Muriel, S. Comment on "It's Tempting to Say That Whoever Asks the Question Has Not Gone Looking Very Hard for an Answer." Matthew Kirschenbaum, "What Is Digital Humanities and What's It Doing in English Departments?" In *Debates in the Digital Humanities,* edited by Matthew K. Gold. Minneapolis: University of Minnesota Press, 2012. http://dhdebates.gc.cuny.edu/debates/text/38.

National Bureau of Statistics. "Nigerian Poverty Profile Report 2010." *Proshare,* November 20, 2012. http://www.proshareng.com/news/16302.

O'Donnell, Daniel. "In a Rich Man's World: Global DH?" *dpod blog,* November 2, 2015. http://dpod.kakelbont.ca/2012/11/02/in-a-rich-mans-world-global-dh/.

Presner, Todd, and Chris Johnson. "The Promise of Digital Humanities: A Whitepaper." November 10, 2015. http://humanitiesblast.com/Promise%20of%20Digital%20Humanities.pdf.

Schnapp, Jeffrey. "A Short Guide to the Digital-Humanities," 2013. An open pdf excerpt from *Digital_Humanities*, by Anne Burdick, Johanna Drucker, Peter Lunenfeld, Todd Presner, and Jeffrey Schnapp, 121–36. Cambridge, Mass.: MIT Press, 2012. http://jeffreyschnapp.com/wp-content/uploads/2013/01/D_H_ShortGuide.pdf.

Stone, Sue. "Humanities Scholars: Information Needs and Uses." *Journal of Documentation* 38, no. 4 (1982): 292–313.

Transcampus Interdisciplinary Research and Study Group. *Transcampus Journal of Research in National Development.* http://www.transcampus.org.

Treviranus, Jutta. "The Value of the Statistically Insignificant." *Educause Review,* January–February 2014: 46–47. https://er.educause.edu/articles/2014/1/the-value-of-the-statistically-insignificant.

Unsworth, John. "What Is Humanities Computing and What Is Not?" In *Defining Digital Humanities: A Reader,* edited by Melissa Terras, Julianne Nyhan, and Edward Vanhoutte, 35–48. Farnham, Surrey, U.K.: Ashgate, 2013.

PART VI][*Chapter 24*

A View from Somewhere

Designing The Oldest Game,
a Newsgame to Speak Nearby

SANDRA GABRIELE

As the media landscape continues to change, studies have suggested that online games as a medium for news can do a better job than traditional news stories in conveying the complexities of systemic issues through experiential play (Bogost, Ferrari, and Schweizer). Newsgames are games that are built around current news stories, though the issue of currency is not a critical factor in gameplay; enduring social issues that routinely come up in news coverage are also excellent fodder for games. Newsgames have the potential to ask players to move beyond the headlines to a more complex understanding of the complicated systems that underlie social issues and are often poorly covered in typical news coverage that focus on events rather than contexts. Newsgames accomplish this focus on systems by simulating a problem or issue. They make suggestions about possible answers through the procedures that are an integral part of their formal structure.

This chapter explores the production of *The Oldest Game: A Newsgame*, a game designed to explore the working lives of sex workers in a new regulatory regime.[1] A research-creation project, it engages with a public policy issue that has enduring presence in the Canadian news cycle. It takes an editorial stand that supports the assertions made by communities of sex workers across Canada that criminalization of sex work and its associated activities actively harms them. Through its game mechanics, it demonstrates the implications of Bill C-36, the *Protection of Communities and Exploited Persons Act* (brought into law on December 6, 2014), for sex workers and those around them.[2]

Newsgames are not objective pieces of journalism. Rather, they take an editorial position through their game mechanics (Treanor and Mateas). They attempt to show particular aspects of a system at work in a given news event, story, or ongoing social issue. Demonstrating how the system works not only requires extensive knowledge of the system itself but requires that designers make choices about how the game play operates, which necessarily foregrounds particular elements of a story. Journalists write stories according to established news values and generic conventions driven by form and medium that favor particular ways of telling stories; similarly, games use rules of game play as part of their storytelling repertoire.[3] For instance, the commonly cited example of *September 12th* uses a simple mechanic to show the philosophy that reckless bombing with collateral damage leads only to more terrorism (Bogost; Bogost, Ferrari, and Schweizer). It is a small one-screen game. It presents an overhead orthogonal view of a section of a Middle Eastern city, complete with tiny people wandering the streets. Most of those people are civilians; some are terrorists. Your mouse places a crosshair over the city. Clicking on the city drops a bomb. Buildings are destroyed. People die. There is crying and wailing. The more dead people and destroyed property, the more the terrorists appear. The point of *September 12th* is its procedural logic. As long as the only way of interacting with a population is through a gunsight, the only result will be more violence. Clive Thompson has described it as "an op-ed composed not of words but of action" ("Saving the World").

As such, video games studies, especially the portion of it that focuses on procedural rhetoric and platform studies, can provide invaluable insights into the nature of newsgames (see Bogost; Bogost and Montfort; Konzack; Montfort, as well as various titles from Bogost and Montfort's Platform Studies series at the MIT Press). However, game studies by itself does not provide the sort of critical context necessary to describe the history and politics of the newsgame form. For that, we turned to the longer history of cultural studies and feminist criticism, especially in light of their welcome invocation in recent significant texts in digital humanities.

Proceeding from the work of cultural criticism within journalism studies and cultural studies (see, for instance, Hall; Hall et al.; Jiwani; Skinner, Gasher, and Compton) and the work of feminist cultural critics (e.g., Balsamo; Nakamura; Nakamura and Chow-White), our project seeks to answer Alan Liu's call to use digital tool-making in the service of cultural criticism ("Where Is the Cultural Criticism"). Liu's challenge to scholars in the field to "extend their critique to the full register of society, economics, politics, or culture" was a turning point in the field, even if it marked a familiar point of departure for games studies scholars (Fernández-Vara). It extends the work of digital scholars committed to a digital humanities that recognizes and demands that we acknowledge the ways difference is marked in the digital spaces we make and tools we use (see, for instance, Cong-Huyen; McPherson; Risam; and Wernimont, "Introduction," "Whence Feminism?," to name only a few). Making a newsgame about sex workers in Canada is explicitly also making an argument about the kinds of subjects that digital humanities can address, and the forms that it can use to address those subjects. It also highlights the terrain journalists routinely must tread as they attempt to represent controversial and extremely complex topics.

Newsgames don't operate like most video games. They don't even have to be fun; discovery through play is a common technique in game design used in a variety of games that attempts to compel players to keep playing long enough to determine why the game operates the way it does. In other words, play is also about understanding how a game builds its argument. This approach leads players to engage with particular news stories rather than remaining disinterested in their outcome. The text that introduces *September 12th* on Games for Change, the site that hosts it, claims, "The game's main goal was not to convince people that the War on Terror was wrong. Instead, it aimed at triggering discussion among young players. Indeed, that's what happened in multiple online forums" (Games for Change). Opinions about the game have always been polarized, but as Bruno Latour points out, controversies are the bread and butter of contemporary scholarship. Indeed, the production of newsgames bears a strong family resemblance to some forms of Actor-Network Theory (a major interdisciplinary paradigm that emerged from sociology to play significant roles in cultural studies and science and technology studies over the last several decades). Both ANT and newsgames begin at the site of controversies, attempt to identify the major actors involved and the connections between them, and identify procedures that would allow the sites of those controversies to be "remapped" into some sort of new, more desirable state (Latour, 21, 23).

In both form and practice, *The Oldest Game* challenges conventional representations of sex work and sex workers in games, and prohibitionist views of sex work, which, as Robin Maynard writes, see it as "inherently violent and exploitative, and propose instead that a carceral, prohibitionist approach must be taken to eliminate [it]" (Maynard).

Incorporating the perspective of sex workers into a game's mechanics is a powerful example of what Bogost describes as "procedural rhetoric" and what Flanagan and colleagues describe as "values-conscious" (or "value-sensitive") game design. Procedural rhetoric is a type of rhetoric that is tied explicitly to the core of what games do: building processes that manipulate symbols according to a set of rules. Through the way that they enact these rules, games can express a rhetoric, a persuasive argument. Much like a political cartoon, a well-designed newsgame encourages critical reflection, mobilizing its formal mechanics to communicate an editorial stance and persuade players to take a position, particularly when faced with purposeful choices about how to handle a given situation (Treanor and Mateas). By allowing players to experience the consequences of choices, games can explore systems and dynamic relationships (Anthropy).

Building immersive experiences can have the effect of eliciting greater empathy (Belman and Flanagan), especially toward the subjects of news stories, many of whom rarely appear as actors in conventional news and are represented in narrow, stigmatized ways (see, e.g., Comella; Hallgrimsdottir, Phillips, and Benoit; Hallgrimsdottir et al.; Jiwani and Young; McLaughlin; Mendes and Silva). Editorial newsgames that have a strong bias have been shown to be particularly successful, and demonstrate a long shelf life: "social comment games often cover highly visible, ongoing public policy issues, thus they remain relevant as long as a situation persists" (Bogost, Ferrari, and Schweizer). Moreover, as Miguel Sicart has argued, newsgames also play a role in participating in the public debate about the issues they cover. Newsgames, then, do not pretend to be neutral bits of news reporting. In the face of a game industry that typically represents sex workers as the abject victims of horrendous violence (Dill et al.), making a game that represents a sex worker as a purposeful agent making choices who perceives neither herself nor her colleagues as victims is already taking a stand.

These ideas about the ideological foundation of games connects with the general principle within science-technology studies, the philosophy of technology and culture, and the critical digital humanities—particularly within the feminist literature—that assert that all technical systems embody values (Drucker, *SpecLab*). Knowing the limited range of representations that existed in both news media and in mainstream games, we set out to design *The Oldest Game* with a mandate to do representation differently. In the methodologies adopted in the game-making process and the scenarios produced in the game, this project has sought to explicitly answer the call put out by Elizabeth Losh ("What Can the Digital Humanities") to develop a "paradigm of process and performance in which the network of power formations moves from ground to figure." From the outset, the team that built *The Oldest Game* (a sex worker hired on contract, undergraduate and graduate students, and two tenured faculty) sought to embody feminist principles of knowledge production by incorporating the expertise of sex workers and advocates themselves through their published research and perspectives on the game's design during playtesting.

We followed a participatory design process where users became participants in the design process by following an iterative cycle of game design between playtesting prototypes. Marilyne, a sex worker who had worked as a massage parlor worker (and became an owner of a parlor during her work with us) and a self-employed escort was hired to act as a consultant on the game. This was a first principle of feminist game design in that we explicitly sought to use our seed funding from the university to hire her for her expertise as a worker with a range of experiences in the fields we were describing and as an advocate for sex worker rights. Paying her for her time was a given. We also explicitly sought out sex workers to be part of the early phases of playtesting and made a point of visiting at least one massage parlor in the city, a visit that Marilyne facilitated, in order to better understand how this type of sex work took place.[4] As Mary Flanagan, Daniel Howe, and Helen Nissenbaum write, "Playtesting can be a time to discover and verify values in a particular game design" ("Values at Play," 754). However, we quickly learned from our playtesting with sex workers that the values our playtesters wanted to see were far from uniform, sometimes conflicted with good game design, and were sometimes simply impossible to represent.

A game exploring sex work and Bill C-36 is a ripe target for further controversy. GamerGaters are always ready to attack explicitly feminist games, while abolitionist feminists were very active in the debates leading to the passage of the bill and even have much of their language enshrined in the legal text of the bill.[5] This chapter explores our team's iterative design process, describing the risks inherent in such a project, particularly at a historical moment when a misogyny, vitriol, hate, and doxing were common practices online, especially directed at feminists and feminist game designers and players. Our process was an explicit attempt to valorize the experiences of sex workers, who often challenged us to do better. It continually forced us to reconsider our categories of knowledge and practices of knowledge making based on the feedback we received (Alcoff; McPherson). The process also forced us to confront issues implicit in the digital representation of knowledge.

If the practice of making newsgames involves shaping topical stories according to the contours of an appropriate procedural rhetoric, it could arguably be described as part of the field of knowledge representation. As John Unsworth argues, knowledge representation is "an interdisciplinary methodology that combines logic and ontology to produce models of human understanding that are tractable to computation" ("Knowledge Representation"). Following the work of John Sowa, Unsworth describes a three-part structure to this methodology, consisting of logic, ontology, and computability. "Logic disciplines the representation, but is content-neutral. Ontology expresses what one knows about the nature of the subject matter, and does so within the discipline of logic's rules. Computability puts logic and ontology to the test, by producing a second-order representation that validates and parses the ontology and the logic of the knowledge representation" ("Knowledge Representation"). Unsworth contends that the value of such a project for humanities scholars lies in its heuristic function: "because the rigor it requires will bring to our attention undocumented features of our own ideation" ("Knowledge Representation"). Subjecting the experiences of sex workers to the logic of game code—how much value a "risky" choice has over a "safe" choice, weighing safety over health or financial security—forces the design team to confront the situatedness of the variables of the constructs themselves: what is risky in one context changes in another; what is risky for one body type, skin color, or ethnicity is not the same for another.

If the use of computers and the programming that it entails is novel, Unsworth's closing sentiment is not; it is, in fact, a very familiar, Innisian notion: the idea that close attention to the bias of a given media form, especially an unfamiliar one, might allow us to locate our own critical blind spots through the application of a comparative framework. Inevitably (and Unsworth acknowledges this too), this will also be lost, but that's how media bias works. A newsgame will make some aspects of a complex story visible while obscuring or ignoring others. Our wager is that the process of fitting our research on sex work (ontology) into the procedure of the game form (logic) in a way that makes it playable by others (computation) adds a dimension to the story that has been obscured until now. Certainly the ongoing process of making the game has been useful for us in terms of identifying our own blind spots. After a brief review of conventional representations of sex work and sex workers in news and mainstream games, we explore two issues that arose through our test sessions with self-identified gamers and sex workers.

Sex Work in Journalism

A goal of the project from the outset has been to engage the problem of how to tell the story of sex workers differently and engage in a public dialogue about sex work differently than conventional news coverage has historically. Media accounts for the most part have adopted a neutral viewpoint that sought to balance arguments for the legalization of prostitution with arguments against it, providing the reader with little guidance as to how to evaluate the validity of each side in relationship to the lived experiences of sex workers. The classic limitation of neutral reporting—what media scholar Jay Rosen has described as the "view from nowhere" ("View from Nowhere")—is that it produces news coverage that leaves the readers themselves disengaged from the issue under scrutiny. This is especially problematic when dealing with the issue of sex work, since the discourses surrounding it are often couched in a moralizing discourse that either infantilizes sex workers who require rescuing or dismisses sex workers' needs, since they are not seen as virtuous women and thus in need of basic protections (Hallgrimsdottir, Phillips, and Benoit; Hallgrimsdottir et al.; Jiwani and Young; McLaughlin). Other key findings from research on news representations of sex work have found that street sex work is overrepresented in the news media, leaving citizens with a fairly narrow sense of the range of work entailed in sex work (Jiwani and Young; Van Brunschot et al.; see also Grant). Violence is almost always associated with sex work, and it represented rare moments when sex workers' voices were actually heard (though this level of representation shifted in coverage of Bill C-36). Generally speaking, sex workers are not sources of expertise in news stories, but rather are called on for their personal experiences. Sex workers are often seen as vectors of contagion, whether of community or psychological malaise, disease or criminality. Hallgrimsdottir and colleagues found that there has been a shift over time from focusing on the risk sex workers pose to the public, to sex workers' "risky" behavior. This conveys the message that sex workers are to blame for the dangers they face, "offering them up as the appropriate target for legal and moral intervention" ("Sporting Girls" 133).

Sex Work in Games

In games, one of the central issues with how sex workers are typically represented is that they are almost always non-player-characters (NPCs) and therefore lack any agency of their own beyond the game's built-in artificial intelligence. Their presence in the game is exclusively as something to be interacted with, and often even more reductively, something to be acted upon. These portrayals are often sensationalist, clichéd, and heavily coded in violence.

Representations of sex workers in video games date back at least to the 1980s. *Leisure Suit Larry in the Land of the Lounge Lizards* and *PimpWars,* a 1987 version of the venerable *Star Trader* arbitrage game, present the most stereotypical end of the spectrum of sex-worker representation in video games, as "hookers" to be bedded or "hoes" to be infested with diseases or stolen from your enemies with crack. *Porky's,* the unlikely Atari 2600 tie-in of the Canadian teen comedy film of the same name, featured a level set in the eponymous bar that required the player to avoid foes such as strippers while planting dynamite to blow up the club.[6]

The most well-known contemporary examples of portrayals of sex workers in video games comes from the *Grand Theft Auto (GTA)* series. It is possible for players to hire a sex worker, then recuperate their money by killing her, in no fewer than four titles: *Grand Theft Auto III, Vice City, Liberty City Stories,* and *Vice City Stories.* In later games, more choices are introduced: players have options in how they respond to solicitations; interactions are longer and more complex (including specifying services); and multiple voice actors play a wider range of sex worker characters. Yet, if a player stands near a sex worker too long without interacting with her in *GTA V,* she will ask him to leave. But not respecting her request is rewarded with a "star," a metric that will positively alter interactions between police and player.

In *Hitman: Absolution,* women who work at the Vixen bar are forced into prostitution by bar owner Dom Osmond, who controls them with threats of violence. The threat of violence is real, as players can kill sex workers throughout the game and then distract the police by strategically disposing of their bodies. *Red Dead Redemption* offers the player the option to rescue these women: in one scene, a man is beating a sex worker outside a saloon and the player can intervene; in another, a man is pictured carrying off a hogtied sex worker and a player can intervene then too. However, should a player put that hogtied sex worker on nearby train tracks and allow a train to run her over, the player earns a secret achievement known as the "dastardly" trophy. Sex workers—or "hos," as they're called in *Saints Row: The Third*—are often portrayed with their pimps, and kidnapping them is often central to several missions. In virtually all Triple A games we surveyed, when sex workers appear, they are never represented with agency, they are frequently the subject of violence, and actions done to them are often a mechanism for unlocking secret game play or points. No matter the game, she (and, she is overwhelmingly female) is never represented with dignity.

Designing The Oldest Game

Given the limited range of representations of sex workers in games, it was crucial that we offered an alternative to these portrayals of sex workers in *The Oldest Game.* In particular, we focused on their lack of agency (players typically interact with sex workers or adopt their appearance in games as a disguise but are never asked to play from their character or position), the lack of empathy players are encouraged to have for sex workers (their characters are often used for titillation, plot device, currency, or humor), representing only a single type of sex work (street work) and reducing their work to a simple cost/gain interaction.

In *The Oldest Game,* players assume the role of Andrea. In playing from her perspective, her complexity and agency are reinforced with every decision the player makes. She controls every interaction with clients, and chooses how to respond to every consequence and random event. Rather than the player character walking up to and interacting with a sex worker, the NPCs are the clients; this completely changes the representations of most sex workers' agency in commercial games.

Putting the player in Andrea's shoes was also crucial to developing empathy between her and the player. We also made an effort to develop a sense of Andrea's personality and personal life outside of her job as well—portraying her relationship with her family and colleagues, building in choices around interactions with friends, even giving small glimpses into the potential for romantic relationships. We wanted the player to identify with Andrea, to feel for the choices she is asked to make and be moved to make the best choices possible under the various conditions that she faces.

We also chose to represent sex work in several different forms, each tied to a specific city: in Montreal, Andrea works in a massage studio; in Toronto, she works from home as an independent escort; and in Vancouver, she does street work. Each situation presents different challenges and choices, and the scenarios are structured differently to reflect these. For example, in Montreal, clients are screened for players by a receptionist, while in Vancouver players have to choose to interact with clients before or after getting in their car. But in Toronto, contact is established through email and, after running potential clients through a Bad Date database, players can choose to meet the clients in a nearby hotel. Players must then choose whether to ask their driver to wait for them (thereby incurring greater costs) or send him on his way. By representing different types of sex work and the myriad of choices that are circumscribed by geography and opportunities to evaluate potential dates, we hoped to offer alternatives to the often extremely narrow view portrayed in games, which is generally limited to street work and always with little to no agency given to the sex worker characters.

We equally wanted to present a more robust sense of Andrea as a character not only to elicit more empathy for her but to recognize the fullness of sex workers' lives outside of work. We added a pop-up, for instance, that informs players that it's time to do their taxes. The pop-up provides common tax problems that sex workers who wish to claim taxes face at tax time. At one point, players have the option to spend money to buy a present for a sister's birthday, to take a night off and go on a date (or have a coffee in the afternoon), or spend a night with a friend watching Netflix, and we included dialogue with other sex workers, particularly in the massage parlor, where socialization happens frequently between clients. We used these scenarios as well to recognize the intersectional and varied nature of sex work. Dialogue between these characters (who are all named) and Andrea reference fears of being caught without legal papers to work, opportunities to take drugs, the presence of pimps, issues of doing sex work while transgender, and a fear that an indigenous colleague has gone missing.

What ended up being most complicated, however, was how to handle the actual mechanics of the game in a way that also served these goals and dissuaded the player from metagaming, or "gaming the game." Initially, we did this by removing any traces of traditional systems of metrics from the game entirely. Aside from keeping track of money earned and spent, there were none of the bars or meters to indicate progress, resources, or health status that games typically use as an index of success and progress. These were represented only in Andrea's changing expression (a nod to the original *DOOM*'s method of indicating injury through facial expression), which would become more haggard and stressed when she was tired or in debt. The idea was to privilege the emotive and narrative connection over one developed through interaction and to keep the focus on Andrea's story rather than making the players feel as though they wanted to "win." We wanted to discourage playing to the metrics, rather than playing for Andrea's well-being (which wasn't always the same thing).

Through playtesting, however, we found that the lack of metrics actually hindered the player's ability to identify and empathize with Andrea. In our first feedback sessions, playtesters noted that the lack of clearly visible metrics prevented them from evaluating a sense of how they were "progressing in the game."[7] More importantly, what we discovered was that the metrics served an important pedagogical function: they helped us to demonstrate what was in Andrea's best interests or what were typical consequences for particular kinds of choices. One playtester noted that their lack of presence encouraged them to care about Andrea less, noting "there is no sense of urgency, I never need to spend money on food, or pay my debt off, or incur unexpected costs" and "when bad things happen there are no long-term or cumulative effects," which led to no pressure to make any risky decisions at all. Conversely, we also heard that "the lack of irreversible consequences" made it more likely for players to engage in risky behavior. This feedback led to our choosing to put these metrics back in, to engender empathy and give a sense of measurable consequences when it came to choices made. That is, money often comes at the cost of health and well-being.

Another area of *The Oldest Game* that presented challenges in terms of bringing balance to our representations of sex work was the element of risk. One of the elements that Marilyne, our sex work consultant, insisted on from the outset was that the interaction not skew overwhelmingly toward the negative. Her instruction, based on her own experiences and perspective on sex work, was that most interactions with clients generally proceed without incident, are occasionally banal, often neither traumatic nor exciting, with exceptionally good or bad clients in the minority.

Based on the feedback that we received from the last round of playtests, however, we had swung the pendulum too far toward the positive. Sex workers who later played the game referred to the "lack of consequences" as a barrier to both the realism and enjoyment of the game. In not wanting to portray sex work as sensationalist and negative, we eliminated the sense of urgency and real risk that is necessary to create a sense of tension in gameplay but also to give a sense of the specific work-related challenges experienced by the sex workers we sought to represent. Subsequent revisions of the game have introduced additional challenges and consequences, especially when health and happiness metrics get too low, to create a more nuanced portrayal of the difficult choices sex workers are often forced to make. For example, we added a random number generator to both Toronto and Vancouver in order to recognize the constant potential for police surveillance. One script in Vancouver involving a police officer specifically referenced helping Andrea get "cleaned up":

OFFICER. The street is no place for you, honey. Why don't you let me take you somewhere you can get yourself cleaned up and off the street?
ANDREA. Are you kidding me? I certainly don't need any help from those people! I can take care of myself.
OFFICER. It's never too late to change your mind. I'll ask you next time I see you. If you're still alive, that is.

This randomized scenario was an important addition for recognizing the explicit bias toward "saving" sex workers, both in terms of common attitudes among the general population and law enforcement and explicitly within the language of Bill C-36. The final revisions to the game will include a pop-up that will reference the recent coverage of police assaulting sex workers, which led many to call for discussion of the issue at the federal inquiry into Missing and Murdered Indigenous Women (Macdonald).

Adding numeric values to the metrics was a key way to demonstrate consequences. After our last round of playtesting with sex workers, we added a scenario where Andrea gets a sexually transmitted infection. A pop-up informs players that they have lost money because of time off work to go to the health clinic and to purchase the needed medication. There is also a hit, however, in terms of mood and health. In addition to giving the option to have intercourse without a condom, we provided other opportunities to engage in risky behavior such as being hired for group sex. Should a player choose to take the clients, the financial gain is substantial; however, there is a slight consequence in terms of mood and health in order to recognize the toll that the stress and worry of the *potential* for violence pose and the fatigue that comes with this kind of work. Emerging out of our iterative game design process, these changes to the mechanics of the game forced recognition of our knowledge assumptions and ontological choices that prescribe a particular point of view in the game.

Many sex workers do not believe sex work is inherently violent; rather, they point to criminalization, stigmatization, and misogyny as sources of violence (Benoit and Shumka). The difficulty of representing the lack of consequences for systemic misogyny and police indifference, let alone (sexual) assaults and abuse committed by police, have posed a particular design challenge for our team. One respondent's feedback was particularly instructive. When asked what was the one thing they would change about the game, the respondent wrote,

> More consequences. One thing I appreciate is that the actual sex acts weren't porn-ified and the game focused on the before and after. It was appreciated, trust me. I really appreciated that my character wasn't raped.
>
> But in general, there just weren't any consequences—jail? STI's? Threats of violence? If you don't "choose" well, you're at risk. And it's not the work that puts you at risk, it is the complete lack of protection for sex workers' rights. The government and law enforcement doesn't do anything to protect us so we have to be hyper-vigilant. For someone like me, it was easy because I just "got it" but for many sex workers, it can be very difficult. There are men out there who know how difficult to can to [sic] prosecute crimes against sex workers and they exploit the sex workers because of it.
>
> It's not the work that puts us in danger, it is the fact that there are no consequences. Men think they can rape us or beat us up and get away with it and the sad fact is, they can.

This respondent was a self-identified frequent game player and thus, the respondent's comments about not being raped clearly reference the common tropes found in typical game play that involve sex work. But as a newsgame, the target demographic here is not dedicated game players specifically, though they will obviously be part of the audience for the game. Though we have adjusted our metrics to better reflect the possibility of experiencing some negative consequences when engaging in risky behavior, we also wanted to leave the variability in place because this is precisely the point. Even as sex workers establish a wide range of best practices to ensure the health and safety of sex workers, like any workplace, there are no guarantees that all safeguards will succeed. Further, when faced with the very real need to engage in risky behavior because of lack of funds, not all chances taken end badly. Variability, then, is as much the point of trying to represent the everydayness of these experiences. With the added unpredictability of game play, the experiences and "messages" taken from game play may vary from player to player and length of game play (Consalvo, *Cheating*).

We know that the wide range of perspectives and experiences of sex workers can never be fully represented in one game. Yet the unpredictability and variability of game play also mean that there won't be a singular game experience on the other end. At some level, we must proceed with our design and representational considerations while remembering Hall's aphorism that in this attempt to represent sex work in a game, we are practicing "politics without guarantees" (Hall, *Representation and the Media*).

We want to highlight that the risks embedded in the game extended outside the game too, especially to the team: our sex worker consultant had not yet revealed her profession to her family. We held off on releasing the trailer on YouTube until she had told her family because she was named as the "consultant" at the end, using her given name. The students working on the project also faced attacks online, especially at the height of GamerGate, but also from virulent antifeminist and anti-sex work public discourse, especially online. Though this risk is nothing like that experienced by sex workers themselves, it's part of what responsible designers must confront in a time of hate. By challenging the classic approach to news reporting through a guise of neutrality (the "view from nowhere," Rosen; Haraway), we've discovered that designing with a "view from somewhere" has meant confronting goals that often conflict.[8]

As a contribution to the creation of a genuinely critical digital humanities, our project strikes at the core of the impossibility of a politics of representation grounded in truth claims. This game cannot be the definitive display of sex work. It cannot show every challenge sex workers face in their intersectionality; it cannot succeed at showing lived experience for everyone. It engages with a very specific piece of legislation from a very specific moment in Canadian history, and the effect that that legislation has had on a portion of the Canadian labor force. Though we have aimed to represent a wider range of racialized and gendered bodies, we worried continuously about charges of tokenism (and rightly so). We still don't know what it means to win at the game, or what it means to lose. We've added some dialogue with a fellow sex worker who references the missing and murdered women in the Vancouver area because it was problematic *not* to recognize this terrifying context for many sex workers in this region. Further, those risks are not even for all sex workers. We know that trans workers (especially trans women) face higher risks for abuse and violence, and that First Nations, Métis, and Inuit women are disproportionately disappeared across the country (Benoit and Shumka). But at the same time, putting it into the game runs the risk of reifying that all street work ends up in murder and violence. In other words, once we take seriously Johanna Drucker's imperative to recognize that signification is always done on behalf of someone somewhere (2009), it points to the risky business of gamifying variously marginalized bodies.

At the same time, however, our process and design also lead to specific questions about the promises of newsgames to address issues of representation in journalistic practice itself: is it possible to produce games that capitalize on the currency of news events; avoid the same traps of conventional, stereotypical news coverage; and pay attention to the deep dynamics of game mechanics in a rapid prototyping model? Though the production time of this game has been exceptionally long, how can a feminist commitment to public (or civic)-oriented journalism that seeks to work alongside community groups fit into a model of more rapid game design like typical journalistic production?[9] Will an iterative prototyping model that works with the communities being represented have any impact on other forms of journalistic practice?

While one outcome of this project has been to question if journalism in any of its forms can fully represent the experiences of such marginalized populations precisely because their social, political, and economic contexts are so precarious, we have come to realize this perhaps shouldn't be our goal. As Trinh Min-Ha has so eloquently suggested, rather than speak for, one true contribution of a project like this to the larger project of expanding knowledges within the digital humanities may be to find a multitude of ways of "speaking nearby": "In other words, a speaking that does not objectify, does not point to an object as if it is distant from the speaking subject or absent from the speaking place. A speaking that reflects on itself and can come very close to a subject without, however, seizing or claiming it. A speaking in brief, whose closures are only moments of transition opening up to other possible moments of transition" (Chen, 86–87). A truly feminist contribution to a digital humanities that engages marginalized communities seeks not moments of closure in its acts of representation; it, in fact, resists closure as a goal. Yet, though we value games and other immersive journalistic forms for their ability to create empathy, we have also become acutely aware of how readily the game can slip into a state of knowingness whereby singular experiences become generalized, like in much conventional journalism. "Speaking nearby" has meant making space for a dialogue about leaving sex work, even though the government framed the legislation, with the support of abolitionist feminists, as promoting this end state as the only desirable outcome. "Speaking nearby" has meant making space for violence, pleasure, flirtation, and abuse in uncomfortable ways, in unpredictable ways. It's meant providing a view from somewhere recognizable, even if not fully knowable from the outside.

Notes

The author wishes to thank the reviewers for their generous and thoughtful comments on this essay; this essay is stronger for their efforts. The author also wishes to thank Concordia University for seed funding for this project.

1. The project is led by Sandra Gabriele at Concordia University. Lisa Lynch, formerly of the Department of Journalism, was a co-investigator on the project in its earliest stages. The project was possible only because of the amazing work of a group of talented students who researched, coded, designed the graphics, wrote the scenarios, created the soundscapes, ran the play tests, and contributed to the overall design of the game: Martin Desrosier, Jennifer Sunahara, Natalie Zina Walschots, Amanda Feder, Eileen Holowka, Sadie Couture, Esther Splett, Marilyn Sugiarto, Stephanie Goddard, Rebecca Waldie, and Ben Spencer. See theoldestgame.com for a trailer of the game and the latest blog posts.

2. Bill C-36 is formally known as the "Protection of Communities and Exploited Persons Act. An Act to amend the Criminal Code in response to the Supreme Court of Canada decision in Attorney General of Canada v. Bedford and to make consequential amendments to other Acts." It arose after the Supreme Court ruled that the laws surrounding sex work (selling sex itself was not, and is still not, illegal) were unconstitutional because they made it impossible for sex workers to avoid breaking the law. Chief Justice Beverley McLauchlin wrote in the 9–0 decision, "Parliament has the power to regulate against nuisances, but not at the cost of the health, safety and lives of prostitutes," further noting, "it is not a crime in Canada to sell sex for money" (CBC News, "Supreme Court"). Three laws in particular were struck down and formed the basis for game play in *The Oldest Game*: prohibitions against keeping a bawdy house, living on the avails of prostitution, and communicating for the purposes of prostitution.

3. For example, stories that appear in the pages of the daily newspaper often follow an inverted pyramid style, while weekend newspapers offer a variety of writing styles and layout that are distinct from their weekday counterparts.

4. One issue that came up with playtesting done in spring 2015 was paying sex worker playtesters for their time. Though our budget was limited, we were prepared to pay these playtesters for their time using a similar logic to hiring Marilyne as a consultant on game design. Unfortunately, the university research ethics committee determined that paying the playtesters would constitute a major revision to our Ethics Certificate and would warrant an application to alter the conditions of our ethics approval. In the interest of proceeding with the playtesting, we opted not to pursue this avenue, but are doing so for the final playtesting session as a way of recognizing the expertise of sex workers and that their time should be compensated.

5. For those unfamiliar with the Gamergate phenomenon, see Lewis, "Gamergate," for a brief introduction; Consalvo, "Confronting," and Chess and Shaw, "Conspiracy of Fishes," among others, explore its implications for feminist game scholars.

6. *PimpWars* should not be confused with *Pimp War* published by Happy Empire Inc. Launched in 1999, it now has over a million "pimps" registered on the site. As the website explains under the watchful gaze of a racialized pimp conventionally dressed: "You will become a master at the art of pimping your hoes, commanding your thugs and battling your enemies to protect what you have and to help your empire grow. This game is NOT for whiners. PimpWar players have 5000 ways to call you a bitch ass. So if you think you can handle it we suggest you get a couple friends together so you are not alone in this bad bad place and then bring yo bad self." (*Pimp Wars* [video game], http://www.pimpwar.com/).

7. Losh, "In Country," describes the development of a trust meter in *Tactical Iraqi*, a military training game designed to enhance language acquisition of spoken Arabic to facilitate deploying soldiers. The trust meter was developed by the game designers in order to provide immediate feedback to the player, yet also had the effect of teaching the critical skill of establishing trust in dialogue.

8. Though Rosen is describing journalistic practice specifically, my point here is highly indebted to Donna Haraway's specific mobilization of the phrase to describe the political implications of speaking from situated knowledges.

9. The long production time in many ways is a product of building games within an academic and professional context: Lisa Lynch left Concordia; our student team members graduated or left their programs of study, necessitating hiring new students; our sex work consultant purchased her own massage parlor with her partner and subsequently had a child; and the lead investigator was maintaining a demanding service position as chair of her department, and now as a senior administrator.

Bibliography

Alcoff, Linda. "The Problem of Speaking for Others." *Cultural Critique* 20 (Winter 1991–92): 5–32.

Anthropy, Anna. *Rise of the Videogame Zinesters: How Freaks, Normals, Amateurs, Artists, Dreamers, Drop-outs, Queers, Housewives, and People like You Are Taking Back an Art Form.* New York: Seven Stories, 2012.

Baldwin, D., and Treena Orchard. "Representation and Reflections of Two Former Sex Trade Workers Covering the Pickton Trial in Vancouver, British Columbia." *Feminist Media Studies* 9, no. 4 (2009): 505–9.

Balsamo, Anne. "Feminism and Cultural Studies." *Journal of the Midwest Modern Language Association* 24, no. 1 (1991): 50–73.

Belman, Jonathan, and Mary Flanagan. "Designing Games to Foster Empathy." *Cognitive Technology* 14, no. 2 (2010): 5–15.

Benoit, Cecilia, and Leah Shumka. "Sex Work and Violence." *Sex Work in Canada* (2015). Accessed August 15, 2017. http://www.understandingsexwork.com.

Bogost, Ian. *Persuasive Games: The Expressive Power of Videogames.* Cambridge, Mass.: MIT Press, 2010.

Bogost, Ian, Simon Ferrari, and Bobby Schweizer. *Newsgames: Journalism at Play.* Cambridge, Mass.: MIT Press, 2010.

Bogost, Ian, and Nick Montfort. "Platform Studies: Frequently Questioned Answers." *Digital Arts and Culture. After Media: Embodiment and Context.* December 12, 2009. Accessed October 31, 2016. http://www.escholarship.org/uc/item/01r0k9br.

CBC News. "Supreme Court Strikes Down Canada's Prostitution Laws." cbc.ca, December 20, 2013. Accessed January 15, 2014. http://www.cbc.ca/news/politics/supreme-court-strikes-down-canada-s-prostitution-laws-1.2471572.

Chen, Nancy N. "'Speaking Nearby:' A Conversation with Trinh T. Min-Ha." *Visual Anthropology Review* 8, no. 1 (1992): 82–91.

Chess, Shira, and Adrienne Shaw. "A Conspiracy of Fishes, or, How We Learned to Stop Worrying about #GamerGate and Embrace Hegemonic Masculinity." *Journal of Broadcasting & Electronic Media* 59, no. 1 (2012): 208–20.

Comella, Lynn. "Representing Sex Work in Sin City." *Feminist Media Studies* 9, no. 4 (2009): 495–500.

Cong-Huyen, Anne. "Thinking Through Race (Gender, Class, & Nation) in the Digital Humanities: The #transformDH Example." Prezi.com, January 4, 2013. Accessed October 29, 2016. https://prezi.com/ysz-t5mc7hyu/thinking-of-race-gender-class-nation-in-dh/.

Consalvo, Mia. *Cheating: Gaining Advantage in Videogames.* Cambridge, Mass.: MIT Press, 2007.

Consalvo, Mia. "Confronting Toxic Gamer Culture: A Challenge for Feminist Game Studies Scholars." *Ada: A Journal of Gender, New Media & Technology* 1 (November 2012). http://adanewmedia.org/2012/11/issue1-consalvo/.

Dill, Karen E., Douglas A. Gentile, William A. Richter, and Jody C. Dill. "Violence, Sex, Race and Age in Popular Video Games: A Content Analysis." In *Featuring Females: Feminist Analyses of the Media,* edited by Ellen Cole and Jessica Henderson Daniel, 115–30. Washington, D.C.: American Psychological Association, 2005.

Drucker, Johanna. "Humanities Approaches to Interface Theory." *Culture Machine* 12 (2011): 1–20.

Drucker, Johanna. *SpecLab: Digital Aesthetics and Projects in Speculative Computing.* Chicago: University of Chicago Press, 2009.

Fernández-Vara, Clara. *Introduction to Game Analysis.* New York: Routledge, 2015.

Flanagan, Mary, Jim Diamond, Helen Nissenbaum, and Jonathan Belman. "A Method for Discovering Values in Digital Games." dans Proceedings of DiGRA (2007), 752–60.

Flanagan, Mary, Daniel C. Howe, Helen Nissenbaum. "Values at Play: Design Tradeoffs in Socially-Oriented Game Design." CHI '05 Proceedings of the SIGCHI Conference on Human Factors in Computing Systems, 751–60. New York: ACM. 2005.

Frasca, Gonzalo, and Newsgaming. *September 12th: A Toy World,* 2003. Accessed May 12, 2015. http://www.gamesforchange.org/play/september-12th-a-toy-world/.

Games for Change. "September 12th: A Toy World: Synopsis." Accessed May 12, 2105. http://www.gamesforchange.org/game/september-12th-a-toy-world/.

Grant, Melissa Gira. *Playing the Whore: The Work of Sex Work.* New York: Verso, 2014.

GT Interactive. *DOOM* (video game). Developed by id Software. Tom Hall, director; Shawn Green and Sandy Peterson, designers. Released 1993. New York.

Hall, Stuart. *Representation and the Media* (video tape). Directed by S. Jhally. Northampton, Mass.: Media Education Foundation, 1997. 55 mins.

Hall, Stuart, ed. *Representation: Cultural Representations and Signifying Practices.* London: Sage, 1997.

Hall, Stuart, Chas Critcher, Tony Jefferson, John Clarke, and Brian Roberts. *Policing the Crisis: Mugging, the State and Law and Order.* London: MacMillan, 1978.

Hallgrimsdottir, Helga K., Rachel Phillips, and Cecilia Benoit. "Fallen Women and Rescued Girls: Social Stigma and Media Narratives of the Sex Industry in Victoria, BC, from 1980 to 2005." *Canadian Review of Sociology & Anthropology/Revue canadienne de sociologie et d'anthropologie* 43, no. 3 (2006): 266–80.

Hallgrimsdottir, Helga K., Rachel Phillips, Cecilia Benoit, and Kevin Walby. "Sporting Girls, Streetwalkers, and Inmates of Houses of Ill Repute: Media Narratives and the Historical Mutability of Prostitution Stigmas." *Sociological Perspectives* 51, no. 1 (2008): 119–38.

Haraway, Donna. "Situated Knowledges: The Science Question in Feminism and the Privilege of Partial Perspective." *Feminist Studies* 14, no. 3 (1988): 575–99.

Jiwani, Yasmin. *Discourses of Denial: Mediations of Race, Gender & Violence*. Vancouver: University of British Columbia Press, 2006.

Jiwani, Yasmin, and Mary Lynn Young. "Missing and Murdered Women: Reproducing Marginality in News Discourse." *Canadian Journal of Communication* 31 (2006): 895–917.

Konzack, Lars. "Computer Game Criticism: A Method for Computer Game Analysis." In *Proceedings of Computer Games and Digital Cultures Conference*, edited by F. Mäyrä, 89–100. Tampere: Tampere University Press, 2002. http://www.digra.org/wp-content/uploads/digital-library/05164.32231.pdf.

Latour, Bruno. *Reassembling the Social: An Introduction to Actor-Network-Theory*. Oxford: Oxford University Press, 2005.

Lewis, Helen. "Gamergate: A Brief History of a Computer-Age War." *The Guardian*, January 11, 2015. Accessed November 30, 2017. https://www.theguardian.com/technology/2015/jan/11/gamergate-a-brief-history-of-a-computer-age-war.

Liu, Alan. "Where Is the Cultural Criticism in Digital Humanities?" In *Debates in Digital Humanities*, edited by Matthew K. Gold, 490–509. Minneapolis: University of Minnesota Press, 2012.

Losh, Elizabeth. "In Country with *Tactical Iraqi*: Trust, Identity, and Language Learning in a Military Video Game." *Proceedings of the Sixth Digital Arts and Culture Conference, 2005*. Accessed October 28, 2016. https://eee.uci.edu/faculty/losh/virtualpolitik/DAC2005.pdf.

Losh, Elizabeth. "What Can the Digital Humanities Learn from Feminist Game Studies?" *Digital Humanities Quarterly* 9, no. 2 (2015). Accessed August 23, 2016. http://www.digitalhumanities.org/dhq/vol/9/2/000200/000200.html.

Macdonald, Neil. "Justice for Families Requires MMIW Inquiry Investigate Role of Police." CBC News, September 1, 2016. Accessed September 1, 2016. http://www.cbc.ca/news/politics/murdered-missing-inquiry-macdonald-1.3743744.

Martino, Paul J., author, and J. Coyle, developer. *PimpWars* (video game). Released 1990. Description at MobyGames. http://www.mobygames.com/game/pimpwars.

Maynard, Robyn. "Carceral Feminism: The Failure of Sex Work Prohibition." *FUSE Magazine* 35, no. 3, ABOLITION (July 2012). Accessed November 30, 2017. http://robynmaynard.com/writing/carceral-feminism-the-failure-of-sex-work-prohibition/.

McLaughlin, Lisa. "Discourses of Prostitution/Discourses of Sexuality." *Critical Studies in Mass Communication* 8, no. 2 (1991): 249–72.

McPherson, Tara. "Why Are the Digital Humanities So White? Or Thinking the Histories of Race and Computation." In *Debates in the Digital Humanities*, edited by Matthew K. Gold, 139–60. Minneapolis, University of Minnesota Press, 2012.

Mendes, Kaitlynn, and Kumarini Silva. "Introduction: Sex Workers in the News." *Feminist Media Studies* 9, no. 4 (2009): 493–95.

Montfort, Nick. "Combat in Context." *Game Studies* 6, no. 1 (2006). Accessed November 1, 2016. http://gamestudies.org/0601/articles/montfort.

Nakamura, Lisa. *Digitizing Race: Visual Cultures of the Internet.* Minneapolis: University of Minnesota Press, 2008.

Nakamura, Lisa, and Peter A. Chow-White, eds. *Race after the Internet.* New York: Routledge, 2011.

Risam, Roopika. "Beyond the Margins: Intersectionality and the Digital Humanities." *Digital Humanities Quarterly* 9, no. 2 (2015). Accessed October 29, 2016. http://www.digitalhumanities.org/dhq/vol/9/2/000208/000208.html.

Rockstar Games. *Grand Theft Auto: Liberty City Stories* (video game). Released 2005. Dan Houser and James Worrall, writers. San Diego, Calif.

Rockstar Games. *Grand Theft Auto: Vice City* (video game). Released 2002. Dan Houser and James Worrall, writers. San Diego, Calif.

Rockstar Games. *Grand Theft Auto: Vice City Stories* (video game). Released 2006. Dan Houser and David Bland, writers. San Diego, Calif.

Rockstar Games. *Grand Theft Auto III* (video game). Released 2001. James Worrall and Paul Kurowski, writers. San Diego, Calif.

Rockstar Games. *Red Dead Redemption* (video game). Released 2010. Dan Houser and Michael Unsworth, writers. San Diego, Calif.

Rosen, Jay. "The View from Nowhere." *Press Think: Ghost of Democracy in the Media Machine,* September 18, 2003 (weblog). Accessed April 23, 2013. http://archive.pressthink.org/2003/09/18/jennings.html.

Sicart, Miguel. "Newsgames: Theory and Design." In Entertainment Computing - ICEC 2008. ICEC 2008. Lecture Notes in Computer Science, vol. 5309. Edited by S. M. Stevens and S. J. Saldamarco, 27-33. Springer, Berlin: Heidelberg, 2008.

Sierra On-Line. *Leisure Suit Larry in the Land of the Lounge Lizards* (video game). Released 1987. Chuck Benton and Mark Crowe, directors, Al Lowe, writer. Oakhurst, Calif.

Skinner, David, Mike J. Gasher, and James Compton. "Putting Theory to Practice: A Critical Approach to Journalism Studies." *Journalism* 2, no. 3 (2001): 341–60.

Square Enix. *Hitman: Absolution* (video game). Released 2012. Tore Blystad and Peter Flekenstein, directors, Greg Nagan and Tore Blystad, writers. Tokyo, Japan, 2012.

Thompson, Clive. "Saving the World, One Video Game at a Time." *New York Times,* July 23, 2006. Video Games. Accessed July 21, 2016. http://www.nytimes.com/2006/07/23/arts/23thom.html.

THQ. *Saints Row: The Third* (video game). Released 2011. Keith Aram, director, Steve Jaros, lead writer, Jeffrey Bielawski, writer. Agoura Hills, Calif.

Treanor, Mike, and Michael Mateas. "Newsgames: Procedural Rhetoric Meets Political Cartoons," *Proceedings of DiGRA 2009* (2009), 1–8.

20th Century Fox. *Porky's* (video game). Released 1983. Los Angeles, Calif.

Unsworth, John. "Knowledge Representation in Humanities Computing." Accessed August 26, 2016. http://people.virginia.edu/~jmu2m//KR/.

Van Brunschot, Erin Gibbs, Rosalind A. Sydie, and Catherine Krull. "Images of Prostitution." *Women & Criminal Justice* 10, no. 4 (2008): 47–72. doi:10.1300/J012v10n04_03.

Wernimont, Jacqueline. "Introduction to Feminisms and DH Special Issue." *Digital Humanities Quarterly* 9, no. 2 (2015). Accessed August 23, 2016. http://www.digitalhumanities.org/dhq/vol/9/2/000217/000217.html.

Wernimont, Jacqueline. "Whence Feminism? Assessing Feminist Interventions in Digital Literary Archives." *Digital Humanities Quarterly* 7, no. 1 (2013). Accessed August 23, 2016. http://www.digitalhumanities.org/dhq/vol/7/1/000156/000156.html.

PART VI][*Chapter 25*

Playing the Humanities

Feminist Game Studies and Public Discourse

ANASTASIA SALTER AND BRIDGET BLODGETT

Both game studies and the broader digital humanities value the public scholar: the intersection of games academic spaces with games journalism and online communities offers lots of valuable opportunities for debate and shared knowledge. However, participation within these communities comes at very different potential costs for scholars based on their identities, and the currency of one network becomes fuel for a witch hunt from another. Acting as a public scholar brings with it risk that is inherently tied to a scholar's identity and position: gender, race, sexual identity, and other elements of identity not only bring intense scrutiny but often invite harassment, trolling, and silencing. Thus, the privileging of public scholarship in the games and digital humanities research communities can come at a high price for already marginalized participants, with important ramifications for whose voices are heard and recognized within the field.

Game studies and the digital humanities are fields with significant overlap: game studies can be found in departments ranging from English, media studies, and American studies to communication, digital media, and computer science. While the field is inherently interdisciplinary, many game studies scholars hold a home department and disciplinary training from a humanities background. The technical nature of both the games under study and the methods required to effectively analyze them connects with some digital humanities methods. It is thus unsurprising that game studies also suffers from some of the challenges facing the digital humanities community, including the privileging of coders and "makers" and a push toward public scholarship that comes with significant risk, as observable in the experience of pushback against feminist scholarship at the Digital Games Research Association documented by Shira Chess and Adrienne Shaw ("We Are All Fishes Now"). By examining the parallel experiences of researchers working on bringing feminist discourse to these two spaces of technical-humanities intersection, we can better understand the larger challenge facing both fields.

Being Public

Public scholarship in both game studies and the digital humanities is centered on community and practices of sharing and amplification, and one of the most important networked publics (defined by danah boyd as a space constructed as a public through networked technologies and the collective emerging from this construction) for both is Twitter (boyd, "Social Network Sites"). As a social network, Twitter was created in 2006 and provides a platform for sharing content limited to 140 characters (which might include links, videos, and/or images) that has been significantly popular with academics thanks in part to its model of following, rather than friending, which allows for nonmutual connections, unlike the reciprocal model of Facebook. This is particularly helpful for new and emerging scholars, who can follow significant voices in the field while establishing themselves. As sava saheli singh notes, "practices like this are even becoming part of academic professionalization—the things a grad student or early-career scholar must do to develop a reputation as a scholar and academic" ("Tweeting to the Choir"). These expectations are becoming the norm in any technologically related or dependent field, as participation is a sign of both technical literacy and relevance, and may also be key to networking, promoting publications, and finding a job.[1] Lisa Spiro has gone so far as to define digital humanities as a field of public scholarly practices, noting that "how the digital humanities community operates—transparently, collaboratively, through online networks—distinguishes it" ("'This Is Why'"). Such rhetoric, while compelling, leaves little room for opting out of those networks. It is notable that Spiro's discussion tackles this head-on, suggesting a need for explicit shared values and codes of conduct within digital humanities, both of which have yet to be truly realized.

Participation in this sort of collaborative online field comes at a cost. Game studies shares similar values: the field's main journal, *Game Studies,* is open access, and many of the field's most noted scholars regularly share and collaborate through Twitter and other networks. Given these similarities, events from 2010–2017 in the game studies community offer a powerful case study for the risks inherent in public acts of scholarship, particularly on Twitter. As a network, Twitter is highly regarded in the digital humanities community: as Matthew Kirschenbaum observes "Twitter, along with blogs and other online outlets, has inscribed the digital humanities as a network topology, that is to say lines drawn by aggregates of affinities, formally and functionally manifest in who follows whom, who friends whom, who tweets whom, and who links to what" ("What Is Digital Humanities"). Digital humanities practices value the public scholar: as Bonnie Stewart notes, "Going online and talking to people you don't know about areas of shared interest . . . opens up your capacity to build communities of practice" ("What Counts"). However, the consequences of online participation in these communities of practice (with the digital humanities broadly construed as one such community) have been strongly felt by women, persons of color, and other marginalized voices. By putting the experiences of games scholars and digital humanists in dialogue, we can better understand why calls for public scholarship can be marginalizing and silencing even as they seek to strengthen their respective disciplines. Humanist and social science games scholars, particularly those addressing inequities and inclusivity, have in many ways served as the canary in the coal mine for academia at large: the same forces and institutions that have been marshalled in the games culture wars are as of 2017 a dominant part of the academic landscape (Bernstein). The real and immediate dangers (particularly to those from marginalized identities) have never been greater (May).

Both games and digital humanities suffer from a similar challenge of being adjacent to science, technology, engineering, and math (STEM), but not part of the discourse of STEM. This challenge was particularly crystallized in a highly circulated op-ed in the *New York Times* in November 2017 by Cathy O'Neil with the provocative title "The Ivory Tower Can't Keep Ignoring Tech." This idea that academia was "ignoring" tech was particularly exhausting thanks to a line that drew the immediate ire of researchers in both the digital humanities and game studies: "There is essentially no distinct field of academic study that takes seriously the responsibility of understanding and critiquing the role of technology—and specifically, the algorithms that are responsible for so many decisions—in our lives" ("Ivory Tower"). One researcher, Victoria Massie, responded aptly on Twitter with the observation that "the ivory tower isn't ignoring tech. Rather academia, like tech, suffers from the same structural inequalities. And if tech, like academia, didn't ignore the folks at the margins who have been about this work, we wouldn't be in this mess" ("@vmmassie"). Massie's comment is particularly insightful, as it serves as a reminder that scholars fundamentally driven by understanding and critiquing the inequities emerging from technology through the lens of gender and race are also frequently those whose voices are least likely to be amplified.

While many expressed understandable frustrations that O'Neil's op-ed appeared to ignore the rich history of entire fields of academia, the oversight is neither new nor unexpected. A hierarchy of fields is inevitable, and STEM research has traditionally been far more visible. Both game studies and digital humanities are STEM adjacent, but participants in those fields contributing outside the technical center are frequently marginalized. Even scholars with significant personal capital note the challenges facing scholars outside these central disciplines. In his "Year Fifteen" report on the field of game studies, Ian Bogost noted, "The truth is, as a critical and pedagogical concern, game studies is hardly a powerful actor. Games are, I'm sorry to report, a joke that have managed nevertheless to eke out a place in the study of arts and culture" ("Game Studies"). The centering of these debates over identity and cultural value on code and public contributions is itself inherently gendered. Within the games industry, there are defined tiers of participation, and while game design is interdisciplinary by nature, the procedural aspects of game design are often most recognized as being the primary work. These mirror the common discursive constructions of the fields of science and technology where the more technical and mathematically based focuses are seen as the higher-status positions, which likewise echo debates in the digital humanities over the technical barriers to entry and participation. We will examine the parallel threads of academic representation and community silencing within games studies and digital humanities discourses, with particular attention to how these self-selected gatekeepers determine who participates and who is heard in forming scholarly publics.

The co-location of these outbreaks on a primary medium of digital humanities discourse, Twitter, brought with it a huge intersection with academic speech and debate. The overlap between academia and fandom (a concept Henry Jenkins refers to as "aca/fan" brings with it huge overlaps in discourse communities between academics who study and develop games and the larger games industry and gamer communities.[2] Defining the space of game studies is difficult: games programs and courses have emerged as part of computer science and engineering departments, English and literature programs, art and design schools, and interdisciplinary studies. While games can be identified as part of STEM disciplines, the study of games has often been more closely aligned with media studies, and games are often found occupying the same spaces as the digital humanities.

Such programs also frequently align themselves with media creation and procedural knowledge as a means toward greater relevance within the institution and in relationship to the games industry, as Austin C. Howe criticized: "scholars, who struggled to establish game studies as a discipline within academia, chose to focus on procedural styles of play as a strategy for establishing an independent and legitimate field of study, but it was still a hard sell.... By combining play studies with programming and animation, a games curricula emerged that focused on games that are designed around both ludocentric and tech-fetishistic rhetorics" ("On the Ghost"). This debate has allegories in the digital humanities, as Miriam Posner writes: "As digital humanities winds its way into academic departments, it seems reasonable to predict that the work that will get people jobs—the work that marks a real digital humanist—will be work that shows that you can code. And that work is overwhelmingly by men" (*Some Things*).This criticism holds echoes of the code-obsession that often surrounds digital humanities programs and conferences, with the expectation that procedural (rather than humanities) literacies are the saving grace offered by the introduction of the digital. As existing trends already continually reaffirm the systemic challenges that women and other marginalized communities face in STEM-based institutions, programs with a code-centered curriculum risk reproducing the same trends in representation and student bodies.

Similar risks accompany the privileging of crowdsourced, "open source," and public scholarship movements. The inherent challenges of meaningful discourse in such spaces are increasingly being recognized. Confronted with a wealth of meaningless debates and misinformation in its own comments section, *Popular Science* made the decision to give up on moderation and shut the whole forum down (LaBarre). The availability and public nature of discussion on the web raises questions about who may participate in discussions of academic topics and how different voices should be valuable as providing insight or feedback to the academic community. Even in more academic venues, the idea of crowdsourcing knowledge rarely leads to an amplification of women's voices, as Elizabeth Losh points out in an article addressing explicitly what digital humanities can learn from feminist game studies: "Collaborative authorship in the digital humanities cannot be similarly strongly correlated with feminism. Only one of the ten authors of the critical code studies book *10 PRINT* was female, and women made up only a fraction of the multiple authors of the "crowdsourced" book from the University of Michigan Press *Hacking the Academy*. Perhaps this is not surprising given the machismo sometimes associated with multiple authorship in other forms of digital textual collaboration, such as when hackers generate code or Wikipedia editors produce pages or computer scientists rack up publications with the multiple authorship that defines their scholarly networks" ("What Can the Digital Humanities"). As Losh observes, in game studies collaboration between women authors is more common, perhaps in part thanks to the challenges inherent to feminist discourse within game studies as a space.

Contextualizing Gendertrolling through GamerGate

Both digital humanists and games scholars, and indeed many tech-savvy academics in the community at large, rely on corporate-run media networks as platforms for collaboration and discourse. Among those, Twitter has been dominant for nearly a decade, and has thus had a dramatic impact on the networks and discourse of both fields. The same aspects that make Twitter so inviting to scholars make it dangerous to marginalized participants. Twitter's use of asymmetric friendships and public-facing content make the tweets of scholars available for use and critique by anyone, and those people in turn can easily reply, amplify, or harass the writer. Twitter as a platform has proven to be particularly suited for what Karla Mantilla calls "gendertrolling," or misogynist harassment with a focus on silencing and driving women away from participation in public social media platforms ("Gendertrolling"). The games and game studies communities have proven particularly volatile to this type of harassment, with a series of major incidents on Twitter drawing attention to the dangers of participating in public space and discourse. This tension within games studies (and now, academia at large) place scholars in a no-win scenario: participation on networks such as Twitter is valued as academic currency, but participation is also an invitation to overt gender-based harassment. These incidents have been fueled by questions of identity: Who gets to claim the title of gamer? Whose voices will be heard (and, importantly, silenced) in conversations surrounding games and games culture?

The most widely recognized and publicly noted incident of gendertrolling and campaigns of harassment and silencing within the games community on Twitter is

GamerGate, a hashtag started in August 2014 by the ex-partner of a game designer (Zoe Quinn, as chronicled in her powerful memoir *Crash Override*) that was marketed as a fight against what members of the movement perceived as a lack of ethics in games journalism and a move toward "political correctness" that they saw as threatening their gaming culture. This was far from the first outbreak of misogyny-driven conflict within the games community on Twitter: several previous events had forewarned of the coming storm. In 2010, the publication of a comic featuring rape as punchline by industry convention leader Penny Arcade spurred a dispute over the appropriateness of rape as a subject, which escalated as Twitter accounts with names like "Dickwolvington" and "TeamRAPE" threatened rape and violence against any woman who criticized the comic (Salter and Blodgett). In 2012, a pivotal hashtag #1ReasonWhy begun with women answering a male designer's tweeted question, "Why are there so few lady game creators?," with frank discussions of the experience of being a woman in the games industry and community.[3] We previously examined this Twitter conversation through analyzing a number of tweets and found that they revealed a number of trends among the problems experienced by women: "Rape and Sexual Harassment, Overt Sexualization, Harassment, Silencing, and Gendered Assumptions" (Blodgett and Salter). This tension has escalated in both visibility and impact over time, as Leigh Alexander captures in her examination of gamer as an identity: "'Games culture' is a petri dish of people who know so little about how human social interaction and professional life works that they can concoct online 'wars' about social justice or 'game journalism ethics,' straight-faced, and cause genuine human consequences. Because of video games" ("'Gamers' Don't Have to Be"). These themes offer insight into the experiences of women and marginalized members of the community, and the problem of silencing holds particularly problematic implications for both the gaming community and those who study games.

The GamerGate movement has much more explicitly engaged game studies and particularly women academics as targets for silencing, gendertrolling, and other threats. One of the most powerful tools of silencing is doxing, a practice of outing someone's real information (including address, names of partners and children, telephone numbers, employers, etc.) for the explicit purpose of harassment. Doxing is a powerful weapon in the hands of internet trolls and particularly when used against women, as it can quickly be amplified to include threats of rape and death. Several women subjected to campaigns of harassment have left the games industry completely, while others have had to take extreme measures invoking the FBI and at times fleeing their homes. The public attacks against such figureheads serve as a warning to others who would risk inflaming the anger of the movement. Other tactics simply shut down free speech, such as the threats of a massacre if Anita Sarkeesian (media critic and creator of a series of videos examining the depiction of women in video games) followed through with an invited speaking engagement at Utah State. Informed that security could not prohibit firearms at the event or provide any assurances of safety for herself or the students, Sarkeesian canceled the talk.

For academics working on GamerGate, the public visibility and attacks on scholarship became quickly personal. Adrienne Shaw chronicled the challenges she faced when her work unexpectedly was caught in the spotlight: at first, she wasn't expecting the problem, as "although feminist game scholars follow, research, and sympathize with the targets of this kind of coordinated hate campaign, it is rare that academic work becomes a target itself" (Chess and Shaw, "Conspiracy of Fishes"). Yet the intersections between academia and the games industry have brought academic work into the battlefield. Many scholars found their personal information, blogs, Twitter comments, and the like being taken out alongside their professional writing for analysis. This was not the analytic discourse of peer review; it was often accompanied with intensely personal and gendered attacks, often with attempts to professionally discredit academics by destroying their reputations or sense of security. As Katherine Cross explains the maelstrom: "Almost immediately we—and I must include myself in this, for as a feminist academic and writer, I was quickly targeted as well—were all, as a class, deemed guilty by association: guilty until proven innocent, with no proof ever seeming to satisfy the braying mobs. Suddenly our names began to appear in spider charts, sinful stars in senseless constellations of conspiracy" ("'We Will Force Gaming'"). The implications of being included on such lists could be frightening, from harassment on Twitter to the ever-present threat of the escalation or fulfillment of tweeted threats.

Conferences with a tradition of public scholarship were confronted with the challenge of unexpected public scrutiny and hostile outside attention: in the case of one communications conference, this escalated rapidly. Several scholars in the community had turned their gaze to GamerGate, but rather than evoke the name in public reference, they opted to use the term "Death Eaters" in reference to Harry Potter's villainous and bigoted enemies. However, a mistaken tweet revealed the game, drawing attention to the conference and the work of one woman PhD, Natalie Walschots, whose dissertation focuses on the movement. As she explains, "There have been calls to attend future conference panels that I am presenting on, to contact the dean of graduate studies at Concordia in an attempt to get me expelled, to buy up all the domain names associated with my name and handle to ruin my SEO for future employers" (Goodyear). In the current academic job market, such threats can be lasting attempts to silence a feminist voice.

Katherine Cross captured the difficulty these constant attacks pose for gamers researching in the space in a roundtable on GamerGate: "As a researcher, you are in the midst of this maelstrom, implicated in it, and it is almost impossible not to be directly emotionally involved . . . because as the researcher you are directly under attack. So many of GamerGate's conspiracy theories and its general weltanschauung about the gaming space positions academics as being part of the problem, especially if you study gender. So any attempt to theorize about them or write about them is to make yourself a target, and some might argue that biases you" (Veen).

This problem is not unlike that of any public scholars whose identity makes them a target, from black academics handling the criticism of movements such as Black Lives Matter alongside the rest of their Twitter feed to transgender scholars caught by arbitrary encoded rules such as Facebook's "real" name policy (Steele et al.). In each of these cases, the idea of academic distance and the avoidance of bias can make it impossible for those who are by their identity and research participants in a happening to be taken seriously when they stand to address it.

The International Communication Association was one of many academic organizations to publish a statement on GamerGate, and in doing so the association captured some of the greatest challenges it presents for not just this field but for all of academia and particularly humanities discourse: "You might feel that these events do not relate to your research area, your position, or your students. You are wrong. The harassment members of our community have experienced is a problem that can have chilling effects on academia—both in and out of the communication field. Already, graduate students (and even some colleagues) have conveyed to us that they are frightened to speak up or study video games. When fear enters academia it is the research that suffers as all of our research becomes suspect and 'under investigation'" (Chess, Consalvo, et al.). This observation is essential to understanding the harm that GamerGate and similar forces can deal to academic discourse, and particularly the digital humanities idea of the public scholar, which demands continual participation in spaces of scrutiny and against forces that demand silence or submission.

Digital humanities and game studies scholars are an overlapping group: while digital humanities is traditionally defined as examining humanities works through digital methods, game studies scholars are often examining digital works with toolsets drawn from humanities and other disciplines. The two disciplines are now facing similar challenges thanks to this grounding in technical culture, which itself has been undergoing increasing scrutiny for reinforcing a "brogrammer" culture that silences diverse voices and reinforces an insular way of thinking.[4] Both digital humanities and game studies communities have continually demonstrated a tendency to privilege the procedural and the public, a mindset that can ignore the very real differences in risks and privilege faced by women and other marginalized groups in seeking to be heard.

The attacks on women academics in particular seeking to broaden definitions of games and advocate for greater inclusion serve as a warning for the digital humanities at large. It is impossible to guess at what scholarship has been silenced thanks to the looming threats on those who participate: the self-censoring of the term "GamerGate" at conferences and in public discourse is just one obvious example of a complex network of decision making and risk analysis for public participation. The reliance of the digital humanities (and "public scholarship" as constructed within this and other disciplines) on networks such as Twitter becomes particularly questionable when viewed through this lens, as such networks are also home to some of the most aggressive trolling and forces demanding silence. When identity gate-keeping and evaluation of influence are conducted in part on metrics such as a presence on these networks, the results must skew in favor of those whose presence in public spaces is more accepted, and whose mere visibility does not immediately make them a target for harassment.

Notes

1. This type of claim is advanced in many advice columns to graduate students, such as Bekker, "Why You Should Use Twitter."
2. Described on Henry Jenkins's online bio: Jenkins, "Who the &%&#."
3. See Blodgett and Salter, "Hearing."
4. See Lobo, "Silicon Valley's Sexist Brogrammer Culture."

Bibliography

Alexander, Leigh. "'Gamers' Don't Have to Be Your Audience. 'Gamers' Are Over." *Gamasutra,* August 28, 2014. Accessed November 16, 2017. https://www.gamasutra.com/view/news/224400/Gamers_dont_have_to_be_your_audience_Gamers_are_over.php.

Bekker, Sherree. "Why You Should Use Twitter during Your PhD." *The Thesis Whisperer,* October 22, 2014. http://thesiswhisperer.com/2014/10/22/why-you-should-use-twitter-during-your-phd/.

Bernstein, Joseph. "Here's How Breitbart and Milo Smuggled Nazi and White Nationalist Ideas into the Mainstream." *Buzzfeed,* October 5, 2017. Accessed November 6, 2017. https://www.buzzfeed.com/josephbernstein/heres-how-breitbart-and-milo-smuggled-white-nationalism?utm_term=.enWVZBWL4#.byyNqWv10.

Blodgett, Bridget, and Anastasia Salter. "#1ReasonWhy: Game Communities and the Invisible Woman." *Foundations of Digital Games,* 2014. Association for Computing Machinery. http://www.fdg2014.org/papers/fdg2014_paper_02.pdf.

Blodgett, Bridget Marie, and Anastasia Salter. "Hearing 'Lady Game Creators' Tweet: #1ReasonWhy, Women and Online Discourse in the Game Development Community." *Selected Papers of Internet Research* 3 (2013).

Bogost, Ian. "Game Studies, Year Fifteen." *Ian Bogost* (blog), February 2, 2015. Accessed October 12, 2017. http://bogost.com/writing/blog/game-studies-year-fifteen/.

boyd, danah. "Social Network Sites as Networked Publics: Affordances, Dynamics, and Implications." In *Networked Self: Identity, Community, and Culture on Social Network Sites,* edited by Zizi Papacharissi, 39–58. London: Routledge, 2010.

Chess, Shira, Mia Consalvo, Nina Huntemann, Adrienne Shaw, Carol Stabile, and Jenny Stromer-Galley. "GamerGate and Academia." *International Communications Association,* November 2014. Accessed August 4, 2015. https://web.archive.org

/web/20150214094817/http://www.icahdq.org/membersnewsletter/NOV14_ART0009.asp.

Chess, Shira, and Adrienne Shaw. "A Conspiracy of Fishes, or, How We Learned to Stop Worrying about #GamerGate and Embrace Hegemonic Masculinity." *Journal of Broadcasting & Electronic Media* 59, no. 1 (2015): 208–20.

Chess, Shira, and Adrienne Shaw. "We Are All Fishes Now: DiGRA, Feminism, and GamerGate." *Transactions of the Digital Games Research Association* 2, no. 2 (2016).

Goodyear, Sheena. "Meet the Woman Getting a PhD in Gamergate and the Death Eaters Trying to Stop Her." *Mary Sue,* June 15, 2015. Accessed August 20, 2015. http://www.themarysue.com/phd-in-gamergate/.

Cross, Katherine. "'We Will Force Gaming to Be Free': On GamerGate and the License to Inflict Suffering." *First Person Scholar,* October 8, 2014. Accessed November 19, 2015. http://www.firstpersonscholar.com/we-will-force-gaming-to-be-free/.

Howe, Austin. "On the Ghost of Formalism." *Haptic Feedback,* January 31, 2015. Accessed July 9, 2015. http://hapticfeedbackgames.blogspot.com/2015/01/on-ghost-of-formalism_62.html.

Jenkins, Henry. "Who the &%&# Is Henry Jenkins?" *Henry Jenkins,* n.d. http://henryjenkins.org/aboutmehtml.

Kirschenbaum, Matthew. "What Is Digital Humanities and What's It Doing in English Departments?" In *Debates in the Digital Humanities,* edited by Matthew K. Gold, 3–11. Minneapolis: University of Minnesota Press, 2012.

LaBarre, Suzanne. "Why We're Shutting Off Our Comments." *Popular Science,* September 24, 2013. Accessed August 6, 2015. http://www.popsci.com/science/article/2013-09/why-were-shutting-our-comments.

Lobo, Rita. "Silicon Valley's Sexist Brogrammer Culture Is Locking Women Out of Tech." *New Economy,* June 5, 2014. https://www.theneweconomy.com/technology/silicons-sexist-brogrammer-culture-is-locking-women-out-of-tech.

Losh, Elizabeth. "What Can the Digital Humanities Learn from Feminist Game Studies?" *Digital Humanities Quarterly* 9, no. 2 (2015). http://www.digitalhumanities.org/dhq/vol/9/2/000200/000200.html.

Mantilla, Karla. "Gendertrolling: Misogyny Adapts to New Media." *Feminist Studies* 39, no. 2 (2013): 563–70.

Massie, Victoria M. "@vmmassie." *Twitter,* November 14, 2017. Accessed November 14, 2017. https://twitter.com/vmmassie/status/930464657722171392.

May, Charlie. "A College Professor Criticized Trump. Now the White House Wants an Investigation." *Salon,* October 10, 2017. Accessed November 12, 2017. https://www.salon.com/2017/10/10/a-college-professor-criticized-trump-now-the-white-house-wants-an-investigation/?source=newsletter.

McCrea, Christian. "The Play Machine: Game Studies Keynote." *CODE Conference,* Swinburne University of Technology, 2012. https://web.archive.org/web/20150110070845/http://www.academia.edu/2543071/The_Play_Machine_Game_Studies_Keynote_from_CODE_Conference_November_2012.

O'Neil, Cathy. "The Ivory Tower Can't Keep Ignoring Tech." *New York Times,* November 14, 2017. Accessed November 20, 2017. https://www.nytimes.com/2017/11/14/opinion/academia-tech-algorithms.html.

Posner, Miriam. *Some Things to Think About Before You Exhort Everyone to Code.* February 29, 2012. Accessed November 17, 2015. http://miriamposner.com/blog/some-things-to-think-about-before-you-exhort-everyone-to-code/.

Quinn, Zoe. *Crash Override: How Gamergate (Nearly) Destroyed My Life, and How We Can Win the Fight against Online Hate.* New York: PublicAffairs, 2016.

Salter, Anastasia, and Bridget Blodgett. "Hypermasculinity & Dickwolves: The Contentious." *Journal of Broadcasting and Electronic Media* 56, no. 3 (2012), 401–16. doi:10.1080/08838151.2012.705199.

singh, sava saheli. "Tweeting to the Choir: Online Performance and Academic Identity." *Selected Papers of Internet Research* 14.0 (2013). Denver, Colo.: AoIR.

Spiro, Lisa. "'This Is Why We Fight': Defining the Values of the Digital Humanities." In *Debates in the Digital Humanities,* edited by Matthew K. Gold, 16–34. Minneapolis: University of Minnesota Press, 2012. http://dhdebates.gc.cuny.edu/.

Steele, Catherine Knight, Kishonna L. Gray, Jenny Korn, and Sarah Florini. "#BlackLives Matter: At the Intersection of Racial Politics and Digital Activism." *Selected Papers of Internet Research* 15 (2015). Phoenix, Ariz.: Association of Internet Researchers.

Stewart, Bonnie. 2014. "What Counts as Academic Influence Online?" *The Theoryblog,* April 27, 2014. Accessed August 3, 2015. http://theory.cribchronicles.com/2014/04/27/what-counts-as-academic-influence-online/.

Veen, tobias c. van. "Safeguarding Research: A Scholarly Roundtable on Gamergate." *First Person Scholar,* December 10, 2014. Accessed August 8, 2015. http://www.firstpersonscholar.com/safeguarding-research/.

Contributors

BABALOLA TITILOLA AIYEGBUSI holds an MA in English from University of Lethbridge with a focus on digital humanities.

MOYA BAILEY is a scholar of critical race, feminist, and disability studies at Northeastern University.

BRIDGET BLODGETT is associate professor in the Division of Science, Information Arts, and Technologies at the University of Baltimore.

BARBARA BORDALEJO is assistant professor in digital humanities, Department of Literature, KU Leuven in Flanders, Belgium.

JASON BOYD is associate professor and codirector of the Centre for Digital Humanities, Ryerson University.

CHRISTINA BOYLES is assistant professor of culturally engaged digital humanities at Michigan State University.

SUSAN BROWN is professor of English and Canada Research Chair in Collaborative Digital Scholarship at the University of Guelph.

LISA BRUNDAGE is director of teaching, learning, and technology at Macaulay Honors College at the City University of New York.

MICHA CÁRDENAS is assistant professor of Art + Design: Games & Playable Media at the University of California, Santa Cruz.

MARCIA CHATELAIN is Provost's Distinguished Associate Professor of History and African American Studies at Georgetown University.

DANIELLE COLE graduated from Brandeis University with an MA in sociology and works as a youth mentor to support children with mental illness or trauma history.

BETH COLEMAN is associate professor of experimental digital media at the University of Waterloo.

T. L. COWAN is assistant professor of media studies (Digital Media Cultures) in the Department of Arts, Culture, and Media (UTSC) and the Faculty of Information (iSchool) at the University of Toronto.

CONSTANCE CROMPTON is assistant professor in the Department of Communication at the University of Ottawa.

AMY E. EARHART is associate professor of English at Texas A&M University.

NICKOAL EICHMANN-KALWARA is assistant professor and digital scholarship librarian at University of Colorado Boulder.

JULIA FLANDERS is professor of the practice in English and director of the Digital Scholarship Group in the Northeastern University Library. She directs the Women Writers Project and is editor in chief of *Digital Humanities Quarterly*.

SANDRA GABRIELE is vice-provost, Innovation in Teaching and Learning, and associate professor of communication studies at Concordia University.

BRIAN GETNICK is an artist and facilitator of contemporary performance in Los Angeles.

KAREN GREGORY is a digital sociologist, ethnographer, and lecturer in the Department of Sociology at the University of Edinburgh and program director of the MSc in Digital Society.

ALISON HEDLEY is an SSHRC Postdoctoral Fellow at the McGill University .txtLAB and editor of the Yellow Nineties Personography.

KATHRYN HOLLAND is a faculty member in English at MacEwan University and senior research fellow for The Orlando Project.

JAMES HOWE holds an MLIS with a focus on academic libraries and digital technology and works at Rutgers University.

JEANA JORGENSEN is a folklorist, writer, dancer, and (sex) educator teaching at Butler University.

ALEXANDRA JUHASZ is chair of the film department at Brooklyn College, City University of New York.

DOROTHY KIM is assistant professor of English at Brandeis University.

KIM BRILLANTE KNIGHT is associate dean of graduate studies and associate professor and area head of critical media studies in the School of Arts, Technology, and Emerging Communication at the University of Texas at Dallas.

LORRAINE JANZEN KOOISTRA is codirector of the Centre in Digital Humanities (CDH) and professor of English at Ryerson University.

SHARON M. LEON is associate professor of history at Michigan State University, where she develops digital public history and digital networking projects related to enslaved communities in Maryland.

ELIZABETH LOSH is associate professor of English and American studies at The College of William and Mary. She is author of *Virtualpolitik: An Electronic History of Government Media-Making in a Time of War, Scandal, Disaster, Miscommunication, and Mistakes* and *The War* on Learning: Gaining Ground in the Digital University; coauthor of *Understanding Rhetoric: A Graphic Guide to Writing* with Jonathan Alexander; and editor of *MOOCs and Their Afterlives: Experiments in Scale and Access in Higher Education*.

IZETTA AUTUMN MOBLEY is an American studies doctoral candidate at the University of Maryland. She has been a facilitator and social justice educator specializing in youth and diversity issues.

PADMINI RAY MURRAY is the course leader for the postgraduate program in digital humanities and teaches at Srishti Institute of Art, Design, and Technology.

VERONICA PAREDES is a media arts scholar and practitioner at the University of Illinois.

ROOPIKA RISAM is assistant professor of English, coordinator of the secondary education English undergraduate program, and coordinator of the digital studies graduate certificate at Salem State University.

BONNIE RUBERG is assistant professor of digital media and games in the Department of Informatics at the University of California, Irvine.

LAILA SHEREEN SAKR (VJ UM AMEL) is assistant professor of film and media studies and faculty affiliate in the feminist studies department at the University of California, Santa Barbara.

ANASTASIA SALTER is assistant professor of digital media at the University of Central Florida.

MICHELLE SCHWARTZ is research fellow at the Centre for Digital Humanities at Ryerson University.

EMILY SHERWOOD is director of the Digital Scholarship Lab at the University of Rochester's River Campus Libraries.

DEB VERHOEVEN is a film and media studies scholar and associate dean of Engagement and Innovation at the University of Technology Sydney.

SCOTT B. WEINGART is program director of digital humanities, core faculty of humanities analytics, and librarian at Carnegie Mellon University.

JACQUELINE WERNIMONT is the Distinguished Chair of Digital Humanities and Social Engagement and associate professor of gender, women's, and sexuality studies at Dartmouth College. She is the author of *Numbered Lives: Life and Death in Quantum Media*. Her work on digital feminist media has been published in *Digital Humanities Quarterly*, Slate.com, IEEE, *Debates in Digital Humanities*, and elsewhere. She codirects HASTAC, a transdisciplinary scholarly network.

Index

AAUP. *See* American Association of University Professors
Abbate, Janet, xi, 11, 266
abortion, 5–6, 12
access, xvi, 9, 16, 29, 33, 48, 78, 87–88, 110, 122, 133, 140, 142, 144–45, 151, 153, 163, 166, 181–82, 186–87, 192–94, 213, 220, 232, 239, 242, 247, 250, 254, 297, 299, 345, 348, 356, 371–72, 378, 383, 387, 411, 413, 421–22, 425–27, 435, 437–38, 444
activism, 58–60, 62, 73–74, 76–77, 95, 101, 134, 141–42, 144, 150, 173–75, 180, 182, 185–86, 188–89, 191–95, 197–98, 204, 207, 224, 369, 372, 381, 386, 391–92, 394–401, 404–6, 413, 419
Actor-Network Theory (ANT), 187, 449
ADHO. *See* Alliance of Digital Humanities Organizations
Advanced Research Consortium (ARC), x
AEME. *See* Archive of Early Middle English
affect, xii, xvii, 18, 57, 60, 82, 203, 206–12, 214–16, 218–20, 225, 232, 238, 265, 267, 274–75, 310, 313, 315, 394, 406
affective labor. *See* labor
African American. *See* Black identity
Agamben, Georgio, 197, 406
Ahmed, Sara, xxiii, 85, 237
AIDS. *See* HIV/AIDS
alchemy, digital, 59, 375
Alexa, 34
Alliance of Digital Humanities Organizations (ADHO), ix–x, xv, 73–74, 77, 79–80, 83, 86–87, 89, 261, 322, 341

All India Dalit Mahila Adhikar Manch (AIDMAM), 195
alt-ac employment, xviii, 266, 306–17, 375
alternative academic employment. *See* alt-ac employment
Amazon Mechanical Turk, 44–45
American Association of University Professors (AAUP), 311, 314
American Council on Learned Societies (ACLS), 93, 309, 346, 352
American Historical Association (AHA), 345, 349–50, 252, 360
American Indians. *See* indigenous peoples
American Memory. *See* Library of Congress American Memory
American Studies Association (ASA), xxii, 30, 96
Anzaldúa, Gloria, 26–27, 29
appropriation, 221, 226, 267, 271
Archive of Early Middle English (AEME), 231–32, 235–39, 242–50
archives, x–xii, xvii, 14–15, 110, 132, 135–37, 139–41, 151, 169, 177, 188, 192, 203, 221–22, 226, 230–31, 238, 242–44, 246, 250–53, 354–58, 371–72, 374, 383, 429; digital archives, 110, 186, 193–95, 198, 230–31, 241, 243, 249–53
archive stories, 230, 250–53
Arduino, xiv, 9–10, 20
Aristotle, 42, 279
Armed Forces Special Powers Act (AFSPA), 192–93

[481]

artificial intelligence, xiv, 34, 40–44, 46, 50, 116, 452
artistic communities, 158, 160–61, 168–69, 413–15
assemblage, xiv, xvii, 11–13, 25–26, 29, 32, 47, 187
Atwood, Margaret, xviii, 269–70
autoethnography, 306

Bailey, Moya, xii, 59–60, 94, 109, 293–96, 370, 375, 419–20
Balsamo, Anne, xxiii, 213, 223, 270–71, 275, 448
Barad, Karen, 43, 233, 273, 275
Barnett, Fiona, xxii, 114
Battlestar Galactica, 30, 36
Beardsley, Aubrey, 159, 162, 166
Bianco, Jamie "Skye," xxii, 94, 108, 122, 386, 411
bibliography, xi, 120, 134–40, 143, 150, 297, 410, 418, 420, 424
big data, xx, 7, 13, 15, 46–47, 234, 251–52, 375, 391–92, 397, 406, 436, 440–41
"big tent" digital humanities, xii, 72, 76, 88
binary characteristics. *See* nonbinary characteristics
Black communities, 17, 376–79, 382, 393, 396–97, 403
Black digital intelligentsia, xi–xii, xvi, 180, 375, 405
Black feminism. *See* feminism
Black history, 381–82, 396
Black identity, x–xii, xvi, 26–27, 29–30, 44, 51, 57, 60, 79, 173–80, 196–97, 394, 406, 473
Black Lives Matter (BLM), xx, 174–75, 180, 195–97, 391–406, 473
Black news media, 399
Black press, 346
Black Twitter Project, 384–85
Bland, Sandra, 393
Blank Noise, 189, 192, 194

Blas, Zach, 40, 111, 117, 124
BLM. *See* Black Lives Matter
Bogost, Ian, 447–50, 468
Borgman, Christine, 58, 392
boundary objects, xiii–xiv, xvi, xxiii, 276–77
Bowker, Geoffrey, 276
boyd, danah, ix, xii, 467
Brown, Michael, 174–74, 177, 393–94, 397–402, 406
Brown, Susan, xvii–vii, xx, 143, 157, 322
Browne, Simone, xii
Brown University, 264, 357, 376, 412
Burroughs, William S., 215
Busa, Roberto, x, 344
Butler, Judith, 191, 392–93

Cambridge University, 41, 252, 409, 424–25
Camptown Cemetery, 381–82
Canadian Writing Research Collaboratory (CWRC), x, 143, 425–27
cárdenas, micha, xiv–xv, 59, 111, 116
care work, ix, xx, xxii, 15, 85, 190, 222, 227, 250, 268, 315, 317, 323, 327, 331, 337, 349, 371
Cartesianism, xiii, 185, 233, 292
caste, xvii, 185–86, 192, 194–98
Castile, Philando, 374, 391, 393, 404–6
Center for Civic Media, 195
Center for Solutions to Online Violence (CSOV), 58–60
centers. *See* digital humanities, centers
Centre for Internet and Society, 187
Chang, Edmond, 111
Chicago, Judy, 429
civil rights movement, 394, 396, 401
classification, xiv, 149, 151, 158–60, 165–65, 169, 296–97
Clement, Tanya, 58, 354
COBOL (Common Business-Oriented Language), 300, 302, 303

code literacy and codework, xi–xii, xiv, 10, 26, 30, 32, 43, 45, 48, 72, 114, 117, 121–22, 138, 144, 165–67, 237, 241, 243–44, 266, 272–73, 277, 290–91, 293–96, 299–301, 303, 413, 418, 428, 451, 459, 466, 468–70

Cohen, Dan, 344–45, 354, 358, 430

collaboration, xv, xxii, 27, 33, 58–67, 81, 111–12, 135, 157, 170, 195, 203–13, 220–23, 226, 254, 265–66, 300, 306, 309, 315–16, 335, 347, 349, 351–55, 357–59, 375, 378–79, 381–85, 409, 418–22, 426–27, 442–44, 467, 470

Collaborator's Bill of Rights, 354, 358, 371

colonialism, xxi, 4, 32, 36, 44–45, 50–51, 88, 145, 187, 247, 251, 292, 295, 358, 396

Columbia University, 188

community. *See individual communities*

community partnerships, xxii–iii, xv, xix–xx, xxii, 5, 17–18, 32–33, 57–67, 94–96, 141–42, 176–78, 193–94, 197, 208–15, 219–20, 375–84, 419, 447, 449, 459–60

Companion to Digital Humanities, 215, 262, 269, 278, 344

conferences, xxi, 72–88, 182, 241, 261, 264, 308–9, 321, 331, 436, 441, 444, 472–73

cookbooks, 272

corpus linguistics, 240–41, 346

Council on Library and Information Resources (CLIR), 308–9

counterpublics, xiv, 10, 20, 405–6

craftwork, 5, 9, 11–12, 298

credit, 86, 162, 166, 170, 252, 310, 314, 351, 354, 358, 373, 375, 384, 419, 421, 425–26

Crenshaw, Kimberlé, xxiii, 154, 331–32, 386, 394

crowdsourcing, xxiii, 174, 421, 430, 438, 469–70

cultural cloning, 332–34

cut and paste, 206, 208, 212, 214–16, 220–23, 225

cut and sew, 237

cut-ups, 215

cyberfeminism. *See* feminism

cyborgs, xiv, 25–26, 35, 39, 42, 166, 168, 185, 204–6, 208, 222, 224, 275

Dakota Access Pipeline, 30

Dalits, 193–98

Dalit Women Fight (DWF), 195–97

Danger, Jane Roe!, xiv, 5–8, 12–13

Darwin, Charles, 42, 88

database queries, 347, 360

databases, 17–18, 44, 48, 87, 100, 102, 119, 142–44, 157–58, 164–66, 169, 206–7, 222, 226, 231, 252–44, 250–53, 292, 344, 375, 424

data mining, 7, 15–16, 39–40, 84, 234, 374

data visualization. *See* visualization

de Beauvoir, Simone, 185

deformance, 5, 12–13, 118

de Lauretis, Teresa, 124

democracy, 19, 50, 93, 102, 109, 181, 194, 197, 345

Derrida, Jacques, 35, 42, 190, 272

Descartes, René, 42

Design for Diversity conference, 301–2

détournement, 5, 19

#dhpoco, xiii, 76

Dibbell, Julian, 189

Dickinson, Emily, 134

Dickinson Electronic Archives, 298, 374

D'Ignazio, Catherine, 18, 421

digital alchemy. *See* alchemy, digital

digital archives. *See* archives

Digital Diversity conference, 157, 426

digital history, 344–59

digital humanities, centers, xxi, 73, 264–65, 309, 346, 354, 434–35

digital humanities, community, 73–77, 79–88, 149, 261, 273, 309, 313–15, 334, 436, 438, 440–41, 466–67, 473

digital humanities, definition, 439–40

digital humanities, labs, ix, 309, 434, 437

digital humanities, politics, 141, 261; conservatism, x, 94, 294, 334, 349, 434; radicalism, xii, xxii, 123, 148, 276, 295, 314, 398, 439

disability, xvii, 19–20, 57, 87, 109, 121–23, 187, 230, 247–49, 296, 324, 327, 331–34, 337, 339, 372

diversity, x, xiii, xv, 71–79, 83–87, 97–98, 100, 102–4, 111, 118, 123, 157 176, 178, 193, 261, 263, 278, 292–95, 301–2, 322–23, 329, 331–36, 411, 426, 429, 436, 442–43

DIY, 8–9, 11, 132, 139, 141, 143–45, 153, 420

domestic labor. *See* labor

doxing, 141, 189, 270, 451, 471

Drucker, Johanna, 118, 232–35, 239–40, 273–74, 278, 450, 458

drugs, 67, 393, 403, 455

Earhart, Amy, xv, xix–xx, 95–96, 139, 153, 261, 420

Egypt, 221, 305

embodiment, xii–xiv, xvi–xvii, 11–15, 18, 20, 29, 43, 46, 109, 122–23, 152, 173, 185–86, 188–89, 191, 197–98, 208, 218–20, 238, 242, 262–64, 269–70, 272–77, 371–72

empathy, 35, 449, 454–55, 459

enslaved labor. *See* labor

equity, xiii, 71, 145, 147–49, 261, 294, 349, 358, 360, 375, 385

essentialism, 4, 9, 14, 26, 50, 116, 371, 428

ethnography, 131, 185, 250

eugenics 371

Eurocentrism, 41, 43, 50

Ev-Ent-Anglement, xvii, 203–27

Extensible Markup Language. *See* XML

Facebook, 180, 188, 190, 193, 195, 205, 216–17, 223, 244, 330, 467, 473; Facebook Live, 404–5

failure, 11, 62, 72, 76, 86, 117, 176, 183, 296, 305, 310, 313, 323

Fembot Collective, 111

feminism: Black feminism, 26, 60, 151, 182; cyberfeminism, 275; radical feminism, 4, 131–33, 141–45, 148–51, 153–54, 230; women of color feminism, 26

feminist communities, 223–24

feminist data visualization, 13, 16–18, 421

feminist digital humanities, xv, xvii, xxi–xxii, 5, 13, 32, 97, 100–101, 111–12, 165, 203–4, 209, 216, 224, 374, 411, 418

feminist game design, 450–51

feminist game studies, xxi, 460, 466, 470, 472

feminized labor. *See* labor

FemTechNet, xiii, 111, 216

Ferguson, Missouri, xiii, xvi, 174–80, 182, 393, 397, 400

#FergusonSyllabus, xvi, 174–82

FLOW-MATIC, 300

Foucault, Michel, 124, 159–60, 250

Fraser, Nancy, 10, 18, 197

Freelon, Deen, 397–401, 404

Froehlich, Heather, 240–41

Gajjala, Radhika, xii, 185–87

Galloway, Alexander, 273, 370

GamerGate, xxi, 113, 189, 451, 458, 460, 470–74

games, xxi, 31, 42, 109, 111–13, 122, 189, 210, 222, 226, 447–61, 466–73

Garner, Eric, 393, 400–404

Gaviria, Andrés Ramírez, 7, 11, 18

gender neutrality. *See* neutrality

gendertrolling. *See* trolling

genres, 242, 253, 409, 415, 417, 429, 439

geographical representation, xiv, 27, 46, 73, 76–77, 79, 83, 86, 439, 441–42

geospatial analysis, 181, 265, 345–46, 352

"Girl Who Was Plugged In, The," 274

GitHub, 144, 209, 231, 252

GLAM (galleries, libraries, archives, museums), 84

glitch, 122, 204, 211
Global Outlook::Digital Humanities (GO::DH), 95, 435–36
Golumbia, David, x, 72
Google, 44, 188, 190; Google Books, 251–52, 296; Google Docs, 203–4, 206–8, 211–13; Google Maps, 292; Google Sites, 383
Grand Theft Auto (GTA), 453
grant funding, xiv–xv, 15, 57–67, 93, 96–98, 100–102, 122, 148, 209, 307, 310, 312–13, 335, 338, 347, 351, 354
"Great Man" theory of history, 348
GynePunk, 8

"hacking" vs. "yacking" debate. *See* "yacking" vs. "hacking" debate
Halberstam, Jack, 109, 116, 124
handmaid, as rhetorical figure, xviii, 268–70, 298
Handmaid's Tale, The, xviii, 270
harassment, ix, xi, xxiii, 109, 112, 150, 175, 190, 192, 270, 334, 466, 470–74
Haraway, Donna, 11, 13, 15, 25–26, 31, 35, 42–43, 116, 185, 275, 458, 461
Harney, Stefano, ix, xiv, 30, 392
HASTAC. *See* Humanities, Arts, Science, and Technology Alliance and Collaboratory
haunting, xii, 151, 190, 396
Hayles, N. Katherine, xiv, 47, 144, 163, 213, 275
Hegel, Georg Wilhelm Friedrich, 50
herstory, 132, 139–41, 150, 386
High Performance Sound Technologies for Access and Scholarship (HiPSTAS), x
Hispanic. *See* Latinx identity
History Matters, 352
HIV/AIDS, 17, 143, 220–21, 223, 228
holdyourboundaries.com, 32–34
homophobia, ix, 111, 145, 150
Hopper, Grace, 299–301

Humanities, Arts, Science, and Technology Alliance and Collaboratory (HASTAC), 58, 73, 436
Humanities Networked Infrastructure (HuNI), x
human subjects research, 371

IBM, x, 42, 344
immigrants, 33, 98, 346
India, xvii, 51, 185–98, 436
Indian women's movement (IWM), 191–92, 194
indigenous peoples, xxiii, 25, 30–32, 50, 102, 185, 188, 197, 225, 291, 331, 357, 365, 369–70, 372–74, 376, 378, 455–56
inequity. *See* equity
information visualization. *See* visualization
infrastructure ix–x, xii–xiii, xvi, xviii, 58–59, 61, 87, 113, 187, 225, 268–69, 293, 316, 356, 383, 401, 410, 425, 437–38
Instagram, 33–34, 195, 206, 217
intellectual property, 187, 314, 372, 384
interdisciplinarity, 4, 82, 174, 214, 226, 261, 263–64, 345, 412, 434–35, 443, 451, 466, 468–69
interfaces, xii, xvii, 13, 110, 115–16, 166–67, 187, 226, 230–35, 237–41, 243, 249, 273–75, 292–93, 296, 410, 415–16, 423–25
International Communication Association (ICA), 473
intersectionality, ix, xi–xii, xxii–xxiii, 18, 26, 32, 94, 102, 108–9, 111, 113–14, 118, 186, 193–94, 198, 251, 290, 301, 332, 370–71, 382, 394, 404, 411, 413–14, 419, 424, 455, 458
intertexuality 236, 414–17
interview data, 82, 153, 221, 398
invisible labor. *See* labor
Irigaray, Luce, 411, 414

Jameson, Frederic, 263
Jim Crow, 173, 394

Johnson, Jessica Marie, xi, xxii, 59
journalism, 59, 161, 179, 447–48, 452, 458–59, 461, 466, 471
JSTOR, 98, 100

Kafai, Yasmin, 8, 10
Kant, Immanuel, 42, 47, 241
Keeling, Kara, 109, 114–15
Kirschenbaum, Matthew, 265, 273, 439–40, 467
Klein, Lauren, 18, 274
Kim, Dorothy, xvii, 59, 254, 374
Koh, Adeline, 123, 247, 249
Ku Klux Klan, 377–79

labor, xi–xiv, xviii–xx, 11, 15–16, 18, 45–46, 62, 66, 72, 75, 82, 85, 117, 119, 162, 166, 180, 207, 222, 231, 251–52, 262, 266–69, 271, 273, 276–78, 294, 298, 305–17, 348, 352–55, 371, 378, 420–21, 430, 458; affective labor, 82, 85, 178, 267, 310, 312, 315; domestic labor, 8, 313; enslaved labor, 16–17, 378; feminized labor, 74, 267, 276; invisible labor, xviii, 117, 162, 252, 310–13; racialized labor, 251–52; reproductive labor, 14, 262, 271
labs. *See* digital humanities, labs
LambaMOO, 189
LaMem, 44–46
Latinx identity, xii, 60, 95, 102, 251, 371, 402–3
Large-Scale Image Memorability. *See* LaMem
legislation, 5–6, 9, 12–13, 143, 176, 194, 393, 403, 458–59
Lesbian and Gay Liberation in Canada, 110, 132, 141–44, 150, 165
lesbian communities, 132–33, 137
Lesbian Herstory Archives (LHA), 132, 139–42
lesbian identity, xvi, 110, 119–20, 131–43, 148, 150–51, 170, 221, 331, 386
lesbian lists. *See* listing
Lewis, Earl, 102–3

LGBT communities, 95, 108, 110, 112, 115, 137, 139–40, 436
librarians, notable, 134, 353
librarianship, 109, 262, 264–67, 274, 313
libraries, 134, 139, 143, 251, 264–67, 330, 355–56, 378, 383
Library of Congress American Memory, 356
Library of Congress Subject Headings (LCSH), 120, 296
LilyPad, xiv, 9–12, 19–20
linked data, 121, 243, 421, 424–25, 430
Linked Open Data (LOD), 428
listing, xvi, 27, 84, 95, 97, 100, 120, 131–44, 150–51, 163–64, 196, 237, 246–47, 314, 335, 354–55, 415, 472
listservs, 252, 264, 268, 330
Liu, Alan, 81, 93–95, 103, 113, 187, 261, 264, 267–69, 278, 429, 448
live coding, 122
Living Net, 14–15
Lorde, Audra, xiv, 26–27, 271, 411, 419
Losh, Elizabeth, 9–10, 213, 262, 405, 450, 460, 470
Lost in Space, 6
lynching, 173, 371–72, 377

Macherey, Pierre, 263
Madwoman in the Attic, The, xix
Mandell, Laura, 278, 322
Manovich, Lev, 45, 234
manuscripts, 221, 230–32, 236–40, 242–54
markup, xx, 119, 142, 153, 157–58, 167–69, 237, 244–45, 249, 290, 356, 410–20, 424, 426, 428, 430
mashup, 215
Massachusetts Institute of Technology (MIT), 9, 11, 44, 195–96
Massive Open Online Courses (MOOCs), 72
material culture, 233, 350
materiality, xiii–xv, xx, xxii, 4, 9, 10–18, 27, 31–32, 35, 43, 47, 61–62, 116, 163, 185, 187–88, 210, 212–13, 215, 217, 230–33,

236, 238–40, 246, 249–50, 252, 268, 270–71, 273–77, 279, 291, 299, 350, 396, 406, 409, 412, 421, 429, 439
McLuhan, Marshall, 4–5, 7, 10, 18
McMaster University, 263
McPherson, Tara, 94, 114, 121, 271, 277, 289–91, 294–95, 298–301, 333, 419, 428–29
MEALS framework, xiii, xxii
Mechanical Turk. *See* Amazon Mechanical Turk
medieval studies, xvii, 230–51, 346
Mellon Foundation, xv, 93, 97–104, 268, 311
Melville Electronic Library, 298
mentoring, 58, 71, 75, 82, 143, 147, 168, 176, 179, 313, 333, 419
messiness, xii, xviii, xix, 9, 17, 94–95, 119–24, 232, 275, 277, 404
metadata, xvi, xx, 113, 119, 121, 157, 245, 291–92, 297, 301, 309, 373, 418, 422, 424
#MeToo, xxiii, 270
Metropolis, 30, 36
midwifery, xviii, 271–72, 275, 351
Mignolo, Walter, xiv, 25, 27
"Millican Race 'Riot,'" 371, 377, 381, 385
mise-en-système, 234, 243, 248–49
misogyny, ix, 16, 75, 85, 183, 269, 395, 451, 457, 470–71
MIT. *See* Massachusetts Institute of Technology
Modern Language Association (MLA), 3, 19, 76, 203, 311, 314, 350, 373
Modi, Narendra, 197
Monáe, Janelle, 30, 36
More Perfect Union: Japanese Americans and the U.S. Constitution, A, 354
Moretti, Franco, 234
Moten, Fred, ix, xiv, 30, 392
Mukurtu, 291, 372, 383
Mukurtu Wumpurrarni-kari Archive, 383
multiculturalism, 134, 325, 335

multilingualism, 78, 84, 235–39, 242–43, 253–54
Mulvey, Laura, 253
museums, 7, 14, 84, 355–58, 370, 372, 375

Nakamura, Lisa, xxiii, 11, 252
naming, xx, 134, 163, 186, 209, 424
National Endowment for the Humanities (NEH), xv, 37, 67, 93, 96–97, 231, 236, 251, 254, 346–48, 360
Native Americans. *See* indigenous peoples
neoliberalism, x, 29, 62, 72, 85, 113, 190, 197, 206
network analysis, 84–85
network graphs. *See* network visualization
network neutrality. *See* neutrality
networks, xii, 14–15, 63, 80–81, 121, 164, 168, 186–87, 208, 211, 214, 217, 221–24, 226, 234, 239–40, 244, 264, 274, 291, 307, 309, 370, 391–401, 404–6, 449, 466–67, 470, 473–74
network visualization, 138, 168, 398–99, 144, 424
neural networks, 40, 43, 46
neutrality, xiii, xxi, 117, 141, 146, 164, 251, 271, 292, 294, 296, 375, 386, 428, 450, 452, 458; gender neutrality, 327; network neutrality, ix
New Maps of Old Lagos, 441
newsgames, 447–51, 457–58
Nigeria, 434–38, 440–43
Noble, Safiya, xii
nonbinary characteristics, xvi–xvii, 7, 18, 42–43, 71, 97, 116, 121, 123, 141, 160, 185, 191, 210–11, 272, 297, 328
No Red Tape, 188
Nowviskie, Bethany, 15, 77, 265–66, 268, 315

Obama, Barack, 40, 97, 405
Oldest Game, The, 447, 449–50, 453–60
Omeka, 265, 278, 377, 383

online communities, 175, 189, 195, 466, 470–73

online violence. *See* violence

open access, 144, 153, 371–72, 383, 421, 467

open data, 411, 425, 427–28

open source, 9, 100, 221, 237, 244, 291, 425, 469

optical character recognition (OCR), 143, 252

oral history data, 373–74, 377, 383–84

Orlando, xviii, xx, 97, 157, 165, 374, 409–30

Orphan Black, xiv, 30

Oxford University, 236–37, 252

Oxygen Editor, 143–44

PAM, 203, 207–9, 212–19, 224–27

Parham, Marisa, xii

patriarchy, x, xiv, xviii, 11, 15, 26, 71, 132, 133, 159, 196, 198, 206, 269, 295, 334–35

pedagogy, xvi, xxii, 73, 84–85, 111, 273–75, 293, 300, 306, 308, 313, 316, 352, 411, 418–21, 424, 455

performance, xvii, 14–15, 26, 29, 12, 203–18, 221–27, 234, 392

personography, 150, 157–70

philanthropy, xv, 100, 102

physicality. *See* materiality

Planned Parenthood, 97

playtesting data, 450, 455–56, 460

pleasure, xvii, 122, 192, 223, 230–33, 239, 241–42, 244–45, 247, 249–50, 253, 259; nonvisual pleasure, 230, 238–40, 250; visual pleasure, 231–33, 239, 241–42, 244–45, 247, 253

police violence. *See* violence

political economy, xii, 395

political unconscious, 262–63

politics. *See* digital humanities, politics

pornography, 205, 457

Porter, Dot, 265–66

Posner, Miriam, xxiii, 78, 88, 132, 142, 148, 268, 276, 292–94, 301, 314, 323, 345, 359, 469

postracialism, 197, 247

praxis, xvii, xxiii, 4, 19, 26–27, 30–31, 35, 63, 113–17, 157, 169, 205–9, 220, 246, 291, 293, 298–99, 315

precarity, 60, 66, 82, 115, 307–8, 310, 312, 392, 406, 459

preservation, xx, xxii, 84, 96, 102, 131–32, 139, 141, 143, 145, 167, 221, 241, 243, 252, 268, 312, 345–48, 354, 356, 373, 379, 420, 438

Presner, Todd, 439

principal investigator role, x, xix, 15, 65, 278, 310, 347–48, 351, 354, 359–60, 375

privacy, 33–34, 57–59, 78, 141, 187, 214, 335, 371, 374, 392

programming. *See* code literacy and codework

programming communities, 117, 144

Project Bamboo, 268–69

prosopography, 150–51, 158, 160–61, 163–65, 168–70, 427

prostitution. *See* sex workers

prototyping, 166, 169–70, 268, 271–72, 417, 424, 436, 450, 458–59

pseudonyms, xvi, 159, 161–64

Puar, Jasbir, 25–26, 29, 198

public humanities, 5, 103, 153, 348, 357

Quantified Self, 15

queer, definition of, 108–9, 158

queer digital humanities, xv–xvi, 108–23

queer game studies, 111–13

Queer OS, 109, 114–15

Queer Technologies, 111, 116–17

queer theory, xv–xvi, 109, 113–14, 117, 276, 297

questionnaires. *See* survey data

Quinn, Zoe, 471

racialized labor. *See* labor
racism ix, xi, 4, 40, 57–58, 133, 145, 148–49, 151, 174, 181–83, 197, 221, 289, 294, 299, 333, 371, 376–78, 387, 391, 393, 395–96, 403
radical feminism. *See* feminism
radical potential of digital humanities.
 See digital humanities, politics
Raid on Deerfield: Many Stories of 1704, 357
Ramsay, Stephen, 269, 293–95
rape. *See* violence: sexual violence
rape culture, 188
RDA. *See* Resource Description and Access
RDF. *See* Resource Description Framework
rejections, 324–26
remix, 204, 215–16, 222, 226, 279
reproduction, xviii, 5–8, 11–13, 17, 26, 97–98, 262–63, 266, 269–72, 275–77, 309, 313
Resource Description and Access (RDA), 297
Resource Description Framework (RDF), 121, 243–46, 427
Reynolds, Diamond, 391, 404–6
Rich, Adrienne, 133–34, 139
Risam, Roopika, xiv, xv, xix, 113, 249, 332, 370, 411, 419
robotics, 6, 9–10, 35, 39–41, 43–44, 47, 205, 251
Robots Reading Vogue, 39–40
Rockwell, Geoffrey, 81, 263, 266, 272, 412
Roe v. Wade, 5–6, 19

Saint-Exupéry, Antoine de, 320
Sammet, Jean, 299–301
Sample, Mark, 19, 375
Sarai, 187
Say Her Name, 196
Scalar, 278
School of Cultural Texts and Records, 187
science, technology, engineering, and mathematics (STEM), xi, 15, 177, 308–9, 468–69

sensorium, human, 238–40
September 11 Digital Archive, 354
serious games, xxi
service, xviii–xix, 82, 85, 175, 180, 261–78, 305, 309–11, 314, 349, 351, 423, 461
sexism, ix, 85, 145, 147–50, 174, 376
sexual harassment. *See* harassment
sexual violence. *See* violence
sex workers, xxi, 132, 193, 392, 447–53, 460
SGML. *See* Standard Generalized Markup Language
Shah, Anushka, 196
Shah, Nishant, xii, 187
Shakespeare, William, 49–50, 222, 235
Shaw, Adrienne, 466, 472
silence, 102, 148, 186, 190, 192, 250, 262–63, 405
silencing, 175, 180–81, 194, 470, 172–74
Siri, 34
situated perspectives, xii–xiii, xviii–xxi, 6, 12–13, 48, 118, 239, 271, 273–77, 369, 371, 378, 384–86, 428, 451, 461
Situationism, 5
slavery, 16, 270, 344, 359, 376, 378, 396
smell. *See* pleasure: nonvisual pleasure
social media, xvi, 31, 33–35, 40, 59, 144, 173–73, 177, 180–82, 188, 192, 195–96, 206–7, 214, 216, 220, 224, 270, 278, 330, 392–401, 404–6, 419, 470
social network analysis. *See* network visualization
Social Sciences and Humanities Research Council of Canada (SSHRC), 231, 422–23
Sofia, 44
Small Wonder, xiv, 39–40
Smith, Martha Nell, 94–95, 276, 290, 333, 374
Smithsonian Institution, 357
social justice, xx, 27, 32, 62, 76, 95–96, 104, 108, 111–12, 132, 175, 178, 180, 182, 261, 292, 295, 302, 369, 375, 386, 397, 399, 404, 406, 471

speculative computing, 118
Spivak, Gayatri, 191
Srishti Institute of Art, Design, and Technology, 188
Standard Generalized Markup Language (SGML), 423, 430
Stanford University, x, xxiii, 76, 244–45, 345
Star, Susan Leigh, xii–xiii, 268, 276
STEM. *See* science, technology, engineering, and mathematics
S.T.I.T.C.H.E.D., 17
Suchman, Lucille, xiii, 273
surveillance, 6, 34, 66, 72, 131, 175, 181, 250, 393, 456
survey data, xv, xviii, 75, 143, 270, 310–11, 320, 323–36, 341, 349, 356, 401, 438, 457
sustainability, xv, xxii, 31–32, 62, 95, 137, 243, 249, 276, 312, 315, 383, 411, 422–26
Svensson, Patrik, 58, 262–63, 278
systemic conditions, ix, xxi, 17, 65, 71, 145, 148, 150, 162, 262, 289–302, 332, 341, 369, 397, 403–4, 419, 457, 469

tacit knowledge, xiii
Tay, 40
teaching. *See* pedagogy
TEI. *See* Text Encoding Initiative
TEI community, 146–47, 153
tenure, 32, 122, 153, 175–76, 179–80, 182, 265, 305–9, 311–14, 316–17, 324, 329–30, 332, 339, 345, 348–51, 356
Terras, Melissa, 76–78, 80, 88, 146, 296, 321, 430
text encoding, 278, 290, 346, 373, 412–13
Text Encoding Initiative (TEI), 97, 119, 142, 153, 237, 243–46, 249, 296, 344, 356, 373, 412, 416, 420, 424, 427, 430
textiles, xiv, 8, 10, 18, 20, 357
Texting Wilde, 110–11
THATCamps, 75–76
Tibetan and Himalayan Library (THL), 372–73

Tiptree, James, 274–76
tools, x, xii–xiv, xviii, xxi–xxii, 25–32, 72–73, 94, 100, 102, 109–13, 119, 121–22, 142, 178, 180, 196, 214–15, 240–41, 246, 268, 270–72, 275–76, 291, 295, 299, 302, 374, 418, 434, 437–38, 440, 448
Toomer, Jean, 49–50
TransAtlantic Slave Trade Database, 435
transCoder, 117, 124
#transformdh, xiii, 76, 95
transgender identity, xii, 10, 27, 34, 132, 150, 297, 325, 328–29, 336, 455, 458, 473
transparency, 47, 85, 117, 292
transphobia, ix, 145, 150
trolling, 40, 112, 175–77, 466, 470–71, 474; gendertrolling, 470–71
Trump, Donald, ix, 30–31, 34–35, 40, 182
trust building, xx, 57, 67, 139, 302, 315, 382–84, 460
Tumblr, 88, 192
Turing, Alan, 39, 115–17
Twitter, xvi, 7, 40, 87, 111, 174–82, 190, 193, 195, 206, 217, 226, 240, 244, 247–48, 249, 321–22, 330, 374, 384–85, 388, 395, 397–401, 404, 467–74

undercommons, ix, xiv, 30, 392
UNESCO DigiArts, 441
universal design, 247–48
universalism, xiv, 27, 40–51, 71, 187, 189, 247–48, 298, 373
University of Maryland, x, 298, 354
University of Victoria, xxi
University of Virginia, x–xi, 265, 352, 356 376
Unix, 271, 294–95, 300, 302
UNSTOPPABLE, 27–29, 32
Unsworth, John, 439, 451

Valley of the Shadow, The, 351–54
Verhoeven, Deb, xv, 147, 268, 278
Vibrant Lives, 14–15

Victorian studies, 45–46, 157–67, 266, 278, 290
violence, xvi–xvii, xxi–xxii, 4, 27, 31, 47, 49, 58–60, 141–42, 148, 174, 178, 182, 185–86, 188–98, 214–15, 217–18, 269–70, 383, 391, 394, 396–97, 399–400, 403, 448, 450, 452–53, 456, 458–59, 471; online violence, xxi, 59, 189, 270, 457; police violence, 174, 176–78, 382, 393–94, 396–406, 456–57, 471; sexual violence, 25, 186, 188–94, 269–70
virtual reality (VR), xiii, 25
visualization, xiv, xv, xx, 7–8, 11–20, 99, 101, 103, 109–10, 167–69, 206, 211, 222, 230, 234–35, 239–41, 248–49, 255, 274–75, 373, 399, 421, 424, 426, 429
visual pleasure. *See* pleasure: visual pleasure
Voyant, 97, 105, 272, 278
VR. *See* virtual reality

Wajcman, Judy, xii, 4, 9, 11, 20, 266
wearable technologies, xii, xiv, 5, 7, 9, 13
Wells-Barnett, Ida B., xvi, 173–74, 180–83
Westworld, 25, 31, 36

Wernimont, Jacqueline, 14–15, 76, 96, 111, 158, 206–7, 261, 271, 278, 371, 374, 411, 429, 448
Whole Cloth, 357
Why Loiter, 192
Wi-Fi, 437
Wilde, Oscar, 110–11, 159, 162
Women Writers Online. See Women Writers Project
Women Writers Project, 96–97, 143, 157, 165, 278, 290, 296, 298, 302, 374, 412–13, 424
Woolf, Virginia, 134, 138, 409–10, 429
WordPress, 203, 206, 244, 383
world-building, 108
Wynter, Silvia, 31, 35

XML, 142, 144, 167–68, 237, 243–46, 249

"yacking" vs. "hacking" debate, 187, 437
Yellow Nineties Online, xvi, 157–70
Yellow Nineties Personography, 157–70
Yik Yak, 395–97
Young Black Twitter (YBT), 398–99, 405

Lightning Source UK Ltd.
Milton Keynes UK
UKHW030743140119
335410UK00002B/44/P